BETWEEN CROSS AND RESURRECTION

Beside Alan's memorial window in the McMillan Building of Austin
Presbyterian Theological Seminary is a plaque which reads:

Stained Glass Window
Given to the Glory of God
and in memory of
Alan E. Lewis
Beloved Professor and Friend
by the
Graduating Class of 1994

The window was designed by Margaret Desmond,
a student of Alan and a member of the class of 1994.

BETWEEN CROSS AND RESURRECTION

A Theology of Holy Saturday

ALAN E. LEWIS

WILLIAM B. EERDMANS PUBLISHING COMPANY
GRAND RAPIDS, MICHIGAN / CAMBRIDGE, U.K.

Wm. B. Eerdmans Publishing Co.
2140 Oak Industrial Drive N.E., Grand Rapids, Michigan 49505 /
P.O. Box 163, Cambridge CB3 9PU U.K.

Paperback edition 2003

Printed in the United States of America

17 16 15 14 13   9 8 7 6 5 4

Library of Congress Cataloging-in-Publication Data

Lewis, Alan E. (Alan Edmond), 1944-
Between cross and resurrection: a theology of Holy Saturday / Alan E. Lewis.
p.   cm.
Includes bibliographical references.
ISBN 978-0-8028-2678-7 (pbk.: alk. paper)
1. Holy Saturday.   2. Jesus Christ — Three days in the tomb.   I. Title.

BT468.L49   2001
242′.35 — dc21

00-069197

www.eerdmans.com

This book is dedicated to

The Reverend Ivor Lewis

(1913-1978)

Contents

PART THREE: LIVING THE STORY

Foreword

Some books come and go quietly; this one will not. You will not be able to put it down. It will stir you, challenge you, trouble you, and widen your horizons. One does not usually speak this way about theological books, but in this case it is justified. Why? For one thing, the silence has been broken — the silence of Easter Saturday. Like the puzzling "silence in heaven" of the Apocalypse (8:1), a literary void has persisted for generations on the apocalyptic hour between Jesus' dying and being raised by God on Easter's first day of the week. Neither the resurrection and historicity debates of 1994-95 in Germany nor the 1997-98 Oxford Press publication of the interdisciplinary symposium on Jesus' resurrection addressed this void. Now, finally, both Good Friday's terror and abandonment and Easter Sunday's impossible new possibility have been lengthened and deepened by the voice from the grave of Easter Saturday. You will never again think of Easter as you did before reading this book.

Not only is Easter Saturday a spellbinding topic, but the encounter with Alan Lewis will hold you fast. Such an explosive style, such unexpected turns of expression, such rich dialogue with the world of academic theological reflection, such disregard for shallow gamesmanship, such a probing reach beyond academia to lived life and lived death, such a careful measuring and articulation of the gaze into the abyss of holy darkness! What you do not know about the author — yet — is that he came to his appointed hour with this topic not only through the spirited shaping of a Welsh/Irish pastor's household and the exquisite rigors of a classical education in Europe and America but also through an Easter Saturday demise of his own. The reader is haunted throughout this book with a growing sense of pathos, with an awareness that this is not merely a topic but a passionate encounter. He or she journeys with the author from Cross to Resurrection through the lived-out death of Easter Saturday. This book is no casual read. The cancer ward, Auschwitz, abandonment, and chaos as well as the grace, hope, glory, and triumph of God are all here to tug and tear at you. You must always keep your wits about you; it does not hurt, moreover, to keep a dictionary close at hand. A further recommendation: the first time through, read Lewis's text only; the second, consult his footnoted dialogue partners. The rewards will be enormous.

The book's structure is simple and forthright: it invites you, initially, to listen to the story of Easter Saturday. Be careful! . . . You are being asked to "hear" about the boundaries between yesterday and tomorrow, the troubling prospects of "God in the grave" and of the Word incarnate and "interred." Then in Part Two you are asked to venture into the war zone of the deadly prospects and vivifying hope of God's union with the Buried One, God's "election" of the grave, moving from God's passion to God's death. Part Three grapples with living this Easter Saturday story in world history, in contemporary society, and — yes — in the mortal transience of our own personal destinies. The structure is simple, but the scope of its vision is not! These are unchartered waters in many respects; yet with vigor the book seeks partners in conversation for the journey. Key theological voices as well as those coming from other disciplines are appreciatively engaged and critiqued with respect and incisiveness. The reader is conscripted too! The dialogue in this book reaches a level of maturity that is rare. It is a model for all of us.

JOHN ALSUP,
a former colleague and friend of Alan Lewis,
Austin, Texas,
February 2001

Preface

Writing in 1993, Alan described the purpose and content of this book thus:

For a considerable numbers of years now, beginning back in Edinburgh, I have been working on a fairly lengthy manuscript on the "theology of Easter Saturday." Its working title is *On the Second Day: God and Humanity between Cross and Resurrection.* It is in fact an attempt to interpret and contribute to the contemporary "theology of the cross," which has enjoyed some prominence, especially in Europe, primarily through the work of Jürgen Moltmann and Eberhard Jüngel, both of them being influenced by their teacher Karl Barth. Their thought is not easy, and part of my aim is to render it somewhat more accessible to the nonacademic reader. The much-ignored theme of Holy Saturday seemed to me very helpful for this interpretative task, since it provides a unique boundary point from which to consider the interconnections between themes of Good Friday and of Easter.

Though it is differently expressed, in many ways my thought is similar to, and not uninfluenced by, Douglas J. Hall, whom I consider by far the most important theologian in North America today.

The volume is very clearly subdivided into three parts, attempting in turn a narrative, a dogmatic, and an ethical approach to "the theology of Easter Saturday." In keeping with that sequence I have tried as best I can to give each part a distinct style, both of writing and of theological discourse. So not all the inconsistencies between the three sections are entirely unintentional! What I have tried to keep uniform throughout, however, is the accessibility of the main text to the general reader. I visualize that reader as a clergy person, or someone with a little theological knowledge, but definitely not an academic or a scholar. I have attempted with some rigor to keep all technical jargon etc., out of the main text. All of that, along with scholarly debate, I have relegated to the footnotes. These are fairly voluminous in places, for the sake of assisting those interested in more academic discussion of the issues; but I think the main text could be read and understood without any reference to the notes at all.

Finally, I cannot avoid a personal reference. Although this has been from the outset a study on the themes of suffering and death, it was never my intention to make it autobiographical, still less one more example of the rather pietistic and exhibitionist discussions of suffering of which the religious market seems so full today. However, in 1987, with this project already well under way, I discovered I had cancer and have been struggling with that condition ever since — which is one reason why my completing of the work has often been postponed. I have in fact, not without some misgivings, made reference to the experience in the final chapter. I am not, as far as I know, under any specific threat of imminent death, though one never knows; but it has been a major goal in recent years to complete my script while I had the time. We are never satisfied in these situations; and now, of course, it has become my dream to live long enough to see the work actually in print.

Alan continued to work on and revise the text until shortly before his death on February 19, 1994. He considered this book to be his life's work; we are grateful that he lived long enough to complete it and that it is being published in its entirety. One of Alan's greatest gifts was his ability to express complex theological ideas in a clear and accessible manner. We trust that this volume will be of interest to academics, clergy, and laypeople alike.

Kay Lewis
Mark Lewis

Austin, Texas
January 2001

Acknowledgments

As Alan indicates in the text, this book was many years in the making. We are therefore indebted to our family and numerous colleagues and friends in Scotland, Northern Ireland, and the United States whose encouragement and support helped make the publication of this book possible.

In Scotland the faculty of New College, Edinburgh University, and The Very Reverend Professor John McIntyre were very helpful. In the United States the faculty of Austin Presbyterian Theological Seminary and Dr. Jack L. Stotts were also very supportive.

Thanks are also due to Dr. John E. Alsup, who read the manuscript; to Lisa Chronis, Alan's research assistant; and to Dr. Donald W. McCullough.

Finally, we are indebted to Austin Presbyterian Theological Seminary and to the Carnegie Foundation for providing financial aid toward the publication of this book, and to all those at Eerdmans who helped produce this volume.

KAY LEWIS
MARK LEWIS

Prologue

> *Now at the place where he had been crucified there was a garden, and in the garden a new tomb, not yet used for burial. There, because the tomb was near at hand, and it was the eve of the Jewish Sabbath, they laid Jesus.*
>
> *Early on the Sunday morning, while it was still dark, Mary of Magdala came to the tomb.*
>
> (Jn. 19:41–20:1, NEB)

But what about the Sabbath, the day between that evening and that morning, over which the storyteller passes so quickly? Faith's supreme drama tells of *three days* which form the center and the turning point of history. Yet, ironically, the center of the drama itself is an empty space. All the action and emotion, it seems, belong to two days only: despair and joy, dark and light, defeat and victory, the end and the beginning, evenly distributed in vivid contrast between what humanity did to Jesus on the first day and what God did for him on the third. None of the evangelists shows any interest in the interval between the two great acts — except for Matthew, who has the priests and Pharisees at Pilate's door on the morning of *Shabbat*, begging for custodial measures to make all the more certain that nothing will happen at the sepulcher that weekend (Mt. 27:62ff.). Otherwise, between the crucifying and the raising there is interposed a brief, inert void: a nonevent surely — only a time of waiting in which nothing of significance occurs and of which there is little to be said. It is rare to hear a sermon about Easter Saturday; for much of Christian history the day has found no place in liturgy and worship it could call its own within the *triduum,* or three-day festival spanning Good Friday and the Day of Resurrection;[1] and it might be thought a bizarre and hopeless starting point for theological reflection. The second day appears to be a no-man's-land, an anonymous, counterfeit

---

1. There have, of course, always been special prayers and readings for "Holy Saturday" in church traditions with fixed liturgies and lectionaries. But torn — quite properly — between contrite memory and expectant hope, the church has often found it impossible to clarify any one particular theme or practice for worship and celebration on this day. Indeed, such is the ambiguity and anonymity of Easter Eve that it has sometimes lost its distinctive, if silent, place in the Christian calendar altogether, and been encroached upon liturgically by the other days of the Easter *triduum,* especially by Easter Day itself. Thus there persisted for centuries a Roman Catholic tradition of chronologically premature celebrations of the Easter Mass, held as early as the Saturday morning. This practice ceased in 1956. It is certainly better for the church to do nothing that is liturgically specific on the second day than to compromise the uniqueness of its position between cross and resurrection by absorbing it as simply an extension of Good Friday or an anticipation of Easter.

The tradition of Paschal Vigil on Easter Eve, which goes back to apostolic times, has been preserved in both East and West, and is now enjoying something of a revival even in some Protestant circles, is a quite different matter, of course, and wholly appropriate. It preserves the integrity of the narrative, and indeed draws attention to its structure, by not anticipating Easter but waiting patiently, through the long, last hours of Saturday night, until the joyous third-day dawn. For a contemporary set of Roman Catholic prayers and liturgies for the three-day festival, which does give Holy Saturday its due, see G. Huck, *The Three Days: Pastoral Prayers in the Paschal Triduum* (Chicago: Liturgy Training Publications, 1981); see also G. Huck and M. A. Simcoe, eds., *A Triduum Sourcebook* (Chicago: Liturgy Training Publications, 1983).

In the theological tradition, as we shall see below, only the Greek Father Gregory of Nyssa has perceived much dogmatic significance in Holy Saturday, while Martin Luther daringly expressed the thought that after Good Friday God's very self lay dead in the grave. In contemporary times, the great Roman Catholic theologian Hans Urs von Balthasar has alone, but profoundly, explored the meaning of Holy Saturday. Though his interests are much more aesthetic and mystical than mine, his influence, sometimes conscious and acknowledged, often subliminal and unreported, permeates this entire project. See esp. H. U. von Balthasar, *Man in History,* trans. W. Glen-Doepel (London: Sheed and Ward, 1968 [= *A Theological Anthropology* (New York: Sheed and Ward, 1968)]); *Mysterium Paschale,* trans. A. Nichols (Edinburgh: T. & T. Clark, 1990), esp. ch. 4; *The Glory of the Lord,* vol. 7: *Theology: The New Covenant,* trans. B. McNeill (Edinburgh: T. & T. Clark, 1989), esp. pp. 228-35; and *The von Balthasar Reader,* ed. M. Kehl and W. Löser, trans. R. J. Daly and F. Lawrence (Edinburgh: T. & T. Clark and New York: Crossroad, 1985), esp. pp. 148ff. See also J. K. Riches, ed., *The Analogy of Beauty* (Edinburgh: T. & T. Clark, 1986), esp. pp. 180ff. Note also J. Moltmann, *The Way of Jesus Christ,* trans. M. Kohl (San Francisco: Harper-Collins and London, SCM, 1990), pp. 190-91.

moment in the gospel story, which can boast no identity for itself, claim no meaning, and reflect only what light it can borrow from its predecessor and its sequel.

Or, alternatively, does the precise locus of this Saturday, at the interface between cross and resurrection, its very uniqueness as the one moment in history which is both after Good Friday and before Easter, invest it with special meaning, a distinct identity, and the most revealing light? Might not the space dividing Calvary and the Garden be the best of all starting places from which to reflect upon what happened on the cross, in the tomb, and in between? The midway interval, at the heart of the unfolding story, might itself provide an excellent vantage point from which to observe the drama, understand its actors, and interpret its import. The nonevent of the second day could after all be a *significant* zero, a *pregnant* emptiness, a silent nothing which says *everything*. We shall have to see.

It needs to be granted immediately, of course, that the events upon which the story of Christ's death, burial, and resurrection is based might comprise an affair of three days only by historical accident, or even by literary design. A day of waiting and inaction belonged to the logic of the historical events themselves. The crucifixion, deliberately timed to precede the Sabbath day (which in John's chronology was the Passover itself), was naturally followed by a pause when nothing would happen, and certainly no visit to the tomb by Mary and the others to anoint the body. And however either faith or unfaith judges the factuality of what is said to have happened when the visit was finally made, and, indeed, the factuality of all the Eastertide appearances, suspicions could never be wholly erased about the neatness of the story's "three-day" structure. Has the gospel narrative of what occurred at the first Easter been constructed to fit a pattern already familiar in the Old Testament, and especially to parallel, however inexactly, the tale of Jonah in the belly of the fish? Some will detect creative, retrospective imagination rather than hard fact, both in Matthew's prophecy that the Son of Man, reliving Jonah's experience, will be "three days and three nights in the heart of the earth" (Mt. 12:40) and in all the other prophecies of Christ's raising and the temple's rebuilding, "on the third day" or "after three days" (e.g., Mk. 8:31; 14:58; Jn. 2:19).[2]

Taking a different approach, one could also say that theologically, as a story of good news about the death of Christ for our sins and his rising for our forgiveness and new life, the narrative does not depend upon its three-day spread either. The story would be no less "gospel," would indeed be the same

---

2. See J. Kasper, *Jesus the Christ* (London: Burns and Oates and New York: Paulist Press, 1976), pp. 146-47.

story of salvation, intrinsically unaltered in its inner content and significance, did it tell of a victory over death on the second day, or on the fourth.

From either of these perspectives, whatever meaning and importance we discover Easter Saturday to have will not lie in the fact that it is *numerically* second, the antecedent of a *third* day and no other, the postlude exclusively of a first. Not its number in the series, but its place, bears its significance, as that day between the days which speaks solely neither of the cross nor of the resurrection, but *simultaneously* remembers the one and awaits the other, and guarantees that neither will be heard, or thought about, or lived, without the other.

Nonetheless, a story is a story; and the fact is that at the center of the extended biblical story which Christians continue to receive and pass on down the generations, and which tells of events from before creation to beyond the end of time, there is a three-day narrative which we find unnecessary to modify and impossible to forget. As Paul put it: "I delivered to you as of first importance what I also received, that Christ died for our sins in accordance with the scriptures, that he was buried, that he was raised on the third day in accordance with the scriptures" (1 Cor. 15:3-4). Christian faith simply would not *be,* did it not hear, believe, and tell what once took place between the sixth day of one week and the first of that which followed.

What keeps the heart of the Christian church beating, and its blood circulating, if not the story of those days, so endlessly rehearsed, with such infinite variety and such steadfast unalterableness? Sketched out by the very first preachers, subjected to profound reflection by the apostles, extended and elaborated four different ways by the evangelists, later reduced again to apothegms by the drafters of countless creeds and confessions, the story of Christ crucified, buried, and risen continues even now to be told and acted out, year by year and week by week. The worship of every Sunday is a fleshed-out echo of what Christians have heard happened that third day, that first day of the week. Likewise the church's hymns, when thoughtful, and her preaching, when faithful, reannounce the first proclamation of death's death and sin's atonement. Each act of baptism dramatizes the dying and rising again of the Savior as well as that of those he died and lives to save; and in every celebration of communion the same story is presented and re-presented with particular intensity and unique effect, red wine refocusing the savagery of execution on Golgotha and the breaking of bread re-releasing the astonished cries of recognition in Emmaus.

Since none of these retellings of the story can be anything but symbolic and abbreviated, the Christian family takes time once a year to replay the events at their original speed — to experience for themselves the somber, then joyous, sequence, moment by moment. Through a few hours of worship and many of ordinary life, they relive annually the growing tensions of the climactic week; the grieving farewells, shameful betrayal, guilty denial, and agonizing fear of the night before the end; the long, dark, deadly day of pain and forsakenness itself; an ecstatic daybreak of miracle and color, song and newborn life; and in between one eerie, restless day of burial and waiting . . . perhaps for nothing: a day which forces us to speak of hell and to conceive how it might be that God's own Son, and therefore God's own self, lay dead and cold within a sepulcher.

Such is faith's story, which we are invited now to hear freshly as if for the first time; to think about with the widest stretching of our minds and our imaginations; and to make our own, as the key to learning how to live and even how to die.

PART ONE

HEARING THE STORY

CHAPTER ONE

The Easter Saturday Story

I. Telling Stories That Tell the Truth

Since the word "story" has long enjoyed prominence, and will continue to do so, some explanation of its use is immediately called for. After all, the telling of stories is commonly reckoned to be the specialty of informers and disinformants, of sneaks and liars. It will be important, therefore, to banish, as promptly as possible, all mental connections between "story" and that which is fictitious, fabricated and fraudulent, or in any sense untrue. Not that that is easy when words of all sorts, but especially those used to tell, or sell, a story, are the object of profound and justified mistrust. In an age of sophisticated propaganda techniques and manipulative advertising, we are becoming increasingly alert to the potential malevolence or phoniness of almost any verbal message. And if we are cynical, doubting that words mean what they say, we are also tired, preferring the visible to the literary as the way to communicate, or fail to. The sickness of the church itself, so closely intertwined with the malaise of Western culture, has been diagnosed as "boredom with language," in contrast to the excitement which "words" generated in Europe at the time of the Reformation.[1] Amid such disenchantment with the verbal, there will inevitably be apprehension that any story heard or told or read is likelier to be false than true. How revealing, how sad, that among the trendiest of clichés in fashionable religious discourse nowadays is "the hermeneutics of suspicion," indicat-

1. G. Ebeling, *Introduction to a Theological Theory of Language*, trans. R. A. Wilson (London: Collins, 1973), pt. 1.

9

ing an axiomatic assumption that words cannot be relied upon to mean what they say.

On the surface at least, this is, therefore, an inauspicious, even perilous, moment for theologians of many varieties and all confessions to agree that it is precisely the genre of story, or narrative, upon which they should concentrate their analysis of how truth is conveyed, and with which they should begin their own attempts at communication.[2] Despite their vulnerability to suspicion and distrust in a postliterary culture, "stories" have recently emerged in much theology as the very means by which the truth of God is understandably received and effectively passed on by the community of faith. It might be, of course, that God's truth is so at odds with human conventions that it *requires* to be told by methods which conflict with the received wisdom and fashionable trends of this or any age. However that may be — and we shall return to this thought later — narrative is now being tested as theology's proper starting point, in response to which, and in reflection upon which, concepts, doctrines, and prescriptions for action may subsequently be constructed.

Among its other purposes, this study might hope to provide some explanation and justification of this current phenomenon of "narrative theology,"[3]

---

2. The present interest in communication through narrative is, in fact, by no means limited to theology, or literary theory. It is coming to play a highly significant role, e.g., in forms of therapy for "mentally defective" persons who are able to express themselves and find a sense of identity through stories as they cannot conceptually. For a fascinating account, see O. Sachs, *The Man Who Mistook His Wife for a Hat* (New York: HarperCollins and London: G. Duckworth, 1985), ch. 21.

3. For very much fuller accounts than can be attempted here of narrative theology, see esp. M. Goldberg, *Theology and Narrative: A Critical Introduction* (Nashville: Abingdon Press, 1982); S. Hauerwas and L. G. Jones, eds., *Why Narrative? Readings in Narrative Theology* (Grand Rapids: Eerdmans, 1989); E. Jüngel, *God as the Mystery of the World,* trans. D. L. Guder (Edinburgh: T. & T. Clark and Grand Rapids: Eerdmans, 1983), sect. 19, "The Humanity of God as a Story to Be Told"; R. F. Thiemann, *Revelation and Theology: The Gospel as Narrated Promise* (Notre Dame: University of Notre Dame Press, 1985); B. W. Anderson, *The Living Word of the Bible* (Philadelphia: Westminster and London: SCM, 1979), ch. 2: "Word of Narration"; S. McFague, *Metaphorical Theology* (Philadelphia: Fortress, 1982 and London: SCM, 1983); G. Stroup, *The Promise of Narrative Theology* (Atlanta: John Knox Press, 1981 and London: SCM, 1984), and "A Bibliographical Critique," *Theology Today* 32 (July 1975); D. Tracy, *The Analogical Imagination* (New York: Crossroad and London: SCM, 1981); and "The Crisis in the Language of Faith," in *Concilium*, trans. J. B. Metz and J.-P. Jossua, vol. 5, no. 9 (1973); D. Cupitt, *What Is a Story?* (London: SCM, 1991); D. Ritschl, *The Logic of Theology* (London: SCM, 1986 and Philadelphia: Fortress Press, 1987), throughout. See also S. J. Grenz and R. E. Olson, *Twentieth-Century Theology* (Downers Grove, Ill.: InterVarsity Press, 1992), ch. 9: "Transcendence within the Story:

and to constitute a concrete, if minor, example of the narrative method in theological procedure. The procedure will be first to hear, in the simplest terms, what it is that the New Testament's gospel story itself declares to us. Only then shall we proceed to more abstract, conceptual reflection, both historical and contemporary, on the story's meaning — how Christians past and present have thought out what they have heard from the story about God, about ourselves, and about reality, and how, conversely, the story has been or should be able to correct and control the church's thinking. Finally, we shall ask what the story implies for the actual living of life and dying of death by individuals, communities, and the world as a whole.

This leaves unanswered the question of just how "story" is, or should be, related to "truth"; and here sides have very decidedly to be taken between the varying approaches which subdivide the current promoters of the narrative genre in theology. The implicit assumption, already apparent here, that it is possible to encounter in the biblical story something of God's own truth, rules out at least one alternative presupposition, namely, that which takes for granted, even before the story is heard, that it is *exclusively* a human story. Of course, no one who is aware that much of the Bible is narrative in form (though there are many exceptions, such as the Psalms and the Wisdom literature) should wish to evade the fact that narrative is an ordinary literary genre, and therefore that the Bible is properly, indeed essentially, subject to the varieties of literary analysis and criticism just as much as comparable "secular" documents, narrative or otherwise in form. This could actually be to press home, rather than deny, the conviction that in the Bible, by the thoroughly human agency of literature, the divine so speaks that, mysteriously, to the ear of faith, the narrative words resonate with "the Word of God." If, however, the definition of Scripture and its stories as literature intends to say that it is "only literature," and that whatever truth the biblical narratives can express is thisworldly truth about the human condition and resides exclusively with their literary form, linguistic structures, or editorial arrangement, then, it would seem, the ears have been prematurely, and illegitimately, stopped to any hearing of the divine Word through human words.

A more subtle and ambiguous approach categorizes the biblical stories, or some components of them, as "myth." A notoriously multiform and slippery notion, resistant to easy definition, myth has sometimes stood, if not bluntly, for the "false," at least for an indirect, unfactual, and generally obsolescent expression of religious aspiration. When first introduced into theological dis-

---

Narrative Theology"; and D. F. Ford, ed., *The Modern Theologians* (Oxford and New York: Blackwell, 1989), esp. vol. 2, ch. 6: W. C. Placher, "Postliberal Theology."

course,[4] myth commonly referred to those accretions by which an originally factual and historical story — about Jesus of Nazareth, for example — came to be overlaid with religious meaning and embroidered with "heavenly" references. Since these embellishments tended to comprise allegedly supernatural beliefs about the world, now known to be scientifically false, modern theology has sometimes attempted to identify and discard these anachronistic, mythical elements of the Bible. To their credit, most of the demythologizers, however questionable their assumptions about what is modern and "scientific," have been anxious not to abandon the underlying *meaning* of the myths. On the contrary, they wish modern men and women to discover for themselves, and interpret in their own terms, the same significance of Jesus which the original mythmakers attempted to convey in theirs.[5] Even so, the assumption has been that the Word of God will be authentically heard in the Bible and in preaching only when the gospel story has been radically pruned, and the ancient mythical husks enveloping its timeless kernel cut away.

In reaction to this negative view of myth, we sometimes witness an enthusiastic embrace of the mythical, as the essential rather than disposable vehi-

4. This happened particularly under the influence of the nineteenth-century German critic D. F. Strauss and his *The Life of Jesus Critically Examined* (1835), reissued, trans. G. Eliot, ed. P. C. Hodgson (London: SCM, 1973). See also H. Harris, *The Tübingen School* (Oxford: Clarendon Press, 1975).

5. This means that in his own way Rudolf Bultmann, who initiated the "demythologizing" program in this century, could be regarded as something of an ally in the present project. Who has ever stripped down the NT more ruthlessly than he to its central three-day story? It is true, of course, that his understanding of Easter, as not a distinct, additional event which corresponds to the crucifixion, but as faith's way of affirming the significance of the crucifixion, means that "for Bultmann, Good Friday and Easter fall on the same day" (H. Zahrnt, *The Question of God: Protestant Theology in the 20th Century,* trans. R. A. Wilson [London: Collins and New York: Harcourt, Brace and World, 1969], p. 234). Moreover, his willingness to distinguish and even disconnect the *kerygma* — the gospel message — from the actual biblical narrative of Jesus' life, death, and resurrection runs quite counter to our intentions here. Even so, Bultmann is one of the few theologians who could be said to have tried consistently to conform his entire thinking to the challenge and mystery of 1 Cor. 1: the Easter word of the cross and the *cruciform* promise of resurrection. See *Kerygma and Myth,* trans. R. H. Fuller, ed. H. W. Bartsch, 2nd ed., vol. 1 (London: SPCK, 1964); R. Bultmann, *Jesus and the Word,* trans. L. P. Smith and E. H. Lantero, 2nd ed. (London: Collins, 1958); and *Faith and Understanding,* ed. R. W. Funk, trans. L. P. Smith (London: SCM and New York: Harper & Row, 1969). For a brief but lucid account of "myth" from Strauss to Bultmann, see A. I. C. Heron, *A Century of Protestant Theology* (Guildford: Lutterworth and Philadelphia: Westminster Press, 1980), ch. 5; also Zahrnt, *Question of God,* ch. 7.

cle for the expression of religious truth. If that, by definition, concerns what transcends us, it will naturally elude the grasp of straightforward statements and intellectual concepts; but it can perhaps be approached indirectly through the imagination. Myth, on this view, is the imaginative use of symbol and parable, of the poetic and the pictorial, to express the inexpressible.[6] Far from false, it is the only way to come close to what is ultimately true. Within limits, these assumptions about the incompleteness and indirectness of religious language coincide with those adopted here. But those who lay hold of "myth" as a solution to the problem of how humans may speak of God run the constant risk that they will speak of humans *instead* of speaking about God. Myth is defined by those who champion it as the articulation of universal human experience. Myths express the lasting values, cyclic events, and rhythmic patterns, the common, universal dreams and dreads which identify us all as human. In the myths of the Bible, it is said, these perennial meanings and values have attached themselves to a unique man of history.[7]

6. See here J. P. Mackey, *Jesus — The Man and the Myth* (London: SCM and New York: Paulist Press, 1979). Among his other achievements in this book, my former senior colleague at Edinburgh has provided the clearest possible exposition and execution of this approach to myth. I cannot convince myself, however, that his distinction between the facts of Jesus and the myth about him avoids in the long run a reduction of Christology, perhaps of all theology, to anthropology. See also J. P. Mackey, *The Christian Experience of God as Trinity* (London: SCM, 1983); and J. P. Mackey, ed., *Religious Imagination* (Edinburgh: Edinburgh University Press, 1986). Cf. A. E. Harvey, ed., *Incarnation, Story and Belief* (London, SPCK, 1981), ch. 2: J. Barr, "Some Thoughts on Narrative, Myth and Incarnation."

7. Though its discourse ranges far beyond the specific category of "myth," there has been a highly publicized and animated theological debate recently, in the United States especially, concerning these universal "religious" experiences. Is the primary task of Christian theology today to contribute to the exploration of the ageless and worldwide "foundations" of religious experience, which all human beings, consciously or unconsciously, share and recognize and about which they are therefore able to converse publicly and coherently with one another, despite their generational, denominational, and other cultural differences? Or is it the task of Christians still to affirm and expound those distinct particularities of faith and concrete, specific truth-claims which make them a unique community of faith over against all other religious traditions? The debate for and against "foundationalism" is often cast, oversimplistically, in terms of a rivalry between the University of Chicago (with particular reference to David Tracy, though there are other equally significant representatives of this approach, including the major Roman Catholic scholars Bernard Lonergan and Karl Rahner) and Yale University (referring to the late Hans Frei and to George Lindbeck). See esp. Tracy, *Analogical Imagination;* and G. Lindbeck, *The Nature of Doctrine* (Philadelphia: Westminster Press, 1984). Lindbeck himself summarizes the dispute — with a regrettable lack of lucidity and accessibility for

Now it is undeniable that every word of the New Testament gives authentic human voice to the faith and hope and love which Jesus of Nazareth has evoked in women and men. Conversely, he would not do that did he and the stories about him not strike chords within human beings of ever-so-many cultures, eras, and personal histories, who recognize his relevance to their inner and outer experience of human life. But does an interpretation which insists that this is what the gospel itself is about actually respect the Jesus narratives for what they are? Hans Frei, among the most notable recent analysts of narrative, has argued influentially that the only interpretations of the biblical stories which do justice to the intentions of those who wrote and told them are those which treat them as *realistic* accounts, whose meaning lies straightforwardly in the unique events they describe.[8] These events may not always be deemed "his-

---

the general reader — as being between the "revisionist experiential-expressive" approach and the "postliberal cultural-linguistic" approach. The present author has considerable reservations about Lindbeck's understanding of the theological enterprise (especially his greater emphasis on the "regulatory" than on the veridical nature of church theology). But it should be abundantly clear that our study here is concerned precisely to interpret Christ's death, burial, and resurrection as unique events in human and divine history, and definitely *not* as merely one culturally conditioned expression of a universal human experience which finds plural and equally valid forms of symbolization. For a very helpful and lucid account of and contribution to this debate, see W. C. Placher, *Unapologetic Theology* (Louisville: Westminster/John Knox Press, 1989). See also C. Gunton, "Knowledge and Culture: Towards an Epistemology of the Concrete," in H. Montefiore, ed., *The Gospel and Contemporary Culture* (London: Mowbray, 1992), esp. pp. 100-101, n. 12.

8. See H. Frei, *The Eclipse of Biblical Narrative* (New Haven and London: Yale University Press, 1974). Frei's argument is that a quite clear and disastrous turning was taken in the history of biblical interpretation in the eighteenth century, when the narratives ceased to be read realistically (as by Calvin and the Reformers, for example), and to be plundered instead for hidden, symbolic meaning attached to, and hence detachable from, the stories themselves. The problems created by this "enlightened" divorce between story and message, fact and interpretation, have plagued theology ever since. In the field of Christology, it has fed the assumption that Christ cannot, on principle, be "God among us," but at most a person of thisworldly history who evokes human experiences describable in the mythical symbols of another world. Frei himself, in *The Identity of Jesus Christ* (Philadelphia: Fortress Press, 1975), attempts, in a slightly obscure way, to pursue a realistic interpretation of the Christological narratives. He is particularly insistent that the resurrection stories are not mythical tales of human hope in the face of death, but "history-like" narratives concerning the unique identity of the "unsubstitutable Jesus of Nazareth," in whose raising God alone has acted (see pp. 135ff., 139ff.). For the same point see O. Weber, *Foundations of Dogmatics*, trans. D. L. Guder (Edinburgh: T. & T. Clark and Grand Rapids: Eerdmans, 1983), vol. 2, p. 67.

The whole issue is clearly discussed by C. Gunton in *Yesterday and Today: A Study of*

tory" in the ordinary sense; but they are "history-like" as they unfold a sequence of interrelated happenings.[9] These specific occurrences themselves constitute the point of the narratives and are not merely pegs upon which some other timeless tale is hung; nor are they a veil concealing a symbolic meaning which the interpreter must discover for him- or herself. In short, the bifurcation of the biblical stories into "fact" and "myth" is one more refusal to listen to them, assuming in advance that they do not mean what they say, and that what they mean is at most an expression or confirmation of some universal truth already

---

Continuities in Christology (London: Darton, Longman & Todd, 1983). He consciously adopts Frei's approach to narrative (p. 60) and convincingly shows that the modern, fashionable, dualistic assumptions about the nature of reality, which keep God out of this world by definition, are neither new nor necessary. Cf. C. Gunton, *Enlightenment and Alienation* (Basingstoke: Marshall, Morgan & Scott, 1985), esp. pp. 121ff.

See also W. C. Placher, "Hans Frei and the Meaning of Biblical Narrative," *Christian Century* 106.18 (1989): pp. 556ff.; and Placher, "Postliberal Theology," in Ford, *Modern Theologians,* vol. 2, esp. pp. 117ff.

On story and narrative in Karl Barth, who greatly influenced Hans Frei, see esp. D. F. Ford, *Barth and God's Story* (Frankfurt: Peter Lang, 1981), and "Barth's Interpretation of the Bible," in S. W. Sykes, ed., *Karl Barth: Studies in His Theological Method* (Oxford: Oxford University Press, 1979), ch. 3; cf. Ford, "System, Story and Performance," in Hauerwas and Jones, eds., *Why Narrative?*; H. Frei, *Types of Christian Theology,* ed. G. Hunsinger and W. C. Placher (New Haven and London: Yale University Press, 1992), esp. pp. 160ff.; Lindbeck, *Nature of Doctrine,* esp. ch. 6; and D. Kelsey, *The Uses of Scripture in Recent Theology* (Philadelphia: Fortress and London: SCM, 1975), ch. 3.

9. For a discussion of the modern debate in the philosophy of history on the question whether history itself is about singular events or about instances of general, universal laws, see W. Pannenberg, *Theology and the Philosophy of Science,* trans. F. McDonagh (London: Darton, Longman & Todd and Philadelphia: Westminster Press, 1976), pp. 58ff. He concludes that "the classical historicist view that history deals with unrepeatable sequences of unique events . . . turns out to be basically correct" (p. 61). But he adds that the historian must also uncover sequences of regular "structure" if the individual event is to be understood. This might illuminate, in the case before us, the relationships between the cross and resurrection event, the rest of the story of Jesus Christ and of the Bible as a whole, and the universal story of nature and human experience about the emergence of life out of death. Would it be right to say that Good Friday–Easter is *not* an instance of a general, timeless truth, but a unique event; that in its uniqueness it clarifies the good news for human beings in the face of death which is conveyed by other NT stories and the Bible as a whole; and that the Bible's message, with the story of cross, burial, and resurrection at its heart, is that we may all universally participate in its truth — that "those who lose their lives shall save them"? To treat that scarcely believable paradox as a natural law of cosmic or human life, which Jesus and the Bible merely illustrate or symbolize, is, among other follies, to sanitize and naturalize what is in fact offered only as a most awkward, unnatural, and unwanted truth, proved only through costly discipleship.

known. Applied to the central story on our agenda, the cross, burial, and resurrection of Jesus Christ, this approach would exclude from the start the possibility of hearing in it a new, unheard-of gospel word, Paul's foolish "word of the cross" (1 Cor. 1:18), which might disturbingly conflict with normal human instinct and experience; might redefine the very meaning of life and its patterns; compel those who listen to rethink all their values and conceptions, hopes and fears; and might readjust the manner of their living and their dying.[10]

There is, however, one way of combating this interpretation of the biblical stories as myth which is itself, perhaps, guilty of not hearing with an open mind what they have to say. The decision that whatever the Bible contains is, and must be, true, even before its contents have been heard, responded to, and interpreted, can sometimes be motivated by the wish to obey uncritically what is believed to be God's own authoritative, even infallible, means of self-communication. Faith here gives allegiance to what is *in* in the biblical witness because of what it already knows *about* the Bible as such: the God-given nature and origins of the documents and their propositions. Yet, ironically, this perhaps quite credit-worthy attempt to respect God by respecting God's Scriptures may in fact neglect and suppress Scripture's own demonstration and affirmation that faith does not precede but comes from what is heard (Rom. 10:17).

If that has any applicability to the nature of the biblical record itself, it surely warns us not to adopt in advance any predetermined external and impersonal factors — such as the inspired, oracular, or dictated nature of a set of books — as the ground for giving attention to the words they contain. Instead, the possibility is promised that if we expose ourselves personally to these words, however fallible and finite, with openness of heart and mind, we will be seized, in that very process, by the knowledge that through them God is indeed addressing us directly.[11] This in turn would mean that we understood and inter-

---

10. See Ebeling, *Theological Theory*, p. 17: "According to Luther, the word of God always comes as *adversarius noster*, our adversary. It does not simply confirm and strengthen us in what we think we are and as what we wish to be taken for. It negates our nature, which has fallen prey to illusion; but this is the way the word of God affirms our being and makes it true. This is the way, the only way, in which the word draws us into concord and peace with God." Cf. A. C. Thiselton, *The Two Horizons: New Testament Hermeneutics and Philosophical Description* (Exeter: Paternoster Press and Grand Rapids: Eerdmans, 1980), p. xx. The same methodologically vital point is made well by Gunton, *Yesterday and Today*, p. 31.

11. This is a summary, and oversimplification, of the long-standing debate within Protestant theology, and indeed the life of the Protestant churches, about the nature of biblical authority. Does that authority derive from what the Bible *is* as inspired and God-given oracles, or from what it *does*, namely, so address us through the power and by the

preted the stories and their message — in effect, formed our theology and shaped our corresponding lifestyle — in obedience to what was thus addressed to us and heard by us, and not within the limits of ideas and assumptions previously arrived at. The latter approach would decide what God was like — for example, the sort of deity who supernaturally inspires human documents (which would tell us much about God's nature in general) — *before* we listened to what the Bible actually had to reveal or say of God. How tempting it would then be, when the moment finally came to do some listening, for the inner ear to filter out whatever in the biblical story failed to conform to the theology (and therefore the lifestyle) already presupposed. How easy to assume that the truth heard and commanded simply confirmed the truth already known and followed. How difficult to be *upset* and *changed.*

In summary, in dealing with Christ's cross, burial, and resurrection, we are to avoid any method which, before we even begin, makes it hard, or even impossible, for us to hear in the three-day story a Word that could confound our intellects, overturn our morality, and shock, surprise, and change us body, mind, and spirit.

This partisan announcement clearly demands a sequel which explains in more positive terms how we are to avoid all these evils of presupposition, and instead to hold open the much-praised possibilities for the destruction of preconceptions and the transformation of mind and life through the hearing of God's story. Can presuppositions be avoided? *Have* they been by those who have decided that the biblical story may not be "only literature," and may be myth neither in the negative nor positive sense, but could be vehicles for hearing the address of God's own self and realizing something of the Trinity's own peculiar truth? They obviously have not. To be prepared to hear a faith-creating Word is an act of faith itself. The "word of the cross" could not encounter me and convince me of its reality and revolutionary power were I hostile or even neutral to that very possibility. God, in other words, can be found only if first allowed to *be there* and then find us; and the fact that we may come to faith (and understanding) only by beginning with faith (and however little understanding) is a circularity in need of no concealment or apology. As Eberhard Jüngel

---

light of the Holy Spirit (what Calvin called the Spirit's "inner witness") that we hear its testimony as Good News, and in that even recognize it as the revelation of Christ, the Word of God for us? For the clearest discussion of the origins and course of this complex and still continuing debate, see J. K. S. Reid, *The Authority of Scripture* (London: Methuen, 1957). See also B. Gerrish, *The Old Protestantism and the New* (Chicago: University of Chicago Press and Edinburgh: T. & T. Clark, 1982), ch. 3, "The Word of God and the Words of Scripture — Luther and Calvin on Biblical Authority."

puts it: "Christian theology does indeed work with a presumption, which is a *presumable presumption*."[12] Without its open and glad presumption, theology would not be theology, taking God's reality seriously, nor listening for the divine Word with dread and expectation.

This, in turn, uncovers a second presumable presumption: that the God who is *there* is a God who *speaks,* and comes to us as Word, in words. We understand full well, even if this is the postliterary age, an essential correlation between words and human personhood. It is by language — not necessarily the sort produced in the larynx, but, if not, by some extension, correlate, or symbol of the spoken word (for the speech-impaired person is no less a human being nor any less a creature and creator of language than any other) — that we discover and define ourselves. As the curious medium of both separateness and togetherness, our words play a primary role both in distinguishing us from everyone around us and in forging and preserving with those around us the relationships without which we would not be ourselves. "In the word, we are together, and yet we distinguish ourselves in such a way that each person is he himself [sic]."[13]

This is another way of saying that speaking words is inseparable from hearing them, and that human personhood creates and relies upon conversation and communication. Our own individuality develops as we prove willing to listen not to ourselves but to others, who address their words to us and ask us to respond with our own words. This mystery of self-identity affirmed through self-forgetfulness and relationship is one that any human being can explore and experience. But it is the particular presumption of faith that fullness of life and personhood depends not only upon encountering and hearing other men and women, but on being addressed by God. And that entails the conviction that the God who is there, and who needs to be heard if we are to be truly human, does *address* us, uses words, is a sort of "speaker" and thus a kind of "person" too — perhaps *the* person par excellence, *more* truly personal than we are.

Naturally, theology cannot possibly know quite what it is talking about when it says such things. Karl Barth has written of "The Speech of God as the Mystery of God";[14] and there is certainly as much mystery, as much incomprehension, as much hopeful but doomed groping for words to describe the indescribable when we say that God is the "Word," or that "the Word was God" (Jn. 1), or that "God says . . . ," as with any of the other metaphors, images, and anal-

12. Jüngel, *Mystery,* p. 161 (italics added).

13. Jüngel, *Mystery,* p. 190.

14. K. Barth, *Church Dogmatics* (hereafter *CD*), ed. G. W. Bromiley and T. F. Torrance (Edinburgh: T. & T. Clark, 1936-69), rev. ed. of vol. I/1 (1975), sect. 5.4.

ogies in theology's toolkit. But Jews and Christians alike[15] take it for granted that the analogy between God and "a speaker of words" is neither arbitrary nor inappropriate, but grounded in and validated by what objectively occurs. The Creator may justifiably be said, and be expected, to *speak,* by dint of having been discovered to do precisely that. To recognize human speakers — the Lawgiver, for example, or the Prophets, or Jesus of Nazareth — as those who in their words and their own persons mediate or reveal something of God's own activity, will, or being means to accept "speech" as an analogy for the Lord provided and thus permitted or even insisted upon by God's own self. Certainly God directs us to the language by which human persons express the truth about themselves in both their uniqueness and their relatedness, as a creaturely reality which bears a reliable correspondence, a far-from-total but still real similarity to the Creator's own nature. That is, a God of utterance who truly expresses the divine identity and activity by *speaking* it, and by *doing* all that the divine Word *says.*[16]

15. It is, of course, a central element in the Christian doctrine of God, expounded as that is in terms of the Trinity, that God the Father of Jesus Christ is Yahweh, the God of the OT. And although popular Christian piety and theology, supported by some dualisms in Lutheranism especially, have too often attempted to contrast the character and will of God in the OT and NT respectively, it is the particular burden of Reformed theology that God is *one* in nature and attitude, a gracious God of mercy already in creation and the giving of the law. This surely must be so if it is true that no gap divides what God says from who God is, but that the Word of God expresses the truth about God's very being. It is just as central to the OT and to the Jewish faith as to the NT and that of Christians, that God is a God who communicates through *speech.* Not only does the OT, even more than the NT, use a range of anthropomorphic images and metaphors to describe God as a speaker, and presents many intermediaries through whom the Lord speaks, but the OT *begins* with God as acting through speech; so that when, in the NT, John 1 describes God as Word it is with an unmistakable echo of Gen. 1. It would posit an impossible divergence between divine Word and divine being were God self-expressive through language in both the "old covenant" and the "new," and yet *say* fundamentally different things in each.

It is a measure of the unanimity of Jews and Christians concerning God's nature as personal Word that the greatest influence upon recent Christian theology in the development of *address* as that which establishes communication between human beings, and between them and God, has been the Jewish philosopher Martin Buber. His understanding of what occurs when persons encounter and address each other as "I" and "Thou" has become standard in the Christian understanding of human nature, and even, ironically enough, as we shall see, in some understandings of the Christian Trinity and its three Persons. See M. Buber, *I and Thou,* trans. R. G. Smith, 2nd, rev. ed. (Edinburgh: T. & T. Clark, 1958); also trans. W. Kaufman (New York: Charles Scribner's Sons, 1970).

16. See Barth, *CD,* I/1, sect. 4, "The Word of God in Its Threefold Form," and sect. 5, "The Nature of the Word of God."

The community of faith is thus surely freed to explore all the uses to which human speech is put, as appropriate and promising means of living out their relationship with a God who, analogously to themselves, speaks *language*. They find words through which to hear God (Scripture), to ponder and pass on what they have heard (theology and preaching), and to speak back to God (praise and prayer). Parable and poetry, dogma and doggerel, all find their uses in this endless discourse with and about the God of the Old Testament and the New.[17]

Why then should it be that "story" has a special place in this divine-human dialogue? For Christians, it is partly that Jesus himself told stories. He used parables as a primary means of expressing literally, in words, that "Word" or truth of God which he embodied in his own person, and in everything that he was and did and said. Long before that, though, as we see in the Old Testament, the Hebrew people of faith found themselves encountered by a God who acted in the events of history; and they discovered that the telling and retelling of historical narratives kept alive their memory of the Lord's past power and grace, and their hopes for God's future faithfulness.[18]

17. I have covered the above ground slightly more fully, and developed it in the direction of the community, i.e., the church, which God creates by being a speaker of words, in "Ecclesia Ex Auditu: A Reformed View of the Church as the Community of the Word of God," *Scottish Journal of Theology* (hereafter *SJT*) 35.1 (1982): 13-31.

18. For some of the rival interpretations of how exactly the events of history constitute a revelation of God in the OT see, e.g., O. Cullmann, *Christ and Time*, trans. F. V. Filson, rev. ed. (London: SCM Press and Philadelphia: Westminster Press, 1962); J. Moltmann, *Theology of Hope*, trans. J. W. Leitch (New York: Harper & Row and London: SCM, 1967); W. Pannenberg et al., *Revelation as History*, trans. D. Granskou (New York: Macmillan, 1968); and G. von Rad, *Old Testament Theology*, 2 vols., trans. D. M. G. Stalker (Edinburgh: Oliver & Boyd and New York: Harper & Brothers, 1962).

On the particular role of narrative in the OT, see von Rad, *Old Testament Theology*, vol. 1, pp. 115-21; and K. H. Miskotte, *When the Gods Are Silent*, trans. J. W. Doberstein (London: Collins and New York: Harper & Row, 1967). See also R. S. Anderson, *Historical Transcendence and the Reality of God* (London: G. Chapman, 1975), ch. 4; and K. Löwith, *Meaning in History* (Chicago: University of Chicago Press, 1949).

See here also G. T. Milazzo, *The Protest and the Silence* (Minneapolis: Augsburg Fortress, 1992). It is strange that, for his own reasons, Milazzo should be so concerned to *contrast* the theology of divine absence, of silence and of protest, which he rightly discovers in the OT, with the whole genre of "biblical theology," which he accuses of ignoring the OT theme of divine absence in favor of a concentration upon God's *activity* in history. Is this a real contrast? Is a theology of divine revelation in history a denial of events and experiences of God's absence? Surely those who detect the mighty acts of God in history are not thereby, as a matter of principle or logic, triumphalistically or optimistically denying the human experience of God's absence from history but bearing witness of the presence of

Up to a point, the stories in both our Testaments prove effective because they are so readily *understood*. Utilizing characters and situations which are familiar, quotidian, and mundane, and events whose sequence can clearly be followed, they communicate with a simplicity and directness which is inevitably sacrificed when the truth they contain is subsequently refined into concepts and propositions — as must, nonetheless, be done, as we shall see below. Yet does not the power of the parables, indeed derivatively of all the biblical narratives, also rest in the fact that *they do not understand too much?* Stories are extended analogies; and by their very nature and form as stories they openly announce that they are *only* analogies, merely approximations and pointers to the truth. The *directness* with which narrative approaches us is matched, therefore, by the *indirectness* with which it approaches God. In consequence, stories both acknowledge that God is beyond all description and comprehension, and yet demonstrate vividly that God *can* be known and understood.

If this liberates us to think through, with all the rational tools at our disposal, the meaning and implication of the knowledge of God which the stories put so simply, it also reminds us that profound concepts and complex doctrines are finally no better match than stories for the heights and depths of the divine. Without rendering further reflection illegitimate or unnecessary, narrative thus has an intrinsic and procedural priority. It declares with "indirect directness" the truth of God, announcing the gospel which theology must then elaborate, while indicating the mystery which theology must not then violate. Was it an instinct for this priority of story which led the compilers of the New Testament canon to place the Gospels, and the history of the early church, before the Epistles, many of which were written first?[19]

Yahweh precisely in the midst of experiences and occurrences which seem devoid of meaning and purpose, hope and presence. That Yahweh acts in the midst of events that conceal God is not the contradiction but the burden of the biblical theology which Milazzo attacks. Miskotte bears witness to this tension between presence and absence, as do S. Terrien, *The Elusive Presence* (New York: Harper & Row, 1983), and S. Balentine, *The Hidden God* (Oxford: Oxford University Press, 1983).

19. It is at best amusing to hear it announced today as first-time news that God can be known only incompletely and obliquely, by metaphor and analogy, in criticism of the church's doctrinal and dogmatic past which naively thought to comprehend God fully and directly (McFague's *Metaphorical Theology* is a good example). In reality, all of the great theological traditions have in some manner built upon the premise of divine ineffability — from the apophatic theology of medieval mysticism to Calvin's doctrine of divine accommodation to the human. Some traditions could more readily be accused of resorting to silence or negation prematurely than of overusing the permission that God gives us to think and speak positively about divine reality. See Jüngel, *Mystery,* esp. pp. 226-45. None-

Now we indicted earlier those who recognize that the biblical stories may tell the truth but uncritically expect the truth they tell to conform to and confirm their own preconceptions of what is true. That amounts to a challenge to take this priority of story over theology seriously — to conform our thinking about God and the world to what we hear in the biblical stories rather than have them conform to what we have already thought. Even after faith's presumptions, such openness to what is heard should not be impossible — though it will not be easy or painless — if the story is as understandable as we have said. For we should then be able to understand that their point and purpose is indeed to surprise and shake us, and compel us to *rethink* our thinking about God in conformity to the new, unheard-of truth about both deity and humanness which they announce. The gospel comprises stories whose genuine, open hearing cannot help but first shockingly disorient, and only then reorient, our minds.[20]

This is most plainly, and at first most acceptably, the characteristic of Jesus' own parables.[21] We may attempt for a while not to notice their offensiveness to *us;* but we can readily recognize how outrageously they flouted the conventions, and short-circuited the expectations, of those who heard them first. We can see so clearly, we imagine, how tales of heartless Levites and compassionate Samaritans, of justified tax collectors and rejected Pharisees, met their intended mark, arousing fury and bewilderment in those days' guardians of ethnic pride and moral purity.

However, the point and effect here are so direct and clear that we can scarcely evade for long the knowledge that it is we ourselves who are under attack, today, from these ancient anecdotes. The costly party for a returning wastrel strikes us, too, as itself wasteful parental overreaction, unfair to the understandably indignant elder brother (Lk. 15:11-32); while equal wages for unequal work seems no more just in a first-century vineyard than in a twenty-first-century factory (Mt. 20:1-16). Yet if we keep faith with such stories these first reactions will not be our last, and they will indeed convert us, change our

theless, it is always good for dogmatics to be reminded of the caution and humility with which this permission must be exercised.

20. See P. Ricoeur, "Biblical Hermeneutics," *Semeia* 4 (1975): 94-112.

21. Among much other literature on the parables, see J. Jeremias, *The Parables of Jesus,* trans. S. H. Hooke (London: SCM, 1954); J. D. Crossan, *In Parables* (New York: Harper & Row, 1973); McFague, *Metaphorical Theology,* esp. pp. 42ff.; R. E. Capon, *The Parables of Grace* (Grand Rapids: Eerdmans, 1988), *The Parables of Judgment* (Grand Rapids: Eerdmans, 1989), and *The Parables of the Kingdom* (Grand Rapids: Eerdmans, 1989). See also A. R. Eckardt, "Divine Incongruity: Comedy and Tragedy in a Post-Holocaust World," in *Theology Today* 48.4 (Jan. 1992).

minds and deeds. Tears of outrage will give way first to those of shame. As stories which condemn the cruelty of rules and the loveless use of law, especially where exercised in the name of God, they continue to convict today the hypocrisy and self-deception of religious zeal and moral censure — indeed, of self-righteousness in all its forms — and to expose the illusion of justice divorced from love and liberty. It is then, however, that the real transformation occurs, and the parables become such subversive, "dangerous stories."[22] Guilt gives way to exhilaration, and shame to tears of relief, when we hear it being said that God's ways are different from the ways of the world and are a threat to every status quo, since the rule of the world by these new and different ways has already begun before our very eyes. In God's kingdom there is a justice which sets free and makes joyful all who stand before it: the guilty are not condemned, the fallen are picked up; nobodies are promoted; the hungry are sated; and the lost are not permitted to remain abandoned. And all of this through a love which knows no sensible bounds and breaks every principle of decorum, prudence, and tradition. As McFague puts it, "the feature which is at the heart of the tension in the parables is their *extravagance*. While the stories are, at one level, thoroughly ordinary and secular, events occur and decisions are made which are absurd, radical, alien, extreme."[23]

What frightens and frees us simultaneously about this new and alien kingdom of God which Jesus preached and told of is the simple fact that it is God's and not our own. That is a dark menace to the complacency and contentment of those who flourish under the kingdoms of this world; a shining vision of release and new beginnings to the victims of the present order; and perhaps also a mocking rebuke to the programs, projects, and pride of those who hope to create a new order by themselves. It is tragic, therefore, that a gospel which promises justice, love, and peace only by insisting that these are God's own gifts, which remain alien, foolish, and impossible except for grace alone, has continually been misconstrued and misappropriated as the goal and burden of human and Christian aspiration. Piously, or politically, we cripple ourselves with the need to *bring about* God's righteousness on earth, failing to hear what Jesus so vividly declares: that we need not shoulder that burden because the goal itself does not need to be accomplished. The goal is a fact, God's fact, the fact of grace and promise. No gap divides what God says from what God does; and the stories of the coming kingdom do not offer dreams and possibilities of what the

22. J. B. Metz, "A Short Apology of Narrative," in *Concilium*, vol. 9, no. 5, pp. 84-96, and "A Short Apology of Narrative," in Hauerwas and Jones, eds., *Why Narrative?*, pp. 251-62.

23. See McFague, *Metaphorical Theology*, p. 46.

Lord might or could do, but speak indicatively, and in the present tense, of what is happening, and of what the future is becoming. The kingdom need not — and cannot — be worked for; it may only be accepted and awaited.

On the other hand, this waiting for God's indicatives cannot be dispassionate or passive. Just as one could not hear the promise of grace and freedom in the stories of the kingdom were one not first gripped and addressed by their all-too-understandable directness, so the only response to these narrated promises is engagement and "entanglement."[24] Having freed us from guilt and self-reliance, the gospel enslaves us again with its imperatives, demanding everything of us by way of repentance and discipleship. "As far as the narration of the story of Jesus Christ is concerned, it is the *truth* which sets free, and then out of that gained *freedom* which derives from *hearing,* there follows the *deed* which moves history further."[25] That is no less true of the stories which Jesus Christ himself narrated.

Because the truth of the kingdom is indeed a truth to be done, the imperative addenda to the story of the new things that God alone is doing must eventuate in human action. Those who become disciples because they have heard the liberating word that they cannot and are not expected to do what God alone can do, are then commanded, with the perfectly foolish logic of the new kingdom, to "go and do likewise"; and their going and doing is the test of whether they have really heard the promise that they can do nothing. However spontaneous and uncalculating must be the action and service which follows Christ and thus enacts the extravagant love embodied in his parables, it is plain that one cannot be entangled in this paradox of freedom and bondage, promise and demand, without *thought and understanding.* Repentance, as every beginner in New Testament Greek knows, is a converting of the *mind* (*metanoia;* see, e.g., Mk. 1:4; cf. Rom. 12:2). And here we glean some early insight into theology's task of conforming truth to story to which we must revert below. That task is a repentant, revolutionary process which allows the subversive, iconoclastic follies of the gospel story, the "word of the cross," to shake up our preconceptions of what is possible or powerful or wise, and forces our thoughts, in reluctant but obedient discipleship, to follow the truth and wisdom of what is heard. The scandal of God's kingdom, which is perhaps even harder for the "clever" theologian to live with than for the "simple" believer, is that folly and rationality are two sides of one reality — if that reality be God's. We come closest to what is really true, and hence most wise and rational, when we subject our ideas of God

---

24. Jüngel, *Mystery,* pp. 303ff., after W. Schapp, *Im Geschichten verstrickt. Zum Sein von Mensch und Ding* (Hamburg: R. Meiner, 1953).

25. Jüngel, *Mystery,* p. 309 (his italics).

and truth to the critical, objective judgment of reality as it confronts us, and painfully align our thinking to that reality, even though by our original standards it was untrue and quite unwise. Only down this intellectual path of disorientation and reorientation, of destruction and remaking, can the point be reached where what we think and say bears some correspondence to what the stories told about God actually convey.[26]

Finally, it must be obvious to those with ears to hear that this power to stop us dead in our tracks and make us recommence our thinking about God, which so characterizes the *stories that Jesus told*, belongs even more uncomfortably to the *story told of Jesus*. The New Testament is not *primarily* about the parables at all, but tells and reflects upon the story of how this narrator of parables and preacher of good news came to be narrated and preached about — the subject rather than the mouthpiece of the gospel. His stories about God take their place within the church's story about him. And the central episode of the story about him, the tridual narrative of cross, burial, and resurrection, describes — though it scarcely explains — the transforming of the preacher into the preached one, and of his parables into a prologue to the proclamation of him.

The story of this transformation is the ultimate iconoclasm, which breaks up our image not only of Jesus — crucified in shame and buried in a grave, then raised in exaltation — but of *God*. How can faith and understanding come to terms with all that this narrative declares about where and who God is? If we are offended by the tales Jesus told and lived out, of pardoned lawbreakers and of untouchables befriended, how must we react to the story of God as the crucified and buried one? To be quite blunt about a matter we must soon think through to its extremity, that story unites the Lord God with a human corpse — with a man who has in some eyes been murdered by criminals, and in others executed as a criminal. The impossible foolishness of this — that after such a

---

26. As words such as "reorientation" and "remaking" here might suggest, this encapsulates a particularly *Reformed* understanding of the way in which faith and theology come to know God — though the claim that this is the only proper way to know God involves the recognition that as a principle of method it may be, has been, and is practiced within *any* theological system or tradition. From their ultimately very different perspectives, Barth and Bultmann, the two dominant figures in twentieth-century Protestant theology, both worked on the Reformation principle that our thinking, like our morality, relies wholly upon "justification by grace." That is, we depend on what God shows us of the truth — know God, i.e., "according to the Spirit" — instead of conforming that truth to our own preconceptions and assumptions "according to the flesh." For the fullest explanation and defense of this whole way of thinking "according to the object," see T. F. Torrance, *Theological Science* (London: Oxford University Press, 1969), esp. ch. 4, "The Nature of Truth."

fate a man should be raised to life with God, and that into such a human fate God's very self, the Lord of glory, should have fallen (1 Cor. 2:8) — is the supreme test of our willingness not to conform story to what we already understand, but to reconform our understanding to the story that we hear.

Even so, this above all others is a story we can understand because it does not understand too much. Its implications for what it means to be God — and equally for what it means to be human — are both too hot to handle and too deep to fathom. Unheard-of things are being said in this story, of which the most we can understand is how little we could ever understand. And that is why from the first moment that the events occurred, they have been told in the *form* of narrative. Women hurried from an empty tomb to tell their friends a story, though "these words seemed to them an idle tale, and they did not believe them" (Lk. 24:11). Later, convinced, a man stood up and repeated the story: "This Jesus you crucified and killed; but God raised him up" (Acts 2:23-24). Likewise, all the evangelists, even the fourth, who had gone furthest in *analyzing* the story,[27] made their confession of the crucified, buried, and risen one in the form of narrative. For Paul, too, the subtle conceptualities of the gospel are grounded, simply and offensively, in the *preaching* of the cross;[28] and as we have said, the church has lived by the telling and retelling of the drama, through word and sacrament, liturgy and action, ever since. All this is because there really is no other medium besides narrative in which to speak about such things as the crucifying of the Lord of glory, the silencing of the Eternal Word, and the resurrecting of a liquidated Galilean. Only story's directness conveys the personal, arresting, entangling demands and promises of such events; only story's indirectness gives anyone the nerve to open the mouth so as to speak of them, or the mind to think of them, at all. Whenever Christ's death, burial, and rising are told or preached, as the story of God's truth, the narrators are admitting that they scarcely understand what they are saying, but are passing on the Word that they have heard; God help them, for they can do no other.[29]

Such an affirmation of what is happening when the story of the cross and grave is repeated is naturally made only in the posture of repentance and confession, that all too often Christians speak of their Lord's death and resurrection in a different spirit entirely: of overconfidence and excessive comprehen-

27. See Tracy, *Analogical Imagination*, pp. 275-81, esp. p. 278.

28. See, e.g., Weber, *Foundations*, vol. 2, p. 63.

29. See, e.g., K. Barth, *The Word of God and the Word of Man*, trans. D. Horton (London: Hodder & Stoughton, 1928), esp. p. 130. On the gospel as that which must be told, see F. Buechner, *Telling the Truth: The Gospel as Tragedy, Comedy and Fairy Tale* (New York: Harper & Row, 1977).

sion. Since it is *the* story of stories, there must be more reflection, more meditation, more theology, about the events between Good Friday and Easter than of anything else in all our Scriptures. And when faith hears the Word of God in that story, it *must* press on toward conceptuality and understanding. The danger is, however, that in our attempt to conceive and understand it we in fact suppress the very revolution that the story embodies, naturalize the alienness of its ideas, tame the violence it does to our logic, and anesthetize its wounding of our pride. For all its power as story — and as a story of powerful resurrection — this is, after all, the most vulnerable of stories, a story of suffering and absence, of negation and of death.

The cross is vulnerable to those who hate its message, its absurdity offering the ultimate grounds for the mocking of faith. And it is vulnerable, too, to those who fear its message, its violence giving a precedent and a weapon to Christians who cannot tolerate the way of peace. It is vulnerable to those who forget its message, its familiarity providing a pretty promise of protection to be worn around the neck. But it is perhaps most vulnerable to those who love it, and who genuinely wish to understand it. Sometimes, in order to honor the cross, we adore, domesticate, possess it, make it *ours,* part of our own experience, in the quietude of mystic oneness or in the exertion of busy emulation. Sometimes, in order to exalt the cross and its outcome, we speculate about its infinite significance and turn it into a metaphysical principle: the negative and positive rhythms of the cosmos, for example. Most pertinent of all here is the risk run when, in the stupendous task of interpreting the cross and its sequels, theology turns to *concepts* to help it fix the story's place at the heart of faith and doctrine. That must be done if the community of faith which believes the story wishes to be coherent in what it does and stands for. But the perennial danger is that of surreptitious import — the unnoticed entry of beliefs and assumptions disconnected with the story, which muffle theology's ear to what the story is in fact saying and predetermine the meaning that is put upon it. As we shall see, the church's understanding of her own central story, about *the unity of God with a human corpse,* has often been determined by concepts which themselves restrict the available meanings of that event by legislating in advance what is and is not possible for God and for humanity.

Mercifully, despite its vulnerability, the cross which is God's *powerful* weakness continues to resist its interpreters,[30] exploding theology's own conceptions and compelling it to suspend its judgments until it has discovered

30. See J. Moltmann, *The Crucified God,* trans. R. A. Wilson and J. Bowden (London: SCM and New York: Harper & Row, 1974), esp. ch. 2, "The Resistance of the Cross against Its Interpretations."

from the story itself what may or may not be true. Whether we here will be half-faithful in following the truth of God and of God's human partners, as seen between the death of Jesus of Nazareth and his rising from the dead, can neither be predicted now nor verified subsequently beyond all dubiety and ambiguity. In any case, the best to be hoped for us is that we reach some precarious balance between understanding and not understanding too much, between the wisdom of the story of the crucified, interred, and risen one and its utter foolishness.

II. The Day between the Days

Theology could learn a great deal from pondering the phenomenon of television reruns! Even if audience figures drop and the number of complaints rises, television channels, it seems, do not always find it commercial suicide to repeat programs previously aired, even several times. Enough of us do not refuse to watch films and plays, comedies and documentaries, which we have seen before to make their reshowing worthwhile. And it is less surprising that this is so than that some viewers find it objectionable. After all, in other spheres of communication and creativity, return to what is already known and familiar is natural and not worthy of note. There is nothing peculiar about attending an opera, hearing a symphony, or reading a book, which we have previously experienced and might know very well. This is to say that, in whatever form it is presented, human beings enjoy and derive meaning from *hearing a story again.* Our passion in childhood to be told again a favorite story we already know by heart never wholly leaves us as adults, and is not simply a mark of immaturity.

This may shed some light on the nature of Christian worship and evangelism; for that, as we have just seen, consists very largely in telling, over and over again — through the reading of Scripture, through song and preaching, through sacramental reenactment, but also through the practice of all these words — faith's many great stories, and its key story of a cross and a tomb. By some indefinable convergence of the Holy Spirit's dynamic and the human spirit's need to rehear the familiar, the Christian story remains a living Word, still powerful to stimulate and to pacify, to elevate and to undermine. Consciously or unconsciously, the church is aware that constant retelling and rehearing of "the old, old story" is not redundant and counterproductive, but essential and effective.

However, this very comfort and familiarity with the spiritual dynamism and missionary necessity of repetition can easily conceal from theology the importance of one question: What is actually happening when one hears or tells, in whatever medium, a story that is already familiar? For clearly to watch a film, read a book, or follow a score for the second time is not identical with the first experience. Particularly when the plot of a story is involved, and even if it is not clearly remembered but merely recognized as it unfolds, a quite different mental and emotional experience is taking place from that in which the events described are fresh and new, and their outcome a secret until it happens. I might very well derive more, even a lot more, from the rereading of a thriller, being able, for example, to notice a detail I previously overlooked through concentration on the story line. But I will never again be able to read it feeling exactly the same suspense, and asking precisely the same questions, as on that first occasion when the mystery really was mysterious. This in turn means that my understanding of the story has subtly altered; for the point of such a book, indeed of most structured stories, is surely that the unfolding of its events should *not* become known in advance, but be revealed only when the author, and not the reader, determines. It is consequently the test of good storytellers, writers, and actors whether they are able to preserve, for the sake of the audience, the full drama, suspense, or mystery, and hence the original meaning, of their material, even though they themselves know what is coming and have passed far beyond the unrepeatable experience of first-time hearing.[31]

All of this should, though it probably rarely does, concern the church greatly. For it raises a question about the way in which Christians repeat and re-enact the story of salvation among themselves, and the way they tell it, in all its familiarity, to outsiders for whom it is really "news." Are we aware that the gospel itself, as a story of unfolding events, becomes a slightly different story when it is familiar, and the events are heard with prior knowledge of their outcome? Continual rehearing of the gospel may well uncover fresh detail and significance, previously missed, and be a source of increasing, not decreasing, insight and stimulation; but as a story it has then lost one essential ingredient: the drama of not knowing what will happen and how or when it will end. This means that a community which depends upon the Word for its life, and lives only in order to proclaim the Word, may without realizing it no longer be hearing and repeating the Word as originally told. Insensitive to the distorting effect of familiarity, we may prove unfaithful stewards of the gospel and poor narrators of its truth, who fail to think through for our own sakes and the world's what the story says and means from the perspective of a first-time hearer. We may misrepresent the pace of the biblical story, hurrying on to the end, impa-

31. Interestingly, the historian Antonia Fraser makes exactly this point with reference to the importance of telling a history story as if one did not know how it was going to end: "although *we* know Henry VIII will marry six times, we must always remember that he did not." A. Fraser, *The Wives of Henry VIII* (New York: A. A. Knopf, 1993), p. 2 (= *The Six Wives of Henry VIII* [London: G. Weidenfeld and Nicholson Ltd., 1992]).

tient with its periods of slowness and waiting; we may silence some of its most painful and puzzling questions because we feel we already know its answers; we may ease its agonizing tensions through foreknowledge of their final relaxation. And in all of this we may suppress the very good news which the story holds for men and women who have to endure life slowly and patiently, who hear no answers to their own questions, or experience tensions with no guarantee of eventual resolution. How might a person in real despair identify with a dissipated prodigal heading homeward from skid row, hoping at best for more exquisite forms of shame? How different the person of dignity or untroubled faith, who hears for the umpteenth time the instructive tale of a young fool who leaves, but hurries back to, the dependable, loving arms of home!

The most glaring and massive example of this temptation to read the story not in terms of its own unfolding but in the light of its ending concerns the Hebrew Bible — the whole of it. As a comparison of Jewish and Christian interpretations of the Old Testament makes so clear, these documents constitute two quite different narratives according to whether or not one has already heard and believed the New Testament as their sequel and conclusion. Of course, believing Jesus Christ to be the fulfillment of the Old Testament and its promises, Christians cannot help but read its stories as in some manner a preparation for and prophecy of the coming of Jesus as the Christ. Yet not to interpret the Old Testament also, indeed first, as the *Jewish* record of faith, belonging to a context which is both historically and theologically antecedent to the recognition of this man from Nazareth as the Messiah, is distorted faith, irresponsible scholarship, and poor storytelling. It treats the historical documents of both Testaments, and the historical sequence of events which runs through them, in a quite unhistorical fashion. Even from a Christian point of view it is essential to the Old Testament story that its promises were given to *faith,* that is, to those who did *not* know what the future was and how the promises would be fulfilled. Conversely, it is essential to the New Testament record that the fulfillment of promise to which it witnesses met with un-faith, since many Jews did not recognize Jesus as the one who was to come but crucified him. In every regard, then, the biblical story is only heard as given when it is heard from the Jewish perspective as well as the Christian, from the standpoint of those who do not foresee or presuppose the story's New Testament conclusion as well as of those who do know and believe it. The New Testament is in part precisely about those who *deny* the continuity of its story with that of the Old.

The need to treat the Old Testament with historical integrity is commonly recognized and easily established. Our concern hereafter, however, is with a story whose hearing and telling is much more subtly — almost indiscernibly — but just as critically vulnerable to the distortions of familiarity. For it is the church's *triduum,* faith's own central event of Jesus Christ crucified, buried, and resurrected, which is par excellence *the* story that is difficult to respect simply for itself. The most important narrative is perversely and dangerously the hardest of all to listen to, identify with, and reenact! As always, the problem lies in the transformation which takes place once the story has been heard. Like any dramatic account, it is no longer quite the same once the sequence of events has been unfolded and the outcome revealed. In this case, because those who really hear the story are themselves transformed by it, they require all the more effort of imagination and thoughtfulness if they are to identify again with a first-time hearer.

The resurrection is the decisive factor here, of course. It is not hard to be puzzled or sceptical about the factuality and meaning of the empty tomb and the Easter appearances. But provided only that one has heard and been open to the story that Christ was raised from the dead, it is supremely difficult — though actually supremely important — still to think of his death in its own right, without or before his resurrection. For that is the only way truly to hear and tell the story of both his dying and his raising in faithfulness to its own structure and plot. As the events of that climactic weekend occurred, and as the gospel story recounts them, this did not *begin* as a three-day happening, destined to end as a story of victory and life. Far from being the first day, the day of the cross is, in the logic of the narrative itself, actually the last day, the end of the story of Jesus. And the day that follows it is not an in-between day which simply waits for the morrow, but it is an empty void, a nothing, shapeless, meaningless, and anticlimactic: simply the day after the end. There is no remarkable tomorrow on the horizon to give that Sabbath special identity and form as the day before the Day of Resurrection. These were anonymous, indefinite hours, filled with memories and assessments of what was finished and past; and there was no reason to imagine that an imminent triumph might render those judgments premature and incomplete.[32] When today we ourselves fail to identify with the

32. Von Balthasar is particularly penetrating on the danger that, as hearers of the Easter Saturday story and observers of its drama, we will simply override the narrative by bringing premature meaning and victory to its palpable incomprehensibility and negativity: "the danger is very real that we, as spectators of a drama beyond our powers of comprehension, will simply wait until the scene changes. . . . The apostles wait in the emptiness. Or at least in the non-comprehension that there is a Resurrection and what it can be. The Magdalen can only seek the One she loves — naturally, as a dead man — at the hollow tomb, weeping from vacant eyes, groping after him with empty hands. Filmed over with an infinite weariness unto death, no stirring of a living, hoping faith is to be found. . . . If one asks about the 'work' of Christ in Hades . . . we must guard against that theological busyness and religious impatience which insist on anticipating the moment of

story of this *Shabbat*, refuse to ponder the death of Christ as seen from this vantage point where death is his only fate, and defeat the only verdict on his life, then do not faith and theology cease actually to hear the very narrative by which the church lives?[33]

Of course, the story then moves on — gloriously. The plot does not peter out on that amorphous, retrospective Saturday but advances with dramatic force to unfold a third day, with its unexpected, exultant conclusion, a humanly impossible and inconceivable finale. *Now* we know the full scenario, and we can see with hindsight that the Friday had not been the last day of Jesus after all, but the first day of a new, unfinished, never-ending history. In its turn the Sabbath was no meaningless period of deflation after a disastrous climax, but a very specific, identifiable *second* day, the day *before* the climax, a time of calm and waiting before the victorious storm. Inevitably, and properly, this knowledge of the end drastically reinterprets everything that has gone before in the story of those days. Christian faith is not that Jesus was crucified, but that Christ crucified was raised; and that throws wholly new light on what his death meant in the first place.

We must ask this, however, as a forceful, critical question: Does the resurrection outcome of this story of the cross and grave actually *negate* what the crucifixion and burial originally were and meant?[34] Are we excused from hear-

---

fruiting of the eternal redemption through the temporal passion — on dragging forward that moment from Easter to Holy Saturday." H. U. von Balthasar, *Mysterium Paschale,* pp. 50-51, 179.

33. For a small but telling example of how easy it is comprehensively to miss the whole point of Easter Saturday by assuming that it is positively to our advantage to have the superior knowledge, unavailable to its participants, of how the narrative is going to end, see T. J. Carlisle, "Holy Saturday and the Annunciation," *The Clergy Journal* 65.4 (1989): 12: "You and I can know the *heart's elation* [his italics] on Holy Saturday in a way impossible to Jesus' close friends because we know about Easter and on that day they did not . . . the fact that nothing can separate us from the power of Jesus, the son of Mary, has done, is doing, and will continue to do for us."

34. "There is no deeper misunderstanding of the *mysterium Christi* than that which insists, against all the evidence, on construing the resurrection as a descent from the cross, publicly and unambiguously visible to all standing around, but made the more overwhelmingly effective by a thirty-six hour postponement. We all of us in different ways, in different situations, have to learn the extent to which we are prisoners of utterly misleading imagery concerning the nature of Christ's victory over the world and the manner of its manifestation." D. M. MacKinnon, "Kenosis and Establishment," in *The Stripping of the Altars* (London: Collins, 1969), p. 37. MacKinnon's observation perfectly sums up the burden of this study: the misreading of the resurrection as the cancellation of the cross, and the misuse of Easter Saturday to reinforce rather than to confront that misconstrual, so fateful to the Christian gospel.

ing and telling the story now as it sounded first, before the ending was known? May we silence and forget, no longer for ourselves and others to identify with, the narrative of Good Friday as a day of defeat and despair, and of Easter Saturday as one of abject misery and forlorn memories? The decisive criterion for every evangelical declaration, for every liturgical reenactment, for every theological intepretation of the cross and resurrection, is this: Does the resurrection free us from thinking of the cross as it was before the resurrection? To answer No is to say that this is a story which must be told and heard, believed and interpreted, *two different ways at once* — as a story whose ending is *known,* and as one whose ending is discovered only *as it happens.* The truth is victim when either reading is allowed to drown out the other; the truth emerges only when both readings are audible, the separate sound in each ear creating, as it were, a stereophonic unity.

This is not so much to admit as to *assert* that the meaning of Jesus' death and resurrection is full of ambiguities. The objective for those who would hear the central story of the Christian faith, understand, proclaim, and live it, must not be to distill a single, simple interpretation out of the different vantage points it offers, and thus transcend all of its ambivalences; but to allow understanding and reaction to emerge out of the tension between rival interpretations and viewpoints. This is to say, in anticipation of our own experiment with that procedure, that the cross must be understood as *both* the disastrous finale to Christ's life as it sounds on the story's first hearing *and* as the first episode in a three-day event of triumph, and thus retrospectively not a disastrous but a saving, resurrecting death.

Conversely, when we first hear of it, the resurrection is a powerful act of glorification for which we have not been prepared by the defeat and ignominy which went before. Yet once we are familiar with the completed story, and reflect upon this contrast between the climax and its antecedents, we have to come to terms with the fact that it is not a powerful but a dead and *powerless* person who has been raised, not a glorious but an ignominious one who has been glorified. The third day, therefore, must be interpreted both as resurrecting in its own right, and as the resurrection specifically and exclusively of one crucified, buried, terminated.

In summary, the complex, multiple meaning of the story will only emerge as we hold in tension what the cross says on its own, what the resurrection says on its own, and what each of them says when interpreted in the light of the other. It would not be impossible to graph the entire history of church doctrine and life by plotting the interpretations which have failed to give due weight to one or other of these essentials in the story by which and for which the Christian community lives. We might discover that the second day, which serves both to keep the first and the third days apart in their separate identities and to unite them in their indivisibility, offers a useful stance from which to make one more effort at a properly multivocal, stereophonic hearing of the gospel story.

We have located the principal threat to such a multivocal interpretation of the death and rising again of Christ in the temptation that those familiar with the story will allow the resurrection to modify the finality of the cross. And it is proposed that the second day, coming between and thus keeping apart, Good Friday and Easter Day, provides a buffer against the premature encroachment of the resurrection upon the cross, and a stance from which to consider the latter on its own as well as in its relatedness to the former. The irony of this suggestion is that this second day has already been recognized as ambiguous itself: a brief and slender, unnoticed and insignificant feature in the original story. Even the New Testament, it seems, does not always pause to allow the finality of the cross to sink in before moving on to the Easter reversal of Christ's deadly and disastrous fate. Indeed, the Gospel of John, with whose telling of the narrative we began, and whom we saw passing over the interval between the evening of Jesus' burial and the morning of Mary's visit with utmost brevity, reinterprets the finality of the cross and gives it a new, "resurrection" meaning. For when, at death, Jesus cries out "It is finished" (Jn. 19:30), John unquestionably understands that not as a cry of defeat and termination, but as a victorious affirmation of what has been done, accomplished, and achieved. There is no need for John to wait through a long Sabbath for the Sunday before Christ can be revealed as Lord of Life. That finale to the three-day story is already present, and worthy of celebration, in its opening; just as, long before his death, the Johannine Christ had spoken, with the most powerful of double meanings, of a "lifting up" in which his physically painful and degrading suspension from a gallows would constitute exaltation and acclamation, the vanquishing of darkness and the manifestation of light (Jn. 12:32ff.; cf. 3:4; 8:28). As John Marsh points out, "it cannot be too strongly emphasized that for John the cross is the instrument and point of victory, not the point of defeat which has to be reversed on Easter morning. Here, as the Lord dies, he conquers."[35]

On the other hand, not even John allows the cross to be swallowed up en-

---

35. J. Marsh, *Saint John,* The Pelican Bible Commentaries (Harmondsworth: Penguin Books, 1968), p. 618. John's distinctive interpretation of the cross is, of course, recognized by very many commentators. Just a few examples out of many observations similar to those of Marsh are: R. Bultmann, *Theology of the New Testament,* 2 vols., trans. K. Grobel (New York: Scribner's, 1951 and 1955), e.g., vol. 2, p. 56; L. Newbigin, *The Light Has Come* (Edinburgh: Handsel Press and Grand Rapids: Eerdmans, 1982), p. 160; and E. Schillebeeckx, *Christ: The Christian Experience in the Modern World,* trans. J. Bowden (London: SCM and New York: Crossroad, 1980), pp. 409ff.

tirely by the resurrection; and he offers no legitimation to anyone else who wishes so to do. His thought is by no means that Jesus did not really suffer; rather, his glory is revealed and accomplished *through* his passion and his death. When the hours of that glory come, Jesus is troubled at the prospect to the depth of his being (Jn. 12:27). John's account of the passion compromises none of its physical horror and terminal mortality; and even though this is a death in need of no "reversal," that does not dissuade John from telling the resurrection story with just as much realism and eye for detail as any of the Synoptists.[36] Above all, although John's narrative disregards the second day as completely as we have seen, he is very far from presenting the death of Christ as an event which would cause no grief and sorrow, and not be reflected upon afterward as a cruel and painful memory. The "Farewell Discourses" of the Fourth Gospel mark exactly that — a farewell, a separation, an imminent bereavement. Jesus explains precisely why his coming again in glory cannot be accomplished without this going away. His disciples will suffer agonies at his departure, like a woman giving painful birth (Jn. 14:2ff.; 16:7; 16:16-22). In a sense, just as John advances the joy and exaltation of resurrection into the crucifixion, so he brings the grief and loneliness and waiting of Easter Saturday forward into the Upper Room.

Despite all these qualifications, the Fourth Gospel clearly remains a decisive biblical witness to the inseparability of the death of Christ and his resurrection, and to the view that the cross, though real and grievous, was not a moment of defeat but the manifestation of eternal glory. If so, there are other New Testament voices which — precisely to announce the same gospel, that Christ's death is for the world's salvation and the source of new life — focus upon the humiliation and abysmal horror of the cross, the more dramatically to offer good news to the broken sinners for whose sake, and in whose company, Christ died. Thus all the Synoptic accounts of the passion, despite their internal variation, stand in some contrast to that of John. They emphasize the great distress and sorrow of Jesus the night before his death (Mk. 14:33ff. and parallels), and highlight the abuse and mocking he receives on the cross itself (Mk. 15:29ff. and parallels). Above all, with amazing frankness, Mark and Matthew report that Jesus died not with a cry of achievement on his lips, but with a howl of desolation (Mk. 15:34; Mt. 27:46).[37]

This Synoptic version of the crucifixion story, with its shocking portrayal of a man at the end of his tether, in both spiritual and physical collapse, surely

---

36. Cf. Newbigin, *Light Has Come,* pp. 263-64.

37. On these and other contrasts between the Synoptics and John in their passion narratives, see von Balthasar, *Mysterium Paschale,* e.g., pp. 70-71, 100ff., 119ff.

needs to be heard simultaneously with John's account if we are to listen "in stereo" to the word of the biblical gospel. And yet the history of reaction to and interpretation of just this portrayal of the cross reveals how difficult the Christian community has always found it to adopt an Easter Saturday vantage point and consider the death of Christ in its own scandalous light. It is not impossible that Luke himself found it unfitting to portray the church's Risen Lord, the Son of God, as having died feeling forsaken by his Father. The so-different sense of confidence with which the Lucan Jesus entrusts his spirit to the Father at the moment of death (Lk. 34:46) could reflect an alternative eyewitness memory from that used by Mark — whose unflattering account of Jesus' godforsakenness and desolation could never have been "invented" by the gospel writers but must be based on history. But even that leaves us asking why Luke *selected* the easy memory for preservation in preference to the scandalous.[38]

Whether or not we may fairly accuse Luke and John of softening the offensiveness of Christ's broken forsakenness, it is beyond dispute that subsequent exegesis has frequently attempted to do so. In particular, appeal has been made to the overall character of Psalm 22, of whose first words Christ's cry of dereliction was a quotation, as an expression not of despair but of righteous trust in Yahweh's faithfulness in the midst of suffering.[39] Yet although it was common in the Judaism of Jesus to evoke an entire Psalm by reference to its opening verse, it strains credibility that Jesus would have uttered words complaining of God's distance if that was the opposite of his true feelings, especially when the same Psalm itself provides some of the most moving expressions of God's attention and closeness to the afflicted (e.g., v. 24).

What we see here, already detectable in the New Testament perhaps, and certainly common ever since, is the church's inclination to look for ways of blunting the cruciform sharpness of Christ's earthly destiny. Instead of listening to its own story of the cross with the ears of first-time hearers, who have no choice but to let events unfold at their own pace, faith, theology, and preaching have taken advantage of what they already know to anticipate the resurrection. Yet it must also be said that it is the Christian tradition itself, especially as that is enshrined in the creeds and confessions of the church, which guards most jeal-

38. See J. Sobrino, *Christology at the Crossroads,* trans. J. Drury (Maryknoll, N.Y.: Orbis Books and London: SCM, 1978), pp. 191ff. Sobrino, though, surely goes too far when he accuses Luke of having "prettified" Jesus' death (p. 185).

39. See, e.g., W. Kasper, *Jesus the Christ,* trans. V. Green (London: Burns and Oates and New York: Paulist Press, 1976), p. 118. See also E. Schillebeeckx, *Jesus: An Experiment in Christology,* trans. H. Hoskins (New York: Seabury and London: Collins, 1979), pp. 289ff. Cf. von Balthasar, *Mysterium Paschale,* p. 125; also J. L. Mays, "Prayer and Christology: Psalm 22 as Perspective on the Passion," *Theology Today* 62.3 (Oct. 1985).

ously and awkwardly the integrity of the cross, and refuses to let it be trivialized, canceled, or absorbed. Again and again, when called upon to define its own faith, explain its gospel, or summarize the tradition of which it is the steward, the church has spoken, implicitly at least, of the second day as marking the death of Jesus Christ off from his rising.

Whereas in the narrative of John, where the cross itself means triumph, and the day between the days is already the day after salvation's climax, Christian dogma resolutely insists upon a break, an interval of both time and meaning, between the darkness and the light. Significantly, the tradition which Paul received, and then passed on to the Corinthians, was that Christ died for our sins according to the Scriptures, *that he was buried,* and that he was raised the third day (1 Cor. 15:3-4). Here resurrection is not permitted to verge upon the cross, instantaneously converting its death into new life, still less to trespass death's own borders and thus to *identify* the cross with glory. Instead, death is given time and space to be itself, in all its coldness and helplessness. Again it is especially typical of the Reformed Confessions that for the Westminster Shorter Catechism the humiliation of Christ, begun in birth under the law, and leading to the cursed death of the cross, consists finally in his "being buried, and continuing under the power of death for a time."[40] The Apostles' Creed, less ancient than its name suggests, yet universally honored and confessed throughout the West and providing a framework for so much dogmatic thinking, is even more careful, in its succinct way, to throw a cordon sanitaire around the cross against the encroachment of Easter. Indeed, it is remarkable that so terse a statement, otherwise so economic with its words, should be so profuse, to the point of pleonasm, when it speaks of the interval between the cross and Easter. Christ was not only crucified but dead; not only dead but buried. And as the Creed narrates it, that burial was neither a passive laying to rest, nor a fleeting, momentary hiatus, before the activity of the third day. On the contrary, the break is significant and occupied — an active interval in which something *happens:* "he descended into hell."

---

40. *The Shorter Catechism* (Westminster, 1648), Q. 27. Cf. *The Scots Confession* (1560), ch. 9: "that he suffered not only the cruel death of the cross, which was accursed by the sentence of God, but also that he suffered for a season the wrath of his Father which sinners had deserved"; *The Westminster Confession of Faith* (1647), ch. 8: "was buried, and remained under the power of death, yet saw no corruption"; and *The Larger Catechism* (1648), A. 50: "Christ's humiliation after his death consisted in his being buried, and continuing in the state of the dead, and under the power of death till the third day, which hath been otherwise expressed in these words: 'He descended into hell.'" These Westminster documents are included in *The Book of Confessions* (Louisville: Office of the General Assembly, Presbyterian Church [U.S.A.], 1991).

It is not important here to decide either what the Apostles' Creed meant to convey when it first spoke of this *descensus ad infernos*[41] or how we might interpret and appropriate such a doctrine now. It is significant, however, that here the church's theology does so graphically interrupt the story's movement from the first day to the third. Time and events are forcefully intruded between the cross and the empty tomb. Here, we are told, we must stop and ponder, must absorb the brutal facts, let the realization sink slowly in that Christ's life is finished and done, that he has drunk the cup of mortality to its last, most hellish drop. Yet, ironically, the clouds of ambiguity roll back over the second day here once again, just when it seemed that a significant, independent territory between cross and resurrection was emerging out of the mists and coming into sharpest focus. For again rival interpretations present themselves of what the "descent into hell" actually means — the one aligning it with the death of Christ, the other with his resurrection. If these alternatives could be held together in tension, then there would be hope, even here, that the story of salvation would be heard both as it sounds upon first hearing and as those familiar with its plot transform it in their minds. But of course competing theories do not tolerate such even-handedness. Each seeks our consent to the exclusion of the other.

As before, it is the cross which faces the greater threat of exclusion — the cross as it stands on its own ground, and its own dark aftermath, before its shadows are lifted by the dawn of Easter's light. To be sure, there have been bold interpreters, especially at the time of the Reformation, willing to take the "descent into hell" at its face value. That did not mean speculating in a quasi-geographical manner about a visitation of Christ to the netherworld of classical mythology, or about the "limbo" in which medieval theology imagined the ancient patriarchs and saints to be awaiting the promised time of Christ's arrival. Rather, the descent into hell was understood to express the fathomless depths of suffering which Christ endured on the cross and in his death. As the victim of divine judgment, he sank into an unimaginable abyss of evil and horror, to a point of measureless distance and unendurable separation from the love of God.[42]

41. Western reference to the descent into hell did not begin to appear in the credal tradition until the fourth century (though it may well have appeared in some much earlier Eastern credal settings), and was not incorporated into the Apostles' Creed until considerably later. See J. N. D. Kelly, *Early Christian Creeds,* 2nd ed. (London: Longmans, Green and Co. Ltd., 1960), pp. 378-83.

42. Thus Calvin, though unwilling to conceive that Christ might have lost his faith as death approached, does insist that the "descent into hell" refers to his spiritual sufferings beyond those of bodily death. For in his death he had to "grapple hand to hand with

38

A more comfortable, and common, interpretation, however, has been that Christ's descent into hell marks the point not where his humiliation is intensified and made most hellishly complete, but, on the contrary, where that humiliation ends, to make way for exaltation. It is a symbol not of Christ's defeat in lowliness but of his exaltation in victory — an expression, therefore, not of the destructiveness of the cross but of its salvation, and the offer of that salvation to all perpetrators of sin and all victims of death.[43]

---

the armies of hell and the dread of everlasting death." See J. Calvin, *Institutes of the Christian Religion* (hereafter: *Inst.*), ed. J. T. McNeill, trans. F. L. Battles (London: SCM and Philadelphia: Westminster Press, 1960), II.xvi.10; see also II.xvi.8-12. This view, which relates the descent into hell with the agonies of the cross itself, had been adopted previously by some of the medieval mystics such as Nicholas of Cusa and Pico della Mirandola, and was to become common in Reformed circles. See, e.g., *The Heidelberg Catechism,* Q. 44: "Why is there added, 'He descended into hell?' A: That in my severest tribulations I may be assured that Christ my Lord has redeemed me from hellish anxieties and torments by the unspeakable anguish, pains and terrors which he suffered in his soul both on the cross and before." Karl Barth has taken a similar line to that of Calvin, interpreting hell as ultimate exclusion from God and the verdict of God upon sin, whose curse can be ended only by God's own bearing of judgment. See, e.g., *Dogmatics in Outline,* trans. G. T. Thomson (London: SCM and New York: Philosophical Library, 1949), pp. 118ff. Luther took a yet bolder line than Calvin, thinking of Christ's endurance of hell as happening at and *after* the point of death, not simply on the cross and before it. Christ is for a time surrendered up wholly into the hands of the Devil and subjected to the full wrath of God's judgment. "He descended into the deepest of all depths, under the law, under the devil, death, sin and hell; and that, I think, is verily the last and lowest depth" (*Sermon,* on Eph. 4:8-10). But as early as Melanchthon, Luther's followers began to interpret the descent into hell in terms of Christ's exaltation rather than his humiliation, and that became standard in Lutheran dogmatics. Cf. A. E. Lewis, "The Burial of God: Rupture and Resumption as the Story of Salvation," *SJT* 40.3 (1987): esp. 344; also Moltmann, *Way of Jesus Christ,* pp. 189ff. The case for an "Easter Saturday" theology based on the descent to hell is well made by G. Sauter, "Jesus the Christ," *SJT* 37.1 (1984): esp. 9.

43. This interpretation, which was common throughout the patristic period, was perpetuated by Thomas Aquinas and adopted by the Council of Trent, but also survives in much Protestant evangelicalism. It is regularly built upon the rather slender exegetical foundation of two texts in 1 Peter. These speak of Christ as going to preach to the spirits in prison (1 Pet. 3:19), and of the gospel being preached to the dead who have been judged in the flesh (1 Pet. 4:6). The accent in this interpretation is thus on both the *completeness* of what Christ has achieved, and its *scope:* the offer of salvation to those who have died before the saving death of Christ. Whether the notion of the "descent into hell" is the most appropriate solution to the alleged problem of the retroactive validity of Christ's death is a matter for personal judgment. The problem itself is created by naive conceptions of time and eternity and by neglect of the *vicarious* nature of our Lord's humanity. For more on the doctrine of the descent into hell and its history, see W. Pannenberg, *Jesus: God and Man,*

What theme could be more impeccably biblical, and more central to the life and mission of the Christian church, than that Christ, by his cross and resurrection, has defeated sin and destroyed the powers of death and hell?[44] Yet precisely because it is not *without,* but *through,* the cross, that newness of life and death's defeat are accomplished — that God uses what is *weak* to overcome what is powerful (1 Cor. 1:27) — the good news of resurrection is itself under threat when the suffering and the folly, the humiliation and the impotence, the godlessness and the finality of the cross of Christ are minimized. This constitutes the core thesis of the study now embarked on. The "descent into hell" can, of course, be certainly heard as a word of victory and power which does *not* minimize the wretchedness and powerlessness of the cross but highlights with the most vivid symbolism what that impotence means for the defeat of the powers-that-be and the victory of grace and love and life. But when the Creed's second-day narrative, that Christ died, was buried, and descended into hell, is heard and told *solely* as a word of victory, in the fear that that victory would be threatened if Christ, or even *God,* really experienced the judgment and the godforsakenness of hell, then we may wonder if the story of salvation has not again been seriously distorted through familiarity. If death and hell are only defeated by the divine submission *to* death and hell, then for the gospel's own sake is it not imperative that nothing cancel out the deadly hellishness of all the Son of God endured?

It would seem once more, then, that if we adopt a second-day vantage point which takes time to regard the death of Christ in all its unabbreviated malignancy and infernal horror, we both protect the cross itself and throw into sharpest relief the *resurrection* gospel: that out of just such a cross as this, and the occupied grave that followed it, come life and joy and hope. And whereas the interval of the second day forces us to hear the first day and the third in or-

---

trans. L. L. Wilkins and D. A. Priebe (Philadelphia: Westminster and London: SCM, 1968), pp. 369-74; and W. Pannenberg, *The Apostles' Creed in the Light of Today's Questions,* trans. M. Kohl (Philadelphia: Westminster Press and London: SCM, 1972), pp. 90ff.; also O. Weber, *Foundations,* vol. 2, pp. 102-4. Cf. von Balthasar, *Mysterium Paschale,* ch. 4; *Glory of the Lord,* vol. 7, pp. 228ff.; and *Credo: Meditations on the Apostles' Creed,* trans. D. Kipp (New York: Crossroad and Edinburgh: T. & T. Clark, 1990), pp. 53-54. See also S. Bulgakov, *The Wisdom of God* (London: Williams and Norgate and New York: Paisley Press, 1937), p. 137.

44. See, e.g., Heb. 2:14; 1 Jn. 3:8; Rev. 1:18; 20:13-14. On the theme that atonement consists in Christ's victorious battles against the satanic forces of darkness and sin, as found in Scripture and developed throughout the history of theology as the "classic" doctrine of salvation, see esp. G. Aulén, *Christus Victor,* trans. A. G. Herbert (London: SPCK, 1935).

derly, narrative sequence, we are thereafter able to hear the drama again in such a way that "the day between the days" unites what first it separated, and allows us to understand the Good Friday story with the pre-knowledge of its sequel, and the Easter tale in the light of its preamble.

We spoke at the beginning of Easter Saturday as a "no-man's-land," and later of the protection it offers to territory on either side. The image thus slowly taking shape can now be recognized: it is a boundary.[45] A boundary, after all, is an invisible line, anonymous and ambiguous, easy to ignore and belonging no-where. Yet it exists to *create* identity and to *assign* belonging. The division it marks — visibly with a wall, invisibly with a map line — actually creates enti-ties on either side, by at once separating and relating them. Neighborhoods, counties, states, countries, hemispheres: all these are what they are because of the borders which keep them apart yet simultaneously make them adjacent. And just because they are so significant in their insignificance, so visible in their invisibility, so creative in their anonymity, boundary points become places of tension, argument — and insight. Though it is at the boundary between them that rivals compete, it is also at their meeting point, and looking both ways, that one can see both sides and secure a bilateral perspective from which to judge between their arguments, and perhaps a balancing point or axis upon which to affirm them both. Possibly we are on the way to some insight into the meaning of Christ's cross and resurrection if and when we can stand — as, in-triguingly, so few in history seem consciously to have done — at the ambigu-ous, invisible, and apparently insignificant boundary between Good Friday and Easter Day. Where better than at the Easter Saturday grave to see with clarity the vivid contrast between the humiliation of the crucified Christ and his glori-

---

45. The term "boundary situation," invented by Karl Jaspers, has been used to great effect in contemporary theology, e.g., by H. Thielicke, who bases his theological ethics on the framework of the conflicts which arise on the boundaries of both personal and public life. But the concept was popularized above all by Paul Tillich, who used it in the title of an autobiographical essay: P. Tillich, *On the Boundary* (New York: C. Scribner's Sons, 1966 and London: Collins, 1967). Tillich attempted to understand his own life, and all of hu-man existence, in terms of the need to live between alternative possibilities, neither of which can be wholly affirmed nor wholly rejected. Cf. Tillich, *The Protestant Era,* trans. James Luther Adams (Chicago: University of Chicago Press, 1948 and 1957); also M. K. Taylor, *Paul Tillich: Theologian of the Boundaries* (London and San Francisco: Collins, 1987). For a famous interpretation of Christ himself as "the boundary," who stands be-tween me and God, and thus between the old and new "I," see D. Bonhoeffer, *Christ the Center,* trans. J. Bowden (New York: Harper & Row, 1966), pp. 61ff. In the United Kingdom this work is entitled *Christology;* cf. 2nd trans. by E. Robertson (London: Collins, 1978), pp. 60ff.

ous exaltation? Where better to find the wisdom which can unite cross and resurrection inextricably, and discover truth in such foolishness as presence-in-absence, powerful weakness, and life-giving death? Where better to hold in equilibrium the first-time hearing of the gospel story and its constant retelling by the people of faith?

CHAPTER TWO

On the Boundary between
Yesterday and Tomorrow

I. A Grave with the Wicked

Those who have heard the central, three-day Christian story and have traversed the path from cross to garden discover at the boundary which the second day interposes between the death of Christ and his resurrection a point of ready access which allows the mind and heart easy movement and a fertile cross-reference between the two. For the first-time traveler, however, the boundary is a frontier-barrier obstructing forward progress. One can go no further, for no more of the story has been told, no territory ahead illuminated. The end, it seems, has been arrived at; and one can only look back, review the steps already taken, and remember the events of yesterday in their own light — or lack of it. This is actually a formidable prospect for contemporary believers. For we have in fact looked over the barrier to the other side and therefore find it difficult now to put ourselves back in the shoes of those who have not. In any case, the Good Friday scene, when observed from the first Easter Saturday, is intrinsically unbearable.

What do we see if we make the effort and muster the courage to examine the cross of Jesus Christ from the second-day frontier, looking back without knowledge of the future? The sight is melancholy, terminal, disastrous. Yesterday a man suffered hellishly and died; was buried; and is now perhaps *in* hell. That makes today a day of godlessness and putrefaction. What are we to make of his death after all he did and said and was in life? What does his dying make of us if he was the Life he said he was?

If there is one word to describe what happened yesterday, it might be "failure" — though at once that seems open to misuse, its sting too easily pulled, made innocuous, even admirable. For failure *can* be grand, heroic, the glorious near-miss of an underdog who goes down fighting, having exerted great and noble efforts against yet greater odds.[1] But yesterday's was different: the ignoble failure one deplores, finds embarrassing or plain despicable, the failure less of the *weak* than of the *wrong*. On Good Friday such guilt is everywhere, the ignominy and disgrace universal.

It has been noticed that Mark's Gospel, in particular, takes pains to implicate all the actors equally — save the principal — in the moral failure of this day. Treacherous Judas; weak disciples, first asleep and then in flight; desperate priests and abusive guards; cowardly Peter and calculating Pilate; violent soldiers and jeering passersby: truly a "solidarity in sin unites all those involved . . . [as] Mark brings the crucified Messiah face to face with the barriers of human guilt."[2] Though each claims innocence, actually all the representatives of humanity are integrated by the passion narrative into collective accountability for the death of Jesus (cf. Rom. 3:23; 11:32). "No one wishes to be responsible. That is why they are all guilty."[3]

This catalogue of universal human failure leaves Jesus alone, isolated, "despised and rejected" (Isa. 53:3), repudiated by the people of God whose mission he sought to fulfill, forsaken by the disciples he chose to follow him. Yet do we not deceive ourselves if we think that the scandal of Easter Saturday is the *innocence* of this man in contrast to the guilt of which he is the victim? Is it not ob-

---

1. See, e.g., Moltmann, *Crucified God,* p. 48.

2. M. Hengel, *The Atonement,* trans. J. Bowden (London: SCM, 1981), p. 67. See Mark 14:17–15:32. The Gospel of Mark is particularly important for us in this context, both because its own character and structure, as the telling of a story, most clearly make it a paradigm and norm for all Christian narrative theology and because the story which Mark tells is, with such exemplary exclusiveness and concentration, a story of temptation, passion, and death: the primordial *theologia crucis,* "theology of the cross." See, e.g., E. Best, *Mark: The Gospel as Story* (Edinburgh: T. & T. Clark, 1983); *The Temptation and the Passion: The Markan Soteriology* (Cambridge: Cambridge University Press, 1965); *Disciples and Discipleship: Studies in the Gospel According to Mark* (Edinburgh: T. & T. Clark, 1986); and "Sermon for St Mark's Day," *Irish Biblical Studies* 15 (Apr. 1993): 63-71; J. Blackwell, *The Passion as Story: The Plot of Mark* (Philadelphia: Fortress Press, 1986); G. G. Bilezikian, *The Liberated Gospel: A Comparison of the Gospel of Mark and Greek Tragedy* (Grand Rapids: Baker Book House, 1977); and W. Telford, ed., *The Interpretation of Mark* (London: SPCK and Philadelphia: Fortress Press, 1985). See, too, W. C. Placher, "Narratives of a Vulnerable God," *Princeton Seminary Bulletin* 14.2 (1993): 134-51. Above all, perhaps, see R. H. Gundry, *Mark: A Commentary on His Apology for the Cross* (Grand Rapids: Eerdmans, 1993).

3. Von Balthasar, *Mysterium Paschale,* p. 115; cf. pp. 112-19.

vious that the failure of *Jesus* dominates the scene, that the outstandingly guilty one is he himself? He is not apart from but implicated in the "solidarity of sin," standing not on the bright but on the dark side of "the barriers of human guilt." The death of Jesus yesterday was the death of a *sinner;* he rests today, dishonored and decaying, "in a grave with the wicked" (Isa. 53:9).[4]

Irresistibly, no doubt, the circumstance of Jesus at this moment evokes such memories of Isaiah's Servant, who suffers for the sin of others, and the all-too-familiar good news that Christ has sinlessly borne the sins of the world. In his innocence he has submitted, first in the foul waters of the Jordan and then in the bloody waters of the cross, to baptism for sin's repentance, becoming cursed for us in order to deliver us and save us from our sin (e.g., Mk. 1:4-9; 10:38; Lk. 12:50; Rom. 6:1ff.; Gal. 3:13; 2 Cor. 5:21). Yet if we are genuinely to hear the gospel as it unfolds, we must ruthlessly postpone all such triumphal, redemptive, saving thoughts and texts which might modify the original, stark, accusatory verdict of the second day. On the day after his death Jesus is no hero, savior, or redeemer. He is dead and gone, convicted as a sinner, a rebel and blasphemer, who has paid the price of tragic failure. He simply died, and his cause died with him, quite falsified and finished.[5]

Theologians today sometimes suggest that the death of Jesus was merely an accident which overtook him: not a conclusion which issued from the logic of his preceding life but an illogical and disconnected catastrophe which befell him.[6] The principal target of that interpretation is the idea that the events of Jesus' life and death were not genuinely open history but the predetermined outworkings of a divine plan for "salvation history." The corollary of that, also subject to attack, is that Jesus was clearly conscious of this plan and went through his life, or at least his years of ministry, willing and securing his own demise and liquidation. In fact, a much more subtle and imaginative analysis will discover no contradiction between Jesus' deliberate choice of firm obedience to his Father's will, which had death as its inescapable conclusion, and his

---

4. We shall return to this theme below, including Martin Luther's uncomfortable but absolutely essential insistence that Christ did not die as a pure, innocent person, but as *peccator pessimus,* the worst of sinners, cursed for our sins with which he becomes totally identified.

5. No one in modern theology has expounded this failure of Jesus with more persistence, poignancy, and eloquence than Donald MacKinnon. See, e.g., D. M. MacKinnon, *Borderlands of Theology* (London: Lutterworth Press, 1963), esp. pp. 103ff.; *Explorations in Theology,* vol. 5 (London: SCM, 1979), ch. 13: "Ethics and Tragedy"; and "The Role of the Doctrines of the Incarnation and the Trinity," in R. W. A. McKinney, ed., *Creation, Christ and Culture* (Edinburgh: T. & T. Clark, 1976), ch. 7.

6. This view is particularly associated with Pannenberg. See his *Jesus,* esp. ch. 7.

involvement in freely developing historical events which were beyond his control even though they meshed with his own intentionality.[7] In other words, the fate of Jesus was neither an accident nor suicide, but the result of actions against him by *others,* who had been provoked by actions of his own. In order to obey the God he believed in, he had entered into conflict; and he died both as victim to those who contradicted him, and in consequence of his own opposition to them.[8]

Can we evade the judgment, however, that this was a conflict which Jesus *lost;* that in both its active and passive aspects the encounter between him and his opponents ended decisively in their favor, massively and tragically to his own discredit? Given this second-day tragedy, Jesus' occupation of the tomb throughout that Sabbath, can we offer other than a quite negative judgment on his controversy? Have his claims not been invalidated drastically? Do all those provocative, hope-inspiring questions that he asked not now demand in answer a curt, disappointed No? Yet the dispute he failed, it seems, to win was fundamental, concerning nothing less than the nature of God and the truth of human life. At issue in the first was the relation of law to gospel; in the second, of power to love.

Jesus was manifestly not opposed to the law as such. Indeed, he both reaffirmed some of its provisions (Mk. 10:19ff.) and removed some of its exemptions (Mk. 10:2-12). And when he summarized the Ten Commandments in terms of love, this abbreviation of their details was anything but a relaxation of their demands (Mt. 22:40). Yet precisely here he excited to bitter debate some who saw themselves as standing sentinel over the law. For the law could not consist of love unless it were itself an instrument and tool of love — unless, that is, the God of righteous, holy love were as such a God of grace and mercy, whose justice embraced the very ones whom the judgments of the law excluded. Yet how could religion and morality tolerate such inversions of their logic, such blows to their values and anticipations?[9] For God to judge sin and yet welcome and forgive those so judged was an offense to sense which would tear the fabric of social and religious life, would marginalize the righteous keepers of the law and subversively, intolerably, give priority to those who were the "out-lawed."

7. This interaction of active obedience and passive victimization, of power and helplessness, epitomized in the accusation "he saved others, himself he cannot save," is profoundly analyzed by Frei in *Identity,* ch. 10. See also R. S. Wallace, *The Atoning Death of Christ* (London: Marshall, Morgan & Scott and Westchester, Ill.: Crossway Books, 1981), pp. 93ff.

8. See esp. Moltmann, *Crucified God,* pp. 126ff.

9. See Moltmann, *Crucified God,* pp. 120ff., 128ff.; Pannenberg, *Jesus,* pp. 251ff.; and Sobrino, *Crossroads,* pp. 204ff.

Nevertheless, in the logic of what Jesus preached, precisely this folly was the delight and fulfillment of God's law. Intolerance, legalism, and self-righteousness were *not* the true purpose of Torah — itself as much an expression of God's faithfulness and gracious, covenantal mercy as any conception of justifying grace in the New Testament. Yet in the hands of some authorities that law had been hardened and distorted, made vindictive and unpardoning, the antithesis of grace. But, said Jesus, the imminent rule of God would reveal and restore the truth about the law. It would mete out justice by having compassion upon the poor and the weak, the outcast and the fallen; it would not lay heavy burdens on those who must be righteous but could not, but would accept the unrighteous as they were, without condition, and then tell them to go in gratitude and sin no more.[10]

10. Not all interpreters would agree that in attacking legalism and the harshness of the law, Jesus was affirming the law as truly the expression of love and grace. It has been traditional both in systematic theology and in NT studies to see grace as the antithesis and abolition of the law and thus to endorse the negative assessment of the law often attributed to Paul. Yet Jesus is clearly portrayed in the Gospels as challenging the Pharisees' understanding and exercise of the law, not in order to destroy but to fulfill the law (Mt. 5:17); likewise it can be shown that Paul was not hostile to the law as such when he asserted that Christ was the end of the law (Rom. 10:4), since righteousness comes by faith, apart from the law. The law follows rather than precedes the gracious covenantal promises of God, and acts like a schoolmaster on behalf of grace (Gal. 3:15-29). Those set free from the law through faith must still fulfill the whole law as that is summed up in the commandment to love one's neighbor (Gal. 4:13-14). Alternative interpretations of Paul and Jesus with respect to the law divide Luther and Calvin, and their respective traditions. For Luther, the law is the opposite of grace since we cannot fulfill it, yet in trying to do so we rely on our own righteousness, not that of Christ's. Law is thus the Devil's instrument, though controlled by God's "left hand" to compel us to accept the graciousness of the "right." See G. Wingren, *Creation and Law,* trans. R. Mackenzie (Edinburgh: Oliver & Boyd and Philadelphia: Fortress, 1961); and *Credo,* trans. E. M. Carson (Minneapolis: Augsburg, 1981), ch. 2; also Bultmann, *Theology of the New Testament,* vol. 2, pp. 259ff. For Calvin, on the other hand, the law reflects God's own nature and determines the pattern of life even, or rather especially, for those justified by the grace of Christ. See *Inst.* II.vii. The view that Paul had a positive, robust understanding of the law, even while convinced that not the law but the person of Christ was the basis of God's salvation for Jews and Gentiles alike, has emerged with great conviction recently, on the basis of studies of Judaism at the time of Jesus. From there, the rethinking extends to the view that the NT distorts the attitudes of "the Pharisees" and "the Jews" with polemically negative caricatures, falsely suggesting that the Judaism of Jesus' day was uniformly legalistic, petty, and self-righteous. See esp. K. Stendahl, "The Apostle Paul and the Introspective Conscience of the West," *Harvard Theological Review* 46 (1963): 199-215; also in Stendahl, *Paul among Jews and Gentiles* (Philadelphia: Fortress, 1976 and London: SCM, 1977); and E. P. Sanders, *Paul and Pales-*

Far more than the words of Jesus, it was, of course, his pointed deeds which provoked such fury and retaliation. In the name of gracious law he scandalously acted out his challenge to the harshness of the law, embodying in concrete action his claim that the Sabbath law should serve humanity, not enslave it (Mk. 2:27); that unforgiving judgment on those who broke the moral code simply exposed hypocrisy in the accuser (Jn. 8:3ff.); and, above all, that God's coming kingdom, already inaugurated, would welcome and uplift the insignificant, the downtrodden, the despicable (Mk. 10:14; Lk. 19:1ff.). This was a dispute about God, but also about Jesus himself and his authority: Did the severe, meticulous law of "the Pharisees" (as the evangelists, perhaps less than accurately and objectively, depict them) express and execute the truth of God and the real nature of God's law, or did this son of the carpenter, who forgave the sins of tax collectors and malefactors?

Even to pose and practice such a question, however, was foul, intolerable blasphemy. Anybody who claimed to speak for God (for whom — holy, transcendent, sovereign — surely no one else may speak) and to reinterpret God's law (which surely never could be altered) stood self-convicted as the enemy of God and the breaker of God's law. And that conviction could be no less visible and concrete than the actions which provoked it. Beyond mere words of provocation, he had acted out his challenge to the law and its interpreters; likewise, the guardians of that interpretation had actively vented their outrage and their insecurities. And whatever the technical purity of the process by which they tried him and accomplished his disposal,[11] there can be no doubt that in the death of Jesus the law of these "Pharisees" had done its work, had triumphed over this rival to its authority. Blasphemy had been exposed for what it truly was — a challenge to the God they worshiped and to the law they cherished. And since no credible agent of God's righteousness and rule could come to

---

tinian Judaism (Philadelphia: Fortress Press and London: SCM, 1977), esp. pp. 474ff.; *Paul, the Law and the Jewish People* (Philadelphia: Fortress Press, 1983 and London: SCM, 1985); and *Jesus and Judaism* (Philadelphia: Fortress Press and London: SCM, 1985). See also J. Riches, *Jesus and the Transformation of Judaism* (London: Darton, Longman & Todd, 1980), esp. ch. 6; S. Westerholm, *Israel's Law and the Church's Faith* (Grand Rapids: Eerdmans, 1988); J. D. G. Dunn, *Jesus, Paul and the Law* (London: SPCK and Louisville: Westminster/John Knox Press, 1990); J. H. Charlesworth, ed., *Jesus' Jewishness: Exploring the Place of Jesus within Early Judaism* (New York: Crossroad, 1991); and H. Räisänen, *Jesus, Paul and Torah,* trans. D. E. Orton (Sheffield: Sheffield Academic Press, 1992).

11. For the view that Jesus' death was not "judicial murder," but that the Sanhedrin's judgment was in accordance with its own law, see, e.g., O. Weber, *Foundations,* vol. 2, pp. 196ff. Doubts on this are expressed by, among others, Pannenberg in *Jesus,* pp. 253ff. See also Schillebeeckx, *Jesus,* pp. 312ff.

such a scandalous fate as this, the cross and the grave that Sabbath day were proof enough of the justice of their charge. In the excruciating circle of legalism's logic, the sentence this man endured ratified the verdict he sustained: his accursed, godless death confirmed the godless sacrilege of his offense. With double certainty, then, his cause against the law had failed.

Although convincingly exposed as a breaker of the law, Jesus lay dead in the grave of the wicked, not strictly as a blasphemer but as a rebel and subversive, a usurper and pretender. Stoning was the punishment of the Jews for blasphemy; crucifixion that of Rome for sedition. This man had preached the imminence of God's new rule, had been hailed by some as the Messiah, had refused to reject unambiguously the vaulting sobriquet "King of the Jews." Thus with understandable misunderstanding the imperial occupiers of Palestine had perceived and liquidated a threat to their authority and peace.[12] But what had they misunderstood, and what had they perceived?

They failed to understand that no violence, no hatred, no resistance which met oppression on its own terms and fought it by its own rules could possibly be the policy or goal of this "King," who preached, and claimed to found, the reign of love. What damage could be done to the mighty structures of the empire by one who gave Caesar his due, who scorned the bigotry which hated an infidel and punished the ungodly, and who pictured a kingdom of freedom, peace, and love in which the distinction between friend and foe would lose all meaning? Yet, with their unseeing eyes, the Romans had rightly perceived a radical and dangerous subversion — with clearer intuition, it seems, than those who still characterize the preaching of Jesus as spiritual and therefore not political. What, in fact, could be more "political," a more complete and basal challenge to the kingdoms of this world, to its generals and its lords, both to those who hold power and to those who would seize it, than one who says that his kingdom is not of this world, and yet prays that the kingdom of his Father will come and his will be done *on earth*. This is an aspiration for the world more revolutionary, a disturbance of the status quo more seismic, an allegiance more disloyal, a menace more intimidating, than any program which simply meets force with force and matches loveless injustice with loveless vengeance. Here is a whole new ordering of human life, as intolerable to insurrectionists as to oppressors. It promises that forgiveness, freedom, love, and self-negation, in all their feeble ineffectiveness, will prove more powerful and creative than every system and every countersystem which subdivides the human race into rich and poor, comrades and enemies, insiders and outsiders, allies and adversaries. What could an earthly power, so in love with power as to divinize it in the per-

---

12. See Moltmann, *Crucified God*, pp. 135ff.; and Sobrino, *Crossroads*, pp. 209ff.

son of its emperor, do with such dangerous powerlessness but capture and destroy it? It could change everything were it not extinguished, and speedily.

So destroyed and extinguished it was. That happened yesterday. And now on the day after, on the boundary, with "the King of the Jews" stripped of his absurd crown and mock purple panoply, lying stiff in the impotence of death, who can deny to human power the smug satisfaction of such sweet success? The potentates of the world have conquered that "other" kingdom and its king, have satisfied themselves that God is power and that power is God. Until the last moment he has had his chance to prove things otherwise, to verify that there really is some divine enigma by which the vulnerability of love can mightily conquer everything, provide miraculous escape from the tightest of tight corners. But the "Son of God" has not come down from the cross; his brand of nonresistance has, after all, proved no match for military might or the politics of fear. He has failed against the politicians and soldiers as against the priests and moralists; and beside him in the grave has been laid to rest the naive dream that the meek shall inherit the earth.

Even though it was obviously a defeat for himself that the controversy between Jesus and the forces of law and of power came to such pathetic closure, it would almost trivialize the grim reality of Good Friday and the day that followed to describe this as a "personal failure." Many women and men, after all, put heart and soul into their beliefs and projects, only to see their mission come to nothing, their resources prove unequal to their vision. By giving such a denouement as that on Golgotha so familiar a summation as "personal tragedy," we would give notice that this is an experience we can identify with and readily understand — that it fell within our frame of reference as human beings who ourselves dream dreams and suffer disappointment. Yet that is precisely what is not true of the death of Jesus of Nazareth — whose very identity was at stake in his mission and message in a way quite unparalleled and unfamiliar to our experience.

There are, to be sure, historical problems as well as theological mysteries blocking our understanding of what it means to say that Jesus' preaching and purpose were *himself*. At issue is his relationship as a human being to the kingdom of God whose arrival he promised and announced, and thus his relationship to that kingdom's God.[13] We have no detailed picture of his inner mind or

13. On the enormously complex subject of NT Christology, which involves the attempt to unravel how Jesus thought of himself from how his contemporaries prior to the resurrection thought of him, and to distinguish both from how the post-Easter church developed its understanding of him, among the best introductions are: O. Cullmann, *The Christology of the New Testament,* trans. S. C. Guthrie and C. A. M. Hall (London: SCM

consciousness — how he himself thought of those relations; and we cannot separate with unerring deftness those gospel reports of what he said and did which give reliable evidence of his self-understanding from those colored by the church's later faith in him. There need be no reasonable doubt, however, that in oblique and self-effacing ways, which it often took unnatural perspicacity in others (including, so ironically, the deranged and demonized) to recognize, he did present himself as the focus and embodiment of the judgment he warned about and the good news he proclaimed.

Thus Jesus could refuse to be equated with "the one alone who is good" (Mt. 19:17), and yet speak to the God of heaven with outrageous familiarity and in unheard-of terms of closeness (Mk. 14:36); and he seemed to find an all-satisfying purpose in aligning his will in perfect but costly harmony with his Father's (Mt. 6:9ff.; Lk. 22:41ff.). He could be mystifyingly secretive and evasive if asked about messiahship (Mk. 8:27-38; Mt. 26:63-64) and yet boldly declare that there and then the messianic promise was being fulfilled, as he performed acts of daily healing which could only be interpreted as the signs, long-promised, of the one who was to come (Mt. 11:2-6; Lk. 4:16-21). God's judgment of the world in the final days would do no more than corroborate the decisions and divisions his own ministry created between those who spurned and those who clung to him (Lk. 12:8-10; cf. Mt. 25:31-46); and as "the Pharisees" quite properly had said, his declarations of forgiveness, and his redefinitions of what the law required, were such that God alone could rightly make (Mk. 2:6ff.; Mt. 5:21-48).

So it is that through all the conflicts between Jesus and his contemporaries, and over all the questions he provoked, there stands out one query, supreme in its decisiveness yet stunning in its implications. It is the question of identity: Who is this person, this son of Joseph the carpenter, also called "Son of Man" and "Son of God"? Humble, bent on obedience and service, prepared to suffer, and unassertive when challenged and provoked, he nevertheless thrusts the word "I" into the center of deadly controversy, making his own person the critical test of the credibility of his message. He says, ". . . but I tell you" (Mt. 6:43-44); he asks, "Whom do you say that I am?" (Mk. 8:29); and he compels his

---

Press and Philadelphia: Westminster Press, 1959); J. D. G. Dunn, *Christology in the Making* (London: SCM and Philadelphia: Westminster Press, 1980); R. H. Fuller, *The Foundations of New Testament Christology* (New York: C. Scribner's Sons and London: Lutterworth, 1965 and Collins, 1969); Schillebeeckx, *Jesus;* J. Macquarrie, *Jesus Christ in Modern Thought* (London: SCM and Philadelphia: Trinity Press International, 1990); P. Fredriksen, *From Jesus to Christ* (New Haven and London: Yale University Press, 1988); and Moltmann, *Way of Jesus Christ.* Much more discussion of Christology follows below.

hearers to spell out their own suppressed, gestating question, "Who is this?" (Mt. 21:10).

In the answer to that question, of course, lies hidden the question of who these questioners and critics are themselves.[14] For if this man coming out of Nazareth also comes from God, then (what a scandal and impossibility!) God's own messianic kingdom has arrived before their very eyes (Lk. 4:16ff.), in judgment and deliverance, sifting hearts and minds and deeds, demanding repentance and bestowing freedom. Conversely, if he not be of God, then the future still tarries teasingly and the world's endless unredemption continues unabated, the poor remaining hungry and the mighty proud, sinners still doomed, justice still trampled underfoot, faith and hope still disappointed. So: Is he then the one who is to come, or should they look for someone else (Mt. 11:3)?

What possible alternative does the grave of Jesus that Easter Saturday offer to the verdict that the future must be looked for elsewhere and in some other? Whatever fears he had aroused were needless, whatever hopes illusory. "If you be the Son of God," he had been told, prove your identity and "come down from the cross" (Mt. 27:40). But he had made no escape and secured no heavenly intervention; and in the end all his claims of familiarity with God, directly spoken to "Abba" or obliquely hinted at, seemed hollow, incredible, and unspeakably ironic. Of course, many human deaths are affairs of pain and rank despair. Even today a death in bed, blessed with some dignity, at the natural end of life, or at least with medical aid to mollify the worst agonies of disease, is a luxury denied to many human beings. Dying for millions continues to be violent, unnatural, and grotesque — the malign incursion of natural catastrophe or human bellicosity, the grim harvest of primitive economics or modern means of travel. And in the best or worst of deaths, the final moments of any human being's life may just as easily be filled with loneliness and terror as with serenity and hope. We miss the point of Calvary, therefore, if we quantify its tragedy and locate its uniqueness in the degree of suffering inflicted upon the body of this man, or even on his spirit.

The critical question is not "How much?" but "Who?" Who is this man but a mere mortal, creaturely and finite, and a fool or fraud at that, who, so convinced of the propinquity of God, dies aware only of God's abysmal, utter dis-

---

14. On the Christological question "Who?" in which those who question the identity of Christ are confronted with the question of their own identity, see D. Bonhoeffer, *Christ the Center*, pp. 27-37; Moltmann, *Crucified God*, ch. 3, "Questions about Jesus"; and T. F. Torrance, *Theology in Reconstruction* (London: SCM Press, 1965), ch. 7, "Questioning Jesus Christ."

tance? It is not unknown for men and women to feel abandoned and forsaken, certain that God has departed, if ever present in the first place. But the very person who has called God "Father" and who has staked his life on the promise that the Lord had sent and loved him, and was a God of steadfast grace and flowing mercy? For *him* to die abandoned and rejected, forsaken by the loving, heavenly Father to whose will he had sacrificed his all, surely meant wretchedness unlimited, shattering disillusionment, and hellishness unknown.[15] Yet, forswearing any exegesis that tries to soften this blow, for him or us, are we not forced, by Mark and Matthew at least, to hear the story of how the "Son of God" died in just such godforsakenness as this (Mk. 15:34; Mt. 27:46)?

Who, then, is the ultimately guilty one in this fiasco of the cross? Have we, even now, glimpsed the full dimensions of the crisis hanging over human history on the second day? Clearly, as he hangs alone in desolation on the cross, and then is buried in the cold, malodorous godlessness of the Arimathean's tomb, Jesus of Nazareth has failed — not so much in the collapse of his controversies as in the undermining of his personhood. Perhaps he had been deceiving others, or was perhaps himself deceived, when he claimed the authority of heaven, acting as regent of God's final kingdom and the embodiment of eschatological good news for all the nations. Or perhaps those were indeed his credentials, and he had finally betrayed them — his filial faith and obedient trust weighed and found wanting in the ultimate test? The narrative does not allow us to dismiss this last possibility. On the contrary, it confronts us from the very beginning not with some hypothesis about his origins worth examining, nor with a neutral set of options concerning his identity, but with the uncompromising gospel declaration that this *is* the Son of God, approved, beloved, and sent, and that into his earthly hands had been delivered the authority of the transcendent Father (Mk. 1:1; Mt. 3:16-17; 11:27).

Of course, many theologians would contend that a rational faith today cannot begin with such *assumptions* about the God-relatedness of Jesus Christ, and wish to substitute for such a "Christology from above" a procedure "from below" which assumes only the humanness of Jesus and lets the facts of history direct us, by the rational process of inductive thought, to what may or may not be true of his divinity. Only on the third day, then, from the standpoint of the resurrection, may we look back (according to this method) and see this mortal man's relationship to God retroactively confirmed.[16] But even those who thus

---

15. See, e.g., Moltmann, *Crucified God*, p. 148.

16. For a fuller discussion of these two methods in Christology and the debate between them, see Ch. 6, sect. II, below. For now, see Gunton, *Yesterday and Today*, throughout. As he indicates, the term "Christology from below," in particular, represents a wide va-

stay within the sequence of the narrative, as disclosed to the first-time hearer, and affirm only in retrospect — what had seemed so dubious at the time — that it was indeed the Son of God who had been crucified since it was God who subsequently raised him: even these have not escaped, but rather have intensified, the mystery which molds the cross of Jesus into a cosmic question mark. For if, whether from the beginning or from the end, "from above" or "from below," we are ready to hear that this is a story about God's own Son, and therefore God's own self, we can no longer shut our eyes to the terrible possibility, not that *he* has failed God in his death, but that in his death *God has failed him.* Then this sad Saturday would not be a *Shabbat* of the Lord, still less the final, messianic Day of the Lord, but the worst, most diabolic day in history, truly the day of the Devil.

We are close here to the unthinkable; and we can perhaps begin to see why all of us, not least those otherwise inclined to take all the Bible says at face value, prefer not to treat too seriously Christ's dying cry of dereliction on the verge of hell. For if God is his Father, and if he is truly forsaken in his death, then we are dealing with a *real* and not just a *felt* abandonment. Perhaps God *has* actually abandoned the beloved, only Son, has indeed "delivered him up" (Rom. 8:32)[17] and left him to endure death's agonies and torments all alone? Is

---

riety of approaches and presuppositions; but among its most prominent and careful exponents is W. Pannenberg, whose aim is precisely to establish the resurrection as the historical fact which gives rational ground for a retroactive authentication of Jesus' earlier claims to be the Son of God. Some of the difficulties with this we shall encounter later; but in addition to which is commonly put to Pannenberg, whether the resurrection can really be established according to the "language of facts" rather than that of "promise," there is real doubt whether he takes the scandal of the cross seriously enough. He tends to see the resurrection as canceling out or redeeming the disaster which befell Jesus rather than analyzing, with Moltmann, what it means that precisely the Crucified One was raised, and that the Risen One remains the *crucified* Messiah. See Gunton, *Yesterday and Today,* pp. 18-24; Moltmann, *Crucified God,* esp. pp. 166-78; also Zahrnt, *Question,* pp. 284-91. On Pannenberg's theology see W. Tupper, *The Theology of Wolfhart Pannenberg* (London: SCM and Philadelphia: Westminster Press, 1973); A. D. Galloway, *Wolfhart Pannenberg* (London: Allen & Unwin, 1973); D. H. Olive, *Wolfhart Pannenberg* (Waco, Tex.: Word Books, 1973); C. E. Braaten and P. Clayton, eds., *The Theology of Wolfhart Pannenberg* (Minneapolis: Augsburg, 1988); D. P. Polk, *On the Way to God: An Exploration into the Theology of Wolfhart Pannenberg* (Lanham, Md.: University Press of America, 1989); and S. J. Grenz, *Reason for Hope: The Systematic Theology of Wolfhart Pannenberg* (New York and Oxford: Oxford University Press, 1990); also Ford, ed., *Modern Theologians,* vol. 1, ch. 13; and Grenz and Olson, *Twentieth-Century Theology,* pp. 186ff.

17. Note the unmistakable and unflinching linguistic connections in the NT (*paradosis*) between God "giving up" the Son, and the Son "giving himself up" to death, on

it then the *Father* who has proved a failure in the end, breaking faith with the Son who went from Gethsemane to Calvary staking everything on the filial certainty of heavenly companionship? Has the Father of Jesus pushed through to the end with that terrible, unfatherly betrayal from which the son of Abraham was eventually reprieved (Gen. 22)?[18] Has it indeed been left to the Son of *God* to discover the questionableness of the Psalmist's confidence, that "even though I walk through the valley of the shadow of death, I fear no evil, for you are with me" (Ps. 23:4)?

Only later will we discover how far it is possible to think our way through and perhaps beyond the unthinkability of God's abandonment by God, and to squeeze some meaning and coherence out of its incomprehensibility. But our present lack of understanding does nothing to soften or cancel the accusation against the Father of the crucified on the second day, as Jesus lies entombed. It is finally God, no less, who is under indictment and in the dock. "In the death of Jesus," says Jürgen Moltmann, "the deity of his God and Father is at stake."[19] How could a Father be fatherly and yet forsake the supposedly beloved Son? How could God be God, and good, and yet allow such victory to evil and to death? If it is true that the Son of God has been left to die without God, then he shares a grave with the wicked not only because he has lost in his conflict with the powers-that-be, and been discredited. Much worse, he has died in company with the *godless,* and with those who in their own wickedness have rejected God and been rejected by God; and with those victims of the wicked's godlessness who are left in isolation to suffer without deliverance and vindication.

Is then the absence of God in the death of Jesus the failure of divine *love,* which subjects the Son to unmerited judgment and an outrageous fate? Or is it the failure of divine *power,* which deserts the Son to helplessness before the onslaught of overwhelming evil? Either way, the worst accusation of all, this second day, is that by failing the Son, the Lord of all has failed the world and all who share the Son's humanity. If the Son himself has been delivered up to destruction, what hope is there for the rest of us? Good Friday, it seems, marked not just the last day for Jesus and the end of *his* hopes, but the last day for all hope and for the cosmos as a whole: the apocalyptic end of everything.

---

the one hand, and, on the other, human acts of betrayal and surrender, i.e., the "betraying" of Jesus by his disciples and his being "handed over" and "delivered up" to the Jewish and Roman authorities who destroyed him. See esp. Mk. 9:31; 10:33; 14:10, 41-42; 15:1, 15; Rom. 8:32; Gal. 2:20; 1 Cor. 11:23. See also von Balthasar, *Mysterium Paschale,* esp. pp. 107ff.

18. See, e.g., von Balthasar, *Mysterium Paschale,* pp. 111ff.; Moltmann, *Crucified God,* p. 241.

19. Moltmann, *Crucified God,* p. 151; cf. pp. 175ff.

The Word of God, which creates all things and on which all reality constantly depends, has fallen silent. Has a remorseful, disappointed God said again, as at the Flood (Gen. 6:7), "I repent of all that I have made," and left creation to its sorry fate?[20] How could *we* trust the love of God if even upon Christ, innocent, holy, and divinely cherished, there has been poured out such ruthless curse and wrathful malediction? How could *we* hope in the power of God if not even for the sake of this heavenly victim could God triumph over the earth's ungodly executioners? If at this moment a person who lived so close to God is lying in a criminal's grave, rejected, relationless, and God-betrayed, what reason has the world to believe that even on the best of days God is with *us*, comforting the weak, resisting the tyrants, vindicating the innocent, battling the demonic? And if it is only through the eternal Word and Son that we see, know, and have access to the Father and Creator, then the silencing of the Word and the terminating of the Son hellishly certify the world as an emptiness wherein no God is visible, knowable, or touchable, or quite possibly even present.[21]

So we have not really listened to the gospel story of the cross and grave until we have construed this cold, dark Sabbath as the day of atheism. For now, the solitary sounds to be heard are throaty cries of triumph from the world's satanic despots, and strangulated wails of disbelief from their indignant, disillusioned victims. What we hear from Job in the Old Testament is silently uttered again in the New, on Good Friday and its sequel. It is the outraged exclamation that God is dead. The Lord has forsaken the divine path of righteousness and truth, and relinquished the heavenly throne to the earthly lords of falsehood and injustice. In the death cry of Jesus of Nazareth there resonates the ageless, universal protest of human suffering, affronted by the crookedness of human life, whereby the innocent are tortured and the diabolic flourish. Is the cry of the Crucified, "Why?" not echoed by every victim of oppression, accident, and disease, as they plead for meaning in the midst of the world's absurdity? And the silence that greets his question is the same sorrowing stillness of the cancer ward and the concentration camp. Any present-day Mary who, in the spirituality of the imagination, would revisit the ancient grave of the wicked to anoint its godforsaken corpse, need attend only to the angry pain of her own dying neighbor and to the wretched dispossessed of her own divided world. And those who would hear what the narrative of Christ crucified and buried really says today need simply listen to the alienated disbelief of their own bewildered generation and to the guilty pleadings of their own lonely, disappointed hearts.

20. See von Balthasar, *Mysterium Paschale,* pp. 127ff.; and Barth, *CD,* IV/1, 306.
21. See von Balthasar, *Mysterium Paschale,* p. 49.

II. Raised for Our Acquittal

A new day dawns, however, transforming everything!

Those who have followed the story as it unwinds have not been permitted to anticipate the surprises and inversions of this astonishing daybreak. The barrier of the second day, obstructing any view of the horizon and obscuring the approaching light, has compelled us to "continue under the power of death for a time," enduring the total darkness of the cross, the grave, and their uncompromised finality: the end of Jesus, the end of God, the end of everything. For all we knew the drama had run its course and reached its tragic denouement — the inaction on the stage indicating not that we should wait expectantly for more, but that the play was ended: it was time to go home.

Yet suddenly the curtain rises and the lights come up again; the brightness dazzles eyes grown accustomed to the dark, making it impossible to see and understand exactly what is happening, yet revealing enough to let us know that a new act is taking place, incredible and stunning in its contrast to all that went before.

Many of the traditional — and vital — questions concerning the resurrection event are not our concern here: How are the Easter occurrences to be reconstructed, given the discrepancies of detail between the evangelists? What is the relation between the appearance stories and those of the Empty Tomb (on which Paul, for example, is silent)? What *sort* of appearances were these, and where should they be placed on the interpreter's scale between "events of fact" and "events of faith"?[22] This last question focuses the central issue of the histo-

---

22. Literature on the resurrection in its multiple aspects is, of course, immense; but among the most important discussions are: R. R. Niebuhr, *Resurrection and Historical Reason* (New York: C. Scribner's Sons, 1957); L. Goppelt et al., *The Easter Message Today,* trans. A. Attanasio and D. L. Guder (New York: T. Nelson and Sons, 1964); M. Barth and V. H. Fletcher, *Acquittal by Resurrection* (New York: Holt, Rinehart and Winston, 1964); W. Marxsen, *The Resurrection of Jesus of Nazareth* (London: SCM, 1970); W. Künneth, *The Theology of the Resurrection,* trans. J. W. Leitch (London: SCM, 1965); R. H. Fuller, *The Formation of the Resurrection Narratives* (London: SPCK and New York: Macmillan, 1972); Moltmann, *Theology of Hope,* esp. ch. 3; Pannenberg, *Jesus,* esp. ch. 3; Schillebeeckx, *Jesus,* pp. 320-97; J. E. Alsup, *The Post-Resurrection Appearance Stories of the Gospel-Tradition* (Stuttgart: Calwer Verlag, 1975); T. F. Torrance, *Space, Time and Resurrection* (Edinburgh: Handsel Press, 1976); U. Wilckens, *Resurrection,* trans. A. M. Stewart (Edinburgh: St. Andrew Press, 1977); Mackey, *Jesus: the Man and the Myth,* ch. 3; J. F. Jansen, *The Resurrection of Jesus Christ in New Testament Theology* (Philadelphia: Westminster Press, 1980); P. Perkins, *Resurrection: New Testament Witness and Contemporary Reflection* (Garden City,

ricity of Christ's raising and appearing; and although it is not necessary here to decide between the description of the resurrection as *ordinary* history and some term indicating occurrences on the borderline of history, between the temporal and the eternal, the present and the future, time and the end of time, it is important to recall from Chapter One the insistence of Hans Frei that, as far as the narrators are concerned, the resurrection stories are *"history-like."*[23] They are integrated, that is, into a single sequence of events in which the *quality* of the happenings at the end of the narrative is no different from that of those at its commencement. Between the telling of the story of the cross and the telling of the resurrection, no sudden and unsignaled change of reference and intention takes place, such that the first means what it says, as a temporal incident, while the latter has some *other* meaning, mythic or symbolic, some religious a priori distinct from the events actually described.

Those who choose today to interpret the resurrection as a myth, so that in contrast to the crucifixion we are not dealing in the resurrection with a further, separate event, must at least come to terms with the fact that for the original storytellers this particular contrast between Good Friday and Easter Sunday did simply not exist. On the contrary, it is remarkable with what uniformity the New Testament preachers and gospel writers present the story of the cross and resurrection as a linear chain of homogeneous episodes. For them, these events constitute good news, worthy of proclamation, precisely because they do *not* relate to different worlds and distinct realities at either end of the chain — the one particular and factual, the other timeless, universal, mythical — but constitute a single drama, with continuity of character, setting, and reference, the whole of which they have witnessed and seen happening before their eyes. The simple structure which forms the basis of the early Christian message — later much elaborated — is of two comparable and sequentially connected occurrences whose combined meaning lies in the equilibrium and interrelation between them. The gospel goes simply thus: "This Jesus, . . . whom you crucified and killed . . . God raised up" (Acts 2:23-24).[24]

N.Y.: Doubleday, 1984); G. O'Collins, S.J., *Jesus Risen* (New York: Paulist Press, 1987) and *Interpreting the Resurrection* (New York: Paulist Press, 1988); G. R. Osborne, *The Resurrection Narratives: A Redactional Study* (Grand Rapids: Baker Book House, 1984); P. Carnley, *The Structure of Resurrection Belief* (Oxford: Clarendon Press, 1987); Moltmann, *Way of Jesus Christ,* ch. 5. For a very lucid survey of some of the central issues in current thinking about the resurrection, see the Inaugural Address as Professor of New Testament at Austin Presbyterian Theological Seminary of my esteemed friend and partner John E. Alsup: "Resurrection and Historicity," *Austin Seminary Bulletin* 103.8 (Apr. 1988): 5-18.

23. In this context see esp. Frei, *Identity,* ch. 13: "Jesus Identified in His Resurrection."

24. Cf. esp. Acts 2:32, 36; 3:13-15; 5:30; cf. Rom. 1:3-4; 1 Cor. 15:3-7.

Now, of course, the companion point, which we have in fact already made, is that within this single sequence, with its homogeneity and linearity, the combined meaning of the two episodes lies exactly in the *contrast* between them. It is not in the attachment of a myth to an action, but in the contrast between two very different actions, that the cross and the resurrection comprise a Word to be heard and told. When, from the boundary of the second day, we may finally peer over to the other side and see the territory of Easter, we are met with an entirely new and unexpected vista, astounding in its reversal of the previous tragedy. For darkness there is light; for despair, hope; and for failure, victory. And we see why Scripture and Creed, despite the anonymity of Easter Saturday, have been at such pains to stress the *burial* of Jesus. That intervening time of waiting, that strange, empty territory standing so ambiguously between his dying and his rising, sever those two happenings and keep them disjoined in their very continuity. Unified in quality and structure, as acts in a single drama, they are — at least on first hearing — contrary in content and separate in performance, and only thus do they form a narrative that is worth repeating.

Perhaps the greatest threat to the gospel story, that the Jesus whom Jerusalem murdered God raised from the dead, is the well-intentioned effort of preachers and theologians to make these scandalous, mysterious happenings comprehensible by suggesting that they mirror the familiar. In particular, illuminating analogies are frequently adduced from the phenomenon of the cyclic: the rhythms of sleep and waking, death and birth, which we experience night and morning and observe through all of nature's seasons, as well as in our own passages from infancy to parenthood to death.[25] Above all, the Easter victory over death is domesticated as the supreme instance of a *generic* immortality — the inherent capacity of human beings, or more usually of the human soul or spirit, to survive the grave and achieve eternal unity with our transcendent source.[26] All

25. See esp. Barth, *Dogmatics in Outline,* p. 122. This theme is revisited at slightly greater length on pp. 343-48 and 428-35 below.

26. In a famous little book, which perhaps exaggerates the contrast but nevertheless makes a necessary and all-too-often blurred distinction, O. Cullmann has contrasted the platonic and the Christian views of death in just these terms. Are we essentially immortal because, despite the corruption of our bodies, our souls are indestructible? Or is God alone immortal, and his creatures mortal but offered the *gift* of sharing in God's eternity through his once-for-all act in raising Christ from the dead? See O. Cullmann, *Immortality of the Soul or Resurrection of the Dead?* (London: Epworth, 1958); also in K. Stendahl, *Immortality and Resurrection* (New York: Macmillan, 1965), ch. 1. See also E. Jüngel, *Death: The Riddle and the Mystery,* trans. I. and U. Nicol (Edinburgh: St. Andrew Press, 1975); and M. J. Harris, *Raised Immortal* (Basingstoke: Marshall, Morgan & Scott, 1983 and Grand Rapids: Eerdmans, 1985). Again, see pp. 418 and 434 below.

these attempts to treat the events of Good Friday to Easter Day as particularizing a familiar universal, either anthropological or cosmological, disregard the very narrative which presents them as *history* — as new, unique happenings, involving a particular, unsubstitutable person at an unrepeatable point in time and space.

Still worse, when Christ's resurrection is explicated as following naturally upon his death, evolving out of it in accord with the predictable laws and rhythms of life, *both* the awful finality of Calvary *and* the sheer graciousness and unexpectedness of Easter are compromised. Easter is surely the *ground* of hope for human beings and the cosmos rather than an *example* of life's self-perpetuation; for it identifies God, and God alone, as the one who makes death's defeat possible, and gives new existence to the terminated (Rom. 4:17). Jesus was dead and buried; his life was finished and done with. No rhythm of nature, no innate capacity of humanness, could return him from the grave. Only God's grace and power, accomplishing a new act with and upon a man totally deceased, could win that victory. And although upon reflection it seemed appropriate to the church to say that Christ *rose* from the dead because of what Easter revealed about his own relationship to God, the Lord of Life, the first Christian instincts were to emphasize rather the total passivity of this person in his resurrection, as in his death, and to attribute all the power and action to his God and Father. This Jesus who was crucified and killed *God* has *raised* from the dead.[27]

No doubt the very disciples who stood up boldly in Jerusalem on the Day of Pentecost to narrate this news, risking this antithesis between what the city had done to Jesus in crucifying him and what God had done for him in raising him again (Acts 2:23ff.), are foremost examples themselves of the newness of the gospel drama's second act, and of the transformation it secures. Having loomed large in the catalogue of failure around the cross, they are now changed people. They are visible proof — indeed, once the Risen Christ has again departed, the only visible proof — of the miracle which has overtaken the world. Their courage and their conviction, their love and hope, supplanting in a few short weeks their wretched fear, disloyalty, and doubt, embody and justify their claim that the long-awaited Day of the Lord has after all arrived, and the final reign of God begun. But they are witnesses to this great turning point in history, and evidence for it, precisely because they are *not* the agents of it. Their own words stress that they are not responsible for what has happened, but that God is. Only God's agency and power can provide both the continuity and the contrast which make this single, two-part story what it is.

This is to say that if the ultimate failure confronting our unwilling eyes on the second day was not that of Peter and Judas, Caiaphas and Pilate, or even Je-

27. See Barth, *CD*, IV/1, 299ff.; and Frei, *Identity*, p. 120.

sus, but of *God,* exposed to the charge of forsaking the Son and abandoning the world, then it is God who is supremely vindicated on Easter morning. The one who delivered up Christ to the forces of death has now delivered him out of their clutch. "The same God has turned another page after the first one, has spoken a new word after the first one."[28] And this second word is a resounding Yes to Christ, to us — and even to God's own identity and deity, fatherhood and love, all so questionable while the Son lay buried. Today, after all and at last, despite all those harrowing questions from yesterday, we can be sure that Christ "was not abandoned to Hades, nor did his flesh see corruption"; for the Father raised him up to be exalted at the Lord's right hand (Acts 2:31-33). Whatever abandonment and hell Christ endured for a season — and nothing in the new act cancels that out and makes it not to have happened — was neither God's final word to him nor last transaction with him. Now we know that the final word is precisely what God has said from the beginning: that the victories of sin and evil, injustice and inhumanity, are at worst penultimate; in the end God shall be the conqueror of the conquerors. The Father of Jesus, it is now confirmed, does not allow to the executioners and tyrants, to the satanic and the sordid, a final triumph. As at the first, bringing form out of chaos, calling existence out of nothing, so now the Lord is again self-justified as creative in barrenness, life-giving in the midst of death (Gen. 1:1ff.; Rom. 4:17ff.); and far from being abandoned, we, too, may be persuaded now that nothing in life or death shall finally separate us from God's love (Rom. 8:39). Acquiescing neither in the unrighteousness of which we are guilty, nor in the injustice to which we fall victim, God has been vindicated, proven righteous, powerful, and loving, by raising up Christ for our acquittal and release (Rom. 4:25).[29]

28. Barth, *CD* IV/1, 297; cf. Moltmann, *Theology of Hope,* p. 200; and Pannenberg, *Jesus,* esp. pp. 66ff.; cf. also E. Schillebeeckx, *Church: The Human Story of God* (New York: Crossroad, 1990), pp. 127ff.

29. This is another point at which the present work differs essentially from Milazzo's very profound study of suffering and death in the Bible, *The Protest and the Silence.* While focusing primarily on the theme of God's absence and silence in the OT, Milazzo also discusses the death of Jesus, rightly adopting an "Easter Saturday" perspective which acknowledges the despair, darkness, and godlessness of Calvary which faith must simply confront while waiting for God to speak: "So the cross stands. And with it stands the silence of God . . . that marks the beginning and the end of Christian theology. For about the cross nothing can be said. . . . About God, no word can be spoken. For until God has spoken, until God has emerged from the darkness, only our death and our protest, only the cross and our humanity, only the hiddenness and the absence, remain" (p. 167). All of this is true and in accord with our own theme here — except for the absolutely crucial point that as far as Milazzo is concerned, God has never again spoken. There is no "word of the cross," only the silence; that is to say, there is no resurrection. Yet that, as we

Of course, when God's justice, power, and love justify themselves by justifying us through the raising of the Crucified, they do neither without justifying Christ himself. It was *his* failure and disgrace which were most public and blatant when they made his grave with the wicked. But God's raising of Jesus on the third day announces loudly to the world which killed him that every word spoken by this despised, rejected, and afflicted one was true. Who *but* God, the Maker of all, can bring the dead to life? Thus does the resurrection not only authenticate God's powerful deity and loving fatherhood; it also confirms and vindicates the divine Sonship of the risen one, which was so in doubt while his body lay interred throughout the second day.

Rival interpreters today suggest different forms which this authentication takes. Is Easter merely a *revealing*, a making manifest, of what we could and should have always known about Jesus? Should we not in faith have believed from the *beginning*, like the second and fourth evangelists, that this was God's Word enfleshed, and have heard long since, especially at the Jordan, God naming him as the Beloved Son? Or was it really impossible to be sure until this Easter moment that what he said was true, so that his rising at last *establishes* his Sonship, albeit with retroactive force?[30] In either case, and to a greater extent

---

argue here, both transforms Easter Saturday and reinforces its darkness and silence. Milazzo assumes, it seems, that resurrection *would* inauthentically transcend and deny the silence and godforsakenness of the cross. But that actually constitutes a surreptitious and unintended affirmation of "the theology of glory," which presumes indeed that the resurrection does exactly that to the cross. What we are seeking here is a perspective on the silence and godforsakenness of Easter Saturday which is *not* the last word about the cross but has been followed by the good news of victory — which in turn intensifies the silence of death even in the process of loudly proclaiming the vanquishing of death by confirming indubitably that the death and silence of Good Friday *were God's own*. Not because God has *not* spoken after the cross, but because God has so clearly spoken, is the silence of Easter Saturday literally so deadly serious.

30. See esp. Pannenberg, *Jesus,* pp. 135ff. Despite the weaknesses in Pannenberg's treatment of the cross and the questionableness of his attempt to treat the resurrection as historically verifiable, he is at great pains to assert this *retroactive* nature of Christ's legitimation in the resurrection. He opposes the view of Künneth in *Theology of the Resurrection,* that Christ became divine through the resurrection, insisting rather that from the perspective of Easter we can at last see that Christ has all along been one with God. On the other hand, because for Pannenberg history itself is retroactive, its meaning discoverable only from its end and goal (see esp. *Jesus,* pp. 390ff.), it is important that Christ has only been one with God from the beginning because he was raised from the dead. The authority of God we now know him to have always enjoyed is in fact only an anticipation of the authority the resurrection bestows upon him (p. 137). See also Pannenberg et al., eds., *Revelation as History,* esp. ch. 10: Pannenberg, "Dogmatic Theses on the Doctrine of Revelation."

than the defenders of either sometimes admit, Christ's claim to Sonship was surely questionable and doubtful as it lay buried and disintegrating with him in his failure.[31] But if Good Friday tends to falsify whatever it is we affirm of him at the point of his birth or baptism or resurrection, it is equally clear that Easter stands as a radical counterindication to the cross, confirms indubitably, gloriously, that someone "descended from David according to the flesh [has been] designated Son of God in power according to the Spirit of holiness by his resurrection from the dead" (Rom. 1:3-4).

As before, there is no possibility here of separating the "person" from his message. Indeed, as we have said, it is the resurrection which finally completes what Jesus had himself begun: the identification of the proclamation with its proclaimer. The church would now take his own announcement of the kingdom and reinterpret it as good news about *himself* — that it is in him, crucified and risen, that God's presence has been made manifest and the final rule of grace begun. Yet by identifying the gospel they had to preach with the person who came preaching and teaching and doing good, the first believers were also validating once and for all the things he said and did in his life and ministry as "gospel truth." His own message, subject to conflict and controversy, and seemingly quite discredited and defeated from the perspective of his tomb, is now drastically, triumphantly reassessed. The *emptiness* of the tomb says that if Christ is risen and exalted, his words and deeds are risen and triumphant too, verified and vouched for by the act of God's own power. It was *he* after all who had spoken the truth about the law of God and human power; his adversaries and accusers, who defeated and destroyed him, have been proven blind and wrong, their triumph penultimate and premature.

This sudden, breathtaking reversal of the Good Friday verdict on Jesus' conflict with his opponents is what gives Easter Day its special quality of cele-

---

31. As we noted earlier, if the resurrection retroactively identifies Jesus of Nazareth as the one who is and always was God's Son, that does not eradicate or cancel out the reality, horror, and negativity of the cross, with its tendency to falsify his Sonship. On the contrary, if from the perspective of Easter we know now that Christ had already been proleptically identified and authorized as God's representative throughout his life and ministry from their commencement, this simply (simply!) reinforces the scandal that in the cross there is contradicted and falsified that which God had begun and promised to confirm. Pannenberg cannot *both* argue, against Künneth and others, that Christ does not merely become Son of God at the resurrection *and* discount the indications of the crucifixion that he who in reality always has been the Son has become the godforsaken and rejected one. Apparent here again is Pannenberg's failure to deal seriously with the Christological implications of the cross, esp. in contrast to Moltmann — of whom much more below, on pp. 215-34 and 356-63.

bration and emancipation. The guilty despair and cold forsakenness of the second day give way on the third to joy, relief, deliverance. Today the mood is similar to that of guilty prisoners, sentenced to die, hearing the word "no condemnation" (Rom. 8:1), which means reprieve and pardon; of the terminally ill miraculously restored to health and vigor; of penned-in children at the end of term, spilling noisily out of school, relishing the endless prospect of freedom and of fun. Easter attests, incredibly for those who watched him die, that Jesus is indeed the one anointed by the Spirit to preach good news to the poor, release to captives, and recovery of sight to the blind, to liberate those who are oppressed, and inaugurate the climactic "Year of the Lord" (Isa. 61:1-2; Lk. 4:18-19). The "Pharisees" are falsified, their chains of legalism snapped. The iconoclastic God of Jesus has triumphed over the idols of religiosity and moralism, confirming what the Law and the Prophets had so often announced to deaf, unwilling ears: that Yahweh's justice is merciful and gracious. Now we know for sure that without condoning sin God is a God who loves the sinner, seeks out the lost, embraces the contrite breakers of the law, and elects as friends and chosen people not those who have merited favor through self-righteousness and effort, but cheats and malefactors who are spiritually flawed and bankrupt morally. What Jesus had spoken in daring declarations of forgiveness and practiced in outrageous acts of friendship has now received definitive, divine corroboration. In the impossible, shocking words of Paul, once Saul, whose personal history actually proved their truth, God is "a justifier of the ungodly" (Rom. 4:5) — made manifest as such through the raising of one who hung upon a cross of godforsakenness and was buried in a grave of wickedness.

Likewise the victims of the world's godlessness, those bruised and crushed beneath the heel of the powerful, have cause, on hearing Easter's story, to raise their heads in dignity and hope. In the curious logic of grace, the God of resurrection who welcomes home those who have done evil proves by the same token to be ruthlessly and tirelessly opposed to every form of evil, refusing to be reconciled to sin and the satanic. Easter is God's victory, in particular, over the deadly forces of pride and domination. By raising Christ, the weak and helpless victim of unjust cruelty, the Father not only vindicates the Son but verifies the faith for which the Son died — that the self-promoters who destroy others cannot prove victorious in the end; for the way to life leads only down the path of risky, loving self-expenditure and humble servitude.

The exaltation as Messiah and Lord of one who suffered, was bruised and wounded, and lay dead and buried in company with the powerless and tearful, with the exiled and executed of the world, is God's final affirmation that victory rests not with the earth's victors but with its victims, not with humanity's

64

mighty few but with its impotent many.[32] The day is coming when a Lamb that has been slain, vulnerable and blood-stained, will sit beside the throne, and his triumph will be shared by fellow sufferers who have likewise been abused by injustice, tormented by pain, crushed by sin, and terrified by death (Rev. 5:6-14; 21:1-8). God's indignant, powerful resistance to the evil which destroys humanity, and to the evil by which humanity destroys itself, has secured a decisive victory on Easter morning by giving new life to someone who had tasted the last, most hellish drops of human misery and demonic evil. And those who saw it happen, or hear tell of it now, cannot help believe and hope that in one person's victory lies a promise for us all. "For since death came though a human being, the resurrection of the dead has also come through a human being; for as all die in Adam, all will be made alive in Christ" (1 Cor. 15:21-22, NRSV).

Yet is even this the full measure of the joy and victory of Easter morning? Is the word from the empty tomb — what Karl Barth famously called the "gospel of the forty days" between Easter and Ascension — solely a promise that Christ is the first of many — that after him, at the end of time, others also will be exalted, fulfilled, set free from evil, escape the human and satanic forces which retail death, and see the vision of God's peace and love become reality? That itself, of course, would be stupendous news, which could transform the present by allowing us to anticipate the end. Today must be worth living if tomorrow is worth trusting. The promise that we too, like the glorified "Man of Sorrows" (Isa. 53:3), shall be relieved of sin's burden, released from death's fear, have the tears of pain and loneliness wiped from our eyes, must change the way we deal with guilt and fear and suffering today.

Yet could it be even more amazingly true that this hoped-for, dreamed-of future in a sense arrived today, this first Easter Sunday? Has a mystifying telescoping of time brought the goal and end of history forward into the present, so that — noticed only by a few with eyes to see — God's tomorrow has already taken up residence in humanity's today?[33] Surely the Easter vindication of the

---

32. This biblical, cruciform dialectic of defeat and victory, power and powerlessness, is explored much more fully below. For now, see a series of moving sermons on this theme: J. Moltmann, *The Power of the Powerless*, trans. M. Kohl (London, SCM, 1983).

33. Once again this crystallizes a disagreement between Pannenberg and Moltmann, the two dominant proponents of a "theology of hope." For Pannenberg, the great significance of Easter is that the raising of *one* man from the dead promises, and therefore anticipates, the future general resurrection — the resurrection of *the dead*. It points forward to the imminent end of the world. For Moltmann, "resurrection is no longer the ontic presupposition of the final judgment on the dead and the living, but is already itself the new creation" (*Crucified God*, p. 176). The future is *now*, already arrived in the form of a promise which eschatologically shall be fulfilled when at last God becomes "all in all" at the end

preacher who declared God's kingdom to be close is God's own way of announcing that the new order has indeed dawned as a present reality, though by no means yet completed and perfected — so that those with ears to hear the promise may rejoice already, be acquitted of their guilt and set free from their bondage? What faith hears in the Easter narrative, and passes on to a sceptical and mocking world, is that justice, forgiveness, and reconciliation are not ideals or dreams but realities, facts embodied in a person who lives *now*, who with his words has already been restored to life and reigns in victory. The Risen Christ *is* what he promises and offers; he *is* our peace (Eph. 2:14), our justification (1 Cor. 1:30), and our hope (1 Tim. 1:1). For itself and for the world, the Easter community which lives with and in him asks for a renewal already given, prays for a peace already accomplished, struggles for freedom already guaranteed.

Such are the infinite contrasts, then, between the first day of our story and the third. Looking back from the boundary, Christ's cross and burial seemed the end of him and the end of everything, certainly the end of hope in God's justice, love, and power. Looking forward from the same vantage point, we see another end of the world, the end of its darkness, death, and tears and the arrival-in-advance of heaven. The world of unforgiving legalism and ungodly power, so jubilant and secure on Friday night, is on Sunday morning judged, condemned, and under threat of termination.

We have always said, however, that at the boundary which is the second day it is possible and necessary to look both ways, and that the boundary conjoins what it also divides. But how can these antitheses, these contradictory worlds at either side of their Saturday border, be united and held together in our faith, our understanding, and our ways of life and death? How is it possible for there to be a day in history which is both the day after the end of life *and* the day before the end of death, the day which remembers Christ's failure and his Father's, *and* the day which hopes for his and for God's future and therefore for our own? By now we have felt anguished trauma in the cancer ward and heard

---

(1 Cor. 15:28). But of course that statement of faith is contradicted by the continuing reality of the cross and the world's unredemption; thus the point of the resurrection becomes not one person's restoration to life before the many in the general resurrection, but the fact that it is specifically and uniquely the *crucified* and *forsaken* one who is raised, on behalf of all who suffer, are abandoned, and are unjustly victimized by the world's executioners. See Moltmann, *Crucified God*, pp. 166-78, and Pannenberg, *Jesus*, pp. 66-88. As we shall see below, however, there is a tendency in Moltmann so to emphasize the *eschatological*, not-yet-visible character of God's "kingdom" as to minimize the experience of present liberation amid history's still unrelieved bondage, and so to transcendentalize *God's* future for the world as to contradict and nullify both the present time and the chronological future — that tomorrow which awaits us on the *human*, temporal calendar.

the prognosis of no more pain and suffering in the future; we have had to tolerate the gloating of the executioners and have laughed to see the murdered one vindicated and enthroned; we have recognized the awful loneliness of guilt and have watched the pardoned dance like children in the playground. If the gospel story is that *both* kinds of scenario are serious and true, then it is *in* the very world of sickness, death, and sin that joy and play take place, and Christ is Lord; and it is *only* in the context of injustice, negativity, and despair that we dare to speak of hope. Remaining on the boundary line, we clearly have much more to hear and learn of how the place of crucifixion and the resurrection garden are connected to each other before we can aspire to understand the meaning of the burial ground which divides them like a chasm.

CHAPTER THREE

God in the Grave?

I. The Living among the Dead

It is not really true, a billion words of piety and scholarship notwithstanding, that the Easter morning emptiness of the garden tomb is the pinnacle of Christian faith and its deepest mystery. Rather, if it be true that the tomb is empty now, then the gospel's most luminous affirmation and its murkiest enigma relate to what has gone before — to the fact of the tomb's occupancy yesterday and to its occupant's identity. Who must the crucified have been, and why was he buried, if he is now the Risen One? That is, in the process of answering yesterday's questions and announcing good news for yesterday's world, the story of the third day raises a whole new set of questions. These drive us backward, demanding that we listen again to the story of the first two days if we would fully understand just what the good news of Easter actually is.

To revert from the empty tomb to the filled tomb is thus to cast no doubts whatever on the elation and surprise which its emptiness first evoked, and which we tried to share above. It *is* to doubt once more that "resurrection faith" is exhausted by, and should exhaust itself with, the clarifying of historical facts. Certainly "if Christ be not raised," then preaching is vain, faith futile, and creatures of hope most pitiable (1 Cor. 15:12-19). And if he be not raised in the manner that the narrative asserts, that is, in a "history-like" event along, or perhaps at the terminus of, this world's continuum, where it impacts upon historical, human life, the resurrection of Christ brings no good news to those for whom history is the place where they sin and are sinned against, where they die or are put to death. To bear transformingly upon the world of temporal occurrence, Sunday's vacant tomb and the succeeding appearances must be just as much occurrences of that kind, and as little mere symbols or interpretations, as Saturday's occupied tomb and its preceding passion.

On the other hand, what would be *news,* what would be new and *transforming,* about Easter if the resurrection belonged so exclusively to the world of ordinary occurrence, of sight and sound and science, that it were not about the transcending of that realm, the irruption into the world of suffering and sin, of novel, unimagined possibilities for freedom and forgiveness? On hearing the story of the third day as first-time listeners we have just been overwhelmed by its promise of contrast and discontinuity, the reassessment and reversal of the ordinary world of guilt and godlessness. Did all this not refer to a triumphal re-ordering of life *as we know it,* it would leave the women and men we know, and know ourselves to be, effectively untouched, with no new day to dream of, wait for, and edge toward. Yet exactly the same would be true were faith's new day less than radically *new,* not cast of necessity in the genre of dreams, promise, and anticipation but possessed already by sight, experience, and understanding. In order to be *gospel,* the story of the empty tomb must be a transcending Word, which offers to faith and hope the passing away of what is old and familiar, our passing beyond what humanity only too thoroughly knows and understands. Captive to present reality, we long for a disruption of the here and now, the breaking *open* of the vicious circles which entrap us, the breaking *down* of the limits of what we know and understand, the breaking *in* of the Spirit's fresh winds of new life and re-creation. Would the resurrection of Christ promise such seismic transformations did it register straightforwardly, exactly like his death, on the quotidian graphs of history, visible to finite sight, comprehensible to human understanding, graspable by immanent experience?[1]

Of course, it is tempting to reduce the Easter event to "the language of facts,"[2] confining it within the parameters of sight, understanding, and experience and asking, "What happened on Easter morning?" or "Who moved the stone?"[3] or "Do you believe in the bodily resurrection?" That may be excusable

1. "The rising of Christ cannot be discovered within the old frame of the old conditions of life which by his resurrection he has transcended, or be understood except within the context of the transformation which it brought about. . . . The evidence for the Resurrection can be handled and tested, appropriately, only within the orbit of its impact." Torrance, *Space, Time and Resurrection,* p. 37.

2. Pannenberg, ed., *Revelation as History,* e.g., p. 153; cf. Pannenberg, *Jesus,* esp. pp. 88ff.

3. This is to echo the classic attempt, at least at the popular level, to *prove,* through a kind of investigative journalism, that the tomb was empty, and by no means other than physical resurrection: F. Morison, *Who Moved the Stone?* (London: Faber & Faber, 1930). The fun-

as a reaction against the dissolution of the resurrection into a mythic interpretation of the life and death of Jesus, or the appearance stories into simply internal, subjectivized experiences of the disciples. It may even be intrinsically justifiable as an affirmation that Christ was raised still human, still incarnate, in continuity with and relevance for the known world of space and time and body. But it is also misleading, and may be counterproductive. For it could in fact *exclude* the possibility that the resurrection is so real in its novelty and transcendent otherness as to elude our poor grasp upon reality, and belong gloriously to the realms of mystery, which we cannot see or understand but only dream of.[4]

---

damental question which such empirical studies pose is not whether the evidence adduced amounts to convincing historical reconstruction, or whether the inferences drawn therefrom are logically compelling, but what place *proof* of the historical facts of the empty tomb and of the appearances has in a living knowledge of the Risen Lord. Faith's knowledge, though supremely rational, is also essentially personal and present; and it can surely not stand or fall with historical evidence and logical argument related even to this event of distant ambiguity. As Schillebeeckx puts it (*Jesus*, p. 644; cf. p. 348), "the resurrection of Jesus has often functioned . . . as the great miracle, accomplished in Jesus by God, of course, *yet without any relation to ourselves* [italics added]. It has been envisaged as something empirical and objectivized, as though, given the empty tomb and the appearances, it should really be obvious to believers and unbelievers alike, even if not with mathematical certainty, that Jesus rose." Schillebeeckx goes on to reject the antithetical position, that resurrection is merely "a symbolic expression of the renewal of life for the disciples." Without the subjective "Easter experience of the disciples, expressed in the mode of the appearances," they would have "had no organ that could afford them a sight of Jesus' resurrection. But beside this subjective aspect it is equally apparent that . . . no Easter experience of renewed life was possible without the personal resurrection of Jesus . . . in the sense that Jesus' personal-cum-bodily resurrection (in keeping with a logical and ontological priority: a chronological priority is not to the point here) 'precedes' any faith-motivated experience" (p. 645). This circularity, and the precedence within it, between the objective and the subjective preserves a balance which the approaches of "proof" and "myth," respectively, are at one in destroying. See also Torrance, *Space, Time and Resurrection,* esp. chs. 1 and 4.

4. As noted earlier, Moltmann disputes with Pannenberg whether the resurrection is to be spoken of in the language of historical fact or that of eschatological promise (*Theology of Hope,* pp. 76ff., 172ff.; *Crucified God,* pp. 172ff.; and *Way of Jesus Christ,* ch. 5, esp. pp. 214-15), arguing that the raising of Jesus Christ is not an event within ordinary history but a promise of whole new, eschatological possibilities *for* history which defy empirical description and verification. This, in turn, exposes Moltmann to the criticism that he is offering a *resolution* of the crucifixion less factual, and therefore less credible, than the cross itself. "If Jesus did not rise from the dead with the same historical reality as the historical reality of his crucifixion, then was not after all his despairing cry the truth?" G. Jantzen, "Christian Hope and Jesus' Despair," *King's Theological Review* 6 (Spring 1982): 5. More profoundly, it is often suggested that the suffering and "death" attributed to God in the "theology of the cross" must mean the termination of God if the *facticity* of the Easter vic-

Faith reduced to the knowledge of mere "facts" may betray itself as faith incapable of vision and of hope for what is unknowable and new. Worse still, such faith may undermine itself as trust and self-surrender to the grace of God.

Thus when resurrection faith amounts to a believer's certainty about the miracle of Easter morning, to a confidence defiant of all logic and experience that Jesus walked again in flesh and blood,[5] does it not verge upon *self-*

---

tory is not commensurate with that of the Good Friday defeat. Is it true, however, that the resurrection must be not only "history-like," but "historical" and factual in the identical manner of the crucifixion, in order to be a new act which reverses the despair and overcomes the death of the latter? On the contrary, resurrection as sheer *miracle,* the intervention par excellence of a *deus ex machina,* which canceled the cross and rescued Jesus from death, would be no good news at all. By exposing God as, after all, an omnipotent miracle worker, it would deny that the Creator is such a one as to become incarnate in the weakness of Christ's human flesh and the shameful powerlessness of his cross. It would, in fact, not solve but withdraw the problem of how God can suffer, and be identified with the crucified and buried Christ.

That is why Barth, e.g., for whom Easter actually happened in space and time, but as a unique, singular event of "prehistory," which cannot be grasped historically, insisted that the resurrection was not *miracle* but *revelation.* Resurrection confirms rather than cancels what we see in the life and death of Jesus: a God whose grace and truth are visible in the likeness of sinful flesh and the folly of the cross. And that is a possibility which even after Easter remains hidden from empirical observation and conception, and open only to the hearing of faith and the vision of hope and promise. See *CD,* IV/1, 283-357, esp. 332ff.

5. It is beyond our scope here in any depth to explore the enormous question of "the resurrection of the body," with reference either to Jesus himself or to those who are raised with him to "walk in newness of life" (Rom. 6:4). The narrative presents Jesus as recognizable in his Easter appearances — though not without ambiguity — with nail wounds visible and available to touch, and his capacity for the earthly and earthy unimpaired, to the extent of eating breakfast (Jn. 20 and 21; and see Ch. 4 below). This, like the Pauline hope for "the redemption of our bodies" (Rom. 8:23), attests a degree of continuity and preservation of identity beyond death, which opposes "resurrection" to the world-denying, anti-corporeal "immortality of the soul" associated with Platonism. On the other hand, it is Paul himself who argues that "flesh and blood cannot inherit the kingdom of God" (1 Cor. 15:50) and contrasts the physical body that is sown with the spiritual body that is raised (vv. 40ff.). (Cf. the remarkable juxtapostion in Jn. 6 of texts which seem in turn to emphasize [e.g., vv. 53ff.] and to dismiss [e.g., v. 63], the significance of the flesh of Jesus Christ.) Paul's concept of the "spiritual body," whose actual nature is clearly not yet known (1 Cor. 15:35ff.; cf. 2 Cor. 4:18 and 1 Jn. 3:2), is a hermeneutical reflection upon the Easter narratives, which themselves intersperse moments of unrecognizability and absence with those when the Risen Christ is seen. Such discontinuities between the pre- and postresurrection body of Jesus are in themselves surely enough to confound, on their very own premises, those who equate orthodox biblical faith in the resurrection with straightforward belief that Christ rose "physically" from the grave. I have discussed this at slightly greater length

confidence — that bravado of the intellect, that will to believe, which no longer rests all hope upon the act of God and the surpassing mysteries of love divine and power celestial? As the Risen Christ is known to his apostles no longer according to the flesh but according to the Spirit (e.g., 2 Cor. 5:16; cf. 10:2-3; Rom. 1:3-4; 8:13; 1 Cor. 3:1ff.; Phil. 3:3), might we not permit to the "carnal" intellect its problems, doubt, and difficulties, and trust through the Spirit of hope in the God who has redeemed us from the bondage of human wisdom and mental pride, but promises that those whose knowledge now is only partial shall, in love's future, understand as fully as they are understood (1 Cor. 13:12)?[6]

It is therefore precisely the transcendent newness, the unprepared-for surprise, the irreducible mystery of Easter Day which, without dehistoricizing

---

in A. E. Lewis, *Theatre of the Gospel* (Edinburgh: Handsel Press, 1984), pp. 24ff. Cf. also K. Barth, *CD,* IV/1, 330ff.; Bultmann, *Faith and Understanding,* vol. 1, ch. 3: "Karl Barth: The Resurrection of the Dead"; J. A. T. Robinson, *The Body* (London: SCM and Chicago: H. Regnery Co., 1952), ch. 3; Schillebeeckx, *Jesus,* esp. pp. 329-97; and Cullmann, *Immortality or Resurrection?*

6. A major theme of twentieth-century theology, ever since Barth's dialectical "theology of the Word," has been the epistemological relevance of "justification by grace." That is, the moral tension between works-righteousness and the righteousness of Christ through faith has its equivalent significance for the intellect, and thus for the very method by which faith and theology seek to know the truth. Do we rely on "natural" human understanding and knowledge, or on that which is gifted to us in God's own self-revelation in Christ? See Torrance, "Justification: Its Radical Nature and Place in Reformed Doctrine and Life," in *Theology in Reconstruction,* ch. 9. For Bultmann, we know the Risen Christ not according to the works of the flesh — that is, on the basis of objective historical data about his resurrection, or even his life — but according to the gift of the Spirit, as he encounters us existentially today in the form of proclamation *(kerygma).* (See *Faith and Understanding,* vol. 1, p. 24.) That is a contrast which Bultmann takes too far, with a dualistic polarizing of history and faith, as if the historical reality of the incarnation were quite dispensable, in favor of an ever-contemporary, interiorized encounter with the Christ who is preached. Yet the rationalistic reaction to this, which once again seeks to equate faith with historical knowledge (e.g., Pannenberg), threatens the hiddenness of the gospel, which makes apprehension of the Risen Christ a gift of the Spirit rather than an accomplishment of enlightened reason. Bultmann's protest, in the name of *sola gratia,* against a false objectivizing of the gospel, which in both its Roman Catholic and conservative Protestant manifestations has often taken the form of "salvation through orthodox belief," remains wholly valid and evangelical. "He [sic] who boasts of orthodoxy thus sins against Justification by Christ alone, for he justifies himself by appeal to his own beliefs, or his own formulation of belief, and thereby does despite to the truth and grace of Christ. Once a Church begins to boast of its 'orthodoxy' it begins to fall from grace" (Torrance, *Theology in Reconstruction,* p. 164).

73

the story, properly relativizes the question of what historically took place before dawn that first day of the week. Faith no more requires scientific answers to that question than it depends on scientific knowledge for its praise and wonder at what the Creator did on the first day of the *first* week.[7] And as the original *fiat lux* ("Let there be light!") was an initiating, promissory Word, which brought forth illumination not as an end in itself but to provide pattern and context for all that remained to be created and is being created still, so the Easter Word is itself provisional and proleptic, essentially a promise for the future. We have in fact already seen that the light which shone on the third day, at the new creation's daybreak, casts its rays forward toward the end of days, when it will burn away every form of evil, fully banish darkness, and allow the whole of heaven and earth to enjoy with Christ the tearless, deathless freedom of cosmic resurrection.[8] This in turn identifies neither the past nor the future but the *present* as at least one locus of true resurrection, whereat eternal life commences and faith and hope begin already to trust God's future and to celebrate the coming victories of divine righteousness and transforming love.

Even so, can there be any escape from the fact that the empty tomb, set in the midst of yesterday's history but illuminating the present in the form of future promises for God's tomorrow and the world's end time, also casts dark and bewildering shadows backward upon its own antecedents — not least upon the cross and on the Crucified One whom for two days the tomb contained? The more we look away from the vacant grave to the future it promises, the more we are directed retrogressively to the past preceding it. "For the Easter hope shines not only forwards into the unknown newness of the history which it opens up, but also backwards over the graveyards of history, and in their midst first on the grave of a crucified man who appeared in that prelude."[9] Nothing in the Easter narrative, nothing in Scripture's subsequent reflections, nothing in the church's history or in our own experience, permits us for a moment to cancel the cross, or forget the grave, because of the displaced stone. The gaping wounds in hand and side are still patent in the risen body, pathetic to behold (Jn. 20:27; cf. Lk. 24:39). Likewise a bleeding sheep, bred for slaughter and slain for sin, must pass muster, incongruous yet somehow apt, as the first and final image of sin's victor and the world's redeemer-king (Rev. 5:6; Jn. 1:29; Isa. 53:7). And authentic wit-

---

7. On resurrection as new creation, see, e.g., A. M. Ramsey, *The Resurrection of Christ* (London: G. Bles, 1945), pp. 30ff.; cf. J. Moltmann, *God in Creation,* trans. M. Kohl (London: SCM and New York: Harper & Row, 1985), pp. 292ff.; also Moltmann, *Way of Jesus Christ,* pp. 252ff.

8. See my *Theatre of the Gospel,* pp. 28ff.

9. Moltmann, *Crucified God,* p. 163.

ness, from the catacombs of ancient Rome to the cells of Nazi Germany, has provided endless commentary upon Paul's imperative, that we must suffer with Christ if we are also to be glorified with him (Rom. 8:17; cf. 2 Cor. 12:1-10). Despite every seduction to the contrary of a triumphalistic "theology of glory," it must be insisted that suffering, pain, and death are the marks of resurrection life, just as they marked the body of the Resurrected One (Rom. 5:3; 1 Cor. 2:1ff.; 2 Cor. 1:3ff.; Gal. 4:13; 6:17; Phil. 3:10).[10]

This must be the case; for who else *is* the Resurrected One but he who has been crucified and buried? Surely *this* is the core and scandal of the Christian faith and the ultimate point of its central three-day story: not that one man died and that a human being, one person before the many, was raised to life; but that this particular person, of such a character and fate, crucified and buried as blasphemer and rebel, as convict and sinner, as friend-forsaken and godforsaken, was raised from death to life. The Risen Lord is he who suffered and was termi-

---

10. In addition to being clearly set out in narrative form in the Gospels, especially in Mark, as we have seen, the biblical "theology of the cross" is supremely the expression of Pauline thought, most clearly expounded in Galatians and the Corinthian Epistles. What Paul has to say about the cross and death of Christ not only has abundant social and political consequences through its iconoclasm of all "human" concepts and usages of power; it also bears directly upon the meaning and content of individual Christian existence. Paul's "theology of the cross" in particular challenges those individualistic and pietistic church traditions which use Scripture — including Paul — to justify a triumphalistic "theology of glory." This proposes that the truly Christian life be normatively identified with intense "spiritual" experiences, "signs and wonders," faith healing, "speaking in tongues," and the like. In fact, though a "charismatic" himself, Paul clearly propounds a "pneumatology of the cross," subjecting all the gifts of the Spirit and their application to the radical critique of Christ's own experience of suffering, weakness, and crucifixion. See, e.g., F. D. Bruner, *A Theology of the Holy Spirit: The Pentcostal Experience and the New Testament Witness* (Grand Rapids: Eerdmans, 1970), esp. ch. 7; C. H. Cosgrove, *The Cross and the Spirit: A Study in the Argument and Theology of Galatians* (Macon, Ga.: Mercer University Press, 1988); and C. B. Cousar, *A Theology of the Cross: The Death of Jesus in the Pauline Letters* (Minneapolis: Fortress Press, 1990). See also F. D. Bruner, and W. Hordern, *The Holy Spirit — Shy Member of the Trinity* (Minneapolis, Augsburg, 1984), esp. chs. 3 and 4; Moltmann, *Way of Jesus Christ*, e.g., pp. 151ff., 196ff.; and J. Moltmann, *The Spirit of Life*, trans. M. Kohl (London: SCM and Minneapolis: Fortress Press, 1992); also E. Käsemann, "The Pauline Theology of the Cross," *Interpretation* 24 (1970): 151-77. Douglas J. Hall, whose thought has been particularly influential for the present writer, has done much more than anyone else specifically to apply the "theology of the cross" to North American culture and church life. See esp. D. J. Hall, *Lighten Our Darkness: Toward an Indigenous Theology of the Cross* (Philadelphia: Westminster, 1976); *God and Human Suffering: An Exercise in the Theology of the Cross* (Minneapolis: Augsburg, 1986); and *Thinking the Faith: Christian Theology in a North American Context* (Minneapolis: Fortress Press, 1991).

nated, and the Crucified and Buried One who has risen and appeared.[11] According to Luke (24:5), the first question on Easter morning was "Why do you seek the living among the dead?" For Christ had been removed from the place of the dead to a new place, of deathlessness and life eternal. Yet the corollary of this is that "among the dead" is precisely the place where the Lord of life has been, so that he remains forever, even in his glory, *the Living One who has been dead.* Conversely, as we shall see Jüngel explicate it later, the Christian gospel attempts to speak and think about and live in correspondence to "the death of the Living God." Easter dawn therefore bequeaths to us the sharpest of retrospective questions, leaving us to wonder what kind of life it is that comes to birth among the dead, and what kind of death could yield up its defeated victim to victorious life.

As such conundrums indicate, simply to make the daring identification between him who lay in the grave and him who triumphed over the grave is in fact to explain nothing. Rather, it is to raise gigantic questions of new complexity and depth: *Who* is the Risen Lord if he is also the one who died in shame and was delivered to the dust? And how could there be a cross and grave for one who would be manifested as the Lord of righteousness and life? If death is the human destiny, and resurrection the act of God, how can there be an *identity,* and not solely a contradiction, between the buried and the risen? Could a *mortal* be filled with resurrection glory, or *God* succumb to human fate? Could, at least at this one point, human death and divine power resist our compulsion to distinguish them as incompatibles? Has God come to glorious self-fulfillment through human shame and perishing? Can it be in God's own death that humanity has found its liberty and fullness?[12]

In raising questions of this sort, all of which depend upon the oneness of the risen and the crucified, we are indicating that the time has come to permit what for most of us is the instinctive and only natural hearing of the three-day story: that is, as a *familiar* tale whose ending is known from its beginning. Narratives, we said above, however different once familiar, are made for repetition; good narrative invites constant retelling and is enriched thereby. Granted, a story is never quite the same on second or further hearings, when the outcome is not so much revealed as remembered or assumed. Yet the new and different second story has its own identity and meaning. What it lacks in, say, suspense is

---

11. See, e.g., Jüngel, *Mystery,* pp. 307ff., 362ff.; Moltmann, *Theology of Hope,* pp. 197ff.; *Crucified God,* pp. 169ff.; J. Sobrino, *Christology at the Crossroads,* pp. 260ff., and *The True Church and the Poor,* trans. M. J. O'Connell (London: SCM and New York: Orbis Books, 1985), pp. 88ff.

12. "There is a story to be told about a crucified God and a man who has been awakened to a new life." Jüngel, *Mystery,* p. 309. We shall be exploring Jüngel's daring and novel reconceptualizing here in some detail on pp. 234-57 below.

compensated for by poignancy, perhaps, or irony. Watching protagonists from hindsight's privileged position, and knowing what awaits them, we may well have perceptions, sympathies, and insights that are quite impossible to the characters themselves, or to those who must follow their unfolding fortunes at the story's own pace.

How differently might those first-time observers reflect upon a scene of joy if they already knew that tragedy hides just around the corner. How ambivalently we would react to incidents of sorrow if, to our empathetic grief, there were added the certainty of final jubilation. And the confusion of emotion lies not simply in the mingling of pain with premature relief that the pain will not be endless, but more in the additional bitterness of knowing that the final scene of joy cannot be reached *without* the enduring of heartbreak first.

This is precisely the kind of ambiguity which bears, analogously, upon the second-time hearing of the gospel story. Knowing now what happens on the third day, we are bound to have a different, more complex view of what takes place upon the first. And that in turn will add new perceptions of what the third day means itself. On the second day we know now from the outset that more, much more, lies beyond Good Friday. But any relief that the first day is not the end must compete with horror that the final outcome will only be arrived at through the darkness and distress of the penultimate. And that means having to understand how it is that death and darkness *can* turn into life and light, and harder still — why this life and light are only of a special sort, born out of, and determined by, the death of all things, maybe even God.

It is indeed the second day, that indistinct day of nothingness save burial, which reemerges into clarity as the pivot of the oft-told, familiar story. On the initial hearing, the second-day boundary was a barrier. It compelled us to linger with the awful finality of the grave of Jesus, and only then permitted access to a brand new territory of surprise and transformation, where tears give way to laughter, where victims taste victory, and executioners suffer perdition. But now the barrier on the boundary has become the point of contiguity and contact, a two-way vantage point from which we can look both ways, survey and comprehend each territory in relation to its neighbor. Hearing the story the second time around, and every time thereafter, we encounter a grave standing on the boundary where defeat and victory are intimately juxtaposed. This time, on the second day, we are privileged to know already that after yesterday's defeat, victory tomorrow is secure. Yet we are *compelled* to know, too, that it is the finally victorious one who even now lies decaying in defeat; and we must face the shocking truth that the seeds of victory lie in the grave's defeat and nowhere else, that the only flower of victory is one which germinates and grows in the darkness of a tomb.

All of this, of course, will dawn upon us — or bewilder us — only if we remember on the second hearing what the story was about and felt like when we heard it first. What is so lacking in the way that the church normally hears its own decisive narrative is that Christians have forgotten, and make no effort to imagine, what the story *is* when freshly heard, without the benefit of hindsight and the drawback of familiarity. Yet the familiar rendering of the Easter story, heard as it were on "mono," is a hopeless distortion of its true sound. For the comforting joy of Easter morning *already* from the start anesthetizes Friday's pain; the anticipation of Sunday makes casual and phony the waiting of the second day, since there is never any doubt that there *is* a new day coming, to be waited for. It is, we say again, only the "stereophonic" sound of both the first-time story and the familiar which gives the narrative its quality of gospel Word, and its deepest meaning. Perhaps from this perspective the second-day boundary between the cross and the empty tomb is also the balance knob which secures equilibrium between novelty and familiarity, between the original story and the oft-repeated. For it is the grave of the second day which makes that original story what it is — a tale of contrast and reversal; of darkness, night, and finally light; of death and nothing, and only then of life. But once we know about the light and life, the grave becomes the point not of antithesis only but also of unity, not of contradiction alone but of identity: an identity-in-contradiction. For by uniting the first day and the third in a single event, the second suggests that the darkness is itself illuminating, the defeat victorious, and death both the opposite and the source of life. Only as we keep listening to the two stories, attend *both* to the contradiction between the crucified Jesus and the Risen Lord *and* to their identity, can we hope to glimpse what the Scriptures mean when they say that the *cross* is God's greatest power and wisdom, and that only in *dying* may human beings live.

II. The Story Heard Again

In order to hear again the old, familiar story of Christ's death and resurrection, in a way which does not drown the sound or soften the impact of the drama's first telling, let us visit again that dreadful barren scene in which there had seemed to be no drama left at all, but only a story petering out in the dust of pointlessness and death. Center stage is Joseph's rock-hewn tomb, last resting place for its first-ever occupant (Lk. 34:53). And since everyone is at rest on this *Shabbat,* even in this reenactment nothing is happening upon the stage — only a waiting and the imperceptible processes of bodily decay within the sepulcher. On the previous visit, when nothing happened either, it had seemed bleakly certain that nothing was left to happen. Jesus was dead and buried: finished. Every lingering possibility that he was who he had claimed and been acclaimed to be had finally been extinguished, brutally and decisively. Conviction for blasphemy had proved him anything but God's Righteous One; at the same time execution as a rebel, at the whim of empire, had left in mocking letters on a cross any messianic aspirations. Then the lonely godforsakenness of his dying and the hellish godlessness of his burial combined to confirm one of two unthinkable conclusions: either that he had never been God's love and power enfleshed — which left the desperate world still waiting for the coming near of justice and of peace; or, worse still, that this had been God's last, best effort against the tyrants, and that sin's hatred and the power of death had proved impregnable against the fragile flower of grace incarnate. All love and power spent, deity disproved and fatherhood disgraced, God had left the loving Son, and thus the loveless world, to the darkness of destruction. For both, the rest was silence and despair.

Such were the facts we knew, and the inferences we drew, when we were at this tomb before. Yet since then everything has changed. A reversal of that Saturday has taken place, as thorough in its scope as unforeseeable in its surprise. In Paul's synopsis of the drama, the Son of David according to the flesh has been designated Son of God according to the spirit by his resurrection from the dead (Rom. 1:3-4). This new, astounding fact means that the verdict on the Father and the Son has been rewritten, the sentence on the world and humankind revoked. The possibility of incarnation, slipping in and out of focus through the ambiguity of Jesus' life, but finally excluded beyond all doubt by the godlessness of his death, has in his raising returned, with irresistible conviction. He is indeed the Father's favored one, known now for sure, if not before, as the exalted and beloved Son, as he who speaks God's truth, effects God's judgment, shares God's power.[13] And in the process after all of keeping faith with the Son, the God who raised Jesus on the third day out of the godlessness of the second

---

13. Thus one of the major themes of NT Christology is that, by virtue of the resurrection (and ascension), Jesus has been enthroned and exalted as Lord and King, with the power and prerogatives of God's own self. See, e.g., Acts 2:31ff.; Phil. 2:9ff.; 1 Cor. 15:24ff.; Eph. 1:20ff.; 1 Pet. 3:21-22. Of particular interest is the frequency with which the NT gives a Christological interpretation to the text at Ps. 110:1 ("The Lord says to my lord, 'Sit at my right hand, till I make your enemies your footstool,'" NRSV). This Schillebeeckx describes as becoming "the *locus classicus,* the 'Scriptural proof' . . . within a Christian interpretation in which, on the grounds of his resurrection and/or exaltation, Jesus is appointed or acknowledged as 'Christ,' the Messiah" (*Jesus,* p. 501). See, e.g., Mk. 12:35ff.; 14:62; Acts 2:34; Rom. 8:34; 1 Cor. 15:25; Heb. 1:13. See also Cullmann, *Christology of the New Testament,* pp. 88-89; 222ff.; and Dunn, *Christology,* pp. 108-9.

and the godforsakenness of the first, has secured *self*-vindication and regained credibility. If the beloved Son had not been abandoned after all, then neither had God's own righteousness and power been falsified, the Father's Fatherhood compromised, nor the Deity's Godness sabotaged.

This means in turn that having not rejected Christ the Son, God has not rejected us, the sisters and brothers of the Son, but in love and power has delivered us from the guilt and suffering of wintry death into a personal and cosmic summer of grace and life. God's Easter acknowledgment of Jesus, and of all he did and claimed to be, was God's Amen to every fellow man and woman among whom Jesus lived and alongside whom he died. This divine, triumphant Yes to humanity in turn evokes from us our corresponding Yes of recognition. Our confidence and hope restored, we need no more arraign the Lord as the Great Absentee, who left the world to its own devices, but may instead praise the loving Shepherd and King, who kept company with the creatures in their valley of death and proved mightier than the hosts of inhumanity and sin when they threatened to destroy us.

Now let us be quite clear about the consequences of returning to the grave of Jesus armed with this joyful knowledge that tomorrow God will raise him from the dead, vindicating Father and Son alike and revealing both together to be transcendent over all the enemies of life and love and hope. The effect is stunning, though not perhaps in the way one might expect. It is after all — and our new knowledge can never, ever change this — a harrowing scene of human hopelessness and inhuman wickedness. A corpse lies buried: the chilling denouement of treachery and seizure, of mock justice and a mocking mob, and of the cruelest sort of execution. What we know now about this victim, who has suffered as much as any person could, and much more than any should, does nothing to cheer the scene for us, or modify its deadliness for him. What we know is the *identity* of the one who has been buried; and knowing who he is, we know more clearly than the first time we saw this scene what it was that actually was happening in his crucifixion, and in all that led to it. And if knowing what was happening, and to whom, fills us with wonder, and some confusion, it must also cause us shame and shock.

What the resurrection has told us about the man now laid before us in a cemetery, at the end of a life begun in a cowshed and concluded on a cross, is that this is God incarnate. The humiliation and the hunger of this person's life, the hardship and harassment, the homicide and hell — all this has been endured by none other than him who tomorrow, we now know, will be affirmed, exalted, glorified as God's own Son.[14] What the good news of Easter does so

14. See Moltmann, *Crucified God*, e.g., pp. 184ff., 190ff. The clear significance of the

stunningly to the Jesus story is confirm that after all, in this person who lived so *humanly* and with such *inhumanity* was put to death, we have been witnesses to *heavenly* love embodied and enacted. The very circumstances of weakness and failure, of guilt and godlessness, which on our first visit to his resting place proved so conclusively that he could *not* be God's righteous and beloved one, are now revealed to be precisely the conditions to which the Son of God has been made victim, and through which he will pass to victory.

To recognize this is to see how easily we misunderstand the resurrection and look in the wrong direction for its meaning. It was, as we have seen, an event of exaltation and divine *transcendence,* promising that God has irrupted into the godless world and begun to finalize the reign of righteousness and love. Yet it is now apparent that these revelations themselves confirm the *immanence* of God: godly presence, incarnate and incognito, within the present godless world, among its criminals and cripples, its villains and its victims, beside whom and as whom Jesus lives and dies and was interred. The light of Easter, thrown so vividly and hopefully forward upon the future, casts, like any bright light, dark shadows; and the shadows fall backward from the empty tomb upon its erstwhile occupant, the buried one, upon his death and ministry, his youth and finally his birth, indicating that in all of *this* the same God had been present whose presence was made known at Easter. As God's own transcendent act, the event of Easter manifests finally as true what the life of Jesus had always left hanging in ambivalence and shrouded in doubt, and which his death and burial had ruled impossible and false: that with this man from Nazareth God had cho-

---

resurrection for the incarnation, which Moltmann indicates here, is at one level a very proper affirmation of Pannenberg's insights into the Christologically retroactive force of Easter which we noted in Ch. 2. It is by raising Jesus from the dead that God, who alone has power over death, authenticates the prior but questionable claim of Jesus to be the incarnate Son of God. That is absolutely faithful to NT Christology, which often, as we have seen, bases its affirmation of Christ's Sonship, Lordship, etc., directly upon the resurrection (e.g., Acts 2:32ff.; Rom. 1:4). Pannenberg argues, further, that the resurrection has retroactive force, confirming now, in "the order of knowing," that he has *always* been the Son of God in "the order of being." He thus avoids the risk of "adoptionism," for which the man Jesus becomes for the first time Son of God at some point in his history, whether birth, baptism, or resurrection. See Pannenberg, *Jesus,* esp. pp. 133ff., 321ff. Even so, the weakness of Pannenberg is that he overplays the eschatological significance of the resurrection as the raising of one man in a prolepsis of a general resurrection, and actually underestimates the retrospective consideration — that it is the raising specifically of the one who has been *crucified* and thus has died for our sins. It is not just because someone has been already resurrected, but because specifically the Son of God, who died among us and for the sins of the world, has been raised, that there is a universal hope for humanity's future.

sen to be identified. *God* was in Christ; and therefore even in his ambiguous life and godforsaken death, no less than in the clarity of resurrection, this was *God's* humanity. From birth to burial, God has been among us, with this man, in this man, as this man: the self-expression, in the event of a human life, of who God is. Where this person has gone has been God's locus and who he has been, God's identity; what he has done, God's action; what he has suffered, God's passion; and — dare we say and think it? — how he has died, God's perishing.[15]

All of this is Easter "Good News," which we might now prefer never to have heard. Elation gives way to elegy; for by revealing the divine identity of the one who rested in the manger and was laid to rest in the sepulcher, the resurrection simply intensifies the horror, shame, and scandal of all that went before, making the second visit to the scene of Easter Saturday even less bearable than the previous. That was an occasion which ached with disillusionment, when hopes had been unmasked as fraudulent and a thrilling hypothesis dismantled. The dreams which Jesus has inspired, the possibilities he hinted at, had come to nothing — his shameful end proving that he could not be who he might perhaps have been. The world still awaited its salvation. No one, after all, has appeared to liberate the captives or to justify the sinful.

Now, however, that ache of disappointment has become a piercing stab; for we are faced not with the deflating failure of Jesus to prove himself God's Messiah and our redeemer, but with the devastating failure of God's Messiah to be himself, truly to act as our redeemer. We stand now, on Easter Saturday, beside the grave of God's own Son, contemplating the fact that the Son of God has refused to act divinely, to resist his enemies and ours, but has let the forces of destruction overwhelm him. By forgiving human beings their transgressions and by healing their diseases, he had already indicated that the authority of heaven was his; and by raising him at Easter the God of heaven removed all doubt that here was indeed the reign of God personified, the living source of creativity and grace, more powerful than all the powers of sin and evil, of disease and death. Yet in life he had cloaked his messiahship in questionable ambiguity, refusing at times to give the signs and proofs that sceptics asked for, and seeming to associate any unleashed exercise of the power he had less with his

15. We must postpone until Part Two a fuller discussion of the incarnation and personhood of Christ in the light of his raising from crucifixion and burial. For now be it said that the phrase "humanity of God" is intended to affirm, with the classical Christological definition, that Christ is one person, truly God and truly human; but also to see Christ less as a conjunction of two static and contrasting natures than as the *event* in which God's Godness comes to expression precisely in the full humanity of Jesus. God has so entered human life that the occurrence "Jesus of Nazareth" is itself the self-expression and revelation of who God is.

Father's will than with the Devil's wiles (Mt. 4:1-11). And the reluctant verdict on the Sabbath of his burial is that in the critical test his power has proved inadequate, or been suppressed. Willingly, or with no choice, the Messiah has succumbed to evil and the dark. He has failed to resist the deadly tyrannies of law and violence, and human pride. The Son of God has allowed himself to be opposed and contradicted and destroyed, the divine power he embodies rendered weak and powerless in the diabolic conflict. If this man is the humanity of God, then God's humanness has given in to inhumanity. The one who made us has, when human destiny lay in the balance, yielded to those who would unmake us, to the perverters of justice, the corrupters of truth, the annihilators of life. And if the power of God is thus exposed as bankrupt while the acknowledged Son of God lies dead and powerless in the grave, so too his love. The shocking possibility, which could indeed only be a *possibility* when we watched the grave before, without a hope that it might not mean the end of Jesus and the world, is now confirmed as all too actual and real. The Son of God cannot have failed himself, nor surrendered his authority to the powers that destroy his sisters and his brothers, were it not that his Father had failed him and surrendered up the beloved Son to powers that destroyed even him.

Precisely in the shadow of Easter, then, the occupied tomb has become afresh the source of shock and accusation; and in the dock is God's own self, whose love and power have found their limit. Opposed and overwhelmed, God's struggle on behalf of light and life has crumbled in defeat. For if, as Easter says, *God* has become identified with one who has perished and been buried, the corollary can no longer be avoided: that he in whom God dwelled, who did his Father's will and revealed his Father's face, now lies still in the pose of death, abandoned and defeated. God's absence and the tomb's cold godlessness, which seemed so frightening when the grave itself had seemed to prove that it did *not* contain the Son of God, is now a thousand times more chilling when Easter exaltation has assured us that the Son of God is precisely whom the grave contains. "It is really God who assumes what is radically contrary to the divine, what is eternally reprobated by God [and is disclosed] "in the very act of . . . self-concealment."[16]

Nevertheless, who are we to be God's accusers, even, or above all, at this moment? If the verdict has to be that God at the crucial moment, making common cause with godlessness and reprobation, has failed to be a God of love and power, the Father surrendering the Son, the Son surrendering to evil and to death, still the divine absence on Easter Saturday is less a judgment upon God than upon ourselves who brought about that absence. For it is we — humanity,

16. Von Balthasar, *Mysterium Paschale,* p. 52; cf. Ch. 2, throughout.

the world — who have crucified the Son of God, laid him in the ground, and driven him to hell. This must be the bitterest reflection of all as we survey the Sabbath scene, knowing already the identity of the one who has been crucified and buried. The joyous and melodic *Gloria* of exaltation turns once more into a harsh discordant rendering of *Dies Irae,* the Easter manifestation of the Risen One heaping fresh judgment on those who put the Risen One to death. What black irony pervades the story of the death of Jesus, when the now-familiar hearer knows already exactly who this Jesus is. What a grotesque display of inept miscalculation, the boundlessness of human folly, the myopia of hatred! We have to wince, with embarrassment and shame, at the charge of blasphemy, the mock trappings of monarchy, the taunting challenge to prove himself the "Son of God," when we know that the object of this self-righteousness and scorn — which is *our own* — will, on the third day, be vindicated and affirmed precisely as the righteous one of God and his anointed, kingly Son.

However, what judges and appalls us most of all about the cross, as humanity's violent rejection of God and the Messiah, is not perhaps the indignity thus inflicted upon God's majesty, but our arrogant trampling upon God's gentleness. The cross illuminates most vividly the wicked chasms of rebellion and estrangement which separate the human creatures from their Maker, the subjects from their King, by exposing so concretely the contrast between divine humility and human hubris. In Jesus, God has been enfleshed not as a sovereign but as a servant, emptied of grandeur and privilege, coming among us slavelike and self-abasing, solid in his fellowship with the outcast and defenseless, selfless in his capacity for suffering and pain. Yet it is precisely the innocent one, who comes as a lamb to the slaughter, not opening his mouth in self-defense let alone retaliation, who provokes our violence and contradiction (Heb. 12:3), our intolerance and hatred, and our thirst for blood. The gentle embodiment of God's own love proves quite intolerable to the human objects of that love, above all to the guardians of our morals and religion who aspire to legislate for the will of God and to the caesars of our politics and power who yearn to usurp the sovereignty of God. On our behalf the human authorities hurry to destroy this unprotected subverter of our status quo, before, by the sheer force of his emptiness, he destroys our values, overturns our systems, and changes everything. Thus by the cross of Jesus the truth about us is smoked out: we are unmasked, denuded. Convicting truth as blasphemy, mocking the king as an imposter, delivering up to death and the Devil the Son of the living God, we are exposed as idolaters and fools, as hypocritical enemies of peace, as violent allies of the dark.[17]

17. It is very unsatisfactory that Moltmann, so enlightened on the cross as the event of God's suffering *with* us, should dismiss, in so cavalier a fashion, the possibility that he

Are we now, perhaps, ready to face the full awfulness of the story of the second day, when heard as a story told before, viewed as a drama seen before, whose end is known? Because the identity of their victim has already been confirmed, the grave, and the cross that went before, now constitute a catastrophe more complete, an enigma more obscure, than could have been imagined when the story's climax was unknown. Then we could be certain only that *Jesus* had failed, and conclude that God was absent from the cross and grave because the godforsakenness of Jesus' dying and the godlessness of his death disproved the claim that God was with him. Now we know that God *is* with him! Raised by power divine, this is the man to whom from the beginning the Father has said Yes, indicating his flesh as the dwelling place of grace and truth, his life as the enactment of God's love, the installation of his kingdom. Therefore, following the story for the second time, we have had to watch the very Son of God being hung upon a cross and laid inside a tomb — God's living presence in the one who died making God's absence, through his death, doubly strange and shocking. What this human being suffered — reviled and contradicted, tortured and destroyed — must now be seen as a disaster for humanity, human nature at its worst. Only lawlessness could kill the man approved by God (Acts 2:23-24);

---

was also suffering *at our hands,* the victim of our sin (e.g., *Crucified God,* p. 183). He rejects the idea that Christ's dying for our sins means that our sin was the cause of his suffering, and thus the possibility that the cross reveals God's judgment upon us. Yet it is, says Paul, the wrath of God which is revealed by the gospel. God's righteousness is simultaneously that which judges sin and that which sets sin aside, with the free gift of justification apart from the law (e.g., Rom. 1:16ff.; 3:21ff.; cf. 1 Cor. 1:18ff. and the extended Johannine theme that Christ's coming means judgment for the world, e.g., Jn. 1:10-10; 12:3). Both the judgment and the justifying are concluded in the cross. Can an interpretation of the cross claim to be authentic to the broad spectrum of NT theology which dismisses as anachronistic the view that Christ's death is atoning and expiatory, fulfilling — though thereby abolishing — the OT sacrificial cult? That is simply to exclude the element of *guilt* from the problem of human suffering — and jettisons the very idea that Christ accomplishes *reconciliation.* Moltmann rightly sees that God suffers and dies as our partner and liberator, but ignores the fact that the suffering and death from which we need to be liberated are "the wages of sin," the expression of estrangement between God and humanity. (On this, see Jüngel, *Mystery,* p. 225.) Christ's life and death are reconciling precisely because here God crosses over the chasm that separates the Creator from creatures, the Holy One from sinners. We evacuate the divine proximity to us in the suffering and dying Jesus of its point if we forget that God has had to *come* close, across the distance that divides us. Barth is much more perceptive than Moltmann in seeing that Christ can only come as our deliverer if he also comes as Judge, exposing (though only through enduring) our condition as enemies of God. See *CD,* esp. IV/1, sects. 59 and 61. These matters are taken up again in Ch. 6, sect. II.

and his death brings finally into the open light of day the dark, turbulent depths of human sin, the seething rebellion of our pride and disobedience. Our hostility to God and our resistance to God's ways, expressed for generations in rejection of the prophets sent to speak God's truth, has come to its bloody climax in the slaying of God's Son (Mk. 12:1-12).

Yet God has let this happen! The Lord has endured our contradiction and has not resisted it. If the citation against us is that we have destroyed the Son of God, that rebounds once more upon the Son, who has let himself be destroyed, and upon the Father who has left him to that fate. We have conspired to make God absent, rejecting the Messiah and securing his destruction, making his grave the triumph of ungodliness and sin. It is the victory of all who are opposed to God, and who, through pride and prejudice, are the opposite of all God stands for. Yet God, we know, is present in this man; he has established union and identity with the dead and buried Jesus. If we have defeated Jesus' Father and brought about this negation of love and grace divine; if we haved secured the victory over sin and death and demonic evil; then that is a defeat at which God has connived and winked. Divine presence in the diabolic grave simply implicates God as colluding in divine absence. Again the verdict is demanded that in divine humanity God has succumbed to inhumanity, failing to resist the hostility of human sin. Even in Fatherhood, God has surrendered to the death of love, failing in loving faithfulness toward the faithful, loving Son, and forsaking with the Son all his sisters and brothers in the flesh, clothed in whose humanity Christ came.

None of this is canceled — though it is much complicated — by the narrative's established fact that Jesus rose again. The enigmas and disasters of this second day, upon the second hearing of its tale, rest already on the premise that God did *not* abandon Christ, or us, and did *not* fail in Godness or in Fatherhood. It is the *presence* of the resurrecting God in and with the Crucified and Buried One, the fact that death has been inflicted upon nothing less than God's own incarnate presence, which has constituted the puzzle and the shame which we have just encountered. Likewise, because the second day is not, this time, a barrier blocking out the light of Easter from our sight, but a contact point, connecting cross and resurrection in a single, integrated story, we know full well that the grave of God is not by any means the end. Standing here now we can already see that the death and burial of Jesus is merely a staging post upon God's way. All that God is, and does, and suffers here, has point and purpose, for the Creator is dynamically, redemptively engaged, active upon the path of victory. The cross and grave *will* bring the Son to resurrection, us to transformation, and God to vindication. If it is the presence of God in Christ which makes God's absence in the godlessness of Saturday such a shocking episode of shame and failure, human and divine, then that same presence gives new meaning to the absence and forces us to think at deeper levels yet, of who God is and how God works: present-in-absence, and absent where most present; alive in death, and dead when most creative and life-giving.

For one thing, even as we press the charge against ourselves that in the death of Christ humanity was at its worst and sin revealed in all its violent ugliness, we also know that this event, from cross through burial to resurrection, is God's great act for our salvation. If Jesus, crucified and buried, embodies judgment on his human slayers, condemned by the act of their own hands as the enemies of God, we know in Easter's light that the same death has been for our acquittal. The act which judges us is equally the act by which we are no longer judged. For in his death at the hands of guilty, lawless sinners, Jesus has become the guilty one himself, condemned by law, cursed through crucifixion (Gal. 3:1-14; 4:4; Rom. 8:3-4; 2 Cor. 5:21), buried with the wicked. Forgiving those who judge themselves to be justly judged by him, enduring with and for them the hell to which they have consigned themselves, Jesus dies that his executioners might live. And in raising him from death, his Father confirms that in and through the Son there is no more death but life made new, no longer condemnation but forgiveness and fulfillment.

This could be true, in turn, only if the event of human failure, through which we are redeemed, is on the Lord's part, too, a strange, mysterious failure through which he triumphs. We know, even as we watch the Son give up the ghost in dereliction and despair, and see him buried in a tomb, alone and godless, that his Father did not and never could abandon him (Acts 2:31). Remaining faithful to the Son, precisely at the point of direst absence from him, the Father is self-justified as a God of boundless love, who exalts the Son as more triumphant than all the powers of death and darkness. *We* are promised "no separation" from the love of God (Rom. 8:39) because nothing could separate God from Christ the Son, nor obstruct the final fulfillment of eternity's redemptive and transforming will. We have stood now for the second time beside the grave of Jesus, through the long, sad hours of Saturday; and this time it has seemed even more certain than before that this is a day of catastrophe, as the opposition triumphs and God's love and grace have been negated and made absent. Yet we also know this time that a new day comes. The Easter dawn on the horizon assures us that God's Godness has never been more clear, and that in defeat and negativity the Father of the abandoned, buried Son is en route toward the death of death and the ultimate negating of everything not filled with life and hope (Heb. 2:14-15; Rev. 20:13-14, 21:1-4). And our bewildered minds — even more bewildered now after this second hearing of the story — ask, "How can these things be?"

III. The Conundrum of the Grave

The question we are mouthing in this bewilderment is how far, if at all, we can think through and understand such a God as this, whose Godness is effective only in the midst of godlessness. And dare we live (and die) with and by the consequences of such a possibility? For many it is a wholly familiar story, good news so often heard before as to have lost all novelty or shock, that God so loved the world as to send the only-begotten Son. Delivered up for us all, and raised from the dead, that Son has taken away the world's sin and destroyed the power of death. Those who believe in him may have new life that does not perish; and in him all things are being reconciled to God, the day soon coming when everything in heaven and on earth will be made new. But by choosing as far as possible to listen to this story, and hear its gospel word of grace and victory, as an *unfamiliar* story unfolding as it goes, before rehearing it from the perspective of its climax, we have perhaps allowed ourselves some fresh inkling of what mysteries lie hidden, dead center, within the Christian faith.

In brief, the stumbling block we have forced ourselves to take account of, by following the unknown drama before the known, is the utter finality of Jesus' death. Instead of passing over the grave of one brief Sabbath confident that all will soon be well, we let ourselves be stopped, and come to the conclusion that everything had stopped, save the endlessness of suffering and sin. God is not there, only the contradiction of God: human mortality, rampant evil, the reign of death and hell. Moving onward, across the Saturday-boundary into the new territory of resurrection glory, we saw the joyful denouement of the three-day drama with a vividness and clarity denied to those who have not first absorbed the finalness of what has gone before.

If confidence in the resurrection tends to modify the deadliness of Calvary, likewise it is only those who have first looked into the mouth of hell and seen the world abandoned to its godless fate who then can truly see the meaning of the Easter Day reversal. For reversal is precisely what the empty tomb announces: the inversion of everything which the death and burying of Christ implied. That was heaven's spoliation, robbed of sovereignty and fatherhood by that to which God is opposed and of which God is the opposite. But now that death has been defeated, the grave's sting pulled, the Devil's crown of victory snatched away so unexpectedly, what inference is possible but that God has been dynamically in action? Who but God, the source of light and life, could have effected so radical a victory over death and darkness? Where the demonic reigns, can anything less than the Devil's opposite and implacable adversary contest and interrupt the rule of evil? Our pretty pictures of earth reviving annually from the dark of winter into the green of spring, the rhythmic certainties of nature's fertile womb, might have sufficed to illustrate the Easter rising had the death of Christ been at worst a hibernating interval. But the terminal totality of the grave can only mean an Easter victory in which the Lord of life broke through the natural patterns of what we expect and understand, and brought about a mighty act of grace and re-creation. If, on the first-time hearing of the tridual narrative, the grave spells out the world's abandonment by God, that drama concludes with a reversal of the tomb which none but God could bring about, and which assures the world that in the person of the Risen One God is present with us, and has decisively secured our future.

What has happened, however, now that we have listened again to the gospel story, the oft-repeated sequence of Christ crucified, buried, raised, less able than before to modify the finality of Friday by anticipating Sunday, or to quench the ecstasy of Easter by reducing first the shock of Saturday? Unlike the jaded casual hearer, now we are alerted both to the dreadful absence of God while the tomb is occupied, and to God's joyous presence when the tomb is empty. And out of these antitheses there has emerged a new mystery, a scandal and enigma which we still have barely come to terms with. It is a conundrum which, lying at the heart of the church's story, must act as the focal point and test for all we hope to understand and share about the gospel — the truth of Jesus Christ, and of his God and ours, and of ourselves. For what we have learned, hearing the old story while recalling it as new, is that these antitheses of death and resurrection belong together, not apart. It is not that deity is absent in the one and present in the other. If present in the latter, God is no less present in the former. For the Risen One is still the one who died, and it is the crucified and buried person — he and no other — who has been raised to life.

What can this mean but that the grave of Jesus is simultaneously the place where God is undeniably absent and also resolutely present: defeated yet on the way to victory, at once condemning us and securing for us liberty and joy? This must amaze us two times over.

On the one hand, we can scarcely believe that when evil is triumphant and God is far away, there, precisely there, in the depths of human wretchedness, mortality, and sin, even there God is present, a victim of that godforsakenness and thus able to bring the godless and forsaken out of their haplessness and isolation into a new territory of light and joy. How, we ask, could God, eternal and immortal, righteous and holy, be *in* the grave beside the disgraced, the despairing, and the dead?

On the other hand, perhaps we do not want to believe that the resurrection *begins* in the grave — that God is revealed and glorified *only* in the form of one who hungered and was hung? If God is seen as present and powerful on Easter Day, then, unseen and incognito, God was present and powerful too the day before, present and powerful as the one who had no power, and from whom the Father's presence was withdrawn. It is the failed, the lonely, the wounded one, wrapped in grave clothes as once in swaddling cloths, who is the Lord of glory (1 Cor. 2:8); and therefore, as John, of all the evangelists, had realized, the glory of the Risen Christ is the kind that can be recognized only in the earthiness of flesh, the indignity of servitude, and the agony of death (e.g., Jn. 1:14; 12:27-33; 13:1-11). And as Paul could clearly see, this mocks all we think we know, and want to know, concerning what is noble, powerful, and wise (1 Cor. 1 and 2). How, we ask, could the God of glorious beauty and vivifying majesty lie in the malodorous grave of the mortal and the murdered, among the finished and the done for?

From both perspectives, then, the presence of God in the godless grave encounters us as a word we dare not hear and a thought we know not how to think. At once it seems impossible, too good to be true, and intolerable, too painful to be true. That the divine should be present even where manifestly absent, resurrecting and redemptive precisely where our enemies and God's have waxed triumphant, asks us to hope against all hope. That the divine should be absent even where palpably present, resurrecting and redemptive only as one who suffers godforsakenness and has lost all hope, asks us to be foolish against all reason. Between such twin constraints it is not perhaps surprising that theology and faith so rarely succeed in finding God in the grave of Jesus Christ. Either we decide that the place of human death is so demonic and destructive that not even God would have the power to survive and overcome it; or it seems a place too despicable and lowly for the God of power and glory to be found there. Yet human death is the lot of every one of us; for some it comes painfully and tragically, the summation of every form of suffering; for all it comes inexorably and fearfully, the climax and epitome of our fleshly finitude. However strange and shocking, would there be a Christian *gospel* were it *not* true that God has been found among the dying and the dead, where the absence of all life and hope and light proclaims that even God has gone away? Would there truly be forgiveness for the guilty, healing and wholeness for the broken, a home for the rejected, and a coming day of laughter for a world of tears, did God not know how to weep the tears of fear and loneliness, to endure the torments of hunger and disease, and to be identified with godforsakenness and transience?

Conversely, would there be a *Christian* gospel were it not true that God is self-unveiled only *sub contrario,* that is, in the very opposite of Godness, hidden amid the outcasts of the earth who, often in the name of God and of the church, are rejected and despised, and who, by the standards of the world, count for nothing except to live and die that the powerful might become more powerful still? The triumph of God over the grave of Jesus would truly be — as has all too often been assumed — permission for the followers of Jesus to flaunt their plumage of superiority in the face of others, were it not that God in humility ineffable has triumphed *through* the grave, for its many dis-graced, defeated victims and in the form of one of them. That form, seen first in a cradle, later on a cross, and finally as a corpse, is the shape of resurrection, and there is no other. Let others dream of divine salvation for the righteous and the wise, for those able to transcend the flesh and rise to heights of timelessness and sanctity; the gospel of Christ is for the mortal and the carnal, the earthbound and the sinner. For it was just as such a one that Jesus lived, and still as such a one, fleshly, crucified, and buried, that he was raised. In him, concealed in weakness and in death, are God's true power and life at work. It is to Christ's all-too-human family, the fellowship of the weak, the guilty, and the moribund, that God's gracious, loving hands stretch out; and only those prepared to suffer and to die in solidarity with Christ, acknowledging their own neediness and brokenness, truly know the sufficiency of grace and can witness to its healing.

What is so sad and ironic when Christians refuse to face the conundrum of God's presence-amid-absence in the death of Jesus, is that they thus endorse the very objections to the gospel of Christ which unbelief has seen and uttered from the start. The crucified Messiah — God's identification with the Crucified and Buried One — is, says Paul, a stumbling block to the Jews and folly to the Gentiles. For Greeks it was illusory to hope against hope, to imagine that God, changeless and immortal, should so unite with what decays and perishes as to give new life, unending life, to that which death had already swallowed up. That which dies, dies; with what dies — carnal and sordid — deity can have no dealings; and for that which dies there can be no future. For Jews it was blasphemy to mortify the deity, to see the Creator — transcendent, ineffable, holy — hidden among the creatures, humble, lowly, and obedient unto death. Yahweh simply is: "I am who I am" (Ex. 3:14); and this sheer, transcendent, holy being is not to be compromised through confusion with those who are "made," creatures of flesh, daily on their way to the dust from which they come. What for the pagan mind is not possible for God is to the Jews unfitting. And when Christians agree that God could not give hope to those who are beyond all hope by becoming one with them in their godlessness, or that God would not conquer sin and death by first succumbing to them, coming as a *servant* Lord, a *guilty* judge, a *wounded* healer, they simply share with their critics the natural assumption of the human mind that between God and human perishing and frailty there can be no unrestricted dealings. To God's unity with us, and ours with him, there must be limits.

For most of us, those limits have certainly been reached, if they have not come before, at the point of human death. Here the reality of what it means to be temporal and mortal is visible and inescapable, even though we are just as temporal and mortal through every living moment that precedes our last. But in death our humanness is revealed as never before for what it truly is: transient, perishable, finite. Every instinct says, "Here, at least, there can be no place for God, however loving, however strong. How could God, the infinite and everlasting, be one with so vulgar an expression of carnality and time as the *buried* man from Nazareth?" Perhaps this is why we pass over Easter Saturday with such silence and embarrassment.

We may be content to recognize Jesus as the Son of God on the last Thursday of his life, overcoming weakness and temptation, and going to the cross in perfect obedience to his Father's will. We are scarcely able not to see the hand of God in the glory and the power of Easter Day. We perhaps are puzzled by the godforsakenness of Christ on Friday, but relieved to hear the final Johannine shout of victory from the cross, indicative that the mission from heaven has been accomplished, a divine enterprise concluded (Jn. 19:30). But that the God who is in Jesus before his death, and at his resurrection, should be with him in the grave on Saturday — of that there can surely be no question. At most the Eternal Word is quiescent here, or departed for a season.[18] For where all is death and godlessness, how could there be room for life and its creator? Thus we convince ourselves — preferring not to ask how real God's involvement in this man's flesh (and therefore ours) had ever been, if he left the man just at the moment when the real nature of his creaturehood and fleshliness was most apparent and concrete. Was the Word *ever* truly immanent in flesh and time, has the immortal truly promised new life to mortal bodies (Rom. 8:11), if God is *not* "Immanuel: God with us" in the grave, where we are most emphatically temporal, and mortal flesh and blood?[19]

To be fair to ourselves, the reservation we place on God's humanity,

---

18. As we shall see more fully later, it was a standard conclusion of the early Fathers that God the Father did not suffer in the death of Christ, nor the Divine Word as such, however closely that was understood to be united with the suffering human nature of Christ. When Christ died it can only have been in his humanity, the divine nature being either absent or entirely passive. Likewise the weakness and temptation of Christ in his life was regularly attributed to his human nature, the Word as such being inert. Thus Irenaeus: "The Word remained quiescent, that He might be capable of being tempted, dishonored, crucified, and of suffering death." *Adversus Haereses* 3.19.3.

19. On the danger that we will lose hold of *time* altogether, as the condition in which God meets us, and which he redeems, if we do not insist that he encounters us at the point of *death*, see Weber, *Foundations*, vol. 2, p. 91: "God acts in, upon and with the One who suffers, is crucified, and is buried in the grave. God encounters us in the very realm of the 'history of death.' He [sic] makes it important for us just as he qualified time by acting upon us within it. But in his entry into our 'history of death' he encounters us and acts as the Lord" (cf. *Foundations*, vol. 1, p. 457).

which is threatened or implied by our refusal to perceive divine presence in the God-vacated resting place of the departed Jesus, might appear to have its foundation in the first hearing of the gospel story. For that itself was the demonstration of contrast and antithesis between the grave and God. God was demonstrably absent from the scene of death, and brought the dead to life only by breaking in with transcendent otherness, negating death's dark work with the contradicting force of life and love and grace. Where there was death, there was no place for God, and where God intervened, with presence and power, the Devil and darkness had to flee away.

Even then, however, we would have been wrong to interpret God's hostility to death as an incompatibility with those who die, an antagonism to the victims of death as well as to its victory. Contrariwise, by raising Jesus in his body, God has uttered an irresistible "Yes" of love and affirmation to the human creatures who in their bodies suffer, bleed, and die. By contradicting and opposing death, God reveals and verifies an identification with the man who died. And thus we have heard a second story which tells us that God was in and with the very person — the very *Son!* — whom the same God had abandoned and delivered up to death and atheism. God was present with him even in his utter loneliness, defeating the opposing force of death not through intervention against the foe but through union with the foe's defeated captive. The Lord of life triumphs over death, the inimical opposite of life, not by canceling out the adversary but by succumbing to the victory of all that God opposes. Such is the strange story we have heard, the conundrum we find so hard to solve, the shock so difficult to sustain, the abyss we try so hard to bridge, the "scandal of the cross" we would love to render comprehensible and innocuous.[20]

We noted at the outset that, as well as helping us to understand the truth of God which in itself is beyond all human comprehension, parable and story communicate the gospel by their willingness not to understand too much. Only indirectly and in fragments do they open up some windows on God's mysterious ways, preserving the mystery itself which so transcends the limitations of every metaphor, analogy, and concept. It is good to be reminded now, therefore, that to speak of God's humanity, and to recognize in Jesus, crucified, entombed and risen, the Eternal Word made flesh, is to acknowledge him as a living parable of God. Here is an extended, God-provided analogy, in whose human life and person we perceive something of God's reign in action, and can see the face of God as plainly as we can bear.[21] Above all, we should remember that we have

20. Cf. von Balthasar, *Mysterium Paschale,* p. 52.
21. See esp. Jüngel, *Mystery,* sect. 19, "The Humanity of God as a Story to Be Told," to which we shall refer more extensively below.

heard the riddling conundrum of elusive, divine presence amid tangible divine absence, powerfully alive among the weak and dead, not as a celestial truth, lucid and absolute beyond all dispute and ambiguity, but precisely in a narrative. Its story form shields the truth from our eyes and withholds it from our grasp, even while it challenges us to think new thoughts and live new lives by bursting the old wineskins of our understanding. It would be as wrong fully to control and apprehend what the story says as to refuse to follow the parable and let it shake us to the depths of heart and mind and intellect. Indeed, the discovery of God amid the very opposite of God, victorious through defeat, self-affirming through negation, has on occasion been too well understood. Instead of a scandal, which faith can only *hear,* long before it understands, the "identity of opposites" has been made the pinnacle of truth, *our* truth, a mystery penetrated and possessed, a high accomplishment of the human mind — perhaps the very highest. Reality, we say, depends on equilibrium, for example: the constant, balanced strife and tension between opposing forces — hot and cold, light and dark, good and evil, male and female.[22] Or, more dynamically, reality *moves,* in a synthesis of positive and negative — God of necessity realizing self-fulfillment and facilitating ours by overcoming the antithetical resistance of everything nondivine.[23]

22. The idea of the unity of opposites, which recurs both in Eastern philosophy (e.g., the Yin and Yang of Taoism) and in German Idealism (e.g., Schelling, "every being can be revealed only in its opposite, love only in hatred, unity only in conflict"), goes back, in the West, to the pre-Socratics such as Heraclitus, who saw an essential unity in apparent opposites. Beneath conflict there is underlying coherence, and stability in the cosmos depends upon constant strife, battle, or tension between its opposing forces: "God is day night, winter summer, war peace, satiety hunger. . . . It is necessary to know that war is common and right is strife and that all things happen by strife and necessity." See G. S. Kirk and J. E. Raven, *The Presocratic Philosophers* (Cambridge: Cambridge University Press, 1964), esp. ch. 6. It is important to distinguish (more clearly than Moltmann appears to [e.g., *Crucified God,* pp. 25ff.]) the a priori philosophical principle of the unity of opposites *(coincidentia oppositorum)* from the conclusion to which theology is sometimes driven by reflection upon the Christian revelation, that the Father of the crucified Jesus is a God who is hidden in self-revelation and unveiled only in circumstances of hiddenness and contrariness. Thus Luther pressed into service the "coincidence of opposites" in the process of expounding his innovative and profoundly biblical "theology of the cross," which we shall encounter in Chs. 5 and 6 below.

23. This is the dialectical principle of Hegel which, in one of its extensions, underlies the Marxist interpretation of history. For a brief but lucid description of Hegel's use of the coincidence of opposites, and its impact on subsequent theology, see A. I. C. Heron, *A Century of Protestant Theology* (Guildford and London: Lutterworth Press and Philadelphia: Westminster Press, 1980), ch. 2. Useful introductions to Hegel include: J. N. Findlay,

Here rationality and logic have taken possession of the gospel story and made of Good Friday's death, and the life of Easter, an abstract, speculative principle, a universal absolute.[24] The story itself becomes a symbol and example of a higher, general truth; the death of Jesus is no longer history, nor his rising "history-like," unique events along the line of human happening, but illustrative moments in the unfolding of a Divine Idea. And that is precisely to rob the story of its concreteness and its scandal. For once God's unity with that which is not God has become the general and essential truth of God's own life, then the awkward, stunning contradiction in our story has been absorbed, domesticated, divinized. It is no longer human suffering and death — particular, ugly, earthy, datable — to which God has been despicably subjected, but their swallowing up and sanitizing in the universal, the eternal, and the spiritual, that God has triumphalistically accomplished.[25]

Hegel: A Re-examination (London: Allen & Unwin, 1958); and W. Kaufman, *Hegel: A Reinterpretation* (New York: Anchor Books, 1966). See also below, esp. pp. 179-80.

24. On Hegel's concept of a "speculative Good Friday," in which the historical event of the cross is dehistoricized and transcendentalized into an absolute "death of God," see his *Faith and Knowledge,* trans. W. Cerf and H. S. Harris (Albany: State University of New York Press, 1977), pp. 190-91. Hegel's "Good Friday" becomes an expression of the abyss of nothingness which threatens all being. God "dies"; but because through this positing of self-negation God's identity is affirmed, this speculative "death of God" is succeeded by a rebirth of all reality. This makes resurrection a *necessity* for the world, as God the Absolute Idea unfolds itself and pursues its own history. Resurrection is no longer a possibility of *hope,* dependent upon the gracious mighty act of God, upon the world and in *its* history, of raising Jesus from the dead. On this, see Jüngel, *Mystery,* esp. pp. 63ff.; and Moltmann, *Theology of Hope,* pp. 168ff., and *Crucified God,* pp. 253-54; and esp. H. Küng, *The Incarnation of God,* trans. J. R. Stephenson (Edinburgh: T. & T. Clark, 1987), esp. ch. 5. For the criticism of Moltmann's own theology of the cross as too dialectical, with an overrigid contrast between cross and resurrection which prevents a Christian *mingling* of sorrow and joy — "the singing of a song in an alien land" — as God's glory is manifested precisely *in* the cross of Jesus, see David E. Jenkins, "The Liberation of God," in Moltmann, *Theology and Joy,* trans. R. Ulrich (London: SCM Press, 1973), esp. pp. 19-25 (published in the United States as *Theology of Play* [New York: Harper & Row, 1972], without the introduction by Jenkins).

25. See the masterly discussion of the differences between the biblical "theology of the cross" and its philosophical adumbrations in von Balthasar, *Mysterium Paschale,* pp. 56-66: "The Cross and Philosophy." Note esp. p. 65: "Philosophy can speak of the Cross in many tongues; when it is not the 'Word of the Cross' issuing from faith in Jesus Christ, it knows either too much or too little. Too much: because it makes bold with words and concepts at a point where the Word of God is silent, suffers and dies, in order to reveal what no philosophy can know, except through faith, namely, God's ever greater Trinitarian love; and in order, also, to vanquish what no philosophy can make an end of, human dying so

Any such modifying of the contrast between the historical grave of Jesus and the God of resurrecting glory, which in turn trivializes the shock and scandal of their uniting, refuses to hear the gospel story and obey its shape. It was to respect the *antithesis* that we listened to the story as first-time hearers, the more vividly to recognize the *unity* when we heard the tale again. Only this procedure corresponds to the pattern of the narrative, and of the Bible's own reflection on the meaning of the story.

That is nowhere more clear than when Paul dares to *measure* the relationship of grace to sin, of Christ the Savior to the sinner Adam, in Romans 5. Through the sin of Adam death reigned, says Paul (Rom. 5:12ff.); for all humanity sinned in him, and therefore death was everywhere. It was a tyranny of negativity — God's place supplanted by, and lordship forfeited to, the hegemony of the opponent. And God's absence as sovereign of the world was made yet more complete when law was interposed; for it is law which makes sin *count* as sin (v. 13). Thus law increases sin, so that the reign of death is fortified and God's dethronement ratified (v. 20). How, then, is death defeated, and how are law and sin deposed, through Christ's free gift of grace?

Paul is very clear that such a victory occurs not by *denying* the reign of death, nor by pretending that God's absence never happened. Grace *lets sin be* and gives it space and scope; but thereby grace matches it and *goes beyond*. The essential mark of grace and love is their *abundance,* not reducing but surpassing the power and range of negativity and sin. Where sin increased, grace *abounded all the more* (v. 20). So, while the consequence of one human person's sin has been very great, how much greater yet is the result of one such person's righteousness (vv. 15, 17)? There is a parallel and parity between Christ and Adam, each of them one individual who represents the lot of many (vv. 15, 19); but there is in Christ disparity and superfluity, to the extent that life surpasses death, which is the lack of life, a free gift transcends the demands and penalties of law, and pardon outweighs condemnation (vv. 16, 18). Indeed, so fertile, abundant, and expansive is the grace of Jesus Christ that it even surpasses itself, growing and expanding as it reaches out toward its goal. God loves us precisely as rebellious enemies, and accepts the reign of death within us: our revolt and God's deposing; and by showing us a love greater in quality and depth than our lovelessness, God reconciles us and makes us friends. And now that we are friends, God loves us even more, opening up new possibilities of joy and blessedness beyond all measure, the forgiving grace of Christ's death yielding pre-

---

that the human totality may be restored in God. Too little, because philosophy does not measure that abyss into which the Word sinks down, and, having no inkling of it, closes the hiatus, or deliberately festoons the appalling thing with garlands."

eminence to the future, still greater, fruits of his resurrection life (vv. 8-11; cf. Rom. 3:7; 2 Cor. 3:7-8; 8:2).[26]

Do we not see here the essential configuration of the Christian gospel, the scenario of the three-day drama we have been watching? That is a parable about the greatness of sin and the extent of human suffering. The world we know is one in which unjust oppressors too regularly hold sway; in which the innocent suffer through disease, disaster, greed, and war; in which the lifelong threat of death, and the pervasiveness of evil, conspire to make belief in a God of love and power impossible. The parable highlights one moment of this world's history, a day on which it seems that every hope of freedom from guilt and tyranny and pain has been extinguished, every ground for hopelessness and disbelief confirmed. "Sin reigned in death" that day (Rom. 5:21); and no telling of the parable conveys its point if it hurries over the malediction and the emptiness of God's absence in defeat, as the one who raised false hopes for humanity's divine deliverance lay cold in death.

Yet if the godlessness was very great, *how much greater* was God's presence on that day! God was *with* the godforsaken one, was committed to the antithetical, God-abandoned one, absorbing contradiction and even self-negation. God loved this convicted sinner who had falsified God's truth, this unmasked imposter who had claimed but clearly lacked the authority of heaven, this victim par excellence whose death epitomized the impotence of justice and of peace, the cruel and crushing power of Satan. And by remaining *with* the embodiment of godlessness, enduring conditions which trumpeted the overthrow of heaven, the God of heaven wrested from the grave self-vindicating victory, authentication for the Son, and life and hope for the despairing world. How could this be, while the godlessness, so very great, still survived God's new ascendancy, undiminished, uncurtailed, undivinized? Clearly, not by God's *matching* the evil

---

26. For a profound exposition of Rom. 5 and of its central theme that the grace of Christ "surpasses" and achieves "much more" than sin, see K. Barth, *Christ and Adam: Man and Humanity in Romans 5, Scottish Journal of Theology Occasional Papers,* no. 5, trans. T. A. Smail (Edinburgh and London: Oliver & Boyd, 1956). He makes the point very clearly, as we have tried to do both here and below, that the comparison "how much more" between two terms affirms the validity of the first term just as much as it asserts its surpassing by the second. As grace acknowledges the greatness of sin before overflowing its limits, so through the great divine absence in sin's victory, God is even more greatly present in sin's defeat. For Jüngel this "how much more" is central to the concept of "God's unity with perishability" in the death of Christ (see *Mystery,* esp. pp. 184ff., 226-98). Though dissimilar and distant from us, the Creator has in Christ become even more similar to us and more closely identified with us, to the point of sharing our mortality. On Jüngel's startling conceptuality, see esp. pp. 234-57 below.

only, leaving the powers of sin and grace as equal partners, locked in a static equilibrium of cosmic forces. The only way to defeat the power of sin, without denying its reality or reducing its hostility, is to go *beyond* it, surpassing its mighty negativity with yet more abundant creativity, its deadliness with over-flowing life, its emptiness with presence and with filling.

This is surely the core of faith's good news, but also its great difficulty. The protest of unbelief is that the world is godless and unjust, a place of loveless-ness, iniquity, and pain. Faith, by contrast, hears and speaks a word of promise — that nothing, however evil, can separate us from God's love, so that the world's sure destiny is peace and joy. Yet that confidence itself contains the temptation so to proclaim the world's salvation as to take no longer seriously its distancing from God through suffering, sin, and death. There is a "faith" which has forgotten what it is to doubt; a way of hearing which no longer listens to the silence; a certainty that God is close which dares not look into eyes still haunted by divine remoteness; a hope for some glory other than a crown of thorns.

Such supposed but cowardly and inauthentic faith and hope has failed to wrestle with the conundrum of the grave, evading the possibility that God is God *among* the suffering and the dying, and that the King who rules the world is only a wounded lamb that has been slain. Whereas our three-day story — that "word of the cross" to which our faith and hope should be conformed — does indeed portray a God who prevails only by allowing place and recognition to the hostile opposition, saying "Yes" to the guilty and the doubting and the dying. That is divine affirmation of the very persons and realities which em-body the world's great "No" to God, the living expressions of its ugliness, de-structiveness, and sin. But because God acknowledges all this negativity and lets it be, because the word God says is Yes not No, positive not negative, for life not against it, grace surpasses its antithesis, proving more creative than evil can be destructive. Thus, in its very affirmation, death is defeated; and thus the Son of God who lay in death among the godless of the earth rises to new life, and brings them with him: witnesses to God's even greater presence within the ab-sence of that presence, which was great enough.[27]

Have we here, in the story of God's Godness in the grave of godlessness, a revelation of the mystery of love? Is love what it is — fertile, abundant, life-giving and restoring — just because it gives itself away and is prepared to die? And is that because love says Yes to hurt and pain and sacrifice, accepting con-tradiction and rejection, and thus meets opposition and negation with creative, life-promoting affirmation? How could love really die as long as it surrenders

---

27. See E. Jüngel, *The Doctrine of the Trinity: God's Being Is in Becoming,* trans. H. Harris (Edinburgh: Scottish Academic Press, 1976), pp. 107-8.

itself, accepting sacrifice and death? For by that very acceptance love asserts and fulfills itself, and thus outstrips, with yet more life, the destructiveness to which it yields. Likewise, forgiving love can never be defeated: for forgiveness will be met either with love or with rejection. If with love, forgiveness will have found its goal; if with rejection, that can only evoke from true forgiveness more forgiveness still — the pardon abounds even more as the offense increases. And to all of this the corollary is that self-preservation is self-defeating. The refusal to give oneself away is, by its very nature, the denial of affirmation and fertility. By saying No instead of Yes, self-love quenches life and becomes that very victory for death and negativity which the ego fears and tries to protect itself against.

Of course, if it is true that the refusal to accept contradiction is destructive, that loving self-surrender to death and opposition is the dynamic source of life, this is something we ultimately know only — given the poverty of both our love and understanding — because the God who *is* Love has shown it to us. Indeed, it is the one whom faith acknowledges as God incarnate who has told us that those who preserve their lives shall lose them, and they who lose their lives shall find them (Mk. 8:35). But above all it is in the story *about* this man, first crucified, then raised, that we have heard the astounding news that love as self-surrender is the truth for us, because it is first the truth of God's own life and being. We have heard a parable in which the God of heaven has surrendered to contradiction and defeat, bestowing affirmation and identity on one in whom only what is opposed to God is visible and triumphant, while everything that is of God is absent and extinguished. Yet even where negativity abounded and love was given up for dead, the creativity of grace abounded; and where all was death, defeat, and darkness, it transpired that there was much more light and life and victory. God's risky, self-surrendering Yes to the nullity of a godless grave is by the same token a resounding Yes of self-fulfillment in the cause of saving love. Nowhere more than in this self-negation is God's identity so powerfully asserted or so gloriously manifested as the resurrecting Lord of life, triumphant over death.

Once we have seen this happen, however much it puzzles us, we are compelled to ask how it could ever have been otherwise. How could the godless grave and the resurrecting God ever have been kept apart? Could the God we know conceivably refrain from identity with humanity at its lowest, hell-like depths? And could the consequence of such profound self-giving be anything less than the snapping of the deadly power of self-regard and sin? How could the God of *love* not take the path of self-surrender, giving selfhood up to death for the sake of the world the Creator made and loved? How could the *God* of love, going to the inconceivable extremes of life-creating grace, fail to surpass and overcome the demonic opposition when it had gone to unthinkable extremes of life-denying evil? Could the God of resurrection, of whom our story tells, *not* first have been upon a cross and in a grave? Could the God of suffering, death, and burial, of whom our story tells, *not* become at length the God of Easter glory?

Perhaps, then, we have begun to recognize that in the sublime logic of love there is meaning and propriety in a still greater presence amid God's great absence in a godforsaken death. But to acknowledge that is not to indicate that the riddles in our story have been solved, the conundrum of the grave finally decoded. In saying that the things which we have seen are the way things have to be, we are not imposing upon God an extraneous necessity nor subsuming the happenings of Easter within some principle of our own conceiving. The story still conceals more than it reveals; and it demands not to be heard as a comforting narrative which confirms and reinforces what we knew and understood. Rather, like all the church's parables, the Easter story is — we say again — a *dangerous* memory, iconoclastic and disruptive, confounding our conceptions, undermining our understanding, inviting us to grope in thought toward what seems unthinkable.

If that transforming of the mind is a pilgrimage of faith on which we are now set, it is also clear that the journey is only just begun. In the next part of this study much will have to be examined and rethought if even in outline the broad canvas of Christian knowledge is to be so arranged that the fact of God's presence in the grave is its controlling center, governing our perspective on the whole and on all its detail. Certainly, if this is a fact of gospel truth, then it cannot but be a determining criterion and fundamental datum, with which the gospel as a whole must be aligned, on which faith's coherent structures should be grounded, and from which all life and ethics, policies and postures should be derived. As we have heard the startling story, we have, in fact, cast sidelong glances at a range of major questions which the narrative provokes. These now require our attention if our pilgrimage toward an understanding of the filled and empty tomb is to proceed, and if that tomb is truly to be a focal point of Christian comprehension and corresponding lifestyle.

Who, for example, *is* this person, crucified, interred, and raised, from whom, in death, God is so demonstrably distant yet also manifestly close, since the Father who delivered up the Son also delivered him out of death's clutches in world-renewing, life-restoring triumph? Who is this Son of God, who died in godforsakenness, this man from Nazareth from whom, even *in extremis* and descended into hell, God would not be parted? And if these questions of Christology, of the identity of the one who lay in death yet lives, are inescapable, they cannot be asked unless we are also willing to inquire about the identity of God. Who *is* God, this God, this God of love who abandons the only Son, this God of life and creativity who submits to human death and human nullity? What relationship binds the Father and the Son, holding them in even greater unity within the great hiatus of their respective sonlessness and godforsakenness? Can such a mystery be apprehended without an understanding of the *Spirit*, that divine energy which unites in the midst of separation and is creative in the depths of death? And is it only then as *Triune* that we can understand the God who died and rose again, and as a happening of the Trinity that we must interpret the cross and grave and empty tomb?

Of course, it is in these events, above all, apparent that God is not only a God who *is*, but essentially a God who *acts*. Divine being is itself activity, the openness of the self to abandonment and contradiction which mightily delivers us from death. Yet *how* does this God act, what is the logic-defying, experience-denying *modus operandi* of such creative power and saving grace? How can God be the Almighty One, of providence and creativity, if we see in Jesus' expiry the Lord of all abandoning power to human weakness and demonic liquidation? How can there be redemption and renewal from a Creator who accepts defeat at the hands of antagonistic forces which hold the creatures captive? And how, in the end, shall such a God liberate all of history, currently so in bondage to evil and in fear of termination, for a glorious, unending future of freedom and festivity?

Such are some of the questions we now turn to in Part Two, as we analyze the long history of the church's efforts to think through the meaning and implications of its central three-day narrative. Beginning with the New Testament itself, then moving through the early church and the Reformation to the modern era, we shall finally explore in greater depth some extraordinary conceptual developments in our own day concerning "the death of the living God."

Yet not even the questions of thought and understanding which rise out of the grave of the Son about the identity and activity of the living God can be for us the *final* questions. For us, who pose such human queries about divine reality, the final questions — to be confronted in Part Three below — must be about ourselves. Who, in the light of all that God is, and does, are *we*, in our humanity, in our present, our history and future destiny? And how ought we to live as those who seek to follow in God's way? What, in other words, does it mean — globally, socially, individually — to be human if it is true that, even for God, fulfillment of selfhood lies along a path of self-abandonment and death? And, perhaps above all, what does it mean to be *Christian*, to be the *church*, God's people, if even the people's God renounces majesty and safety, risking pain, humility, and death, as the only way to secure on earth the coming reign of justice, grace, and peace? The disturbing, darkening light of the cross and grave must penetrate through the protective atmosphere of thought, conceptuality, and meditation and begin to expose, beneath those clouds, the earthly and earthy reality of how as Christians and as human beings we live and love, serve and die, in a world so full of graves and crosses. Only then shall we be even partly sure that we are truly listening to the indicatives of the tridual Christian story and being obedient to its demands.

CHAPTER FOUR

The Word Incarnate and Interred

I. The Divine Identity of Jesus' Body

Poor Thomas Didymus! For his refusal to believe, without seeing some evidence, that a man was alive and well two days after execution and burial, this sanest of human beings has been forever cast as the patron saint of doubt and scepticism. Did the Fourth Evangelist really intend to diminish the Twin's delayed conviction that Jesus was alive, in contrast to the instant joy of his ten colleagues and the faith of later generations who "not having seen, yet believe" (Jn. 20:19-29)? It is not plain from the text that Thomas's faith in the risen Lord did finally require that touch of his crucified body on which he had first insisted, and which he was certainly offered (vv. 25, 27). We could infer that sight alone of the wounded side and hands proved sufficient to convince and transform this disciple as it earlier had the others (v. 20). If so, then he and they together, believing through what they have been shown, would still stand for John in some contrast to those who would thereafter be blessed with the gift of a faith not based on observation (v. 29). Faith comes by hearing (Rom. 10:17); and whatever historical construction be placed upon the record of the risen Christ's appearances to sight, the unfolding centuries of Easter faith — including quite possibly the generation of the Fourth Evangelist himself[1] — lacked direct vi-

---

1. The most celebrated recent apologia for a very early dating of John's Gospel comes from J. A. T. Robinson, in his *Redating the New Testament* (London: SCM and Philadelphia: Westminster, 1976), and, more expansively, in *The Priority of John* (London: SCM, 1985). He believes that the gospel found its present form well before AD 70. But the major-

sion for either ground or confirmation. To concede, with Kierkegaard,[2] no advantage to the contemporaries of Jesus over his disciples in the present is to insist that all newness of life is conditional not upon the senses but upon the hearing of the inner ear: faith's reception of the Word which tells about, or is, the resurrected one.

However, the priority of hearing over sense notwithstanding, it can scarcely have been John's wish to relativize these visible flesh-and-blood encounters with the post-Easter Christ so as to dishonor any of the disciples, Thomas least of all.[3] He is not so much the last, slowest, and most doubtful of the contemporary disciples as the final and definitive eyewitness of the church's good news for every generation: that Jesus, born in flesh, crucified with finality, and buried in godforsakenness and godlessness, has been raised by God the Father.[4] It is given to Thomas not with tardiness to compromise, but with pas-

---

ity of authorities still prefer a range of later dates. Among the plethora of commentaries and other studies on the Fourth Gospel, the most significant include the following: C. K. Barrett, *The Gospel according to St. John* (London: SPCK, 1955); R. H. Lightfoot, *St. John's Gospel* (Oxford: Clarendon Press, 1956); Marsh, *St. John;* R. Bultmann, *The Gospel of John: A Commentary,* trans. G. R. Beasley-Murray et al. (Oxford: Blackwells and Philadelphia: Westminster, 1971); R. Schnackenburg, *The Gospel according to St. John,* vol. 1 (London: Burns & Oates and New York: Herder and Herder, 1968); vol. 2 (London: Search Press and New York: Seabury Press, 1980); vol. 3 (London: Search Press and New York: Crossroad, 1982); O. Cullmann, *The Johannine Circle* (London: SCM and Philadelphia: Westminster, 1976); and J. Ashton, *Understanding the Fourth Gospel* (Oxford: Clarendon Press, 1991). Also, in keeping with our particular approach here, note two studies on the *narrative* structure of John's Gospel: K. Grayston, *Narrative Commentaries: The Gospel of John* (London: Epworth and Philadelphia: Trinity Press International, 1990); and M. W. G. Stibbe, *John as Storyteller* (Cambridge: Cambridge University Press, 1992).

2. See S. Kierkegaard, *Philosophical Fragments,* trans. H. V. Hong and E. H. Hong (Princeton: Princeton University Press, 1985), ch. 4. Cf. Brevard S. Childs, *The New Testament as Canon: An Introduction* (Philadelphia: Fortress and London: SCM, 1984), pp. 126ff.; also L. Newbigin, *The Light Has Come* (Grand Rapids: Eerdmans and Edinburgh: Handsel Press, 1982), p. 271; and Marsh, *St. John,* pp. 644ff.

3. The weakness of Bultmann's interpretation of faith, e.g., is that he turns the legitimate priority of hearing over sight into a disjunction between the two, commensurate with those between gospel and law, spirit and flesh. To know Jesus according to sight, i.e., according to historical knowledge of Jesus, becomes for Bultmann a false knowledge, to be rejected in favor of the faith which commits itself to the risen Christ without reference to his history. See e.g., *Faith and Understanding,* vol. 1, pp. 273ff. But this is to make the most dubious assumptions concerning what Paul means by living and knowing Christ "after the flesh" (e.g., Rom. 8:4-5; 2 Cor. 5:16) as well as to ignore John's emphasis on the fleshliness of the Christ-event.

4. This importance of Thomas to John would be all the more emphatic if, as is

sionate conviction to encapsulate and finalize, the archetypal Christian confession, naming Jesus eleven days after Calvary as Lord and God. And what evokes that acclamation is demonstrably from the narrative not the fact that Jesus is simply alive, triumphant, and exalted over death, but the fact of gaping wounds which confirm his earlier death. The living one is Lord and God just because he is manifestly none other than the frail and fleshly creature whose final agonies and injuries had emptied him of life and reduced him to a corpse. Like any remains, officially anonymous till named by a relative or friend, it was a familiar body, which had publicly hung from a cross and assuredly occupied a tomb, that was identified by Thomas as the living God (Jn. 20:28). And that naming in turn confirms what John had announced even in his Prologue — that the eternal God, the Word of life, had become identified with mortal flesh, made from the dust of the earth and doomed like every frangible, friable creature to return thereto. In that corruptible, decaying, lowly form, and in none other, had the Creator tabernacled with us, full of grace and truth, unveiling the effulgent glory of the everlasting triune community (Jn. 1:14). From first to last, then, the identity of Jesus is that of one in whom God's presence and splendor are coexistent with their very opposite — with the finitude of creaturehood, the shame of suffering, the finality of termination, the nothingness of sepulture, the relationless nonpresence of extinction. In him the eternal, creating and resurrecting God of heaven and the perishable and finally perished man of Nazareth are one.[5]

It would be premature to nominate without qualification the Johannine Thomas as a representative of the New Testament's entire witness to the identity of Jesus Christ or to assume that all its voices are identical with his in their early Christological confession. Yet confession itself certainly unites them all. Defying those today who would pull out from under Scripture's theological blanket some bare, uninterpreted facts about Jesus,[6] the New Testament writers

widely agreed, John understood the events of 20:19-29 (which include the breathing of the Holy Spirit upon the disciples and their sending out to announce and effect forgiveness, along with Thomas's confession) to have *followed* those now appended in ch. 21, where the men are still at their boats in Galilee, neither expecting nor recognizing Jesus. See, e.g., Barrett, *Gospel according to John,* pp. 471-90; Bultmann, *Gospel of John,* pp. 689-718.

5. This oneness, so characteristic of John, is clearly visible in the double meaning he gives to Jesus' being "lifted up" on the cross — in both execution and exaltation (3:14; 12:32ff.). See, e.g., von Balthasar, *Mysterium Paschale,* pp. 122ff. Von Balthasar also clarifies how distinctively among the evangelists John anticipates Christ's glorification in resurrection and ascension, thereby bridging in advance the hiatus represented by Good Friday and Easter Saturday (pp. 70-71).

6. On this see Gunton, *Yesterday and Today,* pp. 61-65. Like many other exponents of

consistently begin with a conviction, born and nourished through faith's hearing of the three-day story, that in Jesus of Nazareth, crucified and buried, God himself has been actively, savingly embodied.

Christology, Gunton is very clear here about the shortcomings of the "quest for the historical Jesus," which attempted to reconstruct the facts about the historical figure apart from a faith-conditioned theological interpretation of his origins and destiny, identity and purpose. In fact, Albert Schweitzer very effectively brought the original Quest of nineteenth-century Liberal Theology to an end (see A. Schweitzer, *The Quest of the Historical Jesus* [1906], trans. F. C. Burkitt [New York: Macmillan, 1968]); and the "New Quest" in the 1950s and '60s (associated with E. Käsemann, G. Bornkamm, and E. Fuchs, among others) seemed very quickly to peter out (see esp. J. M. Robinson, *A New Quest of the Historical Jesus* [London: SCM and Naperville, Ill.: A. R. Allenson, 1959]). Remarkably, however, and suggesting that theologians as a breed have extremely short memories, yet another flurry of studies in the history of Jesus has recently appeared and attracted considerable attention. Some of these, to be sure, represent fine historical research, making good use of much new sociological data concerning the time and context of Jesus of Nazareth. On that basis there now seems to be some support for the view that Jesus was a Palestinian peasant, actively engaged as an egalitarian "social bandit" in resistance to the oligarchic oppressiveness of both the Jewish religious authorities and those of Roman imperialism. See esp. J. D. Crossan, *The Historical Jesus: The Life of a Mediterranean Jewish Peasant* (San Francisco: HarperCollins, 1991) and *Jesus: A Revolutionary Biography* (San Francisco: HarperCollins, 1993); R. A. Horsley and J. S. Hanson, *Bandits, Prophets, and Messiahs* (Minneapolis: Winston Press, 1985); R. A. Horsley, *Jesus and the Spiral of Violence* (San Francisco: Harper & Row, 1987); and, for a rather less political portrait of Jesus, J. P. Meier, *A Marginal Jew — Rethinking the Historical Jesus* (New York: Doubleday, 1991). See also M. J. Borg, "Portraits of Jesus in Contemporary North American Scholarship," *Harvard Theological Review* 84.1 (1991): 1-22. See also A. R. Eckhardt, *Reclaiming the Jesus of History* (Minneapolis: Fortress Press, 1992).

While historically fascinating in many cases, this resolutely "from below" research, like all the previous versions of the Quest, methodologically brackets off the theologically significant questions about Jesus, including those about his God-relatedness and those concerning his resurrection. The latter is assumed a priori not only to be not historical, but not even to be "history-like" in Hans Frei's sense, but one of countless mythological expressions of a timeless, universal phenomenon of religious experience, somehow inspired in this case by the historical but strictly dead and finished Jesus. Thus, "Emmaus never happened. Emmaus always happens" (Crossan, *Historical Jesus*, p. xiii).

One immensely "successful" account of Jesus is unnecessarily sceptical, driving far too broad a wedge between Jesus and the religion about him allegedly invented by Paul. This is A. N. Wilson, *Jesus* (London: Sinclair-Stevenson, 1992) — a poorly argued book justifiably criticized by, among others, N. T. Wright, in *Who Was Jesus?* (London: SPCK and Grand Rapids: Eerdmans, 1992); cf. N. T. Wright, *Jesus and the Victory of God* (Minneapolis: Fortress Press, 1993). See also B. Witherington III, *The Christology of Jesus* (Minneapolis: Fortress Press, 1990).

The quality of New Testament reflection and conceptualizing about the meaning of this narrative — that earliest *thinking* of the story which is now the object of our story — certainly varied considerably in its complexity, sophistication, and depth. Yet undoubtedly all the post-Easter authors were already embarked upon a journey of theological interpretation later summed up as "faith seeking understanding." They were engaged, that is, in an enterprise of ever deeper exploration into the intelligibility and significance of an event (and person) apprehended as divine in origin and saving in purpose. Their thinking, therefore, had no neutral, detached, presuppositionless point of departure, shorn *per impossibile* of the believer's perspective, commitment, and persuadedness. However primitive or limited at first their understanding, they indeed began with confession: that Jesus Christ, born of flesh and crucified in weakness, was the agent of God's kingdom and the embodiment of God's reality.[7]

It must be granted that the New Testament's variant presentations of this confessional stance and unifying theme display an intriguing diversity of style, memory, and purpose. But this multiformity in the medium surely promotes rather than destroys concord in the message. And it enhances the credibility and authenticity of each, avoiding both the shallowness of the one-dimensional and the superficiality of engineered sameness. It is not illegitimate to indicate — though dangerously easy to inflate — the differences between the Fourth and the Synoptic Gospels. In John, for example, there is a story to be told of the world's redemption from darkness and from death. Though it will quickly become clear that the victory of light and life has been secured in the particularity of one man's time and flesh, that singular existence is set within a cosmic frame, the story beginning before the beginning of everything. For Mark, by contrast, the struggles of light and dark, though equally dramatic, are waged less upon a universal stage than in life's small corners, where little people suffer, bleed, and fail. One of their number, conspicuous only for his mundane familiarity and thus wholly incognito, secretly fulfills the messianic hope for pain's healing and the pardoning of guilt.[8] Thus Mark's good news begins not in eternity but in a wilderness and at a river, and with the secret Messiah's

---

7. One of the most lucid introductions to the nature of the theological task as "faith seeking understanding," takes that phraseology of Anselm for its title; and earlier, so too did Barth's classic, if highly controversial, study of theological method. See, respectively, D. L. Migliore, *Faith Seeking Understanding* (Grand Rapids, Eerdmans, 1991), ch. 1, and K. Barth, *Anselm: Fides Quaerens Intellectum*, trans. I. W. Robertson (London: SCM and Richmond: John Knox Press, 1960).

8. On interpretations of the "messianic secret" in Mark see, e.g., Macquarrie, *Modern Thought*, pp. 75ff.; Childs, *New Testament as Canon*, pp. 79ff.; and Fredricksen, *Jesus to Christ*, pp. 44ff.

subordinate precursor at that, the obscure fulfillment of a small and ancient prophecy (1:1ff.).[9]

When from their different starting points the evangelists converge to portray the things that Jesus said and did and suffered, between his encounter with the Baptist and his departure from his friends, there again can be discerned and again exaggerated — variations between the first three records and the fourth.[10] The Synoptics, for instance, make the imminence of God's kingdom the primary burden of the ministry and message of Jesus, and show him leaving ambiguous and obscure to unbelieving eyes the precise relationship between his own deeds and personhood, and the heavenly Father's reign. Thus in Matthew, Jesus pointedly refuses straight answers both to Caiaphas and Pilate about his own messiahship (Mt. 26:64; 27:11). Yet John, by contrast, punctuates the dialogue of Jesus, which scarcely makes mention of the kingdom, with the uninhibited and shocking self-pronouncement: "I Am." That not only thrust Jesus' own identity and personhood into the very center of the message that he preached; it also evoked oblique, yet unmistakable, connections and identifications between Jesus and the divine and holy One who sent him: Yahweh the God of Israel, self-named as "I am who I am."

9. On the other hand, one of the most stunning features of John's Prologue, which makes so breathtaking a sweep from the life of God before creation to the creaturely enfleshment of the Word, is the seemingly intrusive role played therein (vv. 6ff.) by John the Baptist. Presumably this is aimed polemically at those who have identified the Baptist as himself the promised savior of Israel rather than merely a preparation for the coming Light. But might this also be the evangelist's way of placing the "scandal of particularity" firmly in the path of those who would docetically reduce the incarnation to a timeless, abstract myth? Like Pontius Pilate in the Apostles' Creed, John the Baptist in this Prologue firmly anchors the incarnation in datable, nonrepeatable, unsubstitutable persons and events of historical time.

10. For a useful, popular discussion of the differences and continuities between the Synoptics and John, see J. D. G. Dunn, *The Evidence for Jesus* (London: SCM and Philadelphia: Westminster, 1985), chs. 1 and 2. See, too, his *Unity and Diversity in the New Testament,* 2nd ed. (London: SCM and Philadelphia: Trinity Press International, 1990) and *Christology in the Making.* Whereas Dunn represents a moderate view on the differences between the Synoptics and John (especially in terms of Christology), there are some who go further in distinguishing them (Schillebeeckx, e.g., treated the Synoptics and John in separate books, namely, *Jesus* and *Christ*), and others (e.g., J. A. T. Robinson) who strain to minimize the differences and treat John historically and theologically as *primus inter pares* (first among equals) (see *Priority of John,* p. 35). On the Synoptic and Johannine Christologies, respectively, see also Macquarrie, *Modern Thought,* chs. 4 and 5, and Fredriksen, *Jesus to Christ,* ch. 3; also M. de Jonge, *Christology in Context* (Philadelphia: Westminster, 1988), pt. 2.

Such variations of record and tradition, although significant, are no longer to be explained by a sharp dichotomy between the aims and methods of the Synoptic writings and the Johannine, as if the former were factual biographical history, the latter inventive and symbolic theology. There is a scholarly consensus, as just indicated, that theological creativity has shaped the form and content of the Synoptic narratives also, and a growing recognition that though — or because? — quite sophisticated as a theologian, the Fourth Evangelist is meticulous in his recording of factual detail and works with material from traditions as historically reliable as any. Some have even argued that John is the closest of all to the psychological truth of Jesus — whatever value that may be deemed to have.[11] And any such bridging of supposed gaps in purpose and technique between the different gospel writers serves also to relativize the conflict sometimes alleged to exist between them all and the apostle Paul.

It is obvious that Paul's methods and objectives are not the same as the evangelists'. If the Gospels portray the person and history of Jesus in narrative form, the Pauline and other Epistles generally affirm in more conceptual terms who Christ is, and reflect systematically upon the meaning of his person and history in ways that foreshadow the subsequent postbiblical development of Christian dogma more clearly than anything in the Gospels.[12] However, not even these distinctions are absolute. Quite apart from the idiosyncrasies and high Christology of the Johannine Prologue, Thomas's Christological confession, and others in the Gospels, themselves seem to anticipate those in the later church. Paul, conversely, though not usually constrained, like the evangelists, to quote the record of the words and deeds of Jesus, was faithful to hand on precisely that historical tradition when he deemed it crucial (e.g., 1 Cor. 11:23ff.). Far from discarding the narratives of the history of Jesus, he could offer a digest of the salient events as the very substance of his own preaching and the ground of his claim to be one of Christ's apostles.[13] We owe it to Paul as much as anyone that all Christian worship, proclamation, and reflection is in the end configured to the "simple," tridual narrative of death, burial, and resurrection we have been listening to thus far (cf. 1 Cor. 15:3ff.).

Surely, therefore, it is wrong to assign distinct and conflicting preferences — for facts or interpretation, for story or dogma — to the Synoptists, John, and Paul, respectively? Beneath the diversity of their methods and concerns they

---

11. See Robinson, *Priority,* esp. pp. 352-65.

12. See Gunton, *Yesterday and Today,* pp. 65ff.

13. See Stroup, *Promise of Narrative Theology,* esp. pp. 145ff., referring to 1 Cor. 15:3ff. Cf. E. Schweizer, *Jesus,* trans. D. E. Green (London: SCM, 1968 and Richmond: John Knox Press, 1971), pp. 93ff.

share many fundamentals; and one of them is the assumption that the good news is not susceptible to such polarities as these. For them all, the Christian message is one of scandal and surprise, visible only to the eye of faith. It is credible not to those who close their minds to anything beyond the limits of what might today be considered "ordinary," empirical, or scientific knowledge, but to those who open themselves with courage, obedience, and imagination to the perception and interpretation of transcendent reality. Yet this reality revealed to faith is scandalous and surprising exactly because it locates divine power and presence as immanent in the very world of ordinariness and historicity, the Holy and Wholly Other *in* the mundane and profane. Gospel writers and epistle writers, for all the differences among them and between, uniformly proclaim this mystery: that in a unique and final way the eternal "Maker of heaven and earth" has established identity with the creatures, in and through one human existence which like any others has made the quotidian, mortal pilgrimage from womb to tomb. Neither the affirmations about this person which all these authors make as believers nor the interpretations they offer as theologians have any other point of reference than the stories they all tell of him as narrators. That "faith seeking understanding" which Jesus Christ evoked in the New Testament community is grounded throughout in his history: the record of his words and works, of his birth and baptism, and above all of the events which preceded and succeeded those of his death and burial.

This is to assert, in summary, that all of New Testament Christology, approached from varying starting points and by many different methods, and expressed in a multiplicity of genres, incorporates some common givens. It is presumed that history — the sphere of flesh and time where life flourishes and perishes like grass and flowers — is the arena of God's activity, and that the gospel of salvation narrates a divine history of temporal events, a life lived in flesh, humanly born and inhumanly destroyed. To that extent every biblical confession of Christ shares the same form and the same controlling axiom as that of Thomas; for he, as we have seen, discerned the divine Lordship of Jesus precisely through the fleshly signs of his total, and totally terminated, humanness.

It is still true that to make its common witness to the risen Lordship of the Crucified and Buried One, the New Testament employs the widest range of metaphor and concept, appellation and attribution. There are many Christologies, not simply one:[14] heterogeneous designations for Christ's identity and evaluations of his significance. These can be loosely classified by the degree to which they imply that, without loss of this fully mortal humanness, Jesus Christ

14. See esp. Dunn, *Unity and Diversity,* throughout.

transcends the ordinary bounds of that humanity. Yet the contrasting predications and interpretations of Jesus, with their lesser and greater, simpler and more complex, claims for his relatedness to God, and representativeness for the human race, occur haphazardly throughout the New Testament corpus. Christological diversity yields to no systematic account of its development based on chronology, geography, or milieu. Variations have been attempted on a thesis that ascriptions to Jesus of universality and transcendence are an alien and later accretion to his own teaching, borrowed from pagan culture as the church moved away from him in space and time and thought. But these all shatter against the fact that the New Testament's more complex and exalted affirmations can occur in the earlier of its documents (cf., e.g., Mt. 16:16; Rom. 1:3; 1 Cor. 8:6). They can scarcely be explained except as faithful responses to the impact of Jesus himself on his contemporaries, and as enjoying continuity with his own understanding.[15]

An alternative explanation, therefore, for the New Testament's different estimates of Jesus and the many metaphors for him, to that of alien importation, is one of consistent growth. By a process of organic development from its genesis with Jesus, Christology grew naturally in variety, breadth, and depth. For as the faith of his followers grew, so did their exploration of the full resources of human imagination, language, and conceptuality. Only so could they struggle to give less and less inadequate expression to the unfathomed, inexpressible reality with which they were confronted.

However, both the advocates and the critics of this account may easily miss one (literally) crucial aspect of this reality to which the rich variety of primitive Christology made response. That mystery as a whole demanded and stimulated growth in the church's imagination, thought, and speech; but one dimension of it in particular acted — and still acts — as the final criterion,

---

15. The pagan-influence thesis, originally associated with Harnack (*History of Dogma,* 1897) and Bossuet (*Kyrios Christos,* 1913), and thereafter developed by M. Werner (*The Formation of Christian Doctrine* [London: A. & C. Black, 1957]) and Bultmann (e.g., in *Theology of the New Testament*), came to wider public attention through John Hick, ed., *The Myth of God Incarnate* (London: SCM, 1977). It was contested by some contributors to M. Goulder, ed., *Incarnation and Myth: The Debate Continued* (London: SCM Press and Grand Rapids: Eerdmans, 1979), but with particular effect by C. D. F. Moule, *The Origin of Christology* (Cambridge: Cambridge University Press, 1977). Other studies which embody views contrary to those of Bultmann include: Cullmann, *Christology of the New Testament;* Fuller, *Foundations;* M. Hengel, *The Son of God,* trans. J. Bowden (London: SCM and Philadelphia: Fortress Press, 1976); and I. H. Marshall, *The Origins of New Testament Christology* (Leicester, United Kingdom: Inter-Varsity Press and Downers Grove, Ill.: InterVarsity Press, 1976).

guarding the process of development against assimilation of the extraneous and inconsistent. And it was equally decisive as the fundamental common factor, ensuring unity and coherence among the multiple confessions of Christ's identity. We have said that the New Testament's range of analogies, titles, and embryonic doctrines concerning Jesus represent faith's waxing response to his perceived transcendence of the ordinary bounds of humanness. His humanity was not only particular but representative and universal, that of the Second Adam (e.g., 1 Cor. 15:22, 45ff.; cf. Rom. 5:12-21), the one who on behalf of many both obeyed and paid the price of disobedience. Nor was his humanness exclusive of other possibilities: this was the dwelling place of God's eternal Word, who shared the Father's name and glory (Jn. 1:14; 17:5; Phil. 2:9). But it was no parenthetic piety when we also said that the New Testament witnessed to a transcending of humanity which involved no loss of his total and totally mortal humanness. Here, above all, is the crucial — the cross-shaped — criterion of truth and unifying factor for all Christology. Nothing may be said that compromises this humanity, perishability and actual termination; and it is only because all *this* is to be said and affirmed that there is anything else about Jesus worth saying and acclaiming.

The history of Christological development, even within the New Testament, let alone in later orthodoxy, has often been caricatured as a progressive sacrifice of Christ's humanity to his transcendent God-relatedness. In fact, as we shall later see, the story of patristic dogma can be told to exactly the opposite effect. For now we may assert of the New Testament that every Christological affirmation, no matter how exalted, is governed by one fact, and that by it the whole range of understanding, though so wide, is held together. Jesus Christ is who he is, does all he does, means what he means, not despite but because of his human and wholly unexceptional mortality, and the exceptionally shameful and discrediting manner in which he finally succumbed to that mortality. In all its human loneliness and pain it is the death of Christ, and in its guarantee of that death's finality it is the burial of Christ, which together set the first and final limits on Christology. For they ensure that every attribution of transcendent otherness refers to what faith glimpses within and not outside the parameters of radical, inescapable, and ultimately cursed finitude. Along with the preceding cross, it is the grave of Jesus which, silently and scarcely noticed, supremely constitutes both the problem and the gospel of Christology. And as the last, indelible reminder that Jesus was born and died in human shame and weakness, the three-day interment of his body makes certain that the church's proclamation of his lordship and divinity, far from a mythical accommodation to alien culture, is a scandalous and revolutionary dissent from *every* culture then and now.

II. The Human Embodiment of God's Identity

The original offense of the Christian gospel took shape within, and was felt by, the faith of *Israel*. For it was the Jewishness of Jesus and of those he called and sent which determined the context and content alike of Christology's first problems and earliest proclamations.[16] The subsequent, mostly Gentile, church has always turned its face against exaggerations of discontinuity between the Old Testament and the New, the God of the Jews and the Father of Jesus. Against this "Marcionism," blatant or surreptitious, the humble dependence of the church upon Israel is to be acknowledged, along with the continuity of the former's good news of the grace of Christ with the latter's living testimony to Yahweh's covenantal faithfulness. How could the first community of Christians have recognized Jesus without the antitype of God's salvation, enacted in Israel's history, declared and responded to through Israel's law, celebrated and appropriated in Israel's worship? And how could Jesus be acknowledged without the promises made, the visions painted, the expectations prompted by Israel's prophets? Indeed, not even the early church conviction that in Jesus the Creative Word had been enfleshed, represented unqualified and discontinuous novelty. For the very "logic of the incarnation" can only be followed by those who share presuppositions and inherit precedents which posit an ineffably transcendent God who yet communicates dynamically with the created world and is self-exposed to the wounds and limitations of reciprocity with the elect people and with all humanity.[17]

On the other hand, when the Jews did first acclaim Jesus of Nazareth as the fulfillment of prophetic hope and apocalyptic expectation, hailing him as the center and turning point of covenantal history, the consummation of Yahweh's past salvation and the prolepsis of its completion, they committed themselves to possibilities which their own traditions could only vilify as blasphemy and stumble over as a scandal. Faith in Christ reached its subversive, dangerous conclusion under the impact of the person he was shown to be through the messianic signs he gave: the healing performed, the freedom declared, the justice promised; the forgiveness offered, the repentance required, the discipleship demanded; and above all by the exaltation received, since God alone could raise him from the dead. Yet all this took place and was observed in

---

16. See esp. B. Hebblethwaite, "The Jewishness of Jesus from the Perspective of Christian Doctrine," *SJT* 42.1 (1989): 27-44. See also M.-E. Boismard, *Moses or Jesus: An Essay in Johannine Christology* (Minneapolis: Fortress Press, 1993).

17. See Anderson, *Historical Transcendence and the Reality of God,* pp. 108-45. Cf. Gunton, *Yesterday and Today,* pp. 78ff.

contexts which for Jewish intuitions and traditions negated every expectation, contradicted every axiom, falsified every claim. And the substance of the offense, the ground for rejection, the proof of falsity, was this: that the one identified as the final prophet and as God's Messiah was so ordinary in his humanity, so extraordinary in his shame, weakness, and defeat.

What offended those who watched and heard as Jesus even obliquely identified himself with the arrival of God's long-awaited rule was the local, daily familiarity of him who spoke and acted. Was this not merely the carpenter's boy, Joseph's son, known like his brothers and sisters as one of themselves (Mk. 6:1-6; cf. Lk. 4:16ff.)? Likewise, it was his very earthliness which rendered so outrageous to the keepers of God's law the suggestion that he carried with him God's own authority over human sin (Mk. 2:6ff.). Above all, it was the base contemptibility of his final fate which confirmed his all-too-ungodly earthliness, his vulgar brotherhood in death with criminals and outcasts utterly negating every claim and aspiration to regal status and divine authority. How could he be God's anointed, sent to set the people free from all the fetters of oppression, when he had died, stripped and mocked and fettered at the oppressors' hands? Who could interpret him as the harbinger of final righteousness and power when his mission terminated in abject weakness on a cross, and in a sinner's grave?

Yet that, for those with eyes to see, was precisely his identity. It was their Jewish faith and expectation which had first made possible their tentative association of the Nazarene with God's last prophet and anointed king, sent for judgment and emancipation. Yet a reality encountered them which meant the bursting and replacement of old wineskins, the shattering and reforming of familiar images, the reinterpretation of future dreams and past assumptions. Collectively, the banality of his origins, the scandals of his life, the ignominy of his death, and the evil of his grave canceled former notions; but new conceptions came to birth, revealing the unheard-of possibility of a *crucified* messiah, a human foolishness divinely wise.[18]

How ironic was the very first, post-Pentecost, Christology! For when Jews stood at the farthest distance from other Jews, announcing that he whom Jerusalem had crucified and killed, God had made his Christ, they demonstrated that this unbearable, discontinuous offense lay after all deep in their own scriptures and tradition. The pain and shame which seemed so shockingly to disprove the claims of Jesus were in fact, and had always been, the substance and precondition of messiahship. Though their minds had fought for generations to keep apart the suffering of God's humble servant and the power of his

18. See esp. Hengel, *Atonement,* pp. 39ff., 65ff.; and *Son of God,* pp. 87ff.

anointed king, the ancient truth had now dawned on Simon Peter and later would on Saul. Gallows and grave were indeed the very locus of God's saving power, the chosen path for the elect Messiah. He who would redeem God's people and the world, setting it free from iniquity and anguish, would do so only through the ugliness and grief of lamblike slaughter, and would share a resting place with the foolish and the wicked.[19]

So the scandalous, explosive possibility that the omnipotent God of glory might anoint and send, to reveal and do the will of heaven, a submissive earthly servant destined for terminal humiliation had, it seemed in retrospect, been planted, primed and ready, in Israel's own memory. It waited only to be triggered by events in Israel's history and capital which confirmed as God's Messiah one whose fate had been exactly that. This meant that the faith of Jews in Jesus as the Christ brought to full expression Judaism's long, internal critique of her own nationalistic instincts. The Suffering Servant, now identified with Jesus, was representative of Israel's own vocation as God's uniquely chosen race. They were a people called to serve, and not to dominate, the nations; just as the Father of the Servant-Son wielded sovereign power over the earth not as an absolutist despot but as a caring parent, angered by the children's disobedience yet tearful for their bruises.

If, then, recognition of the crucified Jesus as the embodiment of God's messianic rule caused offense to Jews, it was also the summation of Jewish witness against the tyranny of naked power, the sacralization of imperialistic pride. Certainly Jews and Romans, the keepers of Yahweh's law and the vice regents of Caesar's might, colluded to secure the death and burial of Jesus. But his Easter vindication, though inconceivable to many Jewish expectations, was even more the ultimate protest of Israel's own instincts against the idolatry of arbitrary force to which the Roman Empire gave classical expression. Arising within the covenant tradition, where justice, love, and mercy governed all rule and ordering, human and divine, the exaltation of Pilate's bloody, buried victim as King and Savior signified the "transfiguration of politics" and a subversive revolution in the very nature of authority.[20]

---

19. On the early Servant Christology, identifying Jesus, as Messiah, with the Servant figure of Second Isaiah, see, e.g., Cullmann, *Christology of the New Testament,* ch. 3; Fuller, *Foundations,* pp. 66, 115ff.; Hengel, *Atonement,* pp. 59ff.; Schillebeeckx, *Jesus,* pp. 282ff.; Kasper, *Jesus the Christ,* pp. 104ff.; and esp. M. de Jonge, *Jesus, the Servant-Messiah* (New Haven and London: Yale University Press, 1991); also Moltmann, *Way of Jesus Christ,* throughout. See also J. H. Charlesworth, ed., *The Messiah: Developments in Earliest Judaism and Christianity* (Minneapolis: Fortress Press, 1992).

20. See P. Lehmann, *The Transfiguration of Politics* (New York: Harper & Row, 1974 and London: SCM, 1975).

Indeed, the higher rose the primitive community's acclamations of the crucified Jesus, the deeper penetrated this seismic *bouleversement* of power; and the more radical and dangerous became Christian dissent against the mores and requirements of Rome — and thus against every society which grows fat upon the spoils of its success and worships the symbols of its arrogance. When Jesus spoke of himself as Son of Man, associating his own ministry and the responses it evoked with the future execution of God's last verdict on the rulers and the subjects of this world, he was himself announcing this subversion of private and collective vanity and domination (Mt. 25:31ff.; Lk. 12:8). For the Son of Man enjoyed no ordinary power and glory whatsoever. The heavenly judge would himself bow to the verdict and the sentence upon human sin, enduring pain and persecution, homelessness and helplessness. His path to glory was obstructed by a cross, his way to triumph by a tomb (Mt. 8:20; Mk. 8:31ff.).[21]

At the time, not even the closest of disciples could tolerate or understand the thought of such a denouement to the ministry of Jesus. But faith's perceptiveness came finally to see that his suffering, cross, and tomb *were* Christ's glory and his triumph, the very source and form of his rule and judgment of the world. It was in servitude that his majesty consisted, in humiliation that his glory was revealed. And thus was authority, divine and human, wholly reconceived. Humanity's future and history's end days would be determined not by state hegemony or military clout, but by the imperceptible power of self-abandoned love. Notwithstanding the ascendancy of Caesar, tomorrow's world lay with one of Caesar's crushed and vanquished victims.

Such was the meaning of Christology's development, pursuing the logic of the Son of Man's self-designation. In Jesus, not only had all of God's past promises been fulfilled, but to him God's future had been entrusted, and through him it would arrive. The carpenter of Nazareth, delivered up by Jews and destroyed by Rome, was exalted at God's side as Savior, the object of worship, prayer, and expectation.[22] For he whom imperial power had left sealed

21. On the title "Son of Man," its origins, and its use by Jesus and the NT writers, see, e.g., Cullmann, *Christology of the New Testament,* ch. 6; Fuller, *Foundations,* pp. 34ff., 119ff., 143ff., 229-30; A. J. B. Higgins, *The Son of Man in the Teaching of Jesus* (Cambridge: Cambridge University Press, 1980); Moule, *Origin of Christology,* pp. 11ff.; Schillebeeckx, *Jesus,* pp. 467ff.; H. E. Tödt, *The Son of Man in the Synoptic Tradition* (London: SCM, 1965); Crossan, *Historical Jesus,* pp. 238ff.; and Macquarrie, *Modern Thought,* pp. 36ff.

22. On the Christological title "Savior," see, e.g., Cullmann, *Christology of New Testament,* ch. 8; cf. Bultmann, *Theology of the New Testament,* vol. 1, p. 79; and on "Lord" (*Kyrios*), see Cullmann, *Christology of the New Testament,* ch. 7; Fuller, *Foundations,* pp. 67-68, 119, 184ff., 340-41; Moule, *Origin of Christology,* pp. 35ff.; Schillebeeckx, *Jesus,* pp. 405ff., 499ff.; and Macquarrie, *Modern Thought,* pp. 44ff.

and guarded in a sepulcher, had risen and ascended from death's prostration, and would descend again from heaven's elevation (1 Thess. 4:16). Supreme already over every power and principality, angelic, human, and demonic (Rom. 8:38; Eph. 1:20ff.; Col. 2:10, 15), he would come again to manifest his glory. Then with his suppurating wounds still visible, his lamblike lowliness undiminished, he would sit beside the throne of the Almighty, with every creature gathered round in adoration (Rev. 5:6; 7:9ff.).

John's apocalyptic visions depict Christ's centrality in the last act of the eschatological drama, when heaven and earth will be remade and all things reconciled through him who endured the shame and anguish of a Roman crucifixion. In their first dreaming and recounting these visions brought a promise of comfort and a summons to endurance to those who in Christ's name were themselves suffering persecution and extinction at Caesar's hands. So it was also with the community's archetypal confession which names Jesus as its Lord, the *Kyrios,* and thereby gave to him that name which long had served in Greek as Yahweh's own (Phil. 2:11). This, too, ascribed divine honor and dominion, not to imperial power and imposing greatness, but to a humble slave, and because of, not in spite of, his self-abandoning obedience to a cross. With that audacious affirmation there came, here too, the promise that its inversion of all power would one day be complete — that at the name of God's powerless servant heaven and earth would bend the knee, and of his lordship every tongue would make confession. Yet that promise was itself a call for patience, courage, and the costliest discipleship. The ascription, then, of Lordship to Jesus contained, in some contexts, its denial to Caesar, as it often has since, and still can, to Caesar's many heirs. Refusing to bend the knee to any throne save that of a lamb which had been slain, some early witnesses to the Lordship of the executed one shared their Lord's fate for imperial satisfaction or amusement. The ultimate consequence for those who speak of Christ may, like the originating ground and governing criterion of what they say, be a violent grave.

The confession which could exact so high a price comprised in the first instance, as we saw, a declaration of Christ's futurity. He whom death had so evidently terminated had no less certainly been revealed to faith as the personified prolepsis of time's consummation. Triumphant over the enemies of life, Jesus was now alive beside the Lord of life, sharing the divine glory, until he would come again, destroying every authority and power, that the Father might be all in all in the final reign of justice, peace, and love (1 Cor. 15:24-28). But this participation in God's future, by one who had lived so human a life and dies so finite a death, raised irresistibly a further question for Christology, driving the community of faith to yet more decisive and isolating risks of intellect and heart.

For if the man from Nazareth, once crucified and buried, sits today with God in heaven, and from God will return tomorrow, what was his relation yesterday with God, and from whence did he originally come? As the processes of its language and reflection organically developed, the New Testament church grew in its perception of the starting point of Jesus' God-relatedness. If it was the resurrection through which God identified the crucified as Lord and Christ (Acts 2:36), and by which a son of David was designated Son of God (Rom. 1:3-4), the events of Easter could only be the confirmation of prior affinities and relationships between Jesus and the Father, the disclosure and enactment of shared anterior intentions. And thus the question often asked before Easter, in anger, bewilderment, and doubt, became now faith's own query and conundrum: Where did Jesus come from, and whence did his authority arise (Mt. 13:54ff.; Mk. 6:1-2; Jn. 6:42ff.; 7:25ff., 9:29ff.; 19:8-9)?[23]

In the community's answer to that inquiry lay scandal and offense to match if not transcend that caused to Jews by their confession of Jesus as Messiah and to Rome by their allegiance to him as Savior and as Lord. Intensifying the breach with the guardians of both Torah and the Pax Romana, the church answered the question of Jesus' past with a piece of such folly to the Greeks as to compound the reinterpretation of religion and the reevaluation of politics, with a revolution in philosophy.

What is essentially so disorienting about biblical Christology's answer to the question "Whence?" is its inherent double-sidedness. Apparently conflicting accounts of Christ's beginning are so juxtaposed and held in harmony as to require and assert an understanding of reality inconceivable to Hellenism or its rationalist heirs. This duality is perhaps already visible in the New Testament's "minority report" upon Christ's virginal conception, set in a context where most of its authors show no knowledge of that tradition, and where all of them presuppose and reinforce Jesus' uncompromised humanity.

Of course, the infancy narratives in Matthew and in Luke, each telling independently a story of conception by the Holy Spirit, may in no way be aligned with the presumption of Christ's full humanity so as to plant within the New Testament rudimentary traces of the patristic doctrine of Christ's two natures. That would force the biblical data into the straitjacket of anachronistic categories; and it would beg the question whether the Virgin Birth tradition intends to claim more for Jesus than an ordinary human constitution, or the narrated signs of his normality less than a unique transcendence.

---

23. Cf. Robinson, *Priority of John*, p. 357; cf. K. Stendahl, "Quis et Unde: An Analysis of Matt. 1–2," in W. Eltester, ed., *Judentum–Urchristendum–Kirche, Beiheft zur Zeitschrift für die neutestamentliche Wissenschaft* 26 (1960): 94-105.

However, resistance to such assumptions would also exclude an alternative inference: that instead of a primitive blueprint for the unity of Christ's two natures, the double origination of Jesus, with God and in a human family, betrays the opposition of incompatible Christologies within the New Testament. For the fact is that, no less than Mark and John, the same evangelists who record this miraculous conception also portray Jesus as thoroughly — and scandalously — ordinary. Familiar as one of Joseph's several progeny, he is as unexceptional to his neighbors in genetic descent as he is to us in human emotion (Mt. 13:55ff.; Lk. 4:22; cf. Mt. 26:36ff.; Lk. 19:41-46). In Matthew and Luke it is authorities wholly convinced of Christ's complete entanglement in the normal web and woof of human existence who also record the narrative of divine conception. However evaluated and appropriated by faith today, these narratives scarcely direct us to an abridgement, even partial and fleeting, of Christ's inclusion in the human race. At most (though it could mean everything), they convey an intuition that the very possibility and actuality of Christ's existence, in the fullness of his humanness, was no contingent accident of history, but the specific gift of God's grace and the accomplishment of divine initiative and power. Some see, that is, in the Virgin Birth tradition an invitation or command to consider this absolutely human span, from womb to tomb, governed like any other by the interplay of social, biological, and psychological events, to be the effect of a transcendent will and act, external to that nexus.[24]

Nevertheless, those who are open to such a possibility — and even more, perhaps, those disposed to reject it — are challenged to think through the converse corollary of this interpretation. It is that a human life, which owes its occurrence uniquely to the grace and power of the transcendent God, is, not in

24. On the Virgin Birth issue, see, e.g., K. Barth, *CD*, I/2, 172-202; R. Brown, *The Virginal Conception and Bodily Resurrection of Jesus* (New York: Paulist Press and London: Chapman, 1974) and *The Birth of the Messiah* (Garden City, N.Y., and London: Chapman, 1977); H. von Campenhausen, *The Virgin Birth Theology of the Ancient Church*, trans. F. Clarke (Naperville, Ill.: A. R. Allenson, 1964); Pannenberg, *Jesus*, pp. 141ff.; J. A. T. Robinson, *The Human Face of God* (London: SCM and Philadelphia: Westminster, 1973), pp. 47ff.; H. Thielicke, *Between Heaven and Earth*, trans. J. W. Doberstein (London: J. Clarke Ltd. and New York: Harper & Row, 1967), pp. 59ff.; Weber, *Foundations*, vol. 2, pp. 100ff.; also J. D. G. Dunn and J. P. Mackey, *New Testament Theology in Dialogue* (London: SPCK and Philadelphia: Westminster, 1987), pp. 65-71. Whatever doubts are currently experienced and expressed about the biblical narrative and credal affirmation of the Virgin Birth, it should be remembered that for the early church belief in the Virgin Birth was seen precisely as an antidocetic insistence on Christ's real humanity rather than as a sign that in his sinlessness he was not truly human. For an extreme and highly controversial, but much publicized, discussion, see J. S. Spong, *Born of a Woman* (San Francisco: HarperCollins, 1992); and, among other responses, see Wright, *Who Was Jesus?*, ch. 4.

spite of that but because of it, a life wholly subject to frailty and mortality, defenseless against and willfully exposed to natural and deliberate evil. The cross and the grave govern the Bible's affirmation of the Virgin Birth and modulate its implications. The end of Christ's life casts its shadow backward, insisting that God's very creativity, loosed in all its fertile novelty and initiating power, is directed not toward divine immunity from the peril, pain, and perishing of creaturehood, but to indistinguishable solidarity with createdness. Life as human beings make and live it can be self-serving and self-preserving; life as God purposes it and the Spirit shapes it conforms to fetal vulnerability and filial obedience. He whom the Spirit conceived and formed was, like any other child, born dying; and he, like no other child, was summoned in innocence to die for others' sin.

The virginal conception offers this startling interpretation of the power of God in the form of a narrative probably of limited currency in the early memory of the church. But similar transformations in the concepts of divinity and power are implicit not in a story but in a designation, which is perhaps the most central of all the titles in biblical Christology. The New Testament speaks normatively of the origins of Jesus Christ in terms of his "sending" by the Father. The Galilean son of Joseph, who came from Bethlehem, of David's royal stock, is also he who comes from heaven; and that not of his own accord but at the behest of the Father who has sent him (Jn. 1:45ff.; 6:41ff.; 7:28, 41ff.; Rom. 1:3). Few of the New Testament's many affirmations may more reliably be attributed to Jesus' own awareness and self-interpretation than this — that the earthly mission on which he is engaged, and of which suffering and death are the inescapable consequence, is the execution of a heavenly commission, actualized by a perfect alignment of will and goal between the sender and the sent. Prompted by the unprecedented intimacy and familiarity of Jesus' own language, expressing and addressing as Father the God in heaven who had sent him (Mk. 14:3), the church developed Jesus' consciousness of sonship into a most exalted designation: Son of God.[25]

Scholarship finds ample room for disagreement about the nature and significance of this Sonship as it bears on the question of the origins of Jesus Christ. Are the New Testament writers referring hereby to a temporal, earthly life of such a quality as to function uniquely as the expression of God's activity

25. On the designation "Son of God," see esp. Cullmann, *Christology of New Testament*, ch. 10; Dunn, *Christology in the Making*, ch. 2; Fuller, *Foundations*, pp. 31ff., 65, 68ff., 114, 164ff., 187, 231-32; Hengel, *Son of God*, throughout; Kasper, *Jesus the Christ*, pp. 163-64; Moule, *Origin of Christology*, pp. 22ff.; Macquarrie, *Modern Thought*, pp. 42ff.; and Fredriksen, throughout.

and will? Is Jesus the Son, stamped with God's nature (Heb. 1:3, RSV), because and as he perfectly upholds a human mirror to all that God does and is? Or is his relationship to God ontological and preexistent, so that his earthly birth comprises the event in which a divine person, sharing eternally in the Father's being and activity, and an active agent in divine creation, becomes creaturely, temporal, and human in filial obedience?[26]

It is, of course, impossible historically to reconstruct Jesus' conscious understanding of how the person he was, and the life he lived, bore relation to the eternity of the Father whom he loved and served. But his apparent intuition that such a relationship existed was shared by all in the New Testament who thereafter affirmed him as God's Son, whether they imagined that in this Son, God had become a perfect human, or that in this human, God had found a perfect Son.

Though vital issues are at stake in that dispute, either proposition entails a revolutionary conceptuality. For what form does this life take which so fully embodies or truthfully reveals God's own will and nature as to be acclaimed the perfect discharge of a divine commission or even the very becoming of divine presence? Or what is the content of this existence which evokes so high an estimation of its transparent propinquity to God's own being? The form and substance of the life of God's own Son are servitude, suffering, and surrender. It is not, for the New Testament, that Christ is sent because he is the majestic Son, but that his sending into lowliness constitutes and is the condition of his sonship. He would not be God's Son were he not united with the Father by an active and impeccable submission to the Father's will. Their oneness and equality

26. On the matter of preexistence there is much debate in contemporary theology. Dunn (*Christology in the Making,* pp. 113-28) interprets Phil. 2:6-11 as not asserting preexistence; but he does find it in John, who for him, uniquely in the NT, affirms a full doctrine of incarnation. Robinson accepts Dunn's interpretation of Philippians, but tries to avoid the conclusion that John has preexistence in mind in the Prologue. The exegesis of the Prologue is, of course, tightly bound, both as cause and effect, with one's Christology and understanding of incarnation as a whole. See the early lectures of Karl Barth on John: *Witness to the Word,* ed. W. Fuerst, trans. G. W. Bromiley (Grand Rapids: Eerdmans, 1986). Barth's mature theology, as we shall see, was predicated on God's becoming human in Jesus Christ — the revelation of the Father in the Son — and his *Church Dogmatics* came to its climax in his exposition of "God's Way into the Far Country" (IV/1). But Barth's doctrine of God becoming human embraced the controversial thought that it is not the Logos discarnate but the Word incarnate that preexisted the birth of Christ. See *CD,* IV/1, 52, 181. See also, e.g., Cullmann, *Christology of New Testament,* chs. 9-12; Gunton, *Yesterday and Today,* pp. 67-68; G. Lampe, *God as Spirit* (Oxford: Oxford University Press, 1977); and Pannenberg, *Jesus,* pp. 150ff. A monumental study of preexistence is K.-J. Kuschel, *Born before All Time?,* trans. J. Bowden (London: SCM and New York: Crossroad, 1992).

is not the denial but the accomplishment of a perfectly maintained dependence and subordination, of which the temporal content involves humiliation, servanthood, and death. Thus, even on an interpretation involving preexistence, divine sonship is no otherworldly privilege, signified by supernatural propensities, such as could attach to "Sons of God" in Hellenistic myth.[27] Rather, sending and sonship come to fulfillment in the form of a slave, of one born of a woman under the law, in the likeness of sinful flesh (Rom. 8:3; Phil. 2:7; Gal. 4:4). His identity as Son is publicly declared when he bows in solidarity with other people's sin (Mk. 1:9ff.) and embarks upon a baptism of death (Lk. 12:50). All glorious, let alone magical, prerogatives are rejected as demonically inspired deviations from true sonship (Mt. 4:1-11). He will truly obey his Father's will as he determines to live without divine protection and in the end submit to a cross and grave where even his Father's love is cast in doubt.

So it was that, of a human corpse, awaiting clandestine obsequies after final agonies of soul and body, endured out of pure obedience and self-abandonment, an approximation to faith's own normative confession was wrung from a pagan heart: "truly this man was 'Son of God'" (Mk. 15:39). And the final and strangest inference of all, from the revealing of divine sonship between a crucifixion and a burial, concerns what is thus disclosed about the Father. For if Jesus is the Son, flawlessly embodying in his human life and death God's activity and will, then the extremities of his obedience, which so distance him from God, by the same token perfect and fulfill his mission to bring heaven close to earth and make God plain and tangible. Can it be that in the broken godforsakenness of Jesus, Mary's child and son of Joseph, where we encounter his ultimate self-authentication as obedient Son of God, he is showing us the fullest, deepest truth about his Father's nature also?

That Johannine theme is a reminder of the Fourth Gospel's distinctive place within the pluriform organism that is New Testament Christology. John is unparalleled in his uses of dominical speech and dialogue to elaborate Jesus' identity as the Son and to illuminate both the dependence and the equality of his relation to the Father. In a single context John can reinforce the Father's precedence as greater than the Son (e.g., 14:28) and assert their unity and mutual indwelling (14:10-11; 17:11, 21). The Son is at the service of the Father, obeying the paternal command (14:31), providing access to the paternal home, and making the paternal nature visible and known (14:6ff.). Yet it is conversely true that the Son *is* the revelation, the perfect analogue and repetition of the Father's

---

27. See, e.g., Cullmann, *Christology of New Testament,* 271-72; Dunn, *Christology in the Making,* pp. 13ff.; Hengel, *Son of God,* ch. 5; and G. Stanton, "Incarnational Christology in the New Testament," in Goulder, ed., *Incarnation and Myth,* pp. 151-65.

nature, participant in all the Father is and has, including everlasting glory (16:15; 17:5, 24).

It would be wrong to exclude the possibility that the New Testament elsewhere, though in somewhat different terms, posits a similar relationship between Christ and God's own self. From its earlier to its later letters the Pauline corpus may be interpreted as hazarding the most exalted and extravagant of claims — as when it identifies Christ as the one through whom all things exist (1 Cor. 8:6), who was in the form of God (Phil. 2:6), and in whom the fullness of the Creator of the cosmos has dwelt bodily (Col. 1:19; 2:9). Yet whether or not he surpasses even this exaltation in intention or effect, there is certainly no higher biblical Christology than that which John expresses, both in these Farewell Discourses and supremely in the Logos poem of his Prologue. The latter passage demonstrates as clearly as any why the final break of the New Testament church from Judaism was unavoidable and deep. But it also encapsulates uniquely the revolutionary incompatibility of Christian faith to Hellenism. And it shows how on both fronts, the ultimate definition and constant guarantee of that faith's distinctiveness is provided by the death and burial of Jesus.

Jewish literature, within and outside the Scriptures, had long before John personified as Word or Wisdom that creative, self-communicating power by which God made and ruled the world, saved and addressed the chosen people (e.g., Ps. 33:6; Prov. 3:19; 8:22; Isa. 55:10-11).[28] But no incipient hypostatization of this divine self-disclosure crossed the threshold of God's own monarchy to become an independent entity, more or other than God's self-in-action. It was even less conceivable that the wide ground of holiness and power, guarding God's transcendence from all confusion with the creatures of the Maker's hand, should be trampled and defiled through an identification of Yahweh's eternal act and being with the immanent, mortal clay of human life. Yet for John it was precisely flesh — transient, grasslike, and dependent — that God's eternal, creative Word became.

With shocking implications such as these, John's Prologue decisively confirms the Jewish verdict on Christian faith as intolerably heterodox. But it also shows why the New Testament claims for the "whence" of Jesus, just summarized, constituted a fundamental quarrel between Christians and the Hellenists. And more than anything else it is John's Word or Logos Christology which shows that conflict to turn upon the nature of reality itself.

---

28. On the importance of "Wisdom" for New Testament Christology, see esp. Dunn, *Christology in the Making,* ch. 6; Fuller, *Foundations,* pp. 72ff.; Schillebeeckx, *Jesus,* pp. 429ff.; and R. S. Barbour, "Creation, Wisdom and Christ," in R. McKinney, ed., *Creation, Christ and Culture* (Edinburgh: T. & T. Clark, 1976), pp. 22-42.

For all its conscious echoes of the opening of Genesis, and its crucial extension of the process by which Judaism came to personify God's self-expression, John's Logos poem also betrays by definition a debt to Greek language and conceptuality. Its closest analogies, in fact, occur in Philo, who synthesized the Old Testament "Word" with the Stoic Logos — that divine, all-pervading principle of reason which gives coherence to the cosmos and finds particular expression in human thought, and the language it begets. Philo as a Jew protected God's absolute transcendence by transforming the material, impersonal Logos of Stoic pantheism into a personal, incorporeal expression of divine activity, always subordinate to the God who remains as such unknowable even to the heights of human thought. How doubly contrary, then, John's affirmation that the Logos, who was God, not subordinate but equal to God, has become visible and knowable in the human flesh of Jesus.[29]

Indeed, how contradictory and impossible such an event would be to anyone, Jew or pagan, who shared the axioms of Hellenism. These posit, dualistically, a gulf between the shadowy and impure world of matter, time, and body and the changeless world of beauty, truth, and goodness known to the spirit and the intellect rather than the senses. Assuming such a philosophy and value system, the prolific pagan mythologies which straddled the turning of the eras told diverse tales of a heavenly Logos figure. This intermediary between God and the world descended in disguise to redeem from earth and time and body the enlightened souls of the spiritually eminent.[30] The superficial similarity of such a myth to John's good news of the Word made flesh is precisely what

29. On the possible origins of the Logos concept and its use by John, see, e.g., Cullmann, *Christology in New Testament*, pp. 249-69; Bultmann, *Gospel of John*, pp. 3-83; Barrett, *Gospel according to John*, pp. 125-41; Dunn, *Christology in the Making*, ch. 7; Fuller, *Foundations*, pp. 75-76, 222ff.; Kasper, *Jesus the Christ*, pp. 169ff.; Schillebeeckx, *Christ*, pp. 351-68; and Schnackenburg, *Gospel according to John*, vol. 1, pp. 48-93; also A. H. Armstrong and R. A. Markus, *Christian Faith and Greek Philosophy* (London: Darton, Longman & Todd, 1960), pp. 16-20.

30. On this subject, see Bultmann, *Gospel of John*, pp. 7ff.; Childs, *New Testament as Canon*, p. 136; Cullmann, *Christology of the New Testament*, pp. 252ff.; Fuller, *Foundations*, pp. 223-24; Hengel, *Son of God*, pp. 33ff.; and Macquarrie, *Modern Thought*, pp. 102ff. It is important to note, against Bultmann's argument for the influence of gnostic myth on the NT, that all the extant versions of such a myth postdate Phil. 2 and Jn. 1, so that the influence is much likelier to have been the reverse — the gnostic myths being corruptions of the NT faith. See Dunn, *Christology in the Making*, p. 123; and B. Lindars, *Behind the Fourth Gospel* (London: SPCK, 1971), pp. 20-26. On gnosticism, see H. Jonas, *The Gnostic Religion* (Boston: Beacon Press, 1958); and E. Pagels, *The Gnostic Gospels* (New York: Random House, 1979 and London: Weidenfeld & Nicholson, 1980); and P. Perkins, *Gnosticism and the New Testament* (Minneapolis: Fortress Press, 1993).

casts into high relief all that lacks precedence and conceivability about the incarnation. And it exposes one last time the unseen but determining effect of the grave that held the body of their Lord upon the form and content of the Christian community's early faith.

That even as God's lesser intermediary, the Logos might actually become human and fleshly, subject to bodily passions and conditions, captive to time's decay and destined for termination and decay, would be the antithesis of paganism's possibilities. Its heavenly redeemer could survive his brush with the base world of mortal flesh only because he wore the mask of humanness, deceiving the hostile forces of carnality while secretly releasing from their evil clutches the knowing few who penetrated his disguise. The false appearance of humanity was thus a condition of the Savior's power.

It is quite otherwise with John, for whom no intermediary but *God* has in the Logos truly indwelt the fleshliness of our existence. Of course, God's hidden presence in our real humanity brings to a head the cosmic conflict of dark and light, of falsehood and the truth. Some perversely interpret these polarities in John's soteriology as an endorsement of Hellenistic dualism.[31] Yet John's theme is surely that what differentiates the children of spirit and the light from those of flesh and darkness is that the former see and welcome, as the latter repudiate or miss, precisely God's coming in the profane earthiness of mortal flesh. The sensuous insistence of the Johannine letters — that Christ has truly come in flesh, the Word made audible, visible, and tangible (1 Jn. 1:1ff.; 4:1ff.; 2 Jn. 7) — indicates perhaps that the modern misunderstanding of John as a Hellenizing gnostic perpetuates an unjust fate that befell him from the start.[32] Despite his inattention to the interval of Easter Saturday, John's is, as emphatically and scandalously as any, a passion gospel,[33] which details the human agony of Jesus and the grievous reality of his death. He is risen and above in glory, exalted as the Son of God, not in spite but because of his surrender to the degrading finality of the cross and grave.

John leaves no room either for a Jewish explanation of the third day, that Jesus did not really die on Calvary, nor for a gnostic rationalizing of the first, that his bodily death was a charade played by his immaterial reality. The hard fact of the Word's eventual entombment is anticipated and contained within

31. This position is espoused (against Bultmann) by Käsemann in, e.g., "The Structure and Purpose of the Prologue to John's Gospel," in *New Testament Questions of Today* (London: SCM and Philadelphia: Fortress Press, 1969), pp. 128-67, and *The Testament of Jesus* (London: SCM and Philadelphia: Fortress Press, 1968).

32. See, e.g., Robinson, *The Priority of John,* pp. 381-82.

33. See G. Stanton, in Goulder, ed., *Incarnation and Myth,* p. 161. Cf. D. Senior, *The Passion of Jesus in the Gospel of John* (Collegeville, Minn.: Liturgical Press, 1991).

the extended event of its enfleshment and indwelling. Faith has beheld the glory of the Father's only Son, not in a fleeting instant of earthly genesis, but through the unfolding of a human life. That "flesh" which the Word became was truly human flesh because, like all humanity, it was experienced in existence, extending through time and passing years, and because like all flesh it decayed and succumbed at last to perishing and death. Though anonymous in its sheer nothingness and waiting, the burial of Jesus, even for John, serves to guarantee the reality of his death and thus to give authenticity and content to the flesh in which God has been revealed (Jn. 1:14-18).

Yet if the impending death and burial of Christ are included in all that the Fourth Evangelist intends by "flesh," they thus belong to the very meaning of Jn. 1:14, and help to control our understanding of that and of the poem that precedes it. This would, in turn, exclude each of two common but antithetical interpretations of the Prologue. One of these attests that, though intended to preach an antignostic gospel, of God savingly revealed in body, space, and time, John's work has been cast in gnostic form. For the story of a heavenly redeemer descending and becoming human so as to redeem our flesh is as mythological in essence, however different in its goal, as that of one who descends and puts on humanity's appearance in order to redeem us *from* our flesh.[34] The other deduces from John's manifestly unmythological commitment to the historicity of Jesus that the Prologue cannot tell of a personal, preexistent Word of God becoming human, but only of God's eternal creativity finding uniquely personal expression in and through an independently existent and *solely* human individual of history.[35]

These mutually contradictory Christologies are the obverse results of a mutually shared presumption which identifies the concept and possibility of preexistence with mythology. That in one eternal mode of divine self-differentiation the Creator God should become a creature would, it is assumed, be incompatible with the full humanness of the one that he became. Either no such eternal origin and divine becoming preceded this human being's temporal beginnings; or they constitute not a linear antecedent to those beginnings but an oblique and heterogeneous attachment to them, an interpretative myth of "deity" prefixing his factual, human history.

Yet would a nonmythological interpretation of "the Word becoming flesh" necessarily defame the humanness of Jesus? Ambiguity may attach to other areas of the New Testament from which a doctrine of preexistence has

34. See, e.g., Bultmann, *Gospel of John,* pp. 7ff., 60ff.
35. For example, Robinson, *Human Face of God;* Lampe, *God as Spirit;* and N. Pittenger, *Christology Reconsidered* (London: SCM, 1970).

been induced; but the effort of some to banish that doctrine from John's Prologue are unconvincing. The likelihood remains that here at least biblical Christology wishes to affirm not that in Jesus a human person has been adopted to give expression to God's will and ways, but rather that his humanity is God's own self-embodiment, the Creator becoming one of us. Does this mean that in the enfleshment of the Word, whatever John's intentions, the nature of the flesh must conform to the nature of the Word, so that Christ's humanity yields to the constraints of his preconceived divinity? Does eternal preexistence inevitably compromise or transcendentalize Jesus' finitude, mortality, and temporality?

We have suggested the alternative: that for John, as for the rest of the New Testament, the death and burial of Jesus act as signs and guarantees of his total humanness. They exercise critical control over the meaning of the incarnation, ensuring that the becoming flesh of the preexistent Word be understood from within the presumption of Christ's mortal humanness, precisely so that the humanness not be accommodated to, nor qualified by, his divinity and immortality. To identify preexistence with mythology is to deny the grave and its preceding cross that governing role, their determination and disclosure of what is possible for humanity, the world, and God. Those who presuppose today that divine incarnation and true humanness are incompatible fall over the same stumbling block of foolishness, or perhaps fall into the same crevasse of preconceptions, as the Hellenists whose religion and philosophy were first confronted by the church's faith. At the heart of its gospel was the unheard-of intersection of eternity and time, of "being" and "becoming." If, for John, God's Creator-Logos was everlasting being, all-sufficient, self-originating, then the things which the Word made were creatures not of being but of becoming. Receiving their life as a gift from the Creator, they remained dependent on that source for its persistence and in time yielded it back, returning to the dust and nothingness whence they came. Yet the gospel's staggering assertion, impossible and foolish to Hellenistic instincts and philosophical assumptions, was that the creative source of being had itself "become," had stooped in subjection precisely to that transient dependence characteristic of the world to which it gave existence in the first place.

This unprecedented unifying and co-presence of humanity and God, of the finite and the infinite, of change and changelessness, the community of faith pondered and propounded as they announced and took their good news to the Graeco-Roman world. As we have seen, the church took with it many claims for the person and activity, the future and the past, of Jesus Christ. Together these amounted to an astounding, revolutionary, impossible connection between God's glory and a gruesome grave: that connection intuited by Thomas when he identified as Lord and God one whom he recognized from crucifying wounds as having been a corpse. The development of that association offended Jews as blasphemy, and threatened Rome with its intimations of subversion. But most of all, when John surpassed every "lower" claim with his acclamation of Jesus as the Word made flesh, Christian faith forced upon Greek philosophy whole new possibilities for understanding the nature of existence and of truth. Here, if not before, Christology moved from identifying the crucified and buried Christ with divine activity to raising the question of his relation to God's very being — though it left later generations in the faith to suggest conceptual answers as to how God's union with the cradle and the grave was possible.[36]

As we shall see, the struggle to preserve that possibility was only partially successful. Sometimes the easy preconceptions of the old philosophy triumphed over the daring, imaginative, and rational obedience of those who sought, with Hellenism's tools, to construct a new understanding of divine and human truth. The fragile folly of the gospel remained imperiled by the suffocating wisdom of the world.

So it is, for example, that the ancient metaphysical chasm between the worlds of intellect and sense, of soul and body, of eternity and time, has still not been sealed by all the generations of subsequent spiritual and intellectual development. It still survives in the form of polarities which split asunder our supposedly modern and enlightened perceptions of reality.[37] Theologically, the old dualism is visible even now, in those who shut off a world of history, fact, and science from open reciprocity and interaction with transcendence. And it is equally present in their converse a priori, which denies to that which they call God a dynamic self-negating freedom to identify with the finite world while exercising the powerful leverage of divine otherness upon it.

---

36. Against Cullmann and others, who see in the NT a purely functional Christology, others have insisted that the NT does incorporate affirmations which raise ontological questions, even if it was only later, in the period of classical dogma, that the church attempted to answer them. On the issue see, e.g., Cullmann, *Christology of New Testament,* pp. 3 and throughout; Dunn, *Christology in the Making,* pp. 358-68; Fuller, *Foundations,* pp. 247ff.; Gunton, *Yesterday and Today,* throughout; T. A. Smail, *The Forgotten Father* (London: Hodder & Stoughton, 1980 and Grand Rapids: Eerdmans, 1981); and Macquarrie, *Modern Thought,* pp. 6ff. and throughout.

37. See, e.g., Colin Gunton, *Enlightenment and Alienation* (Basingstoke: Marshall Morgan & Scott, 1985); Lesslie Newbigin, *The Other Side of 1984* (Geneva: World Council of Churches and Grand Rapids: Eerdmans, 1984) and *Foolishness to the Greeks* (Geneva: World Council of Churches and Grand Rapids: Eerdmans, 1986); and T. F. Torrance, "Emerging from the Cultural Split," in *The Ground and Grammar of Theology* (Belfast: Christian Journals Ltd., 1980).

Of course, it is one thing to *say* that reality is not so static, closed, and polarized, to deny that God's possibilities and ours are so restricted, to assert that God can still be God while becoming one of us, and to claim that one of us was fully human while also the one whom God became. To *understand,* defend, and continue to explore such testimony is quite another matter. With their Christology and their concept of the Trinity, the church's "early Fathers," for all their failures, undertook the thought-filled task of comprehending and defending; and with these doctrines theology still today accepts the invitation to further exploration toward the thinkability of the unthinkable That past history and that present challenge now constitute our imminent agenda. But both are predicated on the foundational — and foundation-shaking — affirmation at which New Testament Christology arrived, and which it bequeathed as proclamation and as problem to its posterity. This is the declaration that in Jesus, son of Joseph and of Mary and the church's risen Lord, *God* was incarnate and interred.

PART TWO

THINKING THE STORY

CHAPTER FIVE

God's Union with the Buried One: Doctrine Safeguards Story

I. From Story to Doctrine

"God incarnate and interred" — affirmed post-Easter as a word of victory and salvation, since only in the light of his grave's defeat and his body's resurrection could the buried one be recognized as God: this, we have suggested, encapsulates the central theme of the early church's message and of its written records now constituting our New Testament. This is only an encapsulation, of course, of that community's variegated and complex faith. Yet their gospel, set in its primitive and diverse forms, again and again comes down to this: the identity of a crucified and buried victim with one who has received God's own vindication, who came by God's own sending, who embodies God's own presence. These identifications of the divine with a creature who endured to the utmost humanity's mortality are implicit when Mark announces his stark passion story as the gospel of "the Son of God" (1:1), and John declares the becoming flesh of the eternal Logos (1:14); when Peter announces God's raising up of him whom Jerusalem had killed (Acts 2:23-24); and when Paul summarizes his inherited "tradition" with a three-day story which fulfilled the Scriptures: that Christ died, that he was buried, and that he was raised on the third day (1 Cor. 15:3-4). All these have a story to tell, uniting God with human life and death. Upon the antecedents, the sequel, and the implications of that story the New Testament church elaborated with secondary narratives and memories; with multiple images, metaphors, and titles; and through a variety of literary genres: hymns, parables, sermons, letters, and gospels.

Since from the start the church was obviously compelled to *think* about the meaning of its story and its elaborations, it is clear that rational reflection on the narrative's significance underlies and alone makes possible the New Testament documents. Even so, it is questionable whether even Paul was engaged in the development of systematic doctrine — a coherent set of of intellectual concepts and propositions concerning the story he had to tell and the gospel he proclaimed. Few today are able to detect, as did the Princeton divines, a "system of doctrine" within the pages of the Bible. For some, indeed, the answering of rational questions, especially about the relationship of Jesus to God, such as would require a philosophical or metaphysical conceptuality, was quite alien to the purpose of the New Testament authors. They were content to describe the historical activity and functions of Jesus of Nazareth as God's Messiah, Son, or Word rather than raise abstract, ontological questions about his God-relatedness or "nature."[1]

To this it must be said that at least some of the claims made for Jesus' relationship to God in the New Testament, above all in John's Logos poem, at least raised and left unanswered profound ontological questions. Just what *sort* of identity was this between Jesus of Nazareth and the eternal Logos? And what is the *nature* of this "becoming" which the creative Word has undergone? Such conundrums rendered unavoidable and proper the ontological and philosophical dimensions of the church's subsequent Christological and trinitarian reflections, even if no such conceptual analysis and construction occurred within the scriptural record itself. There the primary and paradigmatic mode of expression was narrative: an accounting of events that happened, to and through whom, and to what purpose — a story of divine and human unity in action for the sake of our salvation.

Be there ever so much more to the New Testament than the bare three-day story of a death, burial, and resurrection, that narrative provides the center and determines the structure of the church's life, the basis of its self-understanding. The People of God in the Old Testament shaped and preserved their community identity by remembering and reenacting stories of divine deliverance and anticipating the fulfillment of the promises those memories contained. Just so, the church lived out its calling and mission through memory's hope-inspiring narration of "salvation history" — a story which implicated God in the tangible

1. A functional approach to NT Christology is shared by such theologically diverse scholars as Oscar Cullmann *(Christology)* and J. A. T. Robinson *(The Human Face),* and also by many of the contributors to *The Myth of God Incarnate.* Others, of course, would insist that a purely functional Christology is impossible: that even functional claims about Jesus's agency on God's behalf entail unavoidable ontological questions about the relationship underlying that agency. See, among many examples, J. Macquarrie, *Jesus Christ,* pp. 7ff., 343-44.

depths of human sin, suffering, and death.[2] And it was in the grip of that history and its narration that they encountered for centuries to come the hostility of Judaism and the seductiveness of Hellenism. Christian confession was then — and surely is still — a narrative to be remembered, a story to be told, a word to be proclaimed. It is the word of the cross and of the grave, folly to the Jews and offensive to the Greeks.

Nevertheless, the experience of the post–New Testament community in relation to their cultural and social milieu demonstrated — what has been continually reconfirmed since — that the church cannot live by narrative alone, the simple telling and retelling of stories.[3] The very word "Logos," central to Scripture's most subtle and developed telling of the story of God's union with human fleshliness, entails the integral connection between speech and thought, language and reason, faith and the intellect. Stories appeal to more than feeling, emotion, or even intuition. Evoking the faith which comes by hearing, and providing the identity which creates and energizes a community, story is an invitation, indeed a demand, to think. In terms adopted later to justify the theological enterprise as the proper outcome of belief and prayer, "faith seeks understanding." Any story which claims to be telling the truth, and through which the hearer intuitively grasps the truth and is in turn grasped by it, initiates a quest of the *mind* for knowledge, wisdom, understanding. Just as children at Passover, hearing the annual retelling of faith's memories, ask "What do these things mean?" (e.g., Ex. 12:26), so the word of the cross, the Christian community's story of God's power and presence in the midst of impotence and death, compels the question of the *meaning* of these strange events. The story, the word, the proclamation may be foolishness to the worldly-wise; but there is indeed wisdom and meaning in the midst of human suffering and death, and a power at work in the world unrecognizable by ordinary norms of influence and might. Above all, there is a rationality in *God,* whose mysterious, discommoding, transfiguring secret is knowable to those who are alive to new possibilities and ready to *change* their minds, even if unknowable, illogical, or impossible by the blinkered norms of preconception and unquestioning assumption. The foolish gospel of the crucified Messiah, the buried Logos, was a summons not just to thinking, but to rethinking — a conversion of the mind to God's own reasoning (cf. Rom. 12:2), the fresh examination

---

2. See G. Stroup, *Narrative Theology,* esp. ch. 5.

3. See D. Ritschl, *The Logic of Theology,* trans. J. Bowden (London: SCM Press, 1986), pp. 14ff. and esp. p. 24. See also D. Hall, *Thinking the Faith* (Minneapolis: Augsburg Press, 1989), pp. 88-89, on theology's need of both story and doctrine (e.g., both the Gospels and the Epistles) — story to guard against doctrinalism, doctrine to provide commentary on the narrative.

of previously fixed conceptions in obedience to the word that has been heard, mental surrender to the sheer force of the story listened to.

Just because, then, it evokes knowledge and brings a challenge to understand what these things mean, faith's story leads appropriately and necessarily to reasoning and rationality, to thinking and rethinking, to theology and doctrine. Far from an alien, desiccating, and ossifying enterprise, intrinsically hostile to the fresh immediacy of narrative, theology's construction of concepts and doctrine is the essential means of bringing to articulation and to order the church's thoughts about its own identifying story. How else but with the tools of reason and conceptuality could the church perceive and conform its mind to the rationality of God, whose ways and thoughts are so different from our own (Isa. 55:8)? And how, without the intellect's ability to shape and order otherwise random reflections, forming patterns and creating "maps and models" of faith's territory,[4] could the community engage in teaching and evangelism, building up its own self-understanding and presenting the gospel, in apologetics and evangelism, to the surrounding culture? Rationality and doctrine are not alternatives to, or evasions of, the church's missionary task but the essential preconditions for doing that task. Without cognitive concepts and their rational ordering the People of God could expound neither to themselves nor to others the meaning of what they had seen, heard, and believed.

Furthermore, in declaring the story which has grasped and been grasped by them to be saving *truth,* the community of faith is necessarily, and however humbly, free of arrogance, drawing *distinctions* between the truth and falsehood. One cannot say Yes to the word of the cross about God's foolishness and weakness without implying a No to other philosophies of life and alternative assumptions of what is powerful and wise. This saying of No necessitates the theological, dogmatic enterprise no less than the task of thinking and ordering the church's positive affirmations. It is supremely by virtue of its task of separating truth from error that theology often claims to be a science; for all science incorporates the examination of data to discover what is actually there, what is real from what is unreal about the object under study, and testing hypotheses and theories for their truthful correspondence to observed reality.[5]

The concepts of theology and their ordering as doctrines play this truth-discerning role in the manner of regulations or grammatical rules.[6] They help

---

4. C. Gunton, *Yesterday and Today,* pp. 150ff. Cf. T. F. Torrance, *God and Rationality* (London and New York: Oxford University Press, 1971), esp. pp. 15ff.

5. See, e.g., T. F. Torrance, *Theological Science,* esp. pp. 119ff.; cf. his *Reality and Scientific Theology* (Edinburgh: Scottish Academic Press, 1985), pp. 25ff.

6. See D. Ritschl, *Logic,* pp. xxi and throughout.

the church determine what may and may not be said by way of expressing and reflecting on its normative stories. Within the church itself there never operates normatively just a single version of the Christian story with a universally agreed meaning, but multiple constructions of the story, with a variety of interpretations and inferences, and rival exegetical methods and results. Theology's regulative function is thus internal as well as external. The rules it makes, the boundaries it erects, make room for, but also set real limits to, diversity of thought and speech, worship and behavior. Some stories, some interpretations and corresponding actions, break these regulations, exceed these boundaries, and are judged by the community as a whole to conflict intolerably with the received tradition, the truth of the story entrusted to its care. For the sake of the whole church and of the gospel itself they must be proscribed as false. Likewise the surrounding culture may threaten to seduce the community with its own stories and corresponding values. Then theology serves the church by helping it discern when those stories are to be affirmed as partial reflections of the truth; when to adopt and adapt them as means of making its own story intelligible and persuasive; and when to reject them as perversions or contradictions of the gospel, hostile to the content and the implications of the church's authoritative story.

It was to meet these regulative needs that theology as early as the second century came to construct a *regula fidei,* a normative summary or "deposit" of the faith. This summarized the tradition inherited from the apostolic generation and functioned as a criterion and canon of intellectual belief. Equally the process of naming and anathematizing heresy, which makes the history of patristic theology so uncongenial to many, giving theology the appearance of hostility to all openness, freedom, and diversity of thought, was in principle, however crudely applied at times in practice, the required antidote to intellectual, moral, and liturgical anarchy. How could the inherited identity of the church, as mediated by its normative story, be maintained if deviations, alien corruptions, and experimental excess were never confronted and rejected? A community unwilling to say No to what was false would have forfeited any claim to be the bearer of truth.

This effort of theology, by means of dogma, ran many risks to distinguish truth from heresy, as we shall see; and it certainly appears in nonauthoritarian times to reek of scholastic narrowness, intellectual arrogance, and a sheer hunger for power on the part of the self-proclaimed "orthodox." Nevertheless, the dogmatic task of distinguishing orthodoxy from its heterodox alternatives may in itself be interpreted precisely as faith's intellectual humility and modesty before the grandeur and mystery of the church's story and its divine subject. Dogmas, that is to say, may be read as essentially *doxological* in character: the

conscious use of the mind's most finely tuned concepts and careful constructions to express the inexpressible and indicate the ultimate unattainability of
God's own truth.[7] In the very effort to formulate the truth through human approximations to its mystery, dogmas use concepts and language in an act of
"noetic self-surrender."[8] Hereby the believing intellect acknowledges the limitations of its understanding and articulation. Reason, in subjection to the given
reality whose meaning and rationality it seeks to understand, confesses, precisely through its dogmas, that even its best statements are partial, penultimate,
and proximate. Instead of quenching and domesticating mystery, dogma is thus
a form of worship, illuminating the transcendent object of its reflections and
confirming the incapacity of finite minds, stretched even to their fullest, to at-
tain God's incommensurable infinity. To no historical construction of Christian theology is this doxological interpretation of dogma more applicable —
despite many resistant criticisms and contrary points of view — than the early
church's struggles with Christology and the doctrine of the Trinity, which
reached a climax with the dogma of Christ's two natures at the Council of
Chalcedon.[9]

There is a case to be made, this is to say, that the patristic development of
doctrine with reference to Christ, and thus to God, was a proper and necessary
evangelical undertaking, required by the questions raised and left unanswered
by the New Testament, and by the missionary context and responsibility of the
early church. Only with thinking and reflection about their story could Christian believers plumb the meaning of their own faith; only with an orderly and
coherent set of affirmations could they teach, defend, and promote their gospel;
and only by differentiating concepts and doctrines and naming some as unacceptable and false could they preserve the veracity of the narrative tradition received from the apostolic generation. Doctrine was constructed in defense of
story: to keep the narrative of salvation alive and true, persuasive and redemptive. The Trinitarian and Christological dogmas which emerged from this period were designed not to deaden faith's story, but exactly to prevent its stifling
or alteration through contact with the cultural milieu, both in the generations
of persecution and in those of Constantinian ascendancy. Despite many threats
faced and dangers run in the course of these developments, was the dogmatic
purpose not largely met? To a considerable extent, we suggest below, the foolish
story of God's union with human flesh and perishing was safeguarded as the
thinking of the church proceeded, wisdom and understanding grew, with the

7. See esp. J. Sobrino, *Crossroads,* ch. 10.
8. Sobrino, *Crossroads,* p. 333.
9. D. Bonhoeffer, *Christology,* pp. 87ff.

rationality of God and of the gospel clarified, concepts refined, doctrines formulated, and falsehoods identified and set aside.

Threat and danger there certainly were, to be sure, throughout this process up to and including Chalcedon, as indeed in the history of dogma until the present day. Concepts do not emerge and develop in a vacuum, but within an intellectual environment — an outlook, a worldview, a dominant philosophy. The church's doctrinal task inevitably involved the use of philosophical notions and intellectual ideas current in the various contexts and generations of its early mission and expansion. To the extent that philosophy is simply the product of refined and ordered thought, early rational reflection on the Christian story could no more avoid philosophy than it could refuse its teaching and missionary imperatives. The former was mandated by the latter. The question was never whether the church should develop concepts and coherent, rational forms of thought, and thus make use of the available philosophy. The issue, rather, was whether the framework used in the development of that thinking altered and perverted the story, or whether, whatever their cultural and philosophical origins, the concepts used by theology were so creatively adapted and given fresh meaning that they served to protect rather than damage the inherited tradition.

Patristic dogmatics certainly *used* a philosophy, namely Platonism and its offshoots, in the refinement of its own thinking; but it did so in a dynamic and critical fashion which preserved the story so offensive to the Greeks and undermined the very presuppositions of Hellenistic thought. The genesis of its concepts in an alien philosophical environment did not prevent the church from turning those concepts on their head and expressing with them new and unheard-of possibilities. Nevertheless, the danger run was that the attempt at such an intellectual revolution would not succeed: that in the interests of accommodation, to make the story less foolish and offensive, more persuasive because familiar and affirming rather than subversive and iconoclastic, the church would allow its borrowed concepts to determine rather than serve the telling of its story, to blunt the sharp edges of its meaning. So it was that at at least one major point, the assumptions of Greek philosophy seduced the church into safe and comfortable waters where it could evade the difficult and dangerous intellectual turbulence generated by the story itself. Since that evasion, as we shall see, concerned the very nature of God and of divine possibility, the seduction of Hellenism came close to perverting the very "word of the cross" which was the church's raison d'être. If, despite that peril, we judge that the story of God's involvement with human life and death finally survived and was preserved by the development of doctrine, it also has to be admitted that not until our own day has theology fully recovered its nerve and come to terms with the stormy implications for the doctrine of God contained in the shocking Easter Saturday story of divine presence in the dead and buried Jesus.

In addition to the danger that in the unavoidable utilization of philosophy the church will avoidably permit philosophical concepts and assumptions to alter and domesticate the story underlying its confession, there is another peril inherent in the doctrinal enterprise. It is that theology will cease to recognize its limitations and penultimacy, so that dogmas, instead of being potential vehicles of doxology and self-surrendering intellectual humility, become instead arrogant claims to final, ultimate truth, more the objects of idolatry than expressions of worship. Doctrine as such, we have argued, is a proper tool, at the church's service, helping it reflect and regulate, while acknowledging its own fallibility and partiality, its falling short of truth itself and thus its own need for further refinement and reform. But doctrine — and those who formulate it and have the power to apply its authoritative norms — can sometimes lose sight of the limitation and penultimacy of theology, that inescapably human, finite science. Dogmas can become fixed and static formulations, infallible propositions abstracted from the dynamic reality of the story and of the story's Subject into compendia of irreformable, lifeless, and legalistic statements. They can then be applied authoritatively precisely not as invitations to reform and further thought, but as barriers to such, in their absoluteness and finality.[10]

The Reformation and its ensuing traditions form a historical and continuing protest against the infallibility and finality of dogma, a critique targeted above all, of course, at classical Catholicism. Yet Protestant and Reformed theology, though committed by self-definition to the continuing reform of the church's thought and life and thus to the repudiation of all self-styled "final words" in the development of doctrine, has its own history of "Orthodoxy" and of "fundamentalism." Here, too, the truth itself has been confused with statements and propositions, biblical or confessional, which in reality rather point to and approximate, than capture or contain, the truth.

How can dogmas, rendered static, finished, absolute, recover their dynamic and be reformed other than by critical subjection once again to the

10. On this, see Karl Barth's foundational discussion of dogmatic science and his distinction between a "science of dogma" and a "science of dogmas" (*CD,* vol. I/1, 11ff., 304ff.; I/2, 758-82, 797-843). Cf. T. F. Torrance, "Karl Barth and the Latin Heresy," *SJT* 39 (1986): 461-82, and Torrance's own extension of Barth's thoughts on the nature of theological truth in *Theological Science,* esp. pp. 337-52. On the *regula fidei* and the temptation to turn it into an instrument of legalistic authoritarianism, see Torrance, "The Deposit of Faith," *SJT* 36 (1983): 1-28. See, too, Douglas Hall's extended critique of the modern, Western church for having absolutized theology, in *Thinking the Faith.*

church's originating, self-identifying story? Whereas the purpose of doctrine is to preserve that story, there are times and instances when it is necessary for the story in turn to critique and reform the church's doctrine, thus exercising its own priority as God-given Word over the reflections, conceptualizations, and formulations of the church. In the case of Christology and the Trinity, we shall later see, what has occurred in recent theology is that a static, dogmatic tradition of orthodoxy which has formally and authoritatively defined the church's belief has been challenged and refined by a new hearing of the gospel story. Under the impact of our own experience of reality, and our fresh hearing through Scripture of the word that tells of God's union with suffering and death, theology today is coming to rethink and reformulate its understanding of Christ's personhood and of the Godhead. Once more concepts are being critically refined, and theology again runs the risk of affirming a story that is strange, foolish, and impossible to contemporary wisdom and subversive of our world's cultural and philosophical assumptions. Having once helped to keep the story alive, the doctrines of Christ and of God are now themselves being brought to life again under the destructive and creative impact of the story of God's union with mortality.

II. The Story and the Trinity

Naturally enough, given its implications for the nature of God and of reality, the post-Easter story of God's identity with one crucified and buried met with external revulsion and internal compromise from the very beginning. Both responses are visible within the New Testament, as both Christians and their opponents trip over the gospel's stumbling block and find intolerable the foolishness of the cross as the revelation and locus of God's own power and wisdom. Clearly one factor contributing to the tension and mutual polemic between Jews and Christians was Jewish offense at the blasphemous exalting of Jesus as one whose origins, destiny, and authority were divine. Some within the church wished to mimimize that offense, reducing the breach with their own tradition required of Jews who believed in the crucified Jesus as God's Messiah. Perhaps these included the "Judaizers" at Antioch and Galatia, who required circumcision of Gentile converts (Gal. 1:6; 2:11-12); and those whom the Gospels sometimes condemn as false believers will not enter the kingdom, despite their outer protestations of "Lord, Lord" (e.g., Mt. 7:21).[11]

11. See P. Fredriksen, *From Jesus to Christ* (New Haven and London: Yale University Press, 1988), p. 39.

Equally visible in the New Testament are Hellenists offended by the notion of God's involvement in carnality and death — and Christians ready to modify that involvement. Such are surely among the targets of the evangelists' unflinching narrative insistence on the realism of Christ's body and feelings, suffering and death, and John's insistence on the tangibility of Christ, denouncing those who by the spirit of antichrist deny that he "was come in the flesh" (1 Jn. 1:1; 4:2-3). Such "docetism," which dismissed the fleshliness and mortality of Jesus as mere appearance, veiling a purely spiritual redeemer, had a powerful impact on the church throughout its early centuries and fueled its earliest doctrinal controversies. Gnosticism mocked the materiality of the church's gospel and seduced not a few into accommodation with its spiritualizing dualism.[12]

Repudiation of this docetism and the need to secure a fully human, truly mortal, Christ helped to occasion the church's first major doctrinal crisis. Here theology was driven to profound intellectual innovation — no less than a new concept of God — in order to protect the community's threatened identifying story. Ironically, though, that crisis occurred when legitimate resistance to Greek docetic denial of Christ's humanness toppled over — in a reflex not uncommon in theological gymnastics — into its polar opposite: quasi-Jewish denial of *divine* presence in the human, mortal Jesus Christ.

The motives and actual opinions of Arius — as opposed to those attributed to him by his enemies — have been much discussed in recent scholarship.[13] Clearly he is not to be dismissed simply as a heretic — still less as a pagan philosopher. Rather, this earnest, spiritually serious Christian thinker sought fidelity to divine revelation and careful, rigorous exegesis of Scripture;

12. See J. N. D. Kelly, *Early Christian Doctrines,* 3rd ed. (London: A. & C. Black, n.d.), pp. 141-42. Some groups, such as the Marcionites, were openly docetic, denying the reality of Christ's passion. The docetic tendencies of others were almost subconscious. Clement of Alexandria, e.g., influenced but yet strongly critical of Hellenistic philosophy, suggested that the divine, spiritual Christ ate and drank not because he needed nourishment but in order to demonstrate to his disciples the reality of his human flesh. See Kelly, *Early Doctrines,* pp. 153ff.; J. Pelikan, *The Christian Tradition,* vol. 1: *The Emergence of the Catholic Tradition (100-600)* (Chicago and London: University of Chicago Press, 1971), pp. 47, 174.

Ignatius, Polycarp, and Irenaeus were among the most significant early defenders of the gospel against docetism and gnosticism.

13. See, e.g., M. Wiles, "In Defence of Arius," in *Journal of Theological Studies,* n.s. 13 (1962): 339-47; R. G. Gregg and D. E. Groh, *Early Arianism: A View of Salvation* (London: SCM Press and Philadelphia: Fortress Press, 1981); R. Williams, *Arius* (London: Darton, Longman and Todd, 1987); F. Young, *From Nicea to Chalcedon* (London: SCM Press and Ann Arbor, Mich.: Books on Demand, 1983), ch. 2.

and while not free from philosophical speculation, he was anxious to present a Christology which secured Jesus as Savior of the world. Out of this soteriological concern Arius opposed docetic reduction of the humanness of Christ, insisting instead, as a necessary precondition of salvation, on a human Jesus like us in all respects — as portrayed in Hebrews, for example, sharing our infirmities and limitations. Not metaphysically sinless by virtue of divinity but a free moral agent capable of change and thus of sinful choices, he progresses through life toward perfect obedience and faith, thus receiving God's gracious favor and acknowledgment as Son. Only so, being our brother, is he also our pioneer, imitating whose obedience we, too, may participate in the Father, as adopted sons and daughters.

This is not outright "adoptionism," the heresy that Jesus became God's Son at his baptism or some other point in time, but an attempt to incorporate the theme of adoption into mainstream thinking. For Arius also insists that the Son who was incarnate in Jesus and lived this life of filial obedience came *from* God. His origins were not solely historical and human.[14] Yet it was precisely the way in which Arius related this Son to God's own being that caused deep conflict in the church, as well as prompting vital theological creativity.[15] For his preconceptions of the divine reality allowed nothing in common, at the level of being or essence, between God's own self and this Son who for the sake of our salvation became fully human, steeped in our moral struggles, subject to flesh and perishing. Arius's inflexible commitment to Jewish monotheism, God's utter oneness and transcendence, was reinforced by the radical dualism of Hellenistic thought, common to Stoicism and all the varieties of Platonism, which separated what is eternal, simple, and immutable from the world of flesh and

14. See Williams, *Arius*, p. 115; cf. pp. 16, 161, 286; also Mackey, *Jesus*, p. 226.

15. It is unnecessary to arbitrate the scholarly debate as to whether Arius's primary impetus was cosmological or soteriological. It is sufficient to acknowledge that both concerns were operative. A presbyter of the church in Alexandria, Arius exhibits a fusion of Jewish and Greek influence. He stands in the Alexandrian trajectory that moves from Philo, the great exponent of Hellenistic Judaism, through the Christian theologians Clement of Alexandria and Origen. But Arius, crucially, denied what Origen asserted, the *eternal* generation of the Son and Logos by the Father. And though his hierarchical triad resembles the cosmology of Plotinus, Arius again denied the Neoplatonic position that the "second principle" (Mind) emanates from the nature of the first, the One. By making the Logos a product of the First Principle's *will*, Arius subordinated the former but at the same time cut off the possibility that the material universe — at the base of the Plotinian hierarchy — is itself an emanation from God's own essence. For that would fatally compromise God's transcendence — so essential to Arius — and the contigency of the world, created out of nothing by an act of God's free grace. See Williams, *Arius*, pp. 117-57, 181-98.

time, mixture and decay. It followed that the Son, deeply involved in just that world, could not be God. Rather, the God who is eternal monad, pure singularity, *became* subsequently a triad by creating the derivate, inferior Son and Spirit.[16] The making of the Son happened before time began — indeed, the Son was the agent through whom all else was brought to being; but the Son was not co-eternal with the God. This was the the core of Arius's "heresy": a pretemporal state of affairs in which the Son did not exist. The Father's essence as eternal, ungenerated source of everything was not something to be shared with any other, not even with the Son. Ontologically distinct from God, the Son exists not as the equal of the Father, sharing the divine *nature,* but in dependence on the *will* of God, who chooses in grace to create the Son, and whose continued favor is contingent on and responsive to the Son's obedience as "servant" and "apprentice" of the Father.[17] This "subordinationism"[18] places the Son firmly on the lower side of the horizontal gulf between God and finite, mortal creatures — albeit as a unique and perfect creature.[19] This, as clearly perceived by the opponents of Arianism, contradicts the inherited tradition that in Jesus Christ it is indeed God who has been involved in our mortal, creaturely existence.

To safeguard this reality of God's involvement, as narrated so scandalously in the Christian story, the church was forced to *think* more deeply than before. Led initially by Athanasius, profoundly enriched by the Cappadocians,

16. See Pelikan, *Christian Tradition,* vol. 1, p. 194.

17. There is thus an analogy between the obedience of Jesus' earthly life and ministry as meriting his gracious adoption into divine sonship and the proleptic obedience of the Son before creation itself in learned servitude to the Father's will. As Gregg and Groh (*Early Arianism,* p. 93) point out, Arius was by no means being innovative or deliberately heretical in emphasizing the Son's dependence on God's will. Such language is present in Justin Martyr, Hippolytus, Clement, and Origen. But Arius's particular use of the notion captured the church's attention and forced it to reflect more fully upon its implications, deeming it unsatisfactory if used in *contrast* to every relation of being and nature between the Father and the Son.

18. It needs to be stressed that though Arius's subordinationism came to be judged heretical, almost none of his claims was without exegetical backing. Central to the debate was Prov. 8:22: "The Lord created me . . . ," which all at the time assumed, as few would now, was speech by the Son referring to the Father, and on that basis confirmed for the Arians the Son's createdness. Again, Gregg and Groh point out scriptural justifications for the insistence that God is singular and alone is true, wise, immortal, etc. See, e.g., Jn. 17:3; Rom. 16:27; and 1 Tim. 6:15-16. Likewise, the soteriological emphasis upon Christ's humanness seems to be well supported in Hebrews, as well as at 1 Tim. 2:5: "one mediator between God and humankind, Christ Jesus, himself human" (NRSV).

19. See Williams, *Arius,* p. 104; and Mackey, *Jesus,* p. 226.

and after many disputes, upheavals, and changes of ecclesiastical fortune between the Council of Nicea (325) and that of Constantinople (381), the church finally turned its face unambiguously against Arianism. The end product of those Councils, which we call the Nicene Creed, represents a major step toward an intellectually credible but genuinely Christian, *sui generis,* understanding of God.[20] That is the doctrine of the Trinity, which stands in contradiction to both Jewish and Greek presuppositions, at once blasphemously identifying a human being with the ineffable, imageless Holy One of Israel and unreasonably reducing eternal and unchanging Being to the level of decay and temporality. Here the church discovers a rational way of saying — what flouts so much human reasoning — that we really are confronted with the presence of the all-transcendent God in the creaturely finitude of Jesus; *and* that we must deal with this ever-so-particular and human Jesus if we would speak of, know, and be delivered by divine reality.

Embodying the Trinity as central among the church's regulative statements, the Creed represents the ecumenical verdict that the Christian community did not recognize the gospel story in the theology of Arius — for all his biblical fidelity, exegetical exactness, and soteriological concern. Missing in Arius is faith's apprehension of God's immediacy and very presence in the person, life, and death of Jesus.[21] That absence was, of course, precisely the consequence, even the intent, of Arius's cleavage between the Son and the being of the Father. Nicene theology, on the contrary, concentrates upon the Son's participation in that eternal and transcendent being, and thus on the presence of no less than God in the incarnation of the Son, which took him to a cross and grave.

Ironically, but in perfect illustration of the need for rational theology and conceptual refinement, the Creed preserves the immediacy of God by means of philosophical vocabulary; and thus, one may judge, served the biblical story with philosophy more effectively in that time and context than had Arius with his scriptural proof-texts. This was more convincingly a Christianizing of Hellenism

---

20. On this period see, e.g., Pelikan, *Christian Tradition,* vol. 1, pp. 200-225; Kelly, *Early Christian Doctrines,* chs. ix and x; A. Grillmeier, *Christ in Christian Tradition,* vol. 1, 2nd rev. ed., trans. J. Bowden (London and Oxford: Mowbray, 1975), ch. 3; Young, *Nicea to Chalcedon,* ch. 2; T. F. Torrance, *The Trinitarian Faith* (Edinburgh: T. & T. Clark, 1988); T. F. Torrance, ed., *The Incarnation* (Edinburgh: Handsel Press, 1981); Mackey, *Jesus,* and *The Christian Experience of God as Trinity* (London: SCM Press, 1983), pp. 135ff.; Macquarrie, *Jesus Christ,* ch. 7; and R. P. C. Hanson, "The Doctrine of God in the Early Church," in his *The Attractiveness of God: Essays in Christian Doctrine* (London: SPCK, 1973), esp. pp. 83-94.

21. See Mackey, *Jesus,* pp. 231-32, and *Trinity,* pp. 123-24.

than the reverse.[22] The key technical phrase, introduced at Nicea and reconfirmed at Constantinople in the Nicene Creed, asserts that Christ, God's begotten Son, is "of one substance with the Father."[23] That unites the Son and the Father precisely through ontology rather than by the Arian transactions of parental will and filial obedience.[24] Being or essence is exactly what the Father in love and self-giving shares with the Son and does not withhold, as Arius had said. All that the Father is and has — glory, eternity, creatorhood — the Son shares in by nature; and, though philosophically expressed, this oneness of being is, from the Nicene viewpoint, soteriologically decisive, rescuing the saviorhood of Christ from the good intentions but disastrous consequences of Arius's doctrine of salvation.

For Athanasius, though it is important that Christ share fully in our humanness since that is the condition needing to be saved — it is equally imperative — what Arius found impossible — that the one so subjected to human flesh and corruption be very God, bringing God's own being and nature all the way into the heart of our condition.[25] What but eternal being can deliver us in our mortality from the threat of non-existence? Who can defeat death but the source and preserver of life?[26] How can sinful humanity be saved other than by

---

22. See Torrance, *Trinitarian Faith,* p. 68; and R. C. P. Hanson, "The Doctrine of the Trinity Achieved in 381," *SJT* 36.1 (1983): 50.

23. The word *homoousios,* "of the same substance," or *ousia* (= being, or essence), introduced by Constantine and adopted at Nicea, and thereafter vigorously defended and expounded by Athanasius, took a generation to gain final acceptance at Constantinople partly because it can be, and by some was, read as implying a strict *identity* between the Son and the Father which blurred the distinction between them. In fact, the mature doctrine of the Trinity wishes to say that the Son and the Spirit share in the one *ousia* or being of the Father precisely in their distinctiveness. God is one only as self-differentiated three ways. In the anathema attached to the Creed of Nicea of 325, *ousia* and *hypostasis* are treated as synonyms for substance or being. Later, in the full refinement of the doctrine achieved by the Cappadocians, *hypostasis* came to signify "person," that of which God is distinctly three, in contrast to the *ousia* which refers to what the three *hypostases* have in common as the one God. See A. I. C. Heron, "*Homoousios* with the Father," in *Incarnation,* ed. Torrance, ch. 3; and on the broader significance of the Cappadocian move to distinguish the previous synonyms *ousia* and *hypostasis,* see C. Gunton, *The Promise of Trinitarian Theology* (Edinburgh: T. & T. Clark, 1991), pp. 9, 96.

24. See Gregg and Groh, *Early Arianism,* p. 173.

25. Cf. Torrance, *Trinitarian Faith,* p. 7; cf. his comment on p. 175 concerning Athanasius's frequent reference to Heb. 2:14-15, with its theme that only by going through death itself could the Son defeat its power.

26. See Athanasius's youthful exposition of creation, fall, and redemption in *On the Incarnation,* in *Contra Gentes and De Incarnatione,* ed. and trans. R. W. Thomas (New York and Oxford: Oxford University Press, 1971).

God's grace and forgiveness, mediated through the Son? Certainly not by our broken efforts at ethical advance, unable as we are, even at our moral best, to earn or merit the favor of the Father? Our adoption as God's sons and daughters is not won through imitation of Jesus' pioneering but as the pure gift of God, who offers to believers a sharing in that love which binds the Father to one who is by nature the eternal Son. Arius's divorcing of God's will and nature made God's love arbitrary, accidental, episodic; for here the Father wills and chooses, not in eternity but in a pretemporal moment, not necessarily expressive of God's abiding nature, to create and favor Christ, and thus ourselves his fellow creatures. Nicene soteriology, by contrast, makes God's grace permanent and trustworthy. Embodied for us in time by the eternal Son, grace is revealed as everlasting: the consistent, unambiguous expression of God's nature. It remains, to be sure, God's free choice to love us and adopt us, not some necessary principle of divine being; but this freely chosen grace confirms and corresponds to God's true nature; and it is a freedom exercised eternally, not in accidental moments.[27]

It is crucial here that theology, while acknowledging the beggarly poverty of its thoughts about the mystery of God, has something to say about eternity. Whereas for Arius, God is eternally pure monad but becomes triadic with the making of subordinates who, lacking full divinity, are capable of contact with the creaturely world, the new doctrine of the Trinity, brought to expression in

---

27. See A. McGill, *Suffering: A Test of Theological Method* (Philadelphia: Westminster Press, 1982), p. 69; also Williams, *Arius,* pp. 238ff. A full accounting of the Nicene *homoousios* would add to its soteriology also its epistemological and doxological significance. In the first case, if Christ is truly God, then the truth that he reveals is God's own truth, accommodated, like Christ's humanity, to finite forms and limitations. As such, it frees theology from speculation and inward subjectivity, where our own feelings and ideas determine what is true for us. In Christ we are graciously brought into "cognitive union" with God (Torrance, *Trinitarian Faith,* p. 59), given objective knowledge and real, though finite and fragmented, understanding of God's own rationality. And if this allows us to think humanly but truly about God, it also makes possible appropriate human speech *to* God. If Christ is one being with the Father, then we may worship God through the Son, and the worship we offer the Son is in turn not blasphemy but fitting adoration of one equal with God who shares fully in God's dignity and glory. One of the accusations against Arius was that he turned the doxology which the church directed toward Christ into the idolatrous worship of a creature. Conversely, the Nicene *homoousios* is a major instance of the *lex credendi,* the rule of belief, following and catching up with the *lex orandi,* the rule of prayer. That is, the doctrine of Christ's deity within the Trinity at last provided a thorough intellectual rationale for that worship, praise, and prayer which generations of the faithful had intuitively been offering to Christ already, without any sense of idolatry or impropriety. See Torrance, *Trinitarian Faith,* esp. chs. 1 and 2.

the latter half of the fourth century, says that God is three eternally. Triple self-differentiation applies not only in "the economy" — God's external actions of creation, rule, and redemption of the world — but "immanently," within the very inner life of God.[28] As an essential step to such an affirmation, the primary development in trinitarian thinking between Nicea and Constantinople concerned the full and equal deity of the Holy Spirit, analogous to and in part entailed by the status of the Son.[29] Within God, therefore, sharing equally and fully in a single, indefinable essence, three distinct "persons,"[30] entities which

28. In addition to rejecting Arian subordinationism, this insistence on the eternal threeness of God was a technical advance beyond the early trinitarianism of Tertullian. He made a vital contribution to the development of the doctrine, not simply by introducing the term *trinitas* but by drawing real distinctions between three "persons" who shared the one divine substance over against the modalists and Sabellians. They effectively identified the Father and the Son and, to preserve the "monarchy" of the one, undifferentiated God, postulated a divine monad who at different times projected different modes of self-expression. Tertullian instead proposed a graded order of distinctions which became manifest as Father, Son, and Spirit in the economy of creation and redemption. Though this was not intended to subordinate the Son — on the contrary, Tertullian's point was that the three together form one equal divine substance — it did allow for discontinuity between what God becomes in the economy and God's inner reality. In fact, though attaching God's threefoldness solely to the economic, Tertullian himself acknowledged that even in eternity God was not entirely alone but accompanied by the Word, a second along with the first. This intuition of immanent self-differentiation, to which the economic distinctions correspond, the mature doctrine of the Trinity brought to expression as the *sui generis* Christian concept of God. See Kelly, *Early Christian Doctrines*, pp. 110ff.

29. Athanasius applied the *homoousios* to the Spirit as well as to the Son — a move strongly criticized by some. See Mackey, *Trinity*, p. 141, and "Doctrine of the Trinity," in *The Westminster Dictionary of Christian Theology*, ed. A. Richardson and J. Bowden (Louisville: Westminster/John Knox and London: SCM Press, 1983), pp. 581ff. By contrast, Basil of Caesarea was content to speak of the Spirit's equality in dignity and glory. It was in these terms, rather than by repeating *homoousios*, that the Nicene Creed, going beyond the bare mention of the Spirit at Nicea itself, affirms the Spirit's deity: "who with the Father and the Son is to be worshiped and glorified."

30. By general consent, modern culture has so substituted psychological for metaphysical ways of thinking that the traditional translation of *hypostasis* by "person" is now highly misleading, suggesting a tritheistic series of centers of consciousness within God. Karl Barth made a decisive break with the trinitarian language of "person," reverting to the pre-Nicene "mode of being." To jettison "person" today would by no means be to minimize the importance of the Cappadocians' distinction between the previously synonymous *hypostasis* and *ousia*. Though their new formulation is not included in the Nicene Creed, it was, as we have seen, their provision of a term for God's triadic, immanent self-differentiation which constituted the major development in the doctrine of the Trinity after Nicea.

manifest individuality and differentness from one another without being separate individuals — who would as such *not* share in one, undivided being.

Despite some exegetical and logical difficulties, especially with reference to the Spirit, and with a humble "apophatic" recognition that here finite human theology speaks all-too-unknowingly of unutterable mystery, the Cappadocians developed a language and conceptuality for securing the distinctiveness of each person while preserving their unity of being. Each has a distinct set of properties and a unique mode of origin (the unbegotten Father, the begotten Son, and the Spirit who proceeds); and each has peculiar works or energies, though not as separate agents but as participants together in one divine activity.[31] Again, though the three are distinguishable because ranged in a given order, such that all things come *from* the Father as the one unique origin and cause, *through* the Son, and *in* the Holy Spirit, yet the second and the third are not thereby inferior to the first. Rather, they are "God from God, light from light" (Nicene Creed), equal to their origin and undiminished by having a source beyond themselves. All of which allows the church to say that as one who shares fully in the being of none less than God, and not as a subordinate and finally dispensable intermediary,[32] the second person of the Trinity has come to us in the flesh of Jesus Christ. In so coming the Son has brought God's own self into our humanity while yet remaining God, not reducing the divine to humanness but *being* God in the midst of humans.

In such a way, then, is the biblical gospel, and its story of the God who in grace goes to the deadly depth of our experience, protected by the Nicenes' radical conceptuality. The essential sharing between the Father and the Son, denied by Arius but permitting theology to conceive of both unity and differentiation

---

31. One of the logical difficulties of the Cappadocians' doctrine is its need simultaneously to secure *both* the uniqueness of the Spirit's activity, as grounds for its distinctiveness with the one Godhead, *and* its sharing with the Father and the Son in the single activity and agency of the one divine being, as the ground for the Spirit's deity. The latter necessity came to predominate in the history of the doctrine, with a consequent threat — which some see as mortal — to the clear status of the Spirit as distinct, third *hypostasis.* The stress on what the Spirit has and does *in common* is present, e.g., in the doctrine of *perichoresis.* This states that though certain "appropriations" of a given divine activity to a given "person" may be made on the grounds of exegesis and salvation history, formally there is a mutual indwelling or interpenetration of the three persons, such that the whole Godhead is always present where one exists and acts. This underlies Augustine's rule that *opera ad extra sunt indivisa:* God's external acts are not to be distributed between the persons. Such a principle makes it particularly difficult to secure the *distinctiveness* of the third person on the basis of works. See Mackey, *Westminster Dictionary,* and *Trinity,* pp. 150ff.

32. See Hanson, "Doctrine of the Trinity," p. 51.

within God, crystallizes a distinct Christian understanding. Through the dynamic activity and interrelatedness of the Trinity, God is able to be present to us, self-emptied and vulnerable, subject to contradiction, without the loss which Arius feared of oneness and transcendent Godness. The bond of unity between the Father and the Son holds firm even while the Son takes on humanity and in our death is forsaken by the Father. This cuts through the dualism shared with Arius by so many subsequent theologies, that true divinity presupposes the absence of relationship, need, and reciprocity. The Hellenized perversion of Yahweh's Hebraic transcendence presumes the absolute self-sufficiency of God, free from all dependence and responsiveness. The Trinity, by contrast, affirms that God exists in community, through the relinquishment of self-containment for the mutual openness, interdependence, and reciprocity of the Father, Son, and Spirit. In that dynamic, fertile fellowship, each needs and depends upon the other; and through their dynamic interweaving of giving and receiving, God is one, and truly God. In the overflow of their love and mutual need the triune family posit reality beyond themselves, creating, sustaining, and redeeming all things through radical involvement with the cosmos, not least its human, mortal creatures.[33]

There is no denying the static quality of the categories — essence, substance, person, nature — with which patristic theology secured its trinitarian and Christological faith. Nor can we minimize the hazards to which these categories — and residual philosophical assumptions from the Greek context whence they were drawn — exposed the dynamic of the biblical story. To those dangers we shall soon return. Clearly something was lost in the shift from historical event to metaphysical being as the church's primary mode of speech about God. Yet something was preserved too, perhaps even gained. In a real sense this was theology's coming of age, bringing its thinking to maturity, expounding and defending with rational concepts its own unique understanding of God in the intellectual marketplace, the public arena of ideas. And did the ideas it offered not keep alive, if only just, the scandalous point of the original gospel narrative? Beneath the seemingly abstract and anemic concept of "one

33. See J. Zizioulas, *Being as Communion* (London: Darton, Longman and Todd and Crestwood, N.Y.: St. Vladimir's Seminary Press, 1985); and Gunton, *Promise of Trinitarian Theology.* Also see McGill, *Suffering,* pp. 70-82, for the argument that this concept of divine need is the crucial distinction between Arian monotheism and the trinitarianism of Athanasius. He makes the important counterpoint to Arius's claim to exegetical fidelity, showing how the trinitarian doctrine, which hangs upon the *homoousios,* corresponds to multiple texts in John's gospel, where the Son acknowledges his need of and devotion to the Father (e.g., 5:30; 8:28; 12:44; 14:13), yet also receives, in infinite self-giving, all that the Father has (e.g., 3:35; 5:23, 26; 16:15). This sharing by the Father and the Son is precisely what Arius denies.

substance" we have found the God of transcendent self-humiliation, who, while remaining God, has embraced our humanness. Here is divinity, ultimate reality, not self-sufficient but existing for the sake of others; not self-preserving but ful-filled through self-expenditure; not invulnerable but exposed to opposition and resistance; not static and immobile but subject to novelty and change!

There is much about the changelessness of God in Greek theology; yet implicit in its identification of the incarnate Son of God as of one substance with the Father is the event whereby God's eternal, changeless being enters into something new: those conditions of body, creaturehood, and time which begin in a womb and terminate in a tomb. The incarnation — not just the birth of Je-sus, to which alone the phrase often gets applied, but everything that followed in life and death and resurrection — represents real change, a new experience for God, new events in the life of the triune community.[34] To this novelty, hid-den in the philosophical language of substance and being, the Nicene Creed also, of course, gives stunning explicit expression when it moves from clipped definitions of the Son's divinity into full narrative cry, declaring in verbal ech-oes of Scripture, including the Johannine Prologue, that he, "for the sake of us humans and for our salvation came down and was made human."

There is something remarkable about this "becoming human" — that theology used Greek concepts to attest both implicitly and explicitly a notion as unplatonic as that God the unchangeable became something different and other, entered new and alien conditions. And it is perhaps equally astonishing — and even more frequently missed — that here the church gave conceptual expression so clearly to divine lowliness and humility, in a context of political success and imperial ascendancy. The charge is sometimes brought against the trinitarian and Christological dogmas, especially in their emphasis on the di-vinity of Christ, that they came to articulation and were ratified after the Constantinian recognition of the church and even, at crucial moments, through the intervention and backing of the emperor himself. The divinity of Christ undoubtedly served as a political device of the established church, as it embraced and was embraced by the very Caesars whose plenipotentiary had liquidated Jesus. A symbol of imperial ideology, the heavenly Lord endorsed the emperor's authority as his earthly analogue and agent.[35] Nor was this the last

34. See Torrance, *Trinitarian Faith,* pp. 88-89. Cf. R. C. P. Hanson, "The Chalce-donian Formula: A Declaration of Good Intentions," in *Attractiveness,* pp. 110ff.

35. See, e.g., D. Cupitt, "The Christ of Christendom," in *The Myth of God Incarnate,* esp. p. 139; J. Pelikan, *Jesus through the Centuries* (New Haven: Yale University Press, 1985 and New York: Harper and Row, 1987), ch. 4; D. Hall, *Thinking the Faith,* pp. 202-3; and J. Moltmann, *The Way of Jesus Christ,* pp. 53-54.

time that God and Christ have functioned as supports of governmental authority and power;[36] and there is certainly no denying the high degree of politics, both ecclesiastical and secular, involved in the formation of the church's dogmas of the fourth and fifth centuries.

If the God to which the doctrine of the Trinity refers is indeed vulnerable, incarnate, immersed in the contingencies of worldly and human affairs, that doctrine itself is correspondingly earthly and carnal, emerging out of complex, often secular, sometimes sordid and certainly historical and all-too-human interactions. Least of all with reference to the Trinity and to Christology was the process by which doctrinal "orthodoxy" came to be established and heresy rejected, a straightforward recognition of preconceived truth — as if perhaps Scripture revealed in seedling form a clear set of absolute doctrines which subsequent theology, discerning truth from falsehood under the guidance of the Spirit, unfailingly brought to full flowering and systematic order. Rather, though clear choices are sometimes to be made which require the naming and rejecting of heresy, by which the church's doctrinal regulations are set, maintained, and rectified, these are always truly difficult, obscure, and fallible decisions where every kind of contingency — including the nontheological — may enter in.

For one thing, real thinking, the strenuous intellectual testing of ideas, is involved in the decision as to what more or less appropriately expresses God's truth in human language. This is a historically open and indeed interminable process, since doctrine, even — or above all — in defense of past tradition, requires constant reforming and fresh thought. Thus "orthodoxy" may even be conceived dynamically as the future goal of theology rather than its static norm, fixed in the past.[37] To this movement of thought in the direction of the future it is often "heretics" who make a vital contribution, probing the boundaries of the church's faith and forcing it to think new and deeper thoughts in response to their own experiments, exaggerations, and innovations.

This uncertain struggle to speak as truthfully as possible, though always fallibly and with penultimacy, happens not in a vacuum of intellectual and spiritual purity, but in the midst of and affected by webs of ecclesiastical, political, and social circumstance.[38] How extraordinary, then, in this case, that it was the

---

36. See, e.g., J. Moltmann, *The Trinity and the Kingdom,* trans. M. Kohl (San Francisco: Harper & Row, 1981) (= *The Trinity and the Kingdom of God* [London: SCM Press, 1981], esp. ch. 6).

37. See Williams, *Arius,* pp. 24ff.; cf. Hanson, "Doctrine of the Trinity," pp. 42-43.

38. For a powerful, sustained statement of the essential contextuality of doctrinal development, see D. Hall, *Thinking the Faith.*

doctrine of the Trinity and thus a God of vulnerability and lowliness to which the church's authorities gave clear endorsement in the years and decades following its triumph — however disastrous that establishment of Christendom may have been for the followers of Jesus, crucified by Pontius Pilate. The church did not stop thinking now about the nature of the gospel, theologically anaesthetized by the elixir of political power.[39] Rather, an understanding of God was sealed which positively challenged the very notions of earthly power and imperial authority which the church in practice was enjoying. If ever there was a moment to preserve for its political effect belief in God as monad it might have been when Constantine brought church and state together under a single dominion: "one God, one emperor, one church." In the face of such a claim upon divine *monarchy*, the ultimate sanctification of earthly sovereignty, the church chose to reject monistic unitarianism for plurality and community within God, the sharing of rule among interdependents rather than its imposition by a single, superior, self-sufficient governor upon inferior subjects. Whatever might be true of the church, of pope and patriarch, of *God* the church's doctrine said that majesty and glory are revealed in the lowliness of mortal being; that almightiness and power are exercised not ultimately from on high but in the powerlessness of a crucified and buried one; that transcendence and distance do not negate but find expression in vulnerability and intimacy, and in the depths of flesh and loss and death.[40] In such contradictions of the external context, and subverting its own bright moment of power and glory, the church of Jesus Christ gave birth to a new doctrine which, in spite of everything, bore witness to the scandalous story of the cross by which foolishness, weakness, and nothingness bring to shame all that has existence, might, and wisdom.

III. The Story and Christology

Manifestly, as we have acknowledged, this witness to the gospel was not unambiguous; and critical questions hang over any interpretation of early church doctrine as effectively safeguarding the biblical story of God's presence in the suffering, death, and burial of Jesus. It may be answered that some of those who criticize patristic theology for surrendering that story take insufficient account of the church's need in every generation to present the gospel in terms germane to its own cultural context, however different from our own. But it must also be conceded that if the gospel is true, it is true for all times and situations, and that

39. See Williams, *Arius,* pp. 236-37.
40. See Torrance, *Trinitarian Faith,* pp. 82-83.

at one significant point at least, classical dogma, attempting to state the truth in its own way, actually said something that is false in any context. What was said poses continuing peril to the church's identifying story, and its correction in contemporary theology has become a confessional imperative.

We may reduce the critical questions to two, and cast them in the categories of the post-Nicene debate itself, namely, Christ's human nature and divine, respectively. Do the formulations of the early church keep the humanity of Christ so concrete and realistic that it is still upon the historically particular *Jesus* that the gospel focuses, and still *our* humanity with which, through this Jesus, God has been identified? And do they leave the participation of Christ's divine nature in the life, and especially the death, of this man so unrestricted that it is still *God's* subjection to a cross and grave which is the heart and scandal of the faith?

It has become a common complaint, especially since the last century, and continuing into the most recent discussions of Christology,[41] that the humanity of Christ — and therefore also of ourselves — was insufficiently attended to by patristic theology in consequence of its preoccupation with Christ's deity.[42] That the church reacted to Arius, who placed such antidocetic emphasis on the struggling obedience of Christ's human will, with a trinitarian response that secured Christ's ontological status as the equal of God, certainly seems to expose this one-sidedness. It suggests that Nicene "orthodoxy" felt little pressing need to safeguard the biblical portrayal of Jesus as a human being, buffeted by temptations, subject to bodily pain, weakness of the will, agonies of soul, and finally death and burial. But that first impression is misleading; and the historical facts cannot suppport the view that the church was simply willing to sacrifice Jesus the earthly, mortal servant to the greater glory of Christ the heavenly, eternal Lord. Indeed, even before the Nicene affirmations of the Trinity and Christ's divinity were ratified, it was plain that the questions raised by Arius and others could not be dealt with at the trinitarian level alone; and the church plunged into a notorious century of ferocious debate precisely about *Christology*.

The question was indeed what it meant for the Creed to say that the Son, of one being with the Father, had been made human. Just in what way — by what kind of union — was the eternal Logos related in incarnation to the hu-

---

41. See, e.g., J. Macquarrie, *Jesus Christ*, pp. 163, 166; and J. Moltmann, *The Way*, pp. 46ff.

42. "All statements about 'the lowliness' of Jesus, his humanity, his suffering, and his death on the cross, are reduced, in favour of statements about his divinity, his exaltation and his triumph, and are integrated into these. . . . What emerges as a whole is the picture of the triumphant Christ in the glory of God." Moltmann, *The Way*, p. 52.

man Jesus? What sort of human being was this, who, born of Mary, was also eternally begotten? How, in particular, were those New Testament events of weakness, temptation, passion, and death to be understood, and the texts that recorded them exegeted, if his whole existence as a human being depended on a movement of God's own self into time and flesh? And could those events save us in our humanity if there was something defective, or celestial, about the humanity of Jesus? Precisely in the course of these debates, in fact, there came to full articulation a principle of salvation intuited and implicitly applied long since: "the unassumed is the unhealed." Only by sharing fully in the condition of our humanness could God in Christ restore those conditions to wholeness and fulfillment.[43] The fraught years leading to the Council of Chalcedon (451), when the debate was provisionally resolved, testify most concretely not to the docetism but to the Christological tenacity of the church: its refusal to let matters rest until a way was found of holding the full humanness of Christ in at least creative tension with his agreed trinitarian status as divine.[44]

In this process, momentary victories for the extremes of one school or the other (commonly characterized as Alexandrian and Antiochene), which failed to maintain that tension proved to be exactly that: temporary proposals and decisions which had later to be withdrawn, or at least winnowed for partial contributions to a final statement.[45] This, though far from a solution, at least held

43. The phrase comes from Gregory of Nazianzus, condemning the Apollinarian heresy which denied the human soul of Christ (see his *Letter,* 101), but the soteriological principle was operative as early as Irenaeus.

44. Among many accounts of this debate, see, e.g., Pelikan, *Christian Tradition,* vol. 1, ch. 5; Kelly, *Early Christian Doctrines,* chs. xi and xii; Grillmeier, *Christ,* vol. 1; F. Young, *From Nicea to Chalcedon;* and Hanson, "Chalcedonian Formula."

45. Those who accuse patristic Christology of surrendering Christ's humanity must in particular account for the repeated refusal of the church, up to and including Chalcedon, to allow an unqualified Alexandrian Christology to prevail. That was always marked by the temptation, sometimes wholeheartedly embraced, to compromise the humanity at the price of ensuring that the Divine Word was the one subject of the incarnation. Even the young Athanasius had betrayed this tendency, when he suggested that the Word used the body of Jesus as its instrument — implying the absence of human mind or soul (e.g., *On the Incarnation,* 44). Athanasius went on later to affirm more clearly the full humanness of Jesus; but when another Alexandrian, Apollinarius, did explicitly deny that Christ had a human mind (on the grounds that that would make him susceptible to sin), but affirmed that he was a "heavenly man" with "one nature," a compound of divine soul and earthly flesh, he was roundly condemned — ultimately by the Council of Constantinople. Likewise the proposal of Eutyches, that at the point of the incarnation the humanity of Christ was fused with the divine to form just one nature, was vigorously excluded at Chalcedon. There the decision of the so-called Robber Synod at Ephesus, 449, which sup-

together in equilibrium all the necessary components of the problem — the mystery that had to be expressed but not dissolved — including, most critically, the full integrity of Christ's humanity. Far from allowing ascendancy to the divine nature, Chalcedon creates a new symmetry, repeating the Nicene trinitarian formula, this time with reference to Christ's identity with *us*: "coessential [of one substance] with the Father as to his deity and coessential with us — the very same one — as to his humanity."[46] Christ therefore exists as "one person" but "in two natures." There is just one personality and individual, Jesus Christ, one subject of the human nature as well as the divine, and that subject is the Word, the second person of the Trinity (this being the main emphasis of Alexandria). But Chalcedon adds the stipulation (meeting Antioch's concern insisted) that the two natures are united "without change, without confusion, . . . the difference between them not removed but the properties of each preserved." In short, Christ's humanity is not diminished by, nor absorbed into, his divinity, but maintains its wholeness in the union.

Of course, the doctrine here of "hypostatic union,"[47] that the humanity

---

ported Eutyches and anathematized "two natures" was overturned, while Leo's Tome of 450, written against Eutyches and emphasizing the unimpaired integrity of each nature, was endorsed and its key language adopted as normative.

46. The Symbol of Chalcedon, in *The Christological Controversy*, ed. and trans. R. A. Norris (Philadelphia: Fortress Press, 1980).

47. The language of "hypostatic union" which Chalcedon adopts ("the character of each nature . . . comes together in one person and one hypostasis, not divided or torn into two persons but one and the same Son and only-begotten God, Logos, Lord Jesus Christ") — meaning that the one subject of the two complete natures is the Word, the second hypostasis of the Trinity — comes from Cyril of Alexandria. It reflects the concern of Alexandrian Christology for the unity of Christ the incarnate Word over against that of Antioch for the duality of his natures and especially the wholeness of his humanness. (On Cyril, see T. F. Torrance, "The Mind of Christ in Worship," in *Theology in Reconciliation* [London: Geoffrey Chapman, 1975], pp. 156-85.) Likewise Chalcedon took from Cyril its repeated phrase "one and the same," which stresses Christ's unity, and upheld the decision of the Council of Ephesus, 431, which had endorsed Cyril against the Antiochene Nestorius in naming Mary as *Theotokos*, the Mother of God. The point here is that the human and divine are so united in Christ that it is proper to attribute divine predicates to that which was human (and the reverse), and thus to describe as God the human child whom Mary bore (the doctrine of *communicatio idiomatum* or "exchange of properties"). Yet Chalcedon was far from an unqualified victory for Cyril and Alexandria. In adopting its "two nature" formula, Chalcedon was rejecting Cyril's language of "one nature" which, without the same "heretical" intent of compromising Christ's humanity, did echo Apollinarius. Chalcedon here was addressing the concern of Antioch that, Christ's oneness of person notwithstanding, at another level he exists in two distinct ways, including that of full humanness. Part of the quarrel about "nature," it is now clear, rested on linguistic am-

of Christ does not exist in independence of the incarnation of the Logos nor have a separate subject of its own, is often regarded as the ultimate threat to the truly human Jesus in classical dogma; for what is real about human nature without a human person? But must we assume the Chalcedonian authors to be disingenuous when they declare that the integrity of Christ's humanity is undiminished? Their goal was to preserve the entire event that was the man Jesus, his constitution, behavior, and experience, as a human, historical existence, while affirming that the sole initiator of this event, without whose coming and becoming nothing would have happened, was God's own self. Jesus did not exist, nor the event of his life take place separately from this *divine* event — otherwise he would be merely a man adopted or indwelt by God, positions Chalcedon for soteriological reasons was determined to reject. Do we really compromise fatally the humanness and historicity of the Christ-event if, viewing it from beyond its finite boundaries, so to speak, we say that this thoroughly human happening only occurred as part of an event in God's own life? Or that "it is in this human life of Jesus . . . perhaps the most human condition of all, that we encounter the one, true God"?[48]

Of course, it was still with philosophical concepts, and ones that seem alien and static in our own intellectual environment, that this defense of the human Jesus and his relevance to all humanity was undertaken. But within that context it was surely at just this level of conceptuality that a battle for the gospel needed to be waged. All along, naturally, Scripture was being read and heard, the church's narratives rehearsed, liturgy celebrated, prayer and worship offered. But while the language of the Bible, of doxology, and of unreflective faith continued unabated, there were cognitive, intellectual threats to the gospel from pagan, philosophical sources. These, with their docetic inclinations, could all too easily have seduced Christian theology into irreparable abandonment of

---

biguity. For Cyril nature *(physis)* connoted individuality, and he was right to say that in Christ we are presented with just one individual. *Physis,* however, could also indicate a set of characteristics — e.g., that human nature shared by all persons regardless of their individual uniqueness. Antioch and Chalcedon had good grounds for saying, on this latter understanding, that Christ existed in two natures, manifesting the full set of properties of both humanity and God. See Mackey, *Jesus,* pp. 243-44. After Chalcedon the concept of hypostatic union was refined by Leontius of Byzantium and John of Damascus in terms of *anhypostasia* and *enhypostasia.* That is, the human nature of Christ lacks its own independent hypostasis, but finds its *hypostasis* in that of the divine Logos (see, e.g., Pelikan, *The Christian Tradition,* vol. 2: *The Spirit of Eastern Christendom (600-1700)* (Chicago and London: University of Chicago Press, 1974), pp. 88ff.; also Gunton, *Yesterday and Today,* pp. 92ff.; and Torrance, *Theological Science,* pp. 217ff.

48. Mackey, *Jesus,* p. 242.

Christ's humanity, his fleshly struggles unto death. It was vital, by means of Hellenism's own concepts — person, nature — to prevent that loss and safeguard the place of human nature beside the divine in the insoluble mystery of Christ's one personhood. In their own way, on their own battleground and with their own terms, the framers of the Chalcedonian Symbol secured not just for themselves but for us, in our own and every generation, the good news that in truly human form God has dwelt among us, has lived our life, died our death, and occupied our grave.

Finally, however, even if we defend classical Christology against the charge of silencing "the word of the cross" by compromising the humanity of the crucified Messiah, it is not so easy to deny that at another point the story was seriously jeopardized. The "hypostatic union" establishes the Logos as the one, sole subject of all that Jesus was, did, and endured. But does this mean that in the life and death of Jesus, God's own self was subject to weakness, suffering, and death? That — the ultimate scandal of the cross — does not find unambiguous protection in Nicene and Chalcedonian theology. On the contrary, almost everyone involved on all sides of the long debates through which that theology took shape held it as a common axiom that even in the incarnation, God as such — the divine nature — did not and could not suffer, still less die. In this context it proved intellectually impossible for the church in this context to muster language, conceptuality, or regulative statements which corresponded to Scripture's own bold attestation that "they crucified the Lord of glory" (1 Cor. 2:8). Here at least the walls of Greek preconception proved impregnable, even as theology wrestled hard to turn that philosophy against itself in defense of the gospel of Christ. Far from being subverted by emergent "orthodoxy," the principle of divine impassibility actually helped to drive the church's thinking forward. What gave birth to the embryonic doctrine of the Trinity devised by Tertullian if not, in part, the need to counteract modalism's identifying of the Father and the Son — with its unacceptable "patripassian" entailment: that the Father suffered in the passion of the Son?

Indeed, the soteriological assumptions which determined further development of the Trinity and of Christology depended on the antithesis of divine to human nature, the latter defined by its capacity for suffering and for change. The condition to which the gospel offers Christ as the sole answer is, for Greek theology, with unmistakable indebtedness to platonic metaphysics, that of corruption and decay, into which humanity has fallen in consequence of sin. Our fleshly nature is unstable and impermanent, threatened by non-being, whose final manifestation is mortality and death. Among the grounds for opposition to Arius was, as we saw, his attributing to Christ a free human will, susceptible to change and thus to sin. Responding at the level of ontology with a Christ who shares in God's own changeless being and is thus immutable before temptation, Nicene theology believed it was securing our salvation: the gracious gift to the human condition of its divine antithesis. Christ brings God's immortality to encounter at its depth, and overcome, our perishability, exchanging our changeableness for his stability. Thus is human nature sanctified, or "deified," restored by Christ to incorruption, as he brings to bear upon the fluctuating disintegration of our lives the divine, redemptive insusceptibility to precisely those conditions.[49]

Now there is, to be sure, a "moment of truth" in the doctrine of impassibility.[50] That may be construed not as a philosophical principle but as the biblical truth that God is not overcome by suffering and death; that the Creator enters into the creatures' pain and weakness in willing freedom, not as the passive victim, as a manifestation, not the denial, of true omnipotence. In free subjection to our condition, God is not reduced to humanness, surrendering divinity, but, remaining God, reveals what Godness means through the ultimate expression of loving self-humiliation. That presupposes no a priori incompatibility between humanity and God since God comes to self-fulfillment precisely by identifying with our otherness — "an even greater similarity within a dissimilarity that is great enough" (Jüngel). However, the axiom of impassibility as it functioned de facto in patristic theology does seem to be predicated on the mutual antithesis of divine and human. God is that which we are not, impervious to the passible condition that defines us. Such dualism, with more or less explicitness, is all-pervasive here. Even Alexandrian Christology, whose primary preoccupation is that the divine Word be the personal subject of Jesus' humanity, regularly draws back at the point of his suffering and death. The passion is not experienced by the Word in its own deity, but by the flesh which that Word assumed.[51]

Yet what really exposes the power in this period of the dualistic polarity between our suffering and God's impassibility is the controlling role it played in the school of Antioch. It tried hardest to be faithful to the biblical narratives of Christ's weakness and suffering, and to give Christological priority to his full humanness of body, mind, and soul — since only in and through a complete human being could the human condition be redeemed. Yet at the same time the

49. See, e.g., Pelikan, *Christian Tradition,* vol. 1, pp. 228ff.; Gregg and Groh, *Early Arianism,* pp. 177ff. On the Greek concept of "deification," see V. Lossky, *The Mystical Theology of the Eastern Church* (Cambridge and London: James Clarke and Co. Ltd., 1957 and Crestwood, N.Y.: St. Vladimir's Seminary Press, 1976), and J. Meyendorff, *Christ in Eastern Christian Thought* (Crestwood, N.Y.: St. Vladimir's Seminary Press, 1975).

50. Gunton, *Yesterday and Today,* p. 101; cf. pp. 92ff.

51. For example, Cyril, "That Christ is One," in *Sources Chrétiennes,* 97, 504.

axiom of impassibility operated to distance God from this condition, turning the necessary *distinction* between the two natures into *separation.* Beginning "from below" with Christ's humanity, even the most moderate of Antiochenes tended to oppose "hypostatic union" with a mere "indwelling" of the divine Word in the independently conceived and "already self-sufficient" man Jesus.[52] This entailed the static juxtaposition of two whole natures in a loose "conjunction" which fell short of the unambiguous unity of Jesus Christ. It partioned off the Word as such from the human nature in which Christ suffered and to which alone the scriptural portrayals of his weakness and passion were to be attributed. Indeed, this detachment served not only to describe but to explain the crucifixion. The death of Christ, in his human nature, happens *because* of the separation of the immutable divine. Far from God tasting human suffering, it was on the precondition of the withdrawal of the immortal nature — in effect a temporary suspension of the incarnation! — that Christ in his humanity could be dead and buried.[53] Here, not for the last time in even "orthodox" theology,

---

52. Grillmeier, *Christ,* vol. 1, p. 429, on Theodore of Mopsuestia; see pp. 421ff.; cf. Pelikan, *Christian Tradition,* vol. 1, pp. 251ff.; and Hanson, "Chalcedonian Formula," p. 108.

53. "The Godhead was separated from the one who was suffering in the trial of death, because it was impossible for him to taste the trial of death if [the Godhead] were not cautiously remote from him. . . ." Theodore of Mopsuestia, *Catechetical Homilies,* 8.9, in *The Commentary on the Nicene Creed* and *The Commentary on the Lord's Prayer and the Sacraments of Baptism and Eucharist,* ed. and trans. A. Mingana, Woodbrook Studies 5 and 6 (Cambridge: Cambridge University Press, 1932-33). Nestorius, the more extreme Antiochene, though probably in the light of modern research (see Grillmeier, *Christ,* vol. 1, pp. 449-63, 501-19, 559-68), not the heretic portrayed by his opponents or the history of doctrine, shares this view. He uses as one proof-text Jn. 2:19: "the third-day burial belonged to this man, not to the deity. . . . It was about this flesh that the Lord said to the Jews, 'Destroy this temple, and in three days I will raise it up'" (Nestorius, "First Sermon on the *Theotokos,*" in Norris, *Christological Controversy,* p. 129; cf. Pelikan, *Christian Tradition,* vol. 1, pp. 252-53). Nestorius takes the temple here to refer to Christ's body and the speaker, "I," to be the Logos, which is not destroyed but rather the power which raised the body in the resurrection. Nestorius's opposition to the description of Mary as *Theotokos* was also predicated on impassibility. Were Mary named the Mother of God, that would imply subjection of the divine Word to the suffering of birth. See Gunton, *Yesterday and Today,* pp. 95-96.

The interpretation of Christ's death in terms of separation of natures was not unique to the Antiochenes, but can be found even in Athanasius (see Grillmeier, *Christ,* vol. 1, pp. 315ff.). Gregory of Nyssa, by contrast, attributes Christ's death to the separation of the body and soul rather than of the divine and human natures, e.g., in *Against Apollinarius,* 30. He goes furthest in this period toward the involvement of God in the cross and grave. See, e.g., "De Tridui inter mortem et resurrectionem Domini nostri Iesu Christi spatio" ("On the three-day interval between the death and resurrection of our Lord

was the "scandal of the cross" compromised by imposition upon the story of preconceived notions of what is possible, and not, for God to be and do.

To be sure, the extremes of Christological dualism were repudiated at Chalcedon, even as Antioch's insistence on the full humanity prevailed. Now the two natures exist in union, "without division, without separation" — the latter phrase perhaps intended to deny the temporary separation of natures at the death of Christ.[54] Yet Chalcedon's other qualifiers of that union, "without change, without confusion," protected the divine nature from the encroachment of our properties, including suffering, as effectively as they prevented the absorption of humanness into deity. Indeed, the Council determined to expel "those who dare to assert that the deity of the Only-Begotten is passible." And though in the sixth-century Byzantine apologists for Chalcedon found it to entail that "one of the Trinity suffered in the flesh,"[55] the Symbol itself — unlike the Nicene Creed — makes no reference to those sufferings, let alone explain precisely who might be their subject. The axiom of impassibility stands uncontested at this acme of Christological refinement and ecumenical agreement — still widely, though not universally, recognized in both East and West.

Whatever its assumptions about impassible divinity, independently considered, the most important point about classical Christology is still its absolute commitment to an event of real union between humanity and God. Any dissolution of that union has been firmly set aside, and no doubt left that, through the Son, God's own being has been present in our history, involved in that finite, perishable, gravebound life which is humankind's estate. Abjuring speculation about this union, and in doxological deference to its mystery speaking only negatively of *how* the natures are related, Chalcedon, we have seen, does seek conceptual correspondence to the biblical account of Jesus Christ, that thoroughly human happening which is also the event of God's self-humiliation into finite flesh.[56] Like every dogma, that of Christ's two natures could not be

---

Jesus Christ"), in *Gregorii Nysseni Opera*, vol. 9 (Leiden: Brill, 1967), pp. 293ff. Gregory also spoke of "God crucified," 'God put to death," etc. *Homilies*, 45. See also Meyendorff, *Christ*, pp. 71, 224; LCC, vol. 3, pp. 121ff.

54. See Grillmeier, *Christ*, vol. 1, p. 553.

55. See Meyendorff, *Christ*, ch. 4.

56. It would be somewhat anachronistic to describe this Christology as "kenotic" — a technical designation deriving from much more recent theology. Yet it is not inaccurate to interpret Chalcedon as attempting to convey in its own forms the Bible's dynamic salvation history, and in particular the model of descent and ascent most fully embodied in the Christological hymn at Phil. 2:6-11, with its key notion of *kenosis* or "self-emptying." On this see Grillmeier, *Christ*, pp. 551-57; Pelikan, *Christian Tradition*, vol. 1, pp. 256-66; von Balthasar, *Mysterium Paschale*, pp. 23ff.; V. Lossky, *Orthodox Theology: An Introduction*

the church's final word but an invitation to further thinking and reform. Likewise the cognate doctrine of the Trinity, which in the West, beginning with Augustine, quickly stagnated and often since has functioned as a veil for de facto unitarianism, requires today profound rethinking and renewal. Yet because they served to safeguard the story of God's union with our life and death it is *reform*, not *repudiation*, that is required of these doctrines: recognition of their permanent signficance along with their incompleteness and provisionality.[57]

Still, in the process of reforming ancient doctrine under the impact of the story that it helped preserve, it is also imperative to dispute its presumption of divine immutability and critically question its dualistic polarizing of God's nature and our own. Could the gospel, for any age or any context, truly contain the conceit that God, by definition, is incapable of sharing in our suffering and pain? For the sake of the proclamation which the early church struggled with such intellectual rigor to protect, theology must struggle again to reconceive the reality of God, not on the premise of a pagan metaphysics but in the light of Jesus Christ himself, the Lord of glory whom they crucified.

(Crestwood, N.Y.: St. Vladimir's Seminary Press, 1989), pp. 100ff.; and Hanson, "Chalcedonian Formula," pp. 111ff.

57. See the verdict of Grillmeier (pp. 555-56), "The formulas of the church, whether they are the *homoousios* of Nicaea or the Chalcedonian Definition, represent the *lectio difficilior* of the gospel, and maintain the demand for faith and the stumbling-block which Christ puts before men. This is a sign that they hand on the original message of Jesus. Nevertheless, the Hellenistic element in them, too, needs a thorough examination and demarcation. . . . They prove the church's desire for an ever more profound *intellectus fidei*, which is not to be a resolution of the *mysterium Christi*. None of the formulas, once framed, should be given up. Yet not one of them can claim to be the church's last word on a divine revelation."

CHAPTER SIX

God's Election of the Grave: Story in Reform of Doctrine

I. The Promise and the Problem of *Kenosis*

The Christian story, we have said, pivots on the axis of Easter Saturday, that boundary between the cross and the empty tomb which reveals the even greater presence of God in the midst of a great absence: the plenitude of divine love's resurrecting power manifest only in and through emptiness, negation, and godforsakenness. Yet this story, so full of strangeness, shock, and scandal, proves constantly disturbing and dangerous to the very community of hearing faith entrusted with its preservation and its proclamation. Prodigious efforts of intellectual courage and conceptual creativity have from the beginning gone into the articulation and the safeguarding of the story; and as we shall see, it is perhaps in our own day that the most profound and daring thoughts of all about God's union with a suffering, dead, and buried one are being brought to mind and thinkability. Yet that contrasts with a tradition — a shaping and handing down of the story in the form of concepts, creeds, and doctrines — often marked by reservation and ambiguity.

We saw this ambivalence above: classical theology's temptation to deaden, if not wholly neutralize, the subversive impact of "the word of the cross"; courage overlaid with caution; an obscuring of the point precisely in the midst of its illumination. The early, but to this day still relatively normative, development of Christian doctrine achieved so much by way of a truly *sui generis* understanding of God. Not least, it attempted to take seriously all that Scripture narrates and affirms of God's identifying with the human, mortal Jesus — in the context of and resistance to other conceptions of God controlled by Greek phi-

163

losophy. That, however, the story of God's presence in the cross and grave was in part conformed to and reduced by the very preconceptions of that philosophy, in the process of its protection from them, proved undeniable.

So what has happened between then and now, the fifth century and our own, to allow or compel this renewing of the mind whereby some practitioners at least of the church's science are thinking the formerly unthinkable, testing impossible possibilities in the doctrine of God? How has it now become possible, even necessary, to speak of God's mortality, of divine abandonment to contradiction and negation, of Easter Saturday as an event in God's own history? What makes dogmatics throw off the cowardice and repent the betrayals of orthodoxy's past, conceptualizing "the word of the cross" with an astringency which the Fathers of Nicea and Chalcedon, for all their achievements in defense of that Word, lacked the tools, or the imagination, or the courage, to hazard? It is crucial to our own theology, *our* understanding of who God is — and therefore who we are — to know something of the process which toppled the barriers of preconception and insecurity that allowed radical reflection upon the cross and grave to be so easily evaded and for so long.

Undoubtedly the sheer force of human experience in the twentieth century has helped to push theology toward the thinking of new thoughts about a suffering, crucified, and buried God. After two World Wars and many "lesser" conflicts, the Holocaust and other genocides, the new palpability of worldwide hunger, poverty and violence conveyed by modern media, and the measurable dying of the planet itself, the stench of death hangs over us all today as perhaps no previous generation. Even without the risk of nuclear destruction — still far from obsolete — which in the minds of many has raised questions about wickedness and folly that are *qualitatively* new, our sheer quantitative exposure to the reality of pain, disease, and death in this century has raised age-old questions of suffering and evil with a new intensity and poignancy, and an urgency not to be resisted by those who speak of faith and hope and give to love a divine dimension and foundation.

How the suffering and evil of our contemporary history has rendered particularly problematic faith's trust in God's loving presence within all of human history, and hope's confidence in the final defeat of evil in history's consummation, are matters to which we must return below. For now, it is enough to say that "after Auschwitz," and in an era so sensitized to the misery endured in gulags and ghettos, prison cells and cancer wards, experience no longer permits theology to support the preaching of a gospel which bypasses the cross and tomb of Jesus as loci of divine suffering and death, or to dismiss as inconceivable the passion and pain of his heavenly Father. How can we do otherwise than speak to our suffering world of a suffering God?

On the other hand, those who seek to think the faith responsibly, like Karl Barth, "with a newspaper in one hand and a Bible in the other," will affirm that it is not simply in response to modern experience in its vividness, still less to fit and appease that experience in its outrageousness, that the church has brought to mind and speech the crucified and buried God. What the hideous contents of twentieth-century news have surely done is return us, of necessity and sometimes in despair, to the Scriptures themselves, alerting us to the presence there from the beginning of a Word that has since been too long silenced and of possibilities — especially divine — which later were too arrogantly pronounced impossible. Empowered by the Spirit, the human words of Scripture (and of preaching) become the means for a creaturely seeing and hearing of God's Word, that is, God's reality in its self-unveiling, self-giving encounter with our world, made ultimate in the incarnate Jesus Christ.[1] The story of that person and event, abbreviated and encapsulated as it is in the triduan narrative of cross, grave, and empty tomb, mediates the dynamic power of Christ himself; and its authority authenticates itself when the story exerts a destructive, reforming impact upon the faith and understanding of the church. For theology is the servant, not the master, of the story; and as we said above (Ch. 5, pp. 136-41), although doctrine can and does vitally safeguard the story by giving it conceptual precision, it may also blunt and betray aspects of the gospel, or allow it to stagnate and ossify within the bonds of absolutized dogma, rigid orthodoxy, or cultural conditioning. The reality, veracity, and power of the Word itself is confirmed when the story breaks free of those chains, subjecting our axioms to critical judgment and creative refinement. Through such a revitalizing and reconstruction of the theological tradition, by the inherent energies of the Word of the cross, and in providential conjunction with our own experience of suffering and death, we have today been liberated for daring new thoughts about the crucified and buried God.

In this living process of critique and reform, the inherited trinitarian and Christological dogmas have by no means been repudiated; but in its respectful reception and continued honoring, aspects of that tradition have been widely questioned — sometimes quite discarded, at others reformulated and supplied with different modes of conception and expression. By some, for example, the static concept of "nature" has been replaced with the category of "event";[2] by

---

1. For a remarkably fresh, still relevant account of "the Word of God," involving the interrelations of Scripture, dogmatics, preaching and Christ himself, see the *Göttingen Dogmatics* of Karl Barth (1924-25); vol. 1, ed. H. Reiffen, trans. G. Bromiley (Grand Rapids: Eerdmans and Edinburgh: T. & T. Clark, 1991); cf. Barth, *CD,* I/1, ch. 1.

2. See, e.g., Gunton, *Yesterday and Today,* pp. 5ff., 11ff.

others, in the illusory hope of disposing with metaphysics altogether — as if non-metaphysical talk about ultimate reality is even meaningful, let alone possible — the language of function has been substituted for ontology. Most pertinent for our purposes has been the blunt refusal in recent years to perpetuate the classical tradition of divine impassibility, as an unbiblical, Hellenistic mistake which betrayed the Christian story. Just how has that story forced upon the Christian intellect recognition and fresh articulation of the passibility and death of God?

It says much for the achievement of patristic theology that despite continuing and increasingly abstruse Christological debate and a succession of subsequent ecumenical councils,[3] the Symbol of Chalcedon for so long retained its normative, dogmatic status through the larger part of the Christian church. That position, perhaps surprisingly, survived the schism between East and West; the proliferation of theologies in the Middle Ages and the Scholastic era; and the upheavals and winnowings, novelties and retrenchments of the Reformation and its counterattacks. Through all of this conflict and diversity Chalcedon retained acknowledgment as a definitive statement of faith's central mystery, which neither domesticated the mystery in Christian reasoning nor allowed its evasion and dissolution by alien philosophical accretions. Yet the very durability of Chalcedon indicates the cessation, or at least discouragement, of creative and imaginative fresh thinking; and in particular it illustrates how unassailable was the highly questionable axiom of impassibility, so hazardous to the Christian story, which permeated patristic theology, including its Christology.[4]

Thus for Thomas Aquinas, God's perfection excludes all passibility. Suffering or change, emotion or need, would indicate defective power or defi-

---

3. On post-Chalcedonian Christology, see esp. Pelikan, *Christian Tradition,* vol. 1, pp. 266ff., and vol. 2, esp. pp. 22ff., 37-90; also A. Grillmeier, *Christ in Christian Tradition,* vol. 2, pt. 1, trans. P. Allen and J. Cawte (London and Oxford: A. R. Mowbray and Louisville: Westminster John Knox, 1987).

4. On impassibility in medieval and Protestant theology, see J. K. Mozley, *The Impassibility of God* (Cambridge: Cambridge University Press, 1926), ch. 1, pp. 104-26. The one aberration from this continuing tradition of impassibility was Luther. He sometimes upheld that axiom, but could also speak audaciously, especially in a Christological context and on the basis of his own, highly "Alexandrian" and almost monophysite understanding of the *communicatio idiomatum,* or "exchange of properties," of the suffering and death of *deus crucifixus.* (See esp. I. D. K. Siggins, *Martin Luther's Doctrine of Christ* [New Haven and London: Yale University Press, 1970]; also W. von Lowenich, *Luther's Theology of the Cross;* and McGrath, *Luther's Theology of the Cross.*) Subsequent Lutheran orthodoxy reaffirmed the changelessness of God, though not without attempting, as we shall see below, to say something new about the event of God's self-emptying.

ciency of being. God loves "without passion" or desire; and in the incarnation it is strictly by reason of his human nature, not his divine, that Christ suffers and dies.[5] Early Reformed theology, though so critical in other ways of the medieval tradition, and while extolling the "wonderful exchange" by which God has assumed our human condition,[6] continued to exempt God from all pain or weakness. Even in the incarnation, where the Son of God is "clothed with our flesh," Christ's suffering and bloodshed "in his human nature are transferred improperly . . . to his divinity."[7] In order to allow his human nature alone to endure the extremity of godforsakenness and death, "His Deity held itself back a little, as if concealed, that is, did not show its power."[8] As with some of the Fathers, this flirts with a temporary suspension of the incarnation, in order to remove God's own self from the cross and grave.

None of this is intended to diminish God's awesome condescension to the depths of our condition and solidarity with us in judgment and death. "The very majesty of God descended to us . . . in such a way that, without leaving heaven, he willed to be borne in the virgin's womb, to go about the earth, and to hang upon the cross."[9] Yet the very structure of "mediation" at the heart of Cal-

---

5. For example, T. Aquinas, *Summa Theologica,* 1.9.1; 1.20.1; 1a.46.12.

6. See Calvin, *Inst.* II.xii.2: "[The Son of God so took] what was ours as to impart what was his to us, and to make what was his by nature ours by grace."

7. *Inst.* II.xii.3; xiv.2. In saying that suffering is not properly ascribed to Christ's divinity, Calvin is characteristically applying the device of *communicatio idiomatum* in a way that corresponds to Antiochene rather than Alexandrian Christology. The properties of one nature are not to be directly predicated of the other, but those of each nature to the one person in whom the natures are united (cf. *Inst.* II.xiv.3). Thus the Mediator may be said to suffer, but not the divine Word as such. For Calvin, the Alexandrian form of the "exchange of predicates" leads ultimately to the heresy of Eutyches (of which he also suspects Luther), whereby the two natures are mingled and confused. To be sure, Calvin also condemns Nestorius, the extreme Antiochene, for going beyond the distinction of the two natures to their pulling part into a double Christ (cf. *Inst.* II.xiv.4); but he intuitively favors the integrity of each nature, including the immutability of the divine, over against the inseparability of their union. It is instructive that in the same breath that he rejects Nestorianism, Calvin almost exactly reproduces Nestorius's exegesis of Jn. 2:19, as indicating the distinctiveness of Christ's body and his divinity (see *Inst.* II.xiv.14; and Ch. 5, n. 53, above). See also Pelikan, *Christian Tradition,* vol. 4: *Reformation of Church and Dogma 1300-1700* (Chicago and London: University of Chicago Press, 1983), pp. 350-58.

8. *Calvin's Geneva Catechism,* 1541, A. 68 (in T. F. Torrance, *The School of Faith* [London: J. Clarke and Co. Ltd., 1959], p. 16).

9. *Inst.* II.xii.1; xiii.4. On the *extra Calvinisticum* here, the Reformed insistence that the eternal Word which united with Christ's human nature remained simultaneously in heaven, not mingled with Christ's human nature nor contained without remainder in the

vin's Christology and soteriology, whereby in the one person of the Mediator God's full nature and our own "grow together by mutual connection," allowed him to distinguish and contrast the two natures in their very union, the power of the one over against the weakness of the other. Thus, ironically, does Calvin protect God from our brokenness while rapt in thankfulness for the divine accommodation to precisely that condition![10]

There was, of course, an admirable sense of fidelity to Scripture as he read it, and to the "orthodox" theological tradition — with a corresponding revulsion from speculation and innovation — underlying Calvin's caution and ambivalence here, and his unwillingness to hazard anything new about God's own subjection to weakness, suffering, and mortality. His profound intuition of God's unchanging faithfulness — which in fact meant constantly changing responses to the vicissitudes of Israel's wayward history — perhaps induced him, like others before and since, to embrace the very different, static changelessness of Greek immutability and thus to recoil from the death of Christ as truly revealing a divine weakness and victimization.

Much the same unwitting beholdenness to alien assumptions in the guise of faithfulness to Scripture undermined what was the boldest attempt between the Reformation and our own day to think the thought of a suffering and humiliated God. This was the theology of *kenosis* — on the surface a courageous and scripturally obedient conceiving of God's own weakness and majestic lowliness. It was prompted by the "Hymn to Christ" in Phil. 2, which speaks of him who was in the form of God but "emptied himself, taking the form of a slave" (v. 7).[11] We have ourselves interpreted Chalcedon as an early "kenotic" attempt to convey the incarnation conceptually as a dynamic event of salvation history,

---

union, and thus not forfeiting its divine, eternal Lordship, see esp. E. D. Willis, *Calvin's Catholic Christology* (Leiden: E. J. Brill, 1966). See also Barth, *Göttingen Dogmatics*, vol. 1, pp. 118ff.; and W. Niesel, *The Theology of Calvin*, trans. H. Knight (Grand Rapids: Baker Book House, 1980), pp. 118ff.

10. See *Inst.* II.xii.1; also xii.3: "he coupled human nature with divine that to atone for sin he might submit the weakness of the one to death; and that, wrestling with death by the power of the other nature, he might win victory for us."

11. Discussion of the proper exegesis of this passage, so influential yet so enigmatic, is superabundant. See esp. E. Käsemann, "Kritische Analyse von Phil. 2.5-11," *Zeitschrift für Theologie und Kirche* 47 (1950): 313-60; R. P. Martin, *Carmen Christi* (Cambridge: Cambridge University Press, 1967); Fuller, *Foundations*, pp. 204-14; Schillebeeckx, *Christ*, pp. 168-77; and the Bibliography on the passage in F. W. Beare, *A Commentary on the Epistle to the Philippians* (San Francisco: Harper & Row, 1959), pp. 40ff. In more recent exegesis it is by no means taken for granted that the passage refers to the incarnation of a pre-existent, heavenly Son of God, as classical interpretation has assumed. See esp. J. D. G. Dunn, *Christology*, pp. 114-21; cf. Macquarrie, *Jesus Christ*, pp. 56ff.

whereby the Son of God descends to our condition in lowliness and ascends again to glory (Ch. 5, n. 56).

The development of *kenosis* as a full-fledged doctrinal theory was occasioned by the introduction into Lutheran dogmatics of a distinction additional to that of Chalcedon between the two natures. This was a contrast between Christ's "two states" — his humiliation succeeded by his exaltation — intended to give dynamic, narrative force to the otherwise static, metaphysical categories of classical Christology.[12] Chemnitz and others expounded this humiliation in terms of *kenosis:* Christ's earthly life was a state of emptiedness. Here, it seems, we verge upon a breakthrough, a new conceptual framework for thinking of Christ's person and work as the event of God's surrender to servitude and lowliness, to contradiction and passion, to death and burial. But who exactly was the subject of this self-emptying, and of what was that subject emptied?

We are so near and yet so far! For once more the rules of Greek philosophy apply, and the Lutherans axiomatically presume that the immutable, eternal Word, God's own self, cannot have been changed or emptied in the incarnation. The tantalizing thought of a *divine* humiliation is thus banished a priori just as it promised to come to thinkability. *Kenosis* is attributed strictly and solely to the human nature of Christ within the incarnate union.[13] That in turn

---

12. On the history of the kenotic theory, see A. B. Bruce, *The Humiliation of Christ* (Edinburgh: T. & T. Clark, 1876), pp. 107-247; Barth, *CD,* IV/1, 180-83; Weber, *Foundations,* vol. 2, pp. 135-42; Pelikan, *Christian Tradition,* vol. 4, pp. 352ff.; H. Küng, *The Incarnation of God,* trans. J. R. Stephenson (Edinburgh: T. & T. Clark, 1987), pp. 538ff.; von Balthasar, *Mysterium Paschale,* pp. 23ff.; E. R. Fairweather, "The 'Kenotic' Christology," Appended Note in Beare, *Philippians,* pp. 159-74. Some early Reformed dogmaticians of the seventeenth century themselves spoke of Christ's twofold state (e.g. Wilhelm Bucanus), but the concept never took hold in Calvinist circles as it did in Lutheran ones under the influence of Martin Chemnitz (1522-86) and Johann Gerhard (1582-1637). These latter were seeking a Christological foundation for the distinctively Lutheran doctrine of Christ's eucharistic presence. For that depended upon a concept of the ubiquity of Christ's body, in, with, and under the elements, and thus a transfer to the human flesh of Christ of an essentially divine attribute. In both its eucharistic and Christological applications, this direct exchange of divine properties to the human strikes Reformed sensibilities as fatally docetic.

13. Reformed Orthodoxy, by contrast, strongly asserting the full humanity of Christ, different from us only in respect of sin, does attribute humiliation, or exinanition, to the divine nature, so that there was indeed a *kenosis* of the preexistent Son of God. But here, too, there is hesitation and ambivalence; for it transpires that once again this is not a genuine renunciation, but only a concealment, of divine attributes, their nonuse or nonmanifestation (cf. Bruce, *Humiliation,* pp. 162-72); and the question which may be put to some of the later Lutheran kenoticists — what could it *mean* for Christ's human nature to

is predicated on a monstrous docetism which quite compromises Christ's humanness and historicity. Surely the humanity of Christ, by definition, does not have *divine* properties to renounce or be self-emptied of. Yet that is precisely what Christ's human nature does have, according to the Lutheran application of the "exchange of properties."[14] For that secures not only a humiliation of the divine nature but also, so questionably, a glorification — in effect a divinization — of the human. By virtue of the incarnation, the humanity of Christ does possess God's attributes of majesty, and it is these that he freely chooses to be emptied of (or on some accounts merely to conceal).[15] Far from allowing Good Friday and Easter Saturday to be the culmination of divine abandonment (in which God remains God), here *kenosis* is a purely human act, but one that renounces properties which could never have been attributed to a truly human Christ in the first place.[16]

A rebirth of German Lutheran kenoticism in the nineteenth century offered a new interpretation of "self-emptying" as indeed God's own act and thus

---

possess but not use divine attributes? — may equally be addressed to the Reformed, with reference to the divine nature itself.

14. On this, see esp. Weber, *Foundations,* vol. 2, p. 136, and Bruce, *Humiliation,* pp. 125ff. The Lutheran use of *communicatio idiomatum* (see above, Ch. 5, n. 47) is enshrined in the Formula of Concord, 1577.

15. On the grounds that Christ's humanity, being united inseparably with the divine, could not strictly renounce the attributes of majesty, a school of Lutherans at Tübingen, following Johann Brenz (1499-1570), taught that Christ even in the state of humiliation did actually possess those attributes, including the kingly rule of the universe, but kept both possession and use concealed from view. That school was accused by an opposing school at Giessen of divinizing Christ's humanity and compromising the reality of his sufferings. But the Giessen alternative — that Christ at least partially refrained from the use of his majesty though he still possessed it — seems scarcely less docetic, and to rest upon a wholly improbable, if not inexplicable, distinction. A formal arbitration between the schools, the Saxon Decision of 1624, found in favor of Giessen, which was generally followed by subsequent Lutheran orthodoxy. See Barth, *CD,* IV/1, 181; and Bonhoeffer, *Christ the Center,* pp. 93ff.

16. Much kenotic discussion, down to the twentieth century, has asked *how* the infinity of God could be "fitted," as it were, into the finitude of Christ's humanity, so that, in the Lutheran case, e.g., the eucharistic body of Christ could enjoy the property of ubiquity. This presupposes a "container" view such that each nature occupies a given magnitude of space and is answered to the effect that God makes room for the infinite in the finite by "expanding" the human nature. But the quantitativeness of that answer exposes and artificiality of the container concept of space; and it reinforces the docetic tendencies of a theory which could foster so grotesque a notion as the enlargement of the receptacle that is Christ's humanity. See T. F. Torrance, *Space, Time and Incarnation* (London and New York: Oxford University Press, 1969), pp. 35ff.

a fresh challenge to the doctrine of immutability; but its results proved once again disappointing and self-contradictory.[17] This time it is clear that the humiliation of Christ in his incarnate life is preceded by that of the very Logos. Becoming incarnate, the divine, eternal Word is humbled and self-denuded, submitting to real change. But in this event of radical mutability, God renounces Godness and deity is self-terminated. The consequence of *kenosis* is not now divinized humanity but — equally problematic — dedivinized divinity. The humiliation of the Word in the mortal Jesus brings not God's even greater presence amid the great absence of godforsakenness and burial, but an absence absolute. This robs Easter Saturday and all that went before precisely of its mystery, as God's "with us" evaporates before our eyes. And indeed who governs and sustains the universe while the Creator is thus divested of sovereignty and power?[18] Far from offering a conceptual breakthrough allowing more re-

17. Here the main contributors were Gottfried Thomasius (1802-75) and Wolfgang Gess (1819-91), who followed the earlier tradition of Giessen against that of Tübingen. Thomasius, attempting to avoid the docetic deification of humanity in earlier kenoticism, was able instead to attribute self-emptying to the divine nature by the device of distinguishing that nature's "immanent" properties, such as holiness and truth, which were retained by the incarnate Word, from those of God's relations to the world, in creation and redemption, such as omnipotence and omniscience, which the self-humbling Word renounced. But this arbitrary classification not only introduces an artificial division into God; it also robs the God revealed to us and involved with us in the flesh precisely of that supposed set of characteristics through which God is knowable by us and related to us. Thus the entire logic of incarnation collapses in self-contradiction. The key section of Thomasius's major work, *Christ's Person and Work,* is included in *God and Incarnation in Mid-Nineteenth Century German Theology,* ed. and trans. C. Welch (New York: Oxford University Press, 1965), pp. 31-101. Gess went beyond the relative restraint of Thomasius, for whom at least the immanent properties of God are not renounced, to a wholesale "deglorification" of the Logos. In this total self-divestiture of Godness, the divine consciousness is extinguished, to regain itself through the slow evolution of the human Christ's spiritual awareness. This reflects the Liberal concern of the time to abandon all metaphysics and restrict the basis of Christology to the developing religious personality of the historical Jesus. And this use of *kenosis* was famously mocked as completing "the *kenosis* of reason . . . to the point of absolute absurdity" (A. E. Biedermann, *Christian Dogmatics,* in Welch, *God and Incarnation,* p. 306). On all of this, see Weber, *Foundations,* vol. 2, pp. 141ff.; Bruce, *Humiliation,* pp. 173-97; Barth, *CD,* IV/1, 182-83; and Macquarrie, *Jesus Christ,* pp. 245ff.

18. The objection that a self-emptied Creator leaves the cosmos at least temporarily without God's sustenance sums up a standard Reformed response to Lutheran kenoticism, nowhere more succinctly put than by D. M. Baillie in his celebrated attack on kenotic theory in *God Was in Christ* (London: Faber and Faber, 1956 and New York: Macmillan, 1980), pp. 94-98. This critique is a further manifestation of the *extra Calvinisticum* — the Reformed intuition that God is not "contained" without remainder in the incarnate union

fined reflection on the Christian story, this maneuver rather jeopardizes the Creator and creation; casts the incarnation into limbo; and cancels the story of God's involvement in human life and suffering, our death and burial. And it unwittingly reinforces the dualistic antithesis of divine and human by assuming that self-humiliation comes so unnaturally to the divine that God can so act only by ceasing to be God! The status quo of impassibility has not been disrupted after all, nor has the story yet renovated doctrine by forcing it to test its preconceptions of what is possible for God to be and do.

At last, however, such reform has begun in our own day, with innovative conceptual responses to "the word of the cross" in modern German Christology, in part anticipated by a further revival of kenoticism, this time British, in the first decades of this century.[19] That early development reinforced the promise of "divine self-emptying" as a concept necessary — at whatever cost to the tradition's axiom of impassibility — to any adequate reflection upon the defining story of Christ's life and death. But it also confirmed, perhaps once and for all, the inherent problems and contradictions of a "kenotic theory" as such, which

---

but that, in dynamic relation to the enfleshed Logos, the Second Person of the Trinity continues "outside the flesh" to "uphold all things by his Word of power" (Heb. 1:3). In truth, the broad lines of Lutheran kenotic thought in the last century were also followed by the Reformed in Germany. Yet it is instructive that their outstanding representative, August Ebrard (1818-88), while affirming the self-restricting of God's omnipotence and omniscience to particular, time-conditioned forms of human power and knowledge, insisted that this was not the termination of Godness. The Word retained its own nature as divine, just as God's majesty was not replaced by lowliness in the incarnation, but rather the lowliness was simultaneous with the majesty and truly revealed whereof that majesty consists. This is, as we shall see, a significant prolepsis of Reformed Christology in the twentieth century, including that of Barth. See Bruce, *Humiliation,* pp. 197-206; and A. I. C. Heron, "An Exchange between Scotland and Germany in 1879: Ebrard of Erlangen and Matheson of Inellan," *SJT* 42.3 (1989): 341-66.

19. The major figures here were P. T. Forsyth (1848-1921) and H. R. Mackintosh (1870-1936), both Scots — though Forsyth exercised his preaching and teaching ministry in England — and embodying the strong links with Scottish and German theology. (There was, to be sure, a brief, distinctively Anglican interest in *kenosis* at the turn of the century, notably in the writings of Charles Gore [1853-1932], including *The Incarnation of the Son of God* [New York: Charles Scribner's Sons, 1891]. Gore emphasized the human ignorance of Christ, in consequence of the willing self-emptying by the Logos of divine knowledge. See Macquarrie, *Jesus Christ,* pp. 249-50.) Though sharing many premises with the nineteenth-century German kenoticists, and subject to many of their weaknesses, the thoughts of Forsyth and Mackintosh about *kenosis* were their own and are not to be simply identified with those of Thomasius and Gess. See Robert Redman's criticism of D. M. Baillie in this regard in "H. R. Mackintosh's Contribution to Christology and Soteriology in the 20th Century," *SJT* 41.4 (1988): 524.

can scarcely avoid implying that in the incarnation God gives up being God. Unlike the first Lutheran kenoticists, Forsyth and Mackintosh are clear that God, and not just the human nature of the incarnate Christ, is the subject of *kenosis;* and in contrast to those of the nineteenth century they seek a premundane self-emptying which is neither partial — whereby only one of two putative sets of attributes is renounced — nor so absolute that it is no longer *God* who is in Christ. "The suicide of God is no part of the kenotic idea, which turns but on self-divestment as a moral power of the eternal Son; who retains his consciousness but renounces the conditions of infinity and its precreate form. . . . [The] Godhead lost nothing in the saving act."[20] The self-retraction of God's infinite properties, from "actuality" to "potentiality" and their concentration within the finite constrictions of the historical Jesus,[21] does not connote the cessation of deity. Rather, God's majesty and power find their fulfillment or *plerosis* through the lowly kenotic act of self-adjustment to human weakness.[22] Progressively through the spiritual, Godward growth of Christ's earthly life, which culminates in post-Easter exaltation, the "life-content of Godhead" becomes completely united with "finite human forms," thus realizing its perfection.[23]

There are, without question, bona fide efforts here to subvert the assumption that God cannot suffer or change, and instead to make dogmatics conform more obediently to the imperatives of the Christ-event itself, as biblically narrated. That bespeaks "the human life of God . . . whose chiefest glory consists in a voluntary descent from depth to depth of our experience."[24] Not diminished but rather fulfilled through self-limitation, God stoops to endure and thus to heal and conquer the most broken, terminal conditions of the human tragedy: that union of the eternal with perishability whose completeness Easter Saturday depicts most starkly.

Yet there are major defects in British kenoticism, like the German, which make it only a stepping stone to further conceptual advance. Their notion of "progressive incarnation,"[25] and interest in the spiritual personality of the his-

---

20. P. T. Forsyth, *The Person and Place of Jesus Christ* (London: Independent Press, Ltd., 1909, 6th ed. 1948), pp. 296, 319; cf. H. R. Mackintosh, *The Doctrine of the Person of Jesus Christ* (Edinburgh: T. & T. Clark, 1912, 2nd ed. 1913), e.g., pp. 473, 485-86.

21. See Forsyth, *Person and Place,* e.g., pp. 307ff.; and Mackintosh, *Person of Christ,* e.g., pp. 476ff.

22. In their respective Christological treatises, both Forsyth and Mackintosh follow their discussion of *kenosis,* self-emptying, with a corresponding chapter on *plerosis* or self-fulfillment. See Forsyth, *Person and Place,* ch. 12, and Mackintosh, *Person of Christ,* ch. 11.

23. Mackintosh, *Person of Christ,* p. 494.

24. Mackintosh, *Person of Christ,* p. 486.

25. See, e.g., Forsyth, *Person and Place,* pp. 330, 349.

torical Jesus, indicates that Forsyth and Mackintosh share with nineteenth-century Liberalism and Kenoticism a revulsion from ontology. Especially they reject all metaphysical Christology, including the allegedly archaic, impersonal, nonexperiential categories of Chalcedon.[26] For them, ontology must yield to the *moral* qualities and impact of God's self-abasement;[27] yet however moving their reflections on that moral act, their reluctance to deal with the act's ontology seems an ultimate refusal to *think* the faith and seek an *understanding* of its deepest mysteries. "Immutability" is overcome here not on its own ground but by retreat from the ontological arena wherein that doctrine operates. To be sure, Forsyth and Mackintosh at times explore the ontological enigmas in Christology — God's own relation to the humble, crucified Jesus, for example — despite themselves;[28] and what is the hypothesis of actual properties reduced to potential if not philosophical? But a polarizing of the moral and the metaphysical evades the conceptual challenge of *kenosis* and leaves the theory of self-contracted attributes unable to say how, in that process, God truly remains God. By refusing ontology, kenoticism is reduced to silence before Baillie's crushing questions: "What became of the Creator and creation while the creative Word was self-emptied of its power?" and "What becomes of incarnation if in taking flesh God ceases to be God?"[29]

Then again, though a significant anticipation of further developments, which will *identify* humiliation with the fullest expression of God's fullness,[30]

26. See, e.g., Forsyth, *Person and Place,* pp. 216ff.; Mackintosh, *Person of Christ,* pp. 213ff.

27. Thus Forsyth writes approvingly of "The Moralising of Dogma" in ch. 9 of *Person and Place,* and emphasizes throughout the ethical significance of God's self-renunciation: "the greatest act of moral freedom ever done" (p. 315). Likewise Mackintosh complains that "ecclesiastical Christology" has not done justice to the moral and spiritual power of the gospel story, whereby "descending into poverty, shame and weakness, the Lord was stripped of all credit, despoiled of every right, humbled to the very depths of social and historical ignominy, that in this self-abasement of God there might be found the redemption of man. . . . There will always be metaphysic in Christology, but it ought to be a metaphysic of the conscience, in which not substance but Holy Love is supreme" (*Person of Christ,* pp. 466-67, 472).

28. See Fairweather, in Beare, *Philippians.*

29. On the need for ontology, in the context of *kenosis,* see Gunton, *Yesterday and Today,* pp. 168ff.

30. "It seems not inappropriate to speak of a self-emptying of God, but only if it is understood in such a way as to be an *expression* rather than a 'retraction' of his deity. The self-emptying is part of God's fullness, for the heart of what it means to be God is that he is able to empty himself on behalf of that which is not himself." Gunton, *Yesterday and Today,* p. 172.

there is something unsatisfactory about the serial juxtaposition of *kenosis* and *plerosis* by these Scots. Though they try to conceive of these as parallel rather than opposed,[31] their progressive, evolutionary reading of the Christ-event forces them to think sequentially. Glory succeeds, indeed "replaces," humbleness,[32] as resurrection follows earthly life and death. The descent of self-surrender yields to the ascent of exaltation, the "redintegration of an old state," where once-resigned attributes of power are now resumed.[33] *Kenosis* thus becomes a past episode, as he who for our sake lost his life regains it; the form of a servant gives place again to the form of God; and the world of his servitude and brokenness is "left behind."[34]

Thus are betrayed, even at this late stage, vestiges of the old immutability, an assumption that only in the renunciation, and not the fullest exercise, of Godness is it possible for God to be subject to our pain and death. And we are left with the nagging impression that God's humility was only a "temporary theophany."[35] In contradiction of John's Prologue, it is not in the midst of the fleshly world, but upon release from it, that God's fullness and glory are revealed. As Weber protests: "The self-humiliation of God in Jesus Christ certainly did happen, but it was not so to speak an intermezzo, but was the gracious and active self-manifestation of God."[36] It was left to Karl Barth to expound this happenedness of *kenosis* so as to secure, better than any kenotic theory of surrendered attributes could, the "unaltered because unalterable deity" of the God so humbled.[37] Barth broke new ground in reflecting on the fullness realized in that emptiedness itself, not merely in its aftermath; the revelation most illuminative amid death's deepest darkness; the power perfected and triumphant not beyond weakness, but at the very point, cruciform and grave-shaped, of radical defeat.[38]

31. See, e.g., Forsyth, *Person and Place,* p. 311.

32. For example, Mackintosh, *Person of Christ,* p. 479.

33. Forsyth, *Person and Place,* p. 311; Mackintosh, *Person of Christ,* pp. 504ff.

34. Mackintosh, *Person of Christ,* p. 494; Forsyth, *Person and Place,* pp. 311, 316.

35. Baillie, *God Was in Christ,* p. 96. Indeed, Baillie (p. 97) accuses kenotic theory of making the incarnation itself only a temporary episode: "He is God and Man, not simultaneously in a hypostatic union, but *successively* — first divine, then human, then God again." That flouts the classical belief in the permanence of Christ's humanity — that it is the incarnate one as such "whose kingdom shall have no end" (Nicene Creed). Cf. *Westminster Shorter Catechism,* A. 21: "[Christ] continueth to be, God and man, in two distinct natures, and one Person forever."

36. Weber, *Foundations,* vol. 2, p. 140.

37. Barth, *CD,* IV/1, 179-80; cf. pp. 179-210.

38. It should be noted that there is a millennium-old tradition of *kenosis* in the spir-

II. From Above and from Below

Why, one might wonder in the light of British kenoticism, was so much modern theology prior to Barth, following in the wake of Liberalism and hostile to ontology, unable to defy completely so ancient and philosophical a taboo as that upon divine suffering? How could the old axiom of impassibility still exert such an influence on the new thinking that began in the West with the Enlightenment? And what was different about Barth, in one sense as modern and post-Enlightenment as his peers, that he could lead contemporary theology at last beyond the impasse of immutability? Part of the answer is surely that modern theology was not as new or modern as it seemed,[39] so that in challenging "modern" assumptions Barth — hailed by some as a "paradigm of the post-modern"[40] — finally broke the shackles of ancient philosophy also.

The point is most clearly made with reference to dualism, by which the platonic tradition bifurcated the world into incompatible realms: eternity and time, goodness and evil, reality and shadow, changelessness and decay. By a process noted above, the early church to some extent absorbed this dualism — which it passed on to the West through Augustine — and allowed its dichotomizing assumptions to taint that Christian thinking about God, Christ, and the cosmos which was actually subverting the Hellenistic worldview. Even in the context of the incarnation, the philosophically impossible "hypostatic union" of the eternal and the mortal, a presumption prevailed that divinity as such was impervious to mortality and change. God's being was shut off from the historical, perishable world of body, time, and pain. While, therefore, orthodoxy endorsed and safeguarded the scandalous news that God had crossed

ituality of Russian Orthodoxy, quite distinct from the Western theory and devoid of its difficulties. Its arena is not dogmatic Christological speculation on the "how" of the incarnation, but Christian piety in imitation of Christ's voluntary self-abasement. That idea has retained a powerful hold upon the Russian religious and literary imagination (see Beare, *Philippians*, pp. 81ff.). In the last century and this, most notably through the work of V. Soloviev (1853-1900) and S. Bulgakov (1871-1944), *kenosis* has also been applied in Russian thought about the Trinity and creation, especially in connection with the figure of Wisdom (Sophia), who represents the feminine principle of selflessness and vulnerability within the Godhead and the agent of God's self-limiting act of creation. See esp. N. Gorodetzky, *The Humiliated Christ in Modern Russian Thought* (London: SPCK, 1938); Baillie, *God Was in Christ*, p. 98; and von Balthasar, *Mysterium Paschale*, p. 35.

39. In what follows I am deeply indebted to Colin Gunton for his discussion of ancient and modern dualism in *Yesterday and Today*, esp. ch. 5.

40. See H. Küng, *Theology for the Third Millennium*, trans. P. Heinegg (New York: Doubleday, 1988), esp. pp. 259-84. Cf. R. W. Jenson, "Karl Barth," in D. Ford, ed., *The Modern Theologians*, 2 vols. (Oxford and New York: Blackwell, 1989), vol. 1, p. 25.

the cosmic gulf between the transcendent and the earthly, the supposition of that gulf survived uncontradicted. How ironic that this dualistic chasm should not be filled in, but rendered even wider, when the Enlightenment thought to throw off the oppressive claims of past authority, philosophical and theological, and propound a modern cosmology based on humanity's autonomous reason and scientific observation. "The 'closed' God of antiquity is answered by the closed world of so much modern thinking."[41]

The Enlightenment's dualism derived surpassingly from Kant's distinction between the world of ideas, "things in themselves" which we cannot know, and that of experience, things we do know through the senses. It posed, in Lessing's imagery, a "big ugly ditch" between the eternal and the temporal as unbridgeable as that in Platonism.[42] The only difference is that now history is absolutized as a self-contained realm, where no place for the transcendent is possible or necessary, whereas the old dualism idealized eternity, the source of truth as knowable by the mind, in contrast to the change, deception, and obscurity of time and the senses. But on both accounts a *meeting* of transcendence and contingency is ruled out a priori; and there can be no *union* of the eternal

41. Gunton, *Yesterday and Today,* p. 207.

42. For a clear and helpful account of the Enlightenment and its impact on theology, including brief surveys of Kant and Lessing, see esp. Heron, *Century,* esp. chs. 1 and 2. See also Barth, *Protestant Theology,* esp. chs. 2-4, 6, and 7; H. Thielicke, *Modern Faith and Thought,* trans. G. W. Bromiley (Grand Rapids: Eerdmans, 1990), esp. chs. 5 and 10; H. Berkhof, *Two Hundred Years of Theology,* trans. J. Vriend (Grand Rapids: Eerdmans, 1989), esp. ch. 1; and J. C. Livingston, *Modern Christian Thought* (New York and London: Macmillan, 1971), esp. chs. 1-3.

In recent years considerable discussion — and a major transatlantic project ("The Gospel and Our Culture") — has developed concerning the tendency of the Western churches to identify the Christian gospel with European culture derived from the Enlightenment. The debate often turns on the dualistic assumption of this culture that religion and faith belong to a private world of moral values over against a public world of scientific verification and historical fact. This latter world is presumed to be nonteleological, not governed by any transcendent power which gives history purpose and direction. See, e.g., L. Newbigin, *The Other Side of 1984* (Geneva: World Council of Churches and Grand Rapids: Eerdmans, 1984); *Foolishness to the Greeks* (Geneva: World Council of Churches and Grand Rapids: Eerdmans, 1986); *The Gospel in a Pluralistic Society* (Grand Rapids: Eerdmans and London: SPCK, 1989); and *Truth to Tell: The Gospel as Public Truth* (Grand Rapids: Eerdmans and Geneva: World Council of Churches, 1991). See also Gunton, *Enlightenment and Alienation;* Torrance, *Reality and Scientific Theology* and *God and Rationality;* A. MacIntyre, *After Virtue* (Notre Dame: University of Notre Dame Press and London: Duckworth, 1981); G. Lindbeck, *The Nature of Doctrine* (Philadelphia: Westminster, 1984); and H. Montefiore, *The Gospel and Contemporary Society* (London: Mowbray, 1992).

and the temporal. Revelation and incarnation, God's *becoming* knowable to human rationality, is impossible to modern thought just as it was scandalous to and threatened by the dualism of the past. Indeed, the universe observable to science and shaped by our own minds would no longer be free and self-contained if guided, let alone indwelt, by transcendent deity; nor would that deity truly be transcendent if related to or present in our immanence and flux.

Thus has much modern theology posed its own internal threat to the gospel story, retaining the axiom of immutability, dismissing God's freedom and power to interact with that which is not God, and assuming that a "hypostatic union" of eternity and time would compromise scientific rationality, human freedom, and history's self-governance. If "incarnation" be spoken of at all, it must be about the growing consciousness of God in Jesus and ourselves, or the moral values inspired by the myth of God's descent.[43] Faith itself is the polar

43. Two major movements of the nineteenth century embody reactions to the Kantian decree that God as such is unknowable. The only way left to speak of God in the light of that decree is in terms of our human religious feelings (Romanticism), or the moral and religious way of life inspired by the man Jesus (Liberalism). These responses may be identified with Schleiermacher, and Ritschl and Harnack, respectively. See, e.g., Heron, *Century,* ch. 2; Barth, *Protestant Theology,* chs. 11 and 29; and *The Theology of Schleiermacher,* ed. D. Ritschl, trans. G. W. Bromiley (Grand Rapids: Eerdmans and Edinburgh: T. & T. Clark, 1983); Livingston, *Modern Thought,* chs. 4 and 9; Thielicke, *Modern Faith,* chs. 7, 8, and 11; and Berkhof, *Two Hundred Years,* chs. 3 and 9. On the recent Myth of God Incarnate debate, see Hick, ed., *Myth;* M. Goulder, ed., *Incarnation and Myth: The Debate Continued* (London: SCM and Ann Arbor, Mich.: Books on Demand, 1979); E. L. Mascall, *Theology and the Gospel of Christ* (London: SPCK, 1977); also M. Wiles, *The Remaking of Christian Doctrine* (London: SCM, 1974), ch. 3, and "Does Christology Rest on a Mistake?" in S. W. Sykes and J. P. Clayton, eds., *Christ, Faith and History* (Cambridge: Cambridge University Press, 1977), pp. 3-12; A. E. Harvey, *God Incarnate: Story and Belief* (London: SPCK, 1981); and A. Thatcher, *Truly a Person, Truly God: A Post-Mythical View of Jesus* (London: SPCK, 1990). Part of the problem with the celebrated "Myth" debate of the 1970s was that the original contributors to *The Myth of God Incarnate,* while united in rejecting Chalcedon's ontological categories in Christology, differed widely in the connotation they gave to the "myth" they would substitute for that ontology. Don Cuppitt, e.g., sees the story of God's incarnation as a *false,* pernicious myth about the uniting of God's world and our own, fatal to Jesus of Nazareth's own message, which posed a radical disjunction between this world and God's transcendent kingdom (see Hick, *Myth,* pp. 140ff.). By contrast, Frances Young upholds the "myth" as real and as conveying "truth." There is no "literal" incarnation, but there is a "story of God being involved in the the reality of human existence with its compromises, its temptations, its sufferings . . . its death." This story challenged her "to trust in God against all odds." Even such an advocate of the myth's nonliteral "truthfulness" is openly committed to Kant's dualism and to the ancient axiom of impassibiity. There are two stories to be told about the man Jesus, one "scien-

opposite of knowledge, a private opinion with accompanying affections and ethical intentions, in contrast to public facts dependably secured by empirical scrutiny.

Admittedly, not every theologian who adopts the Enlightenment's orientation in cosmology and the premises of modern scientific rationalism is so closed-minded as to cut God off from the world or the world from God, deeming impossible the incarnate encounter of eternity and time. The work of Pannenberg, for example, is an impressive modern attempt to state the claims of the Christian faith to be the truth, and theology's credentials to participate in public rational discourse with the other sciences.[44] As we saw in Chapter 3, Pannenberg refuses to assume the divinity of Christ and begins, in modern fashion, "from below," with Jesus' humanness. He contends that by critical analysis, open-minded historical science could infer the factuality even of the resurrection. Thus inductive reasoning, no enemy of faith, would verify the pre-Easter claims of Jesus to be Son of God, and so establish the church's knowledge that in him God had been incarnate, ushering in proleptically at history's midpoint its final destiny and goal.[45]

This moderate form of procedure "from below" presents an admirable challenge from within "modernity" to a scientific outlook (now long outmoded), which assumes the world to be a sealed, deterministic system, self-explanatory and devoid of mystery or transcendent purpose. But it owes more

------

tific," acceptable to modern (public) culture, and the other "mythological," appealing to (private) religious faith. And these two stories, though both necessary, are "incompatible"; for there can be no such actual event as a divine, suffering presence in the human Jesus. Though she claims that it is modernity which has forced her into this unbridgeable chasm, Young in fact accepts without question the ancient platonic presumption that it is impossible for God to be part of human history without loss of Godness and transcendence. Though she finds the myth of the crucified God to be "true," she will not permit the story of the cross to determine what may in fact be possible and true for God (see Hick, *Myth*, pp. 13-47, esp. 33ff.). As Gunton notes (*Yesterday and Today*, p. 89), Schillebeeckx makes the same — supposedly modern — assumption that, being transcendent, God *cannot* be also immanent. See his *Jesus*, p. 627.

44. See W. Pannenberg, *Theology and the Philosophy of Science* (London: Darton Longman and Todd, 1976); *Basic Questions in Theology,* vols. 1 and 2, trans. G. H. Kehm (London: SCM and Philadelphia: Fortress, 1970 and 1971); *Basic Questions in Theology,* vol. 3, trans. R. A. Wilson (London: SCM, 1973 [= *The Idea of God and Human Freedom* (Philadelphia: Westminster, 1973)]); *An Introduction to Systematic Theology* (Grand Rapids: Eerdmans, 1991), and *Systematic Theology,* vol. 1, trans. G. W. Bromiley (Grand Rapids: Eerdmans, 1991).

45. See esp. Pannenberg, *Jesus: God and Man,* ch. 3; and Ch. 3 above. Cf. Gunton, *Yesterday and Today,* esp. ch. 2.

to Hegel's unifying of the Spirit and the world than to their radical divorce in Kant; and it surely exaggerates the identity of faith and reason. Would the resurrection truly be faith's ground of hope for the unseen if it were *only* a temporal, historical event knowable to science like any other? And if the raising of the dead were no scandal to our intellect, what of the crucifying of the Risen One? If Jesus be authenticated retroactively by Easter as having been the Son from the beginning, what sense does that make of his fate on Calvary? The failure, abandonment, and burial of God's own Son remains a foolish word, the contradiction of all wisdom. Could reason, starting from below with a purely human Jesus, ever conclude with the divinity, not just of one who conquered death but of him who succumbed to death and godforsakenness and descended into hell?[46]

So Pannenberg meets the empiricism of our culture by inviting historical science itself to be more open to transcendence than narrow rationalism would allow; yet even he is discomforted by the enigma of transcendence *crucified* in history. How much less ready to question the tradition of divine impassibility are those who react to the Enlightenment's concerns by evading them entirely. There is a procedure "from above" which sets aside the critical-historical difficulties and simply presupposes Christ's divinity and preexistence as revelation's given, with which his humanness is to be reconciled as best it may.[47] But such a starting point proves almost of necessity docetic; and once again it is the scandal of the cross, the humanness of Jesus in extremis, broken and terminated, which mocks the comfortable perception of his Godness. Could faith, starting from above, with a purely divine Christ, ever conclude with the humanity, godforsaken, crucified, and buried, of him who exists from all eternity in heaven's glory?

There is, though, a manner of beginning "from above," letting God be God and not precluding divine presence in human flesh and history, which equally does not assume that Jesus' God-relatedness entails impassibility, nor determine in advance what God can be and do and suffer on the cross and in the grave. Such a method[48] certainly begins with faith, but faith which does not preempt critical and historical engagement nor preconceive God's possibilities and nature. Beginning with an openness to revelation, this faith seeks rational understanding of what it confesses, works with discrimination through his-

---

46. This is the substance of Moltmann's critique of Pannenberg. See *Crucified God,* pp. 166-78; also Ch. 3, n. 26 and Ch. 4, n. 13, above.

47. Some examples of this may be found in M. Green, ed., *The Truth of God Incarnate* (London: Hodder and Stoughton, 1977), essays written in response to *The Myth of God Incarnate.*

48. See Gunton, *Yesterday and Today,* pp. 45-50.

tory's data, and allows the death of Jesus to determine what we may say is possible for God to be and to become within the unfolding and terminating of a human history. This is a methodology of hearing: as Bonhoeffer put it, Christology begun in silence.[49] Instead of posing questions and assuming answers concerning Christ's divinity and human nature, here theology listens to Christ's own questions — "Who do you say that I am?" — and allows the Word of his cross to subvert our preconceptions, making its own discomforting disclosures of what God's possibilities and our own might truly be.[50] Though not a few have followed this procedure in his wake, no one has pursued it in our day with greater rigor or more effectively than Barth. By its means he overcame the dualism of both Kant and Plato, gave quite new content to immutability and, obedient to the word of the cross, traversed a remarkable path from the "total otherness of God" to God's humanity and passion.

III. From Being to Becoming

Barth's is an acoustic method par excellence; and by insisting that dogmatics listen before it speaks, and when it speaks conform its thought and speech to what it hears, he initiated a "new Reformation" which set this century's theology upon a very different path from that taken in the last, and up to World War I.[51] In contrast to a starting point in anthropology — religious experience

49. Bonhoeffer, *Christ the Center,* pp. 27ff.

50. See esp. Moltmann, "Who Do You Say That I Am?" *Crucified God,* pp. 103-7; Torrance, "Questioning in Jesus Christ," in *Theology in Reconstruction,* ch. 7.

51. See F. W. Camfield, *Reformation Old and New* (London: Lutterworth Press, 1947). Accounts of Barth's career, theology, and significance are legion and still multiplying. Particularly helpful as general introductions are Heron, *Century,* ch. 4; Zahrnt, *Question of God,* chs. 1-4; T. F. Torrance, *Karl Barth: An Introduction to His Early Theology 1910-1931* (London: SCM, 1962); and *Karl Barth: Biblical and Evangelical Theologian* (Edinburgh: T. & T. Clark, 1990); E. Jüngel, *Karl Barth: A Theological Legacy,* trans. G. E. Paul (Philadelphia: Westminster, 1986); Jenson, "Karl Barth," in Ford, ed., *Modern Theologians;* G. W. Bromiley, *An Introduction to the Theology of Karl Barth* (Grand Rapids: Eerdmans and Edinburgh: T. & T. Clark, 1979); H. Hartwell, *The Theology of Karl Barth: An Introduction* (Philadelphia: Westminster, 1964); D. L. Mueller, *Karl Barth* (Makers of the Modern Theological Mind, ed. B. E. Patterson) (Waco: Word Books, 1972); H. Frei, *Types of Christian Theology* (New Haven: Yale University Press, 1992). J. Thompson, ed., *Theology beyond Christendom: Essays on the Centenary of the Birth of Karl Barth, May 10, 1886.* See also E. Busch, *Karl Barth: His Life from Letters and Autobiographical Texts* (London: SCM and Philadelphia: Fortress, 1976). More advanced studies include S. Sykes, ed., *Karl Barth: Essays in His Theological Methods* (Oxford: Clarendon Press, 1979); and ed., *Karl Barth: Cen-*

or moral values, intellectual assumptions or a culture's worldview — faith gives an attentive ear to God's own Word, self-positing, self-interpreting. Though often misunderstood by his opponents — and sometimes his supporters — Barth does not mean that first theology presupposes the existence or character of God. That would be one more effort of the human mind to have the first and last word, to control the departure point and thereby everything that followed.[52] The priority of the Word is not a matter of human presupposing but of divine preceding. God is there, speaking to us, acting for us, being with us, in advance even of our supposition or experience that this is so. And while this means that we start with revelation, that signifies God's own self-revealing, not some predetermined principle of our own for interpreting the given truth. Likewise every speculative question concerning what is possible is suspended before the divine self-witness to who God actually is and is therefore capable of being.[53] Because he subjected every question and preconception of God's reality and possibility to the antecedent answers and critical, reforming judgment of God's Word, Barth was able, beyond all precedent, radically to reconceive immutability and divine ontology in the light of the cross and grave of Jesus Christ.[54]

That the one who precedes all theological inquiry is self-interpreting is a

---

tenary Essays (Cambridge: Cambridge University Press, 1989); E. Jüngel, *The Doctrine of the Trinity: God's Being Is in Becoming,* trans. H. Harris (Edinburgh: Scottish Academic Press, 1976); G. Hunsinger, *How to Read Karl Barth* (Oxford and New York: Oxford University Press, 1991); H. U. von Balthasar, *The Theology of Karl Barth,* trans. J. Drury (New York: Holt, Rinehart and Winston, 1971); W. A. Whitehouse, *The Authority of Grace: Essays in Response to Karl Barth,* ed. A. Loades (Edinburgh: T. & T. Clark and Grand Rapids: Eerdmans, 1981); R. W. Jenson, *God after God* (Indianapolis and New York: Bobbs-Merrill, 1969); G. C. Berkouwer, *The Triumph of Grace in the Theology of Karl Barth,* trans. H. R. Boer (Grand Rapids: Eerdmans, 1956); and J. Thompson, *Christ in Perspective: Christological Perspectives in the Theology of Karl Barth* (Edinburgh: St. Andrew Press and Grand Rapids: Eerdmans, 1978).

52. See T. W. Currie III, "The Being and Act of God," in Thompson, ed., *Christendom,* p. 4; also Jüngel, *Trinity,* pp. xix-xx.

53. See S. W. Sykes, "Barth on the Centre of Theology," in Sykes, ed., *Methods,* pp. 33ff.; see pp. 17-54.

54. See Jüngel, *Trinity,* p. xiv. For Barth's Doctrine of the Word, see *CD,* vols. I/1 and I/2; also *Göttingen Dogmatics,* esp. ch. 1, and his major methodological study, so significant for the development from "dialectics" to "dogmatics" (a move already anticipated in *Göttingen Dogmatics;* see n. 69 below); *Anselm: Fides Quaerens Intellectum,* trans. I. W. Robertson (London: SCM and Richmond: John Knox, 1960). Cf. Barth, *The Word of God and the Word of Man,* trans. D. Horton (London: Hodder and Stoughton, 1935); and Torrance, "Karl Barth, Theologian of the Word," in *Barth: Biblical and Evangelical,* ch. 3.

statement about the triune God (though the *concept* of the Trinity is a human construction forged through faith's quest for rational but finite understanding). God is self-revealing through a double reiteration, as the Son makes the hidden Father audible, visible, and knowable, and as the Spirit brings about such hearing, sight, and knowledge as human events in our own experience and history.[55] To whatever extent God becomes the object of human faith and intelligible to human understanding, God as Trinity remains the Subject of that relation and determines the content and meaning of what we understand.[56] It was, he believed, through the Trinity's self-illumination, and especially the unveiling-in-concealment of the Word Crucified, that Barth was constrained in time to acknowledge the actuality and hence the possibility of God's own suffering.

However, to identify the Son as he through whom God speaks a self-defining, self-exegeting Word which the Spirit brings to human hearing is not to deny the role of Scripture in the event of revelation. The Bible becomes God's written Word when through the witness of its human words we hear the Lord's own speech, who is the Word of God incarnate. For Barth, the Scriptures as a whole, but notably their narratives and preeminently the central "trinity" of stories — Good Friday, Easter Day, and Pentecost — mediate creative encounters between the God who speaks and faithful human minds whose doctrines reflect and correspond to the events recounted in the gospel.[57]

This signifies a most Reformed emphasis upon the authority of Scripture (albeit derivative from Christ's own); and Barth's explosive "second Reformation" after World War I, like Luther's first, was detonated by the rediscovered energies of Paul's Epistle to the Romans.[58] But none of this means — again de-

---

55. See esp. *CD,* I/1, sects. 8-12, and *Göttingen Dogmatics,* pp. 325ff.; cf. Jüngel, *Trinity,* pp. 1-41; R. D. Williams, "Barth on the Triune God," in Sykes, ed., *Methods,* ch. 5; Torrance, *Barth: Biblical and Evangelical,* esp. pp 118ff.; J. McIntyre, *The Shape of Christology* (London: SCM, 1966), esp. pp. 157-61; and G. Stroup, *Promise,* esp. pp. 44ff.

56. See *CD,* I/1, 382 and III/2, 176. Cf. James Brown, *Subject and Object in Modern Theology* (London: SCM, 1955), ch. 6; and Jüngel, *Trinity,* pp. 42ff.

57. For Barth's views on Scripture, see *CD,* I/1, 99ff.; *Göttingen Dogmatics,* ch. 2; and on the stories of Good Friday, Easter, and Pentecost, see *CD,* I/1, 331-32, 374, 381. See also Ford, *God's Story* and "Barth's Interpretation of the Bible," in Sykes, ed., *Methods,* ch. 3; G. S. Hendry, "The Rediscovery of the Bible," in Camfield, *Reformation,* pp. 142-56; C. A. Baxter, "The Nature and Place of Scripture in Church Dogmatics," in Thompson, ed., *Christendom,* ch. 3; and D. H. Kelsey, *The Uses of Scripture in Recent Theology* (Philadelphia: Fortress and London: SCM, 1975), pp. 39-50.

58. It was with his stunning commentary (*Der Römerbrief,* 1919), especially in its second edition of 1922, that Barth came to theological prominence, sounding the final death knell for Liberalism and bringing in the revolutionary era of dialectical theology. Here every positive statement about God had to be balanced with a No of divine judgment

spite his critics and all too many of his friends — that Barth was a traditionalist, an antiquarian intent upon recovering the orthodoxy of the past. His ultimate rejection of impassibility and critical reinterpretation of much Calvinist tradition indicate as much.[59] This paradigm of postmodernity, who so subverted the humanistic optimism and narrow scientism of modern, liberal theology, must be understood — as he clearly understood himself — to be an heir of the Enlightenment, who took seriously the questions raised for faith by the modern world.[60] Barth learned — what the Enlightenment itself taught — that theology must stand on its own feet, securing faith's own territory and pursuing the church's own understanding, unwedded to the culture, philosophy, or science of any generation.

Only in the context of the modern secular worldview could anyone distinguish as forcefully as Barth between revealed and natural theology, God's self-imparted knowledge and that derived from human religiosity and reasoning.[61] Indeed, in the early days of his *Commentary on Romans,* Barth seemed to

---

upon humanity's hubristic attempt to know and speak of the transcendent, Wholly Other. See Barth, *Commentary on the Epistle to the Romans,* 6th ed., trans. E. C. Hoskyns (London: Oxford University Press, 1933). The work is full of seismic and incendiary metaphors, befitting its postwar milieu, and was itself famously described as a "bombshell dropped on the playground of the theologians" (see J. McConnachie, *The Significance of Karl Barth* [London: Hodder and Stoughton, 1931]).

59. In this regard the habit, especially in North America, of describing as "neo-orthodoxy" Barth's theology and the broad movement influenced by him is highly misleading and should be scrupulously avoided! Even when Barth expressed respect for and indebtedness to the "fathers" of Protestant orthodoxy, he was highly critical of them and made it clear that he was not concerned with a recovery or repristination of past Reformed dogmatics. See esp. D. L. Migliore's introduction to *Göttingen Dogmatics,* pp. xxxivff., and Barth's introduction to H. Heppe, *Reformed Dogmatics,* ed. E. Bizer, trans. G. T. Thomson (London: Allen and Unwin, 1950 and Grand Rapids: Baker Books, 1978).

60. This is particularly apparent throughout Barth's masterly study of the Enlightenment and its aftermath, *Protestant Theology in the Nineteenth Century.* Especially revealing is Barth's ambivalent attitude to Schleiermacher — in many ways Barth's polar opposite — for the thoroughgoing anthropocentricity of his method and the epitome of all that went wrong in modern Protestant theology. Yet Barth's deep admiration for Schleiermacher's attempt to remain Reformed while adopting a consciously modern standpoint is unconcealed. See *Protestant Theology,* ch. 11, and *The Theology of Schleiermacher.* Also A. I. C. Heron, "Barth, Schleiermacher and the Task of Dogmatics," in Thompson, ed., *Christendom,* pp. 267-84; cf. J. O. Duke and R. F. Streetman, eds., *Barth and Schleiermacher: Beyond the Impasse?* (Minneapolis: Augsburg, 1988).

61. This issue came to a head in the celebrated disputation between Barth and Emil Brunner on "natural theology" in 1934. See Brunner, "Nature and Grace," and Barth, "No!" in *Natural Theology,* trans. P. Fraenkel (London: G. Bles and Berkeley, Calif.: The

force the gospel into the very framework of Kantian dualism, accentuating to excess (though necessarily, perhaps, in correction of the moribund prewar liberalism), the unknowability of God's own self. He gouged the deepest *diastasis* or chasm, an "infinite qualitative difference," between God's Godness and contingent creaturehood, divine righteousness and our unholiness, the inscrutability of heaven and the wretched vanity of our earthly pretensions to the truth.[62]

Be it understood, however, that Barth exploited the Kantian premise — that God, utterly distant from the world of sense experience, is beyond all knowing — so as to turn our "enlightened" assumptions back upon themselves and confront modern culture with the Bible's strange, impossible good news. The eternal Holy One, transcendent and unknowable, has intersected time and finitude, *becoming* knowable to human understanding, though on God's own terms. That is, the God who *precedes,* also *proceeds.* Not surrendering but manifesting Godness and transcendence, God is unchangingly in motion, overflowing the boundless confines of triune being; and in exercising this eternal movement outward God comes even to the "far country" of time and history, visible to human sight, vulnerable to human suffering.[63] Far from unbridgeable, as modern thought including much theology supposes, the gulf between ourselves and God, conceived however widely, has in fact been crossed. In Christ, God comes to us, proceeding into the particularities of one man's history. The assumption, old and modern, that it is not possible for transcendence to be immanent while retaining otherness has been overtaken by the actuality and thus the possibility of incarnation.

This insistence upon Jesus Christ as he in whom God comes, becoming flesh, gives Barth's dogmatics its characteristic and — oddly — controversial

---

Centenary Press, 1946). See also Heron, *Century,* pp. 84ff.; and Zahrnt, *Question of God,* pp. 60ff; also E. A. Dowey, "The Barth-Brunner Controversy on Calvin," Appendix to *The Knowledge of God in Calvin's Theology* (New York: Columbia University Press, 1952), pp. 247-49. It is often not noticed that the later Barth adopted a far less negative assessment of natural theology, especially in *CD,* IV/3. See also H. Bouillard, *The Knowledge of God,* trans. S. D. Femiano (New York: Herder and Herder, 1968); and Torrance, "Natural Theology in the Thought of Karl Barth," in *Barth: Biblical and Evangelical,* pp. 136-59.

62. See Barth, *Romans,* and "The Humanity of God," in Barth, *God, Grace and Gospel,* trans. J. S. McNab, *Scottish Journal of Theology Occasional Paper No. 8* (Edinburgh: Oliver & Boyd, 1959); also trans. J. N. Thomas, in *The Humanity of God* (Atlanta: John Knox, 1960); also Heron, *Century,* pp. 76ff.; Zahrnt, *Question of God,* ch. 1; and Torrance, *Early Theology,* pp. 48-95.

63. See esp. Jüngel, *Trinity,* pp. xx and 1ff.; cf. Torrance, *Barth: Biblical and Evangelical,* p. 97.

"Christological concentration."[64] (How can *Christian* theologians complain about the centrality of Christ? Only those who misunderstand Barth's trinitarian assumptions could take his focus on the Second Person for a slight upon the Third.) God *is* who we see objectively revealed in Jesus Christ. No other God, nor any other undisclosed or contradictory character of God, hides *behind* the back of Jesus — though in one sense God hides *in* Jesus. This man's sheer creatureliness, let alone the ambiguity of his life and the weakness, ignominy, and godlessness of his death, conceals as it discloses and guarantees that revelation remains disguised in hiddenness. God's own majesty and mysterious incognito are preserved in the very event of their jeopardizing.[65]

The cross is foolishness and scandal, and Barth knows that we know only in part, indirectly through a mirror (1 Cor. 13:12). Even so, God's unveiling, mediated through the person and event of Christ, liberates theology to speak truthfully, adequately, and in a way completely, within its finite limits and conditionality.[66] Barth stands in the Nicene tradition on divine knowability, agreeing with Athanasius against Arius that being "of one substance with the Father," Christ seals a cognitive union between ourselves and God. He is "God speaking personally,"[67] the self-impartation of the truth, so that as Son and Father know one another, those who are in Christ share humanly in the circle of divine self-knowing.[68] As Barth moved from "dialectic," and its balancing of affirmations with negations, to "dogmatics," based on the "analogy of faith" (and however

64. See H. U. von Balthasar, *Karl Barth, Darstellung und Deutung seiner Theologie* (Cologne: Verlag Jakob Hegner, 1961), p. 210, and *Theology of Barth*, p. 170; also Zahrnt, *Question of God*, p. 98, cf. 93ff. For Barth on the Spirit, see esp. *CD*, I/2, sects. 16-18. In contrast to P. J. Rosato, who complained about Barth's relative neglect of the Holy Spirit in *The Spirit as Lord: The Pneumatology of Karl Barth* (Edinburgh: T. & T. Clark, 1981), see T. Smail, "The Doctrine of the Holy Spirit," in Thompson, ed., *Christendom*, pp. 87-110. See also H. Berkhof, *The Doctrine of the Holy Spirit* (Atlanta: John Knox and London: Epworth, 1965), pp. 22-29; and Torrance, *Barth: Biblical and Evangelical*, pp. 208ff.

65. That God is not lost in relevation, that *Deus revelatus* remains *Deus absconditus*, Barth sums up by saying that God is self-revealed *as Lord*. God's own sovereignty and freedom are not compromised but affirmed through self-giving and self-disclosure. This, says Barth, is the basic axiom of revelation and "the root of the doctrine of the Trinity." See *CD*, I/1, 304-33; cf. Jüngel, *Trinity*, pp. 19ff.

66. See esp. *CD*, I/1, 166ff. and 187-247; I/2, 52-53 and sects. 25-27; also *Göttingen Dogmatics*, ch. 15. Cf. Jüngel, *Trinity*, p. 51; and Hunsinger, *How to Read Barth*, pp. 78-79.

67. *"Dei loquentis persona," CD*, I/1, 304; cf. Jüngel, *Trinity*, pp. 15ff.

68. Mt. 11:27; Lk. 19:21-22; Jn. 14:7; cf. *CD*, II/1, 252ff. On the continuity between Athanasius and Barth, mediated through Calvin, on the epistemological significance of the antidualist *homoousios*, see Torrance, *Barth: Biblical and Evangelical*, chs. 6-8, and *Trinitarian Faith*, ch. 2; also Hunsinger, *How to Read Barth*, pp. 101-2.

much that shift represents a fundamental change in his own method),[69] he accentuated what the church's science may positively affirm of God. He contended in particular, on the basis of divine knowledge Christologically secured, that of divine salvation we may say that God *elects,* and of divine being that God *becomes.* These themes are the heart of the massive *Church Dogmatics.*[70]

The God who proceeds toward us in Jesus Christ is revealed as one who "loves in freedom," says Barth.[71] The self-giving love which makes, relates to, and enters into creaturely existence to the point of solidarity with human death is freely chosen; and it does not compromise God's sovereignty and lordship. This choice, made manifest in the history of Jesus, is grounded antecedently in God's eternal covenant. In a "primal decision" of grace, "before the foundations of the world" (Eph. 1:4), God elects Christ and in that election chooses us all, whose humanity he assumes, fulfills, and represents. In his own person, Christ is both elected, saved humanity and electing, saving God; the truly human one, by whose life and death in time we are reconciled in grace, and the divine Son who before we are created shares in the Father's sacrificial commitment to our

---

69. A long-standing thesis, much indebted to von Balthasar, is that Barth underwent a radical change of direction in moving to "dogmatics" in response to his study of Anselm (1931). More recent scholarship, especially the bringing to light of the *Göttingen Dogmatics,* suggests that already in 1924/25 Barth was working along the lines that later shaped the *Church Dogmatics.* There remains debate as to whether the positive, analogical statements of dogmatic thinking, however early adopted by Barth, are in discontinuity with the methods of dialectical theology. On all of this, see von Balthasar, *Theology of Barth,* pp. 73-150; Torrance, *Early Theology,* ch. 4; Zahrnt, *Question of God,* ch. 4; Jenson, *God after God,* pp. 77, 202n.51; Hunsinger, *How to Read Barth,* pp. 17, 284n.10; Migliore in *Göttingen Dogmatics,* p. xxxii; and esp. B. McCormack, "A Scholastic of a Higher Order: The Development of Karl Barth's Theology 1921-31" (Unpublished diss., Princeton Theological Seminary, 1989).

By the "analogy of faith" (Rom. 12:6), Barth means the empowerment to speak truthfully of God in human terms that bear a genuine correspondence to divine reality, which is given to us through God's self-revelation. That we may know and speak truthfully of God is a gift of grace, appropriated in faith, and not an innate human capacity expressive of a natural relatedness of the creatures to their Creator through their sharing of a common essence, an "analogy of being." For much of his career, though not perhaps by its end, Barth saw the "analogy of being" as the central falsehood of Roman Catholic theology. See von Balthasar, *Theology of Barth,* pp. 93ff.; Mueller, *Karl Barth,* pp. 90-91; Hunsinger, *How to Read Barth,* p. 283n.2; Torrance, *Barth: Biblical and Evangelical,* chs. 7 and 8; and esp. Jüngel, *God as the Mystery,* pp. 281ff.

70. See the impressive exposition of these themes from *CD* in Jüngel, *Trinity,* ch. 3.

71. See esp. *CD,* II/1, sect. 28; cf. Jüngel, *Trinity,* pp. 3 and 79; Mueller, *Karl Barth,* pp. 94ff.; and Heron, *Century,* p. 93.

reconciliation. Eternally he accedes to that decision and obeys it, as the one to be sacrificed and given up.[72]

Herein lies Barth's profound, if controversial, revision of the Reformed doctrine of "double predestination."[73] For Christ is not only the Elect in whom humanity is chosen and redeemed, but also the Reprobate on whom is laid God's judgment of humanity. His rejection on behalf of all, that all might be accepted, is concluded historically, concretely, in the abandonment of the cross and the hellishness of the grave. Yet as "the lamb slain from before the foundations of the world" (Rev. 13:8), Christ is eternally rejected no less than eternally elect. This means in turn that God has decided "in advance" to be judged and sentenced for the sake of our acquittal.[74] From all eternity God is open to repudiation, the threat of contradiction and negation. The godforsakenness of God, acted out objectively on Calvary, is thus an awesome, mind-transforming revelation of what and who God always is. Exposure to opposition, exclusion, termination, belongs to God's identity. Clearly for Barth, predestination is no extraneous matter but a theme belonging to the doctrine of God; and the question of salvation leads back to that of being.[75]

Theological ontology, as we have seen, has labored in many different contexts and across a wide span of generations, under a dualistic burden which defines God's being as the antithesis of ours. God is all that we are not: eternity the opposite of time; transcendence incompatible with immanence; and immortality with perishing. And the Creator's being is, absolute, unchangeable, indeed it simply *is,* in perfect stability, unlike the flux, contingency, and mutability of creaturely *becoming,* as we stumble from one condition to another, be-

72. See *CD,* II/2, 94-194; cf. Jüngel, *Trinity,* pp. 68-83, esp. p. 72.

73. The Reformed tradition, beginning with Calvin, taught with varying details and different degrees of rigidity that God has eternally decreed the salvation of some human beings and the reprobation of all others (see R. Muller, *Christ and the Decree: Christology and Predestination in Reformed Theology from Calvin to Perkins* [Grand Rapids: Baker Books, 1986]; and P. Jewett, *Election and Predestination* [Grand Rapids: Eerdmans and Exeter: Paternoster, 1983]). But Barth gave a new, christocentric interpretation to this doctrine of double predestination. Christ himself is elected by God to be the reprobate one, who bears God's judgment on the sins of humanity and as such is the elected one through whom all humanity, their judgment borne for them, are chosen in grace for salvation. Most controversial here, of course, is the implication of universal salvation. See *CD,* II/2, chs. 32-35; cf. W. A. Whitehouse, "Election and Covenant," in Thompson, ed., *Christendom,* pp. 87-110; Hunsinger, *How to Read Barth,* ch. 5; Mueller, *Karl Barth,* pp. 96ff.; Thompson, *Perspective,* esp. pp. 20-21, 98ff.; Heron, *Century,* pp. 88-89; von Balthasar, *Theology of Barth,* pp. 155ff.; and Zahrnt, *Question of God,* pp. 107ff.

74. See, e.g., *CD,* II/2, 167; cf. Jüngel, *Trinity,* p. 78.

75. See Jüngel, *Trinity,* pp. 3 and 69.

tween the irretrievable past and the ungraspable future. On the premise of such contrarieties, and in face of Scripture's testimony, God's becoming temporal, carnal, vulnerable, has been deemed impossible. But, says Barth, "such beliefs are shown to be quite untenable, and corrupt and pagan, by the fact that God does in fact be and do this in Jesus Christ."[76]

Though not without precursors and like-minded contemporaries, Barth personally broke with these "pagan" beliefs by daring to conceive of God not on the basis of a general, abstract ontology, an externally determined metaphysic of pure, static essence, but strictly on the grounds of revelation: the actuality of dynamic, triune being as self-unveiled in Jesus Christ. In conformity to that disclosure, Barth constructed a very different doctrine of God's being.

For one thing, since Christ shows God to be among the creatures in finitude and history, and this revelation truthfully corresponds to the way God always is, that gives to God's eternal being the predicates of limitation and duration. God eternally makes space for time.[77] Temporality is not eternity's polar opposite, that is, a pagan notion, a "Babylonian captivity."[78] There is a way of being temporal, involved in the flux of events and happenings as a subject of history, which is not the negation but the expression of God's own manner of existing. "History is a predicate of revelation," since "God's being is constituted through historicality."[79] Far from static and immobile, God's way of being eternal involves that forward movement characteristic of temporal existence,[80] though in God's time the past is not lost nor the future unreachable.[81] Hence Jüngel's summation of Barth's ontology: "God's being is in becoming."[82] Be-

76. Barth, *CD*, IV/1, 186; cf. Jüngel, *Trinity*, p. 85.

77. Jüngel, *Trinity*, pp. 96, 98n.147.

78. *CD*, II/1, 611.

79. Jüngel, *Trinity*, pp. 65n.10 and 67; cf. pp. xiii and 94-95; see Barth, *CD*, I/2, 58-59.

80. See *CD*, II/1, 593-94; cf. Jüngel, *Trinity*, p. 97.

81. On Barth's doctrine of the Time of God, see *CD*, II/1, 608-77; III/2, sect. 47; cf. Jüngel, *Trinity*, pp. 96ff.; R. Roberts, "Barth's Doctrine of Time: Its Nature and Implications," in Sykes, ed., *Methods*, ch. 4; Jenson, *God after God*, ch. 8; and Ford, *God's Story*, ch. 8.

82. See esp. ch. 3 of his *Trinity*; cf. C. Gunton, *Becoming and Being: The Doctrine of God in Charles Hartshorne and Karl Barth* (Oxford: Oxford University Press, 1978). As this latter work indicates, the other major contemporary attempt, besides Barth's, to rethink theological ontology in terms of movement, event, and becoming rather than nature, substance, and static being is that of process theology. Founded upon the process philosophy of A. N. Whitehead, this theology was initiated by Charles Hartshorne and developed thereafter by Schubert Ogden, John Cobb, Norman Pittenger, and others. Suffice it to say here, of an extensive theological movement, that process is a forceful and impressive at-

coming is not what identifies the creature over against the Creator, a restriction and corruption inimical to deity, but a living, kinetic, active existence which is God's way of being God.

This is to propose no disjunction, but thorough mutuality, between God's "being" and God's "act" — a major component of Barth's doctrine.[83] What God does is not separate from who God is, a consequence of or addition to God's own identity. That identity is rather constituted by such action. Divine being is itself a matter and a mode of doing, of initiating and participating in events, in happenings which comprise decisions and their implementation, and thus development and change — vulnerability to the cost and consequences of action undertaken. Indeed, it is necessary — and permissible — to say that God's being is itself *event*,[84] not solitary, motionless existence but a dynamic interaction of relations within the communion of the triune felllowship, in which we who are not God are given to participate, as "secondary, subsequent subjects."[85]

Only such a notion of God's being corresponds to the revelation that God's choice to be with us in our history, which leads to Bethlehem and Calvary, is a primal decision to be with us in advance,[86] to have humanity as faith-

---

tempt to rethink the classical axiom of divine immutability, rejecting the platonic devaluation of time and motion as hostile to the stability of divine, eternal being. In Hartshorne's "neoclassical theism," God is "bipolar": certainly "absolute," transcendent, unsurpassable, but also "relative," conditioned by and suffering in the world, affected and determined by all the events or "occasions" in the evolving process of reality. But this suffering, which elevates the passivity of God, is won at the cost of divine activity. Gunton characterizes Hartshorne as substituting for the classical Unmoved Mover, a Moved Unmover (e.g., p. 41; cf. 47ff.). How can the God, who is in all things and in whom all events occur (panentheism), also be conceived as acting in specific historical events within that process, as not in others? Still more, how can God act against the process? This theology is notorious for its difficulties in rendering justice to the discontinuities and dysfunctions of history, to evil, sin, judgment, and death. Ironically, a theology which innovatively secures God's suffering struggles to account for the cross of Christ as that event in which the relative, passionate God also stands over against history, judging humanity's sin in the very act of self-surrender to it. For all its reworking of the classical tradition in the direction of divine becoming, process preserves a static dimension to God's being which excludes the creator from our death, in clear contrast to Barth's cross-determined trinitarian concept of God's being-in-becoming. In addition to Gunton, see Jüngel, *Trinity,* p. 100n.151; and M. Welker, "Barth's Theology and Process Theology," *Theology Today* 43.3 (1986): 383-97.

83. See *CD,* II/1, 257-72. Cf. T. W. Currie III, "The Being and Act of God," in Thompson, *Christendom,* pp. 1-11; and Torrance, *Barth: Biblical and Evangelical,* esp. pp. 95ff., 124ff.

84. See esp. *CD,* II/1, 262ff.

85. *CD,* II/1, 181.

86. See *CD,* I/1, 383; I/2, 34; cf. Jüngel, *Trinity,* p. xvii.

ful partner and fallen sinner before our own creation.[87] Even in pretemporal eternity God is bound to us in mutual relations, analogous to those between the Father, Son, and Spirit,[88] and is thus exposed to all the menaces and perils, the pain and opposition, which reciprocity with creatures represents. God risks, from the beginning, the threat of nonbeing and negation.

"The God whose being is in becoming can *die* as a human being!"[89] That susceptibility to the caprice of human happenstance and the antagonism of evil, sin, and death which the God who loves in freedom wills to accept even in advance of history is fully realized in the life and death of Jesus. Here, in refutation of every presumption which declares that transcendence cannot be immanent, nor the eternal temporal, is the actuality of "the humanity of God." As an event of divine history, and without loss of Godness, God acts as a subject in *our* history. It is conclusively revealed, through an occurrence of togetherness in which a fully human event is at the same time an act of God's own being, that deity does not exclude humanness. Rather, God's Godness includes and embraces our humanity. This is God's freedom, to be not just our partner in eternity but our fellow creature in time, fulfilling deity within the bounds of a truly finite life.[90] But, furthermore, God's freedom to exist as a creature does not exclude a willingness to be the creatures' victim, to surrender to that "opposition to God which characterises human existence. The consequence of this self-surrender of God is God's *suffering . . .* a suffering even to *death* on the Cross."[91]

Here the nonbeing of annihilation, always a threat to one who moves be-

87. This means that for Barth the incarnate Christ was, in a sense, with God from the beginning. In a highly controversial move, but one consistent with his Christocentricity and understanding of God's eternity as making space for time, Barth refuses to speak of a discarnate Word, prior to and distinct from the Word incarnate. There is no abstract *logos asarkos;* for the Logos of John's Prologue is that very Word which became incarnate and is as such in eternity a "stopgap" or *locum tenens,* making space for Jesus and preserving the place he is to occupy. "Eternity is planned around this Jesus. And in virtue of this plan in the eternal purpose of God the man Jesus *is* in the beginning with God." Jüngel, *Trinity,* p. 81; cf. pp. 80-81 and 98n.147. See Barth, *CD,* II/2, 96ff.; IV/1, 52, 181; IV/2, 33-34, 101; also Thompson, *Perspective,* ch. 8.

88. On this "analogy of relations" — that God's relationship to us corrresponds to and reiterates the triune God's inner self-relatedness, see, e.g., *CD,* I/1, 372; III/1, 49; III/2, 220; IV/1, 186-87, 203. Cf. Jüngel, *Trinity,* pp. xvi and 99-104; Heron, *Century,* p. 92; and Zahrnt, *Question of God,* pp. 100-101.

89. Jüngel, *Trinity,* p. vii.

90. This theme, the substance of *CD,* IV/1 and IV/2, is also put succinctly and with exceptional power in Barth's 1956 paper, "The Humanity of God." See Thompson, *Perspective,* ch. 8.

91. Jüngel, *Trinity,* p. 83.

yond the security of static immobility, becomes the concrete enemy to be confronted and done battle with.[92] In his monumental and imaginative reconstruction of Christology upon the scaffold of the Prodigal Son narrative,[93] Barth conceives of two happenings which simultaneously constitute the one event of Jesus Christ: the way of the Son of God into the far country, and the homecoming of the Son of Man. This seeks to be faithful to Chalcedon's conception of "one Person in two natures," while substituting modern, dynamic, and time-affirming categories for the tradition's metaphysical inertia. But Barth also thereby turns classical Christology on its head, with a chiasmic reordering — attributing humiliation not to human nature but to God, and exaltation not to divinity but to our humanity. "This story is God's own way of defining the two natures, and . . . therefore the story (and not any outside definition) must be allowed to dictate what true humanity and true divinity are."[94] It is God who in Christ is humbled unto death and descended to the nadir of our wretchedness and tragedy. Here God, the Judge, becomes the malefactor, judged and sentenced, and bows to the divine verdict upon human sin and guilt.[95]

On the cross, not only is the Son of God rejected by humanity's violence, our blindness and ingratitude; but the Son sacrificed and delivered up by the

92. "God does not merely give himself up to the risk and menace, but he exposes Himself to the actual onslaught and grasp of evil. . . . He hazarded himself wholly and utterly." *CD*, II/2, 164.

93. *CD*, IV, "The Doctrine of Reconciliation." This is arguably the high point of the *Church Dogmatics* and has at times been hailed as the greatest treatise ever written on Christology and soteriology. Among Barth's other technical innovations in Christology is his superimposition of the Lutheran "two states" of humiliation and exaltation on the Chalcedonian "two natures." But as noted below, Barth overturns the Christological tradition as a whole by interpreting Christ's weakness and humiliation as a *divine* event and his exaltation as a *human* happening. By thus placing *God* in the "far country" Barth bypasses the obstacle of impassibility and is able to carry to its conclusion the thought of divine suffering in the incarnation from which the Fathers at Chalcedon ultimately shrank. Barth's innovation also has the effect of interpreting strictly together, as two perspectives on a single reality, the doctrines of Christ and of atonement, in contrast to past tendencies to separate the Person of Christ from his Work. Here the Person of Christ, as the one in whom God descends and humanity is raised, is itself the Work, or event, of salvation. See Thompson, *Perspective*, chs. 1-8; and "On the Trinity," in Thompson, *Christendom*, pp. 13-32; also Mueller, *Karl Barth*, pp. 120ff.

94. Ford, in Sykes, ed., *Methods*, p. 74.

95. See *CD*, IV/1, 211-357; cf. Thompson, *Perspective*, ch. 5; and H. Küng, *Justification: The Doctrine of Karl Barth and a Catholic Response* (London: Burns & Oates, 1964), esp. ch. 8.

Father endures the heavenly Judge's own rejection of earthly enmity and folly. Yet who is thus the victim of God's malediction but God's own very self? It is the Lord, none other, who has become the humbled servant, the repudiated cornerstone. The Son of the Father gives himself to us, "to suffer in our place the divine rejection, the divine No, the divine judgment, . . . to fulfil the divine Yes, the divine grace."[96] The blow of God's No first of all strikes God's own heart,[97] who "tasted . . . damnation, death and hell" and did "bow before the claim and power of nothingness."[98]

Barth makes much of God's *passion* in this divine encounter with our judgment, mortality, and termination.[99] Who, before him, had gone further in allowing Good Friday and Easter Saturday actually to determine for dogmatics the character and being of God? Undermining every alien supposition of impassibility as God's essential nature, Barth forces theology to conform to the story of crucifixion, death, and burial. The history of Jesus Christ is the revelation and substance of God's being-in-becoming, and the graciousness of that becoming finds its definitive disclosure — amid its murkiest concealment — at the finale of that human history. God *chooses and elects* that cross and grave as the very loci of sovereign, living Godness.[100]

To be sure, Barth is reluctant to attribute *death* as such to God in the light of Jesus' perishing and burial. He rejects as anthropomorphic "the idea of a God who is dead."[101] That is more hesitant, perhaps, than his own logic called for,[102] and certainly more than successors following his own trajectory found possible and necessary. But this reticence reflects Barth's determination to distinguish between an event of divine suffering in which antagonism, death, and

---

96. *CD,* IV/1, 351.

97. See Jüngel, *Trinity,* p. 78.

98. *CD,* II/2, 164; IV/1, 307.

99. See esp. *CD,* IV/1, 174ff., 243ff.

100. "He elected our suffering . . . as His own suffering. . . . The sentence of Pilate He elects as a revelation of His judgment on the world. He elects the cross of Golgotha as His kingly throne. He elects the tomb in the garden as the scene of His being as the living God." *CD,* II/2. 164-65.

101. *CD,* IV/1, 561. Barth does, of course, repeatedly affirm that it is as "true God" that Christ bears our judgment and dies our death (e.g., *CD,* IV/1, 130); and while drawing back from the "death" of God, Barth does boldly confront not just the general tradition of impassibility but the particular proscription upon the *Father's* suffering in the death of Jesus Christ. It is not only the Second Person of the Godhead who suffers. God suffers, too, in the mode of Father. The humiliation of the Son is grounded in a mysterious "fatherly fellow-suffering of God," in solidarity with and substitution for human suffering, realized in the historical event of the cross (*CD,* IV/2, 357).

102. See Berkouwer, *Triumph,* p. 307; cf. Jüngel, *Trinity,* p. 88.

negativity are taken into God, and one which sets the God of life in inner conflict and internal contradiction. Explicitly rejecting the weaknesses we saw in kenotic theories of Christology,[103] Barth insists that in encountering our death God never ceases to be God. Far from dedivinized, God remains Lord over every contradiction, is indeed victorious eternally, "in advance" of the conflict with death,[104] and thus able in a new, creative act to raise the crucified Christ out of death and nothingness.[105]

Barth thus subverts the old and modern dualism which dictated that divine suffering would indeed mean conflict in and with God's being. "In the light of Jesus Christ the empty loveless gods which are incapable of condescension and self-humiliation can be understood only as false gods."[106] The God whose being is in becoming unto death is given to us utterly, but does not give up being God.[107] In that self-forsakenness by which the Father abandons and delivers up the Son, Godness itself is not abandoned, given *away* to the point of cessation, but maintained, revealed, perfected. With stubbornness and perspicacity, Barth takes seriously that what appears impossible for God — to embrace mortality and death while remaining God — is declared by the gospel story to be an actuality and so a possibility. It is precisely in remaining God, while subjected to change and opposition, that God's true immutability consists. So goes Barth's radical *bouleversement* of the ancient and modern axiom of impassibility.[108] Not the divine nature, but all human ideas about the divine

103. See *CD,* IV/1, 180ff.; cf. Berkouwer, *Triumph,* p. 128.

104. See Jüngel, *Trinity,* p. 79. See also Barth's disputation with Berkouwer on the *prevenience* of this victory over death, a triumph already determined in eternity: Berkouwer, *Triumph,* esp. ch. 6, and Barth, *CD,* IV/3, 173ff.

105. See *CD,* IV/1, 185ff., 297ff.; cf. Jüngel, *Trinity,* p. 88. In the light of later reflections, Barth is perhaps to be criticized for prematurely and too cautiously invoking the lordship and power of the Creator here to protect God from the fullest consequences of Christ's powerlessness on the cross. In his defense, it might be pointed out that Barth does indeed speak of God's lordship being hazarded, exposed to the possibility of defeat and loss. There is, in the cross, "a sure and certain risk for God." *CD,* II/2, 162.

106. *CD,* IV/1, 132.

107. Jüngel, *Trinity,* p. 84.

108. *This* impassibility, God's freedom to embrace change, decay, and suffering and to be human unto death, without ceasing to be God, is an "intratrinitarian ability" (Jüngel, *Trinity,* p. 86). Indeed, no one before Barth came this far in conceiving an ontological basis for the bold claim of the early Byzantines that "one of the Trinity suffered in the flesh" (cf. Jüngel, *Trinity,* p. xiv). Barth's achievement depends particularly on his novel, risky but unavoidable decision to speak of a certain "subordination" within God (e.g., *CD,* IV/1, 195-210). What the way of the Son of God into the far country discloses is an obedience, servitude, and bowing to the will of another, which is God's own. It is the Second Person of

nature are contradicted by the cross.[109] It was sinful human pride to reject, on the basis of extraneous philosophical assumptions, the ontological conse-quences of the triune revelation. That uncovers in God's love and grace and power[110] a freedom to visit the farthest reaches of humanity's far country and to do so in fulfillment, not diminution or negation, of who God is.[111] Such is the unheard-of, impossible possibility, the foolish wisdom, of the God who elects to be located on a cross and in a tomb.

the Trinity who so obeys. Thus *within* God, and without disputing but rather confirming the equality of the Father and the Son, there is a second as well as a first, one who sends and one who is sent, one who commands and another who obeys. In that differentiation and interaction within the life of the triune community, we see it manifest that one who is fully God knows how to obey, and how therefore in obedience to be self-emptied, willing as God to be in the far country of suffering and death. Though he is sometimes accused of heretical "subordinationism" here, Barth's explicit point is that in choosing to bow to the will of the Father, Christ is precisely not acting out a status of ontological deficiency or in-feriority but expressing the perfect oneness of the Son and Father. It is just in this mutual-ity of the Obeying and the Obeyed that the unity of God consists (*CD*, IV/1, 201). Like-wise, against ancient and modern Arianism, Barth insists that in Christ's way toward suffering and death "we are confronted with the mystery of the deity of Christ" (*CD*, IV/1, 195), in its utter differentiation "from any notion of supreme, absolute non-worldly be-ing" (*CD*, IV/1, 177).

109. See *CD*, IV/1, 199.

110. It is for Barth the expression of great *omnipotence* that God can be weak and impotent as we are, just as the humiliation of the Son is God's greatest majesty (e.g., *CD*, IV/1, 129).

111. Note how the Roman Catholic Karl Rahner came to follow Barth in this: "God himself goes out of himself, God in his quality of the fullness which gives away itself. He can do this. Indeed, his power of subjecting himself to history is primary among his free possibilities. . . . God expresses *himself* when he empties himself. . . . Otherwise his human-ity would be a masquerade in borrowed plumes." Rahner, "On the Theology of the Incar-nation," in *Theological Investigations*, vol. 4, trans. K. Smyth (Baltimore: Helicon Press and London: Darton, Longman & Todd, 1966), pp. 115-16.

CHAPTER SEVEN

From God's Passion to God's Death

I. The Trinity and the Passion of God

A skull-shaped site of harrowing, diabolic execution and the cold, sepulchral resting place of a victim's cruelly punctured cadaver: what bizarre locations to begin conceiving the being and nature of the universe's Maker, Lord, and Savior! Yet such is the folly and fearlessness of a theology of the Crucified and Buried One — the defining, or redefining, of God from the starting point of Good Friday and Easter Saturday. Breaking through history's long hesitation about conforming faith's reasoning to Scripture's own discommoding "word of the cross," Karl Barth, as we have seen, learned dramatically to rethink the very doctrine of God in the light of Jesus' death and burial. Here the already tottering edifice of immutability collapsed, terminally shaken by the revealed actuality of God's Christomorphic passion. That demanded, and resulted from, a daring retooling of ontology — the replacement of a static metaphysic of pure being with the dynamism of divine becoming and historicality, where temporal activity and change are not the contradiction but expression of God's identity. This notion itself presumes a renovated concept of the Trinity. Only as triune can God be identified with humanness and suffering, while remaining Lord and God; thus when Barth reestablished the primacy of God's triunity he inaugurated "the welcome theme of recent theology that the doctrine of the Trinity is at root a conceptualizing of the event of the cross."[1]

---

1. P. S. Fiddes, *The Creative Suffering of God* (Oxford: Clarendon Press, 1988), p. 123.

As it happens, the most recent theology has gone still further than Barth, treading down to an even greater depth the pathway of trinitarian thought which he traced through Gethsemane, Golgotha, and the garden tomb. While Barth rediscovered on this path the suffering of the triune God, others since, pursuing to the end a logic which Barth himself might consistently have followed, have identified not suffering, but death itself, as the nadir of God's journey into the far country. Thus has the interpretation of the crucifixion as an event in the history of the Trinity moved on from affirming the "passion of God" to conceiving the occurrence of "death in God," and, yet more provocatively, to positing the very "death of God." Such rigorous inferences from the cross and grave of Jesus for our understanding of God and of the world, of history, the church, and ourselves, which presuppose Barth's work but go beyond it, are conditional upon completing that revision of the doctrine of the Trinity which he so profoundly and effectively began but did not, perhaps, quite bring to consummation.[2]

Indeed, it is frequently alleged today that Barth's reinterpretation of the Trinity was only partial, retaining crucial remnants of the very tradition, controlled by the axiom of immutability, to whose overthrow he was making such a contribution. And to be sure, it is easy to perceive the differences between the first volume of *Church Dogmatics,* where Barth formally expounds the doctrine of the triune God, and the last, where all his thinking, including that about the Trinity, is overtly governed by "the humanity of God" as revealed in the incarnation and supremely on the cross. Though it would be absurd to fault Barth for growing in his understanding, the deficiencies of his trinitarian doctrine, which prompted others to continue reconceiving the Trinity to the point of affirming "death in God" or "the death of God," do need to be exposed.[3]

2. By way of introduction to what follows, see esp. R. W. Jenson, *The Triune Identity* (Philadelphia: Fortress, 1982), and "The Triune God," in C. E. Braaten and R. W. Jenson, eds., *Christian Dogmatics,* vol. 1 (Philadelphia: Fortress, 1984); also W. Kasper, *The God of Jesus Christ,* trans. M. J. O'Connell (New York: Crossroad, 1984, 1991), pt. 3. But I am particularly indebted below to Colin E. Gunton, *The Promise of Trinitarian Theology* (Edinburgh: T. & T. Clark, 1991).

3. It does seem perverse to devalue the worth of both Barth's earlier and later formulations on the grounds of their difference from each other. That demands immutability, if not of God, then of those who try to think and speak of God. One major, very influential, and otherwise brilliant analysis of the differences between *CD,* I and *CD,* IV, which seems rather guilty of discrediting both treatments on the grounds of the evolution and thus inner tension between the one and the other, is that of R. Williams, "Barth on the Triune God," in Sykes, *Methods,* pp. 147-93. See also the account of Barth by R. Roberts, in P. Toon and J. D. Spiceland, eds., *One God in Trinity* (London: Samuel Bagster, 1980). More

The contemporary interpretation of the Trinity, initiated if not concluded by Karl Barth, is *modern* and in significant respects unprecedented, not least in its audacious insistence upon the controlling meaning for that doctrine of the cross of Christ. But this new thinking also constitutes a recovery and revivification of *old* thinking, specifically the patristic and largely Eastern understanding of the Trinity which was forged supremely by the Cappadocians, before the Westernization of the doctrine by Augustine and his Latin heirs. Nicene theology, as we saw earlier, discerned from Scripture, and in face of Hellenistic intuitions to the contrary, that God's being may essentially be *shared*.[4] What Arius assumed, and first Athanasius and then the Cappadocians denied, was that God's identity, being that of a solitary monad, would collapse in contradiction and division if the being of the Father was bestowed on any other. The Nicene *homoousios,* "of the same substance," asserts that the Father gives all things, including essence or being, to the Son (Jn. 16:15), and that the Spirit, too, participates equally and fully in everything, uniting the Father and the Son.[5] God is not by definition solitary, but, to the contrary, relational and communal — the oneness of the Godhead not threatened but constituted by the interrelationships and reciprocity of the three in their plurality. Each person is distinctive and unique, yet they have all things in common and find their unity through dynamic mutuality and interaction.

The Cappadocians' trinitarian concept of God as communal being[6] depends upon a particular understanding of what it means to be a person: that is,

---

willing to take seriously Barth's later thoughts in their own right, as a proper correction to and clarification of his earlier, is Jüngel; see, e.g., *God as the Mystery*, p. 351, n. 22. In any case, the contrast between vols. I and IV can be exaggerated. Even though Barth does not speak yet of "the humanity of God," it is clear already in *CD,* I/1, that God is seen strictly in the face of Jesus Christ and not conformed to any preconceived religious or philosophical image. See Jenson, *God after God*, pp. 99ff.

4. See Ch. 5, n. 33 above.

5. See, e.g., Athanasius, *Letters to Serapion*, 3.1, in M. Wiles and M. Santer, eds., *Documents in Early Christian Thought* (Cambridge: Cambridge University Press, 1975), pp. 84-85.

6. This notion has been developed out of its Cappadocian matrix in a highly contemporary and creative way by John Zizioulas in *Being as Communion.* The communal or "social" doctrine of the Trinity avoids tritheism and preserves God's unity, partly through the conception that each person indwells or interpenetrates the other. Such a thought is central to the Cappadocians — reflecting on John's Gospel (esp. 14:10-11) — though the application of classical technical expression *perichoresis* was not accomplished until John of Damascus (c. 675–c. 749); see his *On the Orthodox Faith,* 1.8 (*Nicene and Post-Nicene Fathers,* 2nd series, ed. P. Schaff and H. Wace, vol. 9, pt. 2, esp. p. 11). Cf. Gunton, *Promise,* pp. 139-40.

not an insular, independent individual, but one who fulfills identity in and through relations with another, and finds distinctiveness and individuality not in seclusion and self-sufficiency but in the mutual giving and receiving of inter-dependent fellowship and reciprocating sacrifice.[7] And, of course, such an un-derstanding of the being of God provides grounding for those actions, in cre-ation, incarnation, and salvation, through which God's being is expressed. On a Cappadocian, communal, or family conception of the Trinity, the openness and space between the persons within the Godhead is room held open for others outside the family. Out of the surfeit of mutual love internal to God, external reality is established, affirmed, and given its integrity, and we, God's human partners, our dignity and freedom. So as to heal and fulfill the fractured rela-tions between ourselves and God, the Trinity acts to remove the grounds of our estrangement, reaching out in the Son to take on humanness, destroying our death and removing our sin, so that by the Spirit we might be adopted into the divine family to participate by grace in that love and mutuality which by nature binds the Father and the Son.

However, thanks primarily to Augustine (354-430), a rather different concept of the Trinity, divergent both in presupposition and in consequence, was bequeathed to and enshrined in Western Christianity.[8] It is this tradition which Karl Barth did so much, but not everything, to reform and others since

---

7. See Gunton, *Promise,* esp. pp. 7ff., 173ff.; and Zizioulas, *Being as Communion,* pp. 35ff. As we noted above (Ch. 5, n. 30), the dynamic conception of the Trinity whereby the Godhead consists of distinct persons who nonetheless share a single, indivisible being, is dependent upon the distinction in Greek between *hypostasis* and *ousia,* which were treated as synonyms in the Creed of Nicea, but came to be differentiated in mature trinitarian the-ology. Thus Gregory of Nyssa: "We therefore affirm that while they share *ousia* in common there are characteristics to be seen in the Trinity which are incompatible and not held in common. . . . Each of them is apprehended separately in virtue of his own characteristics and thus . . . we can discover the distinction of the *hypostases.* . . . What we see here is a sort of continuous and indivisible community" ("On the difference between *ousia* and *hypostasis,*" often attributed to Basil of Caesarea and classified as Basil's Letters, no. 38; in Wiles and Santer, eds., *Documents,* p. 34).

8. In addition to Gunton's *Promise,* see, on the difference between Eastern and West-ern views of the Trinity: T. Hopko, "The Trinity in the Cappadocians," and M. T. Clark, "The Trinity in Latin Christianity," in B. McGinn and J. Meyendorff, eds., *Christian Spiri-tuality: Origins to the 12th Century* (New York: Crossroad, 1985), pp. 260ff. and 276ff.; also J. M. Houston, "Spirituality and the Doctrine of the Trinity," in Hart, ed., *Christ in our Place;* Jenson, *Triune Identity,* ch. 4; and Braaten and Jenson, eds., *Dogmatics,* pp. 135ff.; Heron, *Holy Spirit,* chs. 5 and 6; Kasper, *God of Jesus Christ,* pp. 214ff.; and C. M. Lacugna and K. McDonnell, "Returning from 'The Far Country': Theses for a Contemporary Trini-tarian Theology," *SJT* 41.2 (1988): 191ff.

have overtly repudiated, allowing Easter Saturday to become more than ever determinative for the doctrine of God. Augustine did what Eastern, especially Cappadocian, theology did not: that is, abstract and separate the being of God from the threefold relations of the divine community. On the Cappadocian principle of the distinctiveness of each person, the Father uniquely is the source and fount of deity, the Son and Spirit deriving their Godness, without subordination, from the Father.[9] For Augustine, however, the deity of all three persons

---

9. In Augustine's doctrine, this distinctiveness of each person is under threat. Indeed, thinking and speaking in Latin, Augustine admitted not even understanding the Cappadocians' distinction between *ousia* and *hypostasis,* being or substance, and person, which was so crucial for their distinguishing each of the latter (see Augustine, *The Trinity,* trans. S. McKenna [Washington, D.C.: Catholic University of America Press, 1963], vol. 5, pp. 8 and 9; vol. 7, p. 4). The personal identity and uniqueness of the Spirit are particularly compromised by Augustine, who typically describes the Spirit not as a person at all, but as a relation, i.e., the "bond of love" between the Father and the Son. Even the latter two are frequently reduced to the relations in which they stand to each other, i.e., Fatherhood and Sonship; and this identification of person with relation became normative for Thomas Aquinas. But a "person-in-relation," as understood by the Cappadocians, is very different from a mere relationship, as in Western dogma (see Gunton, *Promise,* pp. 39ff. and 169). The latter lacks precisely that *agency* whereby in the communal concept of the Trinity each person *interacts* with the others. That the West has often failed to preserve this personal and distinctive agency of the Spirit has had an enormously negative and impoverishing effect upon our worship, piety, mission, and much else, in comparison with the Eastern churches. The differences between East and West were maximized when, for good or ill, the Western church added the *filioque* clause to the Nicene Creed, asserting that the Spirit eternally proceeds not only from the Father, as in the original Creed, but "also from the Son." This addition owed much to Augustine, who affirmed the double procession, albeit often with the caveat that the Spirit proceeded *principally* from the Father (e.g., *The Trinity,* 15.17). The full ramifications of this church-dividing controversy cannot be discussed here. Suffice it to say that, in the eyes of Eastern Orthodoxy, the procession of the Spirit from the Son, among its other demerits, reduces the former to a mere tool or adjunct of the latter, robbing the Spirit of its own independence and distinctive personhood, as well as the cosmic, rather than purely Christocentric, range of the Spirit's activities and presence. The Western response, not to be lightly dismissed, though increasingly questioned today, is that for a *Christian* understanding of God, creation, salvation, and the church, the eternal, cosmic Spirit is indeed to be identified as the Spirit of *Christ.* For all God's activities express the grace which is revealed in Christ; and it is the very will of the transparent, self-effacing Spirit to find identity and fulfillment in deflecting attention away from itself and precisely on to Christ. For the fullest recent discussion of the *filioque,* see L. Vischer, ed., *Spirit of God, Spirit of Christ* (London: SPCK and Geneva: World Council of Churches, 1981); Gunton, *Promise,* pp. 51ff. and 168ff.; Pelikan, *Christian Tradition,* vol. 2, pp. 183ff., 275ff. and vol. 5, pp. 21-22, 258; Barth, *CD,* I/1, 473ff.; Heron, *Holy Spirit,* pp. 90ff. and 176ff.; and "The *Filioque* Clause," in Toon and Spiceland, eds., *One God in Trinity,* pp. 62ff.;

is derived from an ontologically prior source, that impersonal, indivisible, and impenetrable "substance" which is God's essence or being.[10] Though formally preserving the Christian doctrine of the Trinity over against polytheism, by securing the essential oneness of the deity, the ontological primacy bestowed by Augustine on the one being materially subordinates God's threeness to a de facto unitarianism.[11]

This reverses the Cappadocian insight that the oneness of God is less anterior to the threeness than constituted by the dynamic interactions and togeth-

---

Moltmann, *Trinity*, pp. 178ff.; T. Smail, *The Giving Gift* (London: Hodder & Stoughton, 1988), ch. 5.

10. Gunton makes the telling point that by embracing Augustine's concept of an unknown and unknowable divine essence, in contrast to the Cappadocians' starting point in the economy, where God is revealed and made known as three persons, Western Christianity was preparing the way for its own demise in the form of modern atheism. When the church itself defined God as unknowable, the stage was set for Kant to say exactly the same, ushering in the modern worldview in which God, standing outside the arena of empirical, scientific verification, is by definition unknowable and so redundant and expendable. The true unknowableness of God is not that of an impersonal, abstract substance, on the far side of a Platonic or Kantian cosmic dichotomy, but that of the other *person*, whose identity is irreducible and whose mystery is unfathomable (*Promise*, esp. pp. 31ff. and 163ff.).

11. See Gunton, *Promise*, esp. ch. 3; Moltmann, *Trinity*, ch. 1; Kasper, *God of Jesus Christ*, pp. 290ff.; and particularly K. Rahner, *The Trinity*, trans. J. Donceel (London: Burns & Oates, 1970), esp. pp. 15ff. Here Rahner offers a highly significant and momentous criticism of his own Roman tradition for having effectively divided the doctrine of the Trinity into two discrete parts, the oneness and the three-in-oneness, and giving clear priority to the former. A de facto unitarianism results from this primacy of the impersonal essence. And the bias away from God's communal plurality is further reinforced by the Augustinian-Western principle that *opera ad extra sunt indivisa,* the external works of the Trinity are not to be divided, i.e., not distributed serially among the three persons. In all the activities of the economy the agent is the whole Godhead, not just one of the persons. (Aquinas took this so far as to say in consequence that any of the three persons could have become incarnate — a view vigorously rejected by Rahner, who says that our experience of God would be very different were it not the *Son* who has come to us, revealing the Father and the Father's intratrinitarian relations; see his *Trinity*, pp. 28ff.) Augustine's principle — along with the accompanying doctrine of *perichoresis,* whereby the persons mutually indwell one another, certainly has a role in guarding against tritheism; but it also helps to blur the particularity and uniqueness of each of the persons, further divorcing the economy from the immanent being of God. On the other hand, as Gunton properly argues, it is necessary to apply the concept of *perichoresis* to God's internal relations, which for the Augustinian tradition *are* to be differentiated (*opera ad intra sunt divisa),* so that the immanent threeness of the Godhead is not that of separate and independent individual entities, statically juxtaposed, but of a true community of dynamic exchange and interaction. See Gunton, *Promise*, pp. 3, 137-38, 167-68.

erness of the three. In consequence of that reversal, the Western church, though nominally trinitarian, has in fact been much more monistic in thought and practice than the Eastern, providing — it is increasingly alleged today — dogmatic sanction for authoritarian, hierarchic, and monarchic structures of ecclesiastical and secular government. The oneness of bishop and pope, emperor and king is justified as an earthly analogue of the essential singularity of the heavenly Ruler over all. How different might Western society have been, or might yet become, if modelled on a God whose power is not concentrated in absolute and solitary sovereignty, but dispersed through a community of equals bonded by sharing and mutual dependence?[12]

Indeed, the consequences of the Westernized doctrine of the Trinity, with its bias actually away from God's plurality, are not sociological alone, but more generally anthropological. What does it mean to be human, in the image of God? As we shall see more fully below, axiomatic to the West's monistic or unitarian prejudice is an Augustinian inability to see that "personhood" is an "ontologically primitive" or surdlike reality, not to be reduced to or defined in terms of some other, impersonal principle or substance.[13] It is assumed that being is not fundamentally *relational,* an existence lived out in dependence on, encounter with, and self-giving to others. Rather, behind such relationships we are who we are as discrete, independent, disconnected individuals. The image of God in us is not our human togetherness and mutual reliance as persons, but our separateness and detachment as self-conscious and self-sufficient subjects. God's own supposed oneness and individuality gives theological stimulus and

12. See esp. Moltmann's discussion of "political and clerical monotheism" in *Trinity,* pp. 191-202, and by contrast the liberating political and ecclesiastical implication of a social doctrine of the Trinity, pp. 212-22. See also Kasper's remarks on the dangers of tyranny and totalitarianism when unity swallows up multiplicity (*God of Jesus Christ,* p. 291). A related, but wider, issue, well discussed by Gunton, is the extent to which Western culture since the Enlightenment has alleged that the existence of God would be an intolerable threat to and negation of all human freedom and autonomy. This presupposes — not without justification in the light of much Western theology — that the putative God is a domineering and authoritarian ruler, controlling creation and history with an oppression which does indeed ride roughshod over human choice and freedom. This again, for Gunton, signals the failure of Western trinitarianism, portraying God as a unitary sovereign and not a spacious and liberating community which grants space to creation and establishes, rather than confines, our own relative human and historical freedom. See Gunton, *Promises,* esp. chs. 2 and 8 and pp. 170ff., and his *Enlightenment and Alienation,* throughout.

13. See Gunton, *Promise,* p. 169; also J. Zizioulas, *Being as Communion* and "Human Capacity and Human Incapacity — A Theological Exploration of Personhood," *SJT* 28.5 (1975): 401-47.

sanction to Western individualism, whose obvious benefits, in the form of freedom, rights, and self-expression, so often are perverted by the destructive cognate evils of narcissism, self-gratification, and a privatistic disdain for the other, the neighbor, the community.[14]

This Western disjunction between individual and community is expressive of a wider chasm yet. That is the cosmic dualism we attributed above to Plato, but saw reaffirmed by the Enlightenment and modern scientific culture. It is the polarizing of spirit and body, mind and matter, eternity and time. Strangely, it might seem, although the Eastern Fathers, Athanasius and the Cappadocians included, were imbued with Hellenistic thinking, their doctrines of God, Christ,

14. There is much discussion in contemporary theology about the concept of "the person, as that relates in the first place to the persons of the Trinity, and derivatively to human personhood. The majority view, which dominated the Middle Ages and underlies modern Western individualism, derives from the sixth-century Latin philosopher Boethius, who defines a person as 'an individual substance of a rational nature' *(naturae rationabilis individua substantia)*"; see "Against Eutyches and Nestorius," 3.4-5, in Boethius, *The Theological Tractates,* trans. H. F. Stewart and F. K. Rand (London: Heinemann Ltd. and Cambridge: Harvard University Press, 1918, 1953 [The Loeb Classical Library]). This focuses on the intellect and on the separateness of the individual as the defining characteristics of personhood. But there is a minority view in the Western tradition, associated with the twelfth-century Richard of St. Victor, but also traceable through Duns Scotus, John Major, and Calvin, which is receiving increasing attention today. Richard looks not to the inner soul but to personal relationships for the human image of God. He defines a person as an *existentia;* meaning that persons are not separate from and independent of each other, but relational entities who find their being by "standing over against" others in encounter and reciprocity (see Richard of St. Victor, *On the Trinity,* 4.22 in *Sources Chrétiennes,* vol. 163, G. Salet (Paris: Les Editions du Cerf, 1959). Here, I am who I am not as a separate self-conscious subject but as who I become in the history of my relations and interactions with those around me — as son, e.g., and husband, father, and friend. On this understanding we are truly ourselves only as we engage in mutual love and self-giving with others, after the image of the personal inner relations of the triune God. God and we are communal because love itself cannot be expressed by solitary individuals, but in every case only in the presence of another as the object of one's love. On all of this, see, e.g., Torrance, *Theological Science,* pp. 305ff.; *Theology in Reconstruction,* pp. 85-86; *God and Rationality,* p. 80; and *Transformation and Convergence in the Frame of Knowledge* (Belfast: Christian Journals, 1984); Moltmann, *Trinity,* pp. 171ff.; Pannenberg, *Anthropology in Theological Perspective,* trans. M. J. O'Connell (Philadelphia: Westminster and Edinburgh: T. & T. Clark, 1985), pp. 235-36; Gunton, *Promise,* pp. 43, 91ff.; R. S. Anderson, *On Being Human* (Grand Rapids: Eerdmans, 1982), pp. 6ff.; R. Walls, "The Church — A Community of Persons," in Hart, ed., *Christ in Our Place;* A. J. Torrance, "Can God Suffer?" in Hart, ed., *Christ in our Place,* esp. pp. 362ff., and "Self-Relation, Narcissism and the Gospel of Grace," *SJT* 40.4 (1987): esp. pp. 500ff.; also John Macmurray, *Persons in Relation* (London: Faber & Faber, 1961).

and the Trinity preserve the biblical oneness and wholeness of the universe in defiance of such dichotomies, while the non-Greek Augustine superimposed upon Scripture and dogma the patterns of Platonic dualism, whose alienating effect on Western thought seems well-nigh irremediable. This applies not least to the doctrine of the Trinity, where Augustine did not look, as did the Cappadocians, to the mighty acts of God in history, in flesh and time and matter, and above all to one, specific, mortal life from human womb to earthy tomb, for the revelation of God's triune identity.[15] Instead, Augustine divorced those acts of divine "becoming" in the "economy" from the "immanence" of pure being, the concrete particulars of salvation history from the abstract eternity of divine substance. This substance becomes in effect a fourth and primary member of the Godhead, and God a "quaternity."[16] Moreover, Augustine sought signs and analogies of God's triunity not in self-involving events of incarnation, cross, and resurrection, but in the pure and solitary quiescence of the eternal soul. Created vestiges of the Trinity reside not in the flesh of Jesus Christ, least of all in his crucifixion, but in the invulnerable recesses of private self-reflection. God is not a divine family of self-giving, mutually sacrificial love, but immune, solitary, and independent mind.[17] Thus to the individualism of Western trinitarianism is added our intellectualizing and spiritualizing — the final irrelevance of Christ's humanity, suffering, and death to God's identity as nonrelational, impersonal, immutable, and subjective essence.[18] All this and more had to be challenged before there could develop today's "trinitarian hermeneutic of the cross."[19]

15. See Gunton, *Promise,* esp. pp. 51ff.

16. This has prompted Rahner, in an attempt to overcome the dualism of the Augustinian tradition, especially the bifurcation of the economy of salvation history from God's own immanent being, to propound a controversial thesis, now followed — if sometimes in modified form — by many others. It is that "The 'economic' Trinity is the 'immanent' Trinity and the 'immanent' Trinity is the 'economic' Trinity" (*Trinity,* p. 22). See also Moltmann, *Trinity,* pp. 160ff., and *Crucified God,* p. 240. For Barth and Jüngel on this topic, see below. . . . On the meaning or meanings of "substance" in early trinitarian theology, see G. C. Stead, *Divine Substance* (Oxford: Clarendon Press, 1977), esp. chs. 8-10.

17. See esp. Gunton, *Promise,* pp. 42ff.; and Jenson, *Triune Identity,* pp. 129ff.; also Mackey, *Christian Experience,* pp. 153-63. Augustine finds many triadic analogies or "vestiges" of the Trinity in the working of the self-conscious human mind, but focuses particular attention on that of memory, understanding, and will. See *The Trinity,* esp. bks. 10, 14, and 15.

18. "Augustine has given us little reason to believe that God is to be known . . . in the economy. All the drive of his thoughts is away from that to a knowledge derived from and based on the structures of human mentality: to an essentially singular deity for whom community is epiphenomenal or secondary." Gunton, *Promise,* p. 53.

19. Little happened before the Reformation to alter the shape of Western trinitarian

The challenge from Barth which made this development possible was radical indeed. He vigorously opposed the tradition which treats the oneness of God prior to and separate from the threeness, thus rejecting any notion of quaternity. God's unity is threefold as such.[20] And with his perspicacious instinct for the oneness of God's being and God's act, Barth closes the chasm opened up by Augustinian and subsequent dualisms between God's inner being and the economic acts of self-revealing salvation history. God *is,* not in the mode of timeless immobility, but in that of action and becoming. Eternity and immutability encompass, rather than preclude, temporality and change. So concentrated is Barth, as we saw, upon the history of Jesus Christ for our knowledge of God — there being no other deity nor contradictory character of God, hidden behind the back of Jesus — that in volume IV of *Church Dogmat-*

---

dogma as determined by Augustine. Aquinas followed Augustine closely, finding the same difficulty in establishing the distinct identity of the Spirit, and indeed tending to reduce the Father and Son to a set of logical relations between them (i.e., logically, by the nature of parenthood and sonship, the Father and Son are related to and depend upon each other). This contrasts with the truly personal, immanent interactions of Father and Son, corresponding to their relationship expressed and revealed in the history of salvation. For Aquinas, God is so self-sufficient as to be essentially unrelated to the world; and like Augustine, he makes the events of Christ's history virtually irrelevant to our knowledge of who God is, relying instead for that knowledge on the analogy of the inner structure of the human psyche. Like Augustine, too, Aquinas gives supremacy to God's oneness over the threeness by separating out the dogmatic treatment of each, in effect affirming a double oneness of God — first, that of the divine essence itself, and then that of the triunity. See Moltmann, *Trinity,* pp. 16ff.; and Mackey, *Christian Experience,* pp. 181-90. Calvin, on the other hand, though showing much respect for Augustine on the Trinity, as on much else, still makes significant moves toward the recapturing of some Eastern instincts in correction of Augustine. He places much emphasis upon the distinctiveness of each of the three persons (*Inst.* I.xiii.17-19) and the order in which they stand to one another (I.xiii.20), and praises Tertullian and Hilary, themselves early Western Latin theologians, for preserving the unique particularities of each person, in preference to Augustine, who tended to blur, and preferred in any case to remain silent about, those distinctives (I.xiii.5). Calvin here at least anticipates a truly relational view of God; and he explicitly rejects the possibility of an impersonal essence over against the three persons, which would turn God into a quaternity (I.xiii.25). What Calvin did not do, however, was find a way to relate the Trinity to Christology, above all to the cross. His doctrine concerns the internal structure of the Godhead, not the events of salvation history, including the incarnation and crucifixion. It is that critical link, dependent on a reunifying of the immanent with the economic Trinity, which awaited recovery until the twentieth century, when at last the cross and grave became determinative for the doctrine of the Trinity. See Gunton, *Promise,* pp. 95-96; and Mackey, *Christian Experience,* pp. 192ff.

20. See *CD,* I/1, 295ff., 348ff.

ics he insists that we look directly upon Christ's cross and grave in order to discern the truth of God's nature and the range of divine possibility. That totally reverses the orientation of Augustine's doctrine of God away from this economy, this incarnation, this cross, to the timeless inner structures of the psyche for analogies to God's triunity. For Barth there are no such analogies or vestiges, besides Jesus Christ himself. The only analogy to facilitate a human knowing of God is that provided by God's own self-imparted knowledge.

Barth, we saw, gave priority status to the doctrine of the Trinity in *CD*, I/1, and though his thinking was not yet controlled by "the humanity of God" or the death of Christ as such, he already gave the Trinity a Christocentric content — since the concept itself interprets the structure of revelation, whereby the Spirit brings about the revealedness of the Father, whose revealer is the Son. Nevertheless, this earlier discussion stood in significant continuity with the inherited Western tradition and certainly did not complete its reform or overthrow. Moltmann, a strong critic of Barth here, summarizes the development of Western dogma after Augustine as the era of a "Trinity of substance," followed by that of a "Trinity of subject." At first, that is, on Augustinian presuppositions, God was regarded as a monistic and impersonal "supreme being" or cosmic principle, on which created reality depended, as its uncaused cause and unmoved mover. Subsequently an enlightened, autonomous humanity found this divine explanation of the universe redundant and replaced the God of substance with their own self-conscious egos as the force which shaped reality and moved history toward its destiny. And to this notion of the autonomous human self, Christian theology responded with the claim, also derived from the Augustinian legacy, that God was the ultimate Subject, the archetypal reasoning and willing individual, "no longer the ground of the world [but] the ground of the soul."[21]

It is the tradition of "God as a Self" which Moltmann and others find in Barth's formal exposition of the Trinity. To be sure, God here, as for the Cappadocians — and Calvin — is self-*differentiated;* and the distinctness of each of the three is preserved (even if unsatisfactorily with reference to the Spirit).[22] At the same time, though, this is God's *self*-differentiation, through

21. Moltmann, *Trinity,* p. 15; see pp. 10-19. Moltmann associates the tradition of "God as Supreme Substance" especially with Thomas Aquinas, and the development of "God as Absolute Subject" with Descartes, Kant, Fichte, and Hegel. See also Pannenberg, *Systematic Theology,* vol. 1, pp. 296, 299, and 300ff.

22. Threatening to diminish the personal distinctiveness of each *hypostasis* is Barth's substitution of "mode of being" for the language of "person" to describe that whereof God is triple. "Person" is too anthropomorphic, says Barth, and irretrievably reduced in modern thought from ontological to purely psychological categories, denoting self-conscious personality. "Mode of being" *(tropos hyparxeos)* has its own pedigree as a patristic and

which, in revelation, God is *self*-reiterated and *self*-interpreted. Rather than primordially three, God is more unitary than plural, resembles not so much an interacting community of three as the single, self-interpreting individual, who becomes known not in historical activity but through the unveiling of the self as a sovereign, independent "I."[23] Not even Barth, then, has been able "to reclaim the relational view of the person from the ravages of modern individualism." Missing "one of the glories of trinitarian thinking," he has presented the person as "an individual centre of consciousness [rather than] one whose being consists in relations of mutual constitution with other persons."[24]

Nonetheless, even on occasions when Barth clearly echoes Augustine, upholding "the concept of the one essence of God and of the three persons or modes of being to be distinguished in this essence," he can immediately add "the polemical assertion" that God's triunity is to be found not only in revelation but, because of revelation, in God's own being too, "so that the trinity is to understood as 'immanent' and not just 'economic.'"[25] This reconfirms that God is not simply singular in essence, but that, while one, God's being is also triadic. The triunity of God revealed in the economy discloses and corresponds to the triunity of God's inner self. Thus might our fears be calmed that Barth's God is, in the innermost recesses of deity, an individualistic monad.

Cappadocian trinitarian term. Certainly, for Barth, the three modes of being are to be differentiated by the relationships they enjoy with each other through *perichoresis*. Yet he echoes the Augustinian view that strictly speaking the distinctiveness of the divine persons is ineffable and indescribable (*CD*, I/1, 356); and his use of "mode of being" (*Seinsweise*) strongly indicates an Augustinian priority for the one being, over against the Cappadocians' plurality of the divine community. See *CD*, I/1, 353ff.; also Jüngel, *Trinity*, pp. 25-35. See also Pannenberg, *Systematic Theology*, vol. 1, pp. 299ff.; Jenson, *God after God*, pp. 110ff.; and Gunton, *Becoming and Being*, pp. 140ff.

23. See, e.g., Williams in Sykes, ed., *Methods*, pp. 159 and 158-72; cf. Moltmann, *Theology of Hope*, pp. 55-56, and *Trinity*, pp. 17-18 and 139ff.

24. Gunton, *Promise*, pp. 164-65. This legitimate critique notwithstanding, it is noteworthy that considerable consensus between West and East on the Trinity is now emerging — on a nonindividualistic basis — guided in particular by Barth's work on this doctrine, as extended by Rahner, Torrance, and others. See T. F. Torrance, "Toward an Ecumenical Consensus on the Trinity," *Theologische Zeitschrift* 30 (1975): 337-50; also Torrance, ed., *Theological Dialogue between Orthodox and Reformed Churches* (Edinburgh: Scottish Academic Press, 1985).

25. *CD*, I/1, 333; cf. p. 479: "statements about the divine modes of being antecedently in themselves cannot be different in content from those that are to be made about their reality in revelation. All our statements concerning what is called the immanent Trinity have been reached simply as confirmations or underlinings or, materially, as the indispensable premises of the economic Trinity."

However, in the very process of reading the divine plurality in revelation back into God's internal being, Barth can be seen using that classical distinction between the immanent and the economic which fostered such problems in the Augustinian tradition, threatening to render the temporal acts of creation and redemption finally inconsequential for the constitution of the immanent, eternal Godhead. By continuing to draw this distinction — which he calls "essential . . . deliberate and sharp,"[26] does Barth not unwittingly perpetuate Augustine's dualism and create a gap so large between eternity and time, internal and external, that we can be no longer sure, even in *CD*, IV, that the humanity and death of Christ truly reflect and affect the heart of God's own being? Despite everything affirmed concerning God's election of the cross and grave, and the disclosure there of God's true character and power, is there after all behind that revelation a God, eternally and internally conceived, of whom the weakness, humiliation, and self-surrender of Good Friday and Easter Saturday are not the full and final revelation?

That disheartening possibility seems all the more real when we recall Barth's consistent identifying of God as "one who loves in freedom." God's unconditioned otherness over against creation, without which God would not be God, is not compromised but fulfilled by the love of God for creation, which leads to actions of self-involvement in our createdness and brokenness. God's love is free, the exercise and not surrender of lordship even in the extremities of abandonment and contradiction in our far country.[27] But does this sovereign freedom mean that behind God's actual decision to love, elect, and assume our humanness there stands an open choice, a freedom *not* to love us, a possibility in God's immanence to be other than the loving, self-humiliating God revealed in the economy? If there is no such freedom, what of God's unconditioned lordship? If there is such freedom, is God's love toward us not contingent and capricious — a possibility actually chosen, but which might not have been?[28]

At times Barth seem to risk this inference of an arbitrary grace as the price of safeguarding God's own freedom. It is not "as a matter of course," aris-

---

26. *CD*, I/1, 172; cf. p. 371: "Though the work of God is the essence of God, it is necessary and important to distinguish His essence as such from His work, remembering that this work is grace, a free divine decision, and also remembering that we can know about God only because and to the extent that He gives Himself to us to be known."

27. See esp. *CD*, IV/1, 184ff. See also on this, T. Bradshaw, *Trinity and Ontology* (Edinburgh: Rutherford House Books, 1988), p. 67, and "Karl Barth on the Trinity: A Family Resemblance," *SJT* 39.2 (1986): esp. 148.

28. See Fiddes, *Suffering,* esp. pp. 66-71, 112-23; cf. Jenson, *God after God,* pp. 112-13. See also Moltmann's critique of Barth on this point (*Trinity,* pp. 55-56).

ing from God's internal being, but the result of a free choice and specific act, that God posits and embraces us in revelation.[29] Even in *CD*, IV, Barth can assert that anterior to God's overflowing love which reaches out to us, and preceding ontologically the grace-filled act of self-humiliation which leads to Calvary, there is in God's own inner being a perfect *independence.* "This God has no need of us. This God is self-sufficient."[30]

Of course, that the God who has no need of us should for our sakes become needy (2 Cor. 8:9), that the absolute and unconditioned One should out of that lordly fredom choose to relate to us, be subjected to the mortifying, terminal conditions of our dependency — this sets in sharpest relief God's unimaginable graciousness, humility, and self-abasement. Conversely, though, if in contrast to the outward God who becomes empty, vulnerable, and needy in the incarnation there is an inner, self-contained, invulnerable deity who has no need of us, then it seems that the cross and grave do not after all determine or even correspond to the inmost truth of God's identity. Have we reached "an untouched hinterland in the immanent being of God?"[31] Has the "distinction without separation" of the immanent and economic Trinity, analogous to Chalcedonian Christology's two natures,[32] become a dualistic gap, and the gap become a wedge,[33] between "the passion of God" and a residual element of impassibility? Barth speaks of the God whose "inner life as Father, Son and Holy Spirit cannot be subject to attack or disturbance [and] cannot be opposed," yet who chooses to "enter the sphere of contradiction."[34] Are there here remnants of the old immutability, even as Barth radically reenvisions that doctrine in terms of God's constant and unchanging will to be exposed to the changes and costs of "becoming" and "becoming flesh"?

To be fair, Barth's primary emphasis, as we saw, is precisely on the *correspondence* between the immanent and the economic. What is revealed of God in Christ (and in *CD*, IV, at least, this refers especially to Christ's death) fully and faithfully reflects what is antecedently true of God's own self. Later theologians have followed Rahner's lead in an effort to withdraw the wedge which

29. *CD*, I/1, 172.

30. *CD*, IV/2, 346; cf. II/1, 307-8: "He is the One who is free from all origination, conditioning or determination from without, by that which is not Himself. . . . God is absolute, i.e., utterly independent of everything that is not He."

31. Fiddes, *Suffering,* p. 121.

32. See P. D. Molnar, "The Function of the Immanent Trinity in the Theology of Karl Barth: Implications for Today," *SJT* 42.3 (1989): 367-99, esp. 369-70. See also J. Thompson, "Modern Trinitarian Perspectives," *SJT* 44.3 (1991): esp. 353-54.

33. Fiddes, *Suffering,* pp. 121-22.

34. *CD*, II/2, 169.

Barth occasionally and inconsistently inserts between the two, and assert the *identity* of the immanent and economic Trinity. That development could not have happened without Barth's own creative efforts to overcome Augustinian dualism; and even if that identification is legitimate, putting beyond dispute the significance of the cross for God's inner being, it is still necessary, with Barth, to conceive the distinction between the two in order meaningfully to assert that these are not separate but the same.[35] Without such a distinction, the freedom of God and the sheer graciousness of election as an undeserved and unnecessitated gift would indeed be compromised. Barth's perspicacity here is beyond question, his tenacity impressive. But when he allows this distinction to grow into a wedge he is straying from his own chosen course, drawing back from the logical terminus of his pioneering treatment of the Trinity.

That applies not least to Barth's insistence that there is no going back to abstract possibilities for God behind the actuality of grace revealed in the elect and electing Son. Protecting the freedom of the primordial covenant, which takes the eternal sovereign God into temporality and subjection to creaturely mortality, does not in fact require an immunity to opposition, suffering, and death in God's inner being. The ineffable love which takes God down that path is free and sovereign, even if there is *no* possibility for God to be or act otherwise, no choice to be made internally between this love and some alternative. The necessity for love's journey into the far country is not a coercive requirement imposed on God from outside, but an inner one, grounded in God's own free but unswerving decision to be God, *this* God, of boundless, self-exposing grace.

It is, in fact, Barth's own insight that God's choice of us depends upon and arises from a divine self-choice, whereby God wills and determines simply to be the one who loves, the one who in choosing grace decides irrevocably in favor of self-giving, setting every alternative aside, excluding all other possibilities.[36] God is free, not as one who could do otherwise, but as *the* one above all who can do *no* other. Self-bound to one sole way of being, God is committed, necessarily but thus freely, to the cognate course of action. God's lordship in bowing to the contradiction of the godless cross and godforsaken grace does

<hr/>

35. See E. Jüngel, "Das Verhältnis von 'ökonomischer' und 'immanenter' Trinität," *Zeitschrift für Theologie und Kirche* 72.3 (1975): 353-64; cf. *Mystery,* esp. pp. 368ff. See also J. Thompson, "On the Trinity," in Thompson, ed., *Christendom,* esp. pp. 24-25.

36. See, e.g., *CD,* II/2, 169: "What God does is well done. . . . In all his willing and choosing what God ultimately wills is Himself. All God's willing is primarily a determination of the love of the Father and the Son in the fellowship of the Holy Ghost. How then can its content be otherwise than good?"

not reside, as Barth occasionally and illogically asserts, in a prior self-sufficiency and secure immutability, but — as he more often understood and later followers more emphatically underscored — in the uncoerced impulse to self-consistency: love's determination not to be deflected from its purposes but to flourish and perfect itself through willing self-surrender. What judges us as burdensome imperative illuminates God as free but binding indicative: the truth — for our Creator and therefore for ourselves — that only one who gives up life discovers and fulfills it. On such a basis alone can we understand how the cross and grave truly reveal God's inmost triune life.

This returns us to Barth's daring conception that the God who is shown in the history of Jesus Christ to be "for us" — to the deadliest extremity of finitude and brokenness — is revealed thereby also to be for us *in advance*.[37] The cross reveals who and how God always is, confirming and enacting the "primal decision" of electing, self-giving grace made "before the foundations of the world." When not deviating from his own trajectory, through a sometimes overwrought concern to distinguish the immanent Trinity from the economic, Barth — in his later work especially — delights to thrust the cross of Christ back into eternity. This makes it all the clearer that God's will to be our covenant partner and redeemer, which culminated on Calvary, is not optional, arbitrary, or episodic, but a decision grounded in God's one constant and eternal character as sovereign love. Yet precisely here, over Barth's notion of the eternal cross, the pretemporal slaying of the Lamb, hovers one last question mark concerning his doctrine of the Trinity — a query which had led others to explore still more profoundly the ontological significance of the death of Christ for God's triunity.

We have glimpsed in the notion that "God's being is in becoming," something of Barth's perception that the Trinity is ultimately self-defined as *event,* a dynamic, forward-moving community constituted through action and interaction. Thus God's everlastingness does not negate, but embraces and enters into, temporality and history. That indeed allows us to think of the cross, an historical event anchored in the particularities of space and time, as the realization of a divine movement into the conditions of creaturely finitude and radical mortality which has been willed from all eternity. Many readers of Barth have found themselves asking, however, whether for him the cross is truly this temporal event enacting a pretemporal decision, or rather the mere displaying on time's stage of a decision already acted on and brought to completion as an eternal event before time began. Has the eternal become historical on Calvary? Or has the history of Calvary been eternalized and thus robbed of its own integrity and

37. See above, pp. 181-82.

decisiveness as a contingent happening in time? Has indeed *everything* significant already happened in eternity within the Trinity, needing now only to be recapitulated and revealed so that we might know what has primordially occurred? "No one will object to the way Barth draws together the beginning and the end of the whole historical process in Jesus Christ. But the question is whether in Barth it is still a matter of a historical *process:* does he present anything in history as still *happening?*"[38]

What is in question here is not only the integrity of the cross as a now *past* event in human history which Barth threatens to eternalize and so swallow up. Equally at risk is history's *future,* where Christ's death and resurrection in their redemptiveness still edge the world toward its so-far unreached goal, and where the Trinity, historically active in the cross, will bring to final fulfillment its own still-unfinished life. Barth's frequent portrayal of God in *CD,* I, as a closed, thrice-repeating, self-interpreting I rather than an open community of persons-in-relation; his Augustinian difficulties in defining the Holy Spirit's distinctive personhood and work; and his temptation to widen unnecessarily the Western gap between the immanent and economic Trinity: all these problems come together to raise, in the minds of many, doubts about Barth's *eschatology,* his doctrine of "the last things" in relation to the Trinity.[39]

Perhaps there lurks here the real reason why one who came to flout the classical taboo on mutability, and to perceive instead "the passion of God" upon the cross and in the grave of Christ, still held back from attributing

---

38. Zahrnt, *Question,* p. 113. Here at pp. 112-16 Zahrnt sums up in vivid language the oft-repeated criticism of Barth's dehistoricizing tendencies. See also my unpublished Th.D. dissertation for Princeton Theological Seminary, "The Experience of Grace: The Problem of Sanctification in Contemporary Systematic Theology" (1977), ch. 3.

39. The most trenchant critic of Barth here, who has done as much as anyone to bring about the renaissance of eschatology in recent theology, is Jürgen Moltmann, whose work we examine below. Moltmann's early "theology of hope," though, owes more than perhaps he realizes or acknowledges to Barth's own late efforts to adopt an eschatological perspective. This perspective is particularly visible in *CD,* IV/3, with its treatment of reconciliation in terms of promise and hope. Indeed, a complete final volume of *Church Dogmatics* on eschatology was projected but never written. Also eminent in the struggle to conceive the Trinity in terms of futurity is Robert Jenson. He argues that Barth began, but did not complete, the liberation of the Trinity from the past, and that the doctrine's reinterpretation from the standpoint of the future could not be achieved in sole reliance upon Barth, though not without him either. See his *God after God: The God of the Past and the God of the Future, Seen in the Work of Karl Barth,* esp. pt. 4; cf. *Triune Identity,* pp. 138ff., and "The Triune God," in Braaten and Jenson, eds., *Dogmatics,* esp. pp. 154ff. Jenson closely connects Barth's weakness in eschatology to his neglect of the Spirit within the Trinity. See also Gunton, *Promise,* pp. 130-31.

"death" to God, despite the death and burial of the Son. For only a God of the *future*, who as Trinity can move beyond the totality and finality of opposition and negation to new, creative possibilities (Rom. 4:17), is truly able to sustain, beyond the *suffering* of human life, the termination which is our *death*. Only, that is, through a Trinity and cosmos eschatologically conceived can theology take Easter Saturday with total seriousness as a terminal event which rupture's God's own life, and a silent sign of the continuing bondage of a still-broken world to human unrighteousness and demonic death. Our conceiving of the Trinity must move on from the willingness of a loving Self to be for us and deliver us in advance, through the eternal sacrificing of the Son, to a loving community which endures death in the radical separating of the Father and the Son, and which, through the life-giving Spirit, is still perfecting its being and its act in the slow triumph over evil, until the end of history when the world will be made new and God at last be all in all.

II. The Trinity and Death in God

We have found nothing in the logic of Barth's later thought to prevent him from anticipating some successors in specifying not just the *suffering* but also the *death* of Christ as a trinitarian event, revealing God's inner and eternal being. As it was, Barth allowed the human weakness and humiliation of Calvary to shape our knowledge of God's nature. But he was less willing to allow the godforsakenness and termination of Good Friday to obtrude mortality, separation, and disruption into God's own triune life. Certainly there was no docetic denial here of Christ's real death, and no suspension of the incarnation, withdrawing God at the last moment from the furthest boundary of the far country, as occurred so frequently in previous theology. On the contrary, the God who elects the cross elects also, as we saw, the grave; and it is the Lord as such, become a servant, who endures Good Friday and Holy Saturday, crucified, dead, and buried. Even so, Barth hesitates, illogically, before the ontological implications of Christ's grave as signifying death for God.

One clear, if not compelling, reason for this hesitation was an adamantine refusal on Barth's part to take with total seriousness anything — sin or evil, death or disbelief, darkness or the devil — which contradicts and opposes God's own reality as life and grace and love. Since God is "for us" in advance, the creation of our world and of ourselves is itself an act of covenantal grace. Forming order out of chaos, making light to shine and life to breathe, God already says a No of firm rejection to all that is unruly, dark, and deadly. Such things have only a negative reality, the shadowy existence of spent forces, anachronistic, repudiated from the start, and — when matched against God's overwhelming Yes to light and good — finally "impossible."[40]

Thus our very existence as God's creatures is contingent on the primordial divine defeat of everything demonic, the triumph of grace, forgiveness, and love over wickedness, hostility, and hatred. And what occurs between Good Friday and Easter Sunday acts out an eternal decision against all that challenges God's lordship: our captivating death, the last enemy of the Creator, and our foolish disobedience as ungrateful partners in the covenant of grace. As the humble way of the divine Son into the far country confirms God's No to death and evil, so the obedient homecoming of the truly human Son negates our No of rebellion and distrust. Though only too aware of all the contradictory signs, Karl Barth, enemy of Hitler and witness to the Holocaust, was clear that already and from all eternity death does not reign over us, nor disbelief within us. To the extent that Easter Saturday embodies all those contradictory signs — evil's triumph, the world's abandonment, the collapse of faith, and hope in radical despair — it was impossible for Barth to take that day too seriously, or to linger over its blatant godforsakenness and godlessness.

Others, of course, without denying God's gracious Yes, have found it imperative for the sake of that good news to pay attention to the human and demonic No, to give fullest recognition to evil's tyrannic victories and the strangulated human cry of protest, unbelief, and anger. What distinguishes from Barth such followers along his own trajectory as Jüngel and Moltmann is their search for understanding precisely from the starting point that Easter Saturday represents: the experience of the world as captive to diabolic death, which provokes not faith and gratitude but atheistic anger and bewilderment. How is it possible, they ask, at the end of this millennium and century, *not* to take seriously the world's godforsakenness and humanity's godlessness?[41]

From this perspective, Jürgen Moltmann is preeminently an "Easter Saturday" theologian, committed to testing Christian convictions against the reality of suffering, death, and doubt. Faith must take root, if anywhere, among the cells of the unjustly imprisoned and the graves of the wickedly slaughtered, and in conversation with the indignant and the doubting. We must listen to the testimony of the poor, the forsaken, and the discarded in this and every generation that the world remains in bondage, its longing for divine redemption still unsatisfied.[42]

---

40. For Barth's treatment of these themes, see esp. *CD,* III/1, sects. 41 and 42; III/3, sect. 50.

41. See esp. O'Donnell, *Temporality,* ch. 1: "Contemporary Atheism and Classical Philosophical Theism."

42. For some insight into the faith and hope born in Moltmann as a young German

Indeed, Moltmann came to scholarly prominence precisely by opposing to Barth's masterful "already" of primal decision a more hesitant but profoundly hopeful "not yet" of the world's continued unredemption. There is, indeed, in the eschatology of Scripture, a creative tension between the "already" and the "not yet," the joy of the kingdom coming in our very midst, and hope's patient endurance, waiting for the kingdom's postponed arrival at the end, the *eschaton.* From one angle, Christ has already demolished the walls of estrangement and is *today* our peace, our unity, our righteousness, and our liberation (e.g., Eph. 2:13ff.; 1 Cor. 1:30); from another, creation still groans (Rom. 8:18ff.), and only beyond tomorrow shall evil meet its judgment and death reign no more (Rev. 20–21). Barth represented an eschatology one-sidedly affirming faith's remembrance of God's antecedent election and past acts, through which salvation has already been accomplished, now only to be revealed and recognized. Moltmann's *Theology of Hope,*[43] by contrast, was an exercise of fundamental reorientation in eschatology and the doctrine of God. It put a perhaps equally one-sided emphasis on present incompleteness and future hope — those promises of God for tomorrow which require that we struggle in the present awaiting those things which do not yet appear (e.g., 1 Jn. 3:2; Rom. 8:24; Heb. 11:1), and only at the end of which God will be all in all (1 Cor. 15:28).

One narrative focus of *Theology of Hope* is the Exodus, that paradigmatic, mighty act of divine liberation which is not an end in itself but brings further promises — a land of promise — still to be fulfilled in the future. Before that there lies a wilderness interim of expectation, but also of struggle and suffering,

---

conscript in World War II, amid the hellishness of personal captivity and national collapse, see his deeply moving "Why Am I a Christian?" in J. Moltmann, *Experiences of God,* trans. M. Kohl (Philadelphia: Fortress and London: SCM, 1980), pp. 1-18.

43. See Moltmann's concise critique of Barth's eschatology in *Hope,* pp. 50-58; cf. R. Bauckham, "Jürgen Moltmann," in Toon and Spiceland, eds., *One God in Trinity,* pp. 111ff. For Moltmann's own eschatology, see, in addition to *Hope,* J. Moltmann, *Religion, Revolution and the Future,* trans. D. Meeks (New York: Scribner's, 1969); *Hope and Planning,* trans. M. Clarkson (New York: Harper & Row and London: SCM, 1971); *The Experiment Hope,* trans. D. Meeks (Philadelphia: Fortress and London: SCM, 1975); *Way of Jesus Christ,* esp. ch. 5; Moltmann et al., *The Future of Hope,* ed. F. Herzog (New York: Herder and Herder, 1970). See also D. M. Meeks, *Origins of the Theology of Hope* (Philadelphia: Fortress, 1974); R. Bauckham, *Moltmann: Messianic Theology in the Making* (Basingstoke: Marshall Pickering, 1987) (ch. 1 in this book is particularly helpful on Moltmann's use in *Hope* of ideas taken from the Marxist philosopher of "hope," Ernst Bloch); Bauckham, "Jürgen Moltmann," in Ford, ed., *Modern Theologians,* vol. 1, pp. 293ff.; C. Morse, *The Logic of Promise in Moltmann's Theology* (Philadelphia: Fortress, 1979); Heron, *Century,* pp. 162ff.; Zahrnt, *Question,* pp. 196-201.

and a receding horizon of dreams postponed. The other such focus is, of course, Christ's resurrection, God's clearest fulfillment yet of the promise of redemption. But here, too, fulfillment is leapfrogged by further promises not yet realized: the resurrection and deliverance of all at the end of time. It is clear in *Theology of Hope*, and becomes the more so in Moltmann's subsequent development, that for him Easter Day never cancels out the preceding cross and grave. Rather, he insists, Good Friday, and by implication Easter Saturday, are constant reminders to resurrection faith that the raising of Jesus is *only* the firstfruits, a prolepsis, an anticipation of the end. Much more remains to be accomplished before creation is renewed and the Creator's own life and purpose are finally fulfilled.[44] The raising of the crucified and buried one proclaims that hope is grounded only in suffering and death, and that pain, unrighteousness, and loss still characterize the world whose new future has been promised. Hope therefore stands in an ambiguous, dialectical relation to the present, providing both comfort and critique, affirmation and negation, to the status quo.[45]

On the one hand, every fulfillment-as-future-promise, including the resurrection, assures us that the world's sufferings and injustices are not the last word, will not endure forever. Tears shall end, and the enemies of life and righteousness be overcome. Fired with that ultimate promise, we may and must be involved with the world as God's Exodus people, a pilgrim church protesting the corruptions of this world and bearing witness through *praxis*, active engagement, to the coming, final kingdom. Such action nourishes small, provisional hopes in the here and now in anticipation of the ultimate hope, and squeezes out partial, preliminary victories against disease and poverty, guilt and death.

On the other hand, however, every fulfillment-as-future-promise, including the resurrection, also calls the present into question; for worldly hopes are only that, proximate and penultimate; they are challenged, contradicted, undermined by the greater hope for the messianic kingdom which is not of this world.[46] Turning the traditional, eschatological dialectic of eternity and time onto the horizontal plane, Moltmann conceives the future as a "new paradigm of transcendence."[47] The coming kingdom surpasses, transcends, and subverts

---

44. See esp. *Crucified God*, pp. 166ff., and *Way of Jesus Christ*, pp. 213ff.; cf. R. Bauckham, "Moltmann's Eschatology of the Cross," *SJT* 30.4 (1977): 301-11.

45. See esp. "Resurrection as Hope," in *Religion, Revolution and the Future*, pp. 42-62; see also R. Bauckham, "Moltmann's *Theology of Hope* Revisited," *SJT* 42.2 (1989): 202ff.

46. See, e.g., *Hope*, pp. 84ff.; cf. Bauckham, "*Hope* Revisited," pp. 212ff.

47. See esp. "The Future as New Paradigm of Transcendence," in *Religion, Revolution and the Future*, pp. 177-99; cf. Küng, *Incarnation of God*, pp. 400ff.

the present order, as God's hoped-for *"adventus"* differs from and casts its judgment on the *"futurum"* brought about by human planning and through history's immanent process.[48] The "Exodus Church" may and must engage in politics and encourage social progress;[49] but it trusts in neither, looking ahead to what God alone can and shall do, terminating the present order and making all things new.[50]

What concerns us most directly here is the consequence of such an eschatology for the doctrine of God and of the Trinity, in continuity and contrast with the thought of Barth. For Moltmann, learning from Barth, God is not pure, static "being," but a God of "event" and "becoming"; yet this becoming is marked here even more by temporality, happening, and futurity than in Barth.[51] For it is less that God *is,* through motion and change, than that God "is" not yet. God will be who God will be (one translation of Yahweh), so that only in the future, becoming what God not yet is, will the divine identity be finally fulfilled. That identity is so mediated through activity and time that God's eternal life and being will not be complete until the end of time, when all that God has to do is finally done. If, therefore, for Barth, eternity makes space for time, for Moltmann, conversely, the

---

48. On the distinction between *adventus* and *futurum,* see, e.g., Moltmann, *The Future of Creation,* trans. M. Kohl (Philadelphia: Fortress and London: SCM, 1979), pp. 29ff.; also *Experiment Hope,* pp. 52-53; "Hope and Planning," in *Hope and Planning,* pp. 178-99; "Theology as Eschatology," in Herzog, ed., *Future of Hope,* p. 15; and *Way of Jesus Christ,* p. 317. See also W. Kasper, *Faith and the Future,* trans. R. Nowell (New York: Crossroad, 1982), pp. 8-9.

49. *Hope,* pp. 304-38.

50. In addition to being engaged in *praxis,* active solidarity with the world of suffering, the Exodus Church also lives a life of doxology. The people of hope live in a "messianic intermezzo" between the present and the future and fill out this interim in a messianic lifestyle of openness, festivity, freedom, friendship, and playfulness. See esp. Moltmann, *The Church in the Power of the Spirit,* trans. M. Kohl (New York: Harper and Row and London: SCM, 1977), chs. 5 and 6; also *The Open Church,* trans. D. Meeks (London: SCM, 1978) (= *The Passion for Life: A Messianic Lifestyle* [Philadelphia: Fortress, 1978]), throughout; Moltmann, *Theology and Joy,* trans. R. Ulrich (London: SCM, 1973) (= *Theology of Play* [New York: Harper and Row, 1972]); Moltmann, *God in Creation,* trans. M. Kohl (London: SCM, 1985), ch. 11 and pp. 303-16; see also, O'Donnell, *Temporality,* pp. 142ff.; and Bauckham, in *Modern Theologians,* vol. 1, pp. 296-97. Ironically, in his introduction to the United Kingdom publication *Theology and Joy,* David E. Jenkins asks whether Moltmann, in suggesting that we should "leave the cross out of the game" (p. 50), does not in fact perpetuate something of the dualistic, Augustinian legacy he is attempting to transcend by drawing too sharp a distinction between action and worship, suffering and joy, the realm of work and that of play. See Jenkins, "The Liberation of 'God,'" in *Joy,* pp. 1-25.

51. See esp. O'Donnell, *Temporality,* ch. 4; cf. R. Olson, "Trinity and Eschatology," *SJT* 36.2 (1983): esp. 214-22.

temporal adds to and enriches the eternal.[52] God not only makes time but shares in it, so that through historical involvement the divine life experiences increments of Godhood: greater glory, deeper joy, fuller being.

This daring ontology of divine growth is, of course, wholly predicated upon the reality and primacy of the Trinity.[53] As in other respects, Moltmann here inherits but transcends Barth's conceptuality, completing the critique and replacement of the Western-Augustinian trinitarian tradition begun but not concluded by Barth. Despite the dogmatic priority that Barth assigns to the Trinity, Moltmann accuses him, as we have seen, of being insufficiently trinitarian in practice, perpetuating the concept of God as a single, though reiterating, absolute Self rather than as a true community of three interdependent agents.[54] Moltmann's by contrast is a truly "social" doctrine of divine relations, community, and fellowship, grounded in Cappadocian rather than Augustinian concepts.[55] He relies heavily on the notion of *perichoresis,* the mutual indwelling of the three persons, to ward off (not always successfully in the eyes of some critics) the dangers of tritheism, where the three persons are so distinct and separate as to become in effect three gods.[56] Certainly Moltmann pushes to the lim-

52. See Bauckham, in *One God in Trinity,* p. 129.

53. The wide scope of Moltmann's trinitarian thought gradually comes to view through his foundational trilogy, *Theology of Hope, The Crucified God,* and *The Church in the Power of the Spirit.* Each of these is focused upon a key event in the primary Christian narrative: respectively, Easter, Good Friday, and Pentecost. Barth's doctrine of the Trinity, as we saw above, was also built upon these three stories, though unlike Moltmann he followed the chronological sequence (see Ch. 6, n. 57). Moltmann finally gave systematic structure to his doctrine in *The Trinity and the Kingdom,* trans. M. Kohl (San Francisco: Harper & Row, 1981) (= *The Trinity and the Kingdom of God* [London: SCM, 1981]).

54. See esp. *Trinity and Kingdom,* pp. 16ff., 139ff.

55. "We understand the Scriptures as the testimony to the history of the Trinity's relations of fellowship, which are open to men and women, and open to the world. This trinitarian hermeneutic leads us to think in terms of relationships and communities; it supersedes the subjective thinking which cannot work without the separation and isolation of its objects." *Trinity and Kingdom,* p. 19. This "social" doctrine of the Trinity is not, of course, Moltmann's invention. On earlier versions, see C. Welch, *The Trinity in Contemporary Theology* (London: SCM, 1953), pp. 133ff.; and esp. L. Hodgson, *The Doctrine of the Trinity* (New York: Scribner's, 1944 and London: Nisbet, 1943). For critique of Moltmann's social doctrine, see Mackey, *Christian Experience,* pp. 202-9. See also the important study "Social Trinity and Tritheism," by C. Plantinga, in R. J. Feenstra and C. Plantinga, eds., *Trinity, Incarnation, and Atonement* (Notre Dame, Ind.: University of Notre Dame Press, 1989), pp. 21-47.

56. For Moltmann's use of *perichoresis,* see esp. *Trinity and Kingdom,* pp. 174ff. For the charge of incipient tritheism, see Bauckham, in *One God in Trinity,* p. 130; and O'Donnell, *Temporality,* pp. 149ff.

its the priority of the Godhead's threeness over its oneness. At every point in the history of God there is a "trinitarian differentiation of the divine unity," each person having distinct actions and relations within the fellowship.[57] It is in the very happening of their interactions as Father, Son, and Spirit that the three find cohesion and oneness.[58]

Of course, it was from Barth that Moltmann learned that the Trinity is indeed a happening, or event;[59] but in distinction from Barth, Moltmann locates this event not in the past but in the future. The Trinity is to be conceived not so much from its pretemporal beginnings as from its posttemporal consummation; for the triune community is an *open-ended* event whereby God is moving dynamically toward fulfillment in the future. There is a *missio Dei*, a mission of God, begun in the joy of creation, to be concluded in the doxology of the *eschaton*. Out of the superabundance of their love, their delight in beauty, and as a self-limiting act of "shrinkage," "withdrawal," or "contraction," the divine community "make room" beside themselves for creation and its free response.[60] Suffering and sin corrupt the beauty of the world and of humanity; yet even apart from this estrangement, God yearns for fuller union with us.[61] Thus are

57. Thus in the sending of the Son, e.g.: "The Father sends the Son through the Spirit; the Spirit comes from the Father in the power of the Spirit; the Spirit brings people into the fellowship of the Son with the Father." *Trinity and Kingdom,* p. 75.

58. Moltmann is particularly illuminating and relevant on the social *consequences* he draws from the social doctrine of the Trinity. His insights are in terms of community-based understandings of freedom and authority, the person, the church, and society. See e.g., *Trinity and Kingdom,* ch. 6; also *Open Church,* throughout; Moltmann, *On Human Dignity,* trans. D. Meeks (Philadelphia: Fortress and London: SCM, 1984); J. Moltmann and E. Moltmann-Wendel, *Humanity in God* (London: SCM, 1984 and New York: Pilgrim Press, 1983); also, a source much influenced by Moltmann, L. Boff, *Trinity and Society,* trans. P. Burns (Maryknoll, N.Y.: Orbis and London: Burns and Oates, 1988).

59. See Fiddes, *Suffering,* p. 84.

60. See *Trinity and Kingdom,* pp. 109, 111; cf. pp. 108-11 and 118; *God in Creation,* pp. 86ff.; and *Way of Jesus Christ,* pp. 328ff. In this way Moltmann interprets creation from the viewpoint of the cross. He is sometimes said to compromise thus the omnipotence of God the Creator. But Moltmann sees himself rather as *reinterpreting* omnipotence in the light of the cross — that weakness of God which is greater than human power (1 Cor. 1:25). Even at the human level, the creative act between a man and a woman issues in another person who restricts its parents' freedom, exacts the costs of reciprocity and responsibility, and gives them sleepless nights! This is to be understood in analogy to God's self-limitation, whereby the ineffable act of creation is itself self-handicapping and — restricting — the relinquishment of power understood as isolation, independence, and invulnerability.

61. See *Trinity and Kingdom,* p. 46: "The incarnation of God's Son is not an answer to sin. It is the fulfilment of God's eternal longing to become man and to make of every man a god out of grace; an 'Other' to participate in the divine life and return the divine

God's joys not yet complete, the longings of the divine fellowship still not sated. So it is that the Father sends the Son into the midst of our humanness, our captivity to pain and suffering, and our distance from our Maker. This Son is the messianic one, whose life, death, and resurrection promise the world its liberation and us our intimate place within the fellowship of the Trinity. And God sends the Spirit also, in whose power these hopes for the world's transformation and our own are already being realized, as we look toward the end when, the lordship of the Son a reality at last, the kingdom will be delivered to the Father. Then shall God be all in all, the love of the triune family perfected, and the glory of the Father, which is the Son and Spirit's joy, and that of all redeemed humanity, be complete at last.[62]

---

love" (referring, with apparent approval, to the theology of N. Berdyaev). On God's longing for union with us and bringing that about through the Trinity, see *Church in Power of the Spirit,* pp. 60ff.

62. See *Trinity and Kingdom,* throughout, but esp. chs. 3 and 4. On "glory," see, e.g., *Church in Power of the Spirit,* pp. 57ff., 108ff.; *Trinity and Kingdom,* pp. 124ff., 151ff.; and *Future of Creation,* pp. 88-89; cf. Fiddes, *Suffering,* pp. 78ff.; Bauckham, in *One God in Trinity,* p. 127; O'Donnell, *Temporality,* p. 133ff. Moltmann's concept of the Son handing over the kingdom to the Father is grounded in his highly controversial exegesis of 1 Cor. 15:24-28 (a passage to which he frequently alludes, e.g., *Experiment Hope,* pp. 40, 66, 83, 120; *Hope and Planning,* p. 87; *Crucified God,* pp. 58-66; *Trinity and the Kingdom,* pp. 91-92, 115; Herzog, ed., *Future of Hope,* 25ff.): "then comes the end, when he hands over the kingdom to God the Father.... When all things are subjected to him, then the Son himself will also be subjected to the one who put all things in subjection under him, so that God may be all in all." In order to maximize the distinctiveness of each person of the Godhead (in this case the Father and the Son), and thus to uphold a truly social or Cappadocian Trinity, as opposed to an Augustinian unitarianism, Moltmann risks appearing to affirm an Arian subordination of the Son, as well as the heresy of Marcellus of Ancyra, who denied that the incarnation, and therefore the glorification of Christ's humanity and ours, is permanent (in response to which the Nicene Creed declared that "his kingdom shall have no end"). The Son's reign, suggests Moltmann, is not eternal, for at the end he surrenders his lordship to the Father. In Moltmann's defense it may be said, in keeping with Eastern doctrine, that the handing over of the kingdom need not in fact signify subordination as such, but rather a certain order within the divine community of equals, where the Father alone is the fount of Godhead. Certainly, in positing an eschatological transaction between the Father and the Son, Moltmann flouts the Augustinian rule that the *opera ad extra,* the Trinity's outward works in the economy, are not to be divided. Here the roles of the Father and the Son in the culmination of the economy are sharply distinguished. And, of course, as we shall see in greater detail below, Moltmann not only identified the economic with the immanent Trinity more closely than Barth, but even suggested that it is the economic acts, including the handing over of the kingdom, but especially the cross, which shape and constitute the immanent Trinity, rather than the reverse, where the economy merely reveals in

It should be clear that the grave of Easter Saturday lies silently and invisibly at the very heart of this trinitarian eschatology. For it is specifically as Trinity, a plural community and not a monistic self, that God is able to sustain the radical separation that comprises death and hell, while also remaining united and whole in resurrecting victory over death's disjunctions. Only the Trinity can both experience the rupture of that Saturday and accomplish the resumption which is Easter Day. But equally the cross and grave, as signs of how the world still is today, require that the trinitarian event of the resurrection be understood from a strictly eschatological perspective. The godforsakenness and godlessness of Easter Saturday continue to protest that Easter's victory was a promise only for the future of the world and of the Trinity, not God's instant triumph over death and evil already accomplished and completed.

How precisely, then, may the death of Christ be interpreted as a central event in the history of the Trinity's own life as it moves toward the *eschaton?* For Moltmann, both following and surpassing Barth once more, theology constructs and refines its ontological conceptualities through deep reflection on the gospel's own stories, in this case the "word of the cross" contained in Scripture's reports on the crucifixion and beyond. "The doctrine of the Trinity is no longer an exorbitant and impractical speculation about God, but is nothing other than a shorter version of the passion narrative of Christ."[63]

---

time God's independent, eternal life and nature. The role of the Son in surrendering his kingdom at the end thus belongs to the immanent Trinity as such.

For a full discusion of the text in question, and of the history of its interpretation, see J. F. Jansen, "I Cor. 15:24-28 and the Future of Jesus Christ," *SJT* 40.4 (1987): 543-70 (also in W. E. March, ed., *Texts and Testaments* [San Antonio: Trinity University Press, 1980], pp. 173-97). Jensen judges that Moltmann goes too far in suggesting that for Calvin the crucified Christ becomes superfluous at the *eschaton.* The text itself does not say, and neither did Calvin, that Christ's humanity has a purely functional role in salvation and is relinquished at the end: at most it is implied that Christ's rule is transferred from his humanity to his divinity, allowing perfected humanity to be at last itself, in union with God. Jensen follows the interpretation of Calvin in D. Willis, *Calvin's Catholic Christology* (Leiden: E. J. Brill, 1966), p. 99. For Moltmann himself, despite the risks of subordinationism, it is important that the Son remains the Son, indeed consummates his Sonship in this final act of filial obedience, through which we too enjoy fellowship in the Trinity as adopted daughters and sons. Only in this way is the Fatherhood of the Father also completed, so that God's becoming all in all means the fulfillment of the triune community as a whole, and not its ultimate collapse into a monism of the Father.

63. *Crucified God,* p. 246; see, on what follows below, pp. 240-49; cf. Bauckham, "Eschatology of the Cross," p. 309; "Moltmann," in *Modern Theologians,* vol. 1, p. 304; and *Messianic Theology,* pp. 110-11; also O'Donnell, *Temporality,* p. 115; and Morse, *Logic,* pp. 120-21.

That narrative invites us to interpret the suffering and death, the burying and raising of Jesus, as a trinitarian happening, a sequence of events "between God and God." Indeed, at its heart the story tells of an event in which God is *against* God, though without downright divine annihilation (a possibility which could not be sustained by a unitary Godhead but can be contained and comprehended within a community which continues to love, in the very midst of contradiction).[64] This divine opposition which puts "God against God" is crystallized in the act of self-surrender whereby the Father, for all of us, delivers up the Son to death (Rom. 8:32: for Moltmann a determinative text[65]). "What happened here is what Abraham did not need to do to Isaac: Christ was quite

64. See *Crucified God*, e.g., pp. 152 and 246; also J. Moltmann, "The 'Crucified God': A Trinitarian Theology of the Cross," *Interpretation* 26 (1972): 278-99, esp. p. 294. It is in the first instance a thought central to Luther's theology of the cross (to which Moltmann is clearly an heir: see *Crucified God*, pp. 207ff.; *Trinity and Kingdom*, pp. 65ff.; also Fiddes, *Suffering*, p. 30; and A. E. McGrath, *The Making of Modern German Christology* [Oxford and New York: Blackwell, 1986], pp. 192-93) that, in the death of Christ, God was struggling against God. But the principle which Moltmann invokes here — that only God can be against God *(nemo contra Deum nisi Deus ipse)* — illustrates his particular indebtedness to Hegel. For Hegel, the Christian story of God the Father delivering up to death God the Son gives rise to a "speculative Good Friday," in which the logic of dialectic, the negating of a thesis by its antithesis and the transcending of both in synthesis, applied to the concept of "the death of God," becomes a universal principle explicating the movement of all reality toward fulfillment through a process of dying in order to live. See Moltmann, *Hope*, pp. 168ff.; *Crucified God*, pp. 34ff., 217, 253ff.; also Küng, *Incarnation of God*, esp. pp. 162-74; and Fiddes, *Suffering*, pp. 189ff. Though Moltmann uses this dialectic in his trinitarian exposition of the cross, he does so not on the basis of abstract, logical speculation, but in reflection on the historical narratives of Scripture. Nonetheless, Hegel's dialectic does underlie much of Moltmann's thought, especially his epistemology. Here he substitutes for the later Barth's "analogy of faith" — that we know the divine through God-revealed and created correspondences and likenesses — the opposite principle (again clear in Luther's theology of the cross), that we know things through their contradictory opposites — that God is revealed in hiddenness, present in absence, powerful in weakness, gracious through judgment, etc. See esp. *Trinity and Kingdom*, pp. 25-28; also Bauckham, *Messianic Theology*, pp. 67ff., and "Eschatology of the Cross," pp. 304ff. Such an epistemology does much to explain the difference between Moltmann's interpretation of the death and burial of Christ and Barth's — why, i.e., Moltmann could affirm positively what Barth shrank from: the identification of opposites in the cross and grave, death and God together in the mortal remains of Jesus.

65. See, e.g., *Crucified God*, pp. 191, 241ff.; "The 'Crucified God,'" pp. 291ff.; *Church in Power of the Spirit*, pp. 94-95; *Trinity and Kingdom*, pp. 80ff.; *Way of Jesus Christ*, pp. 172-73; cf. McGrath, *German Christology*, p. 189; and O'Donnell, *Temporality*, pp. 117ff.

deliberately abandoned by the Father to the fate of death: God subjected him to the power of corruption."[66]

To this Pauline concept of the Father giving up the Son — further intensified by the shocking claim that "for us" Christ "became a curse" and "was made to be sin" (Gal. 3:13; 2 Cor. 5:21), there corresponds the evangelists' record of Christ's forsakenness and unanswered cry of dereliction (Mk. 15:34ff.; Mt. 27:46ff.).[67] Here Moltmann takes the conscious risk of pushing the texts — and the elasticity, as it were, of the concept of God's oneness — to the limits, in order to confront us most disturbingly with the separation within God which the Son's death represents. Here is the first Person against the second; the beloved Son torn from, pushed away by, the loving Father; all the world's evil, suffering, and sin rending the divine family asunder. The relationlessness here is truly mutual; for the aloneness and grief of the abandoned Son, thrust into the deadly darkness of fatherlessness, is matched, for Moltmann, by that of the forsaking Father, not spared at the eleventh hour like Abraham from the numbing pain of sonlessness.[68] Nor can there be any passing over of the questionableness into which the Father's own love, faithfulness, indeed very fatherhood and deity, are thrown by the abandoning of the only Son. What kind of Father does such things? What kind of God is this? This disputability of deity, this falsifying of the Father's love, is a kind of "death of Fatherhood" for the one who gave up the Son to death. "Here 'God' is forsaken by 'God'. . . . This is even the breakdown of the relationship that constitutes the very life of the Trinity: . . . the Son does not merely lose his Sonship. The Father loses his fatherhood as well."[69]

Moltmann rightly stops short of assigning death to the Father as such; but there is a dying of the Son which, by the principle of *perichoresis,* mutual in-

66. W. Popkes, *Christus Traditus: Eine Untersuchung zur Begriff der Dahingabe im Neuen Testament* (Zurich: Zwingli, 1967); quoted by Moltmann, *Crucified God,* p. 241; cf. p. 191 and *Way of Jesus Christ,* pp. 175-76.

67. See *Crucified God,* pp. 146ff., 241ff.; "The 'Crucified God,'" pp. 284ff.; *Church in Power of the Spirit,* 93-94; *Trinity and Kingdom,* pp. 77ff.; *Way of Jesus Christ,* pp. 165ff.

68. See, e.g., *Crucified God,* p. 243; "The 'Crucified God,'" pp. 292ff.; *Trinity and Kingdom,* p. 81; cf. pp. 30ff.; *Way of Jesus Christ,* p. 173. Moltmann is insistent that he is not committing here the ancient modalistic heresy of patripassianism — that because the Father and Son are identical, what the Son suffers the Father suffers too, in the crucifixion. Though there is pain, grief, and suffering for the Father in the sacrifice of the Son, it is a different and distinct kind of suffering from that of the sacrificed Son. Likewise Moltmann repudiates the theopaschite formula "the death of God," for that, too, blurs the distinctiveness of the Father and the Son, respectively, in the event of the cross. See Fiddes, *Suffering,* pp. 195ff.; and McGrath, *German Christology,* pp. 190-91.

69. *Trinity and Kingdom,* p. 80; cf. *Crucified God,* 151, 243.

dwelling, intrudes death into the whole Godhead. This, for Moltmann, is not "the death of God," for that would blur the trinitarian distinctions: the Father and the Spirit do not die. But this is death *in* God, since through the cross death and its division does pierce the life and heart of the triune family.[70] How, Moltmann asks in effect, if the incarnation *holds* at the point of the cross, can we avoid the conclusion that here death is taken into God, and radical rupture sustained in God's own life and history?[71]

This, of course, is not the end of the story: as the narrative resumes on Easter morning after the rupture of Christ's passion, death, and burial, so the corresponding doctrine of the Trinity conceives that God is not only differentiated, and thus capable of separation and opposition, but also unified and one. In fact, the oneness of God is being exercised in the very event of Christ's abandonment and death, not only in his later raising. For at the very point of their furthest separation, as "God against God," the Father and the Son are in an embrace of perfect harmony and unity. Christ's sacrifice, after all, by the Abrahamic Father is the Son's Isaac-like self-offering in obedience and submission. In the free giving up of the Son by the Father, and the equally free giving up of himself to the Father, for the world's sake, there is total unity of will between the two. For Moltmann it is revealing that in distinction from Rom. 8:32, where the Father delivers up the Son, in Gal. 2:20 the Son delivers himself up, just as in the Gospels Christ goes voluntarily to the cross.[72]

70. See *Crucified God,* pp. 200ff., 207, 217, 243, 277; cf. Fiddes, *Suffering,* pp. 195ff.

71. Note that in construing the death of Christ as an event for God, Moltmann seeks to retrieve the element of truth in the old *kenotic* interpretation of the incarnation; see *Crucified God,* pp. 205-6, and *Trinity and Kingdom,* 118-19.

72. That the formula "delivers up" occurs in Paul "with both the Father and the Son as subject . . . expresses a deep conformity betrween the will of the Father and the will of the Son in the event of the cross, as the Gethsemane narrative also records." *Crucified God,* p. 243; cf. "The 'Crucified God,'" p. 293; *Trinity and Kingdom,* pp. 81ff.; *Church in Power of the Spirit,* pp. 94ff.; *Way of Jesus Christ,* p. 172. For Moltmann this unity of will between the Father and the Son is not different from, but the same reality as, that affirmed in classical Nicene Christology, which speaks of unity of substance, *homoousios.* See *Crucified God,* p. 244, and "The 'Crucified God,'" p. 293. This total unity of the Father and Son even at the point of their separation in the cross is important for Moltmann's defense against the feminist critique of D. Sölle, who accuses Moltmann of presenting God as a sadistic, patriarchal executioner whose wrath is appeased only by the shedding of the Son's blood. Against this, Moltmann argues that, as the resurrection vindication of Christ shows, the Father is always on the side of the Son, and not against him, in his controversies with the Roman, Jewish, human, and demonic forces that bring about his death; and also that from the Son's side there is a voluntary laying down of his life in perfect harmony with God's loving, saving purposes, and not passive, abject martyrdom to the Father's tyrannical will. See esp.

The medium of this love, conformity, and unity between the Father and the Son is, of course, the Holy Spirit; and in this truly trinitarian hermeneutic of the cross, it is the particular and vital role of the Spirit to hold the divine family together, so to speak, even as the Devil, in the form of death and hell, does its worst to tear the community apart. The Spirit is God not allowing the Holy One to see corruption, raising the Messiah murdered by Jerusalem, and bringing life to the dead and nonexistent (Acts 2:24-36; Rom. 1:3; 4:17; 8:11). Such is the creative power of the love which binds the Father and the Son together in their mutual surrender to disconnectedness and loss (cf. Heb. 9:14). "Whatever proceeds from the event between the Father and the Son must be understood as the spirit of the surrender of the Father and the Son, as the spirit which creates love for forsaken [humanity], as the spirit which brings the dead alive."[73]

Here within the Trinity, God is "for" God in a new act of resurrection in contrast and discontinuity with the former, where "God against God" led to abandonment and death. Now God through the Spirit raises up from death the same one who was given up to death, and restores the sundered (yet still unbroken) union between the Father and the Son. This promises new birth and divine adoption to all the godforsaken in solidarity with whom the Son has died alone (Rom. 8:9-17; Gal. 4:4-7), and justification to the ungodly in company with whom Christ has made his grave (Rom. 4:5; Isa. 53:9).

Nevertheless, a continuity holds the cross and the empty grave together, despite the discontinuity with the past in Easter's new creation. Just as only the crucified one has been raised, so the only risen one remains he who was crucified.[74] The God who suffers pain and grief, death and hell, in the separation of the Father and the Son between Good Friday and Easter Saturday, is still the same suffering, grieving God, who has tasted death on Easter Day. Taking death into the Godhead, as the only way to put death to death (Heb. 2:14), God continues to be subject to the groaning of a captive creation and the mortality of perishing humanity. Only when, through the Spirit, all pain and tears have passed away will God's suffering come to an end, the ascendancy of life over death be uncontested, and what began between Easter's Saturday and Sunday be concluded.[75]

Way of Jesus Christ, pp. 175ff.; cf. O'Donnell, *Temporality*, pp. 153ff.; von Balthasar, *Mysterium Paschale*, pp. 107-12, and *The Glory of the Lord*, vol. 7: *Theology: The New Covenant*, trans. B. McNeil (Edinburgh: T. & T. Clark, 1989), pp. 202-28.

73. *Crucified God*, p. 245.

74. On this unbreakable dialectic in Moltmann's thought between the cross and the resurrection, see esp. Bauckham, *Messianic Theology*, chs. 2 and 3.

75. See esp. *Trinity and Kingdom*, ch. 2; see also Bauckham, in *Modern Theologians*, vol. 1, pp. 298ff.; and Fiddes, *Suffering*, pp. 135ff.

So Moltmann goes much further than Barth here, attributing not just passion but death to the Godhead — and the continuing experience of death at that, through the crucified Son and the Spirit of fellowship and solidarity, until the end of time; for "all human history, however much it may be determined by guilt and death, is taken up into this 'history of God.'"[76] This is a thinkable thought for Moltmann because he is that much more daring in drawing ontological and eternal implications for God from the historical event of the crucifying, burying, and raising of Jesus. Especially in his early work, Moltmann threatened indeed to go too far in connecting divine being and the historical cross. The risk he took was to suggest that this event actually *constitutes* the Trinity, or is the point of the Trinity's "beginning" or "becoming" — as if before or without Christ's death there simply is no Trinity. He "interpreted the event of the cross in trinitarian terms as an event concerned with a relationship between persons in which these persons constitute themselves in their relationship with each other."[77] Indeed, God's very existence as love is "constituted" in the event of the cross. "God's deity is to be developed out of this occurrence."[78]

It is certainly not easy to see how the being of the eternal God may reside in a "becoming" of such extreme temporality and historicality as to have no existence apart from this event of total specificity and particularity. Rarely is even human existence — historical through and through — so episodic and insubstantial. Perhaps wisely, then, Moltmann subsequently reverted to more Barthian language for the relationship between the cross and the being of God. Now, "in this happening God is *revealed* as the trinitarian God."[79]

Yet this position is still an advance upon Barth in its insistence that in the

76. *Crucified God,* p. 246.

77. *Crucified God,* p. 245; cf. p. 255: "the trinitarian God-event on the cross becomes the history of God."

78. "The 'Crucified God,'" p. 296; cf. *Crucified God,* p. 244. Despite some accusations that after *Theology of Hope* Moltmann came to neglect the OT and the God of Israel, he surely is not so ingenuous as to suppose that because God's deity is constituted out of the cross, Yahweh previously was not. Clearly the Father of Jesus Christ and the Holy One of Israel are one and the same (cf. *Crucified God,* p. 150), even though it is in the cross that, from the Christian viewpoint, the divine identity comes most clearly into focus, so that God can never again be known as other than the God of the crucified Jesus. In fact, Moltmann throughout shows his indebtedness to Judaism, to the history of Jewish mysticism, and especially to the OT tradition of divine suffering (cf. esp. *Crucified God,* p. 270; *Trinity and Kingdom,* pp. 25ff.), as interpreted, e.g., by A. Heschel, *The Prophets* (New York: HarperCollins, 1969 and 1971); E. Wiesel, *Night* (New York: Bantam, 1982); and K. Kitamori, *Theology of the Pain of God* (London: SCM and Richmond, Va.: John Knox Press, 1966). See also Bauckham, in *One God in Trinity,* pp. 130-31.

79. *Church in Power of the Spirit,* p. 96 (my italics).

events of cross, burial, and resurrection we are directly and without ambiguity confronted with the character and interactions of God's inner life and being. There is, in short, no reservation here that what is seen at the cross in God's economic history might be other than the immanent constitution of the triune community itself. "The meaning of the cross of the Son on Golgotha reaches right into the heart of the immanent Trinity. From the very beginning, no immanent Trinity and no divine glory is conceivable without 'the Lamb who was slain'. . . . [One] can never think of God in the abstract, apart from the cross of Christ. . . . God is from eternity to eternity 'the crucified God.'"[80]

In thus connecting the death of Christ so directly to God's own being, Moltmann goes as far as anyone could to remove the gap between the economic and immanent Trinity while still retaining their notional distinction. He confirms Rahner's identification of the two,[81] but for himself distinguishes only between the economy as a soteriological concept, where we acknowledge what God does "for us," and immanence as a doxological one, where we praise and worship the Godhead in its intratrinitarian relations for God's own sake.[82] Yet everything we know of these latter relations is still grounded in the former, in God's cross-shaped experience of our pain and death and our own cross-shaped experience of God's salvation.

Moltmann, like Barth, is willing — cautiously — to read back from this economy to God's eternal immanence, to a "Trinity in the origins" where, for example, an eternal generation of the Son and proceeding of the Spirit correspond to the temporal sending of the Son and the Spirit for our salvation.[83] However, this emphatically does not mean for Moltmann that God's activity in time is a mere unveiling of eternity's divine relations and decisions. The Trinity at the beginning is essentially fluid and open to the future,[84] and Moltmann, audaciously and controversially, attributes to the economy a "retroactive effect" upon God's eternal immanence.[85] Who God is inwardly and eternally is thus in part actually shaped and determined by God's own experience of our history — and especially by the cross, and by all that happens through the Spirit until the

80. *Trinity and Kingdom,* p. 159.
81. See *Crucified God,* p. 240.
82. See *Trinity and Kingdom,* pp. 152ff., 160.
83. See, e.g., *Church in Power of the Spirit,* pp. 53ff.
84. See *Church in Power of the Spirit,* pp. 56ff.
85. *Trinity and Kingdom,* pp. 160f. For exposition and critique of Moltmann's relating of the immanent and economic Trinity, see Bauckham in *One God in Trinity,* pp. 112ff., 125ff., and *Messianic Theology,* pp. 110ff.; Olson, "Trinity and Eschatology," pp. 215ff.; O'Donnell, *Temporality,* pp. 124-36; Fiddes, *Suffering,* pp. 135-39. See also Gunton, *Promise,* pp. 21-23.

kingdom of the crucified Son is delivered to the Father. This is the eschatological growth and enrichment of the Trinity through God's pain and suffering in fellowship with us, and joy and delight at loving responses from us.[86] At the end, and only at the end, of this history of suffering and joy will God finally be all in all and fully glorified, having become what the Trinity now is still in process of becoming. Then at last, having shaped God's ultimate identity, "the economic Trinity is raised into and transcended in the immanent Trinity. What remains is the eternal praise of the triune God."[87]

This bold manner of relating the historical happening of suffering and death in the cross and burial of the Son, and the continued sighings of the Spirit, to the inner being of the Trinity, removes any possibility left by Karl Barth that in divine freedom God might have acted otherwise than as actually revealed. That God is gracious, suffering love is not a *choice*, as Moltmann sees it, grounded in a putative freedom not to love; rather, it is "self-evident" and "axiomatic," is simply God's way of being God.[88] And this in turn wipes away any lingering suspicions in Barth's doctrine of God of an inner recess of deity which remains untouched by the economy, impassible, invulnerable, untrammeled. Moltmann's entire project would replace the immutability and "apathy" of Christian tradition and metaphysical theism with a radical theology of divine "pathos."[89] God just *is* that suffering love, that subjection to grief and separation, that embrace and taking in of death and hell, seen on Pilate's bloody cross and in Joseph's chilly tomb.

Moltmann attends closely to the historical uniqueness and particularity of Good Friday and Easter Saturday. These are concrete events of human pain and suffering, of abandonment and loss of hope: a specific moment of our history when the absence of God was tangible and vivid, with the Son of God godforsaken and buried with the godless, and those who looked to Jesus for the coming of God's kingdom deflated and despairing. Here, for Moltmann, amid this episode of divine absence, God was truly *present,* was *in* the one who suffered, was forsaken and discredited, and *with* the hopeless one who cried that weekend in angry protest or bitter resignation at the loss of the Messiah. There-

---

86. See, e.g., *Trinity and Kingdom,* p. 161.

87. *Trinity and Kingdom,* p. 161.

88. *Trinity and Kingdom,* pp. 107-8 and 151. The implicit criticism of Barth's doctrine of freedom here is explicit at pp. 52ff. See Fiddes, *Suffering,* pp. 71-76, 119. For the allegation that Moltmann compromises God's freedom and lordship, which Barth preserved, see esp. Molnar, "Immanent Trinity in Barth," pp. 383ff.; cf. Bauckham in *Modern Theologians,* vol. 1, p. 308.

89. See *Crucified God,* pp. 267ff.; and *Trinity and Kingdom,* esp. ch. 2. See also Bauckham, *Messianic Theology,* esp. pp. 95-113.

fore these datable days and nights in human history can also be charted as happenings in the history of the Trinity itself. Greatly daring, and flouting every principle of changelessness, Moltmann conceives the cross as a distinct and *new* event for God, when the divine experience of suffering takes on a different dimension, a quality unprecedented. Hereafter, until the *eschaton,* God through the Spirit suffers at a level of infinite intensity which did not occur before the incarnation. Though God was self-limited, vulnerable, and reciprocally involved with creation from the beginning, here *kenosis,* self-humiliation, becomes complete, as for the first time "God becomes the God who identifies . . . with men and women to the point of death and beyond." And this new experience, this incarnation unto death and burial, is not temporary or "transitional. It is and remains to all eternity. There is no God other than the incarnate, human God who is one with men and women."[90]

Now this "no God other than the incarnate" gives a two-way significance to the events of Bethlehem and Gethsemane, and above all of Calvary and the garden tomb. These pinpoint in a unique and singular way, we have said, the culmination of God's *kenosis,* the new and final depth of divine humiliation in the Son. But these particularities of divine and human history are also anchor points, for Moltmann, of a much more extensive reality, a cosmic *kenosis* — a self-emptying focused not so much on the Son as on the Spirit, the Spirit immanent through all of time, in all creation.[91] By this Spirit, God is the victim of everybody's pain; takes in not just one death but universal death; absorbs not only the evil done to Jesus but wickedness wherever it occurs: the godforsakenness and godlessness not just of one Saturday, but of every day. That everrepeating "Easter Saturday" experience, at the heart of every generation's suffering and grief, death and hopelessness, also belongs to the trinitarian history of God begun at the cross. "Like the cross of Christ, even Auschwitz is in God. . . . Even Auschwitz is taken up into the grief of the Father, the surrender of the Son and the power of the Spirit." Not before the ending of universal suffering and the cessation of all time's outrages will the history of the Trinity be complete and God fulfilled. "Only with the resurrection of the dead, the murdered and the gassed, only with the healing of those in despair who bear lifelong wounds, only with the abolition of all rule and authority, only with the annihilation of death will the Son hand over the kingdom to the Father. Then God will turn . . . sorrow into eternal joy."[92]

90. *Trinity and Kingdom,* p. 119; cf. pp. 118-19; *Crucified God,* pp. 276-77; cf. Fiddes, *Suffering,* p. 9.

91. See esp. *God in Creation,* p. 102.

92. *Crucified God,* p. 278.

Such a double perspective upon God's suffering and death in the cross and grave, the singularity of these events and their universality, exposes Moltmann himself to double jeopardy. For there are critics who see difficulty in the newness and uniqueness of God's experience in Christ, while others are troubled by the notion that God is the victim of universal suffering. Complaints that, by having the trinitarian history of suffering begin at the cross, Moltmann slights God's constant character as vulnerable love largely miss their target; for Moltmann himself insists on going back from this "beginning" to the creation, interpreting that, in the light of the crucifixion, as an act of self-limitation and exposure to pain, opposition, and death. "At creation itself death enters into God's necessary experience, the death of loved ones. The passion that is at the heart of the world . . . is as much as Moltmann could ever wish, the passion of God."[93] Those who dismiss the uniqueness of the cross for God, on the grounds that God is always vulnerable, even as Creator, surely reintroduce surreptitiously the discredited, static notion of divine immutability, and thus ignore the insight of Barth, Moltmann, and others that the Creator whose being is in becoming is as such open to the posssibility of change, of becoming something new and different, in this case human, mortal flesh.

To be taken more seriously, perhaps, are those who fear that in making God subject to universal suffering, to every Easter Saturday, to all the pain and evil in the historical process, Moltmann makes God a prisoner of that process, dependent on the world, conditioned by it, even identical with it. That, they say, would compromise the divine lordship, denying the freedom of the Creator to stand over against the created order, whether in judgment or salvation.[94] Is Moltmann's suffering, crucified God simply the ultimate, and ultimately helpless, victim? Is this a solidarity with suffering which can do nothing *about* suffering except endure it? In two ways, at least, Moltmann leaves himself open to such questions and critique.

First, there is Moltmann's glaring, and rather inexplicable, weakness on

93. Mackey, *Christian Experience,* p. 261. Fiddes, in *Suffering,* p. 9, reads Mackey in this context as voicing a protest against Moltmann's uniqueness of the cross. But Mackey himself acknowledges that there is nothing in the notion of God being subject to death from the first to which Moltmann would object. Nor would it be inconsistent to move back from the creation again to the incarnation, and say that God's constant exposure to the death of others turns into something qualitatively new when, through the enfleshed Son, God experiences death firsthand, so to speak.

94. See this critique in, e.g., Olson, "Trinity and Eschatology," pp. 221ff.; and Molnar, "Immanent Trinity in Barth," pp. 383ff. The question of whether God is dissolved into history is raised, but answered in Moltmann's favor, in O'Donnell, *Temporality,* pp. 147ff.

the subject of *atonement*. Though he is far from denying the reality of human sin, or of forgiveness as a primary fruit of our salvation, he does deny, as we have seen, that it was for the sake of sin as such that the incarnation and Christ's death took place. Not for sinners so much as for sin's victims, for those more sinned against than sinning, did the Father deliver up the Son. Moltmann is remarkably dismissive of the New Testament's interpretation of the cross as fulfilling the Old Testament cult of sacrifice and theology of expiation.[95] With this he sets aside God's relation to humanity as that of Holy Judge over against guilty and unholy sinners, minimizing Scripture's insistence on a degree of human responsibility for the suffering and evil we endure. God seems so closely identified with our suffering as not to be distinguished from us as the Holy and Wholly Other one, who while enduring our griefs also judges our guilt.[96] If God does not stand apart from the sinful world, as history and humanity's Judge, that also renders questionable God's freedom and power to stand apart from the suffering world, as history and humanity's Deliverer.

Secondly, the suspicion that Moltmann imprisons God within the process of history is hardly allayed by his own flirting with process theology; or, since he declares himself critical of that project, at least his willingness to adopt its principal conception.[97] That is the notion of "panentheism," that all things exist, all events occur, *in* God. For Moltmann this means that not only is God present in all death, but that all death, absorbed by the Trinity, happens in God. "A trinitarian theology of the cross perceives God in the negative element and therefore the negative element in God, and in this dialectical way is panentheistic. . . . To recognize God in the cross of Christ, conversely, means to recognize the cross, inextricable suffering, death and hopeless rejection in God."[98] Thus in addition to thinking of our history of suffering as a human process in which God shares, we must also think of our history as happening in God, such that we, even when victimized by evil, are sharing in God's process. "All human history, however much it may be determined by guilt and death, is taken up into this 'history of God', i.e. into the Trinity, and integrated into the future of the 'history of God.'"[99]

---

95. See esp. *Crucified God,* p. 183; and *Way of Jesus Christ,* pp. 187-88.

96. A penetrating critique of Moltmann (and others) along these lines is contained in D. W. McCullough, "Church and World: The Loss of Distinction in Twentieth Century Theology" (unpublished Ph.D. diss., University of Edinburgh, 1980).

97. See, e.g., *God in Creation,* pp. 78-79; also O'Donnell, *Temporality,* pp. 130ff. Significantly, Moltmann criticizes process thought for the threat it poses to divine transcendence — the very grounds on which his own use of process conceptuality has been questioned.

98. *Crucified God,* p. 277; cf. *Trinity and Kingdom,* p. 19.

99. *Crucified God,* p. 246.

If, however, evil be thus conceived as occurring in God, what becomes of the Creator's apartness from evil, God's power to transcend the world and overcome its unrighteousness and brokenness? Moltmann certainly assures us that through the mutual indwelling of history and God, there is indeed an overcoming of the world: "God in Auschwitz and Auschwitz in the crucified God — that is the basis for a real hope which both embraces and overcomes the world."[100] But if Auschwitz — and all the suffering, death, and evil for which that horror now stands — truly is *in* God, might the final outcome not equally be the opposite — that God is overcome by the world, or at least remains forever indistinguishable from it?

In fact, Moltmann can escape from such conclusions. For despite the appearances fostered by his use of panentheistic language, this is truly not a version of process theology — for which a clear distinction between God and the world proves so hard to sustain. The difference is precisely that Moltmann rests upon, as process thought does not, a robust eschatology in which the present processes of history are radically contradicted and transcended by the discontinuous new creation of the future. If anything, Moltmann is guilty of exaggerating, rather than reducing, the dialectical antithesis seen above between the divine future and humanity's own tomorrow, between God's *adventus* and the world's *futurum*. This can rob eschatological hope of temporal, this-worldly reference and relevance.[101] But at least by contrasting the coming kingdom of God with every form of human and historical dominion, by polarizing the *eschaton* and the process, Moltmann makes it clear that after all the God of the future is neither captive to that process nor merely its indecipherable, immanent dynamic.

There is, as we have seen, growth and increment for God in the final kingdom over the Trinity's present experience of suffering and joy. Indeed, resurrection has already established a "surplus" over the cross, an abundance of grace over the magnitude of evil.[102] The opposition between God and evil is not a stalemate, the equilibrium of commensurable forces. Rather, love triumphs in its confrontation with evil because it flowers, flourishes, increases, precisely by taking up death and absorbing lovelessness. Evil, on the contrary, intent upon destroying life and love, instead destroys itself. "Suffering proves to be stronger than hate. Its might is powerful in weakness and gains power over its enemies in

---

100. *Crucified God,* p. 278.

101. See my own critique of Moltmann along these lines in my Inaugural Lecture, "Apocalypse and Parousia: The Anguish of Theology from Now till Kingdom Come," *Austin Seminary Bulletin,* Faculty Edition, vol. 103 (April 1988): 36-37.

102. See *Way of Jesus Christ,* pp. 186, 214-15.

grief, because it gives life even to its enemies and opens up the future to change."[103] Thus the conflict between life and death resolves itself in favor of creativity and life. The "eschatological surplus of promise,"[104] this 'how much more' of abundant grace (Rom. 5:6-21; cf. 8:34), is our assurance that the victory over evil won proleptically at Easter points forward to a fuller triumph yet: the final disappearance of evil, its causes and its consequences, the end of suffering, unrighteousness and death itself.

Thus Moltmann is clear enough that even though Auschwitz is "in" God, its perpetrators shall not have the last word, nor "the executioners . . . finally triumph over their victims."[105] God is not imprisoned or defeated by our history. Rather, the triune fellowship, which have taken death into themselves, have thereby determined that death and negativity will suffer their own annihilation; for where death increases, life abounds much more. As we shall see, precisely by analyzing more profoundly still the ontological reality of love's surplus, E. Jüngel is able to conceive not only "death in God," but the very death of the still living God.

III. The Trinity and the Death of God

The Death of God! That was the unthinkable thought toward whose thinkability we found ourselves impelled by our listening at the beginning to the three-day Christian narrative which pivots upon Easter Saturday. Having heard "the word of the cross" in the form of a story which locates God in the grave of the crucified Jesus, we have since been learning how indeed it might be possible to conceive the inconceivable things that we have heard, and so to think the unthinkable and say the unsayable as the good news of the Christian gospel. Thus we have traced faith's search for understanding, for thoughts and words appropriate to the story of the cross and grave, from its New Testament origins, patristic development, and conciliar decisions, through its Reformation and modern phases, and — in somewhat greater detail — into our own century.

As we have noted, this history has frequently been marked by hesitancy, ambivalence, and outright denial concerning that "death of God" seemingly announced by the church's defining narrative. Nonetheless, we have seen in these struggles of theology to think the faith a profound conceptualizing of the incarnation, the divine assuming of humanity, with its implied union of God

103. *Crucified God*, p. 249.
104. *Way of Jesus Christ*, p. 215.
105. *Crucified God*, p. 178.

with dead and buried flesh; a thousand years and more of wrestling with assumptions that the story can simply not be true, that God can have no place on a cross or in a grave, could be no longer God if touched by suffering or death; and in our times, at last, the determination to conceive precisely these impossibilities, to affirm God's passion and embrace of death. Now, at the finale of this historical and theological progression, we arrive at a current, flourishing theologian whose project, beyond even "the passion of God" or "death in God," is precisely "the death of God" as that must be thinkable and sayable, indeed be thought and spoken in any address of the Christian gospel to our coevals.

Eberhard Jüngel, interpreter of Karl Barth and Tübingen colleague of Jürgen Moltmann, stands in continuity and some solidarity with both of these, yet is confessionally distinct, highly creative, and resolutely *sui generis*. Unique among all whom we have alluded to or analyzed, Jüngel is *the* theologian of the grave of Jesus Christ. For him, God's death through Easter Saturday *is* the story to be told by the community of faith, the impossible possibility which for our own sake and the world's we must today bring to thought and speech.

Jüngel expounds Barth's doctrine of the Trinity and extends its trajectory, and with Moltmann interprets the very being of the Trinity from the standpoint of Christ's death, burial, and resurrection; yet as a Lutheran he shares in doctrine and hermeneutics the Reformed affinities of neither; and as a contemporary Lutheran he offers a new and even more daunting reading of his own tradition's "theology of the cross." If, like Barth, he stresses more than Moltmann what has already been redemptively accomplished on the cross; and if he sides with Moltmann against Barth in listening to modern atheism's cross-like cry of godforsakenness and disbelief; Jüngel is able more than both of them to identify the cross whereon Christ died, and the grave he occupied, as God's own loci: places where the living God was dead.

Jüngel's major volume, *God as the Mystery of the World*,[106] is subtitled "On the Foundations of the Theology of the Crucified One in the Dispute between Theism and Atheism." That in effect identifies Easter Saturday, the day of the burial of God, as theology's foundational, defining moment. For it is this occurrence, as recorded in the Christian narrative, which maximizes the dispute between faith and non-faith. While the flesh of God's Son lies immured in

---

106. The best introduction to this profound and difficult book is J. B. Webster, *Eberhard Jüngel* (Cambridge and New York: Cambridge University Press, 1986). See also Webster, "Eberhard Jüngel on the Language of Faith," *Modern Theology* 1 (1985): 253-76; "Eberhard Jüngel," in Ford, ed., *Modern Theologians,* vol. 1, pp. 92-106; and Review of *God as the Mystery of the World, SJT* 39.4 (1986): 551-56. See also McGrath, *German Christology,* ch. 8; Küng, *Incarnation of God,* pp. 548ff.; and L. J. O'Donovan, "The Mystery of God as a History of Love," *Theological Studies* 42 (1981): 251-71.

death, the sharpest controversy divides those who see only that God is gone and finished and those who know that in this palpable absence nonetheless God is yet more present, with life-giving resurrecting power. Even so, the God who is present in this absence, whose creative power is at work through the powerlessness of this defeat and death, is no more recognizable to the theist than to the atheist. Faith in God on the day when God is dead is faith of a very different order from the certainties expressed in metaphysics; and it is faith in another God than the distant, immutable, and omnipotent deity of theism, that supreme stranger to suffering and death.[107]

Not only, then, is Easter Saturday the day of mutual contradiction between those who believe in God and those who cannot; it is also the day of shared contradiction for those who believe in the absolute God and those who cannot, by the theology of the Crucified One: faith in the life and power of the God who is dead. To the extent that both these conflicts are occurring *now*, with great intensity, at the end of the modern era, means that today is a cultural "Easter Saturday." And that is the context, where faith hears and opposes both partners in the disputation between theism and atheism, in which theology must work today, and to which the gospel is to be addressed.

Broadly speaking, ours has been an "Easter Saturday" world since the Enlightenment. Present society and culture in the West is the product of that intellectual revolt, ignited by the birth of modern science, which overthrew the authority of God — in all its biblical, credal, and ecclesiastical mediations — and declared the independence of the rational human self. Rehearsing the oft-told tale of this revolution, Jüngel observes that the discoveries of Copernicus and Galileo, which ejected human beings from the center of the universe, induced us ironically to reestablish our place at that very center all the more securely.[108] For we, with our minds, machines, and methods of inquiry, had discovered for ourselves the true shape and movement of the cosmos. Those same masterful resources, unaided by God or revelation, could be applied to every area of

---

107. Though Jüngel is highly critical of "metaphysical theism," which he seeks to replace with a doctrine of God determined by the crucified Christ, he does admit that it contains particles of truth. Theism bears proper witness to the transcendence and otherness of God, as expressed, e.g., in the first part of Jn. 1:18: "no one has ever seen God." But theism fails to go beyond God's unknowability to the good news that in the incarnation God has come close to us, becoming accessible and knowable — as Jn. 1:18 continues: "it is God the only Son, who is close to the Father's heart, who has made him known." See *Mystery*, p. 9. As we shall see below, it is in the light of God's coming to us that Jüngel argues for a view of analogy whereby there is a still greater similarity between God and humanity within a dissimilarity which is great enough.

108. *Mystery*, pp. 14ff.

knowledge. Thus, to calm our insecurities on the edges of the world, we made ourselves the reference point for all reality! This human-centeredness of an uncertain universe was confirmed by Descartes's discovery of the indubitable thinking self: *cogito ergo sum;* and by Kant's discovery of God's incomprehensibility and superfluity, banished from the realm of experience and sense, and thus of knowledge.[109]

All modern problems, anthropological but especially theological, derive, as Jüngel sees them, from this discovery of human autonomy — "this truth . . . received and adopted with a suspicious alacrity," that God is no longer necessary.[110] What was said long ago, that human beings are the measure of all things (Protagoras), now dawns upon the world as self-evidently true. Men and women can understand their world, and more importantly themselves, *by* themselves, without transcendent reference. We "can be human without God."[111] Jüngel, of course, does not endorse the secular inference from this discovery: that because it is possible to live without God it is necessary so to do, and thus be godless;[112] but it is his project to have theology understand, and embrace as its own, the elements of truth in the belief that God is no longer necessary to the world. That would require faith to take atheism seriously as the negation of a false theism, and to acknowledge the partial veracity of its announcement that God is now dead.[113]

There are, of course, many forms of atheism, as Jüngel recognizes. Faith itself, while deriding the fool who says, "there is no God" (Ps. 14:1), knows the questions provoked by God's hiddenness or absence. "'My God, my God, why hast thou forsaken me?' is the most agonizing variant of the biblical question 'Where is God?'"[114] And there has always been the "theodicy question," evoked by "the experience of meaninglessness, absurdity and irreparable injustice."

---

109. *Mystery*, esp. pp. 15, 111ff., 129ff., 193ff.

110. *Mystery*, p. 16. For Descartes himself, in fact, God *was* a necessary being who guaranteed the indisputable existence of the self-conscious ego. But once God was thus *reduced* to being necessary to humanity's sense of certainty, it was a small step to the discovery that we could be certain of ourselves entirely without God as an otherworldly being. God's nonnecessity is thus the conclusion, not the contradiction, of the premise that God is necessary. See *Mystery*, pp. 19ff.

111. *Mystery*, pp. 16, 20.

112. *Mystery*, p. 21.

113. Note Jüngel's comment: "It is not a concern of Christian talk about God to present an apology (defense) over against atheism. The attitude of the Christian faith toward atheism which is preferable . . . would be . . . constant attentiveness to what could be of Christian concern within atheism." *Mystery*, p. 253, n. 15.

114. *Mystery*, pp. 50-51.

That question, cast against God, has taken a specifically modern and ironic form today, when we have in fact deposed God and taken full responsibility for the world upon our own shoulders. "One asks a question about someone whom one no longer knows."[115] And there have been plenty since the Enlightenment whose atheism springs from the presumption that the idea of God is dangerous, a threat to human freedom, a destructive constriction upon our own creative energies and will. Thus Nietzsche defiantly proclaimed, as a fact of European culture — "the most important of recent events" — that "God is dead," murdered by ourselves, so that *Übermensch* or Superman, humanity with its will to power unleashed, might live.[116]

For Jüngel, however, all these forms of atheism, including the perception that God is dangerous to human freedom, are by-products of what is distinctively modern about our culture's unbelief: the discovery that God is simply dispensable to human knowledge and the world's destiny. This "worldly nonnecessity of God"[117] faith itself must recognize.

Jüngel's point is that the theistic God who is necessary, and against whom modern secularity rightly revolts, is a false god who needs to be deposed, is other than the God of faith revealed in the crucified and buried Christ. Nietzsche himself could see that the God of Paul, the God of suffering, weakness, and the cross, is the negation of "God" as humanly conceived — even less tolerable to Nietzsche, but certainly incompatible with the God of metaphysics.[118]

That is the God of pure, impersonal essence,[119] invulnerable and remote, who exercises absolute dominion over the cosmos, and upon whom, theism supposes, the world depends as the coercive, causal explanation of its events and the guarantor of its meaning and destiny. Only static and immutable omnipotence can sustain in being the fluid, perishable world, can supply and uphold its natural laws and preserve it from collapse into purposeless decay and nothingness. Yet, shows Jüngel, for all the power and sovereignty imputed to the Supreme Being, theism's God actually lacks freedom, dignity, and self-determination. A deity necessary to the world is, by the same token, dependent on, conditioned by, grounded in that world — exists not for its own sake but for the sake of that which depends upon it. God is diminished, delimited, and dis-

---

115. *Mystery,* p. 53.

116. See *Mystery,* pp. 63, 146ff., 150ff., 205ff. Note also Feuerbach's contention that the idea of God is now defunct, that theology must be turned into anthropology, and humanity itself into "God." See *Mystery,* esp. pp. 98ff., 141ff., 334ff.

117. *Mystery,* e.g., p. 18.

118. See *Mystery,* pp. ix, 205-6. See Jüngel, "Deus qualem Paulus creavit, Dei negatio," in *Nietzsche-Studien* 1 (1972): 286-96.

119. For Jüngel's critique of the concept of divine "essence," see *Mystery,* pp. 100ff.

honored when labeled "necessary." Instead, acknowledging that the world does not need the "working hypothesis" of the divine as its pseudo-explanation — that it is possible to be *nature* without God, no less than it is to be human — faith must liberate God from demeaning beholdenness to creation. The One whom Christians honor is free, self-determining, unconditioned, groundless, not necessary but "more than necessary" and "interesting for God's own sake."[120]

However, as for Barth, so for Jüngel, God is one who, in freedom, *loves*. This is to say that the God of Christians, truly free and nonnecessary, is not remote and distant like the theists' omnipotent deity of worldly necessity. Rather, this God chooses, through creation, incarnation, crucifixion, and extinction, to be the God of *advent* who comes close, to become — in that foolish weakness which is wiser and more powerful than the world can comprehend — vulnerable, conditioned, and negated. Faith's challenge today is to understand, to make thinkable and speakable, *this* God, while letting go of all past "religious" or metaphysical talk of the absolute, omnipotent deity on which the world depends.[121]

Now while it is a modern discovery, for society and the church, that God is not necessary to the world, for Jüngel it is vital that "the death of God" not be

---

120. See *Mystery,* esp. pp. 21ff., 33ff., 35ff.

121. On the above thoughts, see, e.g., Webster, *Jüngel,* pp. 66-67, and Küng, *Incarnation of God,* pp. 551-52. Note that Jüngel, in addition to referring to the determination of the later Barth to challenge the metaphysical absoluteness of God in the light of God's identity with the crucified Christ (*Mystery,* p. 40), particularly acknowledges his debt to the late, and much celebrated, thoughts of Dietrich Bonhoeffer concerning "religionless Christianity." See *Mystery,* esp. pp. 18f., 57ff.; and D. Bonhoeffer, *Letters and Papers from Prison,* enlarged edition, ed. E. Bethge, trans. R. H. Fuller (London: SCM, 1971 and New York: Macmillan, 1972), esp. pp. 359ff. Bonhoeffer here begins to work out a theological ontology, a doctrine of God's nature, in the light of modern atheism and secularism. Ours is a mature age of human autonomy and worldly independence, in which God is no longer necessary as a hypothesis to account for the existence and workings of the cosmos. Christians, standing "before God," must therefore live *etsi deus non daretur,* "as if God were not a given." This means that secularity is not just pagan disbelief but a cultural development to which God has acceded. For "God lets himself be pushed out of the world on to the cross [and] Christ helps us not by virtue of his omnipotence, but by virtue of his weakness and suffering." *Letters and Papers,* pp. 360-61. The marginalization of God in the modern world, interpreted in the light of the cross, actually reveals God's own vulnerable nature; and God's absence here is a way of being present. The development of this ontology, "which explodes the alternatives of presence and absence" (*Mystery,* p. 62), begun by Bonhoeffer in an embryonic way, could be said to summarize Jüngel's own, more sophisticated objective.

thought of as simply an occurrence in the intellectual evolution of the post-Enlightenment scientific age, "the greatest event of modern history."[122] Although there are sufficient particles of truth in modern atheism for it to be thought faith's "twin" in their shared challenge to the defunct metaphysical tradition,[123] the frequently hostile thrust of today's secularism radically differentiates its antitheological announcement of "the death of God" from the "dark proposition" which Christian faith itself must utter concerning God's death in the light of the cross and grave of Jesus Christ.[124] And when in that light we do proclaim as our own good news "the death of God," we do not in fact pronounce something novel, unprecedented, and fashionably "modern," says Jüngel, but "bring home" a thought which, though long estranged and alien, has actually belonged to theology itself from the beginning.[125]

It is not just that Christians early on were accused of atheism, for preaching a gospel which entailed death for the "gods" of Graeco-Roman culture. Rather, it was always an implicate of the church's own doctrine of the incarnation itself that God had died in the death of the divine Son. However, as we saw, and Jüngel notes, it became quite orthodox, even for such as Athanasius, to recoil from that implication and attribute Christ's suffering and death solely to his human nature, albeit hypostatically united with his divine.[126] Therefore, Jüngel turns to Martin Luther, whose Christology did not so flinch from the meaning of the cross, to show that theology's own "death of God" is not a twentieth-century innovation, but a lost concept now returning home. For Lu-

---

122. *Mystery,* p. 101; cf. p. 44. This is directed not only at the likes of Nietzsche, but also at the "fad" (p. 44) of "the death of God theology" of the 1960s, which Jüngel rightly dismisses as simplistic sloganeering rather than a serious attempt to think through what might be said, by way of positive Christian theology, about "the death of God" in the light of the cross.

123. *Mystery,* p. 102.

124. On theology's own "dark saying of the 'death of God,'" see Jüngel, "Das dunkle Wort vom 'Tode Gottes,'" *Evangelische Kommentare* 2 (1969): 133ff. and 198ff.; also in *Von Zeit zu Zeit* (Münster: Kaiser, 1976), pp. 15ff.; cf. *Mystery,* p. 38. See also Jüngel, "Vom Tod des lebendigen Gottes," *Zeitschrift für Theologie und Kirche* 65 (1968): 93-116; also in Jüngel, *Unterwegs zur Sache* (Munich: Kaiser, 1972), pp. 105-25. The substance of both of these seminal articles is contained in expanded form in *Mystery.*

125. *Mystery,* pp. 55ff.

126. See Ch. 5 above, *passim.* Cf. *Mystery,* pp. 64ff. Jüngel notes that the pre-Nicene Tertullian could say without equivocation that "God was crucified," that "God has died, and yet is alive for ever and ever" (Tertullian, *Adversus Marcionem,* ed. and trans. E. Evans [Oxford: Clarendon Press, 1972], bk. 2, ch. 27, sect. 7 and ch. 16, sect. 3), and that it was not uncommon in medieval mysticism (e.g., Meister Eckhart) to speak of the death of God.

ther, the "exchange of properties" in the Person of Christ required nothing less than that of the crucified Christ, faith should say: "God dead, God's passion, God's blood, God's death"; and linguistic traces of this audacious faithfulness to the divine identity of the dead and buried one remain in the Lutheran hymnodic and confessional inheritance.[127] Hegel, aware of such phraseology in that, his own, tradition, made the concept of "the death of God" pivotal to his own theological and philosophical project. But in this he was, of course, less interested in what occurred on the past, historical Good Friday — "now so long ago as soon to be no longer true,"[128] as in the "speculative Good Friday" where "that special event of long ago has been elevated as a concrete event to the level of a general and enduring truth."[129]

Hegel's thought is that the Idea or Absolute Spirit embraces death and self-negation as a transitional moment in the dialectical process which leads to its self-fulfillment. In this abstract "death of God," the infinite accepts finitude, its frailty, its weakness, its negativity, right up to death itself. But that in turn means the death of death, the negating of the negative, the end of the finite. After self-negation, God is resurrected, everything is reversed, and Life comes to uncontested consummation.[130]

From a biblical point of view, however, Hegel is mistaken here; for it is impossible to distinguish, as the outcome of this radical identity between the infinite and the finite, the humanizing of God from the deifying of humanity.[131]

---

127. See Luther, "On the Councils and the Church" (1539), in *Luther's Works,* American Edition, vol. 41, ed. E. W. Gritsch (Philadelphia: Fortress, 1966); also quoted in the Formula of Concord, the Solid Declaration, Article VIII, *The Book of Concord,* trans. T. G. Tappert (Philadelphia: Fortress, 1959), p. 599. See also the Lutheran Good Friday/Easter Saturday hymn, "O Traurigkeit, O Herzeleid," whose second stanza, by J. Rist (1641), began "O grosse Not! Gott selbst liegt tot" (O great distress, God's very self lies dead). So shocking is this blunt statement of the death of God, however, that Lutherans themselves have tampered with the text, first to make it read, "the Lord is dead," and more recently, "God's Son himself lies dead." See *Mystery,* pp. 64 and 95ff.; "Vom Tod des lebendigen Gottes," pp. 115ff.; and McGrath, *German Christology,* pp. 198, 209, n. 73. See also the Report of the Theological Committee (of which Jüngel was a member) of the *Evangelischen Kirche der Union,* "Understanding the Death of Jesus," *Interpretation* 24 (1970): 139ff., and related papers in the same issue.

128. Hegel, following a Swabian aphorism, quoted in *Mystery,* p. 76. See also Jüngel, "The Effectiveness of Christ Withdrawn," in *Theological Essays,* trans. J. B. Webster (Edinburgh: T. & T. Clark, 1989), pp. 214-31. See, too, Jüngel's extended exposition of "the death of God" in Hegel, in *Mystery,* pp. 63-97.

129. *Mystery,* p. 78.

130. See *Mystery,* esp. pp. 75, 93.

131. *Mystery,* pp. 93-94.

The latter is a contradiction of the gospel, insists Jüngel. In the incarnation and the cross, though God became human to the point of death, the consequence is a clarifying once-for-all of the *difference* between humanity and God. God's willingness to die in solidarity with our death is just what *prevents* humanity from becoming divine — the ultimate idolatry. Rather, the cross releases us from the original sin of wishing to be "Gods" (Gen. 3:5) and liberates us at last to be truly human in our finite creaturehood.[132] Just like Moltmann's, Jüngel's correlation of the cross with God's own life and being is profoundly informed by Hegel's dialectic, yet leads to wholly different conclusions.

The question, then, is how, in completing the "homecoming" to Christian theology and faith of "the death of God," Jüngel can avoid both a Nietzschean, *antitheological use* of the concept and its Hegelian *theological misuse*. How is theology to think and speak truly about "the death of God"? The answer will expose Jüngel's basic starting point as a theologian, and confirm his profound continuity with Karl Barth, whose own starting point we saw Jüngel expound so clearly above.[133] For Jüngel's, too, is a theology of the Word, of revelation, which begins not by positing God's existence as an act of the human mind, but by simply letting God be. There is a presumption here; but it is for Jüngel a "presumable presumption": that God is, and that God is not "speechless," but is to be "taken seriously as one who speaks" in self-revelation.[134] God encounters, addresses, questions us as human persons in "word," inviting us to listen with faithfulness and thoughtfulness, that we might think thoughts "after" God which accord with God's own self-disclosed actuality, thus "interrupting" and "annihilating" our old ways of thinking about deity.[135]

Naturally, the primary event in which this destructive and re-creative Word of God addresses us is the person and history of Jesus Christ, the Word incarnate and crucified. He is himself the ultimate "Word of the cross." But access to that Word lies through the Scriptures, which witness to him with their own "Word of the cross." God's coming near to us in Christ is a "word-event," which gives rise to biblical texts that speak of God, but in human lan-

---

132. See *Mystery,* esp. pp. 94-95; cf. pp. 190, 380ff. In contradistinction from the ultimate identification of the divine and human in Hegel, Jüngel understands the very *proprium* or particular character of the Christian faith to be that in the crucifixion of Jesus, and the unity there of God with humanity, the *distinction* between God and ourselves is established — for the sake of humanity's own authenticity and freedom. See *Mystery,* esp. p. 229; cf. McGrath, *German Christology,* pp. 193, 198ff.; and Webster, *Jüngel,* esp. chs. 5 and 6, and p. 95.

133. See Jüngel, *Trinity,* esp. pp. xixff. and ch. 1.

134. *Mystery,* pp. 160ff.

135. See *Mystery,* pp. 152-69, 175, 246ff.

guage.[136] These texts make it possible for our own words, thoughts, and concepts to be addressed and subverted by God's Word, and thus to be renewed and liberated for the task of thinking humanly about God on God's own terms, that is, as the God identified with the crucified Jesus.

Supreme among the texts that serve this purpose are the New Testament's stories; for the event of God's approach to us in Christ is essentially temporal and historical, extended not momentary, and thus narratable. Only *story* can fully correspond linguistically to *history;* and because of the infinite variety of allusions that a story can make and of the interpretations it can bear, narrative actually gives more and richer meaning to a historical event than was discernible when it occurred. The time surely comes for faith to reflect discursively on the Bible's stories, in ways that lead to concepts and doctrines. But a theology which has made the presumable presumption that God speaks through Christ begins by listening to those stories about him, and above all to the story of his passion, death, and resurrection, toward which all the other stories point. We are not hereby naively restricted, say, to the Synoptic Gospels. Even Paul grounds his doctrine of justification in the narrative of the cross. In effect he uses that story to contradict the Corinthians' postresurrection "theology of glory" with the "dangerous" and iconoclastic word which foolishly proclaims that the only Resurrected One is he who was crucified in suffering and weakness.[137] Like Barth and Moltmann, then, and setting the pattern which we ourselves have followed in this book, Jüngel would have theology first hear and then cogitate upon the story of Christ's death.[138]

---

136. For the notion of "word-event" Jüngel is particularly indebted not only to Barth but also to Ernst Fuchs and Gerhard Ebeling. See, e.g., E. Fuchs, *Marburger Hermeneutik* (Tübingen: J. C. B. Mohr, 1968); G. Ebeling, *Introduction to a Theological Theory of Language,* trans. R. A. Wilson (London: Collins, 1973); *Word and Faith,* trans. J. W. Leitch (London: SCM, 1963), esp. "Word of God and Hermeneutics," pp. 305-32; also "The Word of God and Language," in *The Nature of Faith,* trans. R. Gregor Smith (London: Collins, 1961). Cf. Jüngel, *Mystery,* esp. pp. 9ff., 157ff., 164ff., and "God as a Word in our Language," in F. Herzog, ed., *Theology of the Liberating Word* (Nashville: Abingdon, 1971), pp. 23-45; also Webster, *Jüngel,* pp. 6ff., 11ff., 55ff., and "The Language of Faith," in *Modern Theology,* p. 1.

137. On the above, see *Mystery,* pp. 299-314. Recall, too, our own thoughts about "story" above, considerably indebted to Jüngel. Note, too, the significance acknowledged by Jüngel of the work in this connection by J. B. Metz, especially his renowned article (consistently mistitled in *Mystery*) "A Short Apology of Narrative," in Hauerwas and Jones, *Why Narrative?,* pp. 251-62. See *Mystery,* pp. xi, 302ff.

138. "As with Moltmann, the cross puts everything to the test [for Jüngel], functioning as the foundation and the criterion of responsible Christian discourse concerning God. . . . *Crux probat omnia!*" McGrath, *German Christology,* pp. 202-3.

What the story of the cross requires us to conceive, as a theological necessity, an indispensable thought, is "God's union with perishability."[139] Immediately the conflict between the biblical narrative and the assumptions of metaphysical theism is radicalized; for the metaphysical deity, omnipotent and free of all deficiency, is defined as the opposite of human existence, with its all too great deficiencies and weaknesses. Such a God is therefore supremely immutable, in contrast to human transience, our dustlike frailty, and sinful corruption, our perilous dangling over the canyon between being and non-being, and our final subjection to the grave. So if God and perishability are to be thought together, the imperishable, metaphysically conceived God must die. "Perishability disintegrates [this God]."[140]

Of course, this narrative of the cross concludes in resurrection victory. Spoken in the midst of death's silence and from beyond the grave, "the word of the cross" tells of death's own death. But Jüngel is profoundly aware of the retroactive implications of the resurrection.[141] The empty tomb does not cancel out the cross or the occupied tomb, but rather confirms beyond all earlier doubt that *God* was there, upon that cross and in that tomb. Thus it is precisely Easter Sunday which establishes the shocking story of the Saturday: God's unity with the interred Jesus — "this dead and repulsive man," executed, "scandalously murdered," but above all finished, perished.[142] Here Jüngel goes beyond Barth's thought that in the passion of Christ God is identified with human suffering; and often he echoes Moltmann in interpreting the cross to say that God has here become identified with the crucified, and thus with all who die in godforsakenness and godlessness. But while repeatedly affirming that God is united and identified *with* the dead and buried, perished one,[143] Jüngel also makes shockingly plain his own still more intrepid perception that in this event God's identity is established *as* that of one who died. The cross and grave are — so inconceivable a conception! — loci of divine self-definition. "The being of

139. See *Mystery,* p. 199 and throughout, esp. sect. 13: "God's Unity with Perishability as the Basis for Thinking God."

140. *Mystery,* p. 203.

141. See *Mystery,* pp. 362-63. Jüngel acknowledges here his debt to both Fuchs and Pannenberg (see esp. Ch. 4 above, n. 13), but he is also reproducing the backward movement of Moltmann, from the Risen One to the Crucified One who alone is risen, from "theology of hope" to "the Crucified God." See, too, Jüngel, "Thesen zur Grundlegung der Christologie," in *Unterwegs,* pp. 274-95.

142. E. Jüngel, "What Does it Mean to Say, 'God Is Love'?" in Hart and Thimell, eds., *Christ in our Place,* p. 309. Cf. *Mystery,* e.g., pp. 190, 329, 363; and "Vom Tod des lebendigen Gottes," in *Unterwegs,* pp. 121ff.

143. See, e.g., *Mystery,* pp. 190, 329, 363, 365, 367.

this dead man defines God's own being."[144] Nor is it any more illogical for Jüngel than it was for Moltmann, in his similar case, both to have something new and once-for-all happen to God in this self-defining union with a historical, dead man, and to affirm that God is eternally marked by this union, is always the Creator who brings things into being out of a struggle with nothingness, and enters into death for the sake of life. Only because nothing contrary to the divine being and nature was occurring in this identification with the death and burial of Christ was God able there to confront "the annihilating power of nothingness" without suffering annihilation and self-contradiction.[145]

Nevertheless, a particular *kenosis,* a divine self-emptying, has taken place in the life and death of Jesus Christ, wherein "God's glory subjects itself to perishability for the sake of perishing [humanity]," and whereby God's deity has uniquely been disclosed and defined.[146] God "no longer wishes to be the living God without this dead man."[147] So now it becomes imperative to *think* God through the grave in the light of this identifying with mortality, and so to reconceive God's very being in its unbreakable connectedness with perishing and death.[148] "We can really learn who God actually is only on the basis of this fact. God's life does not exclude death but includes it."[149] All the old metaphysical concepts of God, along with the axioms of absoluteness, apathy, and immutability, "must pass through the eye of the needle of the properly understood concept of the death of God."[150]

Now just as Barth protested, against the old kenoticists, that God's Godness is not lost through self-emptying, but rather fulfilled — that God *remains* God in becoming human, is majestic in that very lowliness — so Jüngel's theme concerning the cross and grave of Christ is that this is the death of the *living* God.[151] God, we have heard Jüngel say, submits to nothingness but is not annihilated or consumed. The struggle God enters between life and death is resolved in life's favor; so while the only Risen One is the Crucified One, it is

144. *Mystery,* pp. 363-64; cf. p. 219.

145. See esp. *Mystery,* pp. 218ff., 225, n. 73; cf. p. 220. See also Fiddes, *Suffering,* pp. 199-200.

146. *Mystery,* p. 191; also pp. 218, n. 64, and 219-20.

147. "What Does it Mean to Say 'God Is Love'?" p. 309.

148. See *Mystery,* e.g., pp. 193, 202; and sect. 13: "God's Unity with Perishability as the Basis for Thinking God."

149. "Das Dunkle Wort vom 'Tode Gottes,'" in *Evangelische Kommentare,* vol. 2, p. 201, quoted in *Mystery,* p. 220, n. 65.

150. *Mystery,* p. 63; cf. p. 373.

151. Again, see his programmatic essay, "Vom Tod des lebendigen Gottes" (On the Death of the Living God).

equally true that the Crucified One — *because* crucified, dead, and surrendered to negation — is raised in victory over negativity and death. In Christ's weakness is the power of God perfected (1 Cor. 1:25ff.; 2 Cor. 12:9; 13:4), and out of nothingness God creates existence (Rom. 4:17). So goes the gospel narrative, and "the word of the cross." The question is whether we can think ontologically about this story of the death of the living God to the point of hazarding a groping answer to the question *how* God conquers death by yielding to perishability.[152]

For Jüngel, the first clue lies in the nature of perishability itself. So governed by Greek assumptions is our theological tradition that we typically attribute only negative connotations to the mortal — to everything touched by time and change and destined to pass away. Only the changeless and eternal is positive and good. Jüngel, however, would free perishability and temporality "from an exclusively negative ontological qualification."[153] For while what is ephemeral and perishable is threatened by non-being, by the tendency to decay away to nothingness, it also participates in being; for though not eternal, the transient does exist, does have life and what Jüngel calls "possibility."

This is the ontologically positive character of perishability.[154] Jüngel's thought is that anything eternal, in the sense of Greek, static changelessness, by definition lacks the possibility of moving forward, of changing, of becoming something new. By contrast, for what is perishable and mutable, it *is* possible to change and become new. When that happens, the perishable does not get lost in the past, but enters the future. In contradiction of the old metaphysics, this makes the perishable, the "becoming," that which struggles between being and non-being, richer, fuller, more pregnant with potential than pure being itself, which is incapable of novelty. "Possibility is the particular distinctive of the perishable . . . understood chiefly as a designation of the future, . . . not . . . as a category of deficiency and defect but rather of capacity and promise."[155]

Of course, this capacity and promise, this openness to newness, is not an inherent power, self-generated by perishable things in their own right. Their very existence is a gift out of nothing, from "the Creator without whom nothing is, no struggle between the capacity of possibility and the undertow toward nothingness. Without God there would be not be any perishability."[156] Moreover, things which "become" and are perishable enjoy their abundant, God-

---

152. See *Mystery,* pp. 209-10.
153. *Mystery,* p. 210.
154. See *Mystery,* p. 213.
155. *Mystery,* pp. 216-17.
156. *Mystery,* p. 218.

given possibilities precisely as they participate in God's own "becoming" (the concept with which Jüngel explicated Barth's ontology of God). As God's raising from the dead of the crucified man with whom God went to death makes plain, God is creative only as the one whose being lies in supreme and infinite becoming, who is not static and atemporal, above the battle, but who enters into the temporal struggle against non-being and so prevails against it.[157] It is God's own limitless abundance of possibility, the divine capacity to flourish and create new life by surrendering to nothingness and death, which grounds the possibility for perishable things to become new too. The victory over death which the resurrection promises us, as perishable creatures, depends wholly upon God's own creativity, which takes on the power of death, draws it into the divine life, and thereby overcomes it. "By making for nothingness a place within divine being, God took away from it [its] chaotic effect. . . . In bearing annihilation . . . God proves . . . victor over nothingness, and . . . ends the negative attraction of 'hell, death and the devil.' . . . God is that one who can bear and does bear, can suffer and does suffer, in [the] divine being, the annihilating power of nothingness, even the negation of death, without being annihilated by it."[158] And to take a little further the question how this can be so, how God is creative by, and only by, absorbing death and negativity, Jüngel, like Moltmann and Barth, fully understands that this is possible not for a monistic deity, but only for the Trinity, the divine community of love.

Having so sympathetically expounded the *Church Dogmatics* from a specifically trinitarian standpoint, Jüngel naturally presupposes and corroborates both the place and the shape which Barth gave to the doctrine of the Trinity. The God who is revealed and self-interpreted through identification with the fleshly, human Jesus is thereby self-differentiated; but equally, in Jüngel's terms, is "self-related," that is, held together as one by the same loving relationships through which the Father, Son, and Spirit are distinct from one another.[159] Moltmann, in fact, accused Jüngel in his early days of following Barth too closely, reproducing the latter's unitarian-Augustinian tendency to conceive God as a single, thrice-repeating Self rather than a genuine community. This meant that Jüngel was interpreting the cross as the death of an undifferentiated

---

157. *Mystery,* p. 218. Cf. "By identifying himself with the dead Jesus, God truly exposed himself to the alienating power of death. He exposed his own divinity to the power of negation. And he did precisely this in order to be God for all men." E. Jüngel, *Death: The Riddle and the Mystery,* trans. I. and U. Nicol (Edinburgh: St. Andrew Press, 1975), p. 109; see also ch. 6: "The Death of Death."

158. *Mystery,* p. 219.

159. See *Mystery,* p. 371, n. 9; cf. Jüngel, *Trinity,* esp. pp. 99ff.

God rather than as a triadic event comprising interactions between the three distinguishable Persons.[160]

However, certainly by the time of *God as the Mystery of the World,* such charges against Jüngel are invalid. Here, viewing the Trinity as a conceptualizing of the statement that "God is Love," Jüngel plainly adopts and enriches a "social" or Cappadocian conception, whereby God's oneness is constituted by the loving relations between the distinct and distinctly ordered Father, Son, and Spirit. And here too, like Moltmann, Jüngel locates the cross as the unique and ultimate point of God's self-disclosure as triune.[161] His interpretation of that occurrence as the event of "the death of God" now maximizes the plurality and openness of the Godhead, and each Person's distinct role and set of relations within the community event that happens to and in God between Good Friday and Easter. Indeed, without this spaciousness and openness within the Trinity, which allows for multiple divine interchange in the death and resurrection of Christ, all the justifying and reconciling purposes of the death of God in the crucified Jesus would be negated. It was "for us," and not for its own sake, that the death of Christ, in his godforsakenness, accursedness, and godlessness, took place; and only the God who is internally open as a community, and not a closed monad, can be open outward also, making space for us, who are not God, to be brought into the divine family, through the death of death and the defeat of all that would exclude us from that fellowship.[162]

Were it not for this question of salvation there would, in fact, be no purpose either, says Jüngel, to the concept of the Trinity itself. Far from being ab-

---

160. See Moltmann, *Crucified God,* pp. 203-4. His critique is particularly directed at Jüngel's article, "Vom Tod des lebendigen Gottes."

161. See *Mystery,* pp. 343, 360ff., and sect. 20: "The God Who Is Love: On the Identity of God and Love." See Webster, *Jüngel,* esp. pp. 71ff.

162. See *Mystery,* e.g., pp. 361ff., 375, 382, 385-86. Note that Jüngel uses virtually the same Synoptic and Pauline texts concerning Christ — "delivered up," "abandoned," "cursed," etc. — as does Moltmann, for his trinitarian interpretation of the cross. On the above, see Webster, *Jüngel,* pp. 74-77. It is hard to accept Webster's criticism that Jüngel lacks a proper soteriology, substituting for the question of salvation that of ontology, of human being. He particularly criticizes Jüngel's reliance on the concept of Christ's vicarious humanity. For Jüngel it is precisely from this Christological standpoint that the questions of salvation and of being are one and the same; for we are redeemed and justified exactly insofar as we are through faith united with Christ in his death and resurrection, and thus able to share ontologically in Christ's own beloved place and loving relations within the Trinity. For the Reformed and evangelical doctrines of grace and of "*Christus solus,*" with which he is inexplicably dissatisfied, Webster would substitute, in an openly Pelagian manner, salvation through our own moral action, independent of the righteousness of Christ. See Webster, esp. pp. 102-3.

stract speculation, as so often alleged, "the doctrine of the Trinity is the dogma of soteriology in an absolute sense." On his reading, the New Testament declares that one denies this dogma, at least in its Christological dimension, at the risk of one's salvation (e.g., 1 Jn. 2:23). Scripture's saving good news is summed up in the story of Jesus Christ presented also as the story of God, which is the story of God's history coming into our history, into our flesh and through our far country to the point of death. This story is epitomized and rendered tellable by the Christian doctrine of the triune God, which "has no other function than to make the story of God so true that it can be told in a responsible way."[163]

The true story which we may responsibly narrate to ourselves and the world may be encapsulated, first, as "the humanity of God," and then, consequent upon the completeness of that humanity, as "the death of God." In the human nature of Jesus Christ, the Creator has come close to us, closer to us than we are to ourselves;[164] for in becoming human, God has shown us the truth of humanness, the way of being fully human, as we never saw or lived it otherwise. Jüngel here extends the later Barth's concept of "the humanity of God," in contrast to Barth's earlier emphasizing of the distance between divine and human being.[165] Barth notoriously criticized the classical, chiefly Roman Catholic, doctrine of "the analogy of being," which postulates continuities between God's being and ours that permit a "natural" knowledge of God's reality drawn from our understanding of ourselves and of our world. That blurs, for Barth, the vast qualitative difference, stressed by Scripture, between ourselves and our Maker, and leads to idolatrous worship of ourselves the creatures, as participants in God's own being (Rom. 1:23, 25).[166]

On the contrary, says Jüngel, the "analogy of being" tends to exaggerate the distance and dissimilarity between God and the world by leaving unknown and undefined the personal identity of the God discovered through experience and observation. Who this God is, is incomprehensible and inexpressible. As formal dogma puts it: "between the Creator and the creature so great a likeness cannot be noted without the necessity of noting a greater dissimilarity between them."[167] On the basis of God's trinitarian coming to humanity in Jesus, Jüngel

163. *Mystery,* p. 344.

164. See *Mystery,* e.g., pp. 182, 298, 300.

165. See on what follows, *Mystery,* sect. 17: "The Problem of Analogous Talk about God"; and sect. 18: "The Gospel as Analogous Talk about God"; also ch. 5: "The Humanity of God as a Story to Be Told."

166. See *Mystery,* p. 282.

167. The Fourth Lateran Council (1215): "*inter creatorem et creaturam non potest tanta similitudo notari, quin inter eos maior sit dissimilitudo notanda.*" H. Denzinger, *Enchiridion Symbolorum* (Barcelona: Herder, 1957), para. 432. See *Mystery,* p. 283; cf. pp. 294, 297.

proposes, instead, an "analogy of advent" which reverses these proportions. Through the incarnation there takes place between God and humanity "the unique, unsurpassable instance of a still greater similarity . . . within a great dissimilarity."[168] In Christ, God is nearer to us than distant from us, more like us than unlike — though still unlike us, to be sure: still God, in and through this humanness. Faith's problem, however, is not that God is so far from us as to be unknowable, but so close to us as to go unrecognized. Still, because God is here among us, near and similar, there is a proper way to think and speak of God in human terms. "There is christological reason to ask whether there is not a God-enabled, a God-required, even a God-demanded anthropomorphism."[169] Such is our freedom, our responsibility indeed, to tell not only the story of "the humanity of God," but also that of "the death of God."

Here the need to tell a *trinitarian* story is all the more acute. For the human life of God which finds its climax in crucifixion and burial is the one "vestige of the Trinity," the only trace or footprint of the divine, the sole earthly sign which illustrates, reveals, and corresponds to the reality and triune identity of the unseen God.[170] In order to be divine, and yet wholly identified with the human, crucified Jesus, God must be capable of clear self-differentiation: "God the Father must be distinguished from God the Son." Yet if God is to remain God in the midst of this distinction, and not collapse into self-contradiction, there must be further distinction yet. "The noncontradictory differentiation of God from God implies the event of God as the Holy Spirit."[171]

Now these self-differentiations, within the abiding wholeness, unity, and self-relatedness of God, become paramount to the conceptualized telling of the story of the cross itself, where "the incarnation of God is . . . taken seriously to the very depths of the harshness of God's abandonment of the Son, who was made sin and the curse for us."[172] In the very cursedness of his death, Jesus is recognized as "truly the Son of God" (Mk. 15:39).[173] Therefore, in this aban-

---

168. *Mystery,* pp. 285-86, 288-89, 294, 298. For a defense of Barth's critique of the analogy of being and the allegation that Jüngel reproduces its errors with his analogy of advent, see Molnar, "Immanent Trinity in Barth," pp. 393ff.

169. *Mystery,* p. 280; cf. pp. 258ff.

170. See *Mystery,* sect. 22: "The Crucified Jesus Christ as 'Vestige of the Trinity.'" The concept of Christ as "vestigium Trinitatis" is very Barthian, given Barth's own anti-Augustinian repudiation of all natural analogies or illustrations of the Trinity; but Jüngel's thought here is much more explicitly cross-centered than Barth's more generally Christological interpretation of the "vestiges." See *CD,* I/1, 333-47.

171. *Mystery,* p. 351.

172. *Mystery,* p. 372.

173. See *Mystery,* p. 362.

donment, Jüngel, like Moltmann, perceives a Godforsakenness of God — a radical separation within God, a rupture in the very relations internal to the life of God's own being as community. No gap is permitted here, any more than by Moltmann, between the economic event of the cross and God's own immanence.[174] Rather, in the death of Christ, where God is both the One who surrenders up the Beloved and that Beloved himself, so surrendered up as to become a dead man, there opens up a "radical antithesis"[175] of infinite proportions. "The divine modes of being, Father and Son, [are] in this death separated into such a great differentiation than which nothing greater can be imagined."[176]

Yet this is not the end of God, in division and self-negation; for it is God's own act, indeed God's act of ultimate self-definition, to surrender up Jesus and be identified with his corpse. And if God brings about this radical self-differentiation between the Father and the Son, then the divine separation and relationlessness in this event cannot destroy God, but is God's own self-expression and fulfillment. God, that is, remains self-related at the extremity of self-distinction. As Moltmann observed, so too Jüngel: in this surrender the Son equally offers up himself, remaining attuned to the Father in his very godforsakenness and hellish isolation. "Pointedly, and yet expressing the heart of the matter, the Johannine Christ says, 'For this reason the Father loves me, because I lay down my life that I may take it again' [Jn. 10:17]. And thus he is the beloved Son who, in the midst of his separation from the Father, relates to him."[177]

Of course, that the Father and the Son hold to each other in mutual love precisely where, for the sake of love, they are radically sundered by death, is the act of the Spirit, that bond or chain of love between the Father and the Son. God's identifying, as the living, resurrecting God, with the dead Jesus expresses and relies upon the triple differentiation of the Father, Son, and Holy Spirit.[178] It is the Spirit, proceeding from the Father and the Son, who both preserves their differentiation and prevents their disintegration. On the basis of Christ's resurrection, those who in death are torn apart by "such a great differentiation

174. See *Mystery,* e.g., pp. 346, 369ff., 372, 375; cf. Jüngel, "Das Verhältnis von 'ökonomischer' und 'immanenter' Trinität." From a staunchly Barthian position, Molnar criticizes Jüngel, as he does Moltmann and others, precisely for closing this gap between the economic and the immanent which, in his opinion, Barth was right to leave open. See Molnar, "Immanent Trinity in Barth," pp. 390ff.

175. *Mystery,* p. 372, n. 11, quoting H. Mühlen, *Die Veränderlichkeit Gottes als Horizont einer zukünftigen Christologie* (Münster: Aschendorff, 1969).

176. *Mystery,* p. 374; cf. p. 362.

177. *Mystery,* p. 328; cf. pp. 368, 372.

178. See *Mystery,* p. 329; cf. pp. 343, 368.

than which nothing greater can be imagined, now so differentiated relate to each other anew in the Holy Spirit." That "Spirit is a third divine relationship, . . . an eternally new relationship of God to God [which] is called, christologically, resurrection from the dead, and is ontologically the being of love itself."[179] Through this Spirit of love the Father is revealed as the one who preserves the Son from the powers of destruction; who awakens the dead; who brings about the new creation; and who says Yes to the world which was judged and put to death with the Crucified Christ.[180]

All of this is to say that it is exclusively as triune — and on an understanding which maximizes the distinctiveness of the Persons in the Trinity and views their unity as maintained by the active love between them — that God can be conceived as surrendering to annihilation without being annihilated. Here, and here alone, in the love of the triune community, is divine possibility: God's "ontological plus,"[181] which Moltmann called the "eschatological surplus," and Paul the "how much more" of grace. In the trinitarian love of God, who has come close to us, lies "the mystery of the world,"[182] the possibility for life in the midst of death, for victory in defeat, for presence in absence and fulfillment through negation; here is the surprise of resumption beyond terminal rupture;[183] and

---

179. *Mystery,* p. 374; cf. p. 388.

180. See *Mystery,* p. 385. Cf. E. Jüngel, "The World as Possibility and Actuality: The Ontology of the Doctrine of Justification," in *Theological Essays,* esp. pp. 108-9. In the light of all the above, it is strange that, like Barth before him, Jüngel should be criticized for weakening the place of the Third Person within the Trinity, reducing the Spirit to an inactive relationship between the Father and the Son, more "a state of affairs" than "a personal agent" (Webster, *Jüngel,* pp. 76-77). In fact, both Barth and Jüngel, stressing the reality and finality of the death of Christ, insist that it takes a radically new act, an act of God alone, to raise Christ and thus resume the interrupted existence of the Son. Certainly for Jüngel, without the *event* and unifying activity of the Spirit (no mere "state of affairs"!), the cross would not represent "the death of the living God," but simply the death, the end, of God. See esp. *Mystery,* sect. 24: "God as Event of the Spirit."

181. *Mystery,* p. 214; cf. p. 298: "What should one call that being which in such great dissimilarity is concerned for the greater similarity, in such great distance is concerned for the still greater nearness, in such great majesty is concerned for the greater condescension, in such great differentness is concerned for the still more intensive relationship? . . . How is that being to be named who counters growing sin with still greater grace (Rom. 5:20)? The answer does not have to be sought. It is both anthropologically and theologically evident and is called *Love.*"

182. See *Mystery,* sect. 25: "The Triune God as the Mystery of the World"; cf. Webster, "Jüngel," in *Modern Theologians,* vol. 1, p. 103.

183. See my article, "The Burial of God: Rupture and Resumption as the Story of Salvation," *SJT* 40.3 (1987): 335-62.

here too — as the Lutheran Jüngel would assuredly add — the good news of justification for the ungodly and the judged.

These mysteries, these impossible possibilities which find realization in us and around us, are all facets of *the* mystery, which is this: that love is weaker than selfishness, but therefore is also more creative. And this mystery is neither some hidden, natural principle on which the universe runs, nor a secret of life unlocked when human ideals and aspirations are attained. Love's mystery is wholly grounded in who *is* the mystery. For however much the world may opaquely manifest love, and human beings, not without ambiguity, receive and give love, only with God may love be identified as such — an identity, for Jüngel, deeply embedded in the Scriptures, supremely the Johannine (especially 1 Jn. 4).[184] Yet even though God *is* love, and as that love, perfectly creative, there are of necessity creaturely analogies to love as divinely defined: God's creative love "needs neither continuation nor perfecting, but it does need human correspondence."[185]

Even when love is only a human correspondence to its divine source, it surpasses nonlove in creativity, we said, exactly through its greater weakness. Love's power *is* its weakness; frail, selfless surrender to the other is the way it flourishes and thrives.[186] "Love carries death within itself" and is "absolutely weak. . . . And yet it is so strong"; for thus are life and death united "in favor of life." The one who dies to self in love is all the more fully alive, and "one thinks

184. See *Mystery,* pp. 325ff.

185. *Mystery,* p. 323, n. 19. Such correspondence is the basis, for Jüngel (as for Barth), of all theological anthropology, the Christian doctrine of the image of God in humanity. See Jüngel, "Humanity in Correspondence to God," in *Theological Essays,* pp. 124-53. On the difference between God's perfect love and human love in its limitations, see "What Does It Mean to Say 'God Is Love'?" esp. p. 309. This article usefully summarizes all that Jüngel says about 'God is Love' at greater length in *Mystery.* Jüngel recognizes the great difference between divine and human love; asserts that only God *is* love and that only God's love can truly overcome lovelessness; and is clearly aware that the human correspondences to God's love, though "needed" by the Creator who loves humanity, are *only* correspondences. In the light of all this, it is strange indeed that Jüngel should be accused of doing a kind of natural theology, offering a phenomenological definition of love which understands God's love in the light of the human experience of love. See Molnar, "Immanent Trinity in Barth," pp. 390-99. How is it possible, given all that Jüngel does to establish the priority of divine love over the human, to accuse him of precisely the reverse priority (p. 398)? Within the priority of God's love, both the indicatives and the imperatives of Scripture do, of course, establish that love is a possibility among human beings, and especially in the church. Molnar's apparent ban on the theological recognition of that possibility would not only silence Jüngel, but — more importantly — excise 1 Corinthians 13!

186. *Mystery,* pp. 319ff., 325ff.

that one has death behind one when one loves."[187] Even in the human arena, then, there is a more abundant resurrection to be won through yielding to the grave.

Though only God's love can fully triumph in such a situation,[188] wherever selfless love meets, not with reciprocating love but with unloving resistance or loveless rejection, there the occasions for love's patience, forgiveness, and self-forgetfulness are simply multiplied; and the floodgates for love's overflow are opened all the wider. To paraphrase Paul (Rom. 5:20), where hate increases, love abounds all the more. Selfishness, by contrast, empties, exhausts, destroys itself — its self-preserving the rejection of self-denial's life-giving creativity and plenitude.

Not only does love's weakness, with inexhaustible strength, overcome its opposite, and triumph through that opposition; the lover's own selfhood is itself affirmed and realized in its very self-negation. Selflessness is neither self-hatred nor self-destruction, but the proper way to wholeness, fulfillment, self-relatedness. I who love give myself away; but in so doing I find myself again, receiving my "self" back in a new and fuller way.[189] Now I am more truly and securely "I" than before I died to self in love; for I have learned to "be," without "having," have learned that in giving up what I have I am free simply to be, to love with truthfulness and realism without the illusions that possessions conjure up.[190] As Scripture promises (Mt. 10:39), "those who lose their lives shall find them." This great mystery of love, Jüngel sums up "as the event of a still greater selflessness within a great and justifiably very great self-relatedness."[191]

We say again that only God *is* love; only God's triune love triumphs and fulfills itself on behalf of the lost and broken, the unlovely and ungodly, and against the world's evil, sin, and death. This God does, precisely by entering into our brokenness and lostness, our lovelessness and godlessness, and by deferring to the powers of darkness. In short, it is true of God before it is true of us, and can only become true for us because it is also and antecedently true for God,

187. *Mystery,* pp. 325-26.
188. See *Mystery,* pp. 329-30; also "What Does It Mean to Say 'God Is Love'?" pp. 309-10. Jüngel here follows Barth. See *CD,* II/1, 278-79.
189. See *Mystery,* pp. 321ff.
190. See *Mystery,* pp. x, 318ff., 321, 379, 390ff., 395-96.
191. *Mystery,* p. 317; cf. p. 391: "the event of love is the most intensive event of self-withdrawal and of new and creative self-relatedness." Note Jüngel's comment that the attempt to love in great selflessness, without concern for self-relation, is akin to "moral castration," while the attempt to love in great self-regard, without concern for selflessness, betokens "moral rape" (p. 319).

that "one who loses life shall find it." Jüngel's great insight, and in effect the central thesis of the present book, is that this promise, from the lips of Jesus, is a true statement about God.[192] *God is the one who knows how to die and knows that in accepting death there is life, and life only through accepting death.* In the Father's surrender of the Son, and the Son's raising by the Spirit, God brings about this life-through-death, this resumption beyond rupture, in self-fulfillment and for the sake of the world.

The closer we have edged to the thinkable thought of "the death of God," the clearer has become the mystery, already disclosed in the narrative of the cross and grave, that God lives, expands, and triumphs through that withdrawal and defeat which is self-surrender unto death. Indeed, says Jüngel, such is the ontology of the triune community that "God is . . . the event of self-surrender itself." That self-abandonment, sustaining opposition and negation through sin's increase, is, in its very impotence, what releases the more abundant increase still of grace, the heightening overflow of divine being which is more present than absent in the midst of godforsakenness and godlessness, which outflanks sin, leaves hate exhausted, and secures the death of death, the negation of non-being.[193]

With this, after tracing some key steps in the development of Christian doctrine from the Bible until now, we have come to and are ready to embrace, perhaps, a thought first triggered by simply listening to a three-day narrative. The thought is still stunning; but is it not now a thinkable thought, one grounded in the Scriptures and expressing good news for the world of life's abundance over the magnitude of evil, sin, and death? It is the thought that on Easter Saturday, in the tomb of Jesus of Nazareth between his crucifying and his raising, God lay dead.

✳   ✳   ✳

To that mystery we must add a closing and prospective reminder that, for Jüngel, the thought of the death of the still living God is a conceptual commentary specifically upon 'justification by grace,' that doctrine by which, for Lutherans, the church herself[?] stands or falls.[194] To say that in dying God lives, so that we who

192. See *Mystery,* p. 368.
193. See *Mystery,* pp. 368-69; cf. Jüngel, *Trinity,* pp. 107-8.
194. For Jüngel's understanding of justification, see *Mystery,* pp. 41-42, 197, 225, n. 73, 231, 307, 339, 343, n. 45, 375, n. 3; also "The World as Possibility and Actuality: The Ontology of the Doctrine of Justification." For his interpretation of Paul's teaching on this theme, see E. Jüngel, *Paulus und Jesus* (Tübingen: J. C. B. Mohr, 1964), sect. B; and on Luther's, E. Jüngel, *The Freedom of a Christian: Luther's Significance for Contemporary Theol-*

die may also live, is to identify the God of Jesus Christ as one who forgives sinners, justifies the ungodly (Rom. 4:5), and promises freedom and life to those held captive by guilt, death, and the demonic. The being of the Trinity, as that community which takes on death and overcomes it in the overflow of love, is the ontological basis of justification, the ground of new, divine possibilities for the sick and sinful, the dying and the dead. In justification we hear God's Yes and we become what we hear, are redefined by the gospel's "word of the cross," which pronounces us forgiven and renewed; but that is the same creative Word by which God raised the crucified Jesus from the grave and has from the beginning summoned existence out of nothing. It is a word not abstractly spoken at a distance, in a vacuum of uninvolvement, but a Word embodied in a fleshly act of divine identity with the godforsaken, the judged, and the dead themselves.

However, this characteristically Lutheran link between the cross and justification arouses, in some Calvinist and Reformed minds, suspicions not wholly groundless, that Jüngel gives too inward and personal a reference to the ultimate significance of "the death of God." Though he speaks of "the mystery of the world," he seems to some, including Moltmann, more intent upon God's relation to the individual than to the world.[195] This is somewhat unfair, for Reformed theology knows, and both Moltmann and Barth have demonstrated, that "justification" need not be individualistic, but embraces all creation from origin to goal.[196] Equally, Jüngel himself consciously indicates the social and

---

ogy, trans. R. A. Harrisville (Minneapolis: Augsburg, 1986). See also Webster, *Jüngel,* pp. 91-92 and ch. 8.

195. See, e.g., Webster, *Jüngel,* pp. 99-100; Gunton, *Promise,* pp. 28, 122-23, 125-26; and Moltmann, *Crucified God,* p. 217. Moltmann's critique here pertains in particular to Jüngel's theology of death (see esp. Jüngel, *Death,* chs. 5 and 6), in which God's identity with the dead Jesus is merely what gives the individual "a tranquil ability to die" with confidence that death's curse has been abolished rather than the gospel's eschatological hope — whose terms must include the sociopolitical — for the dark and deadly processes of the world as such, "the absurdity of existence." In fact, however, Jüngel himself draws attention to the thisworldly and sociopolitical dimension of the Christian understanding of death (see *Death,* pp. 124ff.). And far from giving tranquil hope to individuals, he actually offers a potentially disturbing interpretation of the resurrection. That does *not* promise the survival of the individual, or "continuation of human existence" beyond death (*Death,* p. 119), but is the event whereby the earthly life lived is "eternalized" and "gathered into community" (p. 121). So far from tranquilizing was this to some readers, it seems, that Jüngel was required in *God as the Mystery of the World* to clarify his confidence that Christian eschatology does promise a *personal* future. It was a misunderstanding "that the eternalizing of a lived life meant the setting aside of my person as the subject of my life" (p. 215, n. 58).

196. See, e.g., Barth, *CD,* III/1, 366-414: "Creation as Justification"; and Moltmann, *Future of Creation,* ch. 10: "Justification as New Creation."

political consequences of God's justifying Yes to the poor, the outcast, the inno-cent victim of the murderer.[197] And while he insists against Moltmann on the priority of faith over hope, and emphasizes the "already" over the "not yet" of evil's defeat secured in the raising of the Crucified, he is alert to the universal and eschatological scale of the death of death.[198] There really is hope for the *world* contained in the resumption of possibilities beyond history's caesura in the first and every "Easter Saturday."

How could Jüngel be wrong, in any case, to draw personal inferences from the death of God in Jesus Christ? For all of us are individuals born dying, afflicted with pain, suffering, and tragedy at some intensity of anguish or an-other; and whether we acknowledge it or not, we possess no personal guarantee of enjoying humanity's allotted three score years and ten. How we die, how we live with death, and how we live as though dead and dying (Rom. 14:8; 2 Cor. 6:9; Col. 3:3) are questions above all to be asked in the light of the now think-able story of "the death of God." And at the question how that story may be personally lived, we shall finally arrive. First, though, avoiding any precedence, such as Jüngel sometimes gives, to the individual over the communal and so-cial, we shall ask what it means to live this story in a world that is threatened with death and whose history is captive still to evil and injustice; and what it could mean for the church truly to carry the cross of the crucified God and be, in the dying world, the Body of the Christ in whom the death of God occurred.

197. See, e.g., *Mystery,* pp. xi, 330, 343, 392. See also *Freedom of a Christian,* e.g., pp. 73, 82ff.

198. See, e.g., *Mystery,* pp. 215, 392ff.

PART THREE

LIVING THE STORY

CHAPTER EIGHT

Living the Story in World History

I. Easter Saturday Revisited:
Auschwitz, Hiroshima, Chernobyl

Not the least sobering implication of the triduan story we have now both heard and thought is that the Christian gospel requires of those who live by it unflinching discrimination between hope and optimism. For if our narrative encouragingly promises that at work within us and around us are energies greater than the powers of death and evil which menace and destroy life and empty it of meaning, purpose, and justice, still the story gravely identifies those energies with the wispy, intangible defenselessness of love. And love's power is actually powerless to impede huge triumphs of egregious evil and unrighteousness in the world. Only through vulnerable victimization at the hands of sin and death, and not by blocking, crushing, or annihilating those agents of destruction, does the triune God of righteous love flourish yet more abundantly than the luxuriant barrenness of hate and wickedness.

To hope, therefore, in love as tomorrow's guarantor, as even more creative and enduring than the great destructiveness of lovelessness, is itself to banish shallow optimism for the future of the world. Hope itself embraces the proposition that evil may increase, death have its day of triumph, and history be terminated. Certainly any sunny supposition that the world cannot be lost, nor death be finally victorious, that evil at worst is inept and its successes provisional and passing, is cancelled by a darker hope, grounded in Easter Saturday, which confesses that the only victory of life is won by going beyond, not by thwarting or reducing, the expansive magnitude of death and the surd real-

261

ity of its ascendancy. Faith's assurance of the final consummation of the cosmos does not preclude but makes space of fearsome amplitude for the future loss of history, just as the Son of God's third-day resurrection did not forestall ahead of time, nor cancel retroactively, the end of himself and of the world upon the second day.

Can Christians actually live with so double-edged a narrative, and if so, how? *How* can we sustain an identity shaped by this story which contains within itself such vestiges of despair and fear — at the awful possibility of the loss of everything — as the necessary implication of its promise of the world's salvation through God's ever-so-fragile triune love? We are cast here, theologically, in the realm of theodicy, where questions hang over our faith in providence, our understanding of divine omnipotence, our trust in God's saving Lordship over history; but those queries confront us not as an intellectual conundrum, nor as a speculative teasing of belief, but rather as a crucial test of Christian existence. What does it mean actually to live with the story and the thought of history's termination, in the midst of hope for its deliverance? And how do our memories and nightmares mold Christian lifestyle — our behavior, postures, and relationships — including those with the past and potential victims of that termination whose happenedness or possibility lurks so darkly within hope's great vision of redemption?

Much has happened since the first Easter Saturday to dull the keenness of the questions facing Christian faith and life concerning history and its future. There was, to be sure, for the first generations of believers every reason to distinguish hope from optimism. Though the Day of the Lord, coming like a thief in the night, seemed imminent (1 Thess. 5:1ff.), bringing apocalyptic consummation of the resurrection's proleptic victory over death and the demonic, no such universalizing of Easter's triumph could be expected without reenactments also of Good Friday and Easter Saturday. It was only in the midst of suffering and persecution (Rom. 5:3-5; 2 Cor. 12:10; 1 Pet. 1:6-7), of tribulation and unbridled conflict with God's darkest, deadliest foes (2 Thess. 2:3ff., Rev. 12, and throughout) that faith could anticipate ultimate release from the powers of evil and vindicate its trust in the seemingly weak and powerless cross and death of the lamb that had been slain (Rev. 5:12ff.). If Pontius Pilate's easy prey was indeed to conquer the Babylonian tyranny of the Roman Caesars, that prospect was no instant analgesic but a sobering demand for courage, patience, and endurance (Rom. 8:18-25; 1 Thess. 5:6ff.; 2 Thess. 1:4ff.), through a painful interim of fellowship with Christ's sufferings and concrete identification with him in his own persecution and extermination (Phil. 3:10-11). Thus eager, expectant Christian hope for the apocalypse, when death would be swallowed up by life (2 Cor. 5:4; Rev. 21:4), simultaneously demanded a lifestyle marked by vulnerability, fiery ordeal, resistance and faithful witness unto death (Rom. 8:17; Phil. 1:20ff.; 1 Pet. 4:12ff.; 5:8ff.; Rev. 2:10).[1]

The era of widespread Christian tribulation and martyrdom came to an end, of course, and without the arrival of that Day of the Lord whose expectation had both motivated and rendered endurable so much pain and sacrifice in conformity to the crucified and buried Christ. By stages the delay of the Parousia, the halt to persecution, and above all the official Christianizing of the Roman Empire — though in its own way a fulfillment of Revelation's promises of victory over Caesar — made the church more comfortable in the world and indeed optimistic about its future. History seemed less and less at hazard to the ascendancy of evil; its linear, unimpeded movement toward the triumph of the good and godly much more certain. Jettisoning messianic, apocalyptic, and millenarian expectations,[2] Augustine especially was able to construct a theology of history which gathered all events, whether viewed by their narrators and interpreters as sacred or profane, into a singular, homogeneous, uninterrupted movement toward its guaranteed, eschatological finale. There the terrestrial city, sinful, proud, senescent, would necessarily yield sway to the heavenly and eternal and to the divine, uncontested rule of history's Lord.[3] Though the very intermingling in the present era of the earthly city and the City of God meant that Christians still had to wrestle with evil, sin, and death, the assured penultimacy of those realities encouraged in the church a confidence about the impregnable future that for a thousand years or more often bordered on the complacent or triumphalistic, in contrast to its early embrace of cruciform suffering and death. At times such confidence was interrupted by eras and movements of renewed millenarianism and expectations of apocalyptic struggle for eschatological mastery between the divine and the demonic.[4]

---

1. An outstanding contribution to the recovery of an apocalyptic interpretation of Paul's theology and outlook has been made by J. Christiaan Beker. See esp. his *Paul the Apostle: The Triumph of God in Life and Thought* (Philadelphia: Fortress, 1980) and *Paul's Apocalyptic Gospel* (Philadelphia: Fortress, 1982).

2. On the varieties of millenarianism or chiliasm — eschatological prophecies based on the thousand-year reign of Christ referred to at Rev. 20:4 — see, e.g., A. A. Hoekema, *The Bible and the Future* (Grand Rapids: Eerdmans, 1979), ch. 14; and S. J. Grenz, *The Millennial Maze* (Downers Grove, Ill.: InterVarsity Press, 1992).

3. See esp. K. Löwith, *Meaning in History* (Chicago and London: University of Chicago Press, 1957), pp. 166ff.; R. A. Markus, *Saeculum: History and Society in the Theology of Augustine* (Cambridge: Cambridge University Press, 1970); and C. N. Cochrane, *Christianity and Classical Culture: A Study of Thought and Action from Augustus to Augustine* (London and New York: Oxford University Press, 1944), esp. ch. 12.

4. One such phenomenon, within the "Roman" world, was Joachimism, inspired by

When, however, between the Renaissance and the Enlightenment, Europe threw off its faith in God as the omnipotent, guiding, and saving hand in human and natural events, the autonomous view of history which ensued was unmistakably a secularized version of Augustine's biblical optimism: a belief in progress, the certain triumph of humanity's own power, creativity, and knowledge over all of nature's defects and history's impediments.[5] Subsequent events, philosophies, and ideologies produced two competing visions — the capitalist and the Marxist — of history's secular utopia, its nature, and the means for its achievement — a competition suddenly, though not unambiguously, resolved in our own day, as we shall recall below. And the view of history which has prevailed in the supposed triumph of liberal democracy, itself a secularized version of the Christian drama shorn of apocalyptic crisis, was in turn, in the nineteenth century, rebaptized into Christianity, as a sanguine belief in history and humanity's progressive amelioration. The Liberals of that age, epitomizing "modern" theology, reduced the significance of the Christ-event to the inspirations of a benign, noneschatological founder of a bourgeois, thisworldly kingdom, whose substance would be "the Fatherhood of God and the Brotherhood of Man," and was as such the apotheosis of humane morality and confidence in social betterment.[6]

---

the messianic and pentecostal prophecies of Joachim of Fiore (ca. 1135-1202), whose chiliasm conflicted with Augustinian eschatology and was in turn disputed by Thomas Aquinas. See, e.g., Moltmann, *Trinity and Kingdom,* pp. 203ff.; and Moltmann, *The Spirit of Life,* trans. M. Kohl (London: SCM and Minneapolis: Augsburg Fortress, 1992), pp. 295ff.; also Moltmann, *History and the Triune God* (New York: Crossroad, 1992), pp. 95ff.: "Christian Hope — Messianic or Transcendent?: A Theological Conversation with Joachim of Fiore and Thomas Aquinas." See, too, Löwith, *Meaning in History,* ch. 8; and J. Pelikan, *The Christian Tradition,* vol. 3: *The Growth of Medieval Theology (600-1300 A.D.)* (Chicago and London: University of Chicago Press, 1978), pp. 301-3.

Of course, the Reformation itself was accompanied by and partly predicated on, not least in the mind of Luther himself, the conviction that the Last Judgment had begun, so that history was in its last days, storm-tossed by the terminal conflict between God and Antichrist. See esp. H. Oberman, *Luther: Man between God and the Devil,* trans. E. Wolliser-Schwarzbart (New Haven and London: Yale University Press, 1990 and New York and London: Doubleday, 1992).

5. For accounts of the birth of "progress" and its connections to Christian eschatology, see, e.g., Löwith, *Meaning in History,* ch. 4, "Progress versus Providence"; C. Becker, *The Heavenly City of the Eighteenth-Century Philosophers* (New Haven and London: Yale University Press, 1937); R. G. Collingwood, *The Idea of History* (Oxford: Oxford University Press, 1946); J. Baillie, *The Belief in Progress* (London: Oxford University Press, 1950); and C. Lasch, *The True and Only Heaven: Progress and Its Critics* (New York and London: W. W. Norton and Co., 1991).

6. See esp. Albrecht Ritschl and Adolf von Harnack, along with the long series of

A century later, from the sad vantage point of "postmodernity," how naïve, how alien, how antiquated seems such innocent confidence in the limitless improvability of society and human nature. And how bitter our all-too-knowing disillusionment and rank despair. Our own age, too, has had its brief moments of pride and confidence, bordering on hubris, concerning humanity's capacity, applying "the white heat of technological revolution" (Harold Wilson), to control its own environment and destiny, and shape history to universally benign, just, and prosperous ends. But much more frequently, and with greater justification, we have come to see modern technology as a Sorcerer's

---

contributors to the Quest for the Historical Jesus — a quest dramatically and despairingly concluded by Albert Schweitzer, who, in company with Johannes Weiss (*Jesus' Proclamation of the Kingdom of God*) and M. Kähler (*The So-Called Historical Jesus and the Historic, Biblical Christ*), realized that Jesus of Nazareth was no nineteenth-century bourgeois liberal but a strange, unrecoverable first-century apocalyptic prophet, whose expectations of the end of the world were not only falsified by history, despite his own terminal efforts to trigger its occurrence, but rendered him largely irrelevant to the progressive, scientific, world-affirming culture of modern Europe. See esp. A. Ritschl, *The Christian Doctrine of Justification and Reconciliation*, vol. 3, trans. H. R. Mackintosh and A. B. Macaulay (Edinburgh: T. & T. Clark, 1900); A. von Harnack, *What Is Christianity?*, trans. T. B. Saunders (London: E. Benn Ltd., 1958); A. Schweitzer, *The Quest of the Historical Jesus* (New York: Macmillan, 1968); C. Welch, *Protestant Thought in the Nineteenth Century*, vol. 2 (New Haven and London: Yale University Press, 1985); B. M. G. Reardon, *Religious Thought in the Nineteenth Century* (Cambridge: Cambridge University Press, 1966); A. I. C. Heron, *A Century of Protestant Thought* (Guildford: Lutterworth and Philadelphia: Westminster, 1980); D. W. Lotz, *Ritschl and Luther* (Nashville: Abingdon, 1974); J. Richmond, *Ritschl: A Reappraisal* (London: Collins, 1978); M. Rumscheidt, ed., *Adolf Von Harnack: Liberal Theology at Its Height* (Minneapolis: Fortress, 1991); W. Willis, ed., *The Kingdom of God in Twentieth Century Interpretation* (Peabody, Mass.: Hendrickson, 1987), esp. ch. 1.

Nineteenth-century Liberal optimism survived well into the early decades of the twentieh century in the United States, as evidenced supremely by the "social gospel" movement associated with W. Rauschenbusch. See esp. H. R. Niebuhr, *The Kingdom of God in America* (Chicago: Willett, Clark and Co., 1937).

Though himself a critic of Ritschlian Liberalism for its assumption that there is some kernel of absolute truth in Christianity, Ernst Troeltsch, the founder of "historicism" or the "History of Religions school," who proposed the relativity of every historical religion, also retained vestiges of a Hegelian optimism that history as a whole, being the embodiment of the Absolute Spirit, is moving toward a universal consummation. That came to be discredited in the aftermath of World War I no less than the Liberalism he himself repudiated. The case can be made that by its contemptuous silence about Troeltsch, Karl Barth's seismic *Commentary on Romans* seeks to dispose of the historicist mode of optimism no less than of the liberal. See E. Troeltsch, *The Absoluteness of Christianity*, trans. D. Reid (Richmond, Va.: John Knox Press, 1971); also H.-G. Drescher, *Ernst Troeltsch: His Life and Work* (Minneapolis: Fortress, 1993); and Welch, *Protestant Thought*, vol. 2.

Apprentice: a powerful and complex mechanism unstoppably unleashed upon the world, abetting the worst of human inhumanity and quite possibly threatening our whole existence and our globe's.

In truth the seeds which led to the collapse of scientific optimism into despair and resignation had been germinating from the very inception of the modern myth of progress. For once the eighteenth century finally prised off from the rudder of history the allegedly oppressive hand of a divine creator and redeemer, and declared humanity capable and free to channel its own course toward history's heavenly harbor, it was a small step to the conclusion that history in fact had no rudder and was destined for no harbor, only storms and chaos. That is, the exchange of "salvation history," governed by the providence of a powerful, transcendent but personal God acting in and through temporal events, for a secular history directed by autonomous, enlightened human beings toward a wholly immanent end, itself aided in and prepared for the birth of modern atheism, and its perception that history has no end *(telos)* at all and humanity no power to give it meaning. This loss of teleology, of faith in the purposefulness of historical events as constituting at least a tentative and syncopated advance toward a fitting, rational goal, is for some *the* distinguishing mark of post-Enlightenment Western culture.[7] And it is no comfort whatever, amid society's postmodern pessimism, for Christians to know that some of their own theologians had in the Enlightenment spurred the modern, atheistic loss of teleology by themselves consciously abandoning the question of God's reality to deistic philosophy. That severed the Christian God from Christ and reduced the God of history to a mere impersonal designer and animator of the cosmic mechanism, who promptly became a disposable hypothesis, in favor of a self-generated, self-energizing cosmos going nowhere.[8] So it was that the huge — though by modern standards of catastrophe relatively minor — Lisbon earthquake of 1755, by its evident disproof of God's power or love or both, was enough to topple many European intellectuals of the time from superficial deistic optimism into forthright atheistic despair.

7. See, e.g., L. Newbigin, *The Other Side of 1984,* and *The Gospel in a Pluralist Society* (Grand Rapids: Eerdmans, 1990).

8. The story of this self-alienation whereby Christian theology, embracing a reductive deism, laid the foundations for the modern denial of God, is told with devastating force and magisterial erudition in M. J. Buckley, *At the Origins of Modern Atheism* (New Haven and London: Yale University Press, 1987). See also Löwith, *Meaning in History;* E. Cassirer, *The Philosophy of the Enlightenment,* trans. F. C. A. Koelln and J. P. Pellegrove (Princeton: Princeton University Press, 1951); P. Gay, *The Enlightenment: An Interpretation — The Rise of Modern Paganism* (New York: A. A. Knopf, 1966); and P. Masteron, *Atheism and Alienation* (Harmondsworth: Penguin Books, 1973).

It was, however, the unspeakable carnage of the so-called Great War which decisively punctured the bubble of historical optimism. That vast slaughter subverted both natural and Christian faith in humanity's moral and spiritual resources for cultural and social advance. In the gas-filled, blood-soaked trenches of the Somme and Passchendaele there expired not only the flower of Europe's youth and the bonds of civilized coexistence between its diverse nations, but also the continent's shared, sustaining myth of progress. On some accounting it was now, and no later, that modernity itself came to an end and with it the dream of technological utopia.[9] For it was precisely by harnessing science and its brutal artifacts that humanity perpetrated such demonic self-immolation of body, mind, and spirit. The crater left upon the path to progress seemed to allow no movement ahead nor to the rear. An "end of the world" had occurred. "It is almost impossible even now to describe what actually happened in Europe on August 4, 1914. The days before and the days after the first World War are separated not like the end of an old and the beginning of a new period, but like the day before and the day after an explosion. . . . The first explosion seems to have touched off a chain reaction in which we have been caught ever since and which nobody seems able to stop. . . . [Thereafter] every event had the finality of a last judgment, a judgment that was passed neither by God nor by the devil, but looked rather like the expression of some unredeemably stupid fatality."[10]

The war's *sequellae* of geographic dislocation, of cultural homelessness, of soaring unemployment and inflation, of civil strife and eventual tyranny and genocide: all this would confirm that a new Easter Saturday had occurred, a termination endured when simultaneously humanity's humanness and God's Godness were thrown into radical questionableness. With the ingenuity of its science and the idealism of its spirit badly discredited, humanity's incapacity for self-salvation was cruelly exposed, and the absence of a divine savior rendered all the more obvious and bitter.

To such suffering, disillusion, and despair, the poets, authors, artists, and filmmakers of Europe then and since have given ample, bleak articulation.[11] And,

---

9. See, e.g., H. Arendt, *The Human Condition* (Chicago and London: University of Chicago Press, 1958), p. 6.

10. H. Arendt, *The Origins of Totalitarianism,* new ed. (San Diego and London: Harcourt Brace Jovanovich, 1973), p. 267; cf. p. 478.

11. See, from many examples, G. A. Studdert-Kennedy, *The Hardest Part* (London, 1918); *The Collected Poems of Wilfred Owen,* ed. C. Day Lewis (London: Chatto and Windus, 1963); Robert Graves, *Goodbye to All That,* rev. ed. (London: Cassell, 1957); E. M. Remarque, *All Quiet on the Western Front* (New York: Little, Brown and Co., 1929); A. Solzhenitsyn, *August 1914,* trans. M. Glenny (New York: Farrar, Straus and Giroux, 1972); also the movie "O What a Lovely War!" directed by Sir Richard Attenborough.

of course, theology offered its own response to the almost wholesale rupture which "the war to end all wars" inflicted on liberal Christian optimism. A new epoch of "crisis" (i.e., judgment) and of "dialectic," inaugurated by the seismic second edition of Karl Barth's *Commentary on Romans,* disdainfully dismissed the humanistic pieties of liberalism. A gospel was discovered in Luther and in Paul which addressed God's judgmental, ruthless No to every enterprise predicated on humanity's own moral or religious possibilities — as the necessary precondition for faithful hearing of God's abounding Yes of grace, courage, and forgiveness. And in the swiftest, most ironic reversal of doctrinal history, Barth and his allies in the 1920s wholly reformed and resurrected European theology beyond its postwar ruination precisely on the basis of God's own transcendent, eschatological reign, whose proclamation had made Jesus of Nazareth seem utterly alien and inconsequential to the *fin de siècle* generation which had so recently still believed in humanity's own advance to immanent consummation.[12]

Though Barth's revolutionary theology changed the content and tone of the church's thinking eventually far beyond the German-speaking world, it of course did nothing to halt the twentieth-century's Gadarene descent from early promise into chaos, catastrophe, and eventual *cacotopia,* a veritable demonic terminus. To a second global conflict have been added other local wars, more contained but scarcely less bloody, in the Middle East and Asia, from Central America to Southern Africa to the Persian Gulf; genocidal blood has stained the hands of Turks and Soviets, Germans and Cambodians, Serbians and Iraqis; monstrous tyrants have stamped their vicious seal upon our century — Hitler, Stalin, Pol Pot, Idi Amin; and human life and dignity have repeatedly been crushed, from the Warsaw ghetto to El Salvador, from the Gulag Archipelago to Tiananmen Square. Amid all these falsifications of present complacence and future optimism have three events especially not intensified our fear of the end

---

12. See esp. K. Barth, *The Epistle to the Romans,* 6th ed., trans. E. C. Hoskyns (Oxford and New York: Oxford University Press, 1933). Barth, once a student and convinced follower of Harnack, was particularly shocked and disillusioned by the prominent role which his teacher and many other leading German intellectuals played in support of the Kaiser's declaration of war in 1914. See Barth, "The Humanity of God," 1956; also E. Busch, *Karl Barth,* trans. J. Bowden (London: SCM and Philadelphia: Fortress, 1976), pp. 81ff.; cf. H. M. Rumscheidt, ed., *Revelation and Theology: An Analysis of the Barth-Harnack Correspondence, 1923* (Cambridge: Cambridge University Press, 1972); T. F. Torrance, *Karl Barth: An Introduction to His Early Theology 1910-1931* (London: SCM, 1962); and E. Jüngel, *Karl Barth: A Theological Legacy,* trans. G. E. Paul (Philadelphia: Westminster, 1986).

For this period in general, see J. M. Robinson, ed., *The Beginnings of Dialectic Theology* (Richmond, Va.: John Knox Press, 1968); and H. Zahrnt, *The Question of God,* ch. 1.

of the world? Each in its unsubstitutable particularity, and together in their collective power to symbolize and evoke the world's horror and its dread, these occurrences identify the twenty-first century as a revisitation of Easter Saturday, which in the first instance signaled the end of humanity and history because it meant the end of God. For sequentially, in swelling devilry, our generation has witnessed, in factuality or as fearsome possibility, the end of God's one chosen people, the end of all God's human partners, and the end of God's whole good earth — in Auschwitz, Hiroshima, and Chernobyl.

✳   ✳   ✳

Auschwitz, Poland, has, of course, become a departicularized and ungeographical symbol for all the death camps wherein 6 million Jews and others were exterminated in the Holocaust of World War II. And the term "holocaust" itself has become a mere cipher, increasingly trivialized in political rhetoric to describe any alleged barbarity, often terrible enough in itself, yet often quite different in scale and nature from Hitler's Final Solution. Worst of all, that rhetoric has been interiorized by a popular psychobabble which with nauseating forgetfulness and self-indulgence dares, for instance, to compare all "recovering codependents" and their offspring to Holocaust survivors.[13]

There certainly have been other grotesque acts of genocide in our century: deliberate, large-scale massacres of human beings on mere grounds of their ethnicity or race — Armenians, Cambodians, Kurds, and Balkan Muslims — and other manifestations of totalitarianism besides that of fascism and anti-Semitism.[14] But no universalizing of "holocaust" should be allowed to blunt the

13. This psychological trivialization is mocked, with justifiable outrage, in W. Kaminer, *I'm Dysfunctional, You're Dysfunctional: The Recovery Movement and Other Self-Help Fashions* (Reading, Mass.: Addison-Wesley, 1992).

14. The breadth of modern totalitarianism, embracing leftist forms as well as right, is amply demonstrated in Hannah Arendt's monumental study *The Origins of Totalitarianism.* See also A. Bullock, *Hitler and Stalin: Parallel Lives* (London: HarperCollins, 1991 and New York: A. A. Knopf, 1992), esp. pp. 970-80. On the century's escalating threat to human freedom in general, see esp. A. Huxley, *Brave New World Revisited* (New York and London: Harper and Row, 1958). And on genocides besides the Jewish, see in particular the recent important literature on the slaughter of a million Armenians by the Ottoman government between 1915 and 1918: e.g., R. Melson, *Revolution and Genocide: On the Origins of the Armenian Genocide and the Holocaust* (Chicago: University of Chicago Press, 1993); D. E. Miller and L. T. Miller, *Survivors: An Oral History of the Armenian Genocide* (Berkeley: University of California Press, 1993); Kazemzadeh, *The Struggle of Transcaucasia 1917-1921;* and V. Guroian, "Armenocide and Christian Existence," *Cross-Currents* 41.3 (Fall 1991): 322ff.

specificity and uniqueness of Nazi Germany's liquidation of European Jewry.[15] This thrust a mutilating caesura into an ethnic and religious history which came within a hair's breadth of ending an entire race, and did indeed constitute an irreversible loss, an "end of the world" both for its victims and its survivors (whose own future, too, was murdered in a way). There have indeed been survivors of the Holocaust, and a life beyond termination — most concretely a homeland for a people reduced, as the first act of all totalitarianism, to homelessness and dislocation. Survival and restoration have also been effected by resilient acts of memory — in the form of stories, documents, memorials, and museums, whose witness collectively defies the silencing of so many voices.[16] Nevertheless,

15. Within the vast amount of documentation on the Jewish Holocaust, its origins and aftermath, two comprehensive histories stand out: M. Gilbert, *The Holocaust: The Jewish Tragedy* (London: Collins, 1986 and New York: H. H. Holt, 1987); and L. Yahil, *The Holocaust: The Fate of European Jewry* (New York and Oxford: Oxford University Press, 1990). See, too, N. Levin, *The Holocaust: The Destruction of European Jewry* (New York: T. Y. Crowell Co., 1968); also C. R. Browning, *The Path to Genocide: Essays on Launching the Final Solution* (New York and Cambridge: Cambridge University Press, 1992). Essential reading, as the most significant and sweeping attempt to combine the history of this event with consideration of its theological implications for both Jews and Christians, is R. L. Rubenstein and J. K. Roth, *Approaches to Auschwitz: The Holocaust and Its Legacy* (Atlanta: John Knox Press, 1987).

16. On the importance of testimony see, e.g., S. Shapiro, "Hearing the Testimony of Radical Negation," in E. S. Fiorenza and D. Tracy, eds., *The Holocaust as Interruption* (*Concilium*, no. 175) (Edinburgh: T. & T. Clark, 1984); also J. B. Metz and J.-P. Jossua, *The Crisis in the Language of Faith* (*Concilium*, 5.9, 1973).

On the peculiar and complex qualities of oral as opposed to written testimonies, see esp. L. L. Langer, *Holocaust Testimonies: The Ruins of Memory* (New Haven and London: Yale University Press, 1988); cf. R. G. Lewin, ed., *Witnesses to the Holocaust: An Oral History* (Boston: Twayne Publications, 1990); also H. J. Cargas, *Reflections of a Post-Auschwitz Christian* (Detroit: Wayne State University Press, 1989), pp. 139-46: "On Interviewing Holocaust Survivors." See also A. H. Friedlander, *Out of the Whirlwind: A Reader of Holocaust Literature* (New York: Schocken Books, 1976); J. Glatstein, I. Knox and S. Margoshes, eds., *Anthology of Holocaust Literature* (New York: Athenaeum, 1968); B. Lang, ed., *Writing the Holocaust* (New York: Holmes and Meier, 1988). Outstanding examples of holocaust literature include, of course, the corpus of Elie Wiesel, e.g., *Night* (New York: Avon Books, 1969) and *The Testament* (New York: Summit Books, 1981); cf. the Wiesel bibliography in R. McAfee Brown, *Elie Wiesel: Messenger to All Humanity* (Notre Dame and London: University of Notre Dame Press, 1983); also the work of Primo Levi, including *The Drowned and the Saved,* trans. R. Rosenthal (New York: Simon and Schuster, 1988) (notable for its powerful disquisition on "memory" in ch. 1); and *If Not Now, When?,* trans. W. Weaver (New York: Simon & Schuster, 1985).

See also the extensive work of George Steiner on the ambiguities of language, not the ability of Jews themselves to conceive now of Auschwitz and the Holocaust as lacunae, *inter*-ruptions followed by resumption, permits no one, least of all non-Jews, to forget that in the first instance this truly was a *rupture,* a dagger thrust into the heart of a people's very existence and identity. "The Holocaust is and remains for Judaism a break in continuity of epoch-making extent."[17] After Auschwitz, beyond this hermeneutical as well as biological and historical rupture, nothing can ever be or mean the same. The possibilities for faith, for hope, for the significance of life itself, have abruptly, irretrievably, been changed.[18]

One particularizing mark of "Auschwitz," which requires that the Jewish Holocaust not be simply blended with other manifestations of "ethnic cleansing" or atrocity, is the degree of deliberation, planning, and mechanization invested in this bloodshed. "The Nazi achievement lay in constructing an industry of death never before — or since — seen. An industry of continental size whose raw material was Jews and whose product was corpses."[19] Indeed, the literal architects of this industrialized tyranny and murder were fully conscious that they were engaged in a new, unprecedented, modern enterprise, made possible precisely by advances in engineering and technique.[20] Thus did Auschwitz

---

least in the context of Nazism, including *The Portage to San Cristobal of A.H.* (London: Faber and Faber, 1981).

Note, too, how Hannah Arendt interprets her own study of totalitarianism as an event of speech reborn after an era of silence — her "first chance to try to understand what had happened . . . still in grief and sorrow . . . but no longer in speechless outrage and impotent horror." *Origins of Totalitarianism,* p. xxiii.

The need for continuing language about the Holocaust increases as survivors become fewer and shameful, sometimes willful, forgetfulness sets in. At the time of the opening of the U.S. Holocaust Memorial Museum in Washington, D.C., in April 1993 — the fiftieth anniversary of the Warsaw ghetto uprising — a poll concluded that a considerable minority of Americans are now open to the suggestion that the Holocaust never happened. On the occasion of that opening, see also V. Barnett, "Bearing Witness," *Christian Century* 110.16 (May 12, 1993): 509-10. On the phenomenon of the denial of the Holocaust, see also D. E. Lipstadt, *Denying the Holocaust: The Growing Assault on Truth and Memory* (New York: Free Press, 1993); and P. Vidal-Naquet, *Assassins of Memory: Essays on the Denial of the Holocaust* (New York: Columbia University Press, 1993).

17. H. Küng, *Judaism* (New York: Crossroad, 1992), p. 587.

18. On this rupture, see *inter alia,* S. Shapiro in *Holocaust as Interruption;* D. J. Fasching, *Narrative Theology after Auschwitz* (Minneapolis: Fortress, 1989), esp. pp. 21ff.; D. Cohn-Sherbok, *Holocaust Theology* (London: Marshall Morgan and Scott, 1989), esp. pp. 71ff.; also my own article, "The Burial of God: Rupture and Resumption as the Story of Salvation," *SJT* 40.3 (1987): 335-62.

19. C. Krauthammer, "Holocaust: Memory and Resolve," *Time,* May 3, 1993.

20. Note esp. the speech by Albert Speer, Minister for Armaments in the Third Reich, on this subject as a defendant at the Nuremberg Trials. See, e.g., T. Taylor, *The Anat-*

and the totalitarianism of the 1930s, even more than World War I, effect the collapse of technological optimism and secular millenarianism.[21] It coerced despairing recognition of the true nature of the scientific Trojan Horse so warmly and wantonly admitted into the citadel of modern civilization. Worse disillusion yet, with science, was still to come, however.

To a point, of course, a much-abused truism holds good here, namely, that it is not weapons which kill, but the people who use them. And when the anguished question of *human* responsibility for Nazism and the Jewish Holocaust is unavoidably asked, the searching spotlight thus trained upon *Christians* in particular is not to be extinguished. How can the church avoid its own culpability and complicity, at least in the shaping of the Christian culture in which the Holocaust historically occurred, and in helping to nurture an atmosphere in which Jewish liquidiation came to thinkability? Those whose identity is defined by a narrative which tells of the execution of an innocent Jew, elect of God, have — sometimes by default but sometimes with deliberation — fostered hatred and rejection of all that Jew's sisters and brothers according to the flesh. And in so doing they have surely hastened the historical realization of that "end of the world" for God's chosen people foreshadowed in the murder and burial of that one Jew on Easter Saturday.

The hubris which permitted and perpetuated so blatant a misreading of the New Testament — above all of Romans 9–11 — as the conviction that the once-elect Jews had forfeited their place in heaven, had as its logical and inevitable terminus the inference that they deserved no place either on the earth.[22] Amazingly, it might seem in hindsight, even those most bold to oppose Nazism and "German Christianity" in the name of the sole lordship of Jesus Christ usually had little to say about the particular plight of the Jews in the aftermath of Hitler's rise to power.[23] Penitent rethinking not only of the church's attitude to

---

omy of the Nuremberg Trials (New York: A. A. Knopf, 1992); also Huxley, *Brave New World Revisited,* pp. 43ff.

21. See Lasch, *True and Only Heaven,* pp. 40-41.

22. The impressive insistence of Paul in Romans that God has not irrevocably rejected the Jewish people, despite their rejection of the Messiah, can no longer blind Christians to the fact that the NT itself does contain elements of anti-Semitism and of polemicizing against the early church's Jewish adversaries. Recognition of this is quite necessary to the conduct of meaningful and penitent dialogue of Christians with Jews "after Auschwitz."

23. This silence is especially obvious, and in retrospect embarrassing, in the Theological Declaration of Barmen, 1934, largely composed by Karl Barth — no anti-Semite. Barth was later to regret this silence deeply and to take his share of responsibility for it. See *Karl Barth: Letters 1961-68,* trans. G. W. Bromiley (Edinburgh: T. & T. Clark, 1981), p. 250

Judaism but of its fundamental understanding of the gospel which could allow so diabolic and wrongheaded an inference as this, is a precondition for Jewish-Christian dialogue today and a major component of Christian theology "after Auschwitz."[24]

Nevertheless, the widespread presence of anti-Semitism within the Christian tradition and the church's history, though it has fostered much prejudice and persecution, has not actually led to pogroms and extermination in every "Christian" culture. Something without precedent in quantity and quality happened among the German people to translate that fear and bigotry, and even latent violence, into the specific and unique malignity of the Final Solution. Nor,

---

(letter to E. Bethge); cf. S. Haynes, *Prospects for Post-Holocaust Theology* (Atlanta: Scholars Press, 1991), pp. 54ff. See also K. Scholder, *The Churches and the Third Reich,* vol. 2, trans. J. Bowden (Minneapolis: Fortress, 1989); also K. Scholder, *A Requiem for Hitler,* trans. J. Bowden (London: SCM and Philadelphia: Trinity Press International, 1989); and A. C. Cochrane, *The Church's Confession under Hitler* (Pittsburgh: Pickwick Press, 1971). The way in which Christian convictions, not least in Lutheran formulations, helped to support Nazi ideology and anti-Semitism is apparent in R. P. Erickson, *Theologians under Hitler* (New Haven and London: Yale University Press, 1985). See also V. Barnett, *For the Soul of the People: Protestant Protest against Hitler* (Oxford and New York: Oxford University Press, 1993); and J. Forstman, *Christian Faith in Dark Times: Theological Conflicts in the Shadow of Hitler* (Louisville: Westminster/John Knox Press, 1992).

24. For a very useful account of three major attempts in recent Christian theology to rethink the place of the Jews and Israel within the purposes of God from a post-Auschwitz perspective — by Barth, Moltmann, and Paul van Buren respectively — see Haynes, *Post-Holocaust Theology.* See also K. Sonderegger, *That Jesus Christ Was Born a Jew: Karl Barth's 'Doctrine of Israel'* (University Park, Penn.: Penn State University Press, 1992); and P. van Buren, *A Theology of the Jewish-Christian Reality: Part III — Christ in Context* (San Francisco: Harper & Row, 1988). See also Fasching, *Narrative Theology after Auschwitz;* M. Saperstein, *Moments of Crisis in Jewish-Christian Relations* (London: SCM and Philadelphia: Trinity Press International, 1989); A. J. Peck, *Jews and Christians after the Holocaust* (Philadelphia: Fortress, 1982); D. J. Hall, *Thinking The Faith,* pp. 210ff.; Küng, *Judaism,* pp. 584-609; and the interfaith symposium papers in M. Littell, R. Libowitz, and E. B. Rosen, eds., *The Holocaust Forty Years After* (Lewiston, N.Y. and Lampeter, Wales: Edwin Mellen Press, 1989); also M. Barth, *Israel and the Church* (Richmond, Va.: John Knox Press, 1969); A. Eckardt and R. Eckardt, *Encounter with Israel: A Challenge to Conscience* (New York: Association Press, 1970); and C. M. Williamson, *A Guest in the House of Israel* (Louisville: Westminster/John Knox Press, 1993).

See also S. Sandmel, *Anti-Semitism in the New Testament?* (Philadelphia: Fortress, 1978); J. Koenig, *Jews and Christians in Dialogue: New Testament Foundations* (Philadelphia: Westminster, 1979); S. G. Hall, *Christian Anti-Semitism in Paul's Theology* (Minneapolis: Augsburg Fortress, 1992); and A. T. Davies, *Anti-Semitism and the Christian Mind: The Crisis of Conscience after Auschwitz* (New York: Herder and Herder, 1969).

whatever the Führer's pathologies and personal wickedness, is it adequate to explain the Holocaust by means of a "great man" theory of history which blames Hitler as uniquely evil, powerful, and mesmerizing and so exonerates the German nation in that epoch as a whole from accountability for these events. For many eyewitnesses and interpreters of the Third Reich it has been imperative, often at considerable cost, to call the German people collectively to account for the horrors performed in the name of their national destiny, in which millions of them unprotestingly participated.[25]

Such indictments, however, still do not shine the torch of judgment harshly and deeply enough into the dark realities of this Auschwitz Easter Saturday. Is it possible to stop short of the confession that human nature itself failed here abysmally, the hearts of us all shockingly exposed as capable of bottomless barbarity? While, indeed, it must be asked, and will be soon below, where *God* was in the Auschwitz ovens, a question of equal urgency and possibly more justification asks: "Where was *humanity* in the Holocaust? What terrible truth about us all, our universal, fallen selves, found expression between the gas chambers and the burial pits of Buchenwald, Dachau, and Treblinka?[26] In those living hells how calamitous an end of the world befell our modern, fanciful notions of humanity's moral progress and lofty, spiritual grasp!

That is not to deny the presence of evil and the satanic, powerfully at work in the Holocaust and its preludes. It may well be, as Hannah Arendt argues, that precisely these events, for the first time in human history, have truly taught us the radical nature of evil — while also exposing the mortifying fact that evil at its most radical happens not in dramatic acts of blatant, monstrous savagery, from which we may easily distance ourselves, but in the mundane banality of ordinary, quotidian existence which honesty makes us recognize all too readily as our own.[27]

25. Thus William Shirer, in particular, has insisted throughout his long writing career upon holding the German nation as a whole culpable for the bestiality and brutality of the Nazi years. See W. Shirer, *The Rise and Fall of the Third Reich* (New York: Simon and Schuster, 1960) and *Twentieth-Century Journey,* 3 vols. (New York: Little Brown & Co., 1985-1990). See also P. Levi, *The Drowned and the Saved,* ch. 8; and C. S. Maier, *The Unmasterable Past: History, Holocaust and German National Identity* (Cambridge, Mass.: Harvard University Press, 1988).

26. See, e.g., J. Bemporad, "The Concept of Man after Auschwitz," in Friedlander, ed., *Out of the Whirlwind,* pp. 477ff.; also H. J. Cargas, ed., *When God and Man Failed: Non-Jewish Views of the Holocaust* (London: Macmillan, 1981); cf. Yahil, *Holocaust,* p. 9.

27. See Arendt, *Origins of Totalitarianism,* pp. ix, and the chilling, final chapter to that work, on "Ideology and Terror"; also her *Eichmann in Jerusalem: A Report on the Banality of Evil,* rev. ed. (London and New York: Penguin, 1985). On the unrelieved negativity

Such an acknowledgment simply reinforces the degree of human culpability for this demonic "end of the world." It may indeed be legitimate from a biblical perspective to attribute to sin, Satan, the devil, or the law a third-party role between God and humanity, tempting us, indwelling us, holding us in bondage (e.g., Gen. 3; Rom. 7:13-25). And the hysteria of the Nuremberg rallies, for example, has taught us in new ways that human beings, as if driven by malign, external forces, may act *en masse* as they would never do in isolation. The fact remains that without the human will there would be no instrumentality by which the captivating powers of evil could wreak their nihilistic havoc. The evilness that led to Auschwitz cannot be laid at any Satan's door so as to cancel the charges, in that unspeakable offense, laid upon humanity as such.[28]

Nor, finally, can appeal either to evil or to the guilty verdict on humanity prevent the asking of the most disturbing of all Easter Saturday questions about Auschwitz. That is the question of *God.* If God seemed absent that first Easter Saturday, abandoning to death and hell the Beloved Son himself and therefore canceling all residual hope for the rest of the Creator's children, so too the chill miasma of theodicy hangs over Auschwitz forevermore. Where was God in *this* Easter Saturday disaster, this unmitigated triumph of the executioners over their victims, this surplus of godforsakenness and godlessness over faith, hope, love, and, above all, over righteousness? That question has, of course, brought untold anguish and upheaval to the Jewish people in their post-Holocaust struggle between meaning and futility, between tenuous, enduring faith and rank, indignant disbelief and hopelessness.

For some, the loss of faith in Yahweh's presence would do the Nazis' work for them and grant a posthumous victory to Hitler over Yahweh's people.[29] For other Jews, that abandonment of faith is the only possibility, given God's aban-

---

and evil of the Holocaust, as an awesome, unfathomable *tremendum,* see A. A. Cohen, "In Our Terrible Age: The *Tremendum* of the Jews," in *Holocaust as Interruption,* pp. 11ff.; and *The Tremendum: A Theological Interpretation of the Holocaust* (New York: Crossroad, 1981).

28. This point is well made by D. J. Fasching, "Demythologizing the Demonic," in *Narrative Theology,* ch. 4.

29. This insistence on continued faith is most profoundly and eloquently expressed by Emil Fackenheim, e.g., in *God's Presence in History* (New York: New York University Press and London: University of London Press, 1970) and *To Mend the World: Foundations of Future Jewish Thought* (New York: Schocken Books, 1982). Cf. Rubenstein and Roth, *Approaches to Auschwitz,* pp. 316ff.; and Cohn-Sherbok, *Holocaust Theology,* pp. 43ff. See also V. E. Frankl, *Man's Search for Meaning,* rev. ed. (New York: Washington Square Press, 1985); and E. B. Borowitz, *How Can a Jew Speak of Faith Today?* (Philadelphia: Westminster, 1969).

donment of them, the shocking divine silence, impotence, or absence amid the annihilation of God's people. "We live in the time of the death of God. . . . We stand in a cold, silent unfeeling cosmos, unaided by any powerful love beyond our own resources. . . . After Auschwitz, what else can a Jew say about God?"[30] For Elie Wiesel, torn between these two responses, Auschwitz makes it impossible to understand God, yet it is also impossible to understand Auschwitz without God, without the divine presence in the very midst of its absence. "Thanks to this event, the world may be saved, just as because of it, the world is in danger of being destroyed."[31]

Needless to say, all these Jewish wrestlings with faith, doubt, and unbelief do not supplant but render all the more searching and intense the questions hanging over Christian faith and understanding in the light of Auschwitz. If Christian theology helped even somewhat to bring about the Holocaust, where, if anywhere, was the God of that theology in the midst of that event? A quick, simplistic answer to that mystery would grossly defile the memories of all the victims and survivors. And the slow, deep, self-critical reflection that is required of Christians to honor the legacy of Auschwitz can begin with no other premise than an "Easter Saturday" conclusion — that the Holocaust represents another stunning failure on God's part, a huge discontinuity in the Eternal's promised movement from creation to the *eschaton:* a rupture in *divine* history no less than in human or in Jewish.

※　　　　※　　　　※

30. R. L. Rubenstein, *After Auschwitz: Radical Theology and Contemporary Judaism* (Indianapolis: Bobbs-Merrill, 1966), p. 152. Rubenstein adopts a somewhat less despairing, but still unorthodox, posture in *Approaches to Auschwitz.*

31. E. Wiesel, Foreword to Peck, ed., *Jews and Christians*, p. xi. Though he thus stops short of Rubenstein's original renunciation of faith on grounds of the death of God, and affirms God's presence in the godlessness of Auschwitz, Wiesel has also most notably devoted his whole life to a sustained, elemental, but vivifying cry of protest against God's silence and apparent absence. See esp. McAfee Brown, *Elie Wiesel.*

For illuminating surveys of the various responses to Auschwitz in current Jewish theology, see Rubenstein and Roth, *Approaches to Auschwitz;* Cohn-Sherbok, *Holocaust Theology;* Küng, *Judaism,* pp. 584ff.; and J. K. Roth and M. Berenbaum, *Holocaust: Religious and Philosophical Implications* (New York: Paragon House, 1989).

See also the important and profound reflections of the Jewish scholar Hans Jonas, "The Concept of God after Auschwitz," in Friedlander, ed., *Out of the Whirlwind,* pp. 465ff.; and cf. Jüngel's response to Jonas, "Gottes Ursprüngliches Anfangen als Schöpferischen Selbstbegrenzung," in H. Deuser et al., eds., *Gottes Zukunft — Zukunft der Welt: Festschrift für Jürgen Moltmann zum 60 Geburtstag* (Munich: Kaiser, 1986), pp. 265ff.

Hiroshima, Japan, localizes in an even more shocking "scandal of particularity" than Auschwitz the chronological crater whose gaping, smouldering emptiness marks divine disruption, God's loss of control over history and human destiny. At those precise coordinates there finally intersected, with terminal, apocalyptic portent, the two converging trajectories of modernity: humanity's proud, vaulting lunge for progressive, scientific mastery of nature and ourselves; and our doom-laden plunge into despair — a tardy recognition that the creatures who usurped the Maker's power had lost control themselves and become the impotent, imperiled victims of their own machines.[32]

"You shall be as God" was the primordial serpent's menacing seduction; and on August 6, 1945, that sacrilegious Feast of Transfiguration, gods we became, wielding as never before promethean sovereignty over life itself — only to see in the mirror of atomic light, "brighter than a thousand suns," our transformed faces not effulgent with God's glory but wearing the death masks of the devil. So it was that Robert Oppenheimer, director in Los Alamos of the Manhattan Project, after the earlier blast at the testing site named Trinity (unwitting, blasphemous admission of humanity's assault on heaven), had famously recalled the Hindu *Bhagavad Gita,* "I have become Death, the destroyer of worlds."[33]

Was Easter Saturday and its "end of the world" ever more comprehensively and tragically reenacted? To be sure, the actual death toll in Hiroshima and Nagasaki was tiny compared with the millions of executions in the Jewish Holocaust; and it was matched, on some estimates at least, by earlier, non-atomic bombings of Dresden and Tokyo. Arguably, too, the deployment of the atomic device, by bringing the atrocities of World War II finally to a close, saved far more lives than it cost. Even so, the nature of the death inflicted by the bomb — to say nothing of the misery endured by its accursed survivors and the possibility it presaged for the annihilation of all humanity — identifies Hiroshima not as a quantitative but a qualitative novelty, a *sui generis* lurch of history into

32. On the juxtaposition, indeed contiguity, of Progress and Doom, two sides of a single coin, at the end of the modern era, see Arendt, *Origins of Totalitarianism,* p. vii.

33. See R. Jungk, *Brighter Than a Thousand Suns,* trans. J. Cleugh (Harmondsworth: Penguin, 1960 and San Diego: Harcourt Brace, 1970), p. 183; R. Rhodes, *The Making of the Atomic Bomb* (New York and London: Simon and Schuster, 1986), p. 676. These are the two outstanding histories of the events leading up to Hiroshima. A new study suggests that, for moral reasons, leading scientists may have deliberately obstructed the development of a German atomic bomb in World War II. See T. Powers, *Heisenberg's War: The Secret History of the German Bomb* (New York: A. A. Knopf, 1993). One biographer, however, disputes that claim; see D. C. Cassidy, *Uncertainty: The Life and Science of Werner Heisenberg* (New York: W. H. Freeman, 1991).

a terminal abyss. Not only God's one chosen people, but all the creatures of God's hand are threatened now with liquidation, and the future of the world itself is jeopardized. Here was born the atomic age which has developed the potential, through a third world war, for an infinity of Hiroshimas, raising the bleak prospect of a global "nuclear winter."[34] For half a century the human race held its breath in unthinkable peril, its safety secured only by the hair-trigger logic of deterrence. Not so long ago the highest aspiration for many European, Asian, and American youth was to be near ground zero at the impending arrival of the enemy's missiles, and thus spared the grotesque agonies of nonobliteration. That for now the prospect of nuclear exchange between obscenely over-armed superpowers has disappeared, and small steps begun toward the dismantling of their opposing arsenals, has done nothing to slow the proliferation of destructive weapons which, by design or accident, could still incinerate populations on a continental, if not global, scale.

Thus did the deadly cargo of the *Enola Gay* sever time itself. "The bomb that fell on Hiroshima cut history in two like a knife. Before and after are two different worlds. That cut is more abrupt, decisive and revolutionary than the cut made by the star over Bethlehem."[35] And the day it happened seems to some "the most important date in the history of the human race."[36] Such emotionally understandable hyperbole expresses in its very irreligiousness the deep suspicion of our age that all the grotesqueries of World War II, but transcendingly the evils of its denouement, confirm the modern rumors that God is dead — or else the bitter conviction that God should be, for permitting the demonic such disastrous latitude.

Yet, whatever angry doubts or protests we hurl against the discredited

34. See esp. J. Schell, *The Fate of the Earth* (New York: A. A. Knopf, 1982).

35. H. Wieman, *The Source of Human Good* (Chicago: University of Chicago Press, 1946), p. 37.

36. A. Koestler, *The Observer,* 1 January 1978, quoted in J. Garrison, *The Darkness of God: Theology after Hiroshima* (London: SCM, 1982 and Grand Rapids: Eerdmans, 1983), p. 69. On the epoch-ending, qualitative newness of Hiroshima, see also A. M. Schlesinger Jr., *The Cycles of American History* (Boston: Houghton Mifflin Co., 1986), pp. xiii and 63ff.; D. Aukerman, *Darkening Valley* (New York: Seabury Press, 1981), pp. 33ff.; and Arendt, *Human Condition*, p. 6. But see also my comments in "Apocalypse and Parousia: The Anguish of Theology from Now till Kingdom Come," *Austin Seminary Bulletin* 103.8 (1988): 41, n. 2: "It is, of course, possible to exaggerate this qualitative change. Existentially it is a luxury for the West to be afraid of nuclear oblivion, which is denied to many in the Third World whose preoccupation can only be with immediate and local survival. Their misery is at least a reminder that the fundamental questions of theodicy are the same for any human, as he or she perceives life's injustices and menaces."

Creator naturally rebound upon ourselves. Hiroshima's survivors, certainly no less than those of Auschwitz, demand to know where humanity might have been amid the palpable absence among them of the Lord. And in the decades since, it has made less sense, perhaps, to wonder what has become of God's omnipotence and redemptive purpose than to ask what has become of us, our dignity, vitality, and wisdom, during these years of self-destructive and demeaning madness. Straddling the "evolutionary firebreak of 1945," cleft between our old days and our new, between modernity's ideals and postmodernistic nihilism, between humanness and bestiality, "we are Einstein's monsters, not fully human, not for now."[37]

As with Auschwitz, it has been vital to keep alive the memory of Hiroshima so as to honor and attest the humanity of both victims and survivors, who were consumed in instant conflagration or in creeping, postradiation cancer.[38] Possibly, too, such acts of record and remembrance can help preserve and restore our own diminished and monstrously questionable humanness. Part of what makes us less than fully human now, beyond the nuclear rupture of our times, is the very paralysis of mind which allows us to forget the past, yet leaves us unable to conceive the future. There is about us a "psychic numbness,"[39] a generational and cultural pathology which refuses to face the reality of what we have done with our promethean nuclear fire, or to imagine the awfulness of what we could still do. Without such pathological suppression of the deadly truth would the populations of East and West have with such docility permitted their respective governments to devote immense resources to an escalating arms race, digging a superfluity of silos, amassing ever greater stockpiles, inventing still "smarter" missiles, even after they had brought the world at least once to the precipice of cataclysm?[40] Such popular passivity, and the political irresponsibility it connives at, betray society's self-anesthetizing against intolerable terror. Individually and sociologically we assent with heroic cowardice to the myth of survival, the "denial of death" which promotes the lie that we, our

37. M. Amis, *Einstein's Monsters* (New York: Crown Publishers, 1982), p. 23 and introduction. See also S. H. Dresner, *God, Man and Atomic War* (New York: Living Books, 1966).

38. See, e.g., J. Hersey, *Hiroshima* (London: Penguin, 1946); and R. J. Lifton, *Death in Life: Survivors of Hiroshima* (Durham: University of North Carolina Press, 1991).

39. R. J. Lifton, *Boundaries: Psychological Man in Revolution* (New York: Simon & Schuster, 1963), pp. 31ff. Cf. D. Priestly, *Bringing Forth in Hope* (New York: Paulist Press, 1983), pp. 21ff.

40. See, e.g., M. Beschloss, *The Crisis Years: Kennedy and Khrushchev, 1960-63* (New York: HarperCollins, 1991); and R. F. Kennedy, *Thirteen Days: The Cuban Missile Crisis* (London: Macmillan, 1969 and New York: W. W. Norton, 1971).

family, our nation, or our own elect elite shall scrape through the ultimate apocalyptic crisis to which others shall succumb.[41]

Shamefully, these illusions, which so encourage the very catastrophe they discount, are prevalent among and nurtured by certain forces in the church itself; thus questions of Christian responsibility hang over tomorrow's nuclear holocaust just as they did over the Jewish, yesterday. Is the disingenuous narcissism of survivalism, in the context of the nuclear threat, anywhere more repulsive than in those forms of Christian millenarianism which have posited the deliverance of Israel and/or America and/or the "raptured" saints from humanity's divinely ordained and promised Armageddon? Why are the rest of us not more angry than we seem to be at the pernicious hermeneutical abuse which so blasphemously suggests that a thermonuclear war, so unutterably evil and destructive, would wondrously fulfill Scripture's promises of God's last righteous judgment, the return of Christ the prince of peace, and the triumph of the Spirit, the Lord and Giver of life?[42]

It must be confessed, of course, that this sacrilegious mishandling of biblical apocalyptic, above all by some on the triumphalistic and bellicose Christian fringes, is the price paid for the reluctance of the church at large to take responsibility for the whole Christian canon and tradition, including such difficult and culturally alien books as Daniel and Revelation. Their relative neglect in the mainstream churches has created the vacuum so reprehensively filled by others who, unopposed, manipulate such texts to promote war and sacralize the death of millions.[43] To this failure of nerve on the part of Scrip-

41. See E. Becker, *The Denial of Death* (New York and London: Macmillan, 1973), esp. ch 2. Cf. C. Lasch, *The Minimal Self: Psychic Survival in Troubled Times* (New York: W. W. Norton, 1984); also McGill, *Death and Life;* also, R. Ambler, "Reasons for Not Despairing," in A. Race, ed., *Nuclear Horizon* (London: SCM, 1988), ch. 6.

42. See, e.g., H. Lindsey, *The Late, Great Planet Earth* (Grand Rapids: Zondervan, 1970); and J. F. Walvoord, *Armageddon* (Grand Rapids: Zondervan, 1974). Important historical and cultural studies of millennialism include E. R. Sandeen, *The Roots of Fundamentalism* (Chicago: University of Chicago Press, 1970); T. P. Weber, *Living in the Shadow of the Second Coming,* 2nd ed. (Chicago: University of Chicago Press, 1987); J. H. Moorhead, "Searching for the Millennium in America," *Princeton Seminary Bulletin* 8.2 (1987); and A. G. Mojtabi, *Blessed Assurance: At Home with the Bomb in Amarillo, Texas* (Albuquerque: University of New Mexico Press, 1986). In 1993, the drawn-out siege and its fiery conclusion at "Ranch Apocalypse" near Waco, Texas, home of the "Branch Davidians" and their self-styled messianic leader David Koresh, provided horrifying evidence that irresponsible apocalyptic hermeneutics can still reap a violent, self-destructive harvest, even in a nonnuclear, post–Cold War context. See also M. Barkun, "Reflections after Waco: Millennialists and the State," *Christian Century* 110.18 (June 2-9, 1993).

43. See my booklet *Apocalypse Soon? Christian Responsibility and the Book of Revela-*

ture's exegetes and readers must be added the reluctance of many systematic theologians to speak in realistic, rather than merely symbolic, terms about the Second Coming, the Last Judgment, and the end of the world.[44]

Perhaps surprisingly, in an era dominated precisely by the rescue of eschatology from its nineteenth-century repudiation, contemporary theology has comprehensively shied away from almost all discusssion of the chronological future, in favor of an *eschaton* which wholly transcends time, as in Barth and Bultmann, or even negates and contradicts time, as frequently for Moltmann.[45] This has left the churches ill-equipped to counteract the fashion for literalistic prophecies of an imminent end time, or to address with the good news of God's coming kingdom humanity's amply justifiable fears about what the immediate, temporal future holds. For this evasion, rebuke is well deserved: "the vertical has become the horizontal: the flight 'upwards' from the pressure of reality has now been replaced by a flight 'forward.' The demonstration of the truth of God, whether in space or time, retreats into an indeterminate distance. Conse-

---

tion (Iona Community, Scotland: Wild Goose Publications, 1986). Happily, a responsible recovery of Revelation and its visions' political significance is now underway. Useful recent contributions include: E. S. Fiorenza, *The Book of Revelation: Justice and Judgment* (Philadelphia: Fortress, 1985); A. Y. Collins, *Crisis and Catharsis: The Power of the Apocalypse* (Philadelphia: Westminster, 1987); A. Boesak, *Comfort and Protest: The Apocalypse from a South African Perspective* (Philadelphia: Westminster, 1987). See also D. Aukerman, *Reckoning with Apocalypse: Terminal Politics and Christian Hope* (New York: Crossroad, 1993) and *Darkening Valley*. See also, T. F. Torrance, *The Apocalypse Today* (Edinburgh: J. Clarke and Co., 1960); also C. Beker, *Paul the Apostle* and *Paul's Apocalyptic Gospel;* and R. Bauckham, *The Climax of Prophecy: Studies on the Book of Revelation* (Edinburgh: T. & T. Clark, 1993).

44. By "realistic" is meant here not "literalistic" but based upon a hermeneutic which recognizes the "history-like" quality of biblical narrative, as expounded especially by Hans Frei in his *Eclipse of Biblical Narrative*. Cf. G. A. Lindbeck, *The Nature of Doctrine* (Philadelphia: Westminster, 1984), ch. 6.

45. I develop this critique of Barth, Bultmann, Moltmann and others (including Oscar Cullmann, the great exponent of "salvation history") in my article "Apocalypse and Parousia." All of them most properly exalt eschatology, and in Barth's case especially, Jesus Christ as the *eschatos,* the Last One. But they all tend to turn the *eschaton* into a time-transcending *kairos* at the expense of historical time or *chronos,* and thus lose all interest in the temporal tomorrow. Moltmann, who supremely gave recent theology its eschatological orientation, beginning with his *Theology of Hope,* repeatedly contrasts the eschatological *adventum* of God's kingdom with the temporal *futurum,* suggesting that the former does not so much fulfill as contradict, undermine, and terminate the latter. Yet this seems to leave Christian faith and hope with nothing to say about tomorrow, chronologically concerned, despite our generation's widespread and justified preoccupations with questions about exactly that tomorrow. See above, Ch. 7 (n. 48).

quently, the question raised by modern [humanity], where God is here and now, remains unanswered, as it did in the past."[46]

Nevertheless, not even the best-informed, most responsible reading of Revelation, or the most Christocentric and trinitarian discussion of the "end days," can evade the haunting implications of the church's identifying three-day narrative, centered upon Easter Saturday. For that insists — and nothing in our contemporary experience contradicts its awful truthfulness — that the God of Jesus Christ does not intervene to prevent catastrophe and rupture. As grace abounds only beyond sin's great magnitude and increase, so resurrection and consummation do not cancel or impede but strictly follow after termination and annihilation, for God and humanity alike. The very promise of the *eschaton* confirms rather than refutes God's freedom to be death's victim, the defenseless quarry of predatory evil; and the only hope and power for a divine redeeming of humanity and history rest in a Lamb who has pathetically been slaughtered: the embodiment of hopelessness and helplessness.

Nothing we might proceed to say about the *victory* of that wounded Lamb, an end-of-the-world triumph of grace and love and righteousness, can excuse us from admitting first this benumbing possibility: that as Holy Sabbath preceded Easter Sunday, so the ultimate tomorrow when God shall at last be all in all could follow, not avert, that infinitude of Hiroshimas which would be the holocaust of all humanity. The victorious return of the redeemer who was crucified on a cross and buried in a grave make imminent, not the certainty, but certainly the unprotected possibility, of divine defeat: evil not contained but given fullest scope. Far from fulfilling neatly Scripture's pyrotechnic vision of the Lord's great Day of Judgment, our day of conflagration would be the Devil's own, when God's Godness would again, and finally, be judged inept, mendacious, cancelled.[47]

46. H. Zahrnt, *The Question of God,* p. 201. For a defense of a chronological dimension to eschatological hope, from a Roman Catholic perspective, see K. Rahner, "The Hermeneutics of Eschatological Assertions," in *Theological Investigations,* vol. 4, trans. K. Smyth (Baltimore: Helicon Press, 1966), esp. p. 337. Cf. E. Schillebeeckx, "The Interpretation of Eschatology," in E. Schillebeeckx and B. Willems, eds., *The Problem of Eschatology* (*Concilium,* no. 41) (New York: Paulist Press, 1969), pp. 42-56; see also M. J. Borg, "Portraits of Jesus in Contemporary North American Scholarship," *Harvard Theological Review* 84.1 (1991).

47. The fullest and most provocative attempt to think out an entire theology in the light of Hiroshima and the future nightmares its memory evokes is J. Garrison, *The Darkness of God.* But using the axioms of process theology and panentheism, and its concepts of God's "bipolar" attributes, Garrison sees past and future holocausts as God's own work — the chastisement and wrath of God's shadow side, in equilibrium with the light side of for-

✳   ✳   ✳

Chernobyl, Ukraine, in the eyes of some, at least, extends the case against God's power and love beyond the near extinction of the covenantal, chosen people, and the conceivable perdition of the whole human race, made in the divine image, to the endangerment of the very planet, the Creator's good earth, in its entirety. Thus has our century of escalating doubt and horror learned to put three questions to the Lord of history. First, has Judaism, then has humanity, and now has the globe itself, a future to look forward to?[48] The number of persons killed by the meltdown of the Chernobyl IV reactor on April 26, 1986, compares not at all with the loss of life in the Holocaust or the two World Wars (though it will be a generation, or several, before its effects cease to exact a human toll). Yet the spoliation of the environment close to that power plant, and far, far from it, will endure for millennia. There was, to be sure, a previous near-disaster at Three Mile Island, Pennsylvania; the list of nuclear mishaps around the world keeps growing; and threats to the well-being of the population, of the

---

giveness and grace. Yet this associates God with the doing of evil in a way that regrettably matches that of the fundamentalist prophets of Armageddon, and it supplements God's omnipotence with vulnerability rather than radically rethinking God's power *as* vulnerable love. It thus fails to *subvert* theism's metaphysical tradition of divine coercion and causality, as the present work is seeking to do. Also problematic are G. Kaufman, *Theology for a Nuclear Age* (Philadelphia: Westminster Press and Manchester: Manchester University Press, 1985); and S. McFague, *Models of God: Theology for an Ecological, Nuclear Age* (Philadelphia: Fortress and London: SCM, 1987). More helpful for the rethinking of divine power than these is D. Migliore, *The Power of God* (Philadelphia: Westminster, 1983). Other constructive contributions to the rethinking of theology in the context of the nuclear age include: A. Race, ed., *Nuclear Horizon* (London: SCM, 1988); and J. Moltmann, *Creating a Just Future,* trans. J. Bowden (London: SCM and Philadelphia: Trinity Press International, 1989), sect. 2: "The Nuclear Situation: The Theology and Politics of Peace." See also the Report of the Special Committee anent the Implications for Christian Theology of the Nuclear Threat to Life, in *Reports to the General Assembly* (Edinburgh: Church of Scotland, 1987), pp. 545ff. The present author contributed to the work of this committee. Based on its report is R. Davidson, *Christian Faith in a Nuclear Age* (Edinburgh: Handsel Press, 1989).

48. Mercifully, perhaps, these questions are now being asked even within the White House. In his recent best-seller on the ecological crisis — a remarkably well-informed study theologically and philosophically as well as scientifically, Vice-President Al Gore repeatedly draws parallels between the Jewish Holocaust, Hiroshima, and the unprecedented catastrophe now facing the earth. See A. Gore, *Earth in the Balance: Ecology and the Human Spirit* (New York and Harmondsworth: Penguin, 1993), e.g., pp. 49-50, 55, 177, 205-6, 366; also on the ecological crisis see P. Kennedy, *Preparing for the Twenty-First Century* (New York: Random House, 1993), esp. ch. 6.

natural order, and eventually of this planet as a whole, far surpass those posed by nuclear energy. Bhopal and the *Exxon Valdez*, acid rain and the greenhouse effect, the depletion of the ozone layer, the decimation of the rain forests, and the poisoning of rivers, lakes, and oceans: such disasters and disasters-in-the-making constitute a formidable, now all-too-familiar, catalogue of environmental perils. Even so, Chernobyl itself signals the crossing of a great divide, as did Auschwitz and Hiroshima earlier: a historical rupture which changes everything, including human consciousness.

Like those which started World War I and ended World War II, Chernobyl's explosions ushered in a different epoch, qualitatively new and worse. Its incandescent ruins, concrete-shrouded for an aeon still to come, stand as a global tombstone, memorial, and augury of what has already been deemed "the end of nature."[49] As the Holocaust has taught us of what wickedness humanity is capable, and the bomb of what destructiveness, so Chernobyl exposes the fatal depths of our carelessness and inattention, proving so tellingly Arendt's thesis of the "banality of evil," the fearsome consequences of plain stupidity, shortsightedness, and nonaccountability. No convulsion of overt malignancy nor of demonized authority — from which we ourselves could be so easily distanced — the Chernobyl calamity reminds us that the world's worst perils now may derive from the familiar benign neglect and systemic inertia, the absence of leadership and vacuum of responsibility, so common in our bureaucratized society.[50]

Chernobyl bitingly demonstrates as well that human lassitude and carelessness are most lethal when allied to our most energetic, concentrated, and imaginative advances in science and technology. The end of nature or of the world that disaster symbolizes seems to represent the ultimate collapse of the

49. B. McKibben, *The End of Nature* (New York: Doubleday, 1990). McKibben explains that his title refers not to the end of the world as such, but to the end of an "idea," which respects the integrity and independence of nature (see, e.g., pp. 8, 48). His plea on behalf of that idea is not necessarily to be theologically endorsed since it denies the very *inter*dependence of humanity and the rest of creation which Scripture presupposes and whose recovery is surely essential to the reform of humanity's relationship with nature. But McKibben's elegy for a lost idea, romantic and even antihuman as that can be, is itself predicated on *actualities* which, if unchecked, could indeed hasten the end of the world as we know it.

50. Such is the clear lesson to be drawn from the absorbing account by the chief investigator of the accident and its coverup. See G. Medvedev, *The Truth about Chernobyl*, foreword by Andrei Sakharov, trans. E. Rossiter (New York: Basic Books, 1991). See also Piers Paul Read, *Ablaze* (New York: Random House, 1993). For a shocking account of environmental irresponsibility in the Soviet Union, see M. Feshback and A. Friendly, Jr., *Ecocide in the USSR: Health and Nature under Siege* (New York: Basic Books, 1992).

modern, optimistic expectation that human knowledge shall control nature and perfect the world. Neo-Luddite fearfulness led many in the 1980s to sport the slogan "atomic power — no thanks!" In reality the energy latent in the atom is surely one of nature's most stupendous wonders, the gift of a beneficent Creator which it should be unthinkable for Christians, at least, to be ungrateful for or to decline to use; and the discovery of the means for its release and harnessing ranks among the most creative accomplishment of modern science in its potentiality for good. Yet bitter experience now has taught us the depths of our ability to misdirect God's creativity and ours to demonically destructive ends through folly, arrogance, and irresponsibility.

Modern science, judged by the fruit it bears, has thrown into sharp relief humanity's fateful determination not to remain as creatures, conjoined in mutuality with all creation, but to be our own masterful creators. What began in the Renaissance as a questioning and exploration of the natural order — secular, profane, contingent — with the transcendent Maker's gift of rationality and our own new tools of invention and discovery,[51] quickly degenerated into tyranny and domination. Inquiry became (in the ambiguous but ominous terminology of Francis Bacon) "inquisition," and interrogation, torture.[52] Thus did

51. Though this is to raise critical questions about some of the attitudes adopted and supported by science, it is by no means intended as a repudiation of science as such. How could thinking Christians do that, given the origins of modern science in their own theological tradition. For an excellent recent defense of the scientific exercise against its recent bad press, see esp. P. Kitcher, *The Advancement of Science* (New York and Oxford: Oxford University Press, 1993); and on the Judeo-Christian origins of modern science, see, e.g., S. Jaki, *The Road of Science and the Ways to God* (Chicago: University of Chicago Press and Edinburgh: Scottish Academic Press, 1978); T. F. Torrance, *Theological Science,* esp. ch. 2; *The Ground and Grammar of Theology;* and *Divine and Contingent Order* (Oxford: Oxford University Press, 1981); R. Hooykas, *Religion and the Rise of Modern Science* (Edinburgh: Scottish Academic Press, 1972); I. Barbour, *Religion in an Age of Science* (San Francisco: Harper & Row, 1990); C. Kaiser, *Creation and the History of Science* (London: M. Pickering and Grand Rapids: Eerdmans, 1991); W. Pannenberg, *Theology and the Philosophy of Science* (London: Darton, Longman & Todd, 1976); and A. Peacocke, *Creation and the World of Science* (Oxford: Clarendon Press, 1979); J. Polkinghorne, *One World: The Interaction of Science and Theology* (Princeton: Princeton University Press, 1987) and *Reason and Reality* (London: SPCK, 1991); and D. Allen, *Christian Belief in a Postmodern World* (Louisville: Westminster/John Knox Press, 1989), esp. chs. 1 and 2; also G. B. Deason, "The Protestant Reformation and the Rise of Modern Science," *SJT* 38.2 (1985): 221-40. On the role of invention in helping to shape the methodology of modern science and facilitating its discoveries, see esp. D. Boorstin, *The Discoverers* (New York: Random House, 1983); cf. Arendt, *Human Condition,* esp. ch. 6.

52. See here Torrance, *Theological Science,* esp. pp. 69ff.; Jaki, *Road of Science,* ch. 4;

the Age of Reason spell "the death of nature,"[53] as the disconnection and alienation between humanity and the created order (so vividly portrayed in the primordial narrative of Gen. 3), was dramatically reenacted and fulfilled upon the emergent stage of modern Western culture. The Cartesian dichotomy between mind and body, and the Kantian between what is knowable and what is not, drove a cosmic wedge between science and religion, knowledge and faith, facts and values, allowing society to analyze, exploit, and control nature and its resources without reference to the spiritual meaning and moral consequences of its rapacity and heteronomy.[54]

That "masculine," coercive exercise of reason which alienates humanity from nature also fosters the disconnectedness of human beings from each other. It widens the gulf, so sacralized in contemporary society, between the public and the private, the narcissistic myth that private behavior — or private enterprise — may be pursued to the hilt without reference to its consequences for the human community at large; and it reinforces the major premise of our global economy and ecosystem, which presumes that one community may recklessly maximize its prosperity and comfort now, at whatever cost in damage and deprivation to locations and societies elsewhere or to human persons yet unborn.[55]

Moltmann, *Creating a Just Future*, sect. 3 — "The Ecological Situation: The Theology and Ethics of Creation," esp. pp. 51ff. See also the very enlightening study by Keith Thomas, *Man and the Natural World: Changing Attitudes in England 1500-1800* (Harmondsworth: Penguin, 1983).

53. See C. Merchant, *The Death of Nature: Women, Ecology and the Scientific Revolution* (San Francisco: Harper & Row, 1980). See also E. and G. Strachan, *Freeing the Feminine* (Dunbar, Scotland: Labadum Publications, 1985).

54. On the Enlightenment's dualisms and their consequences for Western culture, see Torrance, *Theological Science, Ground and Grammar, Reality and Scientific Theology* (Edinburgh: Scottish Academic Press, 1985) and "The Making of the 'Modern' Mind from Descartes and Newton to Kant," in *Transformation and Convergence in the Frame of Knowledge* (Belfast: Christian Journals Ltd., 1984), pp. 1ff. See also L. Newbigin, *Gospel in a Pluralist Society*, esp. ch. 2; Gunton, *Enlightenment and Alienation;* and C. Gunton, *Christ and Creation* (Grand Rapids: Eerdmans, 1993), pp. 105-6. The most consistent and hard-hitting theological critique of modern technology is that of Jacques Ellul; see esp. his *The Technological Society*, trans. J. Wilkinson (New York: A. A. Knopf, 1964), and *The Technological Bluff*, trans. G. W. Bromiley (Grand Rapids: Eerdmans, 1990).

55. See, e.g., H. Montefiore, ed., *The Gospel and Contemporary Culture* (London and New York: Mowbray, 1992); also my article, "Keeping Our Nerve: AIDS and the Doctrine of Sin," *Austin Seminary Bulletin* 105 (1989): 23ff. Perhaps the most profound and imaginative attempt yet to overcome by means of *relational* concepts the deep-seated dualism in modern thought is J. E. Loder and W. J. Neidhardt, *The Knight's Move: The Relational Logic of the Spirit in Theology and Science* (Colorado Springs: Helmers and Howard, 1992).

Because modern science grew out of a biblical perception that the natural order is indeed profane, not sacred, and therefore legitimately studied, it has been fashionable in some quarters to blame Christianity in particular for the inquisitorial and exploitative attitudes to nature which have precipitated our ecological peril. Inviting humanity to fill, subdue, and dominate the earth (Gen. 1:26ff.), and portraying the Creator, in whose likeness we are made, as a despotic, masculine oppressor, the Scriptures themselves, it is alleged, have mandated and motivated the West's technological abuses.[56]

Is it credible, however, that those who have most ruthlessly and greedily exploited the earth and its resources have had foremost in their minds the wish to obey every word of Scripture and meticulously do the will of Scripture's God? The problem rests with disobedience, not obedience! For the truth is that the Bible enjoins not thoughtless subjugation but responsible stewardship of the created order, and that both Old Testament and New themselves constitute, for those with eyes to see, the most radical subversion of doctrines and images of God as patriarchal and tyrannical. Faith best serves today's ecological imperatives not by jettisoning but by recovering the God of the Bible. That applies supremely to the first person of the Trinity. Far from exalting the Fatherhood of God as justifying masculine control of nature since the Enlightenment, theology's shortcoming has been precisely the reverse: neglect of God the Father and Creator, in order to concentrate upon the Spirit and the Son.[57]

56. See esp. the famous essay by Lynn White, "The Historical Roots of Our Ecologic Crisis," *Science* 155 (1967). Cf. T. Peters, ed., *Cosmos as Creation: Theology and Science in Consonance* (Nashville: Abingdon, 1989), pp. 258ff.; F. A. Schaeffer, *Pollution and the Death of Man* (London: Hodder & Stoughton, 1970); R. C. Austin, *Beauty of the Lord* (Atlanta: John Knox Press, 1988); and A. E. Lewis, *Theatre of the Gospel: The Bible as Nature's Story* (Edinburgh: Handsel Press, 1984), esp. pp. 19-20.

57. Today, of course, there is a widespread attempt within the Christian community and in theology to recover the once-neglected doctrine of creation and better integrate creation with redemption. See esp. G. Hendry, *Theology of Nature* (Philadelphia: Westminster, 1980); J. Moltmann, *God in Creation,* trans. M. Kohl (London: SCM and San Francisco: Harper & Row, 1985) and *The Spirit of Life,* trans. M. Kohl (London: SCM and Minneapolis: Augsburg Fortress, 1992); H. P. Santmire, *The Travail of Nature* (Philadelphia: Fortress, 1985); D. T. Hessel, ed., *After Nature's Revolt* (Minneapolis: Augsburg Fortress, 1992); J. A. Nash, *Loving Nature: Ecological Integrity and Christian Responsibility* (Nashville: Abingdon, 1991); R. Faricy, *Winds and Sea Obey Him: Approaches to a Theology of Nature* (London: SCM, 1982); W. Pannenberg, *Toward a Theology of Nature,* ed. T. Peters (Louisville: Westminster/John Knox Press, 1993). See also H. H. Oliver, "The Neglect and Recovery of Nature in Twentieth-Century Protestant Thought," *Journal of the American Academy of Religion* 60.3 (Fall 1992): 379-404.

In reaction to the church's patriarchal history and theology, some well-meaning at-

This is surely the theological basis for an anthropocentric worldview which disassociates humanity from the environment and elevates us excessively above the animals and nature. Not by repudiating or revising, but by rediscovering the doctrine of the Trinity (as we have been attempting in this study), re-appropriating the *creatorhood* of God, and of the eternal Word and Spirit, the "two hands" of the Father, might we heal the breach between creation and redemption; and thus might we banish the hermeneutical excrescences of Christians who use the book of Revelation, for example, to render tolerable and divinely blessed, not only a third world war but ecological degradation also — since God will destroy everything in the apocalypse that saves the chosen few.[58]

tempts to rethink the doctrine of God really amount to the replacement of biblical norms and sources with a brand of neo-paganism. That danger is manifest in the much-acclaimed work of S. McFague, for example; see her *Models of God: Theology for an Ecological, Nuclear Age*. For a critique, see A. F. Kimel Jr., ed., *Speaking the Christian God* (Grand Rapids: Eerdmans and Leominster: Gracewing, 1992). See also the important work of R. R. Ruether, *Gaia and God: An Ecofeminist Theology of Earth Healing* (San Francisco: HarperCollins, 1992). Ruether's self-declared intentions are to remain Christian in her understanding of nature and thus to differentiate herself from neo-paganism. For her "the biblical God and Gaia [the living, sacred earth] are not at odds; rightly understood, they are on terms of amity, if not commingling" (p. 240). But despite her admirable attempt to deepen the Christian consciousness and spirituality of the earth, her book merely reinforces the question of how such a development toward the sacredness of the earth itself can possibly keep faith with the origins of the Jewish-Christian tradition, namely, in the radical *contrast* between the transcendent, holy Creator and the good but profane creation, the true worship of Yahweh and the false idolatry of Baal and the other autochthonous deities of Canaan.

Ecological neo-paganism can sometimes manifest appalling sloppiness of thought and outright ignorance. In one article, e.g., the notions that "the Spirit is a natural being" and that "Spirit and earth internally . . . permeate one another" are defended against the charge of pantheism on the grounds that "Christian thought has always maintained that nature and grace, world and God are inseparably interrelated." Interrelated indeed; but precisely because they are *not* identical or indistinguishable. To the same end, the eucharistic "indwelling of the divine in and with everyday foodstuffs" is invoked: "if God can become a loaf of bread or cup of wine, then why can God not become a bird or a beast or a tree or a mountain or a river?" What has become of us when it is seriously offered as a Christian proposition that God *becomes* a loaf of bread? Not even Tridentine transsubstantiation suggested that! See M. I. Wallace, "The Wild Bird Who Heals: Recovering the Spirit in Nature," *Theology Today* 50.1 (1993): 13-28.

58. See here Gore, *Earth in the Balance*, p. 263. Of course, it is equally unsatisfactory to romanticize and idolize nature and dismiss human beings as alien and disposable squatters on the earth. Hence Gore's proper rebuke of the antihuman "Deep Ecologists" throughout his book.

From a different angle, too, that of theodicy, the God of Christian faith still stands under indictment for the terrible possibility of planetary death which Chernobyl has come to represent. Are God's reality and nature any less suspect in the face of an ultimate eco-catastrophe than they would be after a nuclear winter and are already after the Jewish Holocaust? Who and where is God if God's power and love can sustain such losses and accede to such defeats? And would this ultimate defeat and loss — the Creator's forfeiture of all creation (too much an oxymoron to be thinkable) — not provide the final and irrefutable evidence of God's nonreality, the proof that we, demonically divine ourselves, are on our own, as we busily yet carelessly engineer humanity's *Götterdämmerung?* "We are in charge now, like it or not," alleges one weeping observer of nature's ruination. "As a species we are as gods, our reach global. And God has not stopped us. The possibilities . . . include the following. God thoroughly approves of what we have done; it is our destiny. God doesn't approve, but is powerless to do anything about it. . . . Or God is uninterested, or absent, or dead."[59] If God is dead, and planet earth is dying, does Chernobyl date the dawn of the final, *final* Easter Saturday?

II. An Even Greater Hope in History's Great Hopelessness

Such then are among the voluminous grounds for despair and hopelessness which could bring tears to any honest eye surveying the wreckage of the twentieth century and anticipating history's tomorrow as it turns on its millennial axis. Given such a past and present, what hope is there for our historical future? Yet that very question contains the seeds of its own non-despairing rejoinder. What we have just charted briefly is the collapse of optimism about the prospects for world history tomorrow: the apparent incapacity of any agency, natural or mechanical, human or divine, to sustain our assurance that even for a season life shall plainly prevail over the lethal forces at work within us as human beings and through us in our history. Yet this very disappointment effects, we have already seen, a clarifying of the differential between optimism and hope.

For many, to be sure, only despair and pessimism remain to fill the vacuum left by the collapse of confidence; but the abolition of optimism in fact creates the possibility of a subtly but significantly different mien toward tomorrow. That is the posture of hopefulness. For hope, finding space to flourish in

59. McKibben, *End of Nature*, pp. 78-79.

the very absence of optimism, is the courage not to be swallowed by despair but, in frank acknowledgment of rampant evil and negation, to trust in the possibility for life and creativity *amid and beyond* that malign hegemony, though assuredly not in its denial or avoidance. The very realities which banish confidence and legitimize despair also invite a hopeful embrace of love's living power to prevail in history strictly through surrender to the causes of despair and hopelessness which history proves to be immense enough.

However, only with utmost caution dare one ever evoke this hope in the power of God's powerless love, not least in the context of our threefold revisitation of Easter Saturday in recent history. The need for sensitivity and reservation is especially acute, perhaps, when the language of Christian hope is essayed in reference to the Jewish Holocaust. Far too many questions of Christian responsibility and too many promptings of the church's repentance and remorse linger here for us lightly or imperialistically to intrude a hymn of divine victory or Christian hope into the dirge for those ineffably perverse events. We have, to be sure, glimpsed with many Jews themselves intimations of life, faith and reconstruction within the death, despair, and devastation which "Auschwitz" represents. These are the defiant vestiges of memory, resistance, and renewal which deny Hitler his ultimate, posthumous victory. Yet some analysts of these memories and testimonials also bitterly resent, as we have also noted, the superficial enlisting of this residual life-affirming witness in the cause of projecting hopeful and uplifting patterns of redemptive meaning onto a world occurrence which in itself was unambiguously evil, meaningless beyond all qualifying.[60]

When one Jew may give offense by perceiving a heroic triumph of the indomitable human spirit where another sees only catastrophe and the spirit of malignancy, the church would do well to stand back and impose no triumphalistic Christian meaning on the Final Solution; allow the holocaust literature to say no more than it wishes to say, even should that amount only to atheistic protest and despair of human nature; and attribute to Auschwitz no more significance than Jews may determine among themselves to be appropriate. That same reserve, we have already said, would distance us with equal or greater determination from the fatuous blasphemies of Christians who impress a sectarian and supremacist gospel upon a possible nuclear or ecological apocalypse.

60. See esp. the harsh criticism directed by Lawrence Langer against the outstanding Jewish historian Martin Gilbert for concluding his monumental record, *The Holocaust*, with references to the triumphant and heroic human spirit quite unsubstantiated by his own preceding narratives of unmitigated horror and inhumanity. See Langer, *Holocaust Testimonies*, esp. pp. 2, 35ff., and ch. 5.

These caveats should help to regulate how we do and do not attempt to juxtapose with the modern reenactments of Easter Saturday in history, the normative three-day Christian narrative which moves beyond the hopelessness of the cross and grave to the abundant hopefulness of resurrection. Just in what way does "the word of the cross," positing resumption beyond rupture and hope beyond despair, bear upon our repeated experience of abject negation in contemporary world history? It is vital, for one thing, that that Word be heard and passed on as offering an open freedom and *possibility* to discover meaning within history's meaninglessness, and not as an overbearing interpretative instrument which forces rationality onto events of obvious absurdity, and almost insists that they be recognized despite their negativity as inducements to confidence and joy in the future of history and history's God. The gospel certainly makes hope possible; but never *necessary*. Three forms at least of such hermeneutical coercion must be resisted.

The first device is to suppose that the church's memory of Christ's victory beyond the defeat and death of Easter Saturday, that ultimate mighty act of God in history, provides some *historical* assurance that subsequent triumphs in human history of death or unrighteousness are at worst penultimate and must themselves yield, visibly if slowly, to the sway of grace and godliness. In fact, nothing in the raising of the crucified and buried one narrated in the Christian triduum amounts to proof that the victims of Auschwitz shall finally triumph over their murderers, nor that life and creativity are guaranteed ultimate ascendancy over the forces of death and destruction released and typified at Hiroshima or Chernobyl. It is one thing, for those with ears to hear, to exercise faith and trust that the God who raised the divine Son after his Sabbath termination shall in the *eschaton* triumph, too, over every residual power of death and the demonic. It is quite another to find in the hope beyond hopelessness of the first Easter Saturday an irresistible promise that every evil "sabbath" event in subsequent human history shall also realize a sequel of victory and vindication for the good. When we "hope against hope" in the possibility for renewal beyond rupture and purpose beyond nihilism, we are purchasing no false guarantees for happy historical outcomes, but are laying upon God a worthwhile wager, only riskily, though not without some reasons, embracing a prospect for the world's deliverance which contains within itself the cognate possibility, even now, for the continuing success of evildoers, executioners, and all the enemies of life.

Just as faith receives no historical assurances, from the story of divine death, burial, and resurrection, that God shall resolve every temporal conflict with wickedness and death in favor of life and righteousness, neither, secondly, are there any timelesss, ahistorical, *cosmological* certainties that creativity must prevail and justice always vindicate life's victims in the end. This is to repeat an earlier complaint (pp. 88-89 above) that the Christian good news, iconoclastic, unprecedented, *sui generis,* is all-too-often reduced in the church's theology and preaching, hymnology and liturgy — especially in the northern hemisphere, perhaps — to a species of a universal genus: the innate capacity of the cosmos for resumption and regeneration as nature's rhythmic cycles turn day by day, season by season, from dark to light, from death to rebirth, from barrenness to fecundity. This domesticates Holy Saturday's horror, and naturalizes Easter morning's surprise, as instances each of purely natural phenomena, universally conjoined as winter precedes and then concedes to spring. This does no justice to either the dark or the light side of the Christian narrative, but falsely renders predictable and necessary the story's wholly unguaranteed passage from the former to the latter. Such a naturalistic hermeneutic quite suppresses the novelty, unexpectedness, and inconceivability of hope grounded in the raising of the crucified and buried God. For that event confounds every natural law, disrupts every cosmic rhythm, and cancels every fancied analogy between natural regeneration and God's own unique creativeness. On the contrary, the inimitable and primordial act of God, who germinates hope in the midst of hopelessness, actually clarifies the still great dissimilarity between the Creator and the creatures, within their even greater, God-established similarity.

Finally, no less damage is done to the actuality of the events of Christ's death, burial, and resurrection, and to their meaning for world history, when Easter Saturday and Sunday are compelled to provide a *mythological* antidote to despair and hopelessness. Here the events of salvation history are pressed into service as components of a religious myth, one among a profusion of cultural variants, all of which exhibit the ultimate resolution of the timeless, universal struggle between good and evil, eternity and time.[61] It is unnecessary to repeat

---

61. See, as one clear example here, D. Cupitt, *The World to Come* (London: SCM, 1982), and the author's explicit intention there to mythologize Easter Saturday as a component of "the classic mythic dramas of death and rebirth, the end of the world and the coming of the Kingdom of God. . . . Encountering modern nihilism, and experiencing it as Holy Saturday and the end of the world, [*The World to Come*] enacts the pattern of death and resurrection. It seeks to lead its reader to die with Christ, to experience the Nihil, and to come to such a pass that there is no other recourse left him to choose the values of the Kingdom of God on the far side." D. Cupitt, "A Reply to Rowan Williams," in *Modern Theology* 1.1 (Oct. 1984): 27.

Of course, it is not to be denied that there is a generic, recurrent myth in human culture of dying and rising, or of birth, death, and rebirth, nor that it has had immense moral and spiritual impact upon human experience and history. Thus Garry Wills has recently found that form of the myth commonly associated with classical Athens still to be power-our earlier critique of the phenomenon of "foundationalism" in much "post-modern" theology (Ch. 8, pp. 265-69), which seeks to abstract universal religious a prioris from the concrete and nonsubstitutable affirmations and veridical claims of particular theological traditions and communities of faith. It is enough to object that a mythological reduction of Christ's death, burial, and resurrection imposes, again, a coercive, triumphal meaning upon historical events that have themselves reduced humanity to nihilism and despair by treating them as mere episodes in an assuredly redemptive cosmic drama. This in turn concedes that the only answers to historical despair lie beyond history in timelessness, outside that very sequence of events which causes our grief and woe. Here the grounds for hope in the midst of hopelessness are essentially unhistorical and nonchronological; which is to confess that history lacks its own deliverance or deliverer and provides no locus for meaning within its own trajectories, but only in mythic abstraction and removal from them.

Surely, however, only within history are any credible solutions to the problems of history, any meaningful alternative to its chaos to be found. History's redemption must be grounded, if anywhere, within the sphere of history itself and its own brokenness, and certainly not in any cyclic or mythic dehistoricization. That is why all attempts to detemporalize the narrative of the cross and of the occupied and empty grave must be resisted. And one way to keep us mindful of the surd contingency and historical particularity of Good Friday and Easter Saturday, in all their concrete wretchedness, is by repeatedly juxtaposing that story with memories of latter-day world-historical experiences of godforsakenness and termination. That is not, we say, to turn the Holocaust or Hiroshima, for example, into parables of Christian salvation or analogies of natural theology, forcing them to shed meaning and significance today on first-century historical events whose horrendous hellishness the passing centuries have made innocuous. If we allow Auschwitz to breathe fresh life into the story of Good Friday, for example,[62] that would not be to sacralize the Holocaust as a

---

fully latent in Abraham Lincoln's "Gettysburg Address." See G. Wills, *Lincoln at Gettysburg: The Words That Remade America* (New York: Simon & Schuster, 1992), esp. ch. 1. But for Christians to recognize the existence and potency of such a humanistic truism should not mean compromising the absolute uniqueness of the act by which God raised Jesus Christ from the dead, nor the *sui generis* significance of that event for the meaning of human and natural life. Generic "rebirth" bears witness to Easter, not the other way around.

62. See, e.g., H. Frei, *The Identity of Jesus Christ*, p. 170: "I need only remind you of all that we sorrowfully feel in connection with the mention, especially on Good Friday, of the word 'Auschwitz.' . . . The central Christian story in its recited and performed reenactment is the bestower of meaning for other similar events, and yet these other events have to evoke the original and breathe life into it."

vehicle of quasi-revelation and thus to desecrate further the integrity of its victims. But it might disturb the secure faith and clear conceptions of negligent and complacent Christians with the reminder that their own tradition originates in a narrative of speechless termination and boundless tragedy. Too often we forget, and at utmost cost, that redemption was born not in a pretty bed of heroism, loveliness, and rationality, but in the bloody trenches of failure, calamity, and evil, including this impenetrable tragedy: that the price of salvation through a crucified and risen son of Israel has been the very history of anti-Semitism and hatred of the Jew which led to Auschwitz.[63]

Whatever resemblance, then, there might be between the Holocaust and Calvary, whatever light either one might shed upon the other, or darkness of one be intensified through apposition with the other, it is clear that there are *no* retrospective analogies, embedded in the terrible events of the twentieth or any other century, for the mystery and miracle of Easter Sunday whereby the undiminished tragedy of the cross and grave became the genesis of hope for God, humanity, or history. Rather than forcibly transporting the bold festivity of Easter from Jerusalem to Auschwitz, Hiroshima, or Chernobyl, or minimizing there, in Easter's light, our contemporaries' ample grounds for historical despair, all we may do is embody the story of the raising of the Buried One with sufficient credibility that they might recognize with us and through us at least some possibilities for future confidence within and beyond our shared suspicions that the world has already come to a catastrophic end.

That story does encounter us first, as the shape of this whole study has exhibited, in and through the ear, as a "word of the cross" addressing those who would listen out of the very wordlessness of Calvary and the silence of the Saturday. And we have noted how language in our own day burst forth from the ghastly speechlessness of Auschwitz and Hiroshima, bearing life-giving witness to the truth of those events and thus refusing ultimate victory to the muzzling, repressive forces of falsehood and of death. Yet none of this resilient, defiant testimony from the survivors of genocide and mass destruction may be cast against their will as analogous to the joyous torrent of pentecostal words which streamed from those two thousand years ago who broke their stunned and frightened silence of Calvary despair with courageous and missionary declara-

63. These tragic elements of the atonement, including the bitter harvest of anti-Semitism, are a particular burden of Donald MacKinnon. See especially "Atonement and Tragedy," in his *Borderlands of Theology* (London: Lutterworth Press, 1968), ch. 5, pp. 102-3; and cf. his introductory essay to von Balthasar, *Engagement with God*, p. 8; and also his paper on Donald Baillie in Fergusson, ed., *Christ, Church and Society* (Edinburgh: T. & T. Clark, 1992), pp. 118ff.

tions of Easter praise and proclamation. At most, persistent speech from beyond the graves of *modern* liquidation, never to be coerced into proving Christian dogma, may lend some credence to the church's claims for contemporary faith, hope, and love which, we have been proposing, are in fact grounded in the triune God who re-creates all things and gives life to what is not. And it reinforces the mystery that often it is only with words, so impotent in and of themselves, that the most powerful blows are struck against the might of death and wickedness. If only with weak words may the demonic be resisted, conversely words may be all it takes for the God whose word and act are one to vanquish the enemy, bring light out of darkness, and suckle hope at the empty breast of human hopelessness.

The word of the cross, which in its impotence consummates God's creative, resurrecting power, and whose content is the mystery of love — that where sin increases grace abounds much more — effects the creation of a community of listening faith. They not only hear the narrative of vulnerable love's abundant creativity, but are constrained to think that story through, expound and conceptualize its meaning, and by bringing it to thinkability make it a viable stimulus to hope, courage, and engagement for the frightened and despairing of this and every generation. Much of our study, then, has been concerned, beyond the sheer hearing and telling of the Christian story, to explore the theological and conceptual path by which the word about the death of the living God has at last, overcoming much resistance, become a thinkable thought for the contemporary church. So how in particular might this word of the raising of the crucified and buried God, unutterable and inconceivable, yet now becoming a speakable gospel and a conceivable conception, address the multiple terminal crises of world history which are our legacy at the end of our fraught millennium?

✳   ✳   ✳

Even, or perhaps especially, after the Jewish Holocaust and its sequels in our time, not everyone in theology by any means is willing to speak of divine suffering, to locate God upon the cross of Calvary or on the gallows of Auschwitz,[64] or to conceive of the death of Christ as the crucifying of God's own self and thus "the death of the living God." For some it is humanity alone we see suffering in the passion and execution of Jesus, just as it is human suffering *in extremis* we remember or seek reluctantly to imagine in the concentration camps of Europe and the streets of Hiroshima. There is divine redemption from suffer-

---

64. Wiesel, *Night*, esp. pp. 76-77.

ing, atrocity, and guilt, it is said, precisely because, though compassionate for human pain, God does *not* succumb to our weakness and mortality, but rather remains transcendent, and thus triumphant, over all immanent pain and sorrow, sin and death. Of course, for some the language of divine suffering is unhelpful just because it perpetuates an anachronistic tradition, the classical ontology of divine transcendence and objective reality, an outdated myth little improved by the substitution of weakness and suffering for omnipotence and impassibility as the attributes of deity. But there are others for whom that substitution itself abandons rather than reconceptualizes the tradition of divine power, and thus threatens the whole structure of belief in the providential and redemptive agency of God. Perhaps remarkably, Hans Küng, though himself once attracted to Hegel's speculations about the suffering and death of God, has recently veered away from that trajectory, returning to classical conceptions of transcendence supposedly for the sake of a gospel jeopardized by the Hegelian dialectic. For the God reduced to suffering, crucifixion, foolishness, and death is no longer redemptive or even truly compasssionate, but a pathetic God to feel sorry for, and thus not the God of the Bible.[65]

It is plain from our previous two chapters that Barth, Moltmann, and Jüngel are by no means uncritical inheritors of Hegel's speculations concerning divine self-fulfillment through suffering and self-negation. Yet each of these, in defiance of what Küng now claims to be impossible, helped to construct beyond Hegel a biblical and coherent theology of the cross, grounded in a trinitarian ontology which indeed asserts with reason that God becomes and remains transcendent and eschatologically redemptive precisely by being vulnerable and subject to self-negation unto death. Unlike Küng, this trio, among others, have, in the light of Auschwitz or independently, tried to speak and conceive of God's power as the deliverer of humanity and history exactly in terms of that suffering love which hangs upon the cross and on the scaffold; and who thus, and only thus, but truly thus, abounds all the more creatively over sin and death and evil.

Such an understanding of creative suffering in no way *depends* upon the speculative notion in Jewish medieval mysticism of divine "shrinkage," by which God withdraws in order to make room for creation and its infringements

---

65. See Küng, *Judaism,* pp. 592-609, esp. p. 599; cf. his *Incarnation of God,* esp. pp. 413-558. Many of the questions which Küng's recent discussion raises about the biblical and theological justification for the concept of the suffering of God in fact find their answer within the treatment of that theme in his study of Hegel. Küng's remarks are specifically directed to the thought of the Jewish scholar Hans Jonas, whose famous lecture on "the concept of God after Auschwitz," and the comments upon it by Eberhard Jüngel, were referred to above (n. 31).

of Yahweh's holy space.[66] Hans Küng vigorously objects to that conception, but Moltmann especially has adapted it to his Christian conceptualizing of divine vulnerability in the light of Auschwitz. And it is surely possible, perhaps required in the light of the biblical and theological tradition explored above, to conceive of God the Creator as indeed renouncing isolation for companionship and thus freely accepting the handicaps and limitations which the presence of others represents. The God who chooses not to be alone chooses thereby also to forgo the absence of competing fortunes, wills, and needs, and submits instead to both the costs and joys of reciprocity, becoming susceptible to others' pain, rebellion, and ingratitude no less than to the delightfulness of their obedience and happiness.

To create external reality out of nothing, partners out of solitude, is, to be sure, omnipotence supreme beyond all human conceiving, save for the faintest analogies of parenthood, perhaps. Yet this power, not in contradiction of itself but as its truest self-expression (for it is the power of *love*), is also and as such a free act of self-depotentiation, a reduction of one's own space, a handicapping of one's liberties.[67] Not in abdication of lordship and transcendence, but in their perfection and fulfillment, is it the nature of this divine creative love sovereignly to enter into suffering, to absorb the pain and costs of self-expenditure and self-restriction, of relationality and fellow feeling. Thus is it only on the cross and in the grave, where self-limitation reaches its boundary point of self-negation, that the creative power of God is truly and finally revealed; and in the raising of God's buried Son we see at last the boundlessly redemptive and resumptive possibilities of the love that knows abandonment to contradiction.

Conceiving God's creative and re-creative power, then, from the standpoint of the grave, as dynamic surrender to suffering and restriction, can we avoid the conclusion — or should we even wish to? — that in order to be history's omnipotent lord and eschatological redeemer, God must be exposed to

---

66. This is the concept of *zimzum* which featured in Jewish kabbalistic speculations and is particularly associated with Isaak Luria of the sixteenth century. See Küng, *Judaism,* pp. 175ff., 594ff.; G. Scholem, *Major Trends in Jewish Mysticism* (New York: Schocken, 1961); and Jonas, "The Concept of God after Auschwitz." Jüngel treats the concept of "shrinkage" with respectful caution (n. 31 above); Moltmann, though not uncritical, is rather enthusiastic about its utility for the Christian doctrines of God and of creation; see *Trinity and Kingdom,* pp. 109ff.; *God in Creation,* pp. 86ff.; *Way of Jesus Christ,* pp. 328-29; and *Spirit of Life,* pp. 47ff.

67. On what follows, see also my discussion in "The Burial of God," esp. pp. 354-362, and "Apocalypse and Parousia," pp. 39ff. See also B. Russell, "A Nuclear End: Would God Ever Let It Happen?" in A. Race, ed., *Theology against the Nuclear Horizon,* ch. 9; cf. Moltmann, *Creating a Just Future,* esp. pp. 32ff.

the peril, cost, and grief of loss? Indeed, the risk of losing history as a whole and all its creatures is entertained through the abandonment of the beloved Son in whom all things are made and all creation has its being, and whose own loss casts into controversy God's own very being as loving Father of the Son and almighty framer of the universe. To see God self-exposed thus *to* destruction, between Good Friday and Easter Saturday, for the sake of history's deliverance *from* destruction, is to recognize that the creative and redemptive omnipotence of God, far from invulnerable and impervious to opposition is in fact an exquisitely perilous power which does not protect itself against the catastrophe and boundless sorrow which would be creation's devastation and time's annihilation.

Thus does the unthinkable thought become conceivable that the God of Jesus Christ, who surrenders everything for salvation's sake, does not and will not prevent the worst denouements of human, global, or cosmic history. The grace which abounds only *after* sin's increase is not by any means impregnable against the disaster in which that sin expands to the magnitude of an Easter Saturday, of an Auschwitz or Hiroshima, of a third World War or a planetary cataclysm. The Christian story concludes with the pardoning of guilt and the banishing of death, with the redemption of time beyond its rupture and the proleptic dawning of a universal future over the ovens, missile silos, and melting power plants of humanity's hopelessness. Yet the hope which is assured that beyond our worst atrocities and calamities the God of the cross shall still prevail by the flourishing of risky, vulnerable grace cannot and does not exclude, but must allow space for, the most disproportionate and conclusive of historical disasters.

A creator who imperiously and coercively forbade or impeded such damage to creation, humanity, and deity would no longer be the God embodied and revealed in the weakness of the cross of Jesus Christ or in the self-imperiling of his tomb. Rather, in the Friday sacrifice of the Son to destruction and his Saturday surrender to hell and the demonic, all the unrighteousness and crookedness of human history, past and future, of every place and context, is embraced, compacted, and allowed for — given space to increase, to be and do its worst — and only thus transcended and redeemed. The hope which may sustain us in the aftermath of Auschwitz, Hiroshima, and Chernobyl is hope grounded in the harsh and harrowing knowledge that the only love able to triumph over those excrescences of wickedness and folly is the love that bows to their occurrence and makes itself their victim.

There is, of course, an equally important, positive way of saying this, namely that the creative love and providential lordship which yields to such actual or possible defeats as the Holocaust or a nuclear war is an infinitely fructifying and transforming energy which fulfills God's Godness as transcendent over history and redemptive of it. The grace that succumbs to negation and defeat on Easter Saturday truly is the power of resurrection: the hope of the world and the promise of its consummation. Despite Küng's "after Auschwitz" fears that the God of suffering and victimization is in danger of ceasing to be the God of Jesus Christ, we have in fact reviewed the slow, staccato development of a biblical and dogmatic ontology which conceives the very opposite: that the God who suffers pain, resistance, and defeat *remains* God in so doing. Who dies upon the cross of Christ and in his grave but the very God who lives and brings to life? Divine *kenosis* is as such, and with no contradiction, divine *plerosis* and perfecting; and whatever "shrinkage" the self-limiting Maker sustains in creation and on Calvary is the withdrawal of that strangely dynamic love which, because it expresses and perfects itself through self-denial and contraction, actually increases and expands the more it gives itself to opposition and negation.

Thus does God's love harvest a surplus of life, creativity, and wholeness beyond the vast but moribund wastelands of history's foolishness and evil. And that the God who did not prevent the Jewish Holocaust, and will not prevent a nuclear or ecological catastrophe, is still God, still abundantly loving and gracious beyond the unthinkable extremes of tragedy and loss, constantly gives new birth to hope in the living power of the crucified God. Such hope motivates the community of faith, who hear "the word of the cross," to live and struggle by that story so that the worst prospective calamities facing history's future might not in fact take place, and that those who have so far triumphed over the innocent victims of history's most terrible misanthropy shall win no more posthumous victories but be seen in the end to have forfeited the last triumphal word to their presently silenced victims.

Now, as we have seen, what makes the concept of God's victory beyond the defeat of Auschwitz, Hiroshima, and Chernobyl a thinkable thought, and the corresponding lifestyle and ethic a livable option, is at the technical level (though however technical it is the gospel's heart!) the doctrine of the Trinity, whose development we have traced. That is what Küng appears to have forgotten when he supposes that the God who suffers, is crucified, and dies is no longer Scripture's God.

The evolving insight of Barth, Moltmann, and Jüngel has been precisely otherwise: that the divine community of mutual dependence and self-giving is indeed the ontological ground for thinking and living a story which promises the final consummation of time and of the world beyond history's defeat and loss. For the Spirit is revealed between the cross and the grave to be the unifying go-between who holds the Father and the Son together when in self-abandonment to sonlessness the Father gives up the Beloved One to death and hell. And because the eternal Son, fatherless and liquidated, is flesh of our own flesh, God united to the utmost of our perishableness, the Spirit who unites the Father and the Son through their separation also holds together humanity and God, the Creator and the creatures. Thus does death within the living Trinity secure God's even closer union with humanity in its mortality and guilt, on the very boundary of their deepest alienation and furthest separation. Thus too, by the Spirit's unifying act, does the death and burial of the Son, far beyond its falsifying of God's fatherhood and power, become also a healing and authenticating moment in the history of God's becoming, who surrenders to non-being in human history and created time and negates it with even more abundant life.

What, therefore, of the future of the world? It rests not in the linear advance, powerful, unthwarted, guaranteed, as classical eschatology supposed, of God's redeeming purposes toward the final kingdom; nor in its secular, optimistic counterpart, the thrust of human progress toward utopia. For God, the maker and deliverer of history, shall be, until the end, always at hazard to time's outrageous forfeiture of meaning and of purpose, as we lurch through a syncopated series of catastrophes natural and human, of genocides particular and global. Because the omnipotent God of the classical tradition is dead, and the axioms of immutability and causal power no longer credible, Christians today have no metaphysical principles to propound concerning providence and the secure salvation of the world; but they do have a story to share and live about the power of fragile grace.

That speaks of the triune God who creates new beginnings for the world beyond death and cataclysm. But the Spirit of the Trinity opens up such possibilities only by raising from the dead the Father's only Son, in whom death is allowed to work its rupturing effect upon God's very self. Only as the primal victim of sin's increase is the triune God a victor for our sakes over the magnitude of evil and the giver of new life to the Creator's fellow dead among the creatures. Yet through this Easter Saturday love, whose substance is weakness and surrender, the Spirit who raised from death and burial the Father's only Son exceeds our history's plentiful memories of past atrocity and present fears of termination with an even greater hope of future consummation: time's redemption, the glorious liberation of its creatures, and the making new of heaven and earth.

III. The Prayer of Easter Saturday

The only hope this expresses for the future, relying neither on liberalism's self-improvement of humanity, nor the Marxist laws of history's onward march,

300

rests in God's own being, that being-in-becoming which is the dynamic, ontological fruitfulness of suffering and self-restriction. If then, at last, we pay full
attention to the long-surfacing question about Christian lifestyle appropriate to
the hope that is grounded in the living, triune God, and ask what it means to
live the thought-out story of the cross and grave, the answer can only be cast in
terms of an ethic of withdrawal. If God alone defeats death and consummates
the kingdom in which history shall be fulfilled, how can we testify to that hope
and live in correspondence with it except by our own withdrawal, by a self-
renunciation which embodies our own recognition that salvation for the world
is *not* our possibility but lies outside history and humanity's own capabilities.
Only a *kenosis,* a surrender, a shrinkage of ourselves, perhaps, which abjures
self-confidence and abdicates humanity's cherished status as fabricator of reality and determiner of destiny, can make space for the God by whose own space-
making, vulnerable love all things have been made, are upheld, and shall be fulfilled.

The primary description of that lifestyle which repudiates self-sufficiency
and allows God to be the one alone in and through whose dynamism the world
shall be redeemed and the future consummated is: prayer. For what is prayer
but the summary posture of those who foreswear the idolatry of self-reliance
and affirm rather the perfection, primacy, and power of God. Prayer acknowledges and glorifies the name and character of God as the world's sole maker
and redeemer, before whom we are powerless, empty, guilty, but in whose very
grace — in its own way so empty and powerless itself — all human needs are
met, sins forgiven, fears quelled, foes conquered, hopes fulfilled. Our doxology
and confession, our supplications and ascriptions: all these combine to identify
and honor the divine, transcendent possibility to which we must defer and on
which we stake our destiny and our world's.

Of course, that timelessly describes the church's prayer, and summarizes
the content of what Christians always pray and how they give their prayer living
enactment and embodiment. But it is particularly needful today that we illuminate this relationship between prayer and Christian hope for the future of the
world — and that we be as sensitive to the difficulties as the urgency of making
that connection in our contemporary context. For what can it possibly mean
self-effacingly to entrust ourselves in words and corresponding actions to the
power of God alone, rather than any human or historical power, when the very
nature of the God we have been constrained to conceive of in our day, in the
light of Easter Saturday, is a kind of *powerlessness,* a lordship over history
marked precisely by the visible weakness and folly of the crucified and buried
Jesus? How, especially today, attempting to live by the concept of the surplus
creativity of vulnerable love, can we possibly withdraw all self-reliance upon

301

our own resourcefulness in favor of utter trust in this kind of providential im-potence? In fact, nothing better sums up the questions raised by the theology of the cross and grave, in relation to faith's future hope, than the conundrum of prayer and providence from an Easter Saturday perspective. How is it remotely possible to *pray* to a crucified and buried God? What can be achieved by en-trusting the future of our world and of ourselves to a self-emptied servant, cru-cified in weakness and buried in extinction? To what effect might we ascribe all the kingdom, power, and glory to one whom death destroyed, hell swallowed up, and evil annihilated?

This, at least in part, is a new problem for theology and Christian living. Our various past traditions spoke easily and in significant accord about God's sheer omnipotence and providential sovereignty exercised over all human and inanimate life, conspiring to bring not just individuals or communities or na-tions but universal history to a sure, appointed goal: the triumph of God's sov-ereign grace and perfect will. So total seemed that lordship, so secure the des-tiny of the elect, that at times it could be asked — albeit rhetorically, the better to understand the mystery — what point there was in prayer to so powerful a God who already knows our needs and has unshakably ordained our future and that of all creation. Why *ask* for anything if God is in control, the divine will ir-resistible, and divine decisions irreversible?[68]

Of course, the contemporary theological developments we have traced above constitute a massive questioning of the axiom of God's immutability and omnipotence, inviting a thorough trinitarian reinterpretation of Christ's death and resurrection, where God's nature is uniquely and iconoclastically revealed as powerful and lordly to be sure, but only in and through suffering and oppo-sition. The traditional doctrine of providence is among those most rigorously challenged, once it is conceded that theology should not preconceive, on the basis of some philosophical or metaphysical presumption, what it is possible or

---

68. For the classical Reformed exposition of providence see Calvin, *Inst.* I.xvi and xvii. See also B. W. Farley, *The Providence of God* (Grand Rapids: Baker Book House, 1988); and J. Leith, *John Calvin's Doctrine of the Christian Life* (Louisville: Westminster/John Knox, 1982), ch. 3. It is interesting that the rhetorical question about the superfluousness of prayer could be asked by both "Catholic" and Reformed in the days when the omnipo-tence of God was a shared and comfortable axiom; see, e.g., Thomas Aquinas, *Summa Theologiae,* vol. 39, Blackfriars, 2a2ae.83.2: "God's mind is unchangeable and inflexible. . . . Therefore it is not fitting that we should pray to God"; and Calvin, *Inst.,* III.xx.3: "Does God not know, even without being reminded, both in what respect we are troubled and what is expedient for us, so that it may seem in a sense superfluous that he should be stirred up by our prayers — as if he were drowsily blinking or even sleeping until he is aroused by our voice?"

not for God to be and do, but must allow the person of Christ, and the event, supremely, of his death, to reveal and teach us the actualities and possibilities of divine being and doing. Such contemporary rethinking of providence was, in fact, instigated by Karl Barth (the Calvinist!), who, openly and indignantly critical of Calvin's treatment of providence, for confecting an abstract rather than a Christocentric doctrine of God's being, instead interpreted God's almightiness and providential sovereignty over humanity and nature in the light of Christ's own humanity, especially the history of his passion.[69]

Still, this reconceptualizing of providence is just what poses today's radically new problem for prayer. If it was once worth asking why it was not superfluous to pray to an all-knowing and all-powerful sovereign, now it cannot but be asked how one can pray meaningfully and with any confidence to a God of weakness, suffering, and *kenosis*, who flourishes in self-fulfillment only through self-abnegation and power's renunciation. What is the point of praying to the God of the cross whose power and wisdom are only those of impotence and foolishness?

The answer, surely, as discomforting as it is hopeful, makes costly demands even as it liberates. For if the surrender of power is *the* form, and the only form, that God's power takes, and if vulnerable self-abandonment is itself the creative energy which is bringing history powerfully to its fulfillment, that places unbearable demands upon ourselves who in and through words and deeds of prayerful living would align and associate ourselves with the triune history of God, confessing and obeying Christ's cruciform, grave-shaped lordship over all. Such prayer must humanly enact the divine possibility of grace — that those and only those who lose themselves shall find themselves. To pray to the crucified God is, therefore, to affirm and practice radical dependence and surrender to the point of death itself — which may be why so few of us truly know how to pray, or even wish to do so.

That God remains God in self-emptying and self-negation is the core of

---

69. See K. Barth, *CD*, III/3, sect. 48: "The Doctrine of Providence, Its Basis and Form." Cf. W. A. Whitehouse, "Providence: An Account of Karl Barth's Doctrine," in *Authority of Grace*, pp. 33-45. See also McIntyre, *Christian Doctrine of History*, esp. pp. 35ff. For a profound discussion of the providential creativity of the triune God's vulnerability and susceptibility, see W. H. Vanstone, *Love's Endeavour, Love's Expense* (London: Darton, Longman & Todd, 1977), esp. ch. 4. A highly significant discussion of, and contribution to, the reinterpretation of divine power and providence today is A. Case-Winters, *God's Power* (Louisville: Westminster/John Knox Press, 1990). I have elsewhere in this study expressed in brief my reservations about the process theology upon which Dr. Case-Winters's own constructive proposals are based. More promising reconstruction is initiated in D. Migliore, *The Power of God* (Philadelphia: Westminster, 1983).

the trinitarian mystery of Easter Saturday: the creativeness and self-fulfillment of the death of the living God. It is not, then, that the God who primordially in creation and ultimately at the cross and grave surrendered independence is thus rendered impotent without remainder. Rather, this surrender is powerful, this servanthood sovereign, this defeat victorious. And since it is *God's* power, sovereignty, and victory that are thus realized through suffering and contradiction, it remains God alone upon whom our present need relies and to whom our hopes for the future are entrusted. Yet what is this God, who alone is lord and savior — not least upon the cross — doing in and through this renunciation of independence and insusceptibility but determining not to be God alone, in isolated sovereignty whereby the divine will and purpose exercises a solitary, undelegated, unmediated agency.[70] Here, rather, the God before whom in prayer we bow, mysteriously bows to us — finite creatures and sometimes destructive enemies — resolving not to be God without us but with us, exercising lordship only through us. The God who renounces independence declares a longing for us, and is committed to parlous reliance on us, patient waiting for us, and hazardous agency through us, so that not alone but with and through our participation and engagement, the Father of the Son might in the Spirit prove the savior and perfecter of the world.[71]

Even this — God's self-emptying, self-limiting willingness to depend upon us, to be vulnerable to our response and victim of our recalcitrance, hindered by our slowness and thwarted by our cowardice and falsehood — even this is *not* an abdication of God's power, as if this divine weakness and dependence leave it to humanity or to the church to defeat sin, vanquish evil, and complete the harrowing of hell and the liberation of the world. For what this God, who gives up independence, awaits and seeks from us is *our* correspondingly crucified and costly surrender of power and independence, and our acknowledgement of need. *This* is the trigger of God's creative and redemptive power, whereby prayer is granted an earthly instrumentality in heavenly provi-

---

70. See, e.g., C. S. Lewis, *Letters to Malcolm: Chiefly on Prayer* (New York: Harcourt, Brace and World, 1963), pp. 67ff.

71. This particular mystery (and many others concerning prayer and providence) is finely expressed by David Willis in *Daring Prayer* (Atlanta: John Knox Press, 1977), p. 127: "The act of praying is free participation in the process of creation. God wills his creation into existence and elicits free participation, which his own self-limitation makes room for. The creative process is enriched, moved further toward its culmination when part of creation itself expands its consciousness of what it means to be created in the maker's image and to be freely obedient to him. God actually accommodates his purposes to include our acts." See also the excellent study by Peter Baelz, *Prayer and Providence* (London: SCM, 1968).

dence. For as we abandon our image of ourselves as self-made lords and controllers of the future, renouncing pride and self-sufficiency and confessing our dependence on God's own grace, precisely thereby do we humanly share in and release those divine energies by which God makes self-surrendering love the most fertile and redeeming force in heaven and earth.

Our prayerfully acknowledged dependence upon God, in short, frees the God who depends on us to direct the surpassing power of dependent, self-negating love against the dysteleology of self-sufficiency and independence which wreaks such havoc upon history, humanity, and nature. The secret of providence, which the enigmatic logic of Easter Saturday encapsulates, is that though self-preservation is massively destructive, self-expenditure is even more fulsomely creative. And our self-giving to the Lord of history, in response to God's own rejection of solitary despotism, allows Creator and creatures together (bound by the Spirit of mutual dependence and reciprocity) to fertilize and harvest the surplus creativity of selflessness over the barrenness of self-absorption. Prayer, above all, is what enfolds us within this fathomless providential mystery, as we set the God of dependence free to be alone the lord of history, yet find in our servitude to that lordship the grace which unlocks our own enslavement to independence and perfects our emancipation from self-preoccupied inertia to active service and engagement in the world for others' sake and God's through self-abandonment and unconditional commitment.[72]

72. This is to touch upon the conundrum of "double agency," i.e., the search for a conceptual understanding of how events in the world can be simultaneously the effect and evidence of God's transcendent actions on the one hand, and on the other the product of men and women's own creaturely conation. How may there be a conjunction or coincidence of divine and human operations which compromises neither the singularity of a given occurrence nor the involvement and the freedom of both its agents, but constitutes a truly mutual participation of both creatures and the Creator? It would not be apt to explore here the massive theological and philosophical intricacies of this long-standing issue. But it may be worth suggesting that literally crucial to the mystery of "double agency" is the cross of Christ, where God's kenotic surrender to humanity, and humanity's liberation for radical dependence upon God, most perfectly and visibly coincide. For a splendid recent discussion of divine and human action see B. Hebblethwaite and E. Henderson, eds., *Divine Action* (Edinburgh: T. & T. Clark, 1990). This collection of essays is inspired by and amounts to an extended analysis of the thought of Austin Farrer, whose own explorations on this theme were outstanding. See, e.g., A. Farrer, *Finite and Infinite* (Westminster: Dacre Press, 1943; London: A. & C. Black, 1959; and New York: Seabury Press, 1979); *Love Almighty and Ills Unlimited* (Garden City, N.Y.: Doubleday, 1961 and London: Collins, 1962); and *Faith and Speculation* (New York: New York University Press, 1967). See also O. C. Thomas, *God's Activity in the World: The Contemporary Problem* (Chico: Scholars Press, 1983); V. Brümmer, *What Are We Doing When We Pray?: A Philosophical Inquiry*

Adoration and doxology, supremely, articulate this creative recognition of radical dependence upon the God who makes, sustains, and shall redeem humanity and history. Likewise prayerful thanksgiving reiterates our daily need for those boundless resources of grace, utterly beyond our own manufacture or supplying, by which collectively and singly we live in weal or woe, and may die in the hope of guilt forgiven, suffering terminated and evil overcome.[73] Conversely, in confession, we acknowledge and repent our lapses into pride, self-reliance, and idolatry, that worship of the creature in place of the Creator which perpetuates the destructive illusion of human self-sufficiency. Though universal in its scope and ageless in its repetition, this lie has never been promoted and appropriated more gullibly and wantonly, nor with deadlier effect, than in the modern scientific world, shaped by autonomous narcissists whose self-deification bore such demonic fruit at Auschwitz, Hiroshima, and Chernobyl.

It is therefore as audacious subversives, however timid and inchoate their conscious resistance, that believers challenge the dominant smug myth of human self-reliance and our species' mastery of the environment and the future, by entreating the transcendent lord with intercessions and petitions. To ask for things from God, as we witness with constant embarrassment in public displays of self-regarding religiosity as well as in the private recesses of our egos, can be prayer's most sickening falsification and abuse. Yet in a society which idolizes self-sufficiency, has a horror of dependence, and despises those whose misfortunes remind us of our own deep neediness, to petition God for daily bread,

---

(London: SCM, 1984); and W. Pannenberg, *The Idea of God and Human Freedom,* trans. R. A. Wilson (Philadelphia: Westminster, 1973) (= *Basic Questions in Theology,* vol. 3 [London: SCM, 1973]). See also Hunsinger, *How to Read Karl Barth,* pp. 185-224: "Double Agency as a Test Case."

It could be noted in this context that prayer itself is a paradigmatic instance of "double agency"; for it is believers who pray, with manifestly human and finite stumbling words; yet their prayers are possible only because of God's own praying on their behalf. The Spirit intercedes for us when our words fail, liberating us to say "Abba, Father," and uniting us to the only Son, the Great High Priest who precedes us into the Holy of Holies, and through whose own vicarious, filial, prayerful obedience alone we have access to the Father.

73. Though thanksgiving is, of course, a universal theme of Jewish-Christian piety, there is also a special emphasis upon *gratitude,* grounded in the awareness of creaturely dependence upon God, characteristic of the Reformed tradition in particular. It is a distinctive theme, e.g., of Calvin's celebrated treatment of prayer in *Inst.* III.xx. See H. L. Rice, *Reformed Spirituality* (Louisville: Westminster/John Knox Press, 1991), ch. 3. Thankfulness likewise dominates the Reformed practice and interpretation of the Lord's Supper, itself a form of prayer. See esp. B. A. Gerrish, *Grace and Gratitude: The Eucharistic Theology of John Calvin* (Minneapolis: Fortress Press, 1993).

and so acknowledge the limits of our own resources, is an act of defiance against the social and spiritual status quo. So, too, those who intercede for the needs of others, or pray for deliverance from evil, iconoclastically admit that collectively the human race, supposedly so successful and mature, is unable to liberate itself, heal its own diseases, comfort its own fears, solve its own problems, or control its own destiny.[74] And if, in the midst of inadequacy, suffering, malevolence, and death, in despair for ourselves or for our world, Christian prayer peters out into speechlessness and mumbling, leaving God's own Spirit to sigh ineffably on our behalf, that very silence, human and divine, rebukes the wordy noisomeness and empty rhetoric of our self-promoting age. For supremely in the muteness of unuttered prayer, when all we can do is give up every thought of self-redemption, and all schemes, strategies, and nostrums for personal, political, or cosmic liberation, and confess a defeated defenselessness against the magnitude of sin's increase, then we engage most fully in the prayerful living out of the Easter Saturday story. Then truly, through the Spirit we enter that abyss where the world ended and the Word itself was silenced; and, suspended between patience and resignation, we can only wait for who-knows-what tomorrow might be born out of God's own fresh possibilities.[75]

Yet exactly this abandonment of optimism, this unqualified confession of dependence, is what most effectively and fulsomely releases the potential of the triune God to overcome evil and death, resuming and redeeming history beyond its terminal rupture, by the very power of dependent love. In prayer as word and as wordlessness, both having the content of human self-abandonment and ascription to the crucified but living God of all rule, power, and glory, our participation in the Easter Saturday event unleashes God's own and sole creative, providential, and resurrecting self-abandonment. Our dependence unbridles the God whose own dependence is redemptive and transforming, all the more copiously to expand beyond the vast but sterile territory of evil, and counteract the destructiveness of selfishness with the surpassing creativity of love which shall consummate history and liberate humanity when God is glorified as all in all. Thus do our stumbling, childlike, sometimes not even spoken prayers, the ludicrous epitome of all ineptitude and inefficacy, enable and share in the movement of God's own triune being toward self-fulfillment as the lord

74. See J. Ellul, *Prayer and Modern Man*, trans. C. E. Hopkins (New York: Seabury Press, 1970), esp. pp. 85ff.

75. That prayer, normatively understood as contemplation, is essentially an Easter Saturday experience, which involves our own descent into hell, is, of course, the particular insight of H. U. von Balthasar. See his *Mysterium Paschale*, and *Prayer*, trans. A. V. Littledale (London: G. Chapman, 1961 and San Francisco: Ignatius Press, 1986). Also, on Christian existence as waiting, in radical dependence, recall Vanstone, *Stature of Waiting*.

of history and the savior of the world. "How unsearchable God's judgments, how inscrutable God's ways!" (Rom. 11:33).

However mystifying, such an affirmation needs one codicil, however. For if by praying we may be channels for the providential and transforming dynamic of God's grace, that may occur because neither silent nor spoken is true prayer comprised of words alone. That words do have an instrumental power to create and to redeem is a premise of this exercise in narrative theology. Yet the power of words is inseparable from the actions which give them substance and are the criteria of their sincerity and truthfulness.[76] To live the thought-out story of the God who preserves and shall consummate all history through the cross is to live a life of prayer. But conversely, that prayerfulness, however contemplative or withdrawn, is a *life,* is active and engaged, responsible and busy, embodying sustained reflection on the *consequences* of the lived-out story. In order, then, to delineate the contours of the living of the story of the buried savior of the world we need to sketch out what kind of activity would fittingly correspond to the words of the prayer that renounces self-sufficiency and hallows the name of the crucified God. What shape might such analogous policies and practices take on in our present crisis, as we ponder the end of the world and the triumph of evil which has both already happened and threatens to recur yet more decisively? How shall we *enact* the prayerful life of even greater hope in the midst of such great hopelessness? Or, to put it otherwise, what for us who have heard and thought and prayed the story of the full and empty grave are the contemporary politics of Easter Saturday?

IV. The Politics of Easter Saturday

Speaking formally, to attempt an answer to those questions, even in so preliminary and schematic a manner as occurs below, is to engage in what today is known as "narrative ethics" — though that exercise well predates its current ap-

---

76. No one has propounded more perceptively than Karl Barth the conviction that prayer belongs to ethics, is authenticated and sustained by doing, and is itself a form of responsible human action, albeit devoted to God's sole glory and the displacement of human self-reliance. See esp. Barth, *The Christian Life* (*CD,* IV/4, Lecture Fragments), trans. G. W. Bromiley (Grand Rapids: Eerdmans and Edinburgh: T. & T. Clark, 1981); also Barth, *Prayer,* trans. S. F. Terrien (Philadelphia: Westminster, 1952); cf. rev. ed., trans. B. E. Hooker, in Barth, *Prayer and Preaching* (London: SCM, 1964). Both of Barth's studies incorporate extended analyses of the Lord's Prayer. Dietrich Bonhoeffer, too, illuminated profoundly the relationship between prayer and ethics. See, e.g., E. Bethge, *Prayer and Righteous Action* (Belfast: Christian Journals Ltd., 1979).

pellation.[77] This presumes that we discern the moral norms of our behavior and seek to embody them in practice by reference to the tradition which shapes the community of which we are a part. And access to that tradition, allowing the community to understand itself and be at least partially understood by others, is gained in the first instance through the story or stories that dramatize its meaning, identity, and history.[78] Here, as throughout this present study, "story" in no way connotes the legendary, the fictional, the nonveridical, as if to tell a story were in some way an alternative to telling the truth. On the contrary, since the realities that we experience (or have revealed to us) as *temporal* beings are essentially historical and chronologically extended, story — that is, the narrating of history — is the primordial means by which we may describe reality and truthfully articulate the way things are. And for faith, the stories by which we learn the truth about ourselves and discern the moral consequences of that truth accomplish this by locating our own histories strictly in their relation to the history of God.[79]

Of course, to ground ethics in truth-telling, reality-revealing narrative is to flout daringly the received philosophical conventions of modern, post-Enlightenment culture. For that is a tradition — or a prejudice? — rooted in the dualistic separation we have frequently observed above, between "facts" and "values": the axiom that no "ought" can be derived from "is." Morality embodies arbitrary opinions and private sensibilities, not imperatives consequent upon the veridical indicatives of objective, knowable reality.[80]

Undoubtedly the most prodigious challenge in contemporary theology to this modern divorce of knowledge and morality was mounted by Karl Barth. As we saw, he overcame his own early predilection for Kantian dualism with a pro-

---

77. I am much indebted here to a beautifully lucid and succinct account of narrative ethics by my cherished friend and colleague Duncan Forrester, in his *Beliefs, Values and Policies: Conviction Politics in a Secular Age* (Oxford: Clarendon Press, 1989).

78. See esp. A. MacIntyre, *Whose Justice? Whose Rationality?* (Notre Dame and London: University of Notre Dame Press, 1988). One of the dominant figures in moral philosophy, MacIntyre juxtaposes the principal moralities in Western cultural history in terms of their competing, and internally conflicted, narrative traditions: e.g., the Homeric, Platonic, Aristotelian, and Biblical/Augustinian. See also S. Hauerwas and D. Burrell, "From System to Story: An Alternative Pattern for Rationality in Ethics," in Hauerwas and Jones, *Why Narrative?* pp. 158-90.

79. See S. Hauerwas, *The Peaceable Kingdom: A Primer in Christian Ethics* (Notre Dame and London: University of Notre Dame Press, 1983), chs. 2 and 3.

80. See here, in particular, A. MacIntyre, *After Virtue* (Notre Dame: University of Notre Dame Press and London: G. Duckworth, 1981); also Newbigin, *The Gospel in a Pluralist Society,* esp. ch. 3.

found reintegration of existence, grounded in the incarnate unity of humanity and God, in correspondence to God's own oneness of "being" and of "act." Insistent that humanity must *do* that which is appropriate to all we are revealed in Christ to *be,* Barth would not separate the disciplines of ethics and dogmatics; but showed instead that ethics is theology as such, an articulation of the injunctions laid *upon* us by the disclosure of God's graciousness *toward* us. And in so refusing to disjoin the indicative task of dogmatics from its consequential ethical demands, Barth also reversed the characteristically Lutheran order of salvation which placed the gospel second to the law. The costly commands of God, for Barth, are not other than, nor a precondition of, preparation for the gospel of free grace — as if we could know what God requires of us before we even know who God is, and therefore who we are ourselves, in the light of Christ's electing grace.[81]

Now as it happens, in so ordering gospel and law, and so uniting dogmatics and ethics, Barth was establishing the closest connections between *story* and *politics.* Recall that for him, God's self-revealing in Jesus Christ is not effected absent the Word of God written, Scripture's testimony to the triune God; and that that witness comes to clearest focus in a threefold narrative, the storied events of Good Friday, Easter Day, and Pentecost.[82] Dogmatic science is rational reflection upon God's story, and upon *these* stories, above all, from the history of God's becoming. Ethics likewise, therefore, clarifies the demands upon the community of faith and hearing inherent in the content of these God-disclosing narratives of Jesus Christ. The one so narrated and revealed between Good Friday and Pentecost as God's own Son constitutes the revolutionary subversion of all human thought and expectation, embodying the utter contrast between God's kingdom and our own. Christ thus relativizes all our aspirations and achievements, including the religious and political, where the human ego has so much, and so idolatrously, invested in itself.

Yet the very transcendence of God, to which Barth gave such overwhelming glory in his *Commentary on Romans,* and which required that exaltation of Christ's sole lordship to which Barth directed such radical allegiance in the Barmen Declaration, also constituted for him, with increasing urgency, a this-worldly demand that the church promote provisional, penultimate, but still visi-

81. See Barth, *CD,* esp. vols. II/1 and IV/4, *Christian Life;* also Karl Barth, *Ethics,* trans. G. W. Bromiley (Edinburgh: T. & T. Clark and New York: Seabury Press, 1981). And see R. E. Willis, *The Ethics of Karl Barth* (Leiden: E. J. Brill, 1971); Jüngel, *Barth: A Theological Legacy,* ch. 3: "Gospel and Law: The Relationship of Dogmatics to Ethics"; and T. F. Torrance, *Karl Barth: Biblical and Evangelical Theologian* (Edinburgh: T. & T. Clark, 1990), pp. 23-24.

82. See Ch. 6, sect. III above, esp. n. 57.

ble and concrete human parables of God's grace within the civil realm and the political order. These social analogies, characterized by justice, peace, and freedom, would differ from the present status quo in proportional correspondence to the difference between the human community as such and God's own gracious and transcendent righteous kingdom. To this earthly, but wholly non-idolatrous sociopolitical vision Barth gave a consistently — and often to his less-comprehending admirers, disturbingly — radical, socialist interpretation.[83]

While identifying here a major Reformed source for what since Barth has developed ecumenically as "political" and "liberation" theology, we are also, as indicated, witnessing the anonymous birth of "narrative ethics." In theological arenas far removed from Barth's, as well as some much closer to him, there has developed an integration of story and politics far more self-conscious than his own. Among much else, this has seen a happy convergence of systematic theology and theological ethics.[84] On the one hand, those concerned to define and articulate a "narrative theology" have asked about the consequences for active involvement and discipleship of the narratives by which believers confess themselves to be a community of faith.[85] On the other hand, ethicists have identified narrated memory as the source of the moral goals to which a community aspires, and have thus discovered how it can be that a "mere" *story* can help shape public *policy*.[86]

---

83. See here two vital and much-discussed essays by Karl Barth: *"Rechtfertigung und Recht"* (1938) (= "Justification and Justice," trans. R. G. Howe, in Barth, *Church and State* [London: SCM, 1939 and Greenville, S.C.: Smyth & Helwys Publishing, Inc., 1991]); and *"Christusgemeinde und Burgergemeinde"* (1946) (= "The Christian Community and the Civil Community," in Barth, *Against the Stream* [London: Camelot Press and New York: Philosophical Library, 1954]; also in Barth, *Community, State and Church,* ed. W. Herberg [Garden City, N.Y.: Doubleday and Gloucester, Mass.: P. Smith, 1968]; and in C. Green, ed., *Karl Barth: Theologian of Freedom* [London: Collins and San Francisco: Harper & Row, 1989]). See also G. Hunsinger, ed., *Karl Barth and Radical Politics* (Philadelphia: Westminster Press, 1976); Jüngel, *Barth: A Theological Legacy,* esp. ch. 2; C. Villa-Vicencio, ed., *On Reading Karl Barth in South Africa* (Grand Rapids: Eerdmans, 1988); J. Bentley, *Between Marx and Christ: The Dialogue in German-Speaking Europe, 1870-1970* (London: Verso Editions and New York: Schocken Books, 1982), ch. 6: "The Socialism of Karl Barth." Also, see in particular E. Jüngel, *Christ, Justice and Peace: Toward a Theology of the State,* trans. D. B. Hamill and A. J. Torrance (Edinburgh: T. & T. Clark, 1992), this being Jüngel's profound and personal interpretation of the Barmen Declaration of 1934, inspired and largely drafted by Barth.

84. Witness a major contribution to this field: J. W. McClendon Jr., *Ethics — Systematic Theology, Volume 1* (Nashville: Abingdon Press, 1986), esp. ch. 12: "Why Narrative Ethics?"

85. See, e.g., Stroup, *Promise of Narrative Theology,* ch. 7.4, "Knowing and Doing."

86. See, e.g., K. Lebacqz, *Justice in an Unjust World* (Minneapolis: Augsburg, 1987), esp. ch. 3; cf. Forrester, *Beliefs, Values and Policies,* p. 29.

At such a now-familiar convergence of narrative and ethics do we now ask briefly what particular political demands derive from the three-day Christian narrative centered upon Easter Saturday. What analogies, appropriate to the triune community of God revealed and identified through that story, might be socially constructed among us in these critical days at the apparent end of history? Much more in general will be said in the remaining chapters about the consequences of this thought-out narrative for ecclesial and individual living in contemporary society. For now, though, three characteristics of an appropriate Christian politics might be identified, and each in turn, for illustrative purposes, used to demonstrate the ethical significance of one day in that tridual history for one of the three foci we have examined of history's present peril.

The Politics of Similarity

What finally proved possible in the thought of Eberhard Jüngel, at the climax of the contemporary recovery and rethinking of the doctrine of the Trinity in the light of Christ's suffering and death, was a reversal of the apparently well-justified Protestant protest against the classical Thomist "analogy of being." That at one time seemed, most transparently to Karl Barth, to exaggerate dangerously the ontological continuity between the Creator and the creatures. In short, it made God and humanity too similar, compromising God's holy and wholly otherness, while seducing us into lies and self-idolatry (Rom. 1:25) as creatures who suppose themselves participant in no less than God's own being. However, Barth himself eventually perceived that divine transcendence is not negated, but expressed, through the triune history of God's self-emptying "becoming," that is, becoming human, fleshly, vulnerable, mortal. And by extension of this "humanity of God" to the point even of "the death of God," Jüngel came to reconceive the whole matter of God's distance from us and dissimilarity to us.

That God is God, and different from us, is nowhere plainer than in human beings' demonstrable unwillingness to enter into solidarity and oneness with each other, and especially with those perceived to be different from themselves. We tightly preserve our own identity; we congregate with those we find like-minded and congenial; and we keep our distance from the dissimilar and strange. For Jüngel, divine dissimilarity is a function, by contrast, of the scandalous, unthinkable capacity and will of God to identify and be united with what is alien and different, namely, with us in our mortality and fallenness. We may observe how Jesus of Nazareth manifested his holiness, and God's, by associating with the very outcasts, sinners, and unholy ones whom other human be-

312

ings, attempting fruitlessly to prove their righteousness and purity, shunned and ostracized. No less, says Jüngel in effect, is God's creativity preserved and clarified in the Christ event through the "analogy of advent," as the Creator comes closer to the creatures than they are to themselves, entering self-negatingly into union with their perishability to the point of death. Far from positing too close a resemblance between humanity and God, the old "analogy of being" left them far too far apart, their ontic distance unbridged and their dissimilarity unmodified by the history of God's becoming similar and coming close. It is not that greater dissimilarity than similarity exists between ourselves and God, but that beyond so great dissimilarity (exposed in our incapacity for similarity and solidarity), an even greater similarity was concluded in God's own death upon the cross. If what occurred and was accomplished there may ontologically be described, with Jüngel, as the union of being with non-being for the sake of life, that finds soteriological and biblical expression as "reconciliation through the blood of Christ."

Now this word of the cross has seismic ethical and political effects because the narrative which tells of Good Friday union and reconciliation on the cross makes so little effort to distinguish — and none whatever to separate, but rather the reverse — what are sometimes called the gospel's horizontal and vertical dimensions. The reconciled unity of humanity and God constitutes more, but certainly means no less, than the reconciliation of human beings in their own divisions and dissimilarities (Eph. 2:11ff.). The death which unites humanity and deity also reconciles to God both Jew and Gentile in one body through the cross, and therefore reconciles them to each other, as one new reality out of two. Thus does the event of divine identification with humanity, which also ends the hostility between the circumcised and uncircumcised, become for us the matrix and the model of the politics of similarity.

The cross of Christ no more obliterates every distinction between Israel and the *goyim* than God's incarnation in union with mortality abolished the distinction between the Maker and the made. But what confirms and clarifies that distinctiveness, we have been saying, is an event which makes the dissimilar even more similar. On the horizontal also, therefore, Jews and Gentiles (and by extension men and women, slaves and free — Gal. 3:28) become *more* alike than unlike, their differences not abolished but quite relativized; and what *is* abolished is the friction, the enmity, the barriers between them, to the point where their dissimilarity, though present, scarcely matters. Gender, class, and race are no longer grounds for separation; and such distinctions may even lapse into irrelevance and desuetude, as when, in the light of Christ's promise of a new creation (and how astonishing that Paul, a Jew, could say this!), neither circumcision nor uncircumcision count for anything (Gal. 5:6; 6:15).

313

The present tense, wherewith the New Testament announces that Christ is *now* our peace and reconciliation, since the walls of hatred and division between God's human partners have already crumbled (Eph. 2:14ff.; cf. Rom. 5:11; 1 Cor. 1:30; Col. 1:22), is crucial to a narrative politics of similarity after Auschwitz. How ironic and self-deceptive if, in however sincere and legitimate remorse for the Jewish Holocaust, Christians were to conclude that today at last the alienation between themselves and Jews must end; that past victims and tormentors should finally be reconciled; and that given its dreadful consequence, the church's doctrine that Israel has been superseded as the chosen people needs now to be suspended and disowned.[87] If it is only the memory of Auschwitz that demands of the church harmonious new relationships with Judaism, that disingenuously evades the accusatory fact that those relations were already established by the cross of Christ, through whom Gentiles became humbly indebted "honorary Jews," enabled by sheer grace alone to be engrafted, for Israel's own sake, onto the one elect people of an unabrogated covenant (Rom. 9–11). That makes the history of Christian pride, superiority, animosity, and anti-Semitism a long, shameful anachronism, a failure for two millennia to live by the truth determined once-for-all in the death of Christ. It is of that anachronism that Christians must repent post-Holocaust, returning at last to practices of solidarity and similarity grounded in God's Good Friday union and reconciliation, wherein Christ crucified transcended all distinctions between insider and outside, citizen and alien, those far off and those at hand, the chosen and the reprobate.

Now to evoke the New Testament, the person of Jesus, and the Christian story of his reconciling death might seem — and could easily *be!* — one more attempt of triumphalistic Christians imperiously to impose their own faith and bias upon the Jews and in so doing reinforce the identity of the latter as unbelieving, unelect, willfully unreconciled. To be sure, Christians have no basis on which honestly to speak to Jews which suppresses their conviction about the messiahship of Jesus and the universality and finality of God's salvation revealed and concluded in his person. To propose, upon such premises, a recon-

---

87. See Fasching, *Narrative Theology after Auschwitz,* ch. 1; and C. M. Williamson, *When Jews and Christians Meet* (St. Louis: CBP Press, 1989), esp. chs. 1 and 2. On the question of whether or not the Holocaust, or *Shoah,* should itself be the basis for rethinking the church's understanding of its "mission" to the Jews, see also A. R. Eckardt, "Is There a Mission to Jews?" in C. Williamson, ed., *A Mutual Witness: Toward Critical Solidarity between Jews and Christians* (St. Louis: Chalice Press, 1992), ch. 4; also A. R. Eckhardt, *Jews and Christians: The Contemporary Meeting* (Bloomington: Indiana University Press, 1986), and *Your People, My People: The Meeting of Jews and Christians* (New York: New York Times Book Co., 1974).

ciled harmony and solidarity between the church and Israel can only be meaningful, and be received without offense, if the Christians doing so plainly presume that just because of Christ, as they interpret him, they are more similar to Jews than different from them. That is to say, our faith in redemption by the grace of Christ is not a polemical negation of supposed Jewish legalistic self-salvation; but rather the *same* faith, however differently expressed, as that which Judaism places in the electing mercies and covenantal faithfulness of Yahweh, and in the gracious, liberating, atoning purposes of Torah. Far from polar opposites and inherent enemies, the one elect God-fearers, the other damnable, rejected deicides, Christians and Jews together, though not without their dissimilarities and differences, are more similar than otherwise in their mutual witness to God's reality and nature, and in their common mission in God's name to all the nations of the world.

Rather, then, than engaging in a mode of evangelistic mission designed to convert the Jews by diverting them from faithful Judaism, the Christian church since Auschwitz, as it surely should have from the start, has been learning at a quickening pace to respect the dignity, rights, and equal worth of Jews, and the intrinsic integrity of their own faith and worship. We seek therefore less to preach *at* Jews than to converse *with* them in open dialogue, and to stand *beside* them as we speak together to the world, to the victims and the perpetrators of humanity's millennial tragedies and crises.[88] Only on the lived-out presumption of similarity and oneness, and in the common name of the Creator of the universe, whose Messiah shall in the last days heal the nations and redeem their history, could Israel and the church take significant initiatives against the hate, the rivalry, and the genocide which, not last at Auschwitz but many times since also, have brought a veritable "end of the

88. On all this see Williamson, *Mutual Witness,* throughout, Williamson, ed., *When Jews and Christians Meet,* throughout, and the material referred to above, p. 273, n. 24. One significant example of a major ecclesiastical shift on the question of mission to the Jews is the Report to the General Assembly of the Presbyterian Church (U.S.A.): "A Theological Understanding of the Relationship between Christians and Jews" (Louisville, 1987). See also the collection of recent statements on this question by member churches of the World Council of Churches: A. Brockway et al., *The Theology of the Churches and the Jewish People* (Geneva: World Council of Churches, 1988). See also "Christians and Jews Today," Report to the General Assembly of the Church of Scotland (Edinburgh, 1985). For the remarkable shift in Roman Catholic attitudes since Vatican II, away from its long-standing contempt for the Jews as the "killers of Christ," see Augustin Cardinal Bea, *The Church and the Jewish People,* trans. P. Loretz (New York: Harper & Row and London: G. Chapman, 1966), and John Cardinal Willebrands, *Church and Jewish People: New Considerations* (New York and Mahwah, N.J.: Paulist Press, 1992).

world" to whole peoples of the earth, and edged the human race and its global home to the verge of apocalyptic ruin.

This is to say that mutual respect and shared witness on the basis of their greater similarity than difference, for the sake of ensuring that the Holocaust never be repeated and history's menacing terminations be averted, must take Jews and Christians beyond cozy conversation rooms and convivial ecumenical conventions. Imperative today are indeed politics, not just conferences, of similarity. That would place Jews and Christians in settings local, national, and international, secular and religious, separately or jointly as circumstance dictates, determined to struggle for the transcendence of even greater similarities among human beings over their great and in part God-given differences. Both peoples of the Book would contrive social and political agendas, devise electoral strategies and parliamentary tactics, exercise the optimum leverage and pressure, all designed to encourage authorities and governments to foster community understanding and strengthen bonds of mutual interest and support between parties estranged and reciprocally fearful and suspicious. Without such prompting, how shall neighbors discover that they shall flourish by cultivating their similarities rather than their differences? Only programs of solidarity and commonality can counteract the negative impulse of ethnic memory, racial prejudice, and nationalistic chauvinism which in our day has so easily and disastrously nourished the totalitarian and genocidal spirit. And that sometimes this politics of similarity can actually prove persuasive is currently visible before our eyes, as one recalcitrant and overtly Christian people has finally resolved to abandon the policy and practice of apartheid — surely the ultimate politics of dissimilarity.

Today, of course, nowhere in the world is ethnic, racial, and religious animosity more intransigent and menacing than in the Middle East, and the relations between the state of Israel and its Arab neighbors. If true solidarity can be founded on the similarity of Jews and Christians, that can only be, as is increasingly recognized today, a *critical* solidarity, a willingness, on the basis of firmly established mutual respect, to cajole and criticize and prod each other. This might mean that churches, and nations still subject to Christian public opinion, adopt a critical stance toward the government of Israel with respect to the treatment, and the future, of the Palestinians, insisting that the latter need no less an end to their own displacement, disenfranchisement, and depotentiation than did European Jewry for far too many centuries.[89]

89. On "critical solidarity," see esp. M. Barth, *Jesus the Jew,* trans. F. Prussner (Atlanta: John Knox Press, 1978); and Williamson, ed., *Mutual Witness,* esp. ch. 6; and among a great deal else on the troublesome question of relations between Jews, Christians, and

Equally, however, the strengthening of bonds through such frankly *critical solidarity* would also energize and redirect the efforts of Christians, Jews, and others of good faith who yearn for human dignity and freedom, to demonstrate a *solidarity critical* of society at large, in its capacity for building walls and feeding bigotry and manipulating enmity. Together in our greater likenesses than differences, we can encourage the nations and peoples of the world toward closer contact, more patient listening, and more perceptive mutual recognition, so that the dangerously divided human race at our century's portentous terminus might yet see — what Good Friday, acknowledged or unnoticed, has revealed — the even greater similarities they share than the dissimilarity they so much fear and whose exacerbation is so dangerous to the future of us all?

The Politics of Superfluity

How much more does the reign of God bloom with life-giving creativity than the Devil can expand its sterile, death-dealing suzerainty! That is the joyous hymn of praise with which we have often summarized the Christian gospel and its central three-day story. In the lyrical logic of Romans: where sin increased, grace abounded all the more; so that the God who allows death to have its day and yields to its provisional ascendancy comes to be revealed as the giver of life to the deceased and existence to things that don't exist. This is the gospel of superfluity: the still greater abundance of God's love over the magnitude of godlessness — which opens up new beginnings for the ruptured and the terminated, proliferates life in barren deserts, and nourishes hope in the wastes of hopelessness. While such strange possibilities cannot be inferred from the story of Christ Jesus unless that dwell upon Good Friday and its sequel, rehearsing the penultimate but prodigious growth of sin and death, clearly the strangeness becomes believable and liberating only when the drama reaches its third-day climax: that victory over evil which is no less but all the more a triumph for God's previous defeat by evil. The ethics of superfluity, though meaningless

---

Palestinians, see M. H. Ellis, "Beyond the Ecumenical Dialogue: The Challenge of the Palestinian People," in Williamson, *Mutual Witness,* ch. 5, esp. pp. 109ff.; also M. H. Ellis, *Beyond Innocence and Redemption: Confronting the Holocaust and Israeli Power* (San Francisco: Harper & Row, 1990), and *Toward a Jewish Theology of Liberation* (Maryknoll, N.Y.: Orbis Books, 1987), esp. ch. 6: "From Holocaust to Solidarity"; R. Ruether and M. H. Ellis, eds., *Beyond Occupation: American Jewish, Christian and Palestinian Voices for Peace* (Boston: Beacon Press, 1990); and R. R. Ruether and H. J. Ruether, *The Wrath of Jonah: The Crisis of Religious Nationalism in the Israeli-Palestinian Conflict* (San Francisco: Harper & Row, 1989).

without Good Friday and Easter Saturday, depend upon and correspond most directly to the narrative of Easter Day.

Nothing, of course, is simple, for reasons obvious and quite intractable, about the church's tradition of Christ's resurrection. A myriad of questions, psychological and physiological, historiographical and literary, concerning the Easter narrative was alluded to in Part One above; and we also witnessed directly or indirectly, both there and in Part Two, competing theological instincts, even among those who share a common faith in the resurrected one, about the meaning of his raising, not least for time and history as such. To what extent, for example, is the resurrection past, a concluded temporal event open to memory, whose significance as indicative and imperative is *already* transformingly applicable to human life, personal and social? To what extent, alternatively, has only the barest promise of resurrection been chronologically bestowed, so that primarily Easter faith takes shape as hope, looking to the future and time's ending for the fulfilling, in human life and in divine, of what was proleptically foreshadowed upon Easter Day? We saw in Jürgen Moltmann, especially, this accent upon "the eschatological surplus of promise" — that the superfluity of life beyond death's great expanse is *not yet,* but shall be the consummating event wherein the reign of freedom shall be perfected and God shall be all in all.

Cognate to this dispute, at the forefront of twentieth-century debate, lies another about the meaning of the resurrection which was most energetic and consequential at the Reformation. For Martin Luther, what God has wrought so far through Christ's death and resurrection is a deadlocked equilibrium of forces between law and gospel, the divine and the satanic. God's victory over sin and death and evil, though eschatologically secure, is for now concealed in dialectic and elusive of experience, a reality of justifying grace to be grasped and celebrated by sightless faith alone, barely translatable into empirical transformations of personal or corporate existence. For Calvin, on the contrary, Christ's salvation, in anticipation of its eschatological fulfillment, already effects visible signs of superfluity in human life, concrete advancements of grace over evil and life over death by which justified sinners, as individuals and communities of faith, may be publicly, measurably, albeit only incrementally and incompletely, and not without much ambiguity, transformed and sanctified.

The consequences of this controversy have been immense, and often overtly political, and that far beyond the bounds of purely ecclesiastical affairs. For Lutherans transposed the theological conviction of the unresolved conflict between God and the Devil, in a "two-kingdom" ethic which divided the secular from the spiritual realm and allowed the state, as the instrument of law, uncontested presidency over the community's worldly, temporal events. That encouraged passivity and quietism on the part of the church: a dualistic retreat from mundane responsibility for social life. In the eyes of many that allowed Nazism to flourish in Germany in the 1930s against only minority church protest, and fostered the wicked phenomenon of "German Christians" who thought to distribute their allegiance between Christ and Führer, swastika and cross.

Reformed political instincts were different from the first, finding in God's present victory over evil, as the escalation of grace beyond justification to sanctification, the impetus for Christians to proclaim the unitary headship of the Risen Christ over every sphere of life. That meant accepting responsibility for the state, not directly by theocracy, but through the participation of believers with others in the political process, resisting tyranny and promoting order, peace, and justice in commonwealths analogous to God's coming kingdom. That vision, above all, guided Germany's Confessing Christians in their resistance to Adolf Hitler and his usurpation of the church. And theirs was indeed a politics of superfluity: action hazarded in the conviction that good and evil are not locked in static counterbalance, since the gospel has unleashed dynamic possibilities for transformation far greater than the apparently much mightier, but truly inert and self-defeating, implosive power of wickedness.

To myopic eyes, this Reformed activism is contradictory and confusing, ill-fitting the Calvinist conviction that nothing occurs in history contrary to God's will and sovereignty. But this tradition's doctrines of omnipotent providence and irresistible predestination have not — with some exceptions, to be sure — sacralized social paralysis and political withdrawal. Just because it is God, and not any human force, nor demonic, nor stark chaos, that governs history, because life *has* destiny, purpose, and meaning, we are asked obediently to align our wills to God's and seek to edge society and history toward the divinely appointed and directed goal, busily, responsibly, as faithful stewards and servants, bearing visible witness to the surplus of justice over evil, of new creation over moribund status quo.[90]

In two respects this ethic of superfluity, founded on the story of Christ's raising as that surpasses his death and burial, requires and facilitates political expression in relation to the particular threats of war and devastation which after so bloody a century do and should still haunt us at its millennial end. The narrative of Easter Day determines both the *motive* for and the *content* of Christians' political engagement in the struggle for peace, which took so qualitatively new and urgent a turn after Hiroshima.

---

90. Among much else on the above, see Moltmann, *On Human Dignity*, esp. chs. 4-6; Jüngel, *Christ, Justice and Peace;* Duncan Forrester, *Theology and Politics* (Oxford and New York: Blackwell, 1988); and R. H. Stone, ed., *Reformed Faith and Politics* (Washington, D.C.: University Press of America, 1983).

Fatalism, defeatism, or illusions of survival seemed to paralyze the minds of many, including many Christians, in the Cold War generation: the resigned conclusion that a widescale nuclear war could not be indefinitely averted — though an elect elite might be "raptured" or by some other miracle preserved; or that prevention could only be secured by the MAD logic of "mutually assured destruction." We have indeed ourselves denied above that faith has any grounds to expect that the God of the crucified and buried Jesus would intervene to forestall a third world war, any more than heaven interjected a saving hand to halt the deployment of the deadly weapons that concluded World War II. The narrative of Easter Saturday chillingly convinces us that nuclear annihilation, on the Devil's greatest day, is an open possibility of future history, which God would not choose coercively to thwart. But Easter Day's good news of superfluity attests that even after such unthinkable calamity, the love which puts no limits upon its susceptibility to setback, loss, and grief would still be love, *God*'s capacious and accumulating love which flourishes in contradiction. The God who cares for creatures sufficiently to grant their freedom would be affirmed in that freedom's worst misuse; just as the father of the prodigal proved his love not only when he welcomed back his son but already in releasing him from home for foolish, self-destructive exile.

Easter's promissory demonstration of the superfluity of grace — that love's plenitude always exceeds in creativity evil's ample but barren negativity, is what gives us hope, as opposed to optimism, for a benign rather than a tragic end to history; and it motivates us to ensure that a demonic denouement, though its possibility cannot be excluded, in fact does not occur. That God would still be God after the worst terminus of human destiny, summons God's own people to accountability for their fellows, energizing their struggle to prevent that worst from happening. Those who not only hear and think, but also live the gospel story, are constrained to do all three not only in private, or in the church, but in the political arena at every level, from the United Nations to the civic center in the neighborhood. For the prospect of extinction for the human race is not to be mediated on but rebelled against;[91] and that rebellion must engage us in multiple forms of resistance to the enmity of nations, races, factions — so dangerous a dimension of our current circumstance. And conversely it requires us to support new, healing relationships between communities everywhere, in units small and large, which shall embody the peace-promoting su-

---

91. This is the powerful, recurring plea of Jonathan Schell in *The Fate of the Earth;* see esp. pt. 3. See also the very important anthology, H. Davis, ed., *Ethics and Defence: Power and Responsibility in the Nuclear Age* (Oxford: Blackwell, 1986 and New York: Blackwell, 1987).

perfluity of love, equality, trust, and understanding over rivalry, suspicion, and hostility.

Here the contents of the politics of superfluity come into view: the actual substance upon which such new relationships might arise after the crumbling of the old, which globally depended on at least defensiveness against the menace of annihilation, and sometimes, more perilously yet, upon a "first strike capability." What shall the Christian churches — along perhaps with other communities and institutions which may be said to hum the Christian tune without remembering the Christian words, and others, too, who sing a different song entirely[92] — what shall we say and demonstrate to the great powers and the nations of the world, and to more local groups and gangs and clans and tribes who fear and confront each other on the basis of gender or religion, ethnicity or turf?

Surely this: that trust, defenselessness, and vulnerability are in themselves, despite all appearances, finally more productive and protective than all strategems for aggression or defense, attack or retaliation, self-assertion or self-protection. To be sure, it is difficult enough for any individual to believe and act upon the gospel promise that those who lose their lives shall find them. How much harder for corporate entities, whose very raison d'être seems to lie in self-perpetuation, to be convinced that their own welfare is better served by taking risks, hazarding survival and identity, than by staking all upon security, strength, and the threat of force, whether in offense or in defense. Yet there is a superfluity in love, an even greater power and strength hidden within weakness and defenselessness, says the story of the crucified but risen Christ, than ever resides in sheer omnipotence and invulnerable might. And it is to make that mystery credible, its riskiness worth hazarding, that Christians surely are summoned to peacemaking political activity.[93]

92. On the question of "allies" in the cause of peace, see A. Race, "Christian Involvement in an Interfaith Theology of Peacemaking," in Race, ed., *Theology against the Nuclear Horizon,* ch. 12.

93. The vast literature on "peacemaking" cannot, of course, be catalogued here. It is impressive, not least for its ecumenical scope and its theological breadth, embracing "conservative" and "liberal" starting points and much between. Some examples are Race, ed., *Nuclear Horizon,* ch. 14; G. C. Chapman, *Facing the Nuclear Heresy* (Elgin, Ill.: Brethren Press, 1986); R. S. Sider and R. K. Taylor, *Nuclear Holocaust and Christian Hope* (Downers Grove, Ill.: InterVarsity Press, 1982 and London: Hodder & Stoughton, 1983). Significant contributions from the churches include: *The Challenge of Peace: A Pastoral Letter on War and Peace,* National Conference of Catholic Bishops (Washington, D.C., 1983); "Christian Obedience in a Nuclear Age," Report to the General Assembly of the Presbyterian Church (U.S.A.) (Louisville, 1988); "Report of the Special Committee anent the Theological Im-

Between Hiroshima and the end of the Cold War, the world's peace, so-called (for those decades saw successive theater conflicts all around the globe), was secured by massive systems of attack and defense, retaliation and deterrence. In truth, by such means a sort of "peace" did hold between the superpowers, more effectively than some latter-day unilateral disarmers found it in them to concede. History records the awkward fact that the atomic bomb has only been deployed when one side had it and the other not. Indisputably the West's multilateral policy of weapons builddown was among the factors which brought the Cold War tensions to an end.

Even so, deterrence theory was always both a perilous and a dehumanizing strategy for peace. It encouraged us all to worship at the diabolical high altar of "national security";[94] and it relied upon the threadbare supposition that in a perverse world no accident or miscalculation would ever through untold generations trip the nuclear hair-trigger. As the very phrase "cold war" betrayed, the ideology of security and defense preserved the nominal "peace" by means not of real peace at all, but of belligerence and distrust. Our "nuclear fixation"[95] diminished the humanity of all who sheltered beneath the superpowers' umbrellas, reducing us to fearful dupes and liars, victims and agents, both, of deceit, false rhetoric, and mistrust.[96] How different, how fragile, how disingenuous, were the forty years of nuclear peace after World War II, compared with the tranquility, stability, and integrity of that Jerusalem peace the Old Testament calls *shalom,* and which for Luke-Acts was earthily embodied in that city by the Risen Christ for forty days![97]

In the literal providence of God, it is a little easier now in the 1990s for all to see that even in our crooked, dangerous, and ambiguous world, peace can be more authentic if directly sought and grounded in openness, mutual under-

---

plications of the Nuclear Threat to Life," General Assembly of the Church of Scotland (Edinburgh, 1987); and The Church of England Working Party of the Board for Social Responsibility, *The Church and the Bomb* (London: Hodder & Stoughton, 1982); cf. R. Gill, *The Cross against the Bomb* (London: Epworth, 1984).

94. See R. Rushton, in Race, ed., *Nuclear Horizon,* ch. 13, on "the idols of security."

95. The telling phrase of George Kennan, doyen of U.S. postwar foreign policy. See G. F. Kennan, *Around the Cragged Hill: A Personal and Political Philosophy* (New York and London: W. W. Norton and Co., 1993); cf. G. Kennan, *Sketches from a Life* (New York: Random House, 1989), pp. 294-95.

96. On the "dehumanization" of life, within a "society of enemies," created by the nuclear threat, see Chapman, *Nuclear Heresy,* ch. 8.

97. On *shalom,* in the context of modern war, see, e.g., A. C. Winn, *Ain't Gonna Study War No More: Biblical Ambiguity and the Abolition of War* (Louisville: Westminster/ John Knox Press, 1993), throughout; also Aukerman, *Darkening Valley,* esp. chs. 29 and 30.

standing, and shared interests. Recent history shows that there is indeed a superfluity of safety, a "dividend" of peace to be found in the dropping of defensive postures and the suspending of mutually demeaning threats of annihilation and retaliation. Even so, with the Cold War over and the danger of nuclear holocaust receding, humanity still faces a treacherous tomorrow. The major shifts in global power ironically have multiplied the possibilities for nuclear proliferation among the smaller nations, while reducing the capacity of the great powers to deter their use. Suddenly nuclear terrorism — the use of small-scale but still massively destructive weapons for purposes of international blackmail or localized extermination — looms ever larger as a new configuration of possible disaster: the prospect of Hiroshima revisited, perhaps on its original scale, at the close of the first atomic century.

All the more urgent, then, is the Christian imperative at once to reach out to humanity's antagonistic ethnic groupings and rival traditions of tribal memory and religious fervor, with the Easter promise that trust, defenselessness, and powerlessness surpass the well-being and security achievable for persons and communities through naked power, defensiveness, and violence. Can we make credible, as the basis for pragmatic politics, the story which tells of the living God who yielded nonresistingly to death? of the power of the powerlessness of the cross and grave? of the victory of the lamb they led to slaughter?

Above all, with that story and through corresponding lives, can we persuade governments and other powers-that-be that there can be no peace where there is no *justice?* The shortest, most effective path to the pacifying of feuds and antipathies earthed in color, ethnicity, or creed is to remove the injustices and inequities which stimulate grievance and keep hatred and hostility alive. Only in a more just world will humanity begin to learn how much more rewardingly postures and practices of peace and trust may prosper beyond the impressive but abortive efficaciousness of force.[98]

98. On justice in relation to peace, amid a huge literature, see, e.g., Moltmann, *Creating a Just Future*, esp. pp. 38ff.; and Jüngel, *Christ, Justice and Peace*, throughout. Note the concentration today of the World Council of Churches on the triad of interconnected themes: justice, peace, and the integrity of creation. These were the subjects of a WCC world convocation in Seoul, South Korea, 1990, and of the 7th General Assembly of the WCC, Canberra, Australia, 1991. See esp. D. P. Niles, ed., *Between the Flood and the Rainbow: Integrating the Conciliar Process of Mutual Commitment (Covenant) to Justice, Peace and the Integrity of All Creation* (Geneva: World Council of Churches, 1992); also G. Limouris, ed., *Justice, Peace and the Integrity of Creation: Insights from Orthodoxy* (Geneva: World Council of Churches, 1990). See also "Restoring Creation for Ecology and Justice," Report to the General Assembly of the Presbyterian Church (U.S.A.) (Louisville, 1990).

The Politics of Surrender

In conclusion, what politics might derive from the Christian narrative in its reference to Easter Saturday as such? The movement of God's triune history from Good Friday until Easter Sunday calls us into solidarity with the least of our neighbors and into similarity with the alien and different. Nurtured through this reconciliation shall be a surplus in God's final kingdom of peace and justice over violence and unrighteousness — concrete, visible signs of which can and must be fashioned within our social ordering today. Here mutual trust and risky undefensiveness already exhibit a strange capacity not to weaken but to strengthen the sinews and fabric of community relations, proleptic of the *eschaton's* human unity and harmony within the perfected community of the Trinity itself. But at the heart of this movement of the Trinity, of course, on the boundary we have patrolled throughout this study, between God's similarity to us in death upon the cross and God's superabundance over death in the empty tomb, stands the cold, silent day of Sabbath waiting. That boundary point, that presence-in-absence both divine and human, that significant zero and pregnant vacuum, so dense and tangible in its insubstantiality, serves both to conjoin and to separate the Friday cross and the Sunday garden, preventing at once both rank despair and cheap triumphalism, both the nonoccurrence and the premature arrival of a resurrection sequel to the crucifixion.

This is to say that though there *is* an Easter victory, a fecundity of life in the midst of death which shall redeem and transform history, the only way to that future and to its temporal anticipations here and now passes through barrenness and negativity. God can no more come to the divine tomorrow of consummation and fulfillment than we can to ours, without first embracing suffering, defeat, and death. More specifically, our non-optimistic hopes of participating in history's future of justice, peace, and freedom cannot be separated from the imperative upon us, as upon the God of history's own self, to countenance the varieties and costs of *surrender:* the pain of giving away, of giving up, of letting go.

For that is *how* God flourishes, how the Trinity asserts and fulfills itself, securing the superfluity of grace over sin: by venturing, indeed surrendering, its own identity. Easter Saturday, we have proposed above, is that moment when *God* is present-in-absence, fulfilled through self-negation. As God's own Son lies buried in the grave and descended into hell, Holy Saturday speechlessly announces that the Logos which creates the world has been laid to rest, and the Word which upholds the cosmos silenced. The one who loves in freedom is now captive to the Devil and its hatefulness, the divine love rendered questionable by the sacrifice of the Beloved Son. God's very being as trinitarian community has on Easter Saturday been delivered up to contradiction and falsification: the Godness of the Father who gave up the only Son; the Godness of the Son who gave himself away; the Godness of the Spirit who, it seems, allowed death to sever the divine fellowship's eternal bonds of unity.

Our reflections on this divine crisis would lack all coherence if they did not reiterate in relation to every circumstance of human life — global, social, personal — the conundrum of God's self-surrender: the truth that holds for God before it is true for us, and is only true for us *because* it is God's own truth — that those and only those who lose and give themselves away shall find and fulfill themselves. From the narrative which shows how it might be that God lives by giving up to death — which is, as Jüngel says, *the* mystery of the world — derives an ethic of surrender possessing universal application and instant urgency.

Paradigmatically these ethics translate, once more, into a new politics of Christian-Jewish relations after Auschwitz, demanding that though Gentile Christians do not have to give up being the church, the chosen people of the Lord, we can discern and obey the meaning of that identity only if, consciously and all-too-belatedly, we abandon our self-appointed standing of superiority and supersession. Instead, we shall with humility and gratitude surrender ourselves to relationships with Israel of derivation and dependence, indebtedness and servanthood, our election being quite gratuitous and wholly enacted for the sake of theirs.

Likewise if a world-historical catastrophe post-Hiroshima is to be averted for all time, the new policies and orderings required of the nations of the world will have to embody decisions and deeds of institutional self-surrender, however painful, politically impracticable, or even at this moment inconceivable. An "end of the world" different from the violent, cataclysmic extinction we have learned so well to fear will require costly, courageous, collective acts of giving up and giving away. Certainly to be abandoned, we have just said, are the arsenals of aggression and defensiveness, those expansive but so duplicitous idols of security which governments east and west have sacralized. In that process, elements at least of national identity and sovereignty will also have to be relinquished, in favor of new treaties and bondings of mutual trust, cooperation, and obligation: a yielding of authority which recent turmoil in the European Community shows even the most secure and sophisticated of democracies to find barely tolerable. Some even say, in contradiction of the post-Soviet *Zeitgeist*, which has newly invigorated the myths and released the demons of nationalism with so barbaric an effect in many places, that a peaceful future for Europe and the world depends upon our modifying, if not totally abandoning, the very concept of the nation-state. It may be true that the peoples of the world will establish lasting peace and security among themselves only if they are persuaded to give up their attachment to national identity and their perilous beholdenness to its competitive and disuniting logic.[99]

However, it is surely to an ecological ending of the world, the impending threat to the future of world history and nature post-Chernobyl, even more than to the ruptures of Auschwitz and Hiroshima, that the politics of surrender most urgently apply for now. What deep, wide-ranging changes in values and lifestyles, behavior and policy — all of them involving surrender of many past customs and not a few comforts — will be asked of the developed countries now commonly identified as "northern," if the world's worsening environmental crisis is to be responsibly confronted and in time.

Promisingly, given the political malaise in so many of just those countries, where a majority of citizens feel alienated from and powerless toward their own governments and bureaucratic structures, there is much by way of a new politics of surrender that allows every individual and family, community and city, to contribute to such changes on a global scale. By practicing conservation and recycling, for example; by means of lobbying, boycotts, and selective purchasing; by modifying consumption and adopting different transportation patterns, we all have it in us to help save endangered species, slow the exhaustion of nonrenewable resources, replenish and repurify the supply of water, reverse deadly damage to the atmosphere. Responsible stewardship at the personal and local level can do much to harmonize our complex ecological and economic interrelations with one another and with nature — though not without the quite conscious exercise of prudent surrender and calculated sacrifice.[100]

On the other hand, it is quite imperative for the future of the human race and its global home that a new ethic of restraint and sacrifice for the sake of the earth *not* be privatized and domesticated — as if our crisis could be resolved purely by local, small initiatives and the moral heroism of individual visionar-

---

99. See here P. Kennedy, *Preparing for the 21st Century,* ch. 7; and R. Rhodes, *The Making of the Atomic Bomb,* pp. 781-88.

100. Current literature on the measures necessary to avert the ecological crisis is, of course, vast. It certainly includes signifcant works referred to above, including Gore, *Earth in the Balance,* and Kennedy, *Preparing for the 21st Century.* In addition, Douglas J. Hall has developed a profound and timely biblical theology of stewardship, sacrifice, and discipline, precisely in the light of the cross of Christ as advocated here. See D. J. Hall, *The Stewardship of Life in the Kingdom of Death* (New York: Friendship Press, 1985); *Imaging God: Dominion as Stewardship* (Grand Rapids: Eerdmans and New York: Friendship Press, 1986); *The Steward: A Biblical Symbol Come of Age,* rev. ed. (Grand Rapids: Eerdmans and New York: Friendship Press, 1989); and *Thinking the Faith,* esp. pp. 219ff.; cf. Gore, *Earth in the Balance,* ch. 9: "Self-Stewardship."

ies. Such might be the preference of authorities desperate to postpone hard and unpopular decision making. In fact, however, nothing needs more to be a matter of *public* policy, a major if not *the* major item on the agenda of those governments at national and international levels, as well as on the leaders of industry and commerce, of agriculture, and of many technologies including the medical and genetic.[101]

In this public sphere, what the Christian churches must in particular commend to secular society is the thinkability of surrendering today's all-pervasive myth of limitlessness: the supposedly emancipating, but in reality enslaving supposition that limitations, restrictions, and contractions, especially material and economic, are by definition inimical to human well-being, freedom, and prosperity. As a world community we shall in fact be *more* free — because more able equally and justly to share in life's good things, to maximize our wondrous capacity for invention, discovery, and adaptation, and to reduce the terminal menace to our common planetary home — if, surrendering the pipe dream of existence without limits, we collectively accede to some constraints and regulations, boundaries and restrictions governing our interactions with our habitat, commensurate with our finitude, creaturehood, and cosmic tininess.[102]

Such a goal requires that Christians and their allies who seek leverage upon public policy be prophetically vocal in favor of some limits upon human autonomy, especially its modern interpretation as radical individualism, and against the anthropocentric lie that nature is amoral and inert, properly passive to humanity's domination and rapacious exploitation. That means being:

> *for* real limits to economic growth, and *against* the secular dogma that national and supranational economies, to be healthy, must always be expanding, never contracting nor in stasis.[103]
>
> *for* limits upon technological development, and *against* the assumption that all scientifically feasible projects — in the highly ambiguous field of genetic engineering, for example — should in fact be undertaken without reference to moral and social consequence.

101. On the need for Christian involvement in public policymaking and not just in private choices, with references to the environment, see esp. Nash, *Loving Nature,* ch. 8; cf. the current church literature on the integrity of creation on pp. 287-88, n. 57 above.

102. See esp. Nash, *Loving Nature,* ch. 2: "Dimensions and Dilemmas of the Ecological Crisis: Exceeding the Limits"; cf. McKibben, *End of Nature,* e.g., p. 214.

103. On how we might begin politically to resolve the tensions between ecological and economic desiderata, see Nash, *Loving Nature,* pp. 197ff.; cf. Gore, *Earth in the Balance,* ch. 10.

for limits upon agricultural and livestock productivity, and *against* the myopic denial of Sabbath rest to the exhausted earth[104] and greedy unconcern for the effects of adding chemicals and hormones to our foodstuffs-in-the-making.

for limits to the depletion of resources and the loss of biological diversity, and *against* the lust to consume whatever lies in the earth or lives upon it, subject only to profitability and not to the fortunes of other species or the long-term welfare of our own.[105]

Most delicate of all today, given the cherished democratic traditions of the "enlightened" West, are the moral and political minefields being quite properly laid by those who argue with increasing vehemence and specificity that some much-vaunted freedoms of the individual citizen may have to be regulated or curtailed if the global community as a whole is to achieve equality and equilibrium, and thus some equanimity about its doubtful future. The dilemmas thus raised extend beyond the marketplaces of acquisition and consumption, and the highways of private transportation, to that most holy temple of modern, secular existence: the private bedroom. What limits may need to be placed upon our reproductive freedoms in particular if the rapidly reduplicating human population is not to outdistance all conceivable parameters of sustainability, economic and social, nutritional and medical?[106]

Of course, the demographic explosion, though it threatens everyone, represents many times over a more serious crisis in the Third World than elsewhere. With the discommoding consequence that the peoples of those nations must be told, perhaps, that the global future hangs upon *their* renouncing some of the very rights and liberties which for two hundred years the West has considered sacrosanct, more precious, sometimes, than life itself. Such is the irony and the fearsome instability of the world's predicament today. And in fact, despite some bold initiatives in the developing world toward a slowing of the

104. See Moltmann, *Creating a Just Future,* ch. 3, sects. 3 and 7, and *God in Creation,* pp. 5ff., 276ff. See also *While the Earth Endures: A Report on the Theological and Ethical Considerations of Responsible Land-Use in Scotland,* Science, Religion and Technology Project (Edinburgh: Quorum Press, 1986).

105. See esp. Gore, *Earth in the Balance,* ch. 11: "We Are What We Use."

106. See here two very important studies calling for restraint on private freedom for the sake of the globe's emancipation: G. Hardin, *Living within Limits: Ecology, Economics and Population Taboos* (New York and Oxford: Oxford University Press, 1993); and D. Worster, *The Wealth of Nature: Environmental History and the Ecological Imagination* (New York and Oxford: Oxford University Press, 1993). See also Kennedy, *Preparing for the 21st Century,* ch. 2.

birthrate, by and large the disposition of the South, not unexpectedly and all-too understandably, is much more to emulate the materialism and license of the North than to adopt patterns of discipline, austerity, or spirituality different from our own indulgent exercise of unbridled freedom in pursuit of gratification and instant happiness.

Thus, to be honest, real hope for the future felicity of the human race, grounded in "justice, peace, and the integrity of creation," might seem as ephemeral a dream as ever. The ecological dangers facing human history in the twenty-first century appear as intractable and mortal as the totalitarianism and bellicosity which so scarred and demonized the twentieth. All the more reason, then, eschewing optimism and despair alike, for those with ears to hear and intellects to think the story of the future of the dead and buried God, to live their narrative with courage, conviction, and a proven readiness to surrender everything, in the hope that they and the whole imperiled world may live.

CHAPTER NINE

Living the Story in Contemporary Society

I. The Close of the Age: An Easter Saturday Culture

1989, the *annus mirabilis* of recent times, was and remains a huge and rapturous rebuke to historical fatalism. That was the end-of-a-decade year when the Berlin Wall was torn down and the Iron Curtain fell; when the totalitarian governments of Eastern Europe suddenly toppled at gathering pace, till it was observed that what had taken Poland ten years took Hungary ten months, East Germany ten weeks, Czechoslovakia ten days, and Rumania ten hours; and when decisive dies were cast which ensured the very disappearance of the Soviet Union soon after. Thus a whole generation now knows, from immediate experience and vivid memory, that no power is impregnable nor history inexorable, inhospitable to surprise, novelty, and the almost miraculous, to swift reversals of direction and major triumphs over evil and despair. Our world is not, after all, set on an uninterruptible path toward disaster and closure. The nuclear calamity whose fearsome possibility we confronted in the last chapter is not inevitable, nor even, for now, remotely likely. Tyranny sometimes yields helplessly to freedom, and the grip of evil on human events and communities can be prised off — with remarkable ease when appropriate conditions conjoin.

In the justifiable euphoria of that year and its sequels, the West declared itself victorious in the Cold War, its leaders promised a "new world order," and some of its prophets projected upon the approaching new millennium unprecedented growth, prosperity, and peace for the human race.[1] And there were

1. See, e.g., J. Naisbitt and P. Aburdene, *Megatrends 2000* (New York: Avon Books,

even those who substituted for the suddenly vanished demonic nightmare of an apocalyptic "end of the world," a benign, glorious, triumphalistic "end of history."[2] There was happening before our eyes, it was proposed, the final resolution of Hegel's dialectic of the historical Spirit: the struggle for social order concluded in the ascendancy of liberal democracy over both its modern rivals, fascism and communism. This triumph of "the Western idea" throughout the globe was bringing ideological conflict, and in that sense "universal history" itself, to an end. To be sure, this termination was not altogether to be welcomed; and it would certainly not bring instant utopia. Though future large-scale conflict was deemed unlikely, it was — with some bitter prescience — foreseen that ethnic and nationalistic violence might well increase; and with the conflict of ideas at an end, society would forfeit the courage and vision such struggles nurture, lapsing into the tedium of bureaucracy, consumerism, and soulless technology, and feeling a powerful nostalgic tug toward the days when history still existed.[3]

Such qualifiers notwithstanding, the putative "end of history," even when understood in its technical, Hegelian sense, was an implausible thesis, oblivious to the fact that liberal democracy no less than communism contains internal flaws and contradictions which could lead to its own collapse, or at least radical modification. It is by no means yet clear whether capitalism can "succeed" for society as a whole, or must necessarily perpetuate an unbridgeable gap at some level of the community, between the economically successful and socially powerful on the one hand, and poor, disenfranchised failures on the other. Can the wealth of the developed nations be truly shared with the underdeveloped, or must it remain, as now, dependent upon the impoverishment and subservience of the latter? Far from a settled question, then, it remains to be seen whether liberalism and economic justice can be made compatible, in theory or in practice.

In any case, much was actually occurring in 1989, and has been since, to falsify the optimists as well as the fatalists in their rival estimates of history's culmination. After all, even as the beneficent, liberal "end of history" was being trumpeted, a hideous massacre in Beijing's Tiananmen Square was exposing the ruthless resilience of democracy's supposedly defunct ideological antithesis.

1990). For a different prognostication, see G. Mestrovic, *The Coming* Fin de Siècle (London and New York: Routledge, 1991).

2. F. Fukuyama, "The End of History?" *The National Interest* (Summer 1989), and *The End of History and the Last Man* (New York: Free Press, 1992).

3. Nor, to be fair, does Fukuyama propose that the human suffering endured in the process of history's violent dialectic is justified by the ultimate resolution of that conflict. "A Universal History is simply an intellectual tool; it cannot take the place of God in bringing personal redemption to every one of history's victims" (p. 130).

Subsequently, the grotesque slaughter of the Gulf War, which supposedly helped America again "feel good about herself," the exchange of genocidal atrocities in the Balkans, the nasty surge of xenophobia, neo-fascism, and anti-Semitism in several parts of Europe, the resurfacing of ethnic hostilities in the erstwhile Soviet Union, and the cynical neglect of Africa and other Third World regions once they ceased to be useful pawns in the Cold War between the super-powers — all of this, and much else, has made a gruesome joke of the conceit that history has already evolved by some rational process toward a harmonious and unified conclusion. Can the relative peace now existing between the fortu-nate minority of democratic states really be projected so soon onto the human race as a whole, as the prolepsis of an imminent and terminal abeyance of con-flict, in favor of universal justice, freedom, and peace?

Indeed, quite apart from the intractable dilemmas and sufferings of the developing and underdeveloped nations — problems no less severe and deadly for the trend toward rudimentary, indigenous forms of democracy emerging in many of them — the peaceable and developed nations of the West itself are more realistically seen as moribund and decaying, in possibly terminal decline, than as reaping the fruits of vindication and success at the apex and finale of an historic struggle. "We stand at what feels like the end of a period of extraordi-nary brilliance. The feeling of being 'at the end' is . . . the feeling that our culture has no future and the life therefore has no meaning."[4]

Is it not apparent, for example, that Europe, for all its growing economic cohesiveness and strength, is a deeply tired continent — with the United King-dom, drained by empire, war, and class struggle, perhaps the tiredest of all? Eu-ropeans to a great extent exhausted their moral energies in the conflicts of the twentieth century; and despite their political progress of the last fifty years, to the point where warfare between the old antagonists now seems inconceivable, the once visionary prospect of European unity has become hostage to persis-tent nationalisms, ethnic and cultural rivalries, economic self-interest and bu-reaucratic heavy-handedness.[5] Ruinously materialistic, and with old, atavistic fears and hatreds seething close to its mature, sophisticated surface, contempo-rary Europe faces the end of the century — which also brings an end to its own magnificent millennium of staggering power, expansion, and civilization —

4. Newbigin, *The Other Side of 1984*, p. 25.

5. For a rather fuller, if now dated, reflection upon modern Europe, see my pam-phlet "Humanity between the Cross and the Resurrection: The Word of God and the Real-ity of Europe Today," Edinburgh, Church of Scotland Board of World Mission and Unity, Occasional Paper No. 2, 1986. On contemporary Europe, see also S. Rostagno, "Europe be-tween Secularization, Renewal of the Sacred and the Quest for New Values," *Metanoia* 1 (1991).

directionless, decadent, and shallow. And it does so, of course, as a a profoundly secular, de-Christianized culture; so that the end of Europe's epoch also effectively marks the end of Christendom.

Our approaching *fin de siècle* means also the closing of what has often been called "the American century." But behind the rhetoric of Cold War victory, and of a *novus ordo,* not only, as in 1776, for one nation but now for the world as a whole under an American aegis, there are again stark indicators of senescence and disintegration, of a society and people in demise, suggesting that the next century may belong elsewhere.[6] It is not just that America is forfeiting its economic domination, to Japan especially, nor that its military power had already passed its apex before the dismantling of its defense structures became politically imperative with the collapse of the Warsaw Pact.[7] A reduction in economic and military power could actually help America to nurture a different set of national priorities which made for a stronger, more cohesive, and compassionate society. But in fact the opposite seems to be emerging: a more and more fragmented, greedy, bigoted, and manipulative society where violence, drugs, poverty, disease, and the breakdown of families, all symptomatic of "savage inequalities"[8] in housing, education, and health care, have quickened "the fraying of America,"[9] the shredding and decomposition of its social fabric. There seems here to be a society, cynical, disillusioned, and sick of soul, groping nostalgically for a lost past and confusedly for a future role, obsessed with the trivial, the ephemeral, the selfish, and watching its dreaming self-image as a global haven of freedom, justice, and progress fade into bathos on its own TV screens.

Actually, as always, American society is the clarifying microcosm of Western culture as a whole, almost universal as that now is in its range, in a world in-

---

6. For a brilliant analysis of the rise and fall of "the American century," and of the question what will happen next, see D. Halberstam, *The Next Century* (New York: W. Morrow and Co. Inc., 1991). Among the best analyses of contemporary North American society in its state of decay is Douglas Hall's *Thinking the Faith: Christian Theology in a North American Context,* a ground-breaking attempt to think through the Christian faith afresh within the particular context of Canada and the United States today; see esp. pp. 158-234. See also C. Lasch, *The Culture of Narcissism: American Life in an Age of Diminishing Expectations* (New York: W. W. Norton, 1978); D. W. McCullough, *Waking from the American Dream* (Downers Grove, Ill.: InterVarsity Press, 1988); and R. N. Bellah et al., *Habits of the Heart* (Berkeley: University of California Press, 1985).

7. See the provocative thesis on the decline of U.S. power in P. Kennedy, *The Rise and Fall of the Great Powers* (New York: Random House, 1987). See, too, his *Preparing for the Twenty-First Century* (New York: Random House, 1993).

8. See J. Kazol, *Savage Inequalities* (New York: Crown, 1991).

9. See R. Hughes, "The Fraying of America," *Time,* Feb. 3, 1992.

creasingly homogenized, despite the fashionable rhetoric of diversity and plu-ralism.[10] It is an entire cultural epoch in world history which appears to be close to, if not already beyond, its end, and an end not of Hegelian resolution and triumph but of disintegration and breakdown. Generically this is the end of the "modern" age — an epoch which could come to be regarded as a brief blip on the screen of human history — and we inhabit the time and culture of "postmodernism" (that fashionable term so variously defined and hugely over-taxed as to have outgrown almost all utility).[11]

The "modern" era may be said to be the child of the Enlightenment, of human autonomy, rationality, and the "scientific worldview." The burgeoning technology which it spawned gave birth to boundless optimism for material progress, social amelioration, and the flowering of humanity's noblest instincts and most creative energies. There are multiple calendars by which to chart the ending of this modernity, the revising of the liberal, optimistic, and rationalis-tic vision. For some, it coincided with World War I, when technology, adapted for mass carnage, exposed not our lofty humanness but our bestial inhumanity; and for others it occurred in the Holocaust, the final, incontrovertible falsifica-tion of those who believed that human nature was improving and society mak-ing progress.[12] For many, the world "ended" with the making and deploying of the atomic bomb;[13] for others, with the assassination of a youthful, visionary President, who promised to harness science and technology for a new epoch of

---

10. On this, see C. Gunton, "Knowledge and Culture: Towards an Epistemology of the Concrete," in H. Montefiore, ed., *The Gospel and Contemporary Culture* (London: Mowbray, 1992).

11. On postmodernism, see, e.g., H. Küng, *Theology for the Third Millennium* (Lon-don: Collins and New York: Doubleday, 1988), esp. pp. 1-11; D. Allen, *Christian Belief in a Postmodern World* (Louisville: Westminster/John Knox Press, 1989); and H. Cox, *Religion in the Secular City: Toward a Postmodern Theology* (New York: Simon & Schuster, 1984). See also E. Gellner, *Postmodernism, Reason and Religion* (London: Routledge, 1992); and R. Bellah et al., *Postmodern Theology: Christian Faith in a Pluralist World*, ed. F. C. Burnham, ed. (San Francisco: Harper and Row, 1989).

12. For a penetrating study of the Enlightenment's myth of progress and of the con-temporary exhaustion of the progressive tradition, see C. Lasch, *The True and Only Heaven: Progress and Its Critics* (New York: W. W. Norton, 1991).

13. For a distinction between the ending of the modern, scientific "age" with the First World War and the birth of the modern political "world" after the Second, see H. Arendt, *The Human Condition* (Chicago and London: University of Chicago Press, 1958), p. 6. See also A. M. Schlesinger Jr., *The Cycles of American History* (Boston: Hough-ton Mifflin Co., 1986), pp. xiii and 63ff.; W. H. Wieman, *The Source of Human Good* (Chi-cago: University of Chicago Press, 1946), p. 37; and R. Rhodes, *The Making of the Atomic Bomb* (New York: Simon & Schuster, 1987), esp. pp. 778ff.

freedom, exploration, and peace; and for others again, it occurred in the sober 1990s, after the mercenary, deficit-financed intoxications of the Reagan 1980s.

At all events, across a wide spectrum of our common life in "Western civilization," the post-Enlightenment era is coming to a close in disillusionment, discord, and displacement. Technology, once the stimulus for such utopian dreams, has become a dehumanizing and demonic monster. We have learned to fear our own machines, unable, like the Sorcerer's Apprentice, to control what we have begun. The threat of world destruction through weaponry has been minimized for now; but we have also learned terrible lessons about the devastating consequences of nuclear technology even when dedicated to peaceful goals, if handled irresponsibly by an apathetic, inept, and unaccountable bureaucracy.[14] So it is that while our fears that modern science might destroy the earth through warfare, deliberately pursued or triggered accidentally, have mercifully subsided, our fears, ironically, have simultaneously augmented at the gross, possibly terminal, damage being done to the natural environment through technology's greedy and unjust exploitation of the earth's resources and damage to our global habitat. Now we know that the fruits of modern progress, even without another global war, might not be the utopia once imagined, but the slow, insane agonies of planetary self-strangulation.

The inertia which seems forever to postpone daring decisions and sacrificial actions by the world's governments to deal with the environmental crisis is a significant cause of our cultural malaise in its political dimensions. To varying degrees, all the Western nations, not to speak of others, now manifest a disturbing alienation of the "grass roots" from government, of citizens from the civic order. Even as the triumph of democracy is heralded as the end of history, the democratic process seems critically sick, and the social contract nullified. Distanced from and disillusioned by their own governments, the public admit to a loss of faith in democracy as a mechanism of rational discourse and community action for the common good — an estrangement creating perilous vacuums ripe for the irruption of undemocratic and totalitarian alternatives.[15] Explanations of this political alienation and frustration range from the thesis, on the one hand, that ideological conflict between left and right, both now ex-

14. See esp. G. Medvedev, *The Truth about Chernobyl* (San Francisco: HarperCollins, 1991); Z. A. Medvedev, *The Legacy of Chernobyl* (New York: W. W. Norton, 1990); and D. H. Hopper, *Technology, Theology and the Idea of Progress* (Louisville: Westminster/John Knox, 1991).

15. The brief but spectacular emergence of a nonpolitician, Ross Perot, as a serious contender for the U.S. presidency in 1992 was one symptom of this political disaffection. Another is the consistently low voter registration and turnout among Blacks, Hispanics, and the poor in American elections at all levels.

hausted, has paralyzed a "politics of remedy" directed to the concrete solving of problems,[16] to the widespread perception, on the other, that holders of public office are cynical, self-serving pragmatists, more concerned with the perpetuation of their own power and rewards than with championing either ideals or ideas. But in either case, political leadership seems ineffective, dishonorable, and elitist, a vocation from which citizens of true stature, integrity, and vision, and certainly those of limited means, turn away in disgust. So crumbles the democratic culture and the vision of politics as the means by which a community extends the range and depth of its compassion, justice, and equality at home and abroad. And with the entrenchment of inequality in particular, the healthy, dynamic diversity of cultures, such as in the United States, falls increasingly into static rivalry, atavistic animosities, and sometimes violent competition, deepening rather than bridging religious, racial, gender, and ethnic fissures.[17]

The stridency, demagoguery, and superficiality of so much political discourse today, the triumph of image over substance, of sound bite over debate, of negative slur over positive proposal, contributes much to our disillusionment with and disengagement from public life; and it is indicative of our society's *fin de siècle* crumbling at a deeper stratum still: in the life of the mind. This is a bitter denouement indeed for a post-Enlightenment culture grounded in the rule of reason and the freedom of the individual to think.[18] We are witnessing today a legitimate and fructifying concern for "multiculturalism," that is, the recognition, especially in the academic world, that the art, literature, music, and philosophy of Christian Europe, the aesthetic and philosophical heritage of the Renaissance, the Reformation, and the Enlightenment, is not the only civili-

---

16. See esp. E. J. Dionne Jr., *Why Americans Hate Politics* (New York: Simon & Schuster, 1991).

17. See, e.g., A. M. Schlesinger Jr., *The Disuniting of America* (New York and London: W. W. Norton, 1992).

18. The diagnosis of our intellectual malaise by Jacques Ellul is particularly biting and perspicacious. See, among much else, J. Ellul, *The Betrayal of the West*, trans. M. J. O'Connell (New York: Seabury Press, 1978); *The Humiliation of the Word*, trans. J. M. Hanks (Grand Rapids: Eerdmans, 1985); and *The Technological Bluff*, trans. G. W. Bromiley (Grand Rapids: Eerdmans, 1990). An equally scathing and yet more prominent critic of our present intellectual pathology is, of course, Aleksandr Solzhenitsyn. He views the relativizing and negativity of postmodernism the fitting nadir of the whole century's cultural illness, manifest not only in his native Russia but also in the West as "a general coma of all culture." See his January 1993 address published in the *New York Times* of February 7, 1993, under the heading "The Relentless Cult of Novelty and How It Wrecked the Century."

zation of value, and that other cultural treasures deserve to be opened up, honored, and appropriated. But too often the dislodgment of the Western intellectual tradition conceals a virulent anti-intellectualism: the polemical judgment and repudiation of ideas and creativities precisely on the basis not of their content and intrinsic worth, but of their context and origins, so that how one thinks, writes, or paints is judged in terms of one's age, gender, race, or nationality. The ultimate bogey of this debased multiculturalism is the "dead, white, European male," whose ideas, it is now decreed, can by definition have no worth. Here a deep irrationality infects philosophical and aesthetic discourse. Does this idolatry of context and disregard for content not signal the arrival of the barbarian at our gates, the detour of modern rationalism into a cul-de-sac of unreason, the bankruptcy, beyond recovery, of our entire worldview?

The contemporary pathology of the intellect has been predicated, no doubt one-sidedly and with elitist exaggeration, upon "the closing of the American mind," as evidenced by the ejection of Western classical texts from the curricula of the country's seats of higher learning.[19] But the mental malaise is by no means confined to one side of the Atlantic. Some of Europe's most refined minds have hastened the West's cultural sickness by engaging in bizarre acts of intellectual self-destruction: the rational proposal of nonrationality, the use of language to announce the emptiness and impotence of language. The academic fashions of structuralism and deconstruction are founded on the premise that language, the very vehicle of human communication, in fact conveys no meaning beyond that embedded in the structural relations of words to one another. Such an introversion of meaning allows for no relationship between words and the world of external reality. The task of interpretation is secondary and negative: to view with suspicion and to subvert the false presumption that the text is meaningful and mediates a primary encounter between author and reader. Hereby rationality resorts obscenely to self-cannibalism, consuming itself in its own nihilism.[20]

Since a relational view of reality is grounded in the relationality of God's own triune being, the intellectual crisis in contemporary culture is profoundly theological in nature. Its ultimate source is the loss of transcendence, the solipsistic abandonment of all reference to reality beyond our selves, or even

---

19. A. Bloom, *The Closing of the American Mind* (New York: Simon & Schuster, 1987); cf. his *Giants and Dwarfs* (New York: Simon & Schuster, 1990). See also G. M. Marsden and B. J. Longfield, eds., *The Secularization of the Academy* (Oxford and New York: Oxford University Press, 1992).

20. See, e.g., J. Begbie, "The Gospel, the Arts and Our Culture," in Montefiore, ed, *Gospel and Culture*, pp. 68-69.

beyond our texts. Intellectually, ours is an Easter Saturday culture, not just bereft of a sense of divine presence, but even indifferent to the divine absence. Hence the intuition of a contemporary Jewish polymath and prophet "that where God's presence is no longer a tenable supposition and where [God's] absence is no longer a felt, indeed overwhelming, weight, certain dimensions of thought and creativity are no longer attainable."[21]

Equally unattainable, of course, is any objective grounding for morality, which now is undermined by the swirling sea of ethical relativism and historicism. Gone, in our moral collapse, are the foundations for a rational, publicly debatable set of values as the substratum of a community's common life. "The very language of order and disorder" has become unavailable; for "the integral substance of morality has to a large degree been fragmented and then in part destroyed."[22] Of course the Enlightenment, though a protest against divine authority, in no way brought an end to religion, but rather ushered in a new theological era, grounded in its anthropocentricity precisely upon reason, morality, or religious experience. But in many respects the secularity of contemporary culture has brought even that accommodation with religion to an end (except to the extent that our secularity be construed as a new paganism and thus a rebirth of earth religion).[23] Certainly the cultural death of God now marks the

21. G. Steiner, *Real Presences* (Chicago: University of Chicago Press and London: Faber and Faber, 1989). This is perhaps the most brilliant and influential critique of deconstruction. Though no orthodox believer, Steiner affirms not only that words do indeed refer to realities beyond themselves, establishing immediacy between author and reader, but that all art and literature is grounded in a "wager" on divine, transcendent reality. "I sense that we shall not come home to the facts of our unhousedness, of our eviction from a central humanity in the face of the tidal provocations of political barbarism and technocratic servitude, . . . if we do not re-experience the life of meaning in the text, in music, in art. We must come to recognise . . . a meaningfulness which is that of a freedom of giving and of reception beyond the constraints of immanence. . . . Any argument on our inward and our social being, with particular reference to the encounter with immediacy and transcendence in the aesthetic, is, of necessity, an argument on *Logos* and word" (pp. 49-50).

22. A. MacIntyre, *After Virtue,* 2nd ed. (Notre Dame: University of Notre Dame Press, 1984), pp. 4-5. This sweeping critique of the relativism which derives no "ought" from an "is," no "value" from a "fact," and is the consequence of the failure of the Enlightenment project to ground morality on nonteleological and nontheological foundations, is widely regarded now as a major milestone in modern moral philosophy.

23. The most vocal and visible advocate of the recovery of paganism in contemporary culture and a new Dionysian deification of sexuality and nature is Camille Paglia. See her *Sexual Personae* (New Haven: Yale University Press, 1990) and *Sex, Art and American Culture* (New York: Random House, 1992).

terminating point for the liberal Christian experiment in religiosity, which reached its zenith in the last century.

To be sure, Christianity as such is not dead; quite the contrary, especially in the United States, still a far more religious nation, sociologically speaking, than any other in the West. Religion, especially of a conservative color, plays today a major role in American political and moral debate — on abortion, homosexuality, education, "the family," etc. — and in presidential electioneering. Thus it could be said that the end of Christendom has not happened in the United States, despite its constitutional separation of church and state from the beginning, as it has in Europe. There, certainly, society has become radically secular, and effectively post-Christian, displacing the churches even in countries where they are territorially deployed, constitutionally established, or state-supported, and where major political parties are nominally Christian. In the United States, the religious right became powerful in the 1980s when conservative Christians imitated the social involvement and political activism of liberals in the 1960s and 1970s; and while the so-called "mainline" churches are being marginalized, evangelicals and fundamentalists and pentecostalists flourish.[24] Yet here, too, there is surely taking place the ending of a religious era, the close of Constantinianism in its American form, along with the end of the enlightened modernity which itself posed such a challenge to the status and authority of the churches.[25] No longer does society accommodate itself to the church or acknowledge it as a central force and forum in its intellectual, cultural, and social affairs. The radical privatization of faith has expelled the churches from the now "naked public square,"[26] leaving committed Christians increasingly

24. See esp. R. Wuthnow, *The Struggle for America's Soul: Evangelicals, Liberals and Secularism* (Grand Rapids: Eerdmans, 1989); also G. Wills, *Under God: Religion and American Politics* (New York: Simon & Schuster, 1990); Dionne, *Why Americans Hate Politics,* ch. 8; W. C. Roof and W. McKinney, *American Mainline Religion* (New Brunswick, N.J.: Rutgers University Press, 1987); also A. B. Seligman, *The Idea of Civil Society* (New York: Free Press, 1992). The Presbyterian Church (U.S.A.) has produced a fascinating and comprehensive case study of "mainstream decline": *The Presbyterian Presence: The 20th Century Experience,* ed. M. J. Coulter, J. M. Mulder and L. B. Weeks, 7 vols. (Louisville: Westminster/John Knox Press, 1990-92). Not all, of course, on the theological right have endorsed the emergence of the politically powerful "Religious Right." See the significant protest by the well-known conservative and ex-politician Charles Colson that evangelicals have betrayed their own biblical cause in favor of the kingdom of God by pursuing mundane political leverage and status: C. Colson, *The Body* (Waco, Tex.: Word Books, 1992).

25. See Hall, *Thinking the Faith,* pp. 200ff.

26. R. J. Neuhaus, *The Naked Public Square* (Grand Rapids: Eerdmans, 1984); also *America against Itself: Moral Vision and the Public Order* (Notre Dame: University of Notre Dame Press, 1992). On this privatization of religion see also M. Marty, "Religion in Amer-

tempted, perhaps justifiably, to see themselves as a colony in a strange neo-pagan land, "resident aliens" in a hostile or — still worse — an indifferent territory.[27]

Through a kaleidoscope of perspectives, then — scientific and ecological, political and moral, intellectual and educational, religious and ecclesiastical — there are perhaps grounds for the admittedly sweeping generalization that we are witnesses to and participants in a cultural terminus, the close of an age, the end of the modern world. All around us is the loss of authority and of meaning, the collapse of institutions, the flight from public life, and dissatisfaction with a worldview. Naturally, change, renewal, and revivification for a moribund culture are not impossible, making this a time of waiting and suspension rather than a terminus as such, an inter-ruption, not a rupture; and that is indeed predicted for our culture by some who hold a cyclical view of history.[28] For now, though, dislocation, polarization, triviality, and negation characterize society, suggest its decline, and set us on the edge of a cultural abyss. If "Easter Saturday" connotes rupture and termination, a sense of darkness and disintegration, the loss of meaning, hope, and creativity, then our culture is surely to a significant degree an Easter Saturday society, in the throes, wittingly or not, of its own demise. And that is to say, not only that the distinctive features of "modern" society are perishing or have perished, but that "society" itself, the very existence of a cohesive and ordered community, is in peril. Are we any longer a "society"

---

ica 1935-85," in D. W. Lotz, ed., *Altered Landscapes* (Grand Rapids: Eerdmans, 1989). See also the recent corpus of Lesslie Newbigin on the privatization of faith in post-Enlightenment culture, to which we shall refer below: *The Other Side of 1984, The Gospel in a Pluralist Society,* and *Truth to Tell: The Gospel as Public Truth;* also his pamphlet *Mission and the Crisis of Western Culture* (Edinburgh: Handsel Press, 1989).

27. S. Hauerwas and W. Willimon, *Resident Aliens: Life in the Christian Colony* (Nashville: Abingdon, 1989). See also S. Ahlstrom, *A Religious History of the American People* (New Haven and London: Yale University Press, 1972), ch. 63. On the "disestablishment" of the church in the United States, see R. T. Handy, *A Christian America,* 2nd ed. (New York and Oxford: Oxford University Press, 1984), and *Undermined Establishment: Church-State Relations in America, 1880-1920* (Princeton: Princeton University Press, 1991). See also H. Bloom, *The American Religion: The Emergence of the Post-Christian Nation* (New York: Simon & Schuster, 1992); J. Habermas, *The Structural Transformation of the Public Sphere,* trans. T. Burger (Cambridge, Mass.: M.I.T. Press, 1989); and J. Carroll and W. C. Roof, eds., *Beyond Establishment: Protestant Identity in a Post-Modern Age* (Louisville: Westminster/John Knox, 1993).

28. See, e.g., A. Schlesinger, *The Cycles of American History;* also C. Clifford, *Counsel to the President: A Memoir* (New York: Random House, 1991), pp. 664ff. For a less sanguine view of history's cycles and the moment of suspension between them, see Hall, *Thinking the Faith,* esp. p. 194.

at all? Is the social quality of human existence, the unvarying essence of community as such, surviving the damage being done to the foundations and structures of our public life?

The most obvious ground for doubting our sociality now resides in the individualism and privatism so manifest in this "culture of narcissism" — the hedonistic pursuit of individual freedoms and gratifications without accountability to or interdependence with any wider community.[29] At the same time, however, jeremiads against individualism, however frequent and justified, do not wholly address the dimensions of the collapse of "society." To be sure, one experimental alternative to individualism has been depotentiated and in many cases has disappeared entirely: the totalitarian state which destroys individual freedom and identity even more directly and effectively than does the deification of the individual and the idolizing of personal freedom in many liberal societies. But the vacuum left by the collapse of the collectivist state has not been wholly filled with Western privatism and consumerism. Rather, what we see, alongside and often superimposed upon an individualistic ethos, is indeed a community culture, but one that is demonized and potentially — sometimes actually — genocidal, and threatens to turn the end of our age into the beginning of a "new barbarism."[30] These are the now rampant ethnic, tribal, and nationalistic forms of community which flourish in their hostility to cognate but different groupings over against which they find their own identities. Mocking the sentimentality of those who see "community" as a panacea for all individualism, insularity, and partisanship, there are communities defined by shared and exclusive racial, tribal, or religious memories and dreams, which are themselves denials of true "society." Protestants and Catholics in Northern Ireland, Serbs, Croats, and Muslims in the Balkans, Jews and Palestinians in Israel, all constitute "communities" which legitimately preserve cultural traditions and identities but are also capable of degeneration into alienated tribes who refuse social togetherness, mutual respect, and peaceful coexistence. Any recovery of "community" beyond its current Easter Saturday rupture will require not only the overcoming of individualism and the demons of private license and acquisitiveness; it will also need the exorcism and redemption of societal existence turned hateful, intolerant, and thus profoundly antisocial.

29. The sociology of this phenomenon has been superbly described and analyzed in R. Bellah et al., *Habits of the Heart: Individualism and Commitment in American Life* (New York: Harper & Row, 1986).

30. See J. Lukacs, *The End of the Twentieth Century and the End of the Modern Age* (New York: Ticknor and Fields, 1993).

II. The Buried Body: Catholicity and Participation

There is one community on earth summoned and able — able, that is, to the limited extent that it obeys its summons — to be a creative critic of our era's Easter Saturday loss of community, a judgment upon, but thereby also a re-demptive agent within, our social brokenness and cultural collapse. That com-munity is the church of Jesus Christ — according to the Nicene marks, one, holy, catholic, apostolic — which is his "body" in the world. This spiritual yet visible gathering of women and men from all the nations of the earth has the task and possibility of being itself an Easter Saturday community, fully partici-pant in the world and therefore set in multivalent relations to the terminal so-cial conditions of our world and present age. Embedded deeply within our pro-fane and moribund Easter Saturday society, it is yet sharply differentiated from that society's profanity and morbidity, while, in this very differentness, also en-ergetic in prayer and labor for society's renewal.

The church, we say — tautologously in fact — is a summoned commu-nity: the *ecclesia* called out of the world by God's free but costly word of covenantal choice which, as profligate, surprising, unwarranted, and risky grace, elects one people for the sake of many and demands that their gratitude take the form of obedience, responsibility, and service to the many.[31] It is this Word of God, of which our hearing and obeying is called faith, and not any human vi-sion, energy, or instigation, that alone creates and sustains the being of the church. And as we have seen, the Word of God has come to its most concrete and definitive articulation in the scandalous flesh of one crucified and buried. So that the church is not only — as Reformed tradition properly but sometimes too cozily defines it — the "creature of the divine Word," but is more pointedly, dis-concertingly, and often beyond its seeming capacities for obedient response, the creation of the *incarnate, crucified, and buried* Word of God.[32] It is indeed our

---

31. On the church as "called," see esp. H. Küng, *The Church*, trans. R. R. Ockenden (London: Burns and Oates and New York: Sheed and Ward, 1968); Barth, *CD*, IV/1, 651ff., and IV/3, 681-762; P. T. Forsyth, *The Church and the Sacraments* (London: Independent Press, 1917); Moltmann, *The Open Church*, trans. D. Meeks (London: SCM, 1978) (= *The Passion for Life: A Messianic Lifestyle* [Philadelphia, Fortress, 1978], ch. 6); C. Schwöbel, "The Creature of the Word: Recovering the Ecclesiology of the Reformers," in Gunton and Hardy, eds., *On Being the Church* (Edinburgh: T. & T. Clark, 1989); W. M. Alston Jr., *Guides to the Reformed Tradition: The Church* (Atlanta: John Knox Press, 1984); and A. E. Lewis, "*Ecclesia Ex Auditu*," *SJT* (1982).

32. On the trinitarian ontology of the church, see Gunton, in Gunton and Hardy, *On Being the Church*, esp. p. 75, and Ford, in the same collection, p. 244; also E. L. Mascall, *Christ, the Christian and the Church* (London: Longmans, Green and Co., 1946), ch. 6.

familiar story of the cross and grave which shapes, directs, and animates the church. The ecclesial question which that story raises is whether the community of the Word is willing, like the Word of God itself, to be incarnate, crucified, and buried.

This is the community of those who hear and think and therefore live that story at whose heart, between a cross and an empty grave, was a day of emptiness, defeat, and death. And precisely because those who hear and think this story are required in and through those acts to repeat the story, not only by its retelling and repreaching, but by its reliving in the Spirit through material and active embodiments of the narrative, the church of Christ crucified, buried, and raised cannot be itself except in intricate and intrinsic relations with our present world's Easter Saturday culture. Carrying the marks of Jesus branded in its body (Gal. 6:17; cf. 2 Cor. 4:10), through many kinds of suffering and death in conformity with Christ's own cross and grave, the church is itself an Easter Saturday community, sharing as God's called and chosen people in God's own identification with the sorrows, ruptures, and expirations of the world's people, communities, and cultures. Thus does the Word and story of the cross create an Easter Saturday church, sent by the Easter Saturday God into the Easter Saturday world, for the sake of that world's new, Easter life and eschatological renewal.

The Easter Saturday church naturally bears the marks of Christ crucified on its body because it *is* the Body of Christ who was crucified in the trinitarian history of God. That the church, according to the fecund image so variously deployed in the New Testament, *is* Christ's body (e.g., Rom. 12:3ff.; 1 Cor. 10:17; 12:12ff.; Eph. 3:6; 4:4, 11ff.; Col. 5:23) is not to be dismissed either as a platitude of ecclesiological correctness, too static and timeworn to startle back to life the often dormant missionary zeal of the Christian community today, nor as a metaphorical device whose potential for reinvigorating the church rests upon the inherent power of symbols sometimes to stimulate the imagination and fire the enthusiasm of a new generation. The "Body of Christ" is neither ancient doctrine nor inspiring metaphor, but the way things are: the church's ontological identity. The Body of Christ is just what the church *is*. "It is almost impossible to exaggerate the materialism and crudity of Paul's doctrine of the Church as literally now the resurrection *body* of Christ."[33] Christians, in their multiplicity

---

33. J. A. T. Robinson, *The Body* (London: SCM and Philadelphia: Westminster, 1952), p. 51; cf. Barth, *CD,* IV/1, 666 and see pp. 662-68. On "the Body of Christ" see also Bonhoeffer, *Cost of Discipleship,* ch. 29; A. M. Ramsey, *The Gospel and the Catholic Church* (London: Longmans, 1936); L. S. Thornton, *The Common Life in the Body of Christ* (London: Dacre Press, 1941); G. MacGregor, *Corpus Christi* (Philadelphia: Westminster Press,

as members or membranes of Christ's body, are that organism which constitutes Christ in his new humanity on earth, "the earthly-historical form of the
existence of Jesus Christ," that is, the *form* that Christ takes in the world
through the interim between ascension and return.[34] In that time given to the
church to be the church, the Christian community is, not metaphorically but in
concrete actuality, the worldly shape and presence of its Lord.[35]

If this be not symbolic but concrete and real, neither is it merely traditional but contemporary. Consider the clarity with which the "Body of Christ"
conceptuality drives away today all glorying and triumphalism in Christology
and ecclesiology alike. Karl Barth, always remarkably ready to bring us down to
earth, for one so frequently accused of elevating theology to heavenly discourse,
revoltingly identifies the starting point for affirming the church as Christ's own
body. In the first instance, he recalls, "body" *(soma)* biblically refers to a corpse,
a dead and lifeless body. For Christ himself was body and became a crucified,
dead body and a buried corpse, that "body of death" (Rom. 7:24) which bore
and destroyed the "body of sin" (Rom. 6:6; cf. Col. 1:22; 2:11; Eph. 2:16; 1 Pet.
2:24). And of just *this* Christ, bodily and buried, the church is told: "*You* are the
body of Christ" (1 Cor. 12:27).[36]

So the church is that organism, that one community of many members,
which makes present, visible, and concrete in the world — where it once lay
buried, cold, and lifeless in its bleeding and exhausted expiration — the body of
Christ, God's very Son, he who now is risen and ascended, yet who offered up
his body to death once and for all (Heb. 10:10). Where and how is this Christ
now in the world, but in and as the church? And how can the church be Christ's
body now within the world if not as his body which once lay subject to sin, corruption, and destruction in the deadly tomb: God's own life in union with our
impotence and perishing?

1958); E. L. Mascall, *Corpus Christi* (London: Longmans, Green & Co. Ltd., 1953), esp. ch. 1;
L. Newbigin, *The Household of God* (London: SCM, 1953 and New York: Friendship Press,
1954); H. Küng, *Church* (New York: Doubleday, 1976), pp. 203-60; A. Dulles, *Models of the
Church* (New York: Doubleday, 1978), pp. 54ff.; Barth, *CD,* IV/2, sect. 67 and IV/3, 856ff. See
also *Lumen Gentium* (Dogmatic Constitution on the Church), *The Documents of Vatican II,*
ed. W. M. Abbott (London: G. Chapman and New York: The America Press, 1966).

34. Barth, *CD,* IV/1, 710. See also Bonhoeffer, *Christ the Center,* pp. 59ff. (Bowden
trans.), and *The Communion of Saints* (New York: Harper & Row, 1963) (= *Communio
Sanctorum* [London: Collins, 1963]); also J. A. Phillips, *The Form of Christ in the World: A
Study of Bonhoeffer's Christology* (London: Collins, 1967); also E. Schillebeeckx, *Church:
The Human Story of God* (New York: Crossroad, 1990).

35. See esp. Barth, *CD,* IV/1, 725-39: "The Time of the Community."

36. Barth, *CD,* IV/1, 662ff.

Of course, this is the body, too, that was raised and glorified; and as Christ's Easter Body the church indeed is that community which has itself been brought from bondage to emancipation, from burial to new life (Rom. 6:4ff.), from humiliation to exaltation, proleptic promise to all humanity and to the cosmos of its own deliverance and eschatological fulfillment. Yet just as there was no risen Jesus Christ who was not first, and remains forever (Heb. 5:6ff.), the Crucified and Buried One, so there is no glorious church, no triumphant, chosen people, who are not by that very token those whose new, joyful life is hidden in suffering and death, and whose glory is the majestic humility of servitude and self-abandonment to others in conformity with Christ.

Above all to be resisted are the docetic seductions of such a concept as "the body of Christ," which tempt dogmatics to spiritualize or even divinize the church, imbuing it with the mysterious and mystic properties of a heavenly society, supernaturally purified and sustained on earth, and thus extending there God's incarnation as "another Christ."[37] The Easter Saturday history of Christ's own fleshly body brutally and insistently secures the humanness of the church. Not despite but *because of* the Holy Spirit, which creates and sustains the *ecclesia* in union and communion with Christ the Crucified and Buried One, the church is not spiritiualized or deified, but constantly returned, however recalcitrant, otherworldly, and escapist, to the humanity it shares with him. By the Spirit, that is, we participate in God's own humanness, whose divine history intersected the worldly historicity of crucifixion and burial; and thus are we kept true to our earthly and earthy identity and calling, the church's human and historical pilgrimage which passes strangely through Gethsemane, Calvary, and the garden on the way from Pentecost to *parousia*. How can the church participate in the triune fellowship of God without also sharing in God's own participation, through the history of the Trinity, in the world's suffering, godforsakenness, and death? Truly, the Body of Christ, commissioned to baptize in the

---

37. The high point of this ecclesiological docetism came remarkably late in the history of Catholic dogma, namely, the encyclical *Mystici Corporis* of Pope Pius XII in 1943. On this, see, e.g., Küng, *Church,* pp. 12, 240, and *Structures of the Church,* trans. S. Attanasio (New York: Nelson, 1964 and London: Burns & Oates, 1965), pp. 305-51, esp. p. 321; also Dulles, *Models of the Church,* ch. 3; and Barth, *CD,* IV/1, 659ff. See also "Church," in K. Rahner, ed., *Sacramentum Mundi,* vol. 1 (New York: Herder & Herder and London: Burns & Oates, 1968). In Küng's view (*Church,* pp. 234-41), the church is not to be divinized nor conceived as a "continuing Christ," nor placed above the Word of God, but is to be seen as that community which serves the Word, humbly obeying and accepting Christ's authority. That is admirable, but it is scarcely persuasive as a reading of much of the actual Roman teaching he is expounding, at least as it stood prior to Vatican II. See also Schillebeeckx, *Church,* pp. 189-95, 210ff.

triune name (Mt. 28:18), was "born on the cross from the side of the savior" whence flowed the water and the blood (Jn. 19:34).[38]

Likewise, to say that the church is commissioned and sent, that is, "apostolic," is indeed, despite some traditions to the contrary, not to deify the church as glorified body, nor to idealize its continuity, in order or in doctrine, with the apostles; rather, it is to reinforce the humanness of the church, as the *buried* body of Jesus Christ. Apostolicity itself betokens a church which does not exist or act for itself, any more than it is self-created and self-sustaining. The "called" community is as such the *sent* community: sent by the Son as was the Son by the Father (Jn. 20:21),[39] and therefore sent by Another and to others, and for those others' sake commissioned for self-giving and self-forgetfulness. "It builds up itself . . . in the common hearing of the Word of God, . . . in common prayer, in baptism and the Lord's Supper, in . . . inner fellowship, in theology, [not] simply for its own sake but only in the course of its commission — only in an implicit and explicit outward movement to the world with which Jesus Christ and in His person God accepted solidarity, for which he died. . . . It can never consider its own security, let alone its appearance. As His community it is always free from itself. . . . Its mission is not additional to its being. It is, as it is sent and active in its mission."[40] This means that participation and involvement in the world is the only way for the church to be itself. How can the church be for the world without entering into its condition?

Indeed, the insidious but historically ineradicable presumption that the "apostolic" church exists for itself could not more blatantly and heretically falsify its true identity as the body of Christ, inasmuch as Christ is primordially the One for others, in whom God's own triune life is for others given up to suffering and to death. Only as the church that exists for the world, comes close to the world, and enters into it, can the church be the body of Christ, whose divine identity was fulfilled in coming close to us, subject to the world's weaknesses and hungers and finally surrendered up to its killing fields and burial grounds. It is therefore into our own decaying world, hanging as it does by an Easter Saturday thread of despair, dislocation, and dissolution, that the Christian community today must go, letting itself be the sent and buried church which makes its grave with the wretched and the wicked, the victims and the perpetrators of our culture's termination and society's collapse. "Solidarity with the world means that

38. See Barth, *CD,* IV/1, 667.

39. See Barth, *CD,* IV/3, 768-69. See also my article "All Things New: Foundational Theses on World Mission," in *Austin Seminary Bulletin* 103.4 (1987): 5-13.

40. Barth, *CD,* IV/1, 724-25; on the "apostolic" church, see *CD,* IV/1, 712-25; cf. IV/3, 762-95: "The Community for the World."

those who are genuinely pious approach the children of the world as such, that those who are genuinely righteous are not ashamed to sit down with the unrighteous as friends, that those who are genuinely wise do not hesitate to seem to be fools among the fools, and that those who are genuinely holy are not too good or irreproachable to go down 'into hell' in a very secular fashion."[41]

But how exactly is this apostolic participation unto burial and hell to be envisioned and enacted? What must the church do and be to become and remain truly the buried body of Christ at the turn of our millennium, the form now to be taken by the one who two thousand years ago was crucified and dead, buried and descended into hell?

III. The Servant Body: Catholicity and Presence

Could the church of Jesus Christ, his apostolic, buried body in the world, more sharply distinguish itself from today's dominant culture, or bear clearer witness to the difference between the Spirit of the cross and our own beginning-of-millennium *Zeitgeist,* the spirit of our decaying age, than by declaring itself "catholic" and so acting? What potential countercultural forces surreptitiously await release — if only Christians dared to set them loose — within their deceptively harmless self-definition as "the catholic church." For "catholicity" denotes the connectedness, the sameness and the universality not only of Christ's church but — since that body exists not for itself but for the world — of the human race entirely. Thus does "the church catholic" embody a subversion of and a proleptic deliverance from the pathological individualism, polarization, and sectionalism of our terminal society.

Theologically, the predicate "catholic" is of course synonymous with and derivative of another: "Christocentric." Catholicity is the product, not the precondition, of being Christ's body in the world. The church is not anointed as that body because independently or by logical priority it is already universal and organic. Rather, they are catholic who by the Spirit are united with Christ and in consequence comprise the interconnected totality of all through space and time who share that common identity which is himself, in whom all are one.[42] Likewise "the catholic truth," though classically defined as that which all Christians everywhere at all times believe, does not reside in the orthodoxy or

41. Barth, *CD,* IV/3, 774.
42. On catholicity, see esp. Küng, *The Church,* pp. 296-319; Barth, *CD,* IV/1, 701-12; Ramsey, *Catholic Church;* also S. Louden, *The True Face of the Kirk* (London: Oxford University Press, 1963), ch. 2.

harmony of the church's doctrines or traditions, but rather in Christ himself the living truth — to whose fullness and veracity the believing community aspires to correspond in thought and word.[43]

However, this in turn means that the church can only be true, and truly catholic, when actually conformed to the Christ in whom it finds its being, purpose, and identity, and that means Christ as he actually is, namely, the Crucified and Buried One, whose Easter glory and exaltation are expressed through, and not polarized with, the humiliation of his suffering and death. Since the church, flinching from Christ's cross and grave, fails repeatedly to be itself and fulfill its own identity, the catholicity of the Christian community which so critically judges and undermines our worldly society can only do so creatively, for that society's redemption, by first judging the church itself and calling it to penitence and to reform.[44]

As a catholic "body," the church is organic and interdependent in the image of the Trinity itself. All its many parts in their great diversity are equally important, mutually reliant, and integrally connected, and each affects and is affected by the others (1 Cor. 12:12-26). How profoundly the concept and reality of such connectedness and reciprocity contradicts our prevailing cultural mores and assumptions! Our age elevates private, solitary individuals as the focal unit of our social ordering, whose independence and private pursuit of happiness is not to be constrained — though it mightily compounds in practice their loneliness and sadness. The stimulating and gratifying of their needs and wants drives our national and even global economic mechanisms. Deplorably, however, a pandering to the religious experience, emotional preoccupation, and social preference of private, disconnected persons characterizes much of the Christian community itself today. This reduces the function of the church to providing therapeutic settings where individuals may volunteer to nurse their grievances and pursue their dreams while rubbing congenial shoulders with others like themselves.

True ecclesial catholicity, by contrast, betokens not the voluntary association of insular, like-minded individuals, but the unconditional connectedness

---

43. On the classical definition of catholicity *(ubique, semper, ab omnibus)*, which derives from Vincent of Lérins, see Küng, *Church,* p. 298; cf. Barth, *CD,* IV/1, 712; also Pelikan, *Christian Tradition,* vol. 1, ch. 7.

44. See here my paper "Catholicity, Confessionalism and Convergence," in *Reformed World* 38.8 (1985). See also Moltmann, "The Ecumenical Church under the Cross," in *The Open Church.* Also, for some fine insights into the "ecclesiology of the cross" in relation to Paul's Corinthian epistles, see D. Ford, "Faith in the Cities: Corinth and the Modern City," in Gunton and Hardy, eds., *On Being the Church,* esp. pp. 238ff.; and F. Young and D. F. Ford, *Meaning and Truth in 2 Corinthians* (London: SPCK, 1987).

of those commandeered for discipleship and togetherness by a common Lord who chooses his friends — not they him (Jn. 15:16) — and demands that they follow him as one body, bound ineluctably to one another in chains of love and mutuality. Thus is the church no agglomeration of atomistic members who decide to be together for reasons of self-interest, on the basis of whatever variant — color, age, location, class, or race — set them apart from other human groupings. Rather, Christ chooses our neighbors for us — including the uncongenial and quite unlike us, socially, ethnically, temperamentally — and connects us to them, his brothers and sisters and therefore ours, in an integrated fellowship which transcends both time and space and every boundary between races, classes, nationalities, and generations. To practice such connectedness in the church is not only to be set in conflict with this era's highly individualized piety and with its ecclesiastical cognate of radically independent congregationalism. It is also to provide to the privatized and factionalized secular culture of the postmodern world an alternative understanding and enactment of humanness as such.

For what happens in the church of Christ, as human beings corporately discover their own ligaments of solidarity and mutual reliance, is that the created truth of all humanity is thereby disclosed and realized. The truth is, as we have seen — definitively from the standpoint of the cross and grave — that we model the image of God's own triune community not as solitary, independent islands of personal existence, but essentially together, connected and relational, primarily as male and female, but in countless other forms too, of relationality and cohumanity which unite us to the different in bonds of equality and reciprocal dependence.[45]

Where is this truth about ourselves as human creatures visible, and where is there a preview of the eschatological vision wherein the Creator's purpose for our togetherness in the triune image shall be fulfilled and realized and God be all in all? In the catholic church. For that is summoned by the cross and grave of Christ, of whose very body it is now the earthly form, to devise and live by concrete structures and public styles of true connectedness fit to persuade a sad society, lonely and divided, that there are possibilities worth hoping for and working for toward redemption from its self-destructive idolizing of the individual and its disastrous pursuit of sectional concerns.

---

45. "Original sin" is that condition whereby, in the self-deluding wish to deny this connectedness and be alone, sovereign, and independent, we all universally and inescapably confirm that we are in fact all the same, discomfortingly locked in the very solidarity with one another that we foolishly prefer not to acknowledge. See my article, "Keeping Our Nerve: AIDS and the Doctrine of Sin," *Austin Seminary Bulletin* 105.1 (Fall 1989).

How the church should assess society's preoccupations now with group identity, and attempt to mediate our hardening group conflicts, is, to be sure, a matter demanding the greatest sensitivity and insight. Here, too frequently, well-intentioned Christians adopt and reinforce the ascendant secular ideology, instead of speaking and acting on the quite distinctive basis of their Christocentric catholicity. In fully justified revulsion at social and political imperialisms of the past — the hegemony of Eurocentric over other cultures, for example, and of men over women and white over black — a historical reversal of prejudice is being sought in our society through the conscious elevation of pluralism. This rightly affirms the value and propriety of racial and sexual diversity, and of cultural and linguistic multiplicity; and seeks entrée to the corridors of power for minority groups previously and grieviously excluded from them. Yet by its very logic, this social strategy can foster not greater unity but more disintegration; for it may reinforce a sense of victimization and exclusion, keep alive memories of old hurts, resentments, and rivalries, and highlight still today the very differences of race, color, gender, and history which were the basis for yesterday's injustices. Thus, some fear, does the new American ideology of multiculturalism threaten to replace the search for unity out of plurality *(unum e pluribus),* with a cult of plurality *per se,* which renders unity and cohesiveness even less realizable than before.[46]

Unfortunately, today's churches often seem unable to distinguish this ill-fated, secular pluralistic project from the far more profound, revolutionary but unifying inclusiveness of the Christian gospel. The "word of the cross," as we have heard, declares the radical humanness of the God who has, in Jüngel's terms, come closer to us than we are to ourselves, more similar to us than dissimilar from us, and become united with us in the most concrete particulars of our humanity, including mortality and death itself. Since no human being is excluded from the created dignity, or fallen wretchedness, of the creaturely condition made the Creator's own between Mary's womb and the garden tomb, the oneness of humanity assumed, endured, and redeemed in Christ is absolute and total. To this totality, the catholicity of the church bears witness.[47]

This essential sameness and oneness of all whose relationship to Christ is grounded in his incarnation, death, and burial has now in faith and through the Spirit been sealed with the sign of baptism in the universal church. Given this absolute and unconditioned oneness of all those so baptized, proleptic representatives of all humanity, no one in the church can be excluded or subordinated; for in the unity of the Spirit all fleshly, worldly barriers of inquality and

46. See Schlesinger, *The Disuniting of America.*
47. See here esp. Küng, *The Church,* p. 302; and Barth, *CD,* IV/1, 701.

rivalry have been removed; and differences of gender, class, nationality, and race not dramatized, as in "multiculturalism," but radically relativized and robbed of consequence (Gal. 3:27-28; cf. Col. 3:10-11). Here male and female, Jew and Greek, free and slave are all the same, equally included in Christ's one baptismal body. Within this sameness, tasks and responsibilities, including those of leadership, are distributed precisely not according to worldly differentials of status and position but on the basis of the varying gifts of Christ's own Spirit (Rom. 12:3-8; 1 Cor. 12:12-31; Eph. 4:7-13). Authority within the church goes, therefore, neither to those who enjoy nor, *simpliciter,* to those who are excluded from worldly power or position, but to those appropriately marked out for it by the Holy Spirit.

Certainly in most instances such persons will include many from whom both the world and the church of the past have wickedly withheld authority. But the rectification of that injustice in the church is to be grounded upon an inclusiveness more complete and nonnegotiable than anything that society could engineer; for it is based precisely not on who one is according to the flesh, but on who one is in Christ and how one has been graced and gifted by his Spirit.

The imperative upon us is surely not to construct on earth the supposedly ideal church by setting quotas of inclusion and targets of representativeness which in fact revivify past rivalries and divisions, paying more attention yet to the sin-exaggerated differentials of skin and sex, accent and ability. Is it not rather that we witness through our structures and methods of empowerment to the undifferentiated sameness of all Christ's baptized members, and so of all God's human partners? That would allow the church to be reformed anew, shaped by "the word of the cross" into Easter Saturday communities, not of pluralism and self-assertion but of common discipleship and self-surrender, guided by women and men of every sort, identified not by their places in the world, past or present, marginal or central, powerful or victimized, but by their Spirit-given capacity for leadership in Christ-like suffering and service.[48]

Among much else, such radical inclusiveness, grounded not upon social ideology, "political correctness," or ecclesiastical kingdom-building, but on the ontological identity of the church as one in Jesus Christ, would represent a plangent protest against the tribalism and barbaric nationalism resurgent now in the aftermath of the "cold war" and in the older polarizing of the earth into affluent North and poor South, the old and new worlds and the "third." What

48. See esp. the brief but telling observations on "inclusiveness" in D. M. McCullough, "The Diversity of Gifts," *Presbyterian Outlook* 173.39 (Nov. 11, 1991). See also J. P. Burgess, "Conversation, Conviction and the Presbyterian Identity Crisis," in *The Christian Century* 110.6 (Feb. 24, 1993).

more vividly contradicts the atavistic ethnic hatreds and the yawning gaps of global inequity in our crumbling Easter Saturday world than the good news that in Christ Jesus there is one humanity and one world only? The walls of hostility between Jews and Gentiles,[49] and all the nations of the earth, have been demolished, Christ having made peace between enemies and strangers through the blood of his cross, ending the distinction between insiders and outsiders, citizens and aliens (Eph. 2:11-22). This is the universality to which catholicity refers, though it denotes a wholeness of humanity in Christ transcending differences of locality and context broader than the merely geographical spread of one institution across the inhabited world, under a single see, to which the notion of "the catholic church" was too long reduced, and for which "ecumenical" has been widely adopted as far too shallow an equivalent.[50]

On the basis of the cross, Christians may truly affirm that through all times and places there is one human race, whose reconciliation, integrity, and indivisibility entirely transcend all differences of nation, race, or tribe, and thus credibly embody alternatives to the rivalry of cultures, nation-states, and ethnic groups which currently rend the fabric of our world. Yet to do this the church must first repent of its own history, wherein Christ's gospel has itself been falsely wedded to the fortunes, identities, and destinies of separate nations, races, and cultures.[51]

---

49. On the particularly sensitive and difficult question of what "catholicity" means with reference to relations between Christians and Jews, see esp. Moltmann, *Church in the Power of the Spirit* (Minneapolis: Augsburg Fortress, 1993), pp. 350ff., and *Way of Jesus Christ,* ch. 1; also H. Küng, *Judaism,* trans. J Bowden (New York: Crossroad, 1992); Barth, *CD,* esp. II/2, sect. 34; and P. van Buren, *A Theology of the Jewish-Christian Reality,* 3 parts (San Francisco: Harper & Row, 1980-88).

50. For the complaint that "ecumenical" is too geographical a predicate to be a satisfactory substitute for "catholic" in such contexts as "the ecumenical movement," see Küng, *The Church,* pp. 303, 306-7; and Barth, *CD,* IV/1, 702-3. If there is something contradictory in prefixing "Roman" to the universal "catholic" church, something arrogant about denying full ecclesial reality to those not in communion with the Bishop of Rome, and something unidimensional in reducing the church to such "a sociological and juridical criterion of what is apostolic" (*CD,* IV/1, 713), Barth equally and rightly deplores the willingness of Protestants to abandon the term "catholic" or to treat "catholic tendencies" as a matter for guilt and accusation (p. 702). Likewise, Küng regrets that "at the time of the Counter-Reformation some Catholics were thoughtless enough to accept this [Roman] label which threatened the whole concept of catholicity" (p. 306).

51. See esp. R. H. S. Boyd, *India and the Latin Captivity of the Church* (Cambridge: Cambridge University Press, 1974); also B. Stanley, *The Bible and the Flag: Protestant Missions and British Imperialism in the Nineteenth and Twentieth Centuries* (Leicester: InterVarsity Press, 1990).

Actually, it is relatively easy now to deplore the blasphemy of a "German Christianity," and perhaps too its contemporary cognates — South African or Irish, North or South — or even the subtler marriage of the Christian faith to the mores and values of the British Empire or the American Dream. It is far harder to recognize, and takes more courage to counteract, liberations from these "babylonian captivities" which unwittingly repeat the idolatries of old in newer forms. It is one thing strenuously to affirm that the Christian gospel must be interpreted for and by South Americans, Africans, and Asians no less than for the Western, developed nations. It is another to suppose that the acculturation of the gospel in new, non-Eurocentric, settings is necessarily protected from the dangers of cultural conditioning which that process seeks to overcome. In principle, an "African Christianity" is as open to abuse as a European, Afrikaner, or American. Christ, surely, may no more be held captive to Asia's indigenous cultures, for example, than to the imported values of its earlier imperialistic history.

The cosmic range of Christ's crucified lordship means that, on the one hand, he may be found and followed in every society, and his gospel and his church live in symbiosis with every culture; and, on the other hand, that no culture whatsoever may be sanctified or idolized, identified as the embodiment of truth on which his church depends.[52] Thus some cultural fashions in the worldwide church today, though properly devoted to the rectifying of Western dominance, are no less subject to the judgment of the cross and grave, which expose misunderstanding and distortion of God's truth in every form of human wisdom and experience, than are the assumptions and prejudices of the church's colonialist, missionary past.

What is true about this dual affirmation and relativizing of all cultures geographically, in the light of Christ's universality and the church's catholicity, also applies chronologically. The Spirit may inspire any and every generation to truthful articulation of the mystery of Christ through its own worldview and forms of thought and speech. But no language, philosophy, or epoch can comprehend the Trinity itself, any more than the Holy Spirit may be identified with the spirit of any age or culture. That is why, however disasteful, unfashionable, or perilous the task, the church, for the very sake of the world it serves and addresses, cannot refuse the imperative to reform and purify its preaching in every generation and be prepared to draw fresh lines between falsity and truth, heresy and gospel, authenticity and apostasy.[53] For the truth is Christ himself, and he, the crucified, is always at risk to bondage, manipulation, and distortion through cultural conditioning, historical shortsightedness, or sheer perversity.

52. See esp. Barth, *CD*, IV/1, 703.
53. See esp. Barth, *CD*, IV/1, 701-2.

Therefore the church which bears Christ's name and identity, while declaring the end of every other barrier, cannot refrain from separating the true, "catholic" church from the schismatic and the false, distinguishing everything which promotes and serves his salvation from that which corrupts and contradicts it. Such is the continuing particle of truth even in so misused and rightly suspect a maxim of traditional catholicity as that "outside the church there is no salvation."[54] While far beyond the visible boundaries of the Christian church there arches over all humanity, through the universal Spirit, the good news of Christ's redemption and God's coming rule, there repeatedly flourish falsifications of that saving word which the church must reject with a resounding No and keep outside its borders. Thus it was that to confess Christ's lordship and refuse idolatry, Christians in recent generations distinguished the true church from the false by saying No to such heresies as "German Christianity" and the scriptural defense of apartheid.[55] Likewise today, only a church can render pure and audible the saving word of the cross, God's Yes to all humanity, which does not flinch from banishing every rationale, inside Christendom or beyond it, for the nationalistic bigotry, ethnic barbarism, and racial ideology which so besmirch our *fin de siècle* global order.

So then, the affirmation of Christian truth is sometimes to be hazarded for the very sake of the world which despises such confidence as gauche, unpersuasive, and triumphalistic. To be sure, catholicity directs our attention more to

54. See Küng, *The Church,* pp. 313-19, for a brief history of this phrase *(extra ecclesiam nulla salus),* its interpretation and application, and its de facto withdrawal by *Lumen Gentium,* the ecclesiological decree of Vatican II — as well as a brief statement of its continued if restricted applicability. See, too, Barth, *CD,* IV/1, 688-89; E. Jüngel, "Extra Christum Nulla Salus," in *Theological Essays;* and K. Rahner, "On the Theology of the Incarnation," *Theological Investigations, IV,* trans. K. Smyth (London: Darton, Longman & Todd and Boston: Helicon Press, 1966), and "Anonymous Christians," in *Theological Investigations VI,* trans. K.-H. and B. Kruger (London: Darton, Longman & Todd and New York: Crossroad, 1982), ch. 23. See also Schillebeeckx, *Church,* esp. pp. xviiff. Schillebeeckx complains bitterly that the new openness shown at Vatican II to the presence of the church and of salvation outside the Roman communion has not been maintained in the subsequent practice of the Vatican's authorities, nor by the Roman Church's recent revisions of canon law.

55. See esp. A. C. Cochrane, *The Church's Confession under Hitler* (Pittsburgh: Pickwick Press, 1976); and J. de Gruchy and C. Villa-Vicencio, eds., *Apartheid Is a Heresy* (Johannesburg: David Philip and Guildford: Lutterworth Press, 1983). For other, highly original discussions of nationalism today from a Christian perspective, see W. Storrar, *Scottish Identity: A Christian Vision* (Edinburgh: Handsel Press, 1990); and K. W. Clements, *A Patriotism for Today: Love of Country in Dialogue with the Witness of Dietrich Bonhoeffer* (London: Collins, 1986).

the center, which is Christ himself, than to the boundaries, requiring the most liberal and irenic recognition of diversity and variations within the church compatible with its Christological center. Nevertheless, the liberating, universal truth of Christ himself sometimes demands cross-based resistance to whatever falsehood divides human beings into first and second class, superior and inferior, and disputes the place of any person, nation, or race in God's coming just and equitable messianic kingdom. This is our reminder, yet again, that catholicity refers finally not to the wholeness of the church, the same across the ages and the world in every location, time, and context, but to the totality of the human race as such in its final fulfillment. The church is truly catholic insofar as it exists not for its own sake but for the world's, and not for some of the world only but for the whole world, which will be redeemed and reconciled in the image of the Trinity at the close of the age.[56]

The concrete question, then, is how, in keeping with its universal, eschatological mission, the Easter Saturday church can *be* catholic today, relating to all humanity and the world in its entirety. In order to serve the whole world must the church, for example, adopt policies of strict neutrality and evenhandedness, favoring all sides equally in every situation of conflict or of need? Or would it not betray a docetic, otherworldly understanding of the church and its worldly task if catholicity precluded all priorities and preferences, all involvements and interventions in specified events and on particular sides in society's affairs. In fact, catholicity does not exclude, but demands, particularity, partiality, and partisanship.[57]

The church of Christ itself, of course, has grossly betrayed its Lord, grotesquely negated its own calling as his body, falsified its catholicity and his, through schism and division, and spintered into rival communions, traditions, denominations, and sects, on the basis of rival competing authorities, confessions, liturgies, orderings, and cultural allegiances. For such a church to attempt catholicity in mission to the whole world without remorse for its sectarian disintegration and active commitment to reconciliation and reunion would simply match hypocrisy with futility.

56. See, e.g., Moltmann, *Church in the Power of the Spirit*, p. 349. Cf. Küng, *The Church*, pp. 302ff.; and Schillebeeckx, *Church*, pp. 168ff. See, too, *Lumen Gentium*, 13. For a distinctly Reformed exposition of the church's catholicity in terms of its mission and witness to the whole world, see J. Leith, *From Generation to Generation* (Louisville: Westminster/John Knox Press, 1990), ch. 6.

57. See here Moltmann's splendid treatment of catholicity and partisanship in *Church in the Power of the Spirit*, pp. 347-52. Of course, the entire phenomenon of "liberation theology" is grounded in the biblically defended premise that God exercises a bias toward and a "preferential option" for, the poor and the oppressed.

On the other hand, the one church of Christ, catholic and universal, surely must embrace reconciled diversity and heterogeneity grounded in the particularities of location and context, of history and culture. The "scandal of particularity" is that God has been united with the perishing humanity of all, precisely in and through the specificity of one man's flesh and unsubstitutable life, one Jewish history from birth under Herod to death under Pontius Pilate. The people of God, likewise, live not in undifferentiated timelessness, but in the concrete, temporal world where contexts vary and where particularitites determine meaning. Thus there may, given full table fellowship and mutual recognition of ecclesial integrity, be many churches, locally diverse and culturally distinct, even confessionally divergent at some points, within the one, universal church of Christ.[58] So it is, too, that in order to be in and with and for the whole world, Christians must interpret and apply the gospel, determine strategy, adopt programs, and exercise choices according to the fluctuations of temporal crisis, geographical setting, and cultural context.[59] Just because God loves all humanity impartially and equally, the cause of divine justice can only be promoted when the victims of human bias and injustice are supported and the structural roots of inequality removed. Can those who are alienated be truly reconciled simply through impartial support of all parties — which would perpetuate the status quo between them — or only by removal of the causes of estrangement through partisan support of the injured and aggrieved and insistence on repentance from the guilty?[60] "Jesus turned to the sinners, tax-collectors and lepers in order to save the Pharisees and the healthy as well. Paul turned to the Gentiles in order to save Israel too. Christian partisan support for the oppressed is intentional and its goal is to save the oppressor also."[61] And as God brings down the mountains and elevates the lowlands, so that all flesh might see God's glory together, how could the church serve the redemption of the world in the messianic kingdom without casting its lot with forces that

58. See my "Catholicity, Confessionalism and Convergence," esp. pp. 425ff.

59. This necessity is clearly analyzed and exemplified by John de Gruchy in his *Theology and Ministry in Context and Crisis* (London: Collins and Grand Rapids: Eerdmans, 1987).

60. The principle that true reconciliation cannot preserve but must remove the grounds of alienation was at the heart of the biblical case raised against the theological supporters of apartheid in South Africa who sought reconciliation with black and "colored" Christians on the basis of spiritual unity but also within the terms of the political status quo. The case for reconciliation through justice is enshrined in the "Belhar Confession" of the Dutch Reformed Mission Church in South Africa. See esp. G. D. Cloete and D. J. Smit, *A Moment of Truth* (Grand Rapids: Eerdmans, 1984).

61. Moltmann, *Church in the Power of the Spirit*, p. 352.

would peaceably overturn the world's social and political landscape (Isa. 40:4ff.; Lk. 1:46-55)? Least of all could the church of the crucified and buried one refuse to reflect God's own strange revolutionary choices revealed on Calvary and in the first community of faith. Of them, "not many were wise according to worldly standards, not many were powerful, not many were of noble birth; but God chose what is foolish in the world to shame the wise, God chose what is weak in the world to shame the strong, God chose what is low and despised in the world . . . to bring to nothing things that are" (1 Cor. 1:27-28). Thus the church of the cross "is related to the whole and is catholic in so far as, in the fragmentation of the whole, it primarily seeks and restores to favour the lost, the rejected and the oppressed."[62]

It exceeds our scope here to judge in detail how such partiality might be practiced in the church's contemporary context in the West. But clearly any missionary strategy biased toward the poor and the marginal cannot be dissociated from the phenomenon by which some churches are themselves being transposed from the center of society. Is this a moment of opportunity for the church of the cross to be reidentified with the crucified Christ in whose death the very God of all surrendered to marginalization and was, in Bonhoeffer's stunning imagery, "pushed out of the world onto the cross"?[63]

There is much discussion, and some not unjustified alarm, surrounding the destiny of "mainstream" or "mainline" churches today which are losing their erstwhile positions of influence, dominance, and power within the religious, political, and social spheres of contemporary society. But is this "decline" unambiguously to be deplored? Of course, it would be unpardonable to react complacently to the loss of members, income, or standing of any church which confesses Christ as Lord; and it would be hideous, even or especially in the name of the cross, to glory in that phenomenon, appealing to some ideology of martyrdom or weakness.[64]

On the other hand, a church with fewer members, but with a higher proportion of them motivated not by social pressures but by a dedication to Christ and to his mission, which might be costly and unpopular among their social peers, is arguably the stronger for being smaller. So that the real question is whether and how it might be true for an institution like the church, no less than

---

62. Moltmann, *Church in the Power of the Spirit*, p. 352.

63. Bonhoeffer, *Letters and Papers from Prison*, p. 360.

64. See the dispute about the celebration of powerlessness and the ecclesial meaning of the theology of the cross, between Stephen Sykes, in *The Identity of Christianity* (London: SPCK and Philadelphia: Fortress, 1984), and R. H. Roberts, in "Lord, Bondsman and Churchman," in Gunton and Hardy, *On Being the Church*, ch. 5.

for the individuals in it, that only those who lose their lives shall find them. What might such saving loss ecclesially entail? Surely the church of Christ, called to conform to the crucified and buried one and to obey the very God who on the cross and in the grave entered the depths of loss and self-negation, is itself summoned to forms of self-surrender and *kenosis*. But *kenosis* of what sort? Such self-abandonment could not be simplistically equated with social or political decline, for that need not be the price of taking the way of the cross but could be the opposite: the consequence of faithlessness and apathy, the abandonment of sacrificial mission. Conversely, those churches which today are growing, however suspect, sometimes, their theology, methods, and appeal, are not necessarily ascendant for disreputable reasons, but may indeed have much to teach the declining "mainline" churches about commitment, passion, energy, and relevance.

Even so, when marginalization happens, through whatever causes, an opportunity arises for the church to reexamine its identity as a church of the cross, and to ask if its preaching and ministry are truly conformed to Christ the crucified. Has it lost favor with the world because its message is a stumbling block to the wise and powerful, or because on the contrary it lacks all conviction and has lost the capacity to challenge and disturb? Do its lifestyle and mission truly take it into fellowship and solidarity with the world's weak and foolish nobodies, the despised and rejected and wicked with whom Christ suffered and beside whom he was crucified and buried? The church's very loss of power and resources may indeed, from one angle, deplorably hamper its ability to meet human need directly, feed and clothe the hungry and the naked, to make its voice heard in the name of peace and justice, and to exercise leverage on governments to pursue humanizing policies among the underprivileged and undereducated, the unemployed and unhoused, the uninsured and unloved. But could it not simultaneously deepen the bonds of solidarity and empathy with the dispossessed and depotentiated of the earth? Perhaps the publicly weakened church may understand afresh that its first task is not be to change the world but to be present in it, quietly, hiddenly, making its dwelling place with its sinners and its outcasts, as the crucified Word itself dwelt among us in the flesh, full of grace and truth to be sure, yet incognito and invisible to those who lacked the eye of faith.[65]

The present loss of prestige and power within the mainstream church in

65. An "Easter Saturday" identification with the sinner and the godforsaken is well exemplified in a small but telling anecdote in the biography of Lord George MacLeod, founder of the Iona Community. At great personal cost, he appeared for the defense in the trial of a highly disturbed Glasgow man accused of murder — the victim himself having been a friend and hand-picked fellow worker of MacLeod. See R. Ferguson, *George MacLeod* (London: Collins, 1990), ch. 18: "Making a Grave with the Wicked."

many Western nations, the voluntary or coerced *"kenosis* of establishment"[66] in our present *chronos,* may represent a Spirit-given *kairos* for the church of Christ, his buried body in the world, to die anew to itself and — less accommodated and accommodating to the mores of the majority — be reborn to the task in the anonymous, incarnate present among the least of its brothers and sisters in the world.

Surely it is not adequate for the Easter Saturday church to speak and preach about, or even to reenact through liturgy and sacrament, the sacrifice and suffering of Christ and the self-emptying of God. To be the church, the form today of Christ's crucified and buried body, and so to participate in the Trinity whose community coheres through mutual surrender and self-giving and whose history is coming to eschatological fulfillment only through a path which embraces death and self-negation, is itself to be concretely and visibly vulnerable to mortification consequent upon the world's hatred or sheer indifference.[67] As Easter Saturday says that the Creator knows and shows the creature how to die, and how to live by dying, so the Easter Saturday church, too, must know how to die, and be ready to practice its own abandonment and self-

---

66. See D. M. MacKinnon, "Kenosis and Establishment," in *The Stripping of the Altars* (London: Collins, 1969); cf. Roberts, in Gunton and Hardy, *On Being the Church,* p. 206. MacKinnon's essay, actually the Gore Memorial Lecture for 1968, is wholly germane to this chapter in its application of the Christology of *homoousios* and *kenosis* to ecclesiology. In particular, he attacks the ecclesiological "fundamentalism" and triumphalism of High Anglicanism. For MacKinnon, the conversion of Constantine was "the greatest single disaster ever to overtake the Christian Church" (p. 15). To remove its effects, abandoning the prerogatives of establishment and institutional power, and repent the arrogance of those who deny even Christian identity to those outside their own communion, the church must radically relearn the way of the cross. "It is in weakness that our strength is made perfect, in genuine weakness, not the simulated powerlessness of the spiritual poseur" (p. 39). To those who argue that the only alternative to establishment is the existence of the ghetto, MacKinnon retorts that perhaps it is precisely in the ghetto, nearer to the center than to the periphery of the world's travail, that Christians ought to be (p. 33). MacKinnon himself is greatly influenced by an even more powerful, this time explicitly Easter Saturday, call for ecclesiastical repentance and kenotic renunciation of power, with particular reference to the Roman Catholic Church: R. Adolfs, *The Grave of God: Has the Church a Future?,* trans. D. N. Snaith (London: Burns & Oates and New York: Harper & Row, 1967), see esp. chs. 4 and 5. Both of these publications are brief, and neither develops the concept of ecclesial *kenosis* or burial very far (though Adolfs does make a number of practical proposals for his own church's self-humiliation). But they are to my knowledge the only serious attempts in recent theology at what might be called an Easter Saturday ecclesiology, and as such they are both greatly to be cherished.

67. See Barth, *CD,* IV/2, 662ff.

surrender.[68] That, of course, does not entail ceasing to be the church, simply giving up the task of being Christ's form and body in the world, nor fleeing irresponsibly from involvement with the world's institutions, structures, and powers-that-be. But it may mean a radical reinterpretation and reform of the church's institutional power, the rigorous transforming of structures and systems, and a ceding of some forms of worldly influence and status in order that, through the Spirit of Christ crucified, the church itself may grow by decreasing (Jn. 3:30),[69] and in its powerlessness prove all the more powerful and creative. Ecclesiastical institutions, no less than the Christians in them, are summoned to discover the yet more abundant creativity of the love that yields to negativity, to learn how much more powerful even a community can be when it is willing to let go of its identity as measured by longevity or magnitude, kudos or cachet.[70]

Perhaps the mainline churches are being called, through their present crises of diminished resources, membership, and influence, to renegotiate their relations to society at large, to accept or even embrace the post-Constantinian era and the new epoch of cultural displacement awaiting churches and traditions not prepared to subordinate the social and political demands of the cross to its purely personal and pious therapy and inspiration. Required to reduce budgets, redeploy staff, and abridge programs locally and nationally, will the churches give priority to salvaging the dreams and expectations of the comfortable, the powerful, and affluent? Or will they seize this historical moment and commit themselves to new forms and strategies for mission which concentrate resources upon society's peripheral minorities, those on the boundaries of the *polis* where pain and need and a sense of impotence and hopelessness are greatest? Will Christians be willing in company with the homeless — those who lack physical homes, or emotional, or political — to endure their own worldly homelessness,[71] strangers and pilgrims themselves among the lost and alien

---

68. See Ramsey, *Catholic Church,* pp. 65-66; and on the church's participation in the descent and humiliation of Christ, the Lamb of God, and the sufferings of the Spirit's labor pains, see L. S. Thornton, *Christ and the Church* (London: Dacre Press, 1956), pp. 33-37.

69. See Barth, *CD,* IV/2, 657.

70. See the very pointed discussion of institutional power (which led to the author's silencing by the Roman Catholic authorities) in L. Boff, *Church: Charism and Power,* trans. J. W. Diercksmeier (New York: Crossroad and London: SCM, 1985), ch. 5: "The Power of the Institutional Church: Can It Be Converted?"

71. As Bonhoeffer above all perhaps has reminded us in modern times, there is a recurrent theme in the teachings of Jesus about the hiddenness, secrecy, and sheer ordinariness of discipleship — along with the sister theme of the extraordinary and highly vis-

and abandoned in our midst — to be, in short, like God, present-in-absence, the church after the era of the church? How ruthlessly did Karl Barth remind the church of its true place within society: despite "the occasional appearance of worldly impressiveness and relevance, it will soon realise that in relation to the rest of the world it can exist only as a small and strangely gesticulating minority driven into a corner."[72]

Where indeed could the Easter Saturday church be the church of Christ crucified and buried, present-in-absence, but in the corners of the world, fulfilled through its own emptiness, seated with, beside, and as the godless and the godforsaken whose human dignity and hope are exhausted and whose world has come to an end? In our day and place is the church catholic truly present anywhere if it is not at least present, suffering, and serving, in our desperate, tumultuous inner cities, in our overflowing public hospitals, in our violent and decaying housing projects, in our AIDS clinics, and in our brutalizing prisons and their shamefully numerous cells along death row?

Easter Saturday proclaims, as we have been hearing and thinking, that God's own true way to consummation and fulfillment goes through self-emptying and negation, a moment of rupture only beyond and through which lies resumption and fulfillment. In order to be at last all-in-all and bring all creation to redemption, God surrenders to humiliation, accepting contradiction and hiatus. Within God's own self, only in emptiness is there fullness; only in sorrow, joy; only in suffering and lowliness, exaltation and glory. For the triune community is constituted and revealed through the way of God's own Son into the far country of servanthood and dereliction, a journey of descent into death and burial. Therefore the church of the crucified and buried Christ cannot but be identified itself as a servant, self-surrendering community, whose primary locus in today's crumbling Easter Saturday culture is on the periphery, cornered among the depotentiated, in solidarity with the godless and the godforsaken.

That surrender of power corresponds to what was classically described as Christ's kingly office, his regal personhood and work which in fact comprised an event of utter servanthood, of the king become a slave. The church's worldly, anonymous presence, akin to God's own, realized in Christ crucified and buried, makes concrete its servanthood in fulfillment of its trinitarian ontology as

---

ible. See esp. *Cost of Discipleship* (New York: Macmillan, 1963), chs. 14-17. See also, on the theme of the homelessness and invisibility of human goodness, Arendt, *The Human Condition*, pp. 74ff. On the presence of the church as that participates in the presence of Christ, including his presence among and as "the least," see Moltmann, *Church in the Power of the Spirit*, pp. 121-32.

72. Barth, *CD*, IV/3, 769.

united to the Father through the Son and in the Spirit. Christ's own historical life and ministry of service to his brothers and sisters in the flesh enacts and corresponds to his intratrinitarian filial obedience. That expresses, as we saw expounded in Barth, Moltmann and Jüngel above,[73] the due subordination of the Son to the Father who sent him, and the free self-surrender of the Second Person and the Third to the First within the triune community, whose history itself embraces a movement of self-limitation and withdrawal for creation's sake.

Could the mission of the church, which is to participate in the mission of God for the creating and redeeming of the world, and which has service and self-surrender as its *modus operandi*, be characterized otherwise than by its own corresponding service and self-giving? Christ himself, the obedient Son whose body the church is, is the great *diakonos* or servant, come among us as one who serves, not seeking to be served but to serve (Lk. 22:27; Mk. 10:45), setting an example of suffering and service. So the church's ministry is defined as service, too *(diakonia)* (e.g., Acts 6:1ff.; 2 Cor. 5:18; 2 Tim. 4:5); and those who share in Christ's ministry and in the church's place within God's mission to the world, even those who lead and bear authority within the community, do so themselves strictly as servants themselves (Lk. 22:24ff.; Mk. 10:42ff.; Jn. 13:12ff.; 1 Cor. 11:1ff.; 1 Pet. 2:21).[74]

How else may the nature of the church, its purpose and its people, be conceived from the standpoint of Easter Saturday, which recalls one who yes-

73. See esp. Barth, *CD*, IV/1, 157-210; Moltmann, *Trinity and Kingdom*, pp. 75ff., 209ff.; Jüngel, *God as the Mystery*, esp. pp. 343-373; and pp. 212-57 above. On the trinitarian basis of the church's ministry, see also C. M. Campbell, "Imago Trinitatis: The Being of God as a Model for Ministry," *Austin Seminary Bulletin* 102.4 (1986), and the response to that paper by G. S. Heyer in the same issue.

74. On service in the church, see esp. Barth, *CD*, IV/2, 598ff., 690ff.; Küng, *The Church*, pp. 388ff.; T. F. Torrance, "Service in Jesus Christ," in J. I. McCord and T. H. L. Parker, eds., *Service in Christ* (London: Epworth and Grand Rapids: Eerdmans, 1966), pp. 1-16; J. K. S. Reid, *The Biblical Doctrine of the Ministry* (*Scottish Journal of Theology Occasional Paper*, no. 4) (Edinburgh: Oliver & Boyd, 1955), ch. 1; E. Ellis, *Pauline Theology: Ministry and Service* (Grand Rapids: Eerdmans and Exeter: Paternoster, 1989), ch. 1; M. Green, *Freed to Serve* (London: Hodder & Stoughton, 1983), ch. 2; E. Schweizer, *Church Order in the New Testament* (London: SCM and Naperville, Ill.: A. R. Allenson, 1961); C. K. Barrett, *Church, Ministry and Sacraments in the New Testament* (Exeter: Paternoster Press and Grand Rapids: Eerdmans, 1985); E. Schillebeeckx, *The Church with a Human Face*, trans. J. Bowden (London: SCM and New York: Crossroad, 1985); Dulles, *Models of the Church*, esp. ch. 6; C. Williams, *New Directions in Theology Today*, vol. 4: *The Church* (Philadelphia: Westminster Press, 1968); also the Reports of the Panel on Doctrine to the General Assembly of the Church of Scotland, on Ministry, 1985 and 1989.

terday gave up his life for all, unless it be as a company of servants called to give themselves to others in costly, concrete acts of self-surrender, and to be among the hungry and the guilty, the rejected, executed, and disposed of? And how may the church consistently and persistently adopt such an Easter Saturday, self-abandoned servant posture externally toward the world in our own day, unless its internal structures and community lifestyle are corrrespondingly shaped and grounded in the practice of mutual servanthood? Must the upbuilding and ordering of this community not be analogous to and continuous with the outreach and mission of the servant body of the crucified and buried one?

Now "by the providence of God and human confusion," and partly at least because of our century's experiences of suffering and death, the church in many communions and traditions has in recent decades been rapidly reexamining and reforming its theology of ministry, precisely with the goal of recovering "service" as the substance of all Christian ministry and the principle of its internal ordering. Much today is said and written, often quite explicitly with reference to the cross and death of Christ, and sometimes, too, to the trinitarian ontology grounded thereon, concerning the diaconal or servant nature of the entire Christian community in its ministry and mission, and therefore also of its leadership.[75]

---

75. Much doctrinal renewal in this area still needs to be done, not least in discussion related to ecumenical reunion or convergence, where the churches seem determined upon a future not much less clerical than their past. Though some useful, and undoubtedly well-meant, deference is now paid to the ministry of the whole people of God, the major ecumenical documents of our time repeatedly revert to the mutual recognition of ministries in the clerical sense as the basis on which the churches might come together in faith and action. The repeated formula for such convergence is the mutual recognition of, and the rectification where necessary of any deficiencies in, a threefold "historic" structure of ministry: bishops, priests/presbyters (or ministers of Word and sacrament), and deacons (who themselves tend to disappear from the serious proposals for convergence, or become the embodiment of ministerial service, while other functions such as authority and responsibility are reserved for bishops and presbyters). This reliance upon the authority of the ordained ministry, distinct from the ministry of the whole baptized people of God, and without defining service as the inner content of all leadership, is noticeable in *Baptism, Eucharist and Ministry,* Faith and Order Paper No. 111 (Geneva: World Council of Churches, 1982); the Final Report of the Anglican–Roman Catholic International Commission (London: SPCK and Catholic Truth Society, 1982); in *God's Reign and Our Unity,* the Report of the Anglican-Reformed Commission (London: SPCK and Edinburgh: St. Andrew Press, 1984). The historic categories of ordained ministry are also at the heart of the most recent "covenanting" proposals of the Consultation on Church Union in the United States: *Churches in Covenant Communion* (Princeton, N.J.: Princeton University Press, 1989). See

The persons of the Trinity themselves, we saw, form a relational community of openness and mutual indwelling *(perichoresis)* bound by correlative self-giving where, through the Spirit of love and unity, all that the Father has is bestowed upon the Son, who in turn subordinates his own will to the glory of the Father. This circle of relationality and reciprocity creates room and freedom for each member of the triune fellowship; and into that space we ourselves are gathered, to enjoy our own relative autonomy and fullness. The church is a corresponding community, a fellowship of freedom within which each is loving servant to the other and all together form a circle of co-responsibility — so illogical to human axioms of authority and control — wherein each is subordinated to and empowered by the others, in a boundless interchange of dependence and autonomy. On this model, ministry is essentially shared, not individualized; power is the expression, not the opposite, of service; and authority emerges horizontally through the exercise of love within the fellowship, rather than bestowed vertically upon the few for the hierarchic governing of the many.[76]

With this reinterpretation and reform of the concept of ministry comes repentant recognition that the church has done precisely what its Lord demanded that it should not do: that is, model its internal relations upon worldly structures of power, status, and domination instead of imitating the example of servanthood and self-abasement he himself provided. "Like the Gentiles, whose rulers lord it over the people and whose great ones act as tyrants" (Mk. 10:42) is precisely how the church's ministry has been shaped and exercised, rather than like Christ, the Lord who serves, whose kingship is not of this world nor like the world's, and whose power and authority are grounded in a love which to the earthly powers seems impotent and foolish.[77]

---

also M. Thurian, *Priesthood and Ministry: Ecumenical Research,* trans. P. Clifford (London and Oxford: Mowbray, 1983); M. Thurian, ed., *Ecumenical Perspectives on Baptism, Eucharist and Ministry,* Faith and Order Paper No. 116 (Geneva: World Council of Churches, 1983); and *Baptism, Eucharist and Ministry 1982-1990,* Faith and Order Paper No. 149 (Geneva: World Council of Churches, 1990).

76. See, e.g., Gunton, *Promise,* esp. ch. 7, and "The Church on Earth: The Roots of Community," in Gunton and Hardy, eds., *On Being the Church,* ch. 2; J. Zizioulas, *Being as Communion;* Moltmann, *Trinity and Kingdom,* pp. 191-222, esp. pp. 200ff.; and C. LaCugna, *God for Us,* esp. ch. 8 and pp. 401ff.

77. By far the most noteworthy, and within its own context revolutionary, rethinking of the doctrine of ministry in recent years has been that of the Dutch Roman Catholic Edward Schillebeeckx. See his *Ministry: A Case for Change,* trans. J. Bowden (London: SCM and New York: Crossroad, 1981), and *The Church with a Human Face.* These books contain a sustained attack not only on the male and celibate exclusiveness of the Roman

Like all repentance, however, remorse for the ecclesiastical past would be inauthentic did it not lead directly, urgently, and intentionally to renewals of practice and actual reshapings of the community, determined by a concrete re-ordering of structures and a converting of the modes of power and authority. Is

---

Catholic priesthood, in doctrine, law, and practice, but also on its underlying ontological sacerdotalism, which bestows a unique "character" and power on the church's bishops (and their derivatively empowered priests) and sets them in a unique, metaphysical relation to Jesus Christ. This development, says Schillebeeckx, contradicts not only Scripture but also the church's own early dogmatic decisions (especially Canon 6 of the Council of Chalcedon, which forbade "absolute" ordinations that would grant priestly power to individuals independently of their leadership functions in worshipping congregations). Against this, and to much Vatican displeasure, Schillebeeckx has proposed acts of "illegality" on the part of a "loyal opposition" as the only viable way forward toward returning authority, leadership, and eucharistic presidency to collegial, locally based, service-oriented male and female pastors.

For other internal critiques of the Roman Catholic doctrine of priesthood, see H. Küng, *Why Priests?*, trans. J. Cumming (London: Collins, 1977) (an argument for a functional view of leadership with a Christian community shaped by "freedom, equality and fraternity"); L. Grollenberg et al., *Minister? Pastor? Prophet?* (London: SCM, 1980 and New York: Crossroad, 1981); J. P. Mackey, ch. 5 in J. D. G. Dunn and J. P. Mackey, eds., *New Testament Theology in Dialogue* (London: SPCK and Philadelphia: Westminster Press, 1987), and ch. 7 in R. Nowell, ed., *Why I Am Still a Catholic* (Glasgow: Collins, 1982); T. F. O'Meara, *Theology of Ministry* (New York: Paulist Press, 1983); and M. A. Cowan, ed., *Alternative Futures for Worship*, vol. 6: *Leadership Ministry in Community* (Collegeville, Minn.: Liturgical Press, 1987).

The acme of the "High Church" Anglican theology of ministry was reached with H. E. Kirk, ed., *The Apostolic Ministry* (London: Hodder & Stoughton, 1946), which argued that bishops are essential to the nature of the church. Since then there has been considerable reaction and rethinking within Anglicanism toward a more shared concept of ministry and authority, with the emphasis on service. Of many examples see T. W. Manson, *The Church's Ministry* (London: Hodder & Stoughton and Philadelphia: Westminster, 1948); A. T. Hanson, *Church, Sacraments and Ministry* (Oxford: Mowbray, 1975), ch. 6; A. T. and R. P. C. Hanson, *The Identity of the Church* (London: SCM, 1987); J. Tiller, *A Strategy for the Church's Ministry* (London: Church Information Office Publications, 1983); M. Green, *Freed to Serve;* P. Baelz and W. Jacob, eds., *Ministers of the Kingdom* (London: Church Information Office Publications, 1985); and L. W. Countryman, *The Language of Ordination: Ministry in an Ecumenical Context* (Philadelphia: Trinity Press International, 1992).

As current debate within the worldwide Episcopalian communion concerning the ordination of women indicates, Anglicans generally continue to hold to the notion of the ordained minister as a priest who plays a role within the church, and especially at communion, uniquely representative of and analogous to Jesus Christ himself. That priestly interpretation is alien to the Reformed theology of ministry, though Calvin certainly maintained a "high" doctrine of the "holy ministry," a fourfold leadership willed and instituted

it not true ecclesially, institutionally, no less than personally, that God's forgiving grace, though free and unconditional, is not cheap, but costly in its unconditional demands? Therefore, our own "Gentile" past can scarcely be forgiven unless our churches are willing to allow their ministry and ministers to be transformed by the Spirit into more recognizably Christ-like, that is, cruciform and grave-shaped, patterns. Which is to say that the way of God into the far country is to be conversely juxtaposed with the way of the churches into the far country, which is now so necessary; and at the intersection of their chiasmic apposition stand the cross and sepulcher, an Easter Saturday meeting point. Christ's way to the fulfillment of his lordship leads through the servanthood and emptiness which culminate in Joseph's tomb. Death and burial are antecedent to his victory and glory. But, by contrast, the church has already had its triumphal history, its long, but passing, epoch of grandeur and prestige, its generations of clerical ministers vested with power and crowned to greater or lesser degrees with superiority, dominance, and glory. The way for us forward now, in our Easter Saturday world, can only be a way back, a return to the cross, from

---

by Christ to govern the church, and he used available models of monarchy and imperial rule for the interpretation of ministerial authority. See esp. H. Höpfel, *The Christian Polity of John Calvin* (Cambridge: Cambridge University Press, 1982). Today a much more functional understanding of ordination prevails in many parts of the Reformed world, where significant attempts have been made to identify service rather than rule and government as the content of authorized leadership. Particularly interesting, here, is the effort to recover the diaconate — one of Calvin's four offices but one routinely subordinated and sometimes wholly lost to sight in Reformed history — as the model on which all ministry should be understood and exercised. See the recent Church of Scotland studies on ministry cited above, and the Report of the Task Force on Ordination of the Presbyterian Church (U.S.A.). In connection with this report see J. Rogers and D. F. Mullen, eds., *Ordination: Past, Present, Future* (Louisville: Presbyterian Publishing House, 1990); also F. Holper, "The Problem of Power and Status in the Ordering of the Church's Ministry," *Insights*, Austin Presbyterian Theological Seminary 106.2 (Spring 1991). See, too, E. A. McKee, *Diakonia in the Classical Reformed Tradition and Today* (Grand Rapids: Eerdmans, 1989), and "The Offices of Elders and Deacons in the Classical Reformed Tradition," in D. M. McKim, ed., *Major Themes in the Reformed Tradition* (Grand Rapids: Eerdmans, 1992); and T. F. Torrance, *The Eldership in the Reformed Church* (Edinburgh: Handsel Press, 1984).

On recent Lutheran discussion of ministry, see T. Nichol and M. Kolden, eds., *Called and Ordained: Lutheran Perspective on the Office of the Ministry* (Minneapolis: Augsburg Fortress, 1990). Cf. the Joint Statements and related chapters on ministry in J. E. Andrews and J. A. Burgess, eds., *An Invitation to Action,* Lutheran-Reformed Dialogue Series 3, 1981-83 (Philadelphia: Fortress, 1984); also W. G. Rusch and D. F. Martensen, eds., *The Leuenberg Agreement and Lutheran-Reformed Relationships* (Minneapolis: Augsburg, 1989).

power to service, from glory to self-giving, from governance to freedom and to sharing, the authority that comes from embracing suffering and service rather than evading it or consigning it to other people's shoulders.[78] This reversionary,

78. Many feminist theologians, and others concerned for the role of women in the church, often understandably, express suspicion and resentment at the themes of service and suffering in contemporary discussion of the church and ministry. They remember the long history whereby women have been cast by the church as the experts in self-denial and service in the image of Christ's humility, while on men has been self-bestowed the burden of corresponding in their ministries to Christ's kingship and lordly power. Clearly a new theology of service which simply reinforced the ideology of abnegation, self-devaluation, or inferiority, and which continued to identify women as the principal embodiments of Christ's servant office, would be intolerable. In the place of service, some have developed alternative interpretations of God and consequent models of leadership and ministry, such as fellowship, friendship, solidarity, companionship, and housekeeping and hospitality. See, e.g., L. M. Russell, *Household of Freedom: Authority in Feminist Theology* (Philadelphia: Westminster, 1987), and *Church in the Round: Feminist Interpretations of the Church* (Louisville: Westminster/John Knox Press, 1992); R. Page, *Ambiguity and the Presence of God* (London: SCM, 1985), ch. 7; L. N. Rhodes, *Co-Creating: A Feminist Vision of Ministry* (Philadelphia: Westminster, 1987); S. McFague, *Models of God* (Philadelphia: Fortress and London: SCM, 1987); E. S. Fiorenza, *In Memory of Her* (New York: Crossroad and London: SCM, 1983); R. Holloway, ed., *Who Needs Feminism?* (London: SPCK, 1991); E. Moltmann-Wendel and J. Moltmann, *Humanity in God* (London: SCM and Cleveland: Pilgrim Press, 1983), and *God — His and Hers* (New York: Crossroad, 1991), esp. ch. 1.

Some of these feminist explorations, it must be said, construct images and doctrines of God which come close to forfeiting the claim to be biblical or Christian; and against that outcome of feminist theology some justified warnings increasingly are being sounded. See esp. A. F. Kimel, ed., *Speaking the Christian God: The Holy Trinity and the Challenge of Feminism* (Grand Rapids: Eerdmans and Leominster: Gracewing, 1992). On the other hand, there is much biblical material itself available for the development of a rich array of models for ministry helpful in overcoming our authoritarian, clerical, and masculine past. Still, is it actually necessary to fear, or biblically possible to jettison, the concept and reality of *service* as the heart of ministry? Surely the good news revealed in the sonship and servanthood of Christ, who obeys the Father within the triune community of God, is that obedience and service need not at all be oppressive or constricting. Rather, the divine truth about obedience is that to give oneself utterly to the other in commitment and obedience is itself liberating and fulfilling. Life truly is creative when let go of, since self-giving love is even more abundant and emancipating than self-preservation is barren and destructive. The reversal of our shameful patriarchal history, which has asked women to specialize in servantlike obedience, lies not in the abandonment but in the reappropriation of the Christian wisdom seen supremely in the foolish cross: that service frees and liberates and is the greatest power of all, the very power which defeats death and creates existence out of nothing. See the very forceful trinitarian argument for the ordination of women in T. F. Torrance, *The Ministry of Women* (Edinburgh: Handsel Press, 1992).

ecclesial pilgrimage, back from resurrection glory to the cross and its humility, must pass through the same grave of Jesus Christ on Easter Saturday, except that now in this reversal of his history interment and crucifixion are the antecedents of humility and service.[79]

What confronts the church today, born between Easter Day and Pentecost, is actually an Easter Saturday challenge: are we willing to enter a historical period of death and burial, a reversal of church history on the way back to the cross? Dare we enter an era when, visibly and concretely, the ministry dies to its old self, cedes its former glories, lets go its prerogatives and perquisites of power, buries its hierarchy, its clericalism, its masculinity and exclusiveness, yields its hold upon jurisdiction and control, and negates its "Gentile" forms of dominance? Thus, and only thus, might we become ready for rebirth, behind Easter Saturday, in a new Good Friday ministry truly conformed to the servitude and suffering of Christ crucified. Only after such an Easter Saturday epoch of termination and surrender, when yesterday's forms of ministry have been laid to rest, could the church truly begin to body forth patterns and practices of ordination and vocation,[80] correspondent to the ministry of Christ the servant,

79. The novelist Martin Amis has recently ventured an extraordinary experiment in the reversal of history: *Time's Arrow* (New York: Random House and London: Jonathan Cape, 1991). By telling a narrative and running a life-history backward, Amis attempts to make sense of the senselessness of human actions, in this case the Nazi holocaust. But how might the church today be challenged to a similar reversal of its own history, in order to expose and repent of its often shameful, guilty past and thus return to the death of Christ, that act of supreme senselessness which is the ground of all meaning, sense, and hope? In a puny way our study here is an attempt to negotiate that reversal, back behind our glorious past to the beginnings of Christian faith, life, and community in shame, defeat, and death.

80. It goes without saying that an Easter Saturday theology of ministry cannot be constructed and enacted without a radical rethinking also of the doctrine and practice of calling and vocation. That would itself have to emphasize the risky vulnerability of the choices which the God of the cross, who chooses the weak and foolish of world, makes in calling women and men to leadership within the people of God. It would need to deal honestly and self-critically with (a) the clerical and monastic constrictions upon "vocation" in our "catholic" past; (b) the privatized interpretation of "the call" in our pietistic, post-Reformation history; and (c) the highly professionalized, status-conscious models of vocation in modern secular society, often imitated in the contemporary church. In contrast, a theology of vocation in the light of the cross must emphasize discipleship, servanthood, and the surrender of power and dignity as the calling of those chosen by the Spirit, working through the public decision-making of the whole community, to shoulder leadership and responsibility within the servant ministry of all the baptized people of God. I have tried to outline a countercultural reinterpretation of vocation in the light of the cross in "Unmasking Idolatries: Vocation in the *Ecclesia Crucis*," in Kettler and Speidell, eds., *Incarnational Ministry* (Colorado Springs: Helmers & Howard, 1990), ch. 7. For an

which the church today now finds it relatively easy to speak of, but still discouragingly difficult to enact.[81]

IV. The Prophetic, Buried Body: Holiness and Protest

Despite appearances, it is no contradiction of the church's Easter Saturday calling to be present but concealed within the broken, godless world, when — to the astonishment or ridicule of that very world — Christians lay claim to sanctity and describe themselves and their community as "holy." The church responsible for inquisition and for schism, for bigotry demonic and hypocrisy perverse, is holy? Yes, holy! and because holy, more not less, identified with the unholy society round about it. Supremely, perhaps, of "the holy church" creeds and confessions speak, "by faith alone," of the unseen, not the visible, not of accomplishment and "works" but of promise and outrageous grace, fully conscious of our perverse ecclesial history of recalcitrance and faithlessness. Yet the sanctification or making holy of the church is no fiction nor a

---

earlier, but far weightier, critique of the modern conforming of ministry and vocation to secular models, see the work of my late friend and colleague R. S. Paul, in *Ministry* (Grand Rapids: Eerdmans, 1965). Paul was highly critical of the most influential discussion of ministry in the American context for a generation, namely, H. R. Niebuhr, *The Purpose of the Church and Its Ministry* (New York and Evanston: Harper & Row, 1956). Those criticisms were somewhat modified in R. S. Paul, "*Ministry* Reconsidered," *Austin Seminary Bulletin* 102.4 (1986): 29ff. A powerful critique, on the basis of the Reformation, of the secularization and bureaucratizing of the ministry is contained in Leith, *From Generation to Generation: The Renewal of the Church according to Its Own Theology and Practice,* ch. 2.

81. That the socially and politically powerlesss may in fact be in a position to realize the transformation of a whole society has been vividly and wondrously illustrated in the collapse of the totalitarian states of Eastern Europe, not least in the now sadly divided Czechoslovakia. There a few and powerless but courageous dissidents eventually were instrumental in toppling the megalithic structures of a coercive state, and their leader became the first president of a new democracy. Václav Havel's understanding of "the power of the powerless" breathes a Christian spirit, without being explicitly a political "theology of the cross." He described in the days of captivity and oppression, and subsequently proved in those of revolution, the potential of people who live internally and existentially according to the truth to subvert the power of a massive system built upon lies. Spiritual and moral authenticity, though structurally powerless by normal expectations, demonstrably has the capacity radically to renew and liberate society. See Havel's eponymous essay in the collection of papers, by himself and others, *The Power of the Powerless* (Armonk, N.Y.: M. E. Sharpe, Inc., 1985). See also Fukuyama, *The End of History*, ch. 24, reflecting on Havel's thought and repeating his title.

fantasy of wishful thinking, but is as real as God is real: the ontological condition of the all-too-human community which the Holy, sanctifying Spirit indwells and joins to Jesus Christ in his own holiness and consecrated wholeness (cf. Jn. 7:17ff.).

Calvin and his heirs have gone beyond Luther and his in their expectation of what this Holy Spirit might accomplish to make the church *become* what it is in Christ: obedient to the imperatives that accompany the indicatives of its new life in him, and thus growing in the practice and the exhibition of a holiness which is in the first and every instance a pure gift of grace.[82] On the other hand, both the Lutheran and Calvinist traditions have kept alive the obvious but painful truth, which some medieval doctrines of the church attempted strangely to deny, that the church, no matter how rigorous its discipline or promising its spiritual and moral progress, remains this side of the *eschaton* a compromised community, subject to the same judgments which the holy God exercises upon the world at large. Eschewing the Roman conceit that the body of Christ itself can be simply holy despite the sinfulness of the members who comprise it, the saints of the Reformation were adamant that, just as of forgiven individuals, so it must be said of the whole church: "righteous and sinful simultaneously" *(simul justa et peccatrix)*. This confession of guilt the Roman Catholic Church itself, since Vatican II, albeit it in its own terms, now seems quite ready to homologate. Ecumenically we can by and large agree now that Christians are a pilgrim people, on the way toward but still far-distant from a Christlike future whose final arrival is certain, but assured by the faithful promises of God's own incontestable grace, not by the community's own efforts at self-preserving progress or innate indestructibility.[83]

What consequences flow from this consensual acknowledgment for the church's sense of identity and purpose and its corresponding actions? It means that the sanctified body of Christ Jesus, God's righteous, holy one, though

82. See esp. Calvin, *Inst.* III.1-10; R. S. Wallace, *Calvin's Doctrine of the Christian Life* (Edinburgh, Oliver & Boyd, 1959); and J. Leith, *John Calvin's Doctrine of the Christian Life* (Louisville: Westminster/John Knox Press, 1989). For a Lutheran view, see, e.g., G. Wingren, *Gospel and Church,* trans. R. Mackenzie (Edinburgh: Oliver & Boyd and Philadelphia: Fortress, 1964). I have discussed the characteristic differences between a Lutheran and a Reformed view of sanctification in my unpublished Th.D. dissertation, "The Experience of Grace: The Problem of Sanctification in Contemporary Systematic Theology" (Princeton Theological Seminary, 1977).

83. On all of this, see esp. Barth, *CD,* IV/1, 685-701; Küng, *The Church,* pp. 319-44; Moltmann, *Church in the Power of the Spirit,* pp. 352ff.; *Lumen Gentium,* esp. ch. II; K. Rahner, "The Church of Sinners," and "The Sinful Church in the Decrees of Vatican II," in *Theological Investigations VI,* chs. 17 and 18; and Dulles, *Models of the Church,* pp. 57ff.

unique and separate, not of the world but radically and ontologically differentiated from it, is at the same time a community which comes from, remains part of, and constantly reenters that world, in all its cross- and grave-shaped brokenness, sordidness, and unbelief. That relativizes the very distinction between the sacred and the profane, the holy and the sinful, which God's holy, judging grace itself creates and clarifies; and it sets the church in relation to the world which Jüngel might describe as an even greater similarity beyond so great a dissimilarity. The church, to be sure, is dissimilar and different: as "wholly other" from the world as is the Holy God who chooses, calls, and sanctifies it. Yet the people of God, just like God's own self, can only be wholly other by being wholly for: manifesting and giving substance to their holiness by their very acts of Easter Saturday solidarity and identification with the world.[84]

Comprised of ordinary human beings who have been chosen, called, and changed by no power or merit of their own but by God's forgiving, justifying grace, and remaining sinful to the end of history even as the new community of saints who dwell and grow in Christ, the church retains inseverable links with the world out of which it has been called. The continuities and connectedness of sin and simple humanness survive the radical discontinuities of grace and judgment, binding church and world together so that the former cannot pursue its own path, for its own sake, toward its own beatitude and fullness, but must be immersed in the very society from which it was removed, exercising fellowship with and a suffering presence in the world, which outstrips the selfish, loveless world's scant capacity for self-giving and involvement. Thus the holy church finally demonstrates its differentness and apartness from the world by its freedom and willingness to engage that world and share its pain and grief and guilt, its godlessness and godforsakenness, with a compassion and recklessness that humanity itself can scarcely muster.

Holiness, then, does not contradict presence, nor difference identification. Rather, the church proves its holiness and difference because its cruciform and Easter Saturday willingness to abandon its own identity and be identified with others shames the worldly ego which stands upon its pride, preserves and preens its own identity, and in Adam-like pretended innocence refuses to be numbered like Christ among the transgressors and the damned. Thus is the church which conceals itself in a worldly incognito actually the unseen salt of

---

84. See D. McCullough, "Holy God, Holy Church," in Kettler and Speidell, eds., *Incarnational Ministry,* p. 29. This essay is a splendid demonstration of how the holiness and ontological distinction of the church can be biblically affirmed without a trace of moralism, superiority, or bogus otherworldliness.

the earth; and in being so is curiously manifested, illumined, and distinguished as the very light of the world, set upon a hill (Mt. 5:13-16).[85]

Obviously, though, it is still required that, as the invisible salt of the earth, the church must *be*, actively and visibly, the light of the world. Within their own even greater similarity, there remains a real dissimilarity which is great enough between the church and its surrounding culture. And that dissimilarity must remain conspicuous, a bright beacon on the hill, even if, or perhaps especially if, the church is relatively powerless, marginalized, a minority reduced to gesticulating in the corner. Perhaps, in particular, the minority church must be today a *vocal* community, even as it lives in muted companionship and presence with the voiceless of the world. Christians' holy but quiet identification with the silenced, the poor and hungry, the despised and disenfranchised, will itself, of course, speak volumes. Yet will there not also be times, *kairoi* of crisis and of opportunity, when the holy, servant church hidden in society must find its own voice and speak out loudly to that society's loud and articulate elite, its prosperous and powerful?

Audacious speech as well as suffering silence is the calling of the Easter Saturday community; for, as we have seen, the one whom by Easter Saturday the world had silenced and liquidated was none other than the Word of God, the enfleshment of that creative *fiat* which gives life to the dead and calls forth existence out of nothingness. Out of the awful, atheistic silence of the first Easter Saturday there burst forth God's death-defeating word of resurrection joy and victory. The terminal hush of unanswered questions and sepulchral speechlessness became the ultimate word-event, the rebirth of language in its triumphal and liberating truthfulness. The burial ground of God's incarnate, silenced Word is also, therefore, the cradle of the gospel, that "word of the cross" which challenges and judges but also creates and reconciles.

So it was that out of the Auschwitz silence, as we saw above, the whispers of resilient language could still be heard and has since become a torrent of words, speech of harrowed memory but not without defiant hope. And so it is, too, that though the church shares in the death of the Word, that "antilogos," so contradictory of human reasoning and speech, whom the world could not tolerate but had to stifle,[86] we are also the community of the Logos, hearing and therefore speaking the story of the cross and emboldened to release that story's destructive and re-creative energies. As such, Christ's ecclesial, buried body,

---

85. See Bonhoeffer, *Cost of Discipleship*, chs. 6-13 and 18-20, on the extraordinariness and separateness of the Christian life, in contrast to his companion theme of hiddenness and ordinariness referred to above.

86. See Bonhoeffer, *Christ the Center*, pp. 29-34.

which shares the quiet, kenotic servitude of his kingly authority, is participant no less in the Lord's wordy and prophetic office. Thereby Christ speaks God's word to the world — gracious and therefore both judging and forgiving — and mediates humanity's response of obedience and responsibiity to God. The Easter Saturday church, the earthly form now of the incarnate, crucified, and risen Word, and filled with the loquacious, pentecostal Spirit, however small and sidelined, however timid or mendacious, has a prophetic voice, the voice of God, no less, and the command, authority, and power of God to give it utterance (Acts 2:4). But have we always the courage to speak with that voice, or the wisdom to discern when and where and how to do so?[87]

Prophets are never popular, of course, and sometimes rightly, since by the logic of their self-defining eccentricity, their subversiveness and unconventionality means that they might as well be false corrupters of the truth, not its defenders or its clarifiers (Mt. 7:15-16; 1 Thess. 5:21; 1 Jn. 4:1). But since the marks of veracity and authenticity include humility and honesty, one test of the spirits and their prophecies is their capacity for self-critique. A church which postured itself as prophetic, yet refused to turn its judgments and indictments back upon itself, would be self-falsified by its blindness and hypocrisy. Contrariwise, the truly prophetic church reveals itself through rigorous self-examination, repentance, and reform. Yet at the same time we need the boldness to face down the charge of cant and arrogance invited by all who speak prophetically to others. Christians cannot permit their abysmal shortcomings and shameful faithlessness to excuse their slowness to challenge the world in Christ's own name. Rather, his disciples, however depotentiated now and muffled in the world, and fully implicated in the failings of the society around them, cannot postpone indefinitely the moment when they confront themselves and the world alike with iconoclastic passion, strengthened by the Spirit "to unmask idolatries in Church and culture,"[88] protesting sin and guilt, violence and injustice wherever they occur in our Easter Saturday society with "the word of the cross," which tells of the God surrendered to impotence and nothingnesss who thereby chooses and redeems society's weak and foolish nobodies. Not in spite of, but because of, God's own Easter Saturday silencing en route to resurrecting self-declaration, the people of God have the power and may seize the courage to address our dying, unjust, and estranged society with the message of God's resurrecting righteousness, justifying grace, and joyful

---

87. Among the most interesting and widely discussed contemporary expositions of the church's prophetic stance toward the world is G. Tinder, *The Political Meaning of Christianity* (Baton Rouge and London: Louisiana State University Press, 1989).

88. "A Brief Statement of Faith," Presbyterian Church (U.S.A.), 1991, line 69.

reconciliation. That gospel may cause disturbance and yet sow the seeds of transformation in our own cities and communities no less than did Peter's in Jerusalem, when he preached that the powerless and godless one whom it had killed, God — no less — had raised to power in vindication.

Preaching itself may indeed be still the most potent and creative means by which the church confronts today's Easter Saturday society — the strangest, most despised but also most salvific of our gesticulations on the margins. To be sure, nothing might seem less promising, more anachronistic or inept than *words* as an instrument of social restoration, the renewal and redemption of community among us. Language itself, we have complained, is in an Easter Saturday crisis of negation, become the weapon of nihilists who use words to deconstruct the very reality and meaning words convey, perversely articulating the triumph of inarticulation, fulsomely and noisily announcing our cultural hollowness and silence. Linguistically, this is the day of the Devil, when words have been demonized in our own ears, made a tool of falsehood and wickedness, disinformation and hysteria, from Hitler's Nuremberg,[89] to Nixon's White House, to the global manipulations of Madison Avenue. In bewildered stasis between verbal feast and famine, we seem overwhelmed by lexical torrents of distortion, rhetoric, and propaganda, yet starved for words — and speakers — that are trustworthy, truth bearing, and humanizing, reduced to a phantom, visual diet of images, photo opportunities, and the cheap illusions of rock video, "cyberpunk," and "virtual reality" on which the younger generation now unnourishingly feeds.

In such a culture, so linguistically debased, what might be the purpose and the point of preaching — a medium for the gospel whose credibility and utility to the Spirit seem surely past?[90] Except that their cultural "incorrect-

---

89. George Steiner, who so trenchantly and explicitly indicts the Easter Saturday nihilism of deconstruction in *Real Presences,* has for long charted and deplored the demonization of language in general, perhaps most vividly in his remarkable novel-turned-play depicting the hellish power of Hitler's rhetoric in *The Portage to San Cristobal of A.H.* (London and Boston: Faber & Faber, 1981). For a chilling, personal account of Hitler's oratory, see W. L. Shirer, *20th Century Journey,* vol. II: *The Nightmare Years: 1930-1940* (New York: Bantam Books, 1992), pp. 118ff.

90. What follows by way of a theology of preaching from the perspective of the cross is more fully explored in my article, "*Kenosis* and *Kerygma:* The Realism and the Risk of Preaching," in T. A. Hart and D. P. Thimell, eds., *Christ in Our Place* (Allison Park, Penn.: Pickwick, 1991), pp. 70-91. See also K. Barth, *The Word of God and the Word of Man,* trans. D. Horton (London: Hodder & Stoughton, 1928), ch. 4: "The Need and Promise of Christian Preaching"; D. Ritschl, *A Theology of Proclamation* (Richmond, Va.: John Knox Press, 1960); T. F. Torrance, "The Word of God and the Response of Man," in *God and Rationality*

ness," their incongruity and apparent impotence, might be just the reason to keep using words to address our Easter Saturday environment, allowing their contemporary weakness and foolishness as such to embody the promises and protests of the gospel so pertinent to the postliterary world. Perhaps medium and message sufficiently coincide that it is primarily with words, and certainly not without them, that "the word of the cross" which speaks of the humiliation of the Word of God may be transformingly addressed to this technological generation which, to its dire detriment, has engineered the postmodern, cultural humiliation of the word.[91]

Of course, today's church should exploit, indeed excel in, every available means of communication in its mission to the world as it exists today. Yet to abandon now the pulpit's unfashionable and demanding mode of speech might be to stumble not over the cultural offense of an outdated medium but over the scandal of the gospel itself, of the crucified and buried Word. That "the preaching of the Word of God is the Word of God"[92] was not intended to justify immodest preachers who boasted that they had God's very truth within their heads and on their lips. Rather, that Reformed axiom presumed the strange and risky graciousness of the crucified God who hazards the gospel to human speakers all too fallible and finite and fully capable of vacuity, sloth, and self-promotion, the freedom not only to preach the truth like Paul, but also to persecute it like Saul, deny it like Peter, and crucify it like Pontius Pilate. And if this be always true about preaching, how much more in this generation, when words are unutterably *passé* and impotent and the arts of speaking and listening both so moribund?

The preaching church, we say, is the historical presence now upon the earth of the incarnate, crucified, and buried Word. He himself, the Servant-King, is also the great Prophet, who from both sides mediates the dialogue between humanity and God; and in anything true the church might say he is as much the proclaimer as the one proclaimed. Yet to the human church it is given to participate in God's true self-declaration through the Son and in the Spirit,

---

(Oxford: Oxford University Press, 1971); Wallace, *Calvin's Doctrine of the Word and Sacrament;* G. Wingren, *The Living Word,* trans. V. C. Pogue (London: SCM and Philadelphia: Fortress, 1960); R. E. C. Browne, *The Ministry of the Word* (London: SCM, 1958); and Leith, *From Generation to Generation,* ch. 3. Also, W. Brueggemann, *Finally Comes the Poet: Daring Speech for Proclamation* (Minneapolis: Augsburg Fortress, 1989).

91. For a devastating Christian critique of our loss of language today see J. Ellul, *The Humiliation of the Word.* See also N. Postman, *Amusing Ourselves to Death* (New York: Penguin Books, 1985).

92. "The Second Helvetic Confession" (1566), ch. 1, in A. C. Cochrane, ed., *Reformed Confessions of the 16th Century* (Philadelphia: Westminster, 1966).

and the task of declaring, by deed but not without words, the judging and justi-fying "word of the cross." Preaching is thus a *form* of that word as much as a medium for its announcement — the foolishness and impotence of the church's words matching and expressing the foolish weakness of the God who lives through dying, triumphs in defeat, and chooses the weak things of the world to confound and shame the mighty.[93]

Why is it, in any case, that from the beginning (Gen. 1:3) faith has found speech to be the most fitting and compelling of all analogies for God's own self-expression, if it is not that with words we most truthfully and wholly identify and expose our personhood? Our bodies are given to us, genetically beyond our own control; but our words we choose for ourselves — which is why we so rightly resent having others "put words in our mouths." Through our own speech — sometimes unawares — we reveal the truth about ourselves in our uniqueness, and address others equally distinct. Thus through words we corre-spond to the image of the triune God's own community of indwelling and mu-tually constituting persons. For thus we break out of the silent, solipsistic pri-vate sphere of thought, where no one else can enter, into the relational world of communication, interaction, and mutual dependence on the other, the Thou without whom I cannot be I.

Perhaps then, words, though culturally now demonized and despised, are precisely what our depersonalized and often demonic Easter Saturday world needs to hear. Through the humanizing relationality of words, the church may hope simultaneously to protest and to heal the narcissistic individualism of our culture and its degradation of communities into actions destructive of togeth-erness and interdependence. Cultural and racial wars at home, religious and ethnic conflicts abroad, all testify to the failure of human beings to speak words of peace and love and mutual need. That is a call for the Easter Saturday church, however hidden among the victims of these catastrophes, to be also vocal, pro-phetic advocates of social healing and community reconciliation.

Of course, here too, as in all else, the Christian churches cannot aspire to be prophetic agents of renewal and reform unless they first subject themselves to the subversive judgment and radical reconstruction of the gospel of the cross and grave. The preaching community is today mired in its own sin and coward-ice of cultural conformity. Its own preaching too frequently degenerates into moralizing, anecdotal trivialization and ministerial exhibitionism which mir-rors the anti-intellectual cult of personality in the political, social, and often

---

93. On the inspired mistranslation in the King James Version of 1 Cor. 1:21 as "the foolishness of preaching," see I. R. Pitt-Watson, *A Kind of Folly: Toward a Practical Theol-ogy of Preaching* (Edinburgh: St. Andrew Press, 1976), p. 1 and throughout.

even academic order. Only by recovering prophetic and objectives modes of preaching, in faithfulness to the gospel of Christ crucified and in contradiction to society's profane habits and priorities, can we truly challenge our dying culture and reveal to it its own possibilities for resurrection.

This is an Easter Saturday demand that the church again die to itself, be crucified to popularity and trendiness and — overthrowing the cultural idols of relevance, effectiveness, and growth — live solely with radical courage and faith in the power of God's crucified and silent impotence. Without such a death, such kenotic but iconoclastic stooping to the lowly vulnerability of language in this culture, how can we credibly address the crisis of our postlinguistic age?

With words, on the contrary, if full of narrative content, cognitive meaning and veridical reference to realities beyond themselves, the prophetic, preaching church may indeed hope to refute and reverse the deconstruction of meaning in Western culture — its loss of objectivity and purpose. Unless we have the audacity, by means not exclusively of preaching but certainly not without it, to tell the story of the cross and grave, rehearsing God's mighty acts of human powerlessness, the history of the Trinity's own way through flesh and death and nothingness to final consummation and the liberation of the universe — how shall the church confront the despairing loss of teleology and providence which so robs our beginning-of-century generation of purpose, hope, and destiny?[94] And how else might we begin to bridge the epistemological dualistic gulf which denies knowability to anything beyond our private, Cartesian self-consciousness? There are indeed, as we have noted, prophets already among us who identify the deep source of our society's malaise, the cancer underlying our multiple pathologies, with this radical privatizing of the truth.[95] The subjectivization, relativism, and privatism of our dominant

---

94. On the loss of teleology and destiny in Western culture, see esp. Newbigin, *Gospel in a Pluralist Society,* chs. 6-9.

95. See, e.g., Newbigin, *Truth to Tell.* Newbigin's much-publicized thinking and writing about "the gospel and our culture" has helped to inaugurate a movement of that name in many parts of the world, including the United States and Great Britain. His work is greatly indebted to the epistemology of the philosopher of science, Michael Polanyi. See Polanyi, *Personal Knowledge* (London: Routledge & Kegan and Chicago: University of Chicago Press, 1958). Another profound influence upon Newbigin, whose own work at overcoming the false epistemological dualism in modern philosophy and culture owes much to Polanyi, is T. F. Torrance. Cf. esp. his monumental *Theological Science.* A further major contribution to the epistemological debate is Colin Gunton's *Enlightenment and Alienation;* also his article "Knowledge and Culture: Towards an Epistemology of the Concrete," in H. Montefiore, ed., *The Gospel and Contemporary Culture* (papers preliminary to the U.K. consultation on "The Gospel as Public Truth," July 1992) (London and New York:

intellectual worldview ultimately denies any locus of truth or foundation of value external to the solitary ego — itself absorbed with its own will for power, gratification, and survival.

Without by any means hoping to reinvent a lost Christendom, or wishing wistfully to reestablish their past authority and dominance within society, the churches at the edges of the world need to contest, with personalizing words creative of relationship and indicative of transcendent community, this philosophical self-centeredness and inwardness. The gospel must be so preached as to challenge society with the possibilities of "public truth" — realities and agencies, demands and gifts beyond the confines of private, self-contemplating consciousness and sensibility. Without a public insistence that truth and reality themselves are public — open at least to discourse, if not to verification, in the civic marketplace — how can Christians resist the self-destructive loss of the transcendent all around us? How else may people of faith today bear witness to the creating and redeeming of our universe and history, our perception and conviction of the otherness of God which is the *sine qua non* for recognizing the otherness, dignity, and needfulness of other persons within the one community of human beings?

Now if the holy church says much quietly about the incarnation of the crucified Word simply by being present in the world of suffering and poverty and the prophetic church says a great deal publicly about the crucifying of the

---

Mowbray, 1992). See also MacIntyre, *After Virtue.* Though challenging the post-Enlightenment dualism between public knowledge and private opinion from another, i.e., Hegelian, starting point, Wolfhart Pannenberg, too, offers staunch resistance to the privatizing and relativizing of truth. See esp. his *Systematic Theology,* vol. 1, esp. chs 1 and 2. For yet another approach to the same cultural relativities (especially in the United States), see R. F. Thiemann, *Constructing a Public Theology: The Church in a Pluralistic Culture* (Louisville: Westminster/John Knox Press, 1991), esp. ch. 1: "Theology in the Public Arena." And for a more practical discussion of the political consequences for public policy of the Christian conviction that theology and faith are not to be subjectivized or restricted to a supposed private sphere of life, see D. B. Forrester, *Beliefs, Values and Policies* (Oxford and New York: Oxford University Press, 1989).

Of course, there stands as an abiding monument in our own generation to the public nature of Christian doctrine and ethics the entire life and work of Reinhold Niebuhr. See, e.g., L. Rasmussen, ed., *Reinhold Niebuhr: Theologian of Public Life* (London: Collins and San Francisco: Harper & Row, 1989). For other recent contributions to the American debate about "public" theology, see, e.g., M. Marty, *The Public Church* (New York: Crossroad, 1981); Tracy, *The Analogical Imagination;* Lindbeck, *The Nature of Doctrine;* W. Placher, *Unapologetic Theology: A Christian Voice in a Pluralistic Conversation* (Louisville: Westminster/John Knox Press, 1989); Hauerwas and Willimon, *Resident Aliens;* Burnham, ed., *Postmodern Theology: Christian Faith in a Pluralist World;* and D. T. Hessel, ed., *The Church's Public Role* (Grand Rapids: Eerdmans, 1993).

incarnate Word simply by preaching in the world that despises language, it is not sufficient for the Christian community either to be simply present for the sake of presence or to simply preach for preaching's sake. The obedience of the church depends on what it preaches: the *content* of its words and thus the *reason* for its presence. What shall the church actually say today in its prophetic protest against society and as the ground of its solidarity with society? What is that message, to which its medium of preaching so aptly corresponds, from the Easter Saturday community of faith in its address to the Easter Saturday world of unbelief? Contexts vary and with them the particulars of the church's single constant gospel of Christ Jesus. There are certainly some loci around the world today, especially contexts of cultural and religious conflict, oppression, and exclusion, where the necessary word for the church to proclaim is one that positively affirms human beings, their dignity and worth, the value of their cultures, and the authenticity of their traditions, faiths, experiences, histories. Here the first imperative of the prophetic church is protest against hatred, division, and dehumanization with the gospel's affirmation of human oneness as the work of God's "two hands," the Creator Spirit, universally enlightening, and the eternal Word who has both made all things and reconciled them through the cross (Jn. 1:1ff.; Col. 1:15-20; Heb. 1:1ff.).

For precisely the same reasons, however — in order to attest the oneness of humanity and the wholeness of the human community worldwide, as created, redeemed, and awaiting consummation by the triune God — there are surely contexts and crises which demand from the church negative and critical, costly and offensive prophecy. Here "the word of the cross" addressed to our idolatrous world must take the form of confessing God's transcendency and sovereign rule and the subordination of every culture, nation, and human institution, and of all politics and ideologies, to the sole and final lordship of Christ Jesus. Sometimes it is only by confronting the worldly principalities and powers which dispute the lordship of the lamb whom Caesar slew that the churches may help to falsify and undermine those ideologies which divide the world so as to conquer it and in so doing rob human beings of their wholeness and equality.[96] In those conditions, the church's path toward the redeeming of the human community lies not in the idealization of diversity and plurality but rather in the relativizing of human differentials, as those are sinfully emphasized and exploited in an unjust world, in favor of humanity's sameness and oneness under the reign of Christ, the world's one Lord.

Thus we have already noted how, at several points of crisis in our century,

---

96. See esp. W. Wink, *The Powers*, vol. 1: *Naming the Powers;* vol. 2: *Unmasking the Powers;* vol. 3: *Engaging the Powers* (Philadelphia and Minneapolis: Fortress, 1984-92).

— so disastrously riven by demonic ideologies of national and racial supremacy — the church has been summoned boldly and without ambiguity to set aside all the convenient and in their own way proper platitudes of diversity and pluralism as to confess one humanity under the authority of the one Creator and Redeemer. Paradigmatically against Hitler and the blasphemies of "German Christianity," and then, following that model, against the heretical "white Christianity" of pro-apartheid Afrikanerdom,[97] it has been necessary to reactivate the Reformation mode of resisting heresies which posed a mortal threat to the gospel by declaring a *status confessionis,* or confessional emergency. Thus have "confessing" churches declared that Christ alone is the way, the truth, and the life, denouncing the false doctrine that other events or powers, figures or truths, could masquerade as God's revelation, that some spheres of life belong not to Christ but to other lords, and that human beings — Jews and Aryans, blacks and whites — may be so separated as to conceal or contradict their reconciliation through the cross.[98]

97. On the German "church struggle," see esp. A. C. Cochrane, *The Church's Confession under Hitler;* and K. Scholder, *The Churches and the Third Reich,* trans. J. Bowden, vol. 2 (Philadelphia: Fortress and London: SCM, 1988); R. P. Ericksen, *Theologians under Hitler* (New Haven and London: Yale University Press, 1985); also J. Moltmann, "Barth's Doctrine of the Lordship of Jesus Christ and the Experience of the Confessing Church," in *On Human Dignity,* trans. D. M. Meeks (London: SCM and Philadelphia: Fortress, 1984).

On the South African "church struggle," see esp. J. de Gruchy, *The Church's Struggle in South Africa* (Grand Rapids: Eerdmans, 1979); also Smit and Cloete, *A Moment of Truth;* and for the relevance of Bonhoeffer and Barth, junior and senior participants in the German Confessing Church, for South African resistance to apartheid, see J. de Gruchy, *Bonhoeffer and South Africa* (Grand Rapids: Eerdmans, 1984); and C. Villa-Vicencio, ed., *On Reading Karl Barth in South Africa* (Grand Rapids: Eerdmans, 1988).

See also G. Hunsinger, ed., *Karl Barth and Radical Politics* (Philadelphia: Westminster Press, 1976); and Barth's own seminal statement on church/state relations in "The Christian Community and the Civil Community," in Barth, *Against the Stream* (New York: Philosophical Library and London: Camelot Press, 1954); also Barth, "Atomic War as *Status Confessionis,*" in C. Green, ed., *Karl Barth: Theologian of Freedom* (London: Collins and San Francisco: Harper & Row, 1989), pp. 319ff.; Boesak and Villa-Vicencio, eds., *Apartheid Is a Heresy;* A. Boesak, *If This Is Treason I Am Guilty* (Grand Rapids: Eerdmans and Trenton, N.J.: Africa World Press, 1987); and A. Dumas, *Political Theology and the Life of the Church,* trans. J. Bowden (London: SCM, 1978).

98. See esp. *The Theological Declaration of Barmen* (1934), in Cochrane, ed., *Reformed Confessions,* Appendix, and the "Belhar Confession" of the Dutch Reformed Mission Church, 1982, in Smit and Cloete, ed., *A Moment of Truth.* See also J. Guhrt, "*Status Confessionis:* The Witness of a Confessing Church," *Reformed World* 37.8 (1983); D. J. Smit, "What Does 'Status Confessionis' Mean?" *Journal of Theology for Southern Africa,* no. 47 (1984); and E. TeSelle, "How Do We Recognize a Status Confessionis?" *Theology Today* 45.1 (1988).

Confession of "Christ alone" is in no way an absolutizing of the Christian religion or a proposal of theocracy; for its critique is directed against the church itself and its infidelities, protesting anything within the church as well as in the state that presumes to glorify the superiority of any race or nation in repudiation of the reconciling death and burial of Christ (Eph. 2). *Status confessionis* directs the critical "word of the cross" precisely at Christians themselves, when they help to demonize the human community by negating the good news that men and women of every race and nation have been redeemed and unified and are being gathered into the solidarity and fellowship of God's coming, final kingdom.[99]

Of course, to declare in the name of the crucified Lord a confessional crisis, which sets prophetic walls between the true church and the false — for the sake of removing false barriers between the peoples of the world — is not a step to be taken lightly or too often, but only when all other means of securing repentance for such falsehood are exhausted.[100] But that does not excuse the church from confessing Christ in every age and situation with matching words and deeds, and in ways fitting and appropriate to the variables of context, time, and place. Must we not always be telling our story to the world — sometimes, at least, in the form of confessions, creeds, and statements, which modestly and now and then, never presuming finality or infallibility but always provisionality and reformability, declare the truth as understood by us for now?[101]

99. Another *status confessionis,* also directed at the false and deadly division of the human race, this time the nuclear policies of West and East, was declared by the Reformed Alliance of West Germany at the height of the Cold War in the 1980s. Also, in the context of religious and cultural conflict in Northern Ireland, where churches Protestant and Catholic have identified the gospel with the political and tribal identities of Ulster "Loyalists" and Irish "nationalists" respectively, there have been small acts of "Barmen-like" confessing, to the effect that the one Word of God relativizes all political and social allegiance. See "A Declaration of Faith and Commitment" (Belfast: Inter-Church Centre, 1986); cf. J. B. Torrance, "The Ministry of Reconciliation," in Kettler and Speidell, eds, *Incarnational Ministry,* pp. 130ff.

100. Hence the decision of the 22nd General Council of the World Alliance of Reformed Churches, in Seoul, South Korea, 1989, not to expand the range of its *status confessionis,* despite some appeals to that effect, in contrast to the decision of its 21st Council, in Ottawa, Canada, in 1982, to declare such an emergency with respect to the theological defense of apartheid and to suspend from membership the then unrepentant Dutch Reformed Church. See *From Ottawa to Seoul* (Geneva: W.A.R.C., 1989); and *Proceeding of the 22nd General Council of the 22nd General Council of the World Alliance of Reformed Churches* (Geneva, 1990).

101. On the self-limitation of Reformed confession-making, see K. Barth, "The Desirability and Possibility of Universal Reformed Creed," in *Theology and Church* (Lon-

Though the particular form and emphasis of Christian confessing and confession making must, at least for some traditions, fluctuate according to circumstance and context, its inner substance will remain the same: "the word of the cross and of the grave." Though there is little enthusiasm, in the United States today, for example, for a new *status confessionis,* and perhaps no singular crisis that would justify it, there certainly are prophets who urgently and perspicaciously insist that the theology of the cross, and of the Crucified One, must indeed be expounded and confessed today, protesting America's dream of beauty and health, success and wealth, its myth of national destiny and self-congratulation as the one surviving superpower. The cross and grave of Christ, their suffering and ugliness, their failure and negation, represent a devastating, iconoclastic critique of such a society and its illusions, and invite it to face its own deep darkness, to intensify its disillusionment and sense of decadence and death, that it might reborn to the true light and life and hope of God's own rule.[102] Can the prophetic church help this culture and society to an Easter

---

don: SCM, 1962), pp. 112-35. See also L. Vischer, *Reformed Witness Today* (Bern: Evangelische Arbeitstelle Oekumene Schweiz, 1982); also *Confessions and Confessing in the Reformed Tradition Today* (Geneva: World Alliance of Reformed Churches, 1982). The provisionality and contextuality of Christian confessing is pointedly embodied in the existence now, in the Presbyterian Church (U.S.A.), not of a single confessional standard as previously (and still in many Calvinist churches — e.g., the Westminster Confession of Faith), but of a *Book of Confessions* representing the major milestones along a still unfinished confessional history. The latest addition to that Book is "A Brief Statement of Faith" (1991), which embodies the same principle of reformable confession. See J. Stotts and J. Dempsey Douglass, eds., *To Confess the Faith Today* (Louisville: Westminster/John Knox Press, 1990); and W. C. Placher and D. Willis-Watkins, *Belonging to God: A Commentary on A Brief Statement of Faith* (Louisville: Westminster/John Knox Press, 1992). See also *Insights: A Journal of the Faculty of Austin Seminary* 106.1 (1990): "On 'A Brief Statement of Faith,'" including my own paper, "From Barmen to Baltimore: Reformed Confessing in the Twentieth Century." In some contrast to Reformed confessing instincts, the Methodist theologians Stanley Hauerwas and William Willimon, while applauding the Barmen Declaration and certainly advocating a confessing posture on the part of the church today, stress not so much the involvement of the confessing churches in taking responsibility for the renewing of society, but more the separation of the Christian community from the world, as resident aliens who stand over against the profane environment. On the possible strengths, but also real weaknesses, of that position, see, among numerous critiques, D. Ottati, "The Spirit of Reforming Protestantism," *The Christian Century* 109.37 (Dec. 16, 1992).

102. This intensification of darkness for the sake of light is the particular burden of Douglas J. Hall's pointed applications of the "theology of the cross" to contemporary North America, in such books as *Lighten Our Darkness* and *Thinking the Faith.* See also A. McGill, *Death and Life: An American Theology* (Philadelphia: Fortress, 1987).

Sunday recovery of community and sociality without confronting in the name of Christ its hollow self-absorption and the menace of its recrudescent racial tension and ethnic rivalry? Can we evade a courageous, perhaps dangerous and costly, countercultural confession from the corner, which denounces the center's idolatry of self-interest and accumulation, its toleration of inequity and prejudice, and envision a new community wherein the Trinity shall gather in, as brothers and sisters of the beloved Son, the poor and ugly, the disinherited and second class?

V. The Priestly, Buried Body: Unity and Prayer

"Where sin increased, grace abounded all the more." The story of the cross and grave, as we have been attempting to hear and think it and to ask about its living out, tells of a contradiction between God and the world, a conflict in which evil triumphs over good, death extinguishes life, and the creatures annihilate their Maker. But the contradiction is not absolute, nor is the conflict finally resolved in favor of negation. For there flourishes even more grace beyond the great magnitude of evil, and a divine fertility beyond the barrenness of the demonic; and out of the mutual opposition of the world and its Creator, there sounds a final and decisive Yes to the creatures, powerful, living and redemptive, which promises them freedom and fullness within the expansive embrace of God's own history and life. To this triumphal Easter Yes, which never cancels but does transcend God's judgmental No to the world on the cross and the world's destructive No to God in the grave, ecclesiology must clearly correspond.

So then, just as the mutual hostility between the world and God which reigns on Easter Saturday is not the final state of their relations, but yields to affirmation, renewal, and redemption for precisely those who secured the death of the living God, likewise the protest of the church, God's chosen, living people, against the sinful, corrupt, and frequently demonic world, cannot be the final word of the Christian community to those around it. Prophetic judgment upon the world and holy separation from it must actively promote and witness to the experiential impact on the world of the greater abundance yet of God's resurrecting grace beyond the increase of its own hostility, foolishness, and brokenness. Whatever opposition the holy church properly directs to the unrighteousness and injustice of its alien, surrounding culture, that resistance itself expresses obedience to the church's calling to be truly catholic, immersed in solidarity and presence in the seemingly godless and godforsaken world. And equally that catholic presence is not a supine, quiescent, inert companionship which does nothing creatively *for* the world in which Christians are quietly em-

bedded. The church's critical posture toward the world is not ultimately negative, nor is its hidden presence in the world quite passive. Rather, we must reaf-
firm that the Easter Saturday church, Christ's buried body, is in essence and
identity *for* the world, and that that identity is realized not just attitudinally or
spiritually, but by way of active engagements with and infiltrations of the
world. Such actions are not designed to supplant or masquerade as God's own
redemptive work; but certainly, through the Spirit of Christ, they are to provide
a humble yet energetic and credible instrumentality for that divine transforming of the world which shall constitute the final kingdom. In that renewal of
heaven and earth, the dynamic, eschatological favor of God's grace toward the
world which rejected, crucified, and buried God's own Son, the church as
Christ's buried but resurrected body cannot but be involved, as servant and
participant.

If, therefore, an Easter Saturday ecclesiology, maximizing the opposition
between worldly power and the weakness of the cross, necessarily casts the
church into relations with the world describable as "Christ against culture," that
counterculturalism is no end in itself, but is ordered toward culture's redemption, its Easter Day renewal beyond its Easter Saturday degradation. This is to
understand the church as concerned, above all, visibly and actively to embody in
society the resurrected, resurrecting Christ who "transforms culture."[103]

That encapsulates the assumption of John Calvin, for example, who, as
we have noted, surpassed Martin Luther in the confidence he felt constrained
by Scripture and experience to entertain in the Holy Spirit's sanctifying power.
Transformation by the Spirit extends beyond individuals — on whose conversion and maturing we shall reflect below — to the church itself, the mother of
believers within whose womb Christian faith is born and nurtured. The Christian community as a whole is shaped by and reflective of God's renewing grace:
a locus of sanctification not only for its own sake but also for the world's. Actively and responsibly engaged in worldly affairs, it penetrates society with the
sanctifying Spirit of God and so enables the social and political order to be
shaped into a godly commonwealth on earth, a far from flawless but still recognizable mirror of the coming kingdom. Thus might there be already a civic
community among us, proleptic of and corresponding to the justice, peace, and
harmony of the final, messianic kingdom.[104]

---

103. See the typology of relations between Christ and culture made famous by H. R.
Niebuhr in *Christ and Culture* (New York: Harper & Row, 1951), esp. chs. 2 and 6; see pp.
217-18 in particular, where Niebuhr identifies John Calvin among others as epitomizing
the view of Christ as the transformer of culture.

104. On Calvin's doctrine of the church in relation to society and the state, which

This relationship of church to world is in fact the ecclesiological implicate of the social doctrine of the Trinity, which we saw to be grounded upon Christ's cross and grave as constituting the history of the triune God. The Trinity is revealed through Christ's death to be a community of mutually dependent, self-giving persons whose reciprocating love creates both freedom on the one hand, and cohesion on the other. Through the Son and in the Spirit it is given to humanity to participate in this divine society; and the *eschaton* is that coincidence of human and divine fulfillment wherein our own sociality, humanly created in the image of the triune family, shall be delivered from its demonic corruptions into individualism and totalitarianism, racism and nationalism, until, redeemed and purified, it is brought into correspondence with the Trinity itself. The church is that community which anticipates, though fallibly and not without much ambiguity and failure, the world's own future of redeemed togetherness wherein shall abide that righteousness and peace, tearlessness and deathlessness often called *shalom* and named the New Jerusalem (e.g., Ps. 122; Rev. 21).[105]

However, to say on trinitarian grounds that the church is *eschatologically* oriented in its relationship to the world and the temporal order of society is by

---

underlay his own activities, especially in Geneva, and many subsequent experiments in social transformation through the history of Calvinism, not least in New England, see, e.g., R. W. Wallace, *Calvin, Geneva and the Reformation* (Grand Rapids: Baker Books and Edinburgh: Scottish Academic Press, 1988); T. George, ed., *John Calvin and the Church* (Louisville: Westminster/John Knox Press, 1990); P. Avis, *The Church in the Theology of the Reformers;* T. F. Torrance, *Kingdom and Church* (Edinburgh: Oliver & Boyd, 1956); J. de Gruchy, *Liberating Reformed Theology* (Grand Rapids: Eerdmans, 1991); W. Bouwsma, *John Calvin: A Sixteenth-Century Portrait* (New York and London: Oxford University Press, 1988); R. H. Stone, ed., *Reformed Faith and Politics* (Washington, D.C.: University Press of America, 1983); A. Boesak, *Black and Reformed: Apartheid, Liberation and the Calvinist Tradition* (Maryknoll, N.Y.: Orbis Books, 1984); K. Barth, "The Christian Community and the Civil Community," in *Against the Stream,* and in W. Herberg, ed., *Community, State, and Church* (New York: Doubleday, 1960); also *Church and State,* trans. G. R. Howe (Greenville, S.C.: Smyth and Helwys, 1991) (= trans. of *Rechtfertigung und Recht* [1938]); Jüngel, *Karl Barth: A Theological Legacy,* esp. pt. 2; C. Villa-Vicencio and J. de Gruchy, eds., *Resistance and Hope: Essays in Honor of Beyers Naudé* (Grand Rapids: Eerdmans, 1985); also S. S. Wolin, *Politics and Vision* (Boston: Little, Brown & Co., 1960), ch. 6.

105. On these relationships and correspondences between the divine community, the human community, and the church community, see esp. D. W. Hardy, "Created and Redeemed Sociality," in Gunton and Hardy, eds., *On Being the Church,* ch. 1; Moltmann, *Trinity and Kingdom,* esp. ch. 6; L. Boff, *Trinity and Society,* trans. P. Burns (Maryknoll, N.Y.: Orbis Books, 1988); Gunton, *Promise,* ch. 4; Zizioulas, *Being as Communion;* LaCugna, *God for Us,* ch. 10; and *The Forgotten Trinity,* British Council of Churches, vol. 1, ch. 6; vol. 2, ch. 6; vol. 3, ch. 10.

no means to attribute an otherworldliness to Christian social and political action, as if such involvement were in fact a charade, a docetic cloak for an essential detachment from the world's concerns and contempt for its historical future. At the same time it does not mean either that the church identifies itself as God's final rule, or endorses any ideology, divinizes any social order, as promising the realization of that reign upon the earth. In fact, far from validating the status quo, or human devices for its alteration, the trinitarian-eschatological premise of Christian political engagement is precisely what animates the church's critical, prophetic protest against the way things are done in temporal society, in the name of the God whom society crucified and buried. As history, perhaps supremely that of Calvinism, demonstrates, the church's penetration of social and political life for the sake of its redemption must often take the turbulent form of opposition to, even revolution against, the present order, at least when its authorities are blatantly evil, unjust, or tyrannical in their trampling of the freedom and welfare of the poor and disenfranchised.[106]

Such subversive actions themselves betray the innate restlessness, homelessness, dissatisfaction in all church engagement with the world, an awareness of the penultimacy of every polity, the ambiguity and inefficacy of all policies and programs, and the danger of idolatry — with its attendant disappointment and disillusionment — in the absolutizing of any social vision. Yet just because no civil order on earth can become or may be ratified as the final kingdom, that also frees the church to support and engage in almost any form of politics which is not tyrannical, makes no claim to absolutism, requires no allegiance incompatible with Christ's Lordship, but does grope for credible, if penultimate and ambiguous correspondences in the civil realm to God's own community and coming rule.[107] For society as such serves God's purposes for peace and

106. The "Magna Carta" of this cautiously revolutionary Calvinism, which simultaneously requires obedience to authority, as divinely ordained, and mandates resistance to authority when egregiously disobedient to God's just law, is Calvin, *Inst.* IV.xx. See also A. Boesak and C. Villa-Vicencio, eds., *A Call for an End to Unjust Rule* (Edinburgh: St. Andrew Press and Philadelphia: Westminster Press, 1986), esp. ch. 11; and C. A. Wanamaker, "Romans 13: A Hermeneutic for Church and State," in C. Villa-Vicencio, ed., *On Reading Karl Barth in South Africa,* pp. 91-104. And for a fascinating if not conventionally theological account of the biblical roots (specifically in the book of Job) of the politics of dissent, see W. A. Safire, *The First Dissident* (New York: Random House, 1993).

107. On the vital political and ethical distinction between the ultimate and the penultimate, see esp. Bonhoeffer, *Ethics,* trans. N. H. Smith (London: Collins, 1952 and New York: Macmillan, 1962), pp. 120ff. And on the restless, Exodus-like pilgrimage that is Christian political engagement, see esp. Moltmann, *Theology of Hope,* p. 22 and ch. 5; also Barth, "The Christian Community and the Civil Community."

justice in the world, and inherits the promise that the political order shall not be negated but perfected, when "the kingdom of the earth has become the kingdom of our Lord and of his Christ" (Rev. 11:15).[108]

Now this ambiguous relationship of the church to the world, grounded in the history of the Trinity whose future both destabilizes and redeems the present, incorporates a specifically Easter Saturday posture, corresponding to the dual relation of Christ, within the Trinity, to the world at the point of his death and burial. For at that boundary, we said, the Son of God, self-humbled to the lowest extremities of humanity's far country, is subject to radical contradiction, all the opposition between God and the world brought to its hellish climax in rejection and annihilation. Yet the divine Son, so demonically negated, is at the same time, on the same cross and in the same tomb, the truly human one on his way home from the far country to the Father's house of healing and reconciliation, vicarious firstfruits of the world's wholeness and redemption in fellowship with the triune community of love. As victim of the world's suffering, target of its sin, and prolepsis of its renewal, Christ is, in the imagery of Scripture and tradition, humanity's Great High Priest, whose self-sacrifice as the unblemished lamb both atones for sin and sanctifies the sinners whom he represents. At the Easter Saturday boundary point the kenotic annihilation of the world's scapegoat is completed and the exalted homecoming of the world's sanctifier is begun.

So it is that the church which is Christ's buried, Easter Saturday body, participant in his regal servanthood within the world, and in his prophetic proclamation to the world, shares also in Christ's priesthood, as sin's victim and its victor, embodying both the mutual opposition between God and the world

---

108. The duality — or frank ambivalence — of this position, which endorses positive involvement in the world but is always critical, at a distance, and never sacralizing, may be traced back to Augustine. For him the earthly city and the City of God are, this side of the *eschaton*, so thoroughly interfused to human eyes that the church itself is "secular," a precarious, worldly institution wherein the elect and the damned are indistinguishably mixed, and thus never to be identified with the pure and abiding heavenly community. Yet sustained by its eschatological hope for the world, the church in its very prophetic and critical tension with that world expressed practical concern for and pragmatic engagement in civil society, however corrupt and profane. See Augustine, *The City of God,* trans. H. Bettenson, ed. J. O'Meara (London: Penguin Books, 1984); also R. A. Markus, *Saeculum: History and Society in the Theology of Augustine* (Cambridge: Cambridge University Press, 1970), esp. ch. 7; K. Löwith, *Meaning in History* (Chicago and London: University of Chicago Press, 1949), ch. 9; Wolin, *Politics and Vision,* ch. 4; and A. H. Armstrong and R. A. Markus, *Christian Faith and Greek Philosophy* (London: Darton, Longman & Todd, 1960), ch. 9.

and divine promise for the world's renewal. And it is to body forth visibly and concretely this promise of sanctifying grace, this abundant, resurrecting power of the lamb of Calvary that the priestly church engages in the world, acting (with all due critical, eschatological reserve) for its transformation while providing provisional indicators of that transformation's reality and imminence.[109] But what in particular are the signs that the priestly church should manifest, and what sort of actions should it undertake for and within an Easter Saturday society?

We have in effect identified disintegration and disunity as the underlying pathology of our Easter Saturday culture. This may take the form of solipsistic individualism which fragments society by severing the bonds of mutual obligation and support which should connect one individual to a community's every other member. Or it may be manifest as a corrupted sociality which certainly makes for groupings of shared interest and common identity but only in ways that exacerbate differentness and antagonism between one such grouping and another. Plagued by both of these phenomena, ours is a society with little experience of a unity connecting all together in a cohesive whole such as permits freedom, respect, and equality for the many groups and individuals within it. In face of these many fractures in modern society, and in humanity as a whole, the church can scarcely fulfill its servant and prophetic roles within the world unless it also becomes through Christ's priesthood a living sign of the possibility of social unity, visible evidence for the gospel's promise that in the triune kingdom the world will indeed be reconciled, its divisions healed, its chasms bridged, its fragments unified.

As Christ's "high-priestly" prayer in the Fourth Gospel makes clear, it is the presumption of John's theology that the promised unity of the world is itself ontologically ground in the oneness of God's triune family, in which, by the

---

109. See esp. J. B. Torrance, "The Vicarious Humanity of Christ," in T. F. Torrance, ed., *The Incarnation*, ch. 6; T. F. Torrance, *Royal Priesthood, Scottish Journal of Theology, Occasional Paper* No. 3 (Edinburgh: Oliver & Boyd, 1955). To this characteristically Reformed theme of Christ's priesthood within his threefold office (see J. F. Jansen, *Calvin's Doctrine of the Work of Christ* [London: J. Clarke and Co., Ltd., 1956]) and its ecclesiological extension, there corresponds in Roman Catholic ecclesiology, particularly since Vatican II, a conception of the church as "the fundamental sacrament," or "the sacramental sign of the world's salvation." This, not unlike the Reformed understanding of the church's relation to the world, can be readily traced back to Augustine. See Markus, *Saeculum*, pp. 183ff.; E. Schillebeeckx, *Christ: The Sacrament of the Encounter with God* (New York: Sheed & Ward, 1963); K. Rahner, *The Church and the Sacraments*, trans. W. J. O'Hare (London: Burns & Oates and New York: Herder, 1963); M. Schmaus, *Dogma 5: The Church as Sacrament* (London: Sheed & Ward, 1975); and Dulles, *Models*, ch. 4.

Spirit's own bonds of unity, the Father and the Son abide in one another — that mutual indwelling which the later church named *perichoresis*. The church's own oneness, in its unity with the Father through the Son and in the Spirit, is the ground on which the fractured world might be convinced of the Father's love and believe that it, too, may participate in the mutuality of the Father with the Son and in the oneness-through-plurality of God's own self (Jn. 17:11 and 21ff.). Likewise in Paul's ecclesiology, the reconciling and unifying of the world is made visible in the oneness of the church, wherein all Christ's many baptized members form one body under his own headship (Rom. 12:4ff.; 1 Cor. 12:12ff.; Gal. 3:27ff.). The church's unity, then, sharing in the oneness of its singular head, corresponds both to the unity of God and to the coming unity of all creation. As there is one God, so there is one Lord, one faith, one baptism, and thus one church; and that unity of the Spirit among all Christians in the bond of peace foreshadows the reconciling of all creation, which shall terminate all stereotyping and segmenting of humanity (Eph. 2:11ff.; 4:3ff.).[110]

Now since God's own unity is that of a community, and Christ himself is comprised of many members, the affirmation that the church is one contains, as we have said, no condemnation of particularity and plurality as such within the church, nor a denial of the diversity and difference of the creatures' "cohumanity" created together in all our variety in the likeness of the triune God (Gen. 1:27). Yet there occur rivalries, secessions, and apostasies within the church which do gratuitously contradict the oneness of God, of Christ, and of humanity. Such disunity within the buried body of the Lord divides up Christ and subjects God's Son again to crucifixion (1 Cor. 1:13; Heb. 6:6). Thus from the beginning has the church been blurring the distinction between the beauty and propriety of diversity and the ugly guilt of disunitedness. Church history is a sorry narrative of discord and disjunction, the dark and shameful side of the church's Easter Saturday identity, our "generations of denominational absolutism,"[111] when we have repeatedly put Christ again to death and buried him in our tombs of triumphalism and prejudice, of schism and sectarianism.

110. Naturally in this ecumenical century the literature on the unity of the church is vast, complex, and beyond summarization here. But a few major treatments of the church as one are: Barth, *CD*, IV/1, 668-85; Küng, *The Church*, pp. 263-96; Moltmann, *Church in the Power of the Spirit*, pp. 342-47; Y. Congar, *Diversity and Community*, trans. J. Bowden (London: SCM, 1984), and *Dialogue between Christians and Catholics*, trans. P. Loretz (Westminster, Md.: Newman Press, 1966); G. Tavard, *The Church: Community of Salvation — An Ecumenical Ecclesiology* (Collegeville, Minn.: Liturgical Press, 1992); Dulles, *Models*, ch. 9; and esp. *Unitatis Redintegratio* (Decree on Ecumenism), in Abbott, eds., *Documents of Vatican II*.

111. Moltmann, *The Spirit of Life*, p. 4.

How might the fissured and fragmented world be expected to believe and know that for their sake God in love has sent the beloved Son, when confronted with the church's endless splinterings into sects, traditions, and denominations, our grotesque concealment of the cohesiveness and sociality in humanity's own createdness and promised transformation? That its quarrelsome history is incompatible with the church's apostolic mission to the riven world, its ministry of reconciliation among the estranged, is incontrovertible; the call for our repentance and the mending of our ways and of our broken bridges are quite irresistible.

There is, to be sure, legitimate debate today about what kind of penitent reunion among the separated Christians of the world would appropriately restore the ancient face of the church and reform us, in the context of our own culture, time, and context, into provisional signs of healing credible to a generation's debased and demonized expressions of community. Some of the distinctions in ecclesiology to which faith-seeking-understanding has learned through time to draw attention may not, in and of themselves, be denials of the unity of Christ and of his buried body. Nuanced contrasts, for example, between the church visible and invisible, militant and triumphant, or between structural institution and local gathering of faithful worshipers, all have their legitimacy — though also their great hazards. Such distinctions may rightly attest that the living community of women and men bound together by the Spirit has through that Spirit's dynamism a scope and shape which wondrously eludes all our legalistic, earthbound, and self-serving efforts to define the boundaries of the church. Yet all such contrasts can also become ossified and manipulative, serving not to liberate the Spirit but to justify our stultifying dualism. How easily, in particular, their deployment can rationalize a docetic, spiritualizing neglect of the structural fissures in the earthly community of faith wherein we have been called to serve the world.[112] That happens, too, when it is proposed that since the oneness of the church is an article of faith, its unity cannot in any case be seen by unbelievers and therefore has no need to be made visible; or that the allegedly "spiritual" unity already binding all Christians around the world renders redundant the organic reunifying of the worldwide church.

112. It has to be said here that Emil Brunner's *The Misunderstanding of the Church,* trans. H. Knight (London: Lutterworth, 1952), which proposes that the true *ecclesia,* the Body of Christ, "is nothing other than a fellowship of persons [with] nothing to do with an organization and has nothing of the character of the institutional about it" (pp. 10-11), is itself based on a gross, spiritualistic misunderstanding, for which he was rightly chided by Karl Barth (cf. *CD,* IV/2, 616). On the role of "base communities" in *reshaping* the institutional church, see esp. L. Boff, *Ecclesiogenesis: The Base Communities Reinvent the Church* (Maryknoll, N.Y.: Orbis Books, 1986).

Our own day sees the waning of the century which gave birth to "the ecumenical movement," when a repentant struggle for visible reunion became for many a missionary imperative. For decades the question was asked: How can we promise in Christ's name reconciliation to the disastrously divided, bellicose and destructive modern world if we ourselves remain patently divided and at odds? Today, despite much progress in attitudes and practices and a few true breakthroughs, with India perhaps providing the model for denominational restructuring, there is much frustration and no little ennui at the slow pace of convergence toward organic union. And in that mood, there is considerable rethinking of the ecumenical goal, not incorrectly in the light of our understanding of the Trinity from the standpoint of the cross. It is increasingly observed that the oneness of God is not itself a rigid, monistic uniformity and singularity, but a community of togetherness and a fellowship of persons who each with an unsubstitutable uniqueness constitute and make space for the others. Perhaps then the unity of the church we seek in the image of the mutually indwelling Trinity is one which acknowledges the irreducible diversity of human beings and so of Christians, and the propriety of particularity and contextual variation. Our oneness, then, would not be a static homogeneity and uniformity, but a unity-in-community, a "perichoretic" *koinonia* of the diverse and heterogeneous within the boundaries of a common apostolic faith.[113]

Whatever the ecumenical future in the next century, however, the pursuit of fellowship between diverse churches must surely not be an excuse to evade or relax the Easter Saturday demand upon the priestly church to remove those dif-

---

113. See *Christ and World: The Unity of the Church and the Renewal of the Human Community,* Faith and Order Paper No. 151 (Geneva: World Council of Churches, 1990); "The Unity of the Church as *Koinonia* and Gift," in M. Kinnamon, ed., *Signs of the Spirit: Official Report of the World Council of Churches, Seventh Assembly, Canberra, 1991* (Geneva: World Council of Churches and Grand Rapids: Eerdmans, 1991), pp. 174-76; A. Keshishian, *Conciliar Fellowship,* Geneva, World Council of Churches, 1992; M. Kinnamon, *Truth and Community: Diversity and Its Limits in the Ecumenical Movement* (Grand Rapids: Eerdmans and Geneva: World Council of Churches, 1988); and esp. K. Raiser, *Ecumenism in Transition: A Paradigm Shift in the Ecumenical Movement?,* trans. T. Coates (Geneva: World Council of Churches, 1991). It is highly significant that shortly after the publication of this work on the paradigm shift from "unity" to "*koinonia,*" Raiser was elected General Secretary of the World Council of Churches. On the movement toward a common confession, as the basis of *koinonia* and reconciled diversity, see esp. *Confessing the One Faith,* Faith and Order Papers No. 153 (Geneva: World Council of Churches, 1991). See also J. Macquarrie, *Christian Unity and Christian Diversity* (Philadelphia: Westminster Press, 1975); and C. S. Calian, *Theology without Boundaries: Encounters of Eastern Orthodoxy and Western Tradition* (Louisville: Westminster/John Knox Press, 1992), esp. ch. 8.

ferences and divisions which rightly scandalize the divided world and for so many render unhearable and unthinkable the reconciling "word of the cross." Can the churches, so manifestly false and hypocritical now in preaching the unity and peace of Christ crucified, keep refusing to submit to the cruciform abnegation and self-sacrifice of denominational *kenosis?* While valuing our traditions and particular identities, and celebrating our diversities in the Spirit, surely the members of Christ's ecclesial body, crucified and buried with him, must be prepared to die to whatever in their past histories and present relationships discredits their attempts to live in visible protest against human division and as viable embodiments of its promised overcoming. That would demand risky, costly sacrifices of all the churches, very different from the pain-free nostrums which politicians too glibly and dishonestly prescribe for the healing of economic, social, and political malaise.

Such renunciations for the world's sake would not, of course, mean the sacrifice of truth; but it may bring, through the process of rethinking, a rediscovery of truth in painful but enlightening new forms.[114] It would certainly require Easter Saturday abandonments of some cherished assumptions and time-honored practice and tradition, and the renegotiating of some nonessentials falsely absolutized. Can there be any true fellowship in and of the church which is not first and foremost and concretely a fellowship — *koinonia* — of Christ's *sufferings,* whereby we become like him in his death (Phil. 3:10)?[115] Must we not therefore allow the God who died on Calvary but lives, to teach the churches also how to die, to stifle their own instincts for self-preservation and abandon their beloved but false identities, in order that in company with Christ they may be raised out of loss, self-negation, and burial to walk before the world in newness of life, as one community proleptic of that world's own resurrection to redeemed, unified togetherness?

Yet to be honest, how few signs there are that we who speak and preach so glibly about Christ crucified and cutely carry round our necks and on our vestments symbols of his death and burial are truly ready to push the churches we belong to down that costly way of the cross toward institutional and denominational *kenosis,* for the sake of our speedily disintegrating world.

In the meantime, we shall all continue to participate regularly, unthinkingly, yet blasphemously, in a huge, collective lie which corrupts the church's life at its very heart — its prayer, liturgy, and worship. For as long as Christians remain divided and the churches separated, the sacraments they celebrate shall be tainted with dishonesty and false consciousness — events proclaiming unity

114. See Küng, *Church,* pp. 289ff.
115. See Moltmann, *Way of Jesus Christ,* p. 155.

and togetherness conducted by the disunited in settings of blatant disconnect-edness.

In the long tradition of Augustine and the Reformers, the sacraments are "visible words," graphic presentations of the gospel's promises which by means of earthly signs set before our eyes God's eternal, covenantal, and redemptive grace which was enfleshed in Christ the divine, self-emptied Word, incarnate, crucified, and buried.[116] One word which the gospel clearly speaks as the eye beholds water, bread, and wine is that of unity: the coming rule of the triune, divine community where God shall be all in all, and all humanity made one. Baptism seals the end of the world's disintegration into rivalries and factions (Gal. 3:27-28); and the Lord's Supper preenacts the future, messianic banquet whereat divisions and distances across the globe shall be transcended and from its far corners women and men shall gather to be at one with God and feast with one another at a table of redemption and reconciliation (Mt. 8:11; Lk. 13:29).

These are far from solely private events, whereby individuals are, for ex-ample, initiated into the church and enriched in spiritual communion with their Lord, and whose meaning therefore hangs entirely upon their meaning-fulness to the psyche or emotions of solitary Christians or gathered congrega-tions. Rather, these sacramental happenings are essentially catholic and com-munal — full of personal significance, of course, but celebrated by the Christian community as the whole of Christ's body in the world, concerning the future of that world, the whole of humanity, and all creation, to whom is promised in Christ a new heaven and a new earth. Thus baptism and eucharist actually liberate us from interior, individualistic preoccupation with ourselves and turn us outward to the world as visualizations of the gospel's communal and global range. They are indeed, in the truest sense, "political" events, which speak visibly to the nature of the social order, its present brokenness and future healing, dramatizing "the word of the cross," the weak power of the crucified God to unify our cities, nations, and the cosmos.[117]

116. The classic exposition of the sacraments as "visible words" is Calvin, *Inst.,* IV.xiv.1-6. See Wallace, *Calvin's Doctrine of the Word and Sacraments;* also R. W. Jenson, *Visible Words* (Philadelphia: Fortress, 1978), esp. pt. 1.

117. The social and political dimensions of baptism and the Lord's Supper and the implications of their essentially eschatological orientation have been a major element in the considerable ecumenical convergence in sacramental theology in recent years. This is evident, above all, in *Baptism, Eucharist and Ministry.* See also M. Thurian, ed., *Ecumenical Perspectives on Baptism, Eucharist and Ministry* and *Baptism, Eucharist and Ministry 1982-1990;* M. Thurian and G. Wainwright, eds., *Baptism and Eucharist: Ecumenical Conver-gence in Celebration,* Faith and Order Paper No. 117 (Geneva: World Council of Churches,

It is just that word which we shamefully contradict and falsify when we enact sacraments of human unity within churches which are themselves unreconciled, and as the body of Christ itself dismembered and recrucified, not one at all but splintered and fractured beyond belief. Thus Sunday by Sunday does the Easter Saturday church, though speaking with its lips and imaging in its liturgy an Easter word of hope to the world, of resurrection from its terminal disunity and brokenness, instead reinforce the world's own Easter Saturday identity. For its very sacramental actions mirror, and too often in its history have added to, the world's fragmentation, by leaving in place barriers which Christ's baptism of death demolished, and by mocking his universal, messianic banquet through withholding table fellowship from one another.

Clearly none of this requires that the churches, even as presently configured, should cease to baptize or break bread. It does mean that every liturgical event, including these, should occur in a mood — actually voiced not too infrequently — of sorrow and remorse. Repentance befits us at the table and the font and in the pulpit, for the sin of our disunity, and confession of guilt for giving the lie by our practice and condition to our audible and visible announcements. Lending authenticity to such acknowledgments will be an accompanying resolve to struggle all the more untiringly and sacrificially for reordered church relations which, however hazardous to our own past traditions and identities, more truly manifest humanity's future unity in the messianic kingdom. Given such resolution we should, despite the hypocrisies involved, display the more enthusiastically before our splintered, moribund society, these Spirit-filled signs of its renewal and reunion. Through the medium of water, bread, and wine, along with the prayer that surrounds them and the preaching and teaching that gives them explication, the church today in the name of Christ may bravely oppose and undermine the structures of division and oppression in the social status quo, both national and global. And by the same means joyfully may we celebrate the impermanence of every Berlin Wall of hatred, fear, and inequality, the promised crumbling of every human barrier through the strange but seismic power of one man crucified in weakness and buried in annihilation.

1984); also G. Wainwright, *Eucharist and Eschatology* (London: Epworth Press, 1971). For a criticism of the developments in *Baptism, Eucharist and Ministry,* precisely for remaining too sacerdotal, hierarchical, and sacramentalist, substituting the church for Christ himself as the focus of the Eucharist and thus preventing it from being truly a meal signifying the oneness of all humanity in Christ, including the Jews, see the important work of Markus Barth, *Rediscovering the Lord's Supper* (Atlanta: John Knox Press, 1988). The objections of Markus Barth may well, as he himself obviously supposes, articulate those which his father Karl might have raised in today's context, given his own nonsacramental interpretation of baptism, especially in *CD*, IV/4.

It should indeed be clear to the church, Christ's priestly, buried body, that Holy Baptism and Holy Communion re-present that death and resurrection at whose boundary stands Christ's Holy Sabbath sepulcher. As water drowns, the Son of God was baptized unto death, so that those who participate through baptism in his new life may only do so as sharers first in his own burial and grave (Rom. 6:3ff.; Lk. 12:50). Though easily reduced to family sentiment and spurious celebrations of childhood innocence and prettiness, baptism is thus a stark reminder of captivity and death — the waters of the Red Sea which open up a way to freedom and new life in a Promised Land of milk and honey only by being first a watery grave for the pursuing, dehumanizing forces of slavery and tyranny, and of the flood which delivered Noah and his family only through the destruction of all things evil (Rom. 6:5ff.; 1 Pet. 3:20-21).[118] Likewise God on Easter Saturday entered into the deadly, hellish waters of estrangement and division, and in so doing triumphed all the more creatively over the demonic powers of hostility and negativity. Thus do we through baptism resist the powers that be, which keep humanity divided and at odds; and we commit ourselves to the replacement of those powers with God's new order on the earth, of peace and reconciliation.

Again, in the frangibility of bread, so easily disintegrated into crumbs, and in the perilous cup of wine, so readily spilt and lost to human use, we see God's own subjection to the tearing of the flesh, the breaking of bones, the spilling of blood, and the snuffing out of life, which so frequently and tragically mark our own society's descent into violent division and ancestral rivalry. Yet these signs of God's self-hazarding to our disunity also voice and symbolize dangerous, disobedient protests which Christians sometimes need to make against the way that things are done and ordered by states, authorities, and governments in the earthly kingdom. Equally, though, they are hopeful, visionary indications of the divine harmony and unanimity which finally shall replace the demonic structures that now torment and alienate so many sisters and brothers of Christ Jesus and ourselves.

It is certainly no accident that the eucharist in its eschatological significance for the renewing of society is such a central focus of today's "liberation theology," nor that under the influence of that movement Jewish theologians, too, have been reemphasizing the political implications of the Passover and its liturgy, or Haggadah.[119] The Lord's own last supper, clearly paschal in its con-

---

118. See esp. D. S. M. Hamilton, *Through the Waters* (Edinburgh: T. & T. Clark, 1989), ch. 3.

119. On the Eucharist in this connection, see, e.g., T. Balasuriya, *The Eucharist and Human Liberation* (Maryknoll, N.Y.: Orbis Books and London: SCM, 1979); G. Gutiérrez,

text and significance, like the church's re-presentation or *anamnesis* of it (1 Cor. 11:24), and the Passover itself, are all remembrances — "dangerous memories"[120] for those who take their subversive implications seriously — of the liberation of Hebrew slaves from political subjugation in Egypt. Who could sacramentally reenact the Exodus and then so privatize and spiritualize the meaning of that liturgy as to suppress its address to the oppressive conditions of our divided sociality and to the despotic powers of death and alienation which, publicly as well as inwardly, hold human beings in their grip of bondage?

Our paschal remembrance of the death of Egypt's firstborn and Pharaoh's hordes seditiously warns humanity's present captors and tormentors that they, too, shall let the people go, not at the say-so of the first Moses but through the cross of the Last, himself the final paschal lamb. At the same time the eucharistic bread and wine promise to the hungry, the poor, and those robbed of equity and justice in the world, of their own future in a land of promised liberty. And while the broken and the sick, the imprisoned and the naked, whom Jesus called his own, await with patience or endurance the coming of the righteous judge into his promised kingdom (Mt. 25:31-46; 26:29; Mk. 14:25; Lk. 22:18, 30), there is abundant paschal manna to sustain them through their desert pilgrimage (Jn. 6:31ff., 48ff.). Real food, for the body as well as for the mind and spirit, will be shared with the world whenever with any authenticity eucharistic food is shared in the church. As Christ himself fed the hungry and ate meals with sinners, told stories of banquets for the flotsam and jetsam on the edges of society, he fulfilled the promise in his mother's song of a new order where the hungry would be fed and the rich emptied of their affluence (Lk. 1:46ff.). So it is that amid the wilderness of our own decaying order, from wretched urban ghettoes to Africa's parched and famished, war-torn deserts and the raped and starving victims of "ethnic cleansing" in "civilized" European cities, the Last Supper continues visibly to proclaim a future of freedom, peace, and plenty in a fellowship of divine and human unity, and commits the

---

Theology of Liberation (Maryknoll, N.Y.: Orbis Books, 1988), pp. 262ff.; R. M. Brown, *Spirituality and Liberation* (Philadelphia: Westminster Press, 1988); B. J. Lee, ed., *Alternative Futures for Worship*, vol. 3: *The Eucharist* (Collegeville, Minn.: Liturgical Press, 1987). See also J. A. T. Robinson, *On Being the Church in the World* (London: SCM, 1960), ch. 3. On the "liberation" significance of Passover, see esp. D. Cohn-Sherbok, *On Earth as It Is in Heaven: Jews, Christians and Liberation Theology* (Maryknoll, N.Y.: Orbis Books, 1987), esp. ch. 4; also J. M. Stallings, *Rediscovering Passover: A Complete Guide for Christians* (San Jose, Calif.: Resource Publications, 1989); and S. Fine, "Passover, Matzah, and Sacred History," in *Explorations*, vol. 6, no. 12 (Philadelphia: American Interfaith Institute, 1992).

120. See B. J. Lee and M. A. Cowan, *Dangerous Memories* (Kansas City, Mo.: Sheed & Ward, 1986).

priestly church to penultimate realizations of that future within the present world.

Of course, those committed, on Christian or other grounds, to a more immediate, humanly engineered overthrow of the status quo might well sneer that the sharing of bread and the pouring out of wine are acts too laughably esoteric, feeble, and inconsequential to disturb the sleep of any government or authority on earth. But that would misinterpret and miscalculate the power of Christ's death and burial of which these sacramental acts give intimation. The "word of the cross" is precisely that out of the very great hopelessness and inefficacy of love resisted and annihilated, there flowers forth reinvigorating and transforming energies which are even greater yet. The visible words of baptism and communion to the earth's poor and empty nobodies is precisely that the crucified and buried God is for them and with them, and has chosen them to confound the ascendent ones of power and substance in the world.

To celebrate with fittingly weak signs this power of the cross and grave is to do nothing other than to pray in confidence and trust for the coming of the kingdom of Christ crucified. The sacraments are forms of prayer, and they share fully both in prayer's mundane ineptitude and in the transcendent potentiality. Prayer is indeed the defining, paradigmatic form of the action which Christ's priestly body takes in and for the world. In their literal prayers, private and public, in their sacraments and ordinances, in every liturgical moment of their cyclic calendar, and in all their deeds outside the sanctuary consequent upon and corresponding to what they do within it, Christians participate in Christ, himself the Great High Priest. Eternally he shares humanity's infirmities as fellow sufferer, and as victim he endures re-crucifixion at their hands. He intercedes for their healing with the Father and pleads their case as advocate, and sends to comfort them the Spirit whose own beseeching, groaning, wordless prayer lifts their pain into the heart of the divine community when their own lips fall dumb in despair and numb bewilderment.

Christ, to be sure, never relinquishes his identity as the only priest, through whom alone humanity finds a place within the welcoming, expansive spaces of God's own triune life.[121] Indeed, the sinful, broken church is no less the object of Christ's prayer, recipient of his compassion, than the sinful, broken communities all around the church. Nevertheless, by faith and in the Spirit, Christians do participate in the obedience, the worship, and the prayer of Christ the Son, as they do in his ministry and mission to all the nations of the world. So it is that we may intercede for the crushed and disunited human be-

---

121. On the prayer of Christ, see esp. J. B. Torrance, "The Place of Jesus Christ in Worship," in Anderson, *Theological Foundations for Ministry,* pp. 348-69.

ings in our midst, and petition the God of love on behalf of all humanity, the victims and the perpetrators of inhumanity, injustice, and insensitivity. And all such supplication by the church, which yearns for God's weak, crucified power to prove more abundant yet than the destructive, sterile power of evil in the world, is itself an act of protest and dissent against the status quo.

Thus by the very act of prayer for daily bread the priestly, interceding church challenges modernity's myth of autonomy and self-sufficiency, our promethean belief in our own capacities to satisfy every need with our own resourcefulness and ingenuity, and secure the future for ourselves and our planetary home without a humble recognition of dependence, fragility, and accountability, or any expression of thanksgiving. And with that prayer, too, the church protests the worldly structures that provide an abundant constancy for a privileged few at the expense of permanent hunger and impoverishment for many. Thus could we shake the very foundations supporting the cruel mechanisms of the present world as a global, eco-economic system.

How might the rulers of this system quake if for a moment they thought that Christians truly meant to live defiantly according to their whispered petitions and strange, simple signs of bread and wine — those seditious words and acts which, in such contrast to the Devil's ways of doing things, invoke the doing of God's will upon the earth no less than high in heaven? Only because they doubt — with all too plausible excuse — our convictions and commitments, do the Pontius Pilates of our present world pay bored regard, if any, to our prayerful pledges of allegiance to a kingdom not of this world (Jn. 18:33ff.), and our attribution of power, glory, and authority only to the crucified God. To be sure, the weak and wounded lamb whom Caesar slew, overthrew the Roman Empire; and at the end, his enemies destroyed, he shall reign forever and ever. Only rarely, though in God's providence not never, were the Caesars and the *Führers,* the oligarchs and tyrants of the twentieth century, astonished at the willingness of that wounded lamb's disciples to challenge their injustices and wickedness, armed only with the weakness of the cross and grave, and with the power of prayer to tilt at the bulwarks of their despotism. Yet such is the constant calling of the prayerful, priestly church: to resist evil and division and promote the unity of Christ's just kingdom with strange gesticulations and quiet words attesting the lordship of the Crucified and Buried Lord.[122]

---

122. On prayer from this perspective, see Barth, *Prayer,* trans. S. F. Terrien (Philadelphia: Westminster, 1952) (also in Barth, *Prayer and Preaching* [London: SCM, 1964], and *The Christian Life* (*CD,* IV/4, Lecture Fragments, sect. 78) (Edinburgh: T. & T. Clark, 1981); J. Lochman, *The Lord's Prayer,* trans. G. W. Bromiley (Grand Rapids: Eerdmans, 1990); L. Boff, *The Lord's Prayer: The Prayer of Integral Liberation,* trans. T. Morrow (Mary-

Perhaps, then, our words of prayer and signs of water, bread, and wine may be as deceptively dangerous today as one long-murdered, buried corpse has proved to be. Yet decisive moments come to the church when it can no longer be enough to say that prayer is active work; and the conviction dawns that the only remaining way is courageously to *act*. Now concrete performance must give embodiment and force even to prayer's most defiant, trusting words. Often the measures which are summoned forth by prayer will take place in the corners of the world, as we have said: small, anonymous servant deeds of love, compassion, and simple presence. At times, however, the church can no longer keep its hands pure and unsullied by the ambiguities of power, but for the sake of the earth and its reunifying it must in the name of Christ, though probably not as Christian parties, enter the political realm and with its resources, influence, and leadership seek to shift the status quo toward a closer approximation to God's reign, which rests on no politics and shall eventuate through no human program and arrive on no human schedule.

Then again, occasionally, *in extremis,* those who would conform their actions to the church's words of preaching, prayer, and liturgy shall be constrained not to take up power for the gospel's sake but to oppose it, with powerful acts of disobedience. Are Christian resistance and civil disobedience not sometimes the only way left to confront, in the name of the crucified God, godlessness and godforsakenness within God's world? Such actions, if obedient to the cross of Christ and meant as signs of his justifying grace, will be truly righteous, however illegal or intolerable to those whose injustice they would thwart. Such righteous action, dissident but prayerful, and costly, perhaps even to the point of death, is the final, liberating possibility for men and women who would truly share in Christ's priesthood, engage in "the fellowship of his sufferings,"[123] as martyrs to his cross, buried beside him in his baptism. Christians who contemplate such worldly unrighteousness in order to oppose the world's unrighteousness must do so with discernment and restraint, in the spirit of the weakness of the cross itself, so that it is not their own moral courage, spiritual heroics, or sacrificial martyrdom that the world admires or they themselves boast of (Mt. 4:5ff.; 1 Cor. 1:31; 2 Cor. 10:17; 12:1ff.).

Equally, however, and by the same token, the church that refuses to coun-

---

knoll, N.Y.: Orbis Books, 1983); and J. de Gruchy, *Cry Justice!* (London: Collins and Maryknoll, N.Y.: Orbis Books, 1986). See also the intriguing exposition of the ethical and political implications of the Lord's Prayer in the context of the nuclear arms race, in "The Report of the Special Committee on the Theological Implications of the Nuclear Threat to Life" (Edinburgh: Church of Scotland General Assembly Reports, 1987).

123. See Moltmann, *Way of Jesus Christ,* pp. 196ff.

tenance such prayerful, righteous action and resistance to the laws and expectations of the world, for the world's own sake, forfeits thereby the name of Christ, the messiah crucified between two bandits, who made his grave with the wicked. In its cowardice and caution, its fearfulness of the worldly principalities, or its carelessness for the wretched of the earth, such a church has surrendered its identity as an Easter Saturday community. For that is a people born out of the grave itself to bear witness even unto death to the buried one by whose blood our fractured sociality has been restored to unity and whose annihilation means life for all humanity.[124]

124. D. Bonhoeffer, of course, provided the twentieth-century church with a paradigm of Christian disobedience. In addition to his own thoughts on such matters in *Ethics* and *Letters and Papers from Prison*, the multiple accounts of his life, his "treachery" against Hitler, and his execution by the German state, see the highly pertinent little book by his nephew and biographer Eberhard Bethge, *Prayer and Righteous Action in the Life of Dietrich Bonhoeffer* (Belfast: Christian Journals Ltd., 1979). And on the case, not a little influenced by Bonhoeffer, for Christian disobedience in the struggle against apartheid in South Africa, see, e.g., *The Trial of Beyers Naudé: Christian Witness and the Rule of Law* (London: Search Press, 1975), esp. Appendix I: "Divine and Civil Obedience"; also C. Villa-Vicencio and J. de Gruchy, eds., *Resistance and Hope;* and A. Boesak, *If This Is Treason I Am Guilty,* and *Walking on Thorns* (Grand Rapids: Eerdmans, 1984).

CHAPTER TEN

Living the Story in Personal Life

I. Malignancy: An Easter Saturday Year

To begin this concluding chapter, may "the author" break his own literary rules and stifle his professorial instincts long enough to become, for a moment, "I" — the better to ask what it means for any human being to be an "I" in the light of Christ's cross and grave? Then let the author say that I embarked upon this study — rather presumptuously, I now suspect — not having undergone in personal life anything that could without hyperbole be labeled an "Easter Saturday" experience; but that I conclude this project no longer in that fortunate (or impoverished?) condition. For somewhere in the middle of its writing (spot the seam!) this volume sustained an interruption of many moons, and the fabric of my personal and vocational history a long, disabling gash. Wistfully now I recall being publicly declared "at the height of my powers," just weeks before whatever creative juices flowed through me were suddenly dammed up. Several years' worth of physical, mental, and spiritual energy drained away in the fatigue of disease, surgery, and therapy. And the impetus of life was arrested by a hiatus of waiting, demonic invasion, and near-termination, which in the circumstances almost demanded to be thought of as an Easter Saturday analogy.

This long, empty Sabbath was filled with the excision and recurrence of a tumorous excrescence of considerable magnitude and menace; the "liberation" of a lung and the slow, puffing process of proving its redundancy; and the exquisite ambiguities of radiation therapy, which seems to incinerate "good" cells at an only slightly slower rate than wicked ones. In the middle of this mid-life crisis (which could yet prove closer to my life's end than to its middle) were

403

twelve months of Easter Saturday writ intense and large: an exact calendar year of hospitalized and homebound harrowing, the suspended, gravelike, animation of high-dose chemotherapy.

This was cancer treatment which would do me good if it did not kill me first; and indeed it meant close shaves with death, as white blood cells perilously plummeted in number; seeming aeons of nausea and wretchedness; cruel rhythms of bodily dysfunction as systems of intake and output alternately collapsed; the oddity — and chill! — of sudden hairlessness; the equally peculiar loathsomeness of food and dread at every meal; ever longer and deeper troughs of debility and enervation; and mercifully brief spells of disoriented panic, unable to hold fast mentally to the day of the week or the spelling of one's name. Such losses of appearance and identity, of dignity, control, and almost life itself, brought "Saturday" moments of farewell, grief, and preparations for the end, consequent upon the disappearance of tomorrow. For like the first Easter Saturday, this was a time of unbounded waiting, of hanging on — sometimes by the hour — without any guarantee of a future to be hung on for, of patiently and otherwise enduring a rupture which might prove no lacunal interruption pending eventual resumption, but cessation pure and simple. This meant in turn my own paschal descent into forsakenness, where sensations and emotions so overwhelmed my powers of description that even the closest loved ones could not understand, and where the comforting assurance of God's presence could teasingly evade my conscious grasp, locking me in the solitude of divine absence and spiritual void, of prayers unanswered, perhaps because unuttered.

All of this spiritual and physical exhaustion brought me close to an agonizing year-end decision, whether to be done with further treatment altogether, to choose however many months of seminormal and productive life, and then perhaps its closure, in preference to the prolongation of a living death: mere survival, bare, enfeebled, uncreative. Sheer grace, however, in the form of positive tests and scans, an encouraging prognosis, and a doctor's own wise sense of timing, intervened to end the therapeutic nightmare and deliver me from decision day. Thus, alive and relatively well for now, even with residual effects in plenty, I can reflect upon my analogous Easter Sabbath as another ending which after all became a new tomorrow; as a year of death transcended, though not cancelled, by a resurrection season; an experience of separation and rupture that gave way to reunion and resumption; a demonic episode where evil increased, but grace abounded even more.

Here, beyond even the surplus of new life over moribund existence, of stabilizing health, returning energies, and quickening activity, there abides a "how much more" of simple thankfulness. Grounds for gratitude multiply: spine-tingling miracles of providential timing — by which malignancy was first detected, financial coverage secured, surgeons and physicians extraordinary discovered, and new "wonder drugs" released; the banter and much laughter that frequently echoed through the valley of my darkness; the discovery with family and special friends of whole new levels of resourcefulness and love, and of wide, unimagined networks of caring and support; and the post-crisis opportunity now, however brief or lengthy, to discard the trivial and shallow and fill every moment and relationship with meaning, intensity, and value.

But above all I must be grateful for the unsought gift of solidarity: solidarity, that is, with the human race in some at least of its universal Easter Saturday afflictions. The question "Why me?" is just too foolish and myopic to be asked in situations such as mine, though one knows it often is. Much more realistic is the question "Why not me?" Why should I expect (because a believer? an ordained minister, perhaps? or maybe a theologian?!) to be exempt from the cancers, or the floods and famines, accidents and disasters, which bedevil sisters and brothers all around me? And by what extravagant mercy have I thus far survived that to which so many others tragically succumb?

How, in any case, was it possible — I now ask myself in retrospect — to contemplate writing of the first and every Easter Saturday, humanity's myriad occasions of godforsakenness and godlessness in company with the God of Jesus Christ, without having known an Easter Saturday myself? Perhaps, even now, I may conclude that it is not a strict prerequisite for hearing, thinking, and living the story of Christ's cross and grave to have oneself approached the grave, and thus to have been able to juxtapose a personal story with the normative narrative of death and resurrection. But such an experience can do no harm, presumably! It is surely no bad thing for those who would meditate upon "the death of God" to confront full face the perishability of humanness, our inexorable decay and transience, by spending time among the dying and those given up for dead.

How many of us would ever explore the dark extremities of our own humanity were we not from time to time thrown into them involuntarily? "Necessity is laid upon me," wrote the apostle Paul; and mostly it is only of necessity, through the inescapability of life's misfortunes, and not in free discipleship or loving service, that we ever enter into solidarity with those who suffer and die, often in despair or unbelief. One there was who set his face toward Jerusalem, a shepherd who of his own accord laid down his life for sheep. For the rest of us, not as volunteers but conscripts, not in freedom but in the chains of accident or sickness, do we make our Easter Saturday graves with the wretched or the wicked.

Yet there, beside our sisters and our brothers, the godless and the godforsaken of the earth, however unwillingly we share their lot, we may indeed find ourselves compelled and enabled so to listen to and think the story of God's burial as to discover that story's livability, the freedom and responsibility that come with acting out Christ's Easter Saturday as the key to selfhood, identity, and personal fulfillment. Certainly with reluctance in my own case, as a passive patient and a hostage to the body's own caprice, I may, through suffering and brushing death in company with others, have freshly discovered who I am, who I could be, and who I shall become in God's good time.

Enough, though, for the moment of this obtrusive, exhibitionist "I." Let "the author" explore further this meaning for our personhood of the Easter Saturday experience — how, mysteriously, it is that in and around the narrow grave which haunts and taunts us daily, which sometimes prematurely captures us but in which the humanity of God was once in history laid to rest, there flowers the broad expanse of abundant human life.

II. Mortality: An Easter Saturday Existence

To live compulsorily or freely through a personal Easter Saturday provides the opportunity to embrace at last the most ambiguous, hideous, but potentially liberating, truth about oneself and all of humankind. That is the truth about mortality, the terrible or beneficient, but in either case ineluctable fact that we shall die. Even those who come to recognize this truth and welcome it as a liberating blessing fear, hate, and avoid it. For we all dedicate stupendous mental, psychic, and physical energy to the postponement, domestication, or outright denial of the surd finitude of our existence. We are terminal and dying from the day of birth, of course, and our death in its magnitude, completeness, and finality is preceded by serial smaller deaths, comprising breakdown, separation, loss, and closure. These discontinuities and ruptures in body, mind, or psyche, relationship, career, or milieu, should keep us constantly alert to the approach of life's last, inevitable terminus. But because, like the author's own, these penultimate Easter Saturdays prove after all, and by definition, to be only interruptions, temporary stoppages and intermissions, which in time give way to further life and movement, to miniature resurrections after miniature deaths, they easily seduce us with the illusion that our staccato progress forward can be indefinitely sustained. There is no guarantee, then, that even in the darkest valleys of human experience, any of us shall grasp the opportunity fully and forever to know the mortal truth about ourselves.

That there is a God-given goodness to this truth, and that human beings, with limitless capacity for falsehood, deny its veracity and thereby convert it to an evil and demonic truth — this wrenching ambiguity of our mortalness is amply exposed in our three-day story of death, burial, and resurrection. But it is just as unmissable in Scripture's originating narratives, which through mythic particularities set the human condition in a universal context. Out of these Genesis stories, too, emerge the major premises of biblical anthropology, the Christian doctrine of creation as it relates to humankind in its finite creaturehood.

In the first instance, the sixth-day verdict of the Creator, confirmed in the rest, satisfaction, and blessing of the seventh, is that the male and female creatures, shaped in their Maker's image, are very good (Gen. 1:31–2:3). And the inescapable inference from the subsequent story of the Garden of Eden is that precisely upon the frail products of dust, whose life and breath are not their own but the gift of Another who can and shall withdraw the gift as easily as give it, has the divine benediction been pronounced (Gen. 2:6). It is good, therefore, very good, to be earthly and finite, mortal and dependent; and it is with that affirmation that a Christian theology of death begins. Even though Christian tradition has, in fact, often bestowed upon the pre-Fall Adam and Eve an immortality, or at least the possibility of never dying, it is the likelier meaning of these stories that even in paradise, the true, intended condition of the human is temporality and transience, not God-like durability, and therefore of benign finitude and boundedness, without the curse which perishability and termination become to those who withhold consent to their own mortality and refuse to embrace it willingly and gratefully.[1]

1. The question whether Adam would have died if he had not sinned has greatly occupied Christian theology from its beginnings. It cannot, of course, be answered, as some would have it, by appealing simply to Paul: "sin came into the world through one man, and death came through sin, and so death spread to all because all have sinned" (Rom. 5:12). For that begs the question of exactly what Paul is referring to as the death that came through sin. His text helps us to ask rather than to answer the question whether there is a natural or physical mortality, a dying or death belonging to creaturehood as such, in distinction from the sin-related experience of "second death" or "spiritual death," death as an unnatural enemy, the effect or punishment of sin. See here R. Niebuhr, *The Nature and Destiny of Man* (New York: C. Scribner's Sons, 1941, 1964), vol. 1, pp. 171ff. Augustine, Aquinas, Luther, and Calvin all in general view every aspect of death as a consequence of sin; but there are grounds for finding a contrary view: in Irenaeus, e.g., and in the contemporary theology of both Barth and Tillich, who, though from very different starting points, reach the same conclusion that humanity is "naturally" mortal. See esp. Barth, *CD*, III/2, 587-640: "Ending Time," and, as an example, p. 631: "Finitude, then, is not intrinsically negative and evil. There is no reason why it should not be an anthropological necessity, a determination of true and natural man, that we should one day have to die, and therefore merely have been." See, too, P. Tillich, *Systematic Theology* (Chicago: University of Chicago Press and London: Nisbet, 1957), vol. 2, pp. 66ff.; e.g., p. 66: "man is deter-

The New Testament story of the cross and empty tomb is the profound and dramatic confirmation of the Creator's Yes to our mortality. It is not just (just!) that in the death and burial of the human Jesus, God's own triune self became identified with and as a dead man, united with and fulfilled through the perishability of our humanity. This soteriological event, the defeat of death through subjection to everything that is corrupt and evil about our humanness, suggests perhaps that mortality itself, as embodied in the crucified and buried flesh of Jesus, is the captivity from which God would deliver us. What must be isolated as a distinct and logically prior dimension of this happening, however, is that this divine, redemptive solidarity with human death is the act of the *Creator.* Who is it, we have asked so many times, that could raise this dead and finished one from the cold finality of Joseph's tomb but the one who makes everything in heaven and earth and summons things into existence out of nothing? It is the one Creator, the same Father in the Trinity who brought forth light and life in the beginning, who now brings forth the crucified Son from his grave.[2] The Easter raising of the human, buried Son thus ratifies and intensifies God's original affirmation of our creaturehood and its mortality. The resurrection of a corpse is the ultimate assurance that it is good to be bodily, carnal, temporal; and that God should say this resurrecting Yes to the human body only by first identifying with that body in the grave confirms that it is good and fitting not only to be fleshly, but for our flesh to perish, to come to termination and ultimate decay.

Thus do the cross and especially the grave sum up scandalously all that we mean by and infer from incarnation: the Creator's own embrace of utter humanness. As Bethlehem affirms our creaturehood in its origins and frail beginnings, so Easter Saturday sanctifies creaturehood in its departures and frail endings. From womb to tomb, God accepts — and therefore bids us also to accept — our dustlike transience and perishing. Perhaps we may therefore find a grain of truth in the fanciful patristic exegesis[3] which saw Christ's burial not

---

mined by his finitude. He is given over to his natural fate. He came from nothing, and he returns to nothing. He is under the domination of death and is driven by the anxiety of having to die. . . . Man is naturally mortal." On this, see also Jüngel, *Death,* pp. 91ff.; K. Rahner, *On the Theology of Death* (New York: Herder and Herder and London: Burns and Oates, 1961), p. 42; Weber, *Foundations of Dogmatics,* vol. 1, pp. 618ff.; R. S. Anderson, *Theology, Death and Dying* (New York and Oxford: Blackwell, 1986), pp. 51ff.; and M. J. Harris, *Raised Immortal* (Basingstoke: Marshall, Morgan & Scott, 1983 and Grand Rapids: Eerdmans, 1985), esp. ch. 7.

2. See esp. von Balthasar, *Mysterium Paschale,* pp. 204-5.

3. See, e.g., Gregory of Nyssa, "In Sanctum et Salutare Pascha" (On the Holy and Saving Pascha), in *Gregorii Nysenni Opera,* ed. E. Gebhardt (Leiden: E. J. Brill, 1967), vol. 9, pp. 309ff.; trans. by S. G. Hall in *The Easter Sermons of Gregory of Nyssa,* ed. A. Spira and

only as the second day of the *triduum,* a day of silence and descent to hell, but also as a day of rest, another, final seventh day, reenacting and fulfilling the Sabbath of the first creation. Thus, as Christ's mortal body lies motionless in death, the Creator rests again, well pleased and satisfied with the finite, passing creature, divinely made in the divine likeness, who is also now the divine beloved Son and our own Second Adam.

Of course, it is precisely the divine truth about his own non-deity, the temporality and dependence of his status as a creature, that the first Adam refuses to concede, and defiantly rebels against. Signs and rationalizations of this universal adamic disobedience and denial, and of its tragic consequences, are all around us. It has found much philosophical expression in the history of human thought and religiosity, not least, for the West, in the Greek tradition to which we have frequently referred. Here the decaying physicality of the body is frankly recognized, but despised as false and evil and abstracted from the essence of our humanness. That which is good and true and beautiful about us is the spiritual, the immortal soul, divine and incorruptible, which escapes from the inessential body at the end point of its decay, and returns to the eternal home which it has always known.

This hellenism has profoundly penetrated Christian thinking, with vast consequences for the church's classical attitudes toward the body and sexuality, toward heaven and eternal life, and not least toward death and dying. The denial of the goodness of the God-created human body, including its decay and temporal boundaries, has often been identified with Christian virtues, though it is in fact quite alien to our biblical roots. And ironically this negativity finds limitless expression in our modern secular culture, which fondly imagines itself to be delivered from the heteronomous shackles of Christianity's moral, doctrinal, and scriptural norms. Many of us inhabit a society profoundly embarrassed and discomforted by death, as an alien intruder upon our facile, optimistic dreams, an intolerable falsifying of our cherished myths of immortality: that youth can be perpetuated, bodies perfected, disease eradicated, death deferred, and every problem solved. Indeed, it seems that our society can deal with death only as something which stands outside of life, to be avoided, resisted, concealed, even survived, rather than acknowledged and embraced as a natural dimension to life, supplying proper and necessary edges to the fabric of existence.[4]

C. Klock (Cambridge, Mass.: Philadelphia Patristic Foundation Ltd., 1981). Von Balthasar, too, conceives of the Word resting from its labors on Holy Saturday, as on the seventh day of creation. See, e.g., *Man in History* (London and Sydney: Sheed and Ward, 1968), p. 283.

4. There is a vast, and quite widely read, corpus of contemporary literature on the place of death, dying, funerals, etc., in modern Western, and especially American, society. It

No one has exposed more ruthlessly the psychic roots of this evasion and dishonesty, not as a modern or North American phenomenon only, but as an intrinsic human response to "the terror" of mortality, than Ernest Becker in *The Denial of Death*.[5] Most human beings, he suggests, maintain a facade of mental health by colluding with the social constructs of denial and adopting a bogus heroism which narcissistically presumes oneself to be invulnerable while all around succumb to death. The condition, by contrast, of those who fail to repress the fearful knowledge of mortality, and cannot play along with society's pretense, is known as schizophrenia. Their honesty and "extreme human creativity" force them "to live on the brink of madness."[6]

For Becker, there is, to be sure, a Kierkegaardian leap of faith to be made — authentically heroic — which entrusts itself to the mysterious life-force and so snaps the chains of our anxious captivity to death. But the object of this trust is undefined and undefinable; and in any case, Becker's diagnosis of humanity's condition is itself a denial of the Christian insistence that, before it is terrible and hostile, our mortality is a welcome, blessed friend. Our faith, that is, comprises a living reminder to ourselves and to our fellow human beings that, anterior to everything rightly regarded as evil, tragic, and destructive about death, there are "seventh day" and "second day" aspects of mortality which beg to be accepted and consented to. To live the Easter Saturday story is to acknowledge and cherish, as the precondition of our self-fulfillment, the limitations, postponements, and terminations that belong to creaturehood. Indeed, it is to let

---

includes such classics as J. Mitford, *The American Way of Death* (Greenwich, Conn.: Fawcett Publications, 1963); E. Waugh, *The Loved One* (Harmondsworth: Penguin Books, 1951 and New York: Little, Brown and Company, rev. ed. 1971); E. Kübler-Ross, *On Death and Dying* (New York: Macmillan, 1969 and London: Tavistock Publications, 1970); and R. A. Moody, *Life after Life* (New York: Bantam Books, 1976). See also P. Aries, *The Hour of Our Death,* trans. H. Weaver (New York: A. A. Knopf, 1981 and Harmondsworth: Penguin Books, 1983). Theologically, no one has more effectively indicted our morbid refusal to grant death an entrance into natural life than Arthur McGill, in his superbly apposite lectures, posthumously published as *Death and Life: An American Theology,* ed. C. A. Wilson and P. M. Anderson (Philadelphia: Fortress, 1987). An equally devastating critic on this continent is Douglas Hall; see esp. his *Lighten Our Darkness: Toward an Indigenous Theology of the Cross* (Philadelphia: Westminster, 1976), and *God and Human Suffering* (Minneapolis: Augsburg, 1986). See also H. Thielicke, *Death and Life,* trans. E. H. Schroeder (Philadelphia: Fortress, 1970), and *Living with Death,* trans. G. W. Bromiley (Grand Rapids: Eerdmans, 1983); also L. O. Mills, ed., *Perspectives on Death* (Nashville and New York: Abingdon, 1969).

5. E. Becker, *The Denial of Death* (New York and London: Macmillan, 1973). For a sympathetic but not uncritical analysis of this amazing book, from a Christian point of view, see Anderson, *Theology, Death and Dying,* pp. 29ff.

6. Becker, *Denial,* p. 63.

oneself be taught to be a mortal creature by the immortal Maker's own self-emptying accommodation to one's condition and one's death. Only through such awesome, humble grace may we learn to be at peace with ourselves and embrace the truth of who we really are.

To be confined for days on end to a hospital bed, caught in a web of wires, tubes and drips, unable to venture far, in any case, because of lassitude, giddiness, and a dominating queasiness, and, above all, in the vulnerability of the horizontal, to see the management of life surrendered up to doctors, nurses, and administrators: these all too familiar experiences of modern sickness provide a hard lesson in the realities of human limitations. Outside such institutional experiences, most of us in the developed world ground our lifestyles in the illusion of limitlessness, and indeed in the actuality of boundless freedoms and resources. In a culture which worships at the altar of "growth" and assumes the desirability and possibility of uninhibited expansion, it is easy to ignore the bleak limitations of food and medicine, security, space, and opportunity by which much of the human race is still grievously constrained. And such forgetfulness of the limits upon others perpetuates denial of the real limits upon ourselves behind the shell of our well-being, liberty, and plenty.[7]

Central to the good news in the Christian three-day story is its demonstration that death does not have the last word upon human destiny: that God sets limits to death, and to death's power to oppress and limit life. But that this Sunday victory over death comes only through a Sabbath when life has been snuffed out by death, is confirmation that the God who limits death also uses death to limit life. And that circumscription is not restricted to the final boundary of literal death. Rather, its exiguity reaches backward into life, setting bounds to and within our existence as a whole. By God's good will, life is not without its demarcations and its borders, its thresholds and its plateaus. There is much, whether we acknowledge it or not in our fantasies of freedom and perfection, that we cannot do: limits to youthfulness and health, to capacities of every kind, and to relationships, which are better conceded than resisted. And there is much that we *should* not do: moral and spiritual boundaries, like those around the tree at Eden's center, marked out by God, which we infringe only at tragic cost to our true humanness. Made in God's own image, with such unique potentiality among the creatures — the infinite array of possibilities, of will and action, vision and imagination, that go with moral freedom and self-transcendence — we find all boundaries arbitrary, contradictory, burdensome. Thus is our freedom fraught intrinsically with ambiguity and tension. And it not only offends the modern, egalitarian, democratic mind, but, as the authors

7. See Hall, *God and Human Suffering,* pp. 55, 58-59.

411

of Genesis so perspicaciously present it, provokes inherent discontent within the human spirit, that with the gift of freedom should come also the requirement of obedience. That others or Another should assume authority over us, imposing limits on us which constrain our thoughts and actions, seems so unjust an imposition upon our will to self-expression, and invites instinctive rebellion and defiance, But death as an authority over us, defiance of which is necessarily inept and ineffective, mocks such rebellion; and it is, if we would only so receive it, a benign teacher of the mystery that precisely in obedience to the just and loving authority of God, who sets our limits, and not in the ego's mutinous autonomy, are true freedom and self-transcendence to be found.

Now few of the limitations of creaturehood are more irksome than those that belong to temporality. If death is the ultimate expression of our boundedness by time, reminding us from birth that we are not only temporal but temporary, destined to pass away and be no more, time also sets penultimate but equally unyielding limits on our lives which mockingly torment us and elude our mastery. We may think, given the frantic pace of contemporary life and its demands for instant gratification, that the power of time to tease us is a modern discovery; but the Scriptures themselves are fully aware of time's duplicity. That is the capacity of minutes and hours, days and years to creep so slowly when we long for them to end as soon as possible, and yet to scurry by in the very situations which we wish might never end. These infuriating variations in time's passage — supposedly so constant — have the Psalmist, for example, reflecting at one moment on the brief elapse of aeons — a thousand of our years like one night to the Creator, and our life span gone "like a sigh" (Ps. 90:4-10) — and at another on the aching, aging slowness of deliverance for the afflicted: "my eyes grow dim with waiting for my God" (Ps. 69:1-3). Indeed, this need to wait, the Bible isolates as the particular burden of the creature's temporal limitations; and the willingness to wait with endurance, patience, and hope as the true mark of faith and means to blessing (e.g., Lev. 3:25-27; Rom. 5:3-5; 8:24-25).

Time as we experience it is by definition a denial of instantaneousness, a requirement to wait; for its units are not punctilious but extended, not concurrent but sequential. This necessity for patience laid upon God's creatures, to which the Creator has become astoundingly and willingly subjected, is graphically portrayed in the narrative of Easter Saturday. For that, as we saw, is precisely a day of waiting, a hiatus and a barrier which prevents a knowing, onward rush to victory and joy by interjecting a painful pause, empty of hope and filled instead with death and grief, with memories of failure and betrayal, of abandonment and anguish. And it is across this motionless, unhurried interstice between yesterday and tomorrow, this deadly stasis of inertia which faith has been constrained to speak of as descent to hell, that God's own self is suspended upon Holy Saturday. Here in horrid captivity to time's protracted sluggishness, the Father and the Son — separated by the sin of our rebellion against limits — must await reunion through the Spirit at humanity's own pace.

It is through participation in the patience of God's Spirit that we learn the gift of waiting which restores us to ourselves from the destructive urgency of our desires and aspirations, and slows the tempo of our intemperance. Where better than in a hospital, one wonders, might a contemporary westerner confront this necessity and fittingness of waiting? Compelled to be *a* patient, however impatient, one might be driven at last to reassess the childishness of modern men and women, reputedly now come of age, who demand the instant satisfying of their hungers and throw tantrums of frustrations when denied — and so deny themselves the more delightful gratifying of desire after postponement and anticipation. Like children, too, we have come to tolerate only the briefest demands upon our concentration and attention span, and in our fears of time's expanses we fill each moment with noise, activity, entertainment, and narcosis, to dull our consciousness of each day's prolongation. Maybe only in an alien environment, whose rhythms — such as those which turn a hospital's nighttime into day — clash with those of regular life, and where much time is spent waiting not for what we shall do next, but for what will next be done for us, and particularly to us, can teach us today "the stature of waiting." That is, the propriety and healthiness of being patient, of waiting for the other and being waited on, in the honest acknowledgment of our dependency and need.[8]

Even in circumstances, medical or otherwise, on the surface most undignified, it is possible to discover a dignity in being passive, patient, and reliant, a calm honesty about the truth of our need for the assistance and resourcefulness of others, which contrasts with the defensive bluster of an ego which must maintain the sham of self-sufficiency. At heart, only those can give who know first how to receive, just as one can truly love only if willing to be loved — which can be so hurtful to our pride. When in humility and maturity we do acknowledge the limits of our own reserves, let ourselves depend on others and be served by them, we are in fact unlocking the truth about relationality which is the image in us of God's own triune being.

8. See the superb study by W. H. Vanstone, *The Stature of Waiting* (London: Darton Longman and Todd, 1982), which, in the light of the passion story of "The God who Waits" (ch. 5), brings out well the connection between waiting and needing. See also his ch. 3: "The Status of Patient." Cf. McGill, *Death and Life,* esp. pp. 61ff. On the ambiguities of "dependence," see my "God as Cripple: Disability, Personhood and the Kingdom of God," *Pacific Theological Review* 16.1 (1982): 13-18, esp. 15-16.

The God exposed to impotence and needfulness on Calvary is, as we have seen, one whose very Godness, as trinitarian community, consists in reciprocity and mutual reliance. God *is* dependence rendered infinite, unable to be Father without the Son, or Son without the Father, just as the Spirit, neither self-generating nor self-regarding, proceeds from the Father of the Son as necessary source, and finds its raison d'être in the glorifying of them both.[9] Likewise it is not as solipsistic, independent egos, but relational, loving members of community, who find meaning in and through others and the exchange of mutual dependence with them, that we come to our true selves, enriched in our humanity, not demeaned, by these limits on our self-determination. We touch upon the mystifying blessedness of those limitations when we feel gratitude rather than resentment toward those around us for help and support without which we know we could not live each day, let alone in times of crisis. So, too, might our years as finite, dependent creatures of an all-sufficient, self-originating Maker constitute extended hymns of praise, that such a God should care for us in our weakness and our need, and of thanksgiving for the sheer gratuitousness of life utterly beyond our own creating, and sustained yet lovingly and lavishly bestowed upon us.

Perhaps it is chief among the grounds of our thankfulness for life that this is a gift which is in time withdrawn. Hallelujah that our lives do not, like God's, endure for aye! Such a doxology, of course, is foolishness to many; yet to understand it is perhaps the sum of wisdom; and it is certainly the precondition of our pastoral caring of the sick, the dying, and the bereaved. Perhaps the greatest lesson that the author learned in recent years is that his birth certificate came inscribed with no contract guaranteeing him a span of threescore years and ten. As the Psalmist knew, even if vitality and health gain one some extension beyond that arbitrary measure, our time will soon be gone and we shall fly away (Ps. 93:10). Brevity is our life's condition, its terminus always approaching and assured; and it is very good. Amid all that is frequently outrageous in the disfiguring and cutting down of lovely human life, there are always grounds for acceptance and for gratitude — for the contents and the quality of life which can far outdo the value of quantity and length; for the enhancement that closure and finale set upon everything that goes before; and for deliverance from the special curse of endlessness.

There is a superfluity of beauty in real flowers, not in spite of but because of their fragility and flimsiness, beyond that of the most convincing but unwithering plastic imitations. And recognition of the evanescent beauty in our precarious dust- and grass- and flower-like existence, is fundamental to the Bi-

9. See, e.g., McGill, *Suffering,* esp. chs. 4 and 6.

ble's anthropology. Likewise, it is grounds not for complaint but satisfaction that our lives, which always tell a story, do have a final chapter, even if sometimes prematurely written. There is for each of us, in the unplumbed mystery of human endings, an unraveling of the plot and a closing of the book, which permits those who remember us, or even, if we are so blessed, ourselves in our last days, to look back at a history completed and complete within itself, to be cherished for the manner and the matter of its passage, regardless of its longitude or the circumstances of its termination.

All too many terminations — from violence, accident, disease — are, of course, cruel, grotesque, and savage, closures demonic not divine, which rightly invoke our indignation at the sullying of God-created beauty and the abbreviating of God-given time. To death's dark, monstrous travesties of God's creative purpose we shall soon return. For now, let the possibility of such malign conclusions simply be acknowledged, along with the certainty that a curtain of one form or another will surely fall upon our stage, and, by any measure, soon. Yet these facts do not summon us to fearful anger or resentment, but to courage for the facing of the truth, and to trust in the one who gave us life and will not leave us separated or unloved in its removal. The sufferer of cancer has surely pondered, probably as profoundly as any, the poignant addendum to death's certainty — which is the total uncertainty of when it will arrive. Humanity may choose to take it as the cruelest joke of a putative creator that we, alone of all the creatures, both know for sure that our end is coming, and are cast upon a sea of deep unknowing about the time and manner of its coming. An alternative, however, is set before us: not to curse this conundrum of our fate but to embrace it daily, grateful for the dignity of reflective consciousness it presupposes, and ready in God's mercy to face with candid courage and with hope both our knowledge and our ignorance of death.

We may be grateful, too, that however accursed may seem this certain and uncertain ending of our lives, its coming contains the promise of release from the even greater curse of endlessness. Not to know of an ending on its way, however unpredictable its timing, is indeed a fate worthy of our malediction. As those who suffer chronic pain, untreatable disease, unassuagable loneliness or grief, know all too well, the hellishness of present suffering might be rendered tolerable if only some fixed end point to their misery could be anticipated. It is not endings but their absence which truly demoralizes and robs us of our humanness. How foolish and hollow sound the protests of the healthy and the wealthy and the safe, against the unjust shortness of their lives, when heard against the cries of those who hopelessly endure the banal monotony of evil, unending cycles of poverty and famine, war, oppression and abuse, and for whom the shortening of life would be good news indeed. Ironically, with the

415

wry humor of the canon, the Scriptures open with humanity's rebellion against finite creaturehood, with its mortality and endings; but they close with Revelation's joy and promise that endings are indeed in sight for a humanity which finds the interminable harder to bear than termination. There shall be an end to pain and hunger, thirst and tears, to darkness, death, and everything accursed (Rev. 21; 22:1-5). But in this *eschaton* all who live forever in God's new creation, set free from the horror of unending, will not be divinized but at last become the creatures they were meant to be, at peace with the limits lovingly set for them by their Creator, whose Son himself embraces boundaries and affirms them, as the Alpha and Omega, the beginning and the end.

✳   ✳   ✳

The time thus comes to move on from all that can be positively said about the goodness of mortality and the propriety of God-provided boundaries, to more direct acknowledgment and exploration of everything blatantly negative, inimical, and baleful about our dying and our death. And where is mortality's duality and ambiguity set more sharply in relief than precisely on the cross and in the grave of this Alpha and Omega, the Lamb slain on Calvary for the world's redemption? For here, on the one hand, is the Second Adam, perfectly obedient, accepting humanity's limits, and sinlessly bowing to the mortal flesh of creaturehood. Unresisting and without denial, Jesus fulfills his humanness and ours through unalloyed consent to human termination. And, as we have conceived it, Jesus' completion of the perfect human life, through total yielding to a human death, is the very act of God's own being, an event in the history of triune deity. Jesus demonstrates divinity and actualizes Sonship, flawlessly enacting his filial obedience to the Father, precisely through his willingness not to act like God, with divine prerogatives and privileges, but, from the wilderness to Jerusalem, Gethsemane to Golgotha, to live, to suffer, and to die in utter humanness, refusing every temptation, including enticements on the cross itself (Mk. 15:29-32), supernaturally to elude our natural ending and refuse the last dregs of our perishable cup. Here, as we have said, does the everlasting Maker, Lord of life, teach us to be creatures and show us how to die.

On the other hand, the same death of this same Christ is the most extreme antithesis to human obedience and acceptance. Here, writ large and bloody, in the violence of crucifixion and its pouring out of hatred, vengeance, fear, is the cosmic climax and universal exposé of human sinfulness, our deadly antagonism against the Lord of life, and our tragic refusal of God's limits. We creatures, despising and rejecting our mortality, rebelliously destroy the Creator come to perfect our creaturehood; and we put to accursed, evil

416

death the truly human and obedient one willing to accept the blessing and goodness of mortality. Once again we are taken back from Joseph's garden to the Garden of Eden, where the story is that mortal human beings, wishing rather, like God, to be immortal — though later God would prove willing to be mortal — gracelessly repudiate the gift and the giver of good, created finitude. Sick irony, gallows humor, is the consequence;[10] for the mortality which the first Adam and his partner will not have cheerfully as gift and friend, they must bear repugnantly as bane and foe. Invited to trust that God will keep them secure in the vulnerability of their finitude, they — representing us — reach out in hubris for infinity and thus are thrown into a vulnerability against which there is no security, subjugations to suffering and death far more unacceptable than the limits they had been unwilling to accept. This tragedy provides a second plank for the construction of our theology of death, which does not replace the first, but must be set beside, however awkwardly, the affirmation of death's blessings.

So shielded are we often — by curtains, cosmetics, and conspiracies of silence — from the fact of death today that there is no guarantee, even in the modern hospital, our normal place of dying, that we shall be publicly, unblinkingly, exposed to the frequent awfulness and ugliness of death's reality. But as everyone with cancer, and even more so those with AIDS, can testify, the embarrassment, euphemism, credulity, even panic which disease can presently evoke betrays a deep awareness of death's anarchy and terror inside a culture which trumpets to itself the mastery of nature and defeat of death. We know more deeply than we dare admit, even to ourselves, the destructive forces at work in our environment, our bodies and our inner selves, and thus the hegemony of death over our supposed autonomy. Suppressed, then, yet all the more alive, is the biblical truth that whatever kind of friend mortality may be to humankind, death is also the last enemy of our Creator and ourselves, the summation of everything irrational, fiendish, and malevolent in our existence. Visible, to those who will look, in cancer wards, AIDS clinics, and children's hospitals, is the truth narrated from Genesis to Revelation, and supremely in the story of Christ's cross and tomb: that death is a demonic foe. Like all its forward troops, little deaths sent out in advance in the form of sickness and disease, death can be a cruel tyrant, harsh destroyer of God's good creation, not to be befriended, denied, or prettified, but rejected and opposed in warfare human and divine.

What has become a commonplace in today's theology of death helpfully clarifies the distinctive Christian honesty about death's evilness and the impla-

10. See here D. Hall, *God and Human Suffering*, pp. 78ff.

cable hostility it summons forth from God and from God's people. That is the familiar contrast, now, between the death of Socrates and that of Jesus Christ.[11] Socrates, as portrayed at least by Plato, embodying the Hellenistic philosophy of immortality but also foreshadowing our present-day denials and mythology, submits to death beautifully, serene at the prospect of fortunate release for his eternal essence from its bodily entombment and entrapment. Jesus, by contrast, prepares for death not with exhilaration that his soul shall soon escape a tomb, but with dread that his body shall soon be placed in one. That prospect means blood, sweat, tears, and agony in Gethsemane, howls of physical pain and dereliction of the spirit upon Calvary. Thus does Christ's death confirm the dimension of horror implicit in all human dying and all too explicit in the actuality of many deaths. The infernal images conjured up for us by Easter Saturday, and the grave's cold, solitary lifelessness, simply reinforce the scriptural perception that death is malign and monstrous, the negation of everything good and beautiful and fruitful about our lives and relationships as God's good creatures.

It is totally unavoidable, however unfashionable, in asking *why* Scripture views death in so negative a light as well as positively, that we trace a close connection between death's hostility and human sinfulness. That link must be drawn both with firmness and the utmost delicacy.[12] A steady nerve is necessary because it is repugnant to society, and to many in the church, it seems, to speak of sin at all today, above all in the context of suffering, disease and sin. Yet often that repugnance is engendered, or rationalized, by the all-too-direct connection which others in the church offensively allege between physical affliction and personal behavior. Hence the need for delicate discernment.

The biblical narrative of the fall, of course, turns upon the relation between death and disobedience. Death is the punishment for transgression, which the Creator threatens, the serpent scoffs at, and Adam and Eve must un-

---

11. See esp. O. Cullmann, *Immortality of the Soul or Resurrection of the Dead?* (London: Epworth Press, 1958); also in K. Stendahl, ed., *Immortality and Resurrection* (New York: Macmillan, 1965), ch. 1; Jüngel, *Death*, ch. 3; cf. Anderson, *Theology, Death and Dying*, pp. 37ff. For Plato's description of Socrates' suicide, see *Phaedo*, trans. H. Tredennick, in Plato, *The Last Days of Socrates* (Harmondsworth: Penguin Books, 1969). The common view in Greek philosophy and religion that the soul is imprisoned in the body is summed up in the play of words *soma/sema* (body/tomb); see, e.g., Plato, *Georgias,* 493a, trans. W. Hamilton (Harmondsworth: Penguin Books, 1960).

12. I attempted such a balancing act in "Keeping Our Nerve: AIDS and the Doctrine of Sin," *Austin Seminary Bulletin* 105.1 (1989): 23-36. Some themes explored there are revisited below. See also here Barth, *CD*, III/2, esp. pp. 596-610; Weber, *Foundations of Dogmatics*, vol. 1, pp. 618ff.; Rahner, *Theology of Death*, ch. 2; Anderson, *Theology, Death and Dying*, esp. ch. 4; McGill, *Death and Life*, pp. 52ff.; and Hall, *God and Human Suffering*, ch. 3.

dergo, beginning with expulsion from the Garden (Gen. 2:17; 3:4, 22-24). As many interpret it, we have seen, all mortality, including its quite physical dimensions, is thus portrayed as consequential upon human disobedience; and all of life and nature, the very ground from which we come, is cursed with toil and pain, hostility and hardship, in intimation and extension of humanity's estrangement (Gen. 3:14-19). Death itself in the Old Testament becomes the place of dark and comfortless aloneness, the self-induced suffocation of those who turn their faces from the fountain and the source of life. Alienated from God, who takes our breath away and returns us to the dust, we die isolated and forgotten, cut off from the land — and the Lord — of the living (e.g., Pss. 88:5, 6, 11; 90:3; 104:29; Jer. 11:19).[13]

The New Testament agrees that death is the price of our estrangement from the grace of God, sin's "wages" (Rom. 6:23). We are dead in our trespasses (Eph. 2:1; Col. 2:13); and in James' ironical reflection on negative fertility, "sin, when fully grown, gives birth to death" (James 1:15). All of this prompts, even within the canon itself, the doubtful but tempting inference that each person's death, or preceding, deathlike suffering, is the direct consequence of his or her own private guilt. There is a "Wisdom" assumption, in Proverbs for example, that since the righteous flourish, misery signals wickedness. Yet what untold misery has been inflicted, sometimes self-inflicted, in the gospel's name, by extrapolations from this presumption. From canting moralizers who wag judgmental fingers at the sick and the diseased for the moral lapses thus being penalized, to the self-tortured victims of illness or bereavement who ask, instinctively it seems, "For what is God punishing me thus?" divine retribution is presupposed, inflicting disease, studiously and imperiously matching personal sin with condign suffering and death.

Scripture in fact raises its own indignant protest against this doctrine of God's vindictiveness — most loudly in the book of Job, which searingly falsifies the bonds between beatitude and innocence, culpability and woe. It is not the deeds and misdeeds of individuals which determine bane and blessing, nor is it in causal responsibility for our misfortunes, but beside us, as companion in their midst, that God is to be found. Jesus himself explicitly declines opportunities to attribute disablement, murder, and disaster to the victims' guiltiness (Jn. 9:3; Lk. 13:1-5). The author can attest that those who struggle with life-threatening disease or gross adversity, and are tempted by cruel external promptings, or the stirring of irrational guilt within, to detect the Almighty's hand in their afflictions, may take refuge in these dominical denials, and in every evangelical

---

13. On death in the OT, see esp. Jüngel, *Death,* pp. 61-80; Anderson, *Theology, Death and Dying,* pp. 38ff., 66ff.

assurance of God's equitable care of the unjust and the just (Mt. 5:45), and loving, inescapable presence in the worst of life and death (Rom. 8:38-39).

Conversely, however — and here one treads softly, with greatest caution,
through the lowlands of spiritual wisdom — though prayer by self and others
for healing or deliverance has its own aptness and scriptural warrant, it should
not reinvoke the discredited principle of divine causality by requesting privileged interventions for healing and protection on behalf of specially deserving
cases. And the same reserve should surely greet the secular, often best-selling,
equivalent of this individualist and elitist view of health and sickness, recovery
and death. What is more compelling in our "culture of narcissism" than theories which align well-being and survival with strength of personality? Popular
manuals of self-help and medical recovery may contain much wisdom, but
their overpsychologized theories that "special persons" and "exceptional patients" avoid or survive sickness also contain the obnoxious implication that
those who succumb to disease or death are simply mediocre![14]

To regard as perverse either the Christian or the secular connection between individual behavior and well-being is by no means to deny the relationship in which Scripture clearly sets sinfulness and death. There *are* life- and
health-destroying "wages" of our antagonism to God's will and grace; and the
same Jesus who refused to attribute one man's blindness to his own sin or his
parents' made the healing of a paralytic almost indistinguishable from the forgiving of his sins (Mk. 2:1-12). Exposed thereby is surely not the disabled person's private guilt, but his solidarity with all humanity, and thus his involvement and responsibility, along with every member of the race, for the massive
distortions and estrangements of the world in its entirety, to which all handi-
cap, disease, and death bears agonizing witness. And here one must insist upon
the much-misunderstood doctrine of "original sin," so constantly maligned, often in the church itself, though in fact an expression of good, humanizing, liberating news.

The underlying function of this dogma is to confirm the God-given integrity and solidarity of the human community. Since animals and objects cannot be held accountable, the accusation against us that we are sinners contains
the positive affirmation of our self-transcendence and responsibility as moral

---

14. The author is here protesting in particular the stupendously "successful" *Love,
Medicine and Miracles,* by B. S. Siegel (New York: Harper and Row, 1986); but there are
countless other examples. The entire current phenomenon of techniques for self-healing is
neatly skewered, though not from a Christian point of view, by Wendy Kaminer, in *I'm
Dysfunctional, You're Dysfunctional: The Recovery Movement and Other Self-Help Fashions*
(Reading, Mass.: Addison-Wesley Pub. Co., 1992).

agents. And by attributing our corruption not to createdness but to fallenness, original sin contrasts what human beings tragically *become* with who they truly *are*, creatures made good in God's own image. Sin, with its folly and rebellion and consequential disordering of human nature and of nature, does not reveal the truth about us but the very opposite. On the other hand, the fact that sin is "original" means that, even in our falsehood and our brokenness as fallen, at least one essential truth about us is preserved and illuminated, not hidden or destroyed: the truth that humanity is *connected*. We are who we are, in righteousness, and fail to be who we are, in sin, *together* not apart.

Granted, original sin appears grotesquely and unjustly to brand all of us as guilty, and necessarily so, before our personal moral histories have begun. But it is in fact our liberation as human beings not to have sinfulness attributed to our private choice and individual decision, but to our "origins" and condition, our sheer existence as members of the human race. It would truly be an intolerable burden, utterly destructive of our humanness, if each of us, alone and solitary, had to bear our moral failures entirely on our own shoulders. Were sinfulness private, its guilt would be unendurable; and the inference that suffering directly penalizes guilt would be irrefutable. Rather, the concept of original sin lifts the weight of private culpability. It is not that we are not responsible for our own actions, but that the inevitability from which our moral and spiritual failure derives is a function not of our individuality but of our corporateness, the nature we share with others, not the decisions that set us apart. There is thus a solidarity in sin reflective of the solidarity of our creation. Made together in the image of the triune God, who lives not in isolation and separateness but in the fellowship and interdependence of divine community, we remain together in our disintegration and our guilt.

This also means that in our human brokenness, we stay bonded, too, with the whole of nature, the created order and the physical realm where diseases disfigure human bodies and flesh decays and dies. Creation, by definition, is not guilty; but it is certainly trapped, says Scripture and our own experience, in the solidarity of judgment and of pain, subjected to futility, suffering, groaning, in company with us whose bodies wait for their redemption (Gen. 3; Rom. 8). Modern culture since the Enlightenment has been built on premises which suppress the truth of our connectedness with all humanity and the whole cosmos round about. Contrasting the public and the private, we sever the individual from the community, and in moral introversion profess no longer to understand how in mutual dependence one person shares responsibility with and for sisters and brothers in society at large. And by dichotomizing the objectivity of "facts" from the subjectivity of "values," the world of scientific observation from that of ethical and religious choice, we polarize morality and nature, supposing that who we are and how we act have no moral bearing on what occurs in our environment and in our bodies. A contemporary disease like AIDS, where private behavior has such a clear and deadly impact not on our own bodies only but on those of countless others, far away and even still unborn, mocks, shockingly, these egoistic, fault-free moralities and wretched fantasies of disconnectedness.

Such illusions are not modern at all, however, or post-Enlightenment, but as ageless and universal, once again, as the narrative of Genesis. For in what does the fall of Adam and Eve consist, if not in the rejection of accountability for fallenness? He blames her, and she the serpent; and the lies of both actually confirm their corporate sinfulness, the collective, mutual attempt to blame another. Thus is the heart of sin exposed as the very refusal to acknowledge sin, as the pretense of innocence, which instead heaps guilt upon the neighbor. In stunning contrast, nowhere more sharply drawn than at his grave, is the sinlessness of Jesus Christ, who died as he lived in innocence, precisely in his willingness to accept the blame, the guilt — the sentence of all sinners. Here on Easter Saturday we see in its full ugliness, the hypocrisy of our imagined blamelessness. As in birth and baptism, so now in death and burial, the innocent makes his grave with the wicked, and the only one with the right to say "it was not I" instead makes confession for us all, vicariously repenting human disobedience and submitting to our judgment and rejection, our godforsaken suffering and godless hell. As Luther graphically put it: Christ the guiltless is so as the chief of sinners, made unrighteous, guilty of the whole world's sin and worthy of the wrath of God — "the greatest thief, murderer, adulterer, robber . . . there has ever been."[15]

All of this means that to *live* the Easter Saturday story means to shake off the solipsistic dream of innocence and in conformity to Christ acknowledge our collective responsibility for human sin, for nature's dysfunctions, and thus for the sickness, disease, and death that bind us together in our common fate. There is, we have suggested, an improper guilt in the face of death, inappropriate inquiries after penal, private explanations for suffering and loss. Yet lying in a radiation center, as virulent, malignant cells in one's own body and machines which harness other of nature's lethal energies do fiery battle in the struggle between life and death, it is perhaps easier than in happier locations to recognize one's membership in a broken universe. Though pain and suffering can sometimes turn us inward, in self-pitying absorption with our own imagined hardships, they can also newly orient us outward, intensifying the awareness of our connectedness to other things and beings which suffer along with us. In the

---

15. M. Luther, *Lectures on Galatians 1535,* in *Luther's Works,* American Edition, vol. 26, ed. J. Pelikan (St. Louis: Concordia, 1963), see esp. pp. 276-91.

personal instance of the writer, the lowest weeks of chemotherapy, with respect to its emotional and mental toll, were those which coincided with war in the Persian Gulf, whose images of savage, senseless slaughter, beamed to a bedside of private combat, seemed to seal one's own tiny place within a diseased, disordered cosmos, convulsed in an orgy of destruction.

Easter Saturday existence, then, lived in any circumstances or conditions, will embrace the suffering of others and one's complicity in the fallenness of which their pain and death are such a bitter harvest. Guilt and judgment do belong to our last encounter with mortality and our skirmishes with little death along the way. As Barth, like few others in the modern church, had the courage to insist, death is rightly perceived as fearful, harsh, and hostile; for in all our endings, penultimate and final, we meet the one who made us and who judges our rebellion and our selfishness, the cowardly denials of our togetherness. Death confronts us with "the severe, remorseless, uncompromising and unsentimental objectivity" of God's judgment upon sin.[16] Yet it is not merely death but God who awaits us with that judgment.[17] It is God, not God's great enemy and ours, whom we should fear in death; and in the cross and grave, Jesus Christ the Judge become the judged, endured sin's condemnation, and removed all grounds for fear. Therefore, with the Heidelberg Catechism, "in all affliction . . . I may await with head held high the very Judge from heaven, who has submitted to God's judgment for me and removed the whole curse from me."[18]

However, the very gospel of God's own death and condemnation, which finally frees us to accept accountability for the corruption that torments us all, simultaneously sets liberating limits upon our own responsibility. Another power, tyrannical and captivating, is the anterior cause of our corruption, pain, and death; and we are sinned against as much as sinning. Therefore Christ's cross and grave are directed not only to the forgiving of our guilt but also to the breaking of our bondage. However we actually conceive of evil, reify, personalize, or neuter the demonic, an Easter Saturday existence acknowledges Christ's death and burial as the Day of the Devil. This is the victory, for a while, of a hideous foe whose misanthropic reign, realized in Christ's death and in our own, is also intimated in every spasm of personal pain, social injustice, or global desecration. Cancer patients, along with many other human beings, *know* about the Devil; we deplore and rage against its unruly incursions, its lurking, surrepti-

16. *CD*, III/2, 605. See also, in a fine article, relevant to our whole discussion here, B. Miller-McLemore, "The Sting of Death," *Theology Today* 45.4 (1989): 426.

17. *CD*, III/2, 608.

18. *The Heidelberg Catechism 1563*, translation adapted from *The Book of Confessions* (Louisville: General Assembly of the Presbyterian Church, USA, 1993).

tious undetectability, its pitiless resilience whereby even its defeats and banishments are never known for sure to be final and conclusive. And our personal, unfinished encounters with the diabolic confirm Scripture's own attesting to the reality and power of evil narratively cast as Satan or the serpent.

Such hypostatizing of evil suggests that sin really is an "other," a discrete and hostile force, a rampant, third-party antagonist between ourselves and God, out to defile the beauty of the Creator's handiwork and pervert God's order into anarchy. So it is that Paul is robust enough in conscience not to be *identified* with sin and death — dead in sin though he knows himself to be — and refuses full responsibility for his own waywardness and weakness. For that is the result precisely of a conflict between himself and an outside power which has invaded and occupied his inner territory, holding him in thrall as Pharaoh did the Hebrew captives yearning for deliverance: "I am of the flesh, sold into slavery under sin. . . . It is no longer I that do it but sin that dwells within me. . . . Who shall deliver me from this body of death?" (Rom. 7:13-25).[19]

Our captivity to death is probably the item of good news least preached about today — and how we enslave ourselves by its suppression! — and "deliver us from the evil one" the most poorly understood clause in our Lord's model prayer. Few generations have had more grounds for recognizing evil than our own — with our hideous wars and genocides, the sheer viewability now of worldwide suffering and wickedness, and our modern understanding of forces and instincts deep within us all over which our conscious selves lack all control. Nevertheless, we in the church, to say nothing of those outside, have largely consigned the diabolic to museums of mythology and ancient superstition, fitting for Luther's medieval world, perhaps, but hardly for our own. This "modernization" we have accomplished without fully explaining, even to ourselves, how it is rational still to believe in God, or the power of grace and love and holiness, but anachronistic to recognize the destructive energies of profanation, unrighteousness, and lovelessness.[20] This loss of the demonic, of a sense of bond-

---

19. Discussion of the proper interpretation of Romans 7 is endless; but few contributions to the recent debate have been more enlightening than that of K. Stendahl, "The Apostle Paul and the Introspective Conscience of the West," in *Paul among Jews and Gentiles* (Philadelphia: Fortress, 1976 and London: SCM, 1977).

20. A brilliant biography of Martin Luther clarifies the vast cultural and theological difference between the Reformation and our own times with regard to serious belief in evil and the Devil — with the strong implication that we today are much impoverished by our avoidance of a realistic demonology: H. A. Oberman, *Luther: Man between God and the Devil* (New Haven: Yale University Press, 1990). A rare contemporary exception to this evasion is the powerful, posthumous volume by Daniel Day Williams, *The Demonic and the Divine* (Minneapolis: Augsburg Fortress, 1990).

age to another party, is impoverishing and enslaving because, if evil not be objectivized, it can only be internalized; and internally it cannot be resisted and defeated by God's reality but is free to master and consume us.

Certainly for one victim of ominous disease, the spirit would finally have been broken the day he consented to be *identified* with the alien presence at work within his body, to be named, and therefore be, a "cancer patient," rather than an independent person victimized by that disease. There is, to be sure, a perverse, inward-looking cult of victimization in our culture, an ideology of passivity whereby we seek identity as victims, the more to be pitied, the less to be held accountable for our own condition. Equally, though, it is vital for true selfhood to insist with Paul that "it is not I, but evil that dwells in me"; to keep the opponent at arm's length and not allow the invader who occupies the body to possess the soul as well. For, able to grapple with the combatant if kept external and not subjectivized, is one still more powerful than evil and who, in the capitulation and seeming catastrophe of Easter Saturday, is actually on the way to defeating death objectively and once for all.

Thus Luther was liberated, not diminished, by his supposedly antiquated sense of the satanic; for he knew that in the weakness of the crucified and buried Christ, the Devil had met its match, had won a battle but lost the war against God's love and grace. For all its seething and malicious energies, the evil tyrant, and thus our sin and death, was defenseless against a single gospel utterance, the word of the cross declaring sinners justified and the dead restored to life. That promise, proclaimed in written word and spoken, was also acted out and rendered visible in baptism and Eucharist, living signs that by broken flesh and spilt blood, and through the waters of death and burial, God had routed the last enemy and put death itself to death. All of this because God, who creates and honors our mortality as such, refuses to bless, or embrace in reconciliation, death as our mortal adversary. The good news of Easter Saturday is that God will not befriend our death in its tragic and destructive aspect. At Christ's grave, as the Father and the Son endure the infinite pain of separation, and Christ is subjected to hell's worst torments, we may see just how perfect, uncompromising, and implacable is God's hatred of death's curse and all it does to us — the lengths to which the triune community will go in the struggle to confront and overthrow that which hurts, disfigures, and destroys the creatures of God's hand.[21]

---

21. "In the person of Jesus Christ God reveals himself as the relentless enemy of destructive powers and thereby also as the enemy of the bad and evil under which we suffer. One doesn't make compromises with evil. The divine opposition against destruction and the suffering it brings *activates* the Son of God and in the end leads him, the Son of God

How foolish, then — though profoundly understandable — is the anger so frequently unleashed in God's direction, when we, or those we love, face pain or grief or tragic termination. Resentment, anger, and indignation are appropriate at the disfigurement of beauty, the foreshortening of hope, the snuffing out of breath. Rightly, with Dylan Thomas, should Christian faith, thankful for the gifts of life and light, feel free and bound to "rage, rage, against the dying of the light." But how misdirected is that anger when targeted against the God and Father of Jesus, as the supposed cause of our suffering and grief, rather than set beside the infinity of God's own pain and anger at the Devil's wicked work. Our tears are but the slightest drop in the ocean of God's own weeping over young lives brutally curtailed, and old extended beyond all meaning, in pain, indignity, and helplessness. The Friday wail of Christ's forsakenness, and his descent to hell on Saturday, provide our final reassurance that God cries out with us in our abandonment to the tyranny of evil, and will go to any lengths that all things and all persons might be delivered from captivity to death.

✳   ✳   ✳

We thus find ourselves in the midst already of a third and final major theme of the theology of death viewed as the foundation for the living of human and Christian life in the light of Easter Saturday.[22] For we are now celebrating and affirming, with that irrepressible song of triumph, always, be it hoped, distinct from triumphalism, which faith sings in the face of death, that mortality — a friend to which we may consent, and a foe which demands divine and human confrontation — has also been conquered, is an enemy still battling but already doomed. Here is "radical comfort," says Barth. "Death may still be the tyrant, but it is no longer an omnipotent tyrant."[23] The tomb once occupied is empty, according to our three-day story; though it is, we have been arguing throughout, equally important, and just as central to the story, that the empty tomb was previously occupied, and that the only one risen from the grave is its still-wounded occupant. There is no other way to the Sunday of his joy and victory, and ours, than through his and our Sabbath of sorrow and defeat.

Still, the promise is that death shall have no longer the last word on our lives and destiny. There is another Word, spoken to us from beyond the bound-

---

himself, into the *abyss of suffering.*" E. Jüngel, "The Christian Understanding of Suffering," *Journal of Theology for Southern Africa* 65 (1988): 10.

22. On what follows, see esp. Barth, *CD,* III/2, 610ff.; Jüngel, *Death,* esp. ch. 6; and Anderson, *Theology, Death and Dying,* ch. 5.

23. Barth, *CD,* III/2, 610-11.

ary of death, a story to be told of a cross and grave powerful in their powerlessness. That story announces the arrival of a new day, the Day of the Lord, after the Devil's Day, the day of waiting. This commences, and promises to consummate (the balance of "already" and "not yet" in this fulfillment being open to debate, as we have seen), the death of death, accomplished in and through death (Heb. 2:14).

Yet even were we to stress to the maximum that Easter's resurrection is only the beginning of God's conquest of the devil, that would not be a beginning without antecedents. The triumphal warfare against death and evil, waged between Christ's cross and resurrection, brings to some climax a conflict long in progress. Barth, for example, as we saw, proposes that ontologically the conflict was fought and its outcome sealed, before time itself began, in the slaying of the Lamb from all eternity, and confirmed with time's own coming into being, in God's definitive Yes to life and light and No to darkness, negativity, and evil. And certainly we must see in the event of incarnation, God's coming into the frailty and decay of flesh, a divine offensive against the powers, physical and psychic, that corrupt and torment human life. This embodied struggle against death and all the little deaths through life of which we spoke, is publicly pursued in the ministry of Jesus, who is "from the very outset engaged in open combat with suffering and sickness in all its forms. Now that the Messiah has come, the immediate and inevitable result is an onslaught against the invasion of the realm of death into the world of life."[24] Christ's healing of the sick, cleansing of the lepers, resuscitating of the departed, all his sobbing, compassionate responses to disease, disablement, and death, and not least, of course, his casting out of devils, are penultimate enactments of the final paschal conflict with the powers of darkness, and its Easter resolution. Even the nature miracles, the calming of the winds and storms, for instance, proleptically intimate the resurrection — signs of the Creator's refusal to be reconciled with the disorder and groaning of creation and determination to liberate the cosmos as a whole from its deadly captivity to evil.[25]

Just so our medical advances against disease and harnessing of nature, humanity's far from finished progress against disorders bodily and ecological, need not always be dismissed as an arrogant, promethean lunge for human mastery of the cosmos, but may be thankfully received as Spirit-filled human mediations of God's own redemptive struggle against all that threatens and de-

24. Barth, *CD*, III/2, 599.

25. See here my "Death in Modern Theology," *Biblical Theology* (Belfast, Northern Ireland), 28:1 (1978): esp. p. 6; and *Theatre of the Gospel: The Bible as Nature's Story* (Edinburgh: Handsel Press, 1983), esp. pp. 23ff.

stroys creation and the creatures. Technology will hardly be denounced as demonic, but blessed as an instrument of divine breakthrough against evil, by anyone who has walked out of a cancer ward alive. Too much of the church's romanticized rhetoric against science, modernity, and progress, medical and otherwise, is thoughtless ingratitude, betraying a culpably shallow theology of creation and of resurrection!

And yet, and yet: the Christian good news of victory over death is not about survival. The very function of Easter Saturday is to prevent the rubbing out of Friday and its grievous memories by the instant and overwhelming exuberance of Sunday. Easter Saturday says that Jesus was gone and finished, subjected to death's power for a season. So Christ himself did not — despite centuries of popular theological and homiletical deceit — survive the grave! He succumbed to death and was swallowed by the grave — his Sabbath rest in the sepulcher a dramatized insistence that his termination was realistic and complete, a proper subject of grief and valediction. This was departure — painful, ugly, uncurtailed; no docetic illusion, no serene transcendence of the spirit high-floating over purely physical distress, no momentary, insignificant hiccup in Christ's unstoppable surge to glory. God's victory over death, as the Christian gospel tells it, is not a matter of smooth, ensured survival but a new existence after nonsurvival — a quite different reality, for us as well as God.

Resurrection hope is not for easy, kind release, that happy, beautiful transition to "a better place" so often triumphalistically and dishonestly proclaimed in some church quarters, even in circumstances of horrible, catastrophic, or untimely death. The song of victory is sometimes only to be chokingly managed in the midst of tears and anger, and may certainly never drown out or replace the sounds of honest grief. No more is resurrection the equivalent of inherent immortality. Our hope is for that "eschatological surplus" after the fact and finality of our extinction, for new possibilities supervening upon discontinuity, a free gift from outside us and beyond us — a share, that is, in God's own triune life. This may in no way be confused with confidence in capacities within our own possession to thwart our blessed or cursed mortality.

Perhaps this niggles or outrages those who sound the trumpet of survival, for themselves or others, in the aftermath of addiction, accident, or sickness. Our culture, we have seen, is pathologically mesmerized with its sense of being victim, and obversely obsessed with the need to survive and with techniques and methods so to do. Not to survive seems the ultimate disaster, a sign of inadequacy, failure, and ineptitude of soul. But to this secular and all too often ecclesiastical idolizing of recovery, the Christian gospel says a definite, uncompromising, yet in its own way joyful No! Easter resurrection, the victory over disease or death, is not a function of our escaping from the devil's clutches, but of the objective defeating of the Devil accomplished in God's own life and history, so that beyond those clutches, after non-escape and termination, there lies a wondrous gift of freedom, victory, and the promise of renewal.

Not long ago the author was constrained to celebrate an Easter as spiritually special, after a Lenten close-run duel with death. And to be sure, the proper impetus to thanksgiving at that moment could not be denied. Yet were the clearest *Christian* instincts finding outlet in that "special" resurrection season? Would the good news of Easter have been less true, less triumphant, even or especially for him himself, if he had *not* survived but been absent from those celebrations, unable to join in those Easter hallelujahs? And will those hymns of praise have to be judged premature in retrospect, too optimistic, if, sooner or later, he becomes a nonsurvivor after all, an eventual victim of the malignant enemy?

Surely not; for the very essence of Easter Saturday existence is recognition that life does end, either gently or abruptly, often with dignity and fittingness but often otherwise, outrageously, unprettily, and far too soon; and yet that just those facts and those events may be squarely faced with candor and courageousness. Whatever the proprieties, discussed above, of prayer in certain circumstances for deliverance from evil, a proper prayer in every circumstance of evil must be for bravery to close with the enemy with the expectation of deliverance, in the knowledge that it has lost its power to determine the final outcome of the war between us. If with faith's pure gift of courage we lose our fear of death, then we are in fact delivered from its evil also; for what is truly demonic about disease and death is less what they can do to us than the fear of what they might or might not do which they poisonously instill in us. Robbed of its fearfulness, death — though it still occurs, and often wickedly — has already forfeited its sting and power. And to lose the fear of death itself is to be delivered, too, from the fear of the other little deaths in life. For in destroying death, God was able "to deliver . . . all those who through fear of death were subject to lifelong bondage" (Heb. 2:15). What penultimates could truly frighten, hurt, or disappoint us — the author has now learned to wonder — once one has walked even halfway down death's dark vale and there received as gift the resolution to live with its ultimate fears and hurts and disappointments? As Victor Frankl, emerging from the infinitely darker, more demonic, valley of concentration camp, concludes his story: "the crowning experience of all, for that homecoming man, is the wonderful feeling that, after all he has suffered, there is nothing he need fear any more — except his God."[26]

26. V. Frankl, *Man's Search for Meaning*, rev. ed. (New York: Washington Square Press), 1985, p. 115.

Since in our story God has stooped to a "wonderful exchange" of death, enduring our death so that we might share in God's,[27] there is nothing left to fear whatever. "In [Christ] alone we may and must seriously reckon with the fact that God is the boundary of the death which bounds us. In Him alone that menacing no-man's-land is stripped of its menace, and invading chaos repulsed."[28] The Easter Saturday fact, for every person with ears to hear, the writer of these words included, is that God's own Son has already died our death and given us his own, so that in no sense which signifies despair or fear do we still have to die. Faith unites us with Christ through the Spirit, allowing us participation in God's own triune life; and that relationship with God allows us in particular to set our death in relation to God's death.[29] The Father and the Son, we have seen, are separated in subjection to death's power, allowing all the world's suffering, sin, and evil to cleave the divine community asunder. Yet we may place our own death into that aching void between the forsaking Father and the forsaken Son, and see it swallowed up, as the waters of the Red Sea enveloped the Egyptian pursuers of the Hebrews. For the Spirit holds the Father and the Son together in their separation, proving still more powerfully creative than death is powerfully destructive, so that in the sundered family's reuniting, the loving arms of God close over our death in an embrace of life, canceling its fearfulness forevermore.

Even amid talk of wonderful feelings and irrepressible songs of joy, this fearlessness, of course, is not to be confused with emotion. Courage is not the same as psychological tranquility, let alone upbeat sensations or an elevated overt spirituality in the face of death, immediate or distant. The Christian victory over death, we say again, rests not in our subjectivity, but in the objectivity of God's mighty acts — mighty in the scandalous impotence and seeming ineffectiveness of the crucified and buried one. Faith in the wisdom of such folly, hope despite the worldly grounds for seeing only hopelessness in Christ's cross and grave, are perfectly compatible with feelings of physical or psychological distress, pain- or drug-induced, and, as in Christ's own case, with the experience of spiritual exhaustion and godforsakenness. It was surely a terrible mistake of our fathers and mothers in the faith to make a person's deathbed state of mind the sole criterion of how he or she would stand beyond the grave before God's supposedly terrifying judgment. We face suffering, distress, and death with courage, faith, and trust, not by maintaining serenity of psyche or buoy-

---

27. See Anderson, *Theology, Death and Dying,* esp. p. 5; cf. Thielicke, *Living with Death,* p. 164.

28. Barth, *CD,* III/2, 615.

29. See Anderson, *Theology, Death and Dying,* esp. pp. 99, 129.

ancy of soul within, but precisely by casting ourselves in all the times of emptiness, aridity, and wordlessness — as well as those still more spiritually dangerous times of optimism or elation — upon the gift of grace outside us and
around us. God promises to do what we cannot do, and go where we need not
go, to enter the dark valley ahead of us and defeat on our behalf the frightening
foe. And the Spirit undertakes to pray for us, and stirs others to intercede on
our behalf, just when we feel awful, overwrought in body or in spirit, when faith
eludes intellect or consciousness and our tongues have lost all utterance.

It should already be absolutely clear, though it is worth reiterating in conclusion, that to trust ourselves in this manner to the objectivity of God's victory
over death is by no means to run, in the last or preliminary crises of our lives, to
"a theology of glory," jettisoning, when times turn difficult, that of the cross
and grave. What we are pursuing is a resurrection gospel which certainly does
not take leave of Good Friday and Easter Saturday amid the proper joy of Easter
Day. That means hope and celebration neither grounded, on the one hand, in a
divine triumph of sheer power, to which divine suffering and death are inciden-
tal or unreal, nor, on the other, in a human triumphalism where our own realities of mortality and suffering are transcended in a soaring spirituality or a
world-denying hope of heaven. Objectivity here signifies neither omnipotence
nor otherworldliness.

In the first case, though it is certainly in God's sole power, not our own,
that we may find refuge, confidence, and hope in the face of hostile, malevolent,
fearful death, this is not, be it said again, the absolute, invulnerable, coercive,
and imposing power of metaphysics, theism, and much classical theology. It is a
very different God, and a very different power, that we have discovered in the
story of divine self-emptying, God's capacity for weakness, the ability — without loss of Godness — to suffer and perhaps to die. This is the triune God of Jesus, fulfilled, majestic, glorified through self-expenditure in the lowly ignominy
of our farthest country. There is power here, resurrecting, death-destroying,
Devil-defeating; but it is the power of love, defying human expectation, which
flowers in contradiction and negation, allowing sin its increase and giving
death its day of victory, but only the more abundantly to outstrip both in the fecundity of grace and life. To live in the face of death an Easter Saturday existence, trusting in the weak but powerful love of the crucified and buried God, is
itself to be objective, turned outward, away from self-reliance and self-
preoccupation, away from our own determination to conquer death, which is
in fact self-defeating and destructive. Instead, we are invited bravely and with
frankness to admit our own defenselessness against the foe and entrust our
selves and destiny to the love of God which in *its* defenselessness proves creative
and victorious.

Our century has seen the reappropriation in theology of the "classical" interpretation of salvation, focused on the power of God against evil and the Devil exerted in Christ's atoning death.[30] And there are real dangers that this tradition of *Christus Victor* will degenerate into a mythic demonology and a despotic soteriology based upon the sheer omnipotence of God in stamping out the enemy, which quite contradicts the "theology of the cross." And there is the temptation that by objectifying and externalizing both the enemy, and the warfare waged against the foe by Christ the Victor, we sanctify diagnoses of the human condition which are shallow and external too, indicting material deficiencies and unjust, outward structures, while ignoring the inner spiritual malaise, individual and social, which is the true source of our tragedy and fear.

Nonetheless, surely the clearest manifestation of our inner sickness, which makes death so frightening and hostile, is precisely our inwardness and solipsism, the self-reliant attempt to keep the enemy at bay through our own interior resources. The answer to an objectifying denial of our inmost pathology is not more subjectivity but less, not more internal effort to conquer the tyranny and the terror of mortality but more trusting dependence upon the weak and foolish power of God's cross, in all its objectivity and historic realism.[31]

Secondly, as God has begun to conquer death not by omnipotent annihilation of the enemy but through submission to its clutches, so we have been liberated thereby to conquer the fear of death, not by rising above our mortality but by yielding to it. Of course, the hope of life eternal, of sharing God's own triune life beyond the nonsurvival of the grave, in that inconceivable fellowship we call heaven, is key to the gospel of the resurrection. "If for this life only we have hoped in Christ, we are of all people most to be pitied" (1 Cor. 15:19).

---

30. The identifying and recovery of this tradition is directly attributable to a controversial landmark text of the twentieth century, G. Aulén's *Christus Victor,* trans. A. G. Hebert, rev. ed. (London: SPCK, 1970 and New York: Macmillan, 1969).

31. Here I am in part responding to and learning from Douglas Hall, friend, colleague, and much admired fellow student of the theology of the cross. His warnings against the danger of "Christus Victor" are well taken: the danger that the objectivizing of redemption will foster the objectifying of sin, which evades the inner sickness of the "collective human spirit" behind our unjust social structures. (Hall has some forms of liberation theology particularly in mind.) Perhaps, conversely, he might agree with me that to speak for these reasons of "conquest from within" runs its own danger — of playing into the very piety and inwardness which is the besetting sickness of contemporary Western Christianity, and which Hall properly deplores. Cultural and religious subjectivity is itself the sign and product of our spiritual malaise. North Americans need no encouragement, least of all in the name of the theology of the cross, to look inward for salvation! See Hall, *God and Human Suffering,* ch. 4.

Easter directs us to the future — in the first instance to the future of the cosmos as a whole, the reconciliation of all things — but also, within that and quite legitimately, to our own future as persons, each uniquely known and loved by God.[32]

This hope, as we have seen, is not for simple continuity, survival through inherent immortality, but for gratuitous renewal after death. The gospel promises that the lives we lived before death shall not be lost to God, in the obliteration of our earthly personhood, but that our identities and lives shall be gathered into God's own life, properly at last established in the perfect relationality of the heavenly community. There personhood and individuality will find true expression and fulfillment, delivered from the egoism and the self-regard which cut us off from one another and so destroy our selfhood in our sinful, fractured, earthly lives. To contemplate the future life, anticipating its freedom, togetherness, and joy, as all God's creatures unite to offer everlasting praise and glory to their Creator, is hope's sublimest vision and faith's rich privilege.

Even so, Christian history is sadly full of grotesque misuses of such dreams and contemplations. Too often has the prospect of heaven served to dull the senses of the poor, oppressed, and suffering to their grievous, earthly burdens — future beatitude offered as recompense or anesthetic for present misery. Therefore must Sunday's life and hope always leave us with one foot still in Sabbath suffering and death — the promise of tomorrow precisely that which offers us the courage to live authentically today, and the motivation and the energy to struggle in the present for the doing of God's will, on earth as it is in heaven. That means acceptance of our creaturely mortality, and penultimate little victories against the demonized mortality of sickness, war, and injustice.

This essential orientation of heavenly triumph toward the here and now, we have already seen, not least in the insights of poor Thomas Didymus, so rightly insistent that the Lord and God who conquers death must still be the wounded, bleeding one, triumphant not over bodily existence but within it. So, too, the Lucan tradition of the risen Lord's time upon the earth, the "gospel of the forty days" (Acts 1:3) prior to ascension,[33] firmly sets the resurrection inside our temporal continuum, in the earthly, earthy world. He who now has walked the earth triumphant over death and the Devil is exactly he who previously spent forty days of wilderness combat against sin, Satan, and the flesh.

---

32. See here Anderson, *Theology, Death and Dying,* ch. 6; H. Küng, *Eternal Life?* (New York: Doubleday and London: Collins, 1984), esp. ch. 5; N. Pittenger, *After Death: Life in God* (London: SCM and New York: Seabury, 1980); also, old now, but still a classic, J. Baillie, *And the Life Everlasting* (London: Oxford University Press, 1934).

33. On this, see esp. Barth, *CD,* IV/1, 117, 301-2, and throughout.

Likewise Peter audaciously and perilously proclaimed the continuity of the Risen One with him whom Jerusalem had murdered amid the griminess of political calculation and religious prejudice; and even Paul who, torn between this life and the next, clearly to be with Christ in heaven, chooses instead to remain in time and in the flesh, in earthly labor with his fellows (Phil. 1:19-24).

This same ambivalence between heaven and earth, resolved in favor of the present world, is deeply embedded in the Reformed tradition. Calvin's celebrated "Meditation on the Future Life," for example, advocates contempt for the world with its vanities and tribulations, longing for the happiness of heaven, and joyful expectation of the Lord's return, "rescuing us from the boundless abyss of all evils and miseries."[34] Yet even Calvin distinguishes contempt from ingratitude. We must give God thanks for earthly life, acknowledge the benefits of mortality, and accept the troubles of the present as "the discipline of the cross."[35] That prevents the hope of heavenly resurrection from shrouding in forgetfulness the reality of earthly crucifixion, and requires, as in Calvin's own ministry and life, the equilibrium of profoundest, heavenward piety and most active engagement in society and world.

Dogmatically, we are alluding here to the distinctive Christian doctrine of "the resurrection of the body," so puzzling since our bodies plainly die and that is that, yet so different from the myth of the immortal soul.[36] This is no bizarre expectation for the future of the physical as such — as Paul's groping, barely comprehending concept of the future "spiritual body" indicates (1 Cor. 15:44). What is sown is perishable, what raised imperishable (v. 42), a new existence after the expiration of the old. Yet there is continuity here as well as discontinuity. Hope is still for "the body," not the soul, for the *person,* that is, who for now is identified with and through the physical body, even though that identity, beyond death, will be held in being without the scaffold, so to speak, of physicality. This future hope for human persons, those now physically embodied, though then spiritually, is a further affirmation of the body's own dignity and worth, the goodness of our fleshly, creaturely existence. The eschatological vision of the human body, redeemed and resurrected, healed of its diseases, freed from tears and pain, raised in glory though sown in weakness, is the gospel's ul-

34. Calvin, *Inst.* III.ix.5 and throughout.
35. *Inst.* III.ix.1.
36. See on this, Cullmann, *Immortality or Resurrection?,* ch. 2; Anderson, *Theology, Death and Dying,* pp. 119-20; Harris, *Raised Immortal,* pp. 114ff.; J. M. Lochman, *The Faith We Confess,* trans. D. Lewis (Philadelphia: Fortress, 1984), ch. 18; L. E. Keck, "New Testament Views of Death," in Mills, ed., *Perspectives on Death,* esp. pp. 70ff.; and Lewis, *Theatre of the Gospel,* pp. 24ff.

timate demand that, while rejoicing in God's victory over death, we accept and not reject, enjoy as blessing and not disdain as curse, our mortality itself.

That same acceptance and enjoyment applies equally to temporality; for it is to creatures of time that God promises resurrection of the body. The gospel hope of everlasting life does not negate our temporal finitude, nor evaporate earthly time in a mist of heavenly timelessness. Rather, the raising of God's eternal Son, who entered time for us and lived his life of glory for forty days upon the earth, signifies the redeeming of our time. Scripture's dream that everything dissipating and decaying, tormenting and demonic, about time shall pass away at last is the affirmation of created temporality along with the bodies with which we live in time. This is good news for all God's mortal creatures, fixed in finitude and destined for an end. But again, they may most fully grasp the import of this news who have themselves almost lost their shaky toehold upon time, and now treasure the pricelessness of every passing moment. Resolved with Kipling "to fill the unforgiving minute with sixty seconds' worth of distance run," to squeeze the last drop of meaning out of every relationship and activity, we who know too well how short our time might be, delight in the promise that time itself has been redeemed and sanctified. No curse to be endured, nor bottomless resource cheaply to be wasted, time is the Creator's first and final blessing on those made in God's image. Joyfully embracing the temporality gifted to us in creation's garden, redeemed in Easter's garden, and awaiting recreation in the garden of the New Jerusalem, we may live an honest, courageous, and abundant Easter Saturday existence through each remaining day or month or year until our earthly time is done.

III. Maturity: An Easter Saturday Identity

Among the most fruitful contributions of "liberation theology" to the church's contemporary understanding of the gospel has been the spotlight it has newly shone upon the story of the Exodus: the paradigmatic event of human need and divine deliverance, and the hermeneutical key which unlocks the meaning of the Bible as a whole.[37] Judeo-Christian faith, says this theology, begins with,

37. See, e.g., G. Gutiérrez, *A Theology of Liberation,* trans. C. Inda and J. Eagleson (Maryknoll, N.Y.: Orbis Books, 1973 and London: SCM, 1974), esp. pp. 155ff. For an excellent summary of the role that the Exodus plays in the liberation theology of Gutiérrez, J. L. Segundo, J. P. Miranda, etc., see J. A. Kirk, *Liberation Theology* (London: Marshall, Morgan & Scott and Richmond, Va.: John Knox Press, 1979), ch. 8. See also D. Cohn-Sherbok, *On Earth as It Is in Heaven: Jews, Christians and Liberation Theology* (Maryknoll, N.Y.: Orbis Books, 1987).

and never departs from, the memory of how Yahweh actually liberated from enslavement a small, downtrodden people who endured a living death of inhumane oppression: political, social, and economic. From this historical, concrete starting point, the New Testament needs to be read as proclaiming a new Exodus and a second, final Moses. Once again, and now definitively, universally, through Jesus the messianic liberator, God has acted to deliver slaves from their captivity and establish the reign of freedom, life, and justice. Indeed, we have ourselves seen above how Paul draws exactly an anthropological and soteriological connection between Calvary and the Red Sea. His own, and all humanity's, condition is that of slavery to sin; but thanks be to Christ, humanity's deliverer, who through his own death and burial has delivered us from the powers of tyranny and death (e.g., Rom. 6:1-11; 7:21-25).

However, "liberation" exegetes would insist here that when the New Testament moves from Pharaoh to "sin" as the oppressor, from Moses to Christ as God's liberating agent, from the particular experience of Hebrew slaves to the universal bondage and emancipation of humanity as such, the social and physical dimensions of slavery and freedom are not transcended or passed by. Faith's memory and hope remain grounded in the story of economic captivity and liberation, while the kingdom of God announced by Jesus and inaugurated in his person, though the inheritance of the poor in spirit, actualizes a divine bias in favor of the literally poor, the politically disenfranchised, the socially despised. To extend its scope beyond the physical and economic is not to spiritualize salvation, or to render the bodily and material an irrelevant distraction from the "real" gospel.

Even so, there is a converse point to be made here, which the "liberation" focus upon Exodus helps to reinforce. It is that, without dematerializing enslavement and deliverance, the gospel does indeed extrapolate from who we are and may become in our physical circumstances and social setting to the question of our identity as persons, of who we are and may become in ourselves and *coram deo*, in our standing before God. Our economic poverty or wealth, political impotence or power, our medical sickness or our health, our nearness to or distance from physical death: none of this is irrelevant to our personal identities (for we have no earthly identity without the body, as we said); yet neither do such factors constitute our identity and personhood without remainder. There is more to living and dying, more to being human, than impecunity, cancer, or their myriad allies in malevolence could possibly determine; for they do not govern our ontology. If we were to say that in the New Testament the literal captivity endured in Egypt becomes a metaphor for the human condition as such, with sin and death now universal, spiritual symbols of an oppression that was at first concrete, material, and particular, that would not permit us to assume either that the literal and concrete now can be forgotten, or that the symbolic or metaphorical is fictional or unreal. We grasp nothing of the New Testament's concern if we think, for example, that the death we might face at life's ending from disease or accident is more real, more Egypt-like, more serious, threatening and deadly, than the death we are all subject to here and now as sinners facing judgment from almighty God. Likewise the freedom that follows on God's gracious word of pardoning is no less real or true, no less Egypt-like or less worthy of exultant celebration, than the news a patient might hear of healing from a menacing disease.

The promise of resurrection on Easter Day is not disconnected from, but cannot be reduced to, victory over death in its physical dimensions, just as Good Friday reveals God's solidarity in a human condition just as estranged, just as distant a far country, on the day of our birth as on the day we die. And between them, Easter Saturday determines not only how we handle our mortality as such, whether we are cowardly or courageous in the face of termination; it is also the measure of our maturity as individuals anywhere upon life's spectrum. To be mature is not just to live authentically with decay, disease, and bodily death, but to be a person who at any age or stage has died already and so been raised to life anew, and who keeps growing, through every age and stage, by learning more deeply how to die each day.

No excuses need be offered for ending our study in this way, with the question of what Easter Saturday means for the individual and his or her identity. Indeed, it would be inexcusable not to end here. The story of God's death and burial, we have suggested, bears upon the whole of human history, in fact on the whole created cosmos in its origins and future, and challenges the way we live upon our perishable, perishing planet. And the story certainly establishes that the only way to live in any circumstances, but including those of our own contemporary society, is together in community, in mutual dependence and reciprocal self-giving. But it is equally and finally true that those who comprise communities are individuals — just as we are "individually members" of Christ's Body (1 Cor. 12:27). Indeed, that which distinguishes community from a totalitarian collective is the way it cherishes and nurtures, rather than crushes and exploits, the individuals who make it up. What the gospel does — not least, we are suggesting, from the perspective of Easter Saturday — is make possible the discovery of authentic selfhood, the living of truly fulfilled individual life which is distinct both from mass existence on the one hand, and on the other from rampant individualism which itself dehumanizes so many individuals and dispossesses others. These perversions have been the respective bitter harvest of communism and capitalism, the two ideologies which singly and in their now largely erstwhile conflict have so dominated recent history. That true individuality has been and remains so under threat in the triumphant social system which, it has been said, now marks "the end of history,"[38] is reason enough to conclude with the question of personal identity. Not in spite of the self-absorption and privatism of so much faith, religion, and theology today, idolatrously conformed to its surrounding culture, but because of that, is it imperative to inquire what the "word of the cross" has to say about authentic selfhood.

Of course, the story of the cross and grave has intrinsic meaning for the human person beyond its present-day, time-conditioned urgency. It is easy, customary, and quite proper to build upon the doctrine of creation an impressive Christian paean to the individual — the uniqueness of every human being made in the Creator's very image and thus infinitely precious to the God who names and calls, cherishes and guards, and welcomes home each one. But actually it is less how and by whom we are made, than how and with whom we end, that exposes the full significance of individuality. Easter Saturday, as the day of death for our Creator and ourselves, even more than the sixth day of creation establishes and illuminates our personal uniqueness. It is central to personhood, as we have often said and shall do so again, that we are created not alone but together, in the image of the trinitarian community; and nothing makes our solidarity and mutual dependence more concrete than that all of us without exception die: we are *connected* in our creaturely mortality and in our fallen subjection to the curse of death. Even so, we have also observed the judgmental quality of the death we must all die, and the fearfulness dependent on the fact that in dying and in death, as in no other circumstance of our existence, we are totally *alone*.

Death is relationlessness and utter isolation,[39] the absence of others and the final severance of those connections with neighbors, friends, and family which have been in an accelerating process of collapse throughout the period of one's dying. By the end, all our relationships are broken, and our solitude is complete, save for the presence of the fearful but all-gracious Judge. No matter how the dying of a loved one might break our hearts and make us wish that we

38. Cf. Francis Fukuyama, *The End of History and the Last Man* (New York: Free Press, 1992). On the proper place of the individual from a Christian perspective, in contrast to both collectivism and privatism, see, e.g., D. J. Hall, "The Theology and Ethics of the Lord's Prayer," in *Princeton Seminary Bulletin,* Supplemental Issue, no. 2 (1992): 130-31. And for a very full discussion of the relationship between the individual and society see W. Pannenberg, *Anthropology in Theological Perspective,* trans. M. J. O'Connell (Philadelphia: Westminster and Edinburgh: T. & T. Clark, 1985), pp. 157-312. See also H. Thielicke, *Being Human . . . Becoming Human,* trans. G. W. Bromiley (Garden City, N.Y.: Doubleday and Co. and London: Collins, 1984).

39. See Jüngel, *Death,* pp. 78ff., and *Theological Essays,* pp. 107-8.

could substitute our lives for theirs, suffering and even dying in their stead, that is one act of selflessness which is denied us. To lay down one's life for one's friends can give them at best a temporary reprieve. The time still comes when they and we, utterly bereft of community or substitutes, must complete a journey which no one else can take. Then, if not before, with the self quite naked and absolutely singular, the question, however much evaded throughout life and theologically perhaps best left to last in any case, will be postponed no longer. It is the final question raised by Easter Saturday, when God's own self, clothed in our humanity lies dead and buried, abandoned, solitary, all alone: the question, "Who am I?"

Truthfully, however, Christ's aloneness in the grave on Easter Saturday actually and savingly contradicts the contention that in our deaths we die alone. In his aloneness of that day, the Son of God keeps company with us in our terminal aloneness, joins us in the solitude of death and judgment, so that we are solitary no longer, and do not have to die alone. In fact, if death means aloneness, and we are not alone after all, then, in the most real sense, because of Christ's own death we do not have to die at all. My lonely, solitary, personal seat before God's judgment throne is occupied by Another, who has taken my place and become my substitute.[40] Easter Saturday says that the impossible thing about our selfhood — that someone else could die in place of us — is, after all, an impossible possibility. The Creator has become in death the creatures' substitute, so that God dies not only with each one of us but also for us. The gospel frees each of us to say, without a hint of self-glorification, but in utmost humbleness and liberation from self-centeredness: this cross, this burial, occurred "for me," for it was the death of "the Son of God, who loved me and gave himself for me" (Gal. 2:20b). Of the crucified Christ, Bonhoeffer asked, "Where does he stand?"; and his answer was, "He stands *pro me*. He stands there in my place, where I should stand, but cannot. He stands on the boundary of my existence, beyond my existence, yet for me."[41] And on that boundary, which is my death, where the dead and buried Christ lies in my place, the only answer to the question of identity is Christocentric: "It is no longer I who live, but Christ who lives in me" (Gal. 2:20a). This is the mystery of Easter Saturday, of presence-in-absence, applied to me: my new self is present precisely where my old self is absent and replaced by Christ.

Now this is strangely, yet consciously and necessarily, to speak of new

---

40. On Christ as "substitute," see esp. Barth, *CD*, IV/1, throughout; cf. T. Hart, "Humankind in Christ and Christ in Humankind: Salvation as Participation in Our Substitute in the Theology of John Calvin," *SJT* 42.1 (1989): 67-84.

41. Bonhoeffer, *Christ the Center*, 1st ed., p. 61.

identity before we have examined the old. The answer to "Who am I" speaks of an "I" who is no longer, but without defining first the "I" that I used to be. Who was it that no longer is? The story of Christ's cross only permits us to answer, or even ask, that question after we have first heard about the new identity, the Christ who is "for me" and "lives in me." Just as patients only understand how sick they were once health has been recovered, and each of us, wedded to self-vindication, finds it hard to acknowledge and repent of guiltiness until a painful word of forgiveness from the wronged one forces recognition from us, so only those who know what they have become in Christ can also confront and confess who they used to be. And both the new identity, and old which is no longer, are revealed most clearly beside the grave of God's dead Son.

As always, there would be no revelation here, no disclosing of God's grace and presence in the midst of absence and unrighteousness, were this not a grave destined to be empty. It is in the resurrection song that we hear confirmed the previously questionable Yes of God — the Yes of affirmation, acceptance, exaltation, addressed to the crucified Messiah, and therefore to all with whom and for whom he was dead and buried. Only by his being raised do we know that this is no failure nor imposter, but indeed the Christ, God's Son, the one who came not to be served but to serve, not to live for himself but to be for others, and supremely to die, not for himself, who had no need to die, but for us while we were sinners (Rom. 5:8). As its Easter Sunday sequel sheds fresh, lustrous light backward upon the dark of Easter Saturday, I may in faith hear the promise that the cross and grave, or rather the crucified and buried person, is *pro me,* the substitute who took my place, and is therefore who my new identity shall be. But the same light, only harsh and cruel this time, also exposes from the vantage point of Easter Saturday who I used to be. Even in the revelation of my self-alienation, the conflict between my "self" and the sin in me (Rom. 7:20),[42] I am identitified as one who put Christ on his cross and laid him in his tomb. Easter Saturday indicts and names me as Christ's crucifier. I belong to the company of those who have rejected salvation's cornerstone, killed God's prophets and then God's Son, and crucified the Lord of glory (Mt. 4:2; 1 Pet. 2:6-7; Mt. 23:21, 33ff., 37; 1 Cor. 2:8). As Jesus lies in the godlessness of hell, making his grave with the wicked, I know myself as estranged and alien to God, perversely ungrateful for the Creator's mercy, love, and grace. It was I who laid hands upon God's servant and led him like a lamb to slaughter (Isa. 53:7), and it is I who still today am implicated in, among much else, the world's injustice, violence, and irresponsibility. Easter Saturday, that day of malediction, allows no more evasion of the fact that God's own Son, and maybe God, died because of me and by my doing.

42. See here H.-M. Barth, *Fulfillment,* trans. J. Bowden (London: SCM, 1980), ch. 4.

Furthermore, if Christ's ungodliness in death exposes mine, his godforsakenness also reveals my own — that as the one who put the Son to death I have been put to death myself, forsaken justly by the God who made me. Easter Saturday, that is, confirms the judgment, verdict, and sentence on my sin. In Christ's abandonment by God to hell, I know myself to be condemned, know that the Father who gave up his Son (Rom. 8:31) also gave up sinners to impurity and degradation for their falsehood and idolatry (Rom. 1:24-25), and that I belong among the malefactors among whom Christ was murdered (Isa. 53:12; Lk. 23:32). In the accursed, forsaken, buried form of Christ, who became *peccator pessimus,* the chief of sinners, I see my own, original identity as sinner and as judged; and having turned the truth into a lie, I am now released, compelled, to return from falsehood to veracity, acknowledging the godforsakenness of who I was, in consequence of godlessness.

To which the jubilant word of the cross and grave and empty tomb is this: that God is the justifier of the ungodly and the giver of life to the dead (Rom. 4:5, 17). Christ died for the ungodly, not the godly; and therefore he died for us who were sinners and unrighteous but now are justified by his blood (Rom. 5:6-11) and raised to walk in newness of life (Rom. 6:5). Justification, the gracious gift and new identity of Christ's own righteousness, for those who are unrighteous, godless, and godforsaken, is the heart of the Christian gospel. It is, as Lutherans rightly insist, the article of faith which determines the integrity of the church, whether it stands or falls.[43] Paul himself saw (e.g., Rom. 3:24) that justification

43. A full discussion of justification, covering its biblical basis and meaning, the history of its interpretation, and its role as a long-standing *casus belli* between Protestant and Roman Catholic theology, cannot be attempted here. Some major texts relevant to such a discussion would include: Barth, *CD,* IV/1, sect. 61, "The Justification of Man"; H. Küng, *Justification: The Doctrine of Karl Barth and a Catholic Reflection,* 2nd ed. (Philadelphia: Westminster and London: Burns and Oates, 1981); Weber, *Foundations of Dogmatics,* vol. 2, ch. 7; A. E. McGrath, *Iustitia Dei,* vol. 1: *The Beginnings to the Reformation* (Cambridge and New York: Cambridge University Press, 1986), and *Justification by Faith* (Grand Rapids: Zondervan, 1988); H. A. Oberman, *The Dawn of the Reformation* (Edinburgh: T. & T. Clark, 1986); Jüngel, "The World as Possibility and Actuality: The Ontology of the Doctrine of Justification," *Theological Essays,* ch. 3; H. G. Anderson, A. A. Murphy, and J. A. Burgess, eds., *Justification by Faith* (Lutherans and Catholics in Dialogue VII) (Minneapolis: Augsburg, 1985); K. Lehmann and W. Pannenberg, eds., *The Condemnations of the Reformation Era: Do They Still Divide?,* trans. M. Kohl (Minneapolis: Fortress, 1990); E. P. Sanders, *Paul and Palestinian Judaism* (Philadelphia: Fortress and London: SCM, 1977), and *Paul, the Law and the Jewish People* (Philadelphia: Fortress and London: SCM, 1983); E. Käsemann, *Perspectives on Paul* (Philadelphia: Fortress and London: SCM, 1971); K. Stendahl, *Paul among Jews and Gentiles,* esp. pp. 23ff.; J. D. G. Dunn, *Jesus, Paul and the Law* (London: SPCK and Louisville: Westminster/John Knox, 1990).

comes by God's grace, as a gift and apart from the keeping of the law (Rom. 3:28; Gal. 3:11); and this freedom and externality of righteousness Luther distinguished from medieval (and subsequent, counter-Reformation), understandings, by which the grace that justified believers was itself divine recompense in responding to our own God-inspired love and moral effort. Thus the Reformers preached that justification is sheer "alien" gift, from quite outside us; and it "imputes" to us (Rom. 4:6) a righteousness which is not our own. Forgiveness and renewal rest not on what we *do,* as "works of the law," but on what we *hear,* the word of the cross which declares us justified and resurrected. But this invited the misunderstanding that the righteousness which comes by faith is fictional or unreal, a verbal change or an arbitrary decision of the Judge to acquit as innocent those who are in fact quite guilty. Against this, the gospel's promise of a new identity rests entirely upon a Christological realism, the "wonderful exchange" of ontological identities between ourselves and Christ, which means that not only the quality but the very subject of our lives is changed.[44]

Christ, who became sin and was accursed for us (2 Cor. 5:21; Gal. 3:13), assumed our condition and identity as godless and godforsaken, and as such was justly judged. But, conversely, he so incorporates us into his own person that by faith and in the Spirit we share in who Christ is and take on his identity. It is not at all that we are truly guilty, but are treated, forensically or verbally, as innocent. Rather, Christ *is* our new ontology; and we become who Christ is, as innocent as he. He is made our righteousness, and we become the righteousness of God, says Paul (1 Cor. 1:30; 2 Cor. 5:21). United with Christ's own perfect humanness, we are clothed in his wholeness and walk in his new life, as he was clothed in our brokenness and endured our death. Despite much distortion, Protestant and Catholic, grace is neither a reified substance poured into the soul nor some external "benefit," detached from Christ's own being. Christ's grace is his own person; and through faith we replace our personhood with his, becoming as righteous and justly uncondemned (Rom. 8:1) as he became unrighteous, properly condemned. Thus is our old identity terminated, finished, gone; and our new reposes in Christ's self. "You have died, and your life is hid with Christ in God" (Col. 3:3). With his self as our own new, hidden subject, we are truly free at last, free to be ourselves and fully human, without the crippling and destructive weight of failure, guilt, and fear of death. For freedom Christ has set us free (Gal. 5:1).

Now this new liberated identity, a subjecthood revealed to be "for us" be-

44. See, e.g., Pannenberg, "A Search for the Authentic Self," in *Christian Spirituality and Sacramental Community* (Philadelphia: Westminster, 1983 and London: Darton, Longman and Todd, 1984), p. 99.

side Christ's grace, where he lies identified with our old enslaved and dead identities, is a free gift, we have said, offered as a word of promise which needs only to be heard obediently, acceptingly, and gratefully. This hearing comes by faith (Rom. 10:17), and has sometimes been described as "justifying faith." That is dangerously misleading if faith be thus conceived as one more "work," a self-justifying leap of spiritual or intellectual heroism, or a moral or religious "decision" of our own which clinches God's decision toward us, adding a requisite, responsive human contribution to what is otherwise an ineffective or deficient gift of God to us. Rather, though the consequential cost and active demands of grace are deep and unconditional, the grace of justification is unconditional too, not dependent on or triggered by any prior qualification, act, or posture of our own. Faith is simply our Amen to God's own Yes to us, and has a passive, humble, self-effacing quality of grateful "acknowledgment, recognition and confession,"[45] rather than being a discrete, autonomous action of our own to secure the new identity. In the asymmetry of faith, we let go of, and allow to die, our old identity, but do not generate or effectuate our new.

Now this letting go of the old self, which goes hand in hand with acknowledging the new, is itself an Easter Saturday event, which corresponds to the mutual letting go of the Father and the Son whch led to God's own experience of Good Friday and of Easter Saturday. To say our human Yes and Amen to God's redemptive Yes to us itself means death for the old subject of our lives, in conformity to Christ's own death for us. As the Father gave up the Beloved Son to death for our sake, and the Son, perfectly obedient to the Father's will and yielded to forsakenness gave up himself for us (Rom. 8:31; Gal. 2:20), and on the cross gave us his very spirit (Mt. 27:50; Jn. 19:39),[46] so our acceptance of Christ's crucified and risen selfhood as our own means "dying to sin" (e.g., Rom. 6:11; 1 Pet. 2:24) and giving up all we used to be, with our cherished, egoistic dreams and self-reliant deceptions and illusions. Faith "abandons the self-sufficiency of [one's] pusillanimity."[47] To be clothed in Christ's own whole and

---

45. Following Barth's highly Reformed exposition of faith as *Anerkennen, Erkennen,* and *Bekennen.* See *CD,* IV/1, sect. 63, "The Holy Spirit and Christian Faith"; also pp. 608ff., "Justification by Faith Alone." See, too, Calvin, *Inst.* III.ii.

46. Note that John here, though not Matthew, uses the same verb, *paradidonai,* for "giving up," "delivering up," "handing over," as that used by Paul of the Father in Rom. 8:31, of the Son in Gal. 2:20, and of Christ's delivering of the kingdom to the Father at the end, in 1 Cor. 15:24. As Arthur McGill suggests, this "handing over" of the spirit in death signifies not merely termination, but the positive communication of *life,* through the act of giving up and self-surrender. So it is that our new, Christocentric identity comes to life when we in faith hand over our old selfhood. See McGill, *Death and Life,* pp. 72ff.

47. Barth, *CD,* IV/1, 605.

full humanity as our own means to be broken and self-emptied in a Christ-like *kenosis* of abnegation and surrender, and does not displace Christ's own "giving up" but is facilitated by it.[48] The good, but costly, news for all humanity is that freedom and fulfillment are possibilities, or rather, in Christ, actualities, for our real existence as women and as men; but that to live within this actuality, to be a participant in the freedom and wholeness of true selfhood, is not possible without the willingness to die. The gospel summons us to align ourselves and our histories directly with Christ's own selfhood which led him through a history of death and burial. Authentic selfhood, a new identity of life and wholeness, means relating one's own story to the narrative of Christ in isomorphic correspondence. He, says our story and our creed, suffered under Pontius Pilate, was crucified, dead, and buried. So we, in identity with him, must suffer with Christ (Rom. 8:17), be crucified with Christ (Rom. 6:6; Gal. 2:20), be dead with Christ (Phil. 3:10), and buried with Christ (Rom. 6:4). And only so shall we also appropriate the promise of being raised with Christ in resurrection and new life (Rom. 6:4-5; Phil. 3:11).

In this Easter Saturday of our own, where in conformity to Christ we give ourselves to death and burial, beside and with Christ there on the way to being with him also in his Easter victory, there is highlighted at last, as a truth and possibility for each of us, that enigma which we recognized above as first and foremost a reality and possibility of God's own being. It is true, mysteriously, of God on Easter Saturday, that one who loses life shall find it, that the very Almighty proves powerful, creative, and abundant only in an ontological surplus which depends upon accepting impotence, defeat, and self-negation. So now it becomes the truth for us as well, that if we would find and fulfill our selves we must first give them up, surrendering our egos, lives, and identities to death. Fullness comes through emptiness and loss, and only thus, says Easter Saturday; this anthropologically means that we become complete and mature as human beings only through giving up the supposed maturity and imagined adequacy of our selfhood, becoming children once again.

Besides the metaphors of death and burial, it is those of birth and infancy which Scripture utilizes most to clarify this strange truth about the loss of self that finds the self (Mk. 8:35). It is a deplorable commentary on the theological ineptitude and cowardice of the modern church that, having allowed one particular doctrinal and ecclesiastical faction to appropriate, as its own possession, the Bible's insistence on being "born again," other sizeable sections of Christ's Body, including pastors, preachers, and theologians, have jettisoned wholesale the quotidian Christian language of regeneration. This leaves many in the

---

48. See Pannenberg, "Authentic Self," pp. 103-4.

churches quite unaware that the indicatives and imperatives of rebirth apply to all who would lay hold upon the identity of Jesus Christ. How else can we become identified with Christ's maturity and fullness as the truly human one, without surrendering our own identity, adulthood, and self-sufficiency, so as to enter the kingdom like little children (Mt. 18:3) and be born again (Jn. 3:3-8) as Christ's brothers and sisters, free to call God "Abba" and live with the Son through the Spirit of adoption in the fellowship of the triune community (e.g., Mt. 19:28; Jn. 1:12-14; Rom. 8:14ff.; Gal. 4:4ff.; 1 Jn. 2:29, and throughout; cf. Titus 3:5)? As we explored the doctrine of God from our Easter Saturday perspective, it became increasingly clear that God is not to be conceived of as a solitary monad, but as a family: plural, relational, and mutually dependent; and that the spaciousness within this community of love is room left open for ourselves and all humanity: mansions in the Father's house (Jn. 14:2) where, as God's adopted children and fellow heirs with the Son, we are free to be and to fulfill ourselves, at peace with the God who loves us (Jn. 14:27). Reconciled by the death of the Son, we are brought home by the Spirit to the Father's welcoming embrace, from the far country of our estrangement, where our refusal to be God's sons and daughters and our bid for independence and maturity exact so tragic and intolerable a price. "You must be born again," then, is no sectarian shibboleth, but the truth of humanness itself. Maturity comes from letting go of our self-reliant selves and becoming children who trust in Abba, taking up the free space left for us within the family of the Father, Son, and Spirit.

At a time in history when so much attention is rightly focussed on the child, and all that children suffer — from war, poverty, abuse, and loss of family — it comes as glorious good news that God does not leave us as desolate orphans (Jn. 14:18) but promises each human being, through the Spirit, a home to dwell in of true belonging and abiding love. But it is equally a rebuke to our society, which thinks of itself as come of age, and in which all too many who are disturbed, insecure, and immature try to prove their adulthood by the abusive exercise of power over the vulnerable young, that a child is precisely what each of us must be in order to be whole. And that child, regenerate, adopted, neophyte, on the way at last to maturity and full stature (Eph. 4:13ff.), is what we may become by simply saying Yes to the one who for our sakes risked his Sonship on the cross and yielded to the orphaned grief of Fatherlessness on Easter Saturday.

Another normative element of biblical vocabulary for the letting go of our old identity, which responds to and activates our new, authentic personhood in Christ, and which again, to our great shame, we often now suppress as embarrassing, partisan, anachronistic, is discourse concerning "repentance" and "conversion." Because of the abuse of such language by some Christians, others seem to have torn it from their de facto canon and excised it from their speech. But where is such permission granted to abandon a conceptuality so central to Scripture and tradition, an imperative so nonnegotiable as "repent and be converted" (Acts 3:19; cf. Lk. 5:32)? Repentance *(metanoia),* which itself means a conversion of the mind, is the act whereby I let go of my old identity of sin and lay hold upon my new, of righteousness.[49] Though often cast as the prior condition of forgiveness, true repentance is, as Calvin put it, not "legal" but "evangelical,"[50] not a requirement of the law that needs to be fulfilled to make forgiveness possible, but the response of faith, in gratitude and joy, to the gospel's gracious, prevenient, unconditioned promises. It is the gift of Christ's redeemed humanity which prompts and frees us to repent of our own old ways and be conformed to Christ's. Indeed, it is only because Christ has first repented for us, in the condition of our old humanity, that we ourselves are empowered to repent and be converted, changed in mind and self. Until we hear Christ's promise of justification and forgiveness, we remain immured in the lie of our innocence and need for no forgiveness. By contrast, as we saw, it is Christ the sinless One who has acknowledged human sin, repented of it, and been judged for it, vicariously in his blamelessness bowing to God's verdict on our blameworthiness. "The Son's dealing with the Father in relation to our sins take[s] the form of a perfect confession of our sins. This confession . . . must have been a perfect Amen in humanity to the judgment of God on the sin of [humankind] — a perfect sorrow — a perfect contrition — all the elements of our repentance . . . excepting the personal consciousness of sin."[51]

Now Christ's repentance for our sin, which invites and makes possible our own, clearly belongs to his incarnation itself, becoming truly one of us, bone of our bone, born "in the likeness of sinful flesh" (Rom. 8:3), "of a woman, under the law" (Gal. 4:4). Christ's human existence is itself an event whereby the Son of God has entered into the condition of our humanness and in perfect sinlessness endured the curse of sinfulness before the law, bearing God's judgment on unrighteousness. Only an understanding of Christ's vicarious repentance allows us to make sense of that otherwise puzzling and offensive act with which the public ministry of the incarnate Son begins. For why should one declared in the narra-

49. On *metanoia* in relation to selfhood, see A. J. Torrance, "The Self-Relation," *SJT* 40.4 (1987): 506.

50. See Calvin, *Inst.* III.iii, throughout, and esp. sect. 4.

51. J. McLeod Campbell, *The Nature of the Atonement,* 4th ed. (London: J. Clarke and Co., Ltd., 1959), pp. 135ff. This astonishing work, a classic of Scottish theology, is the Magna Carta of Christ's vicarious repentance and a major milestone in soteriology. See, e.g., G. M. Tuttle, *So Rich a Soil: John McLeod Campbell on Christian Atonement* (Edinburgh: Handsel Press, 1986).

tive of that event itself to be worthy, and well pleasing unto God, publicly submit to the baptism of John, specifically defined as a sign of repentance for the forgiveness of sins (e.g., Lk. 3:1-22)? Here the spotless Lamb accepts the status of the unclean leper, and the pure one asks for washing, repenting our sin, not his own. And this repentant baptism at his ministry's beginning is a prolepsis of what occurred at its end on Calvary and in the tomb. Christ's whole ministry, indeed, was an extended baptism, plunging deeper and deeper into the waters of our wickedness and weakness, which led through the wilderness temptation to climactic violence, trial, and passion in Jerusalem. "I have a baptism to be baptized with; and how I am constrained until it is accomplished" (Lk. 12:50). "Are you able to be baptized with the baptism with which I am baptized?" (Mk. 10:38). Christ's painful, bloody baptism in human sin reaches its nadir in the suffering and death of Golgotha; and his guiltless repentance as a sinner is perfected, its price now fully paid, as he lies in the baptism of hell on Easter Saturday, buried among the wicked and stricken for the sins of many, although he had done no violence and there was no deceit in his mouth (Isa. 53:9).[52]

This brings us finally and directly to our own baptism: the seal of our repentance and rebirth, our death with Christ and union with his resurrection, which is our new identity.[53] Often over several years it has been put to the author of this book that Easter Saturday is a strange, unnecessary topic for reflection, a non-event, a day of no significance for Christian living. Perhaps the best answer to those complaints takes the form of a question and a statement from Paul: "Do you not know that all of us who have been baptized into Christ Jesus were baptized into his death? We were buried therefore with him by baptism into death" (Rom. 6:3, 4a). For the majority of doubters were indeed baptized Christians who, though they seemed not to remember it, had carried on their bodies, usually from infancy, the very sign of Easter Saturday: the burial of Jesus Christ.

To be baptized, and thus appropriate to oneself the historical event in which once and for all one's identity was crucified and buried with Christ Jesus, is itself nothing less than to have an Easter Saturday identity.[54] Baptism confirms our union with Christ, and thus our participation in his repentance which led from the cradle to the Jordan, to the cross and tomb. In this union,

---

52. On the theological relation between Jesus' baptism by John and "The Baptism" of his dying and rising, see D. S. M. Hamilton, *Through the Waters: Baptism and the Christian Life* (Edinburgh: T. & T. Clark, 1989), pp. 47ff. See also G. W. H. Lampe, *The Seal of the Spirit,* 2nd ed. (London: SPCK, 1967), pp. 38ff.

53. See O. Cullmann, *Baptism in the New Testament* (London: SCM and Chicago: Alec Allenson Inc., 1950), pp. 13ff.

54. See, e.g., D. B. Harned, *Creed and Personal Identity* (Edinburgh: Handsel and Philadelphia: Fortress, 1981), p. 71.

sealed with the sign of water that drowns, cleanses, and gives new life, we repent of our old identity, consider ourselves dead to sin and alive to God in Christ Jesus, who himself has died to sin and ended death's dominion (Rom. 6:9-11). For at whatever age this sign is laid upon us, we receive it with empty hands open for the gift of grace, becoming like the little children of whom God's kingdom is comprised. Here it is publicly acknowledged that our old identity has been let go, is finished, dead, and buried, so that we, in and through the crucified and buried Christ, have been reborn.

Thus, despite its seeming unfamiliarity, Easter Saturday, God's day of burial, becomes, for all who are baptized, the event and sign of their old lives' termination and the beginning of their new. Though he did not advocate the baptism of infants, who understood better than Karl Barth, and expressed more vividly, this Easter Saturday identity of Christians as "buried corpses"? "Burial is a renunciation of the deceased. To bury a man is to part from him for ever. Baptism is the burial of a dead man by his community and by the candidate. . . . He died when Jesus Christ died on the cross in place of the legalistic or libertine sinner. But he is now dead in both forms. He can only be buried. He can only be renounced." The baptized confirm thereby their own displacement by Christ's new self, "as in a solemn act of burial . . . in the garden of Joseph of Arimathea . . . they were buried, laid to rest, interred with Him."[55] Only such shocking terms as these, of cadavers and obsequies, of inhumation and disposal, excluding all squeamishness and sentiment, can ensure, perhaps, that we take seriously the death of the old self signified in baptism, which is a reality for all Christ's faithful and the Easter Saturday badge of any who would share in the freedom, maturity, and selflessness of his new life.

Each of us, we said, dies alone, in solitude; and as the sign of our death and burial, baptism is profoundly personal and individual. It is I whom God has created, called, and chosen as a child of the covenant of grace; I whose sin put Christ to death; and I who, dead in my sins, was buried beside him in the tomb and raised with him to a new identity. Nothing could be more personal than the watery sign of Easter Saturday's interment laid upon me in my baptism, along with the name conferred upon me, confirming my uniqueness. And yet, of course, as we shift from once-for-all baptism, the seal of justification, to the life of daily baptism, our growth in sanctification, it is obvious that this personal sign of baptism is given with and binds me to the whole community of faith, and indeed of all humanity. Baptism, though so personal, is the most public, corporate, of acts, even cosmic in its signification.[56] The unique name

55. Barth, *CD*, IV/4, *Fragment*, pp. 79, 160, 91, 197, 117.
56. See, e.g., C. Gunton, "Baptism and the Christian Community," in C. D. Kettler

given me in baptism, which draws me out of anonymity and impersonality, indicating my individuality and unsubstitutable selfhood, is, after all, my "Christian" name. It is in a sense Christ's name, since it betokens I participate in Christ and find my identity in him; it is thus Christ's name for me, as that particular self who, beloved of Abba, Father, has a special, singular place within the fellowship of God's community. Yet it is also true that every other baptized person also has a "Christian" name and bears the name of Christ. If each of us has a unique identity in Christ, it is no less obvious that we all have the same identity, all have Christ, his righteousness and life, as the subject of our own once moribund and sinful lives, and therefore we have just one identity in common.

In the incarnation, God has assumed the flesh of all humanity, through the concrete particularities of one man; thus the humanness of every member of the race is affirmed, honored, dignified, redeemed, through Christ's vicarious humanity, the sin of us all judged and done away with, the death of all endured and overcome.[57] All the worldly rivalries and inequities between God's human partners have thus been transcended, rendered obsolete in Christ, whose birth, burial, and resurrection unite us all and make anachronistic the power of sin, injustice, suffering, and death to separate and divide us from each other. Baptism signifies this oneness of humanity in Christ, this one identity common to all for whom God was enfleshed and died. Here is the Easter Saturday sign of the burial of all God's creatures, who were crucified in fragmentation but raised in unity and commonality.

Of course, the human community continues, beyond Christ's days of death, burial, and resurrection, to be fractured, schismatic, outrageously unequal, so that every event of baptism, celebrating human oneness, is our indignant protest against the failure of humanity to be what it has become in Jesus Christ, in whom there are no distinctions, for the same Lord is Lord of all (Rom. 10:12). But every baptism equally is a sign of hope for God's new, coming kingdom. This act identifies the church as the prolepsis and anticipation of humanity's eschatological reunion: God's baptized, baptizing people, the Easter Saturday community where it is ontologically already true — however concealed and contradicted by our shameful practice — that "all who were baptized have put on Christ; so there is neither Jew nor Greek, slave nor free, male nor female" (Gal. 3:28). In the church, where we have "put off the old nature . . .

---

and T. H. Speidell, eds., *Incarnational Ministry: The Presence of Christ in Church, Society and Family* (Colorado Springs: Helmers and Howard, 1990), esp. pp. 102ff.

57. On the profound concrete, social, and political implications of this reconciliation through Christ's vicarious humanity, see J. B. Torrance, "The Ministry of Reconciliation Today: The Realism of Grace," in Kettler and Speidell, eds., *Incarnational Ministry*, ch. 8.

and have put on the new nature," such differences cannot survive, for "Christ is all and in all" (Col. 3:9-11). And in the final kingdom, made visible among the faithful in advance, all shall know and live the mystifying truth of Easter Saturday existence: that human beings find their personhood and fulfill their sense of self precisely by crucifying and burying along with Christ their egoism and their individualism. We shall be free and whole as persons, having abandoned self-gratification and independence, in exchange for mutual reciprocity and surrender to the other, becoming thus the image of that divine community of love through which God's own self found fulfillment and perfection, in dying on a human cross and being buried in a grave like ours.

✳   ✳   ✳

Now we have been insisting on the utter realism of the new, personal identity sealed for us in baptism, which is Christ's new humanness for us. "Spiritual" is often used in society, and sometimes, unforgivably, within the church, as a synonym for what is ghostly, insubstantial, or just unreal. But if God is real, then what could be unreal about sharing in God's life and by God's Spirit participating in the humanness of God the Son? From faith's perspective, there could be nothing more substantial, actual, and true than the burial of our old identity on Easter Saturday and the birth of our new on Easter Sunday. What is to be admitted, though — a rather different matter — is that our new selfhood, as real as Christ is real, is also as hidden as he himself is hidden between Ascension and the End. "You have died, and your life is hid with Christ in God. When Christ who is our life appears, then you also will appear with him in glory" (Col. 3:3-4). As the history of our past and present identities is utterly isomorphic with Christ's own passage through death and burial to resurrection, our future also is aligned with his and only in his final eschatological visibility shall our new lives in him be totally unveiled, wrapped no more in ambiguity and equivocation. For now, obviously, the new self is, at least in part, an incognito, a concealed and threatened identity, menaced constantly by the all-too-concrete, however anachronistic and "unreal" survival and resistance of our old identity. None of us is solely, unambiguously new. Recidivists all, we wage a daily, often losing, struggle with temptation and despair, engaged in mortal combat between who we have become in Christ and who we used to be and — impossibly — still are. How easy — however foolish — to backslide and having begun with the Spirit to end with the flesh (Gal. 3:3).[58]

58. It was almost certainly a wrong, though a long, tradition to interpret Rom. 7:7-25 as autobiographical analysis on the part of Paul of the dilemma of the Christian,

In understandable deference to this continuing battle between old sin and new righteousness, past burdens and present freedom, acknowledged in Scripture and fully authenticated in the church's experience, there are those who regard ambiguity and combat as the normative mark of the Christian life. Such caution, pessimism even, about the prospects for transcending a conflict of identities was particularly characteristic of Martin Luther. No one was more aware than he of the power of the Devil — of sin and law, conscience and despair — to contest the believer's new justified personhood, received in faith. In fact he was unrivaled also in his confidence that the Devil had once and for all been defeated in Christ's death and resurrection. Luther found refuge from his weakness in the gift of Christ's own righteousness which his baptism had sealed in utter objectivity. The memory that "I am baptized" gave an unshakable security against the demonic ravages of failure, despair, and doubt. Yet equally, for Luther, the Devil never ceases subjectively to challenge the objective and complete reality of faith's new identity, so that the existence of the Christian is by definition double-sided. Each of us is simultaneously both totally justified and totally a sinner; and the Christian life consists of daily baptism whereby, through repeated failures and shortcomings, we constantly surrender the old self and take fresh refuge in God's justifying word of forgiveness and new life.[59]

Luther, to be fair, did not reduce the Christian life to a totally static deadlock, a perfect equilibrium of forces between grace and law which allowed no movement forward in our character. Justification, though primarily consisting

---

tempted still by the old self to do the wrong, which the new self hates and wants not to do (v. 15). Rather, this is probably an understanding, from a Christian perspective, of the plight of those (Jews) who attempt to live under the law as the way to salvation, but find that doing so only exposes and exacerbates their bondage to sin. See, e.g., J. C. Beker, *Paul the Apostle* (Philadelphia: Fortress, 1980), esp. p. 238; and Sanders, *Paul, the Law and the Jewish People,* esp. pp. 73ff. Even so, the many rebukes in Paul's own letters and the rest of the Epistles show that the NT is fully aware of the constant capacity of Christians to "fall from grace," to relapse from the freedom, unity, and Christ-centeredness of their new identity.

59. Accounts of Luther's own experience as a justified sinner, and of his theology of *simul justus et peccator* ("at the same time just and sinful"), are legion. But see esp. P. Althaus, *The Theology of Martin Luther,* trans. R. C. Shultz (Philadelphia: Fortress, 1966), ch. 18 and esp. pp. 242ff.; Oberman, *Luther: Man between God and the Devil,* pp. 184, 320, and throughout; B. A. Gerrish, *The Old Protestantism and the New* (Chicago: University of Chicago Press and Edinburgh: T. & T. Clark, 1982), ch. 4; and the corpus of G. Wingren, including *Creation and Law,* trans. R. Mackenzie (Philadelphia: Fortress and Edinburgh: Oliver & Boyd, 1961); *Gospel and Law,* trans. R. Mackenzie (Philadelphia: Fortress and Edinburgh: Oliver & Boyd, 1964); and *The Living Word,* trans. V. C. Pogue (Philadelphia: Fortress and London: SCM, 1960).

of forgiveness, did have, for Luther, at least, elements of healing, of partial — though only partial, and often well-concealed — growth in the empirical condition of the Christian, away from sinfulness and toward Christ-likeness. And subsequently Calvin, followed by his eponymous tradition, while denying by no means the dialectic of "justified" and "sinner," expressed expectations far more robust than Luther's for the Spirit's power to *sanctify* the sinner and thus allow the justified to mature and grow in their newborn identities. Holiness, as such, is of course as much a Christological reality as is forgiveness. Christ alone is holy: he is our sanctification no less than our righteousness (1 Cor. 1:30). But the Reformed tradition expects of us on this side of the *eschaton* — and this applies to the church and to society at large as much as to the individual — at least increments of some visible, if always limited and never consummated, growth into Christ's vicarious, sanctified humanity, as who we are empirically corresponds increasingly to who we are ontologically already in Christ, the Holy One. And by such openness to the Spirit's sanctifying possibilities, the doctrine of the Christian life aims to do justice to Scripture's indicatives and imperatives of maturity and growth.[60]

With a lovely irony — but also with sobering demands — the New Testament, having required that to be mature we give up our own proud adulthood and be born again as little children, adds that these children must now give up their childishness and grow up into mature adults! Such growth can be set in terms of actuality; for it is the fullness and perfection of Christ himself of which the gospel speaks, and to be in him *is* to be on the way toward maturity. It is for the sake of this growth that the church exists as Christ's Body, nourished with the Spirit's gifts, that "we should all come to maturity, to the measure of the full stature of Christ" (Eph. 4:11-13). But this leaving behind of infancy and coming to full stature, which occurs in Christ, is also a demand: "we must no longer be children, . . . we must grow up in every way . . . into Christ" (vv. 14, 15). It is much, but not enough, to be *in* Christ, to *be* no longer one's old self (Col. 3:3); for that can be too complacent and static an existence. Instead, we must *live* no longer for ourselves, but live *for* Christ (2 Cor. 5:14), and thus grow dynamically in likeness to him. And if we are to "stand mature" (Col. 4:12), and Christ-like, we must move on from our infancy as persons, unlike too many in the church who remain uneducated pupils instead of becoming learned teachers, and are

60. See Calvin, *Inst.* III.vi-x; also W. Niesel, *The Theology of Calvin,* trans. H. Knight (London: Lutterworth Press, 1956 and Grand Rapids: Baker Books, 1980), esp. ch. 10; R. S. Wallace, *Calvin's Doctrine of the Christian Life* (Edinburgh: Oliver & Boyd, 1959); and J. Leith, *John Calvin's Doctrine of the Christian Life* (Louisville: Westminster/John Knox Press, 1989).

restricted to a liquid diet, too immature for meat. "For though by this time you ought to be teachers, you need someone to teach you again the basic elements. . . . You need milk, not solid food; for everyone who lives on milk, being still an infant, is unskilled in the word of righteousness. . . . But solid food is for the mature" (Heb. 5:12-14). Only the mature have the wisdom to comprehend the folly of the cross; and without that wisdom, in their immaturity, the rulers of this age crucified the Lord of glory (1 Cor. 2:6-8; Col. 1:28).

This wisdom of the cross is critical to all true maturity, for the giving up of childishness, having first given up the spurious maturity of self-appointed adulthood, to become a newborn child in Christ means returning constantly, through one's whole lifetime, to the crucified and buried Christ. Human growth in the sanctifying Spirit means taking an ever firmer hold upon one's Easter Saturday identity, a deepening penetration into the life which conforms to Christ's own death and burial. As we first become Christ's own by being buried with him, we develop that identity and grow away from infancy to true adulthood by growing further still toward a Good Friday and Easter Saturday oneness between our selves and him, his cross and burial and our own. We cannot make clearer our new life in Christ unless we also exhibit more plainly his stigmata and marks of death. Thus Paul and his companions are "always carrying in the body the death of Jesus, so that the life of Jesus may be manifested in our bodies. For while we live we are always being given up to death for Jesus' sake, so that the life of Jesus may be manifested in our mortal flesh" (2 Cor. 4:10-11; cf. Gal. 6:17). Thus Paul's discussion of baptism as burial is specifically directed to the life lived *after* baptism, which must correspond to our initiating death and burial in Christ. How can those who died to sin still live in it? Our lives must be appropriate for those who are dead to sin and alive to God (Rom. 6:1-11).

To this extent, Luther was absolutely right: the sanctified life, the growth of our identities in faith, does consist of daily baptism and diurnal death. "I die every day!" (1 Cor. 15:30), says Paul. The Christian life consists in an increasing willingness to die with Christ and in being as content, for Christ's sake, with dying as with living. For "if we live we live to the Lord, and if we die we die to the Lord; so then, whether we live or whether we die, we are the Lord's" (Rom. 14:8; cf. Phil. 1:20). And all of this corresponds, of course, to Jesus' own demands that those who follow him must deny themselves and carry their cross; and to his guarantee that those who lose their lives for his sake and the gospel's shall save them (Mk. 8:34-35) — a promise to which Paul adds his own: "if you live according to the flesh you will die, but if by the Spirit you put to death the deeds of the body you will live" (Rom. 8:13).

Now we are trying here to clarify the peculiarities of Christian living, the special Easter Saturday identity of those who freely make their lives a kind of death, in union and conformity with the self-sacrifice of Jesus Christ. Theirs is a willingness — which may have little or nothing to do with martyrdom or the physical laying down of life for others, though that can never be excluded — to lead risky, unprotected, costly lives, open to others and committed to self-expenditure on their behalf. This they attempt in conscious but unambitious imitation — though never emulation, continuation, or displacement — of the life, and supremely the death, of Jesus. They seek to follow, by increments more closely, after one who gave himself up to murder, judgment, and forsakenness for others, that no one should be victimized, unforgiven, or forsaken. Be it remembered, though, as we insisted in the previous chapter on ecclesiology, that, just like Christ, the church and those who live and die within it exist not for themselves but for the world. The church is holy, separate, different; but it is different in the degree of its solidarity with and inseparableness from the profane world around it.[61] And the truth it knows about identity, personhood, and self-fulfillment is a truth not to be indulgently enjoyed behind church walls, or in the community of Christians only. It is the truth — did they but know it — for all humanity. In their Christian living, believers represent the world: pray and suffer for the world, but also obey, love, and grow mature on its behalf. And they do so not to absolve or exclude those they represent, but with a view to their inclusion, the opening up of the mystery of the world that it may be known, recognized, and practiced as the truth for every man and woman. Christians may identify themselves (and frequently contradict themselves by their inconsistent actions, character, and style of life) as those who uniquely bear the new humanity, making manifest in microcosm, and in prolepsis of the final kingdom, the self-surrender which leads to an ontological surplus of abundant selfhood. But this is in fact a universal truth, the way it is for each creature made in God's own image. The Easter Saturday identity defines not what it is to be a Christian, but what it is to be human. The promise awaits appropriation by everyone who would be fully human that — in Jüngel's terms — within an even greater selflessness there lies a very great self-relatedness. Love, that is, fulfills and humanizes us; and human beings will find meaning, integrity, and completeness in their lives if only they will let go — and not just once, but more and more — to the point of death and self-negation.

Where is it made more manifest that the life of growing conformity to Christ's death and burial, by which Christian individuals mature within the

---

61. See R. S. Anderson, *Historical Transcendence and the Reality of God* (Grand Rapids: Eerdmans, 1975), esp. pp. 260ff.; cf. D. M. McCullough, in *Incarnational Ministry*, pp. 28ff., and p. 31, n. 51.

community of faith, is a life enacted not for its own sake but for the world's, than in the Eucharist? That is the meal which nourishes and amplifies the new life which emerges out of death in baptism; and it is sustenance and manna for the pilgrimage toward maturity and self-surrender, our personal journey as disciples from Galilee to Jerusalem and Calvary. But it is also a foretaste of the celebration that awaits all humankind, when the world as a whole, passing through the wilderness of sickness and disunity, shall come to the Promised Land of unity, healing, and reconciliation in the final kingdom. The sacrament reaffirms continually that the church to which each believer is indispensable as an individual member of Christ's Body (1 Cor. 12:4-31; Rom. 12:4-5; Eph. 4:1-16) is also the visible and structured form which Christ's risen and ascended body takes in the world this side of his return[62] — and thus the presence of his wounded, crucified, and buried body given up and broken for the sins of the whole world. Though the signs and movements in the Eucharist speak less vividly of burial than do those of baptism, they, too, are grounded in the memory of Exodus, of life and death in Passover and the Red Sea crossing.[63] And they constitute a living memorial of the passion and the sacrifice which led to Easter Saturday, thus confirming the identity of all who feed upon and so become the Body of the crucified, as dead to themselves and alive to all their sisters and brothers who share in Christ's humanity. Here our maturity as persons who find selfhood in self-giving is set in its universal context: our solidarity, because of Christ's, with all the world.

Like baptism, the Eucharist is profoundly personal and individual, the promise to each recipient of bread and wine that this is Christ's body broken, his blood spilt, specifically "for you." And communion, like baptism, is by definition communal: we, being many, are one, just as the loaf of many particles is one; for Christ himself, who comprises many members, is one, and we participate in him (1 Cor. 12:16-17). But above all, like baptism, the Lord's Supper is cosmic in its scope. As is understood increasingly today, through an ecumenical deprivatizing of the sacrament, this is a meal for all humanity, a messianic, doxological banquet proleptic of eschatological festivities, when humanity shall come from east and west, north and south, to eat together at one table in God's kingdom (Lk. 13:39; cf. 1 Cor. 11:26; Lk. 22:15-18), and when every creature shall be reconciled and gathered up in hymns of praise and glory to the Maker of heaven and earth (Col. 1:20; Rev. 5:11-14).[64]

62. See J. A. Phillips, *The Form of Christ in the World* (London: Collins, 1967).
63. See, e.g., M. Barth, *Rediscovering the Lord's Supper* (Atlanta: John Knox Press, 1988), ch. 1.
64. See especially the emphasis upon the Eucharist as eschatological and universal

If, however, as a sign of creaturely and human unity, the Lord's Table is always approached with joy, in hope and expectation for the world's reconciliation, we can scarcely partake there without many pangs of sorrow, indignation, and remorse. As with baptism, so with Eucharist, every enactment of the sacrament constitutes a protest at the world's disunity, let alone the church's: the incongruity between heavenly vision and earthly, and ecclesiastical, reality. There must be grief here at the world's refusal to accept God's invitation to the banquet of redemption (Lk. 14:12-24). This is a meal for the poor and maimed, the lame and blind; yet the world, recalcitrant and stubborn, remains outside, broken, crippled, crooked, refusing to accept the truth of its own healing already realized in Christ's rising from the grave of the ugly, the stricken, and the despised (Isa. 53:1-9). And there must be repentance at our meal: shame that the church fails so continuously and comprehensively to provide an empirical foretaste of human wholeness and togetherness; and that while we eat the bread and drink the cup in fellowship and feasting, sisters and brothers go hungry and thirsty, their flesh still torn and blood still spilt by poverty, disease, violence, and war, by manifold evils, human and demonic. And there must be commitment: to live out the costly demands of the Easter Saturday identity, confirmed in every Eucharist, that as participants in Christ's own death and burial we shall struggle, suffer, and make sacrifices, perhaps of life itself, in solidarity with those around us and for their healing and their freedom. The Supper of our Lord, no private retreat of religiosity and piety, drives us to preach and practice Christ's lordship in the public square, in the courthouses and prison cells, the refuges and ghettos, in the corridors of power and towers of opulence — wherever injustices are perpetrated, greed idolized, power centralized, while "the least," who are Christ's sisters and brothers, remain naked, hungry, and forlorn.[65]

And what is the purpose of this Easter Saturday lifestyle, this closeness to

in the ecumenical landmark document *Baptism, Eucharist and Ministry* (The "Lima Report"), Faith and Order Papers No. 111 (Geneva: World Council of Churches, 1982), "Eucharist" section, esp. II, D and E. In this connection, too, see G. Wainwright, *Eucharist and Eschatology* (London: Epworth, 1971 and New York: Oxford University Press, 1981); and for an Eastern perspective on "the Sacrament of Unity," see A. Schmemann, *The Eucharist*, trans. P. Kachur (Crestwood, N.Y.: St. Vladimir's Seminary Press, 1988), ch. 7.

65. Among much else written today, often in the context of liberation theology, though not exclusively, on the link between the Lord's Supper and social action, see T. Balasyria, *The Eucharist and Human Liberation* (Maryknoll, N.Y.: Orbis and London: SCM, 1979); M. Barth, *Rediscovering the Lord's Supper*, ch. 3; B. J. Lee, ed., *Alternative Futures for Worship*, vol. 3: *Eucharist* (Collegeville, Minn.: Liturgical Press, 1987), ch. 3; and Moltmann, *The Church in the Power of the Spirit*, esp. pp. 256-60.

our fellow citizens in the earthly community, however different and distant from us, who are more our real neighbors in Christ than those congenial to us and just like us with whom we happily volunteer to be associated? Of course, in love's logic, response to human need has its own raison d être, without ulterior goal or external rationale. It is certainly not to liberate and unify them by our efforts and ideals that we seek to love our neighbors as ourselves — as if God's kingdom were of our own building or its coming determined by our own schedule. Rather, we love them to make manifest a sign that God is lovingly, redemptively at work among them, having become identified with the godless, the godforsaken, and the dead. The goal of mission and of service is not to improve the world and create utopia on earth; it is that the world may *believe and know*, know that God loves the world and has sent the Son to deliver it from perishing to everlasting and abundant life (Jn. 14:31; 17:21-23; 3:16; 10:10).

As we have seen, the faith which does believe in Christ, the Son whom God has sent and by whom the world and the persons in it are redeemed from perishing, consists precisely in a willingness to die and be reborn. Here the political and the personal are quite inseparable. For public engagement with structural sin — with all the injustices, diseases, and disorders of society — and personal confrontation with inner falsehood, self-righteousness, and pride are conjoint responses to the one demand for vulnerability and courage: the letting go of safety, security, and inauthentic dependency for the risk of loss, humiliation, and destruction.[66] That that is the way to restoration, peace, and freedom, individual and social, is the mystery of the gospel to which our Christ-like Easter Saturday identities bear witness. And how shall they hear without a preacher (Rom. 10:14) or learn without a teacher? The task of newborn but maturing followers and friends of Jesus Christ is to preach and teach, to show humanity how to be human — not by words alone, but by extended and embodied reenactments of the love that took Christ to the cross and grave. How, except by seeing before its very eyes how lives of self-expenditure lead to self-fulfillment, shall a cynical and uncomprehending world find it credible and knowable that in God's superfluity of grace there is indeed a way to wholeness of life and hope and liberty which leads through death and self-surrender? Shall our Easter Saturday solidarity with the world be so transparent in its realism, its depth and fecund power, that a life of self-forgetfulness and mutual dependence becomes for others, too, a risk worth taking, an invitation irrresistible, a mystery that makes some sense?

Let it be repeated, even as we focus here upon the discovery and growth

---

66. On "the political dimension of fulfillment," see H.-M. Barth, *Fulfilment*, ch. 7, esp. pp. 87ff.

of personal identity, that the individual may mediate to society at large the truth about authentic selfhood only in an ecclesial and eucharistic context. On our own we cannot teach the world the secret of true humanness, since to be, by one's own choosing, on one's own is the contradiction of true humanness. Only in and through community, that fellowship *(koinonia)* which is grounded in communion, can we manifest the truth of "being as communion" — that personhood is itself an event of relationality and reciprocity. This we have seen throughout, in the development of a trinitarian ontology from the standpoint of the cross and grave, where God submits to death yet remains God and moves toward becoming all in all, creatively prevailing over nothingness and evil precisely through the interchange of divine, communal relations.

In the Eucharist, where we have fellowship with God's own inner, triune fellowship, there is promised the eschatological fulfillment of this ontology, where human beings, sharing in God's being as communion, will be fully personal themselves, freed from egocentricity, yet for that very reason complete, satisfied, and everlasting, beyond the separation and dissolution of death.[67] Thus we might say that the eucharistic church provides the closest approximation which we have on earth to what life is like "in heaven." The self there, however, is perfected, established at last and unambiguously in its uniqueness and individuality, which is the antithesis of and deliverance from the destructive myopia of individualism. In sin, we human beings concentrate upon ourselves, straining at our own beatitude, indulgently pursuing voyages of self-discovery; and in this introversion we lose ourselves, becoming self-estranged, destroying every hope of happiness and frequently transversing the narrow boundary between self-love and hatred of the self. In redemption, by contrast, to be consummated in the *eschaton,* we discover beatitude by serendipity, on a voyage of self-effacement, turning the self outward toward the other and the Holy Other. Thus we shall come to share God's glory precisely by ceding self-glory and giving ourselves and our attention to the glory of the Father, through the Son, and in the Spirit, in harmony with all God's creatures. The church on earth is the mirror — all too dark and flawed — of heavenly selfhood, fulfilled through worship in the community of bipolarity, mutual dependence, and other-centeredness.[68]

Despite the many cracks in the ecclesial looking-glass, the church is surely a laboratory for testing and developing profane prototypes of celestial existence, the place where we discover for ourselves how to be truly human and mature, the better to show and teach the world. Shaping authentic personhood is

67. See Zizioulas, *Being as Communion,* pp. 59ff.
68. See esp. A. J. Torrance, "The Self-Relation," *SJT* 40.4 (1987): esp. 507ff.

an earthly, earthy task, contingent and experimental, marked, as we have acknowledged, by much calamity and failure. There is no one blueprint applicable to every time and setting, every society and individual, for the realizing of integrity and wholeness. Perhaps we are more aware today than before of the grainy contextuality of Christian, and therefore human, living; of the need to discover, through risk and pain and in great openness, what it means in content, in actual behavior and ordering, for us to lose ourselves within a given context, to die concretely for Christ, and with him to enact mundanely the mature Easter Saturday identity of fulfillment through forgetfulness.[69]

One obvious variant in our existence today, increasingly acknowledged in the church worldwide, is political and economic. It cannot mean quite the same thing, materially, to be a disciple of Christ crucified when penniless, starving, disenfranchised, as it does to bear his cross amid prosperity and power. A theology of the cross and grave which declares the power precisely of love's impotence should certainly not be offered to this world's dispossessed as a sanctified ideology of powerlessness, as if it is good and proper, even in the very eyes of God, for millions to be underprivileged, poor, and disempowered. The gospel of sacrifice and self-denial carries no demand that the dehumanized among us, deemed worthless and expendable by the wealthy and the mighty, should despise and humiliate themselves still further. Rather, they are surely called to undertake the risks of conformity to Christ's own vulnerability and courage, which strengthen self-relatedness through selflessness, by bravely resisting their own oppression and boldly affirming their dignity and worth and creating opportunities to share, not greedily but with greater equity, in the bounty of God's good creation.

Another disjunction upon the path to human selfhood — which has contemporary society, too, convulsively perplexed — is that between the sexes. It is impossible, thankfully, to silence any longer the voices of women in our own and many cultures, who insist that they experience life in all its aspects far beyond the biological, in ways far from identical to those of men; thus the problem of being and becoming human cannot be understood exclusively in categories drawn from male self-understanding or traditions. The church, as the community devoted to learning and showing how to make humanity more human, should (should!) provide the context for the fullest and most open discussion of what it means to be a woman, not a man, and for the wisest, but most courageous, challenges to the worldly status quo between the two. Especially the theological community — including those, be it hoped, who refuse merely

69. Note again the vital and timely discussion of contextuality, for both the thinking and the living of Christian faith, in D. Hall, *Thinking the Faith,* esp. ch. 1.

to conform the gospel to "experience" but seek to interpret experience in the light of God's own word — has a special responsibility here to provide a forum for debate, leadership, and education; and to some extent it has already done so, not least, though not exclusively, in relation to identity and selfhood.

For the pointed question has been raised, especially by women theologians, of wherein exactly sin consists for women — and therefore, by extension, how female new birth and maturity of selfhood should be understood. Is it true, as Scripture might imply, and the tradition certainly affirms, that *pride* is the universal paradigm of fallenness — with humbleness the corresponding Christian virtue, the distinctive posture of all who live by grace alone? Surely, they say, it is not characteristic of women's failings to be hubristic, self-assertive, domineering over others and exploitative of them. That may summarize the indictment against men; but women, by contrast, are marked more by self-devaluation than by self-love, by servile docility and deference rather than assertiveness, by inertia and self-protectiveness instead of hyperactivity and self-advancement. Too often, some women say now, they have tolerated the social roles assigned to them by men, agreeing in the church to be specialists in humility and abnegation, in the image of Christ's servanthood, while men arrogate the privilege of embodying Christ's lordship and authority. Daniel Migliore superbly sums up the feminist critique of those who equate sin with pride: "they have insisted that . . . sin is not only insurrectionary and sensational but is also banal, mediocre, and totally uninventive. . . . Sin . . . is not only titanic, Luciferian rebellion but also the timid, obsequious refusal to dare to be fully human by God's grace."[70]

---

70. D. Migliore, *Faith Seeking Understanding*, p. 131. Probably because much of this discussion has arisen in a North American context, the feminist critique has fastened with particular intensity upon the modern giant of U.S. theology, Reinhold Niebuhr, and his famous analysis of sin in *The Nature and Destiny of Man* (vol. 1, ch. 7). This targeting of Niebuhr is understandable, and it has provided important insights and correctives, but it is rather unfair. For, if anything, it penalizes Niebuhr for the very clarity and succinctness with which he has conveyed a doctrine of sin not of his own invention, but of long-standing tradition. Nor can it really be argued that the tradition he represents and summarizes is biblically unjustified. If the tradition is unscriptural, it is in not noticing the variety of forms which the Bible gives to the generic pride of fallen humanity, rather than in missing a separate category of sin quite distinct from pride. There are, of course, many headings under which the biblical view of sinful pride can be discussed — Niebuhr himself refers to greed and dishonesty, for example. Barth offered a tripartite analysis of sin as pride, sloth, and falsehood (*CD*, IV/1, IV/2, and IV/3), but the latter two are not other than pride, nor connote an absence of it. See esp. A. Saiving Goldstein, "The Human Situation: A Feminine View," *in Journal of Religion* 40 (1960): 100-112; J. Plaskow, *Sex, Sin and Grace: Women's Experience and the Theologies of Reinhold Niebuhr and Paul Tillich* (Lanham, Md.:

This is an important criticism and broadening of the theological tradition, and a justified rebuke to the narrowness of the patriarchal church, including much of its theology. It would, though, be far too heavy-handed to propose that all men are prideful and no women, and that the human condition and its redemption can be analyzed theologically through a static distribution of weaknesses and strengths between the sexes. If there are characteristically masculine and feminine proclivities in human nature or the Christian life, they surely coexist within us all, even if in varying degrees of balance. It is crucial, nevertheless, that human sin not be conceived exclusively as aggression, will-to-power and radical independence; and that the vulnerability and surrender to annihilation of the crucified and buried God not be construed as an undifferentiated call to sufferance, weakness, and abasement. Christ himself rebuked not only those who refused to lose their lives, but just as sternly those who refused to live their lives, to maximize their talents and their opportunities (e.g., Mt. 25:14-30). And the dominical model of mature humanity certainly did not exclude intolerance of what was wrong and a swordlike readiness for conflict and confrontation (Mt. 10:34-36; Mk. 11:12-19). Passivity and lack of daring are no less faults than self-promotion. "Judas's act of betrayal is sin in its aggressive form; the fear and cowardice of the other disciples is sin in its passive form."[71]

Even so, it is not perhaps that Scripture sees pride as one form of sin and cowardly self-depreciation as quite another, nor that, correcting Scripture in the light of feminine experience, we should now do so ourselves. Rather, pride is indeed a generic disposition, but a complex one, which finds variable outlets and expressions, some of which church theology and practice have one-sidedly neglected. Perhaps there is a feminine characteristic of passivity and acquiescence which evades challenges, forgoes opportunities, and may sometimes wallow in victimization, subservience, and abasement. But is this not itself a form of pride, a guarding and indulging of the ego, a preference for safety, control, and false autonomy which would be threatened by the risk of claiming power and taking more initiatives? The self which refuses to affirm itself is, in its own way, still called to self-denial, to the unwrapping of the ego's layers of protection, no less than the self which excessively asserts itself is summoned by Christ's gospel to dash the ego from its pedestal.

Are women and men, despite their differences, not both called by the God

---

University Press of America, 1980); D. Hampson, "Reinhold Niebuhr on Sin: A Critique," in R. Harries, ed., *Reinhold Niebuhr and the Issues of Our Time* (Oxford: Mowbray, 1986), pp. 46-60.

71. Migliore, *Faith Seeking Understanding*, p. 131.

who gives up life to death and nothingness to find rebirth and maturity in becoming vulnerable? For some — men especially, perhaps — that will mean humbly surrendering their hold on power; for some — women especially, perhaps — it will mean taking hold of power, with all its costs and risks. For the latter, too, that means letting go of pride and becoming vulnerable in a new way, exchanging the imposition of weakness upon designated specialists in servanthood for the chosen weakness, the true bearing of a cross, of those who understand the Easter Saturday mystery that any power worthy of the name is dangerous and costly, mortifying in its exercise. The two sexes are challenged equally to understand the wisdom of the cross, the equation of self-relatedness and selflessness, the even greater presence of the self in its great absence and renunciation. That is, we cannot be ourselves except in relationship and dependence upon others — yet true relationality and dependence are nourishing and not destructive to the self. "The task for men is thus to learn to find themselves *in relationship;* the task for women to find *themselves* in relationship."[72] On both sides, maturity consists in giving up, at one and the same time, autonomy and anonymity, aggressiveness and facelessness. It is to acknowledge need, abandon isolation, and exercise mutual reliance, and yet to find in that community one's very own identity, irreducible selfhood, and unique vocation. Different human beings may need to travel different paths toward such maturity as this. But we may pursue our separate journeys in partnership, respect, and mutual support. For our togetherness as male and female, and in all the other configurations of our diversity, is the image in us of God's own triunity, and our single human nature was raised to wholeness and new possibilities from the one grave wherein it lay on Easter Saturday.

72. D. Hampson, in Harries, *Reinhold Niebuhr,* p. 55.

Epilogue

We conclude in silence — which is where we started and where, in a sense, we have been all along. We began by listening — to a story, scriptural and credal, which itself told of silence. For our narrative described a day of emptiness and speechlessness, of waiting (for what?) and of termination: the end of God's Son and the end, therefore, of God, and so of everything including hope and possibility. Yet in the story's own silence we also heard language, a word of promise, of new beginnings and of life, divine and therefore human. Beyond the death of God, said the story, there is still God, resurrecting and creative; beyond the void, out of the nothing, comes new existence, where despair makes way for joy and defeat for victory. After listening to such a story, to its silence and its word; after thinking what the story means and how it might be understood; and after asking how the story should be lived, in history, society, and within ourselves, it is time to listen to it one last time, not in narrative now, but in prayer — a form of words which itself has much more to do with listening than with language, more with silence than with speech.

For surely it is only in the mode of prayer — in meditation, reflection, and straining of the heart and ear for a word of God beyond human speechlessness, that one could finally do justice to a narrative like ours which at its center point has God buried in a grave on Easter Saturday. What is there left to do *but* pray, if the story of God's own death and burial be true?

How can one *hear* such a story, which constitutes the collapse of human language, without the wordless prayer which sighs for hope beyond all hope? How can one *think* such a story, which transcends the limits of human reasoning, without the thought-less prayer which gropes for a conception of the in-

463

conceivable, the thinkability of the unthinkable? How can one *live* such a story, which imples exhaustion of the human spirit, without the helpless prayer which begs for resources of life, energy, and vision beyond one's own supplying?

The end of God on Easter Saturday would mean also the end of the world, confirming our generation's despair and doubt, the sense that history is pointless and anarchic, that evil's control is uncontested and the future for humanity and for its planet perilous, hostage to disastrous folly, myopia, and greed. Yet what could one do for such a godforsaken world but pray for a *Messiah* to deliver it from evil? Likewise the end of God would also mean the end of the church, the collapse of its foundations, the falsifying of its proclamation and the rendering pointless of its mission, its service, and its suffering for the sake of God's new kingdom. Yet what could one do in such a moribund community but pray for a *Spirit* to give it direction, steadfastness, and vigor? And the end of God would also mean the end of the person, the loss of dignity and worth, of meaning to existence; unconsolable aloneness; and inescapable entrapment in guilt and fear and death. Yet what could one do as such a terminable self but pray for a *Father* to bring pardon, courage, and regeneration?

All three prayers, and many more, for a God whom the story says is buried would, of course, be grounded in despair, made against the odds, silently addressing silence. But such is the world we live in, no different now from the first Easter Saturday, the day of divine abandonment and absence, Yet is not all prayer designed for Easter Saturday, the product of confusion, emptiness, and grief? Prayer is desperation translated into daring — the risk of letting go of confidence, eloquence, and that "spirituality," so fashionable now but so seductive. To pray is to confess not the abundance but the exhaustion of one's verbal, intellectual, and spiritual resources. It is surrender to one who prays for us when we have no prayers left and can only do so only when we acknowledge our own bankruptcy of spirit. The One who truly prays is the Spirit of the Father, whose unutterable cries, by their very nature, begin when we have ceased to speak; and the Spirit also of the Son, whose high-priestly intercessions depend upon our abject willingness to approach the Father not in our own proud name but exclusively in his. Prayer then, the sound of silence upon Easter Saturday and every day which reenacts it, is the last breath of our self-relinquishment, the freedom we give God at last to *be* God, gracious, holy, and creative, precisely in those crises where our bodies, intellects, and souls cry out in tears of anger and bewilderment that God is dead.

However, because God lives, in and beyond God's death, present in the absence, praying and responding in the silence, the Easter Saturday story which leaves us mute is also our empowerment for utterance and prayer. The extraordinary mystery of faith, that it is God who lies buried in the grave, may drive us to despair; but at the same time it frees us for doxology, since buried there in death is love incarnate, with the power to conquer death and summon forth what is, out of what is not. Again, what is there left to do *but* pray if the story of God's death and burial be true? How else can we respond to the actuality of such impossibilities as life beyond annihilation and the justifying of the godless? Prayer is astonishment translated into adoration — the risk of letting go of caution, inhibition, doubt, for the spontaneity of thankfulness and awe before God's ontological surplus and surprise.

How can one *hear* such a story, which restores and sanctifies one's language, without the fulsome prayer of praise to the God of resurrecting hope? How can one *think* such a story, which transforms the mind and gives the intellect new, explosive concepts, without the rational prayer of supplication for the understanding and illumination of God's foolish wisdom? How can one *live* such a story, which promises new personal identity, without the rejuvenated prayer of invocation for the Spirit, who creates new life and gives one energy, incentive, and maturity?

God's new beginning, after the end of God on Easter Saturday, would mean resumption and redemption for the world, hope for history's deliverance from the tyranny of evil for the reconciling of the cosmos, and the coming of a future not frightening and deadly, but alluring and full of unimagined possibilities. Therefore the story bids us pray for the coming soon of God the messianic Son, savior of humanity and history: *Maranatha.*

Likewise, God's new beginning would mean the redintegration of the church, the fresh authenticating of its message, new and deeper consecration of its mission of suffering and servanthood, of solidarity and intercession, the reinvigoration of its membership and leadership. Therefore the story bids us pray for the power of God's pentecostal Spirit, the healer of society and church: *Veni, Creator Spiritus.*

And God's new beginning would mean the regeneration of the person, a homecoming to the Father who welcomes each of us as precious and unique, sets our sin aside, and lets us die with courage, be born again to the righteousness that comes by grace alone, and grow in womanhood and manhood through the self-surrender which means wholeness of the self. Therefore the story bids us pray for the love of God the gracious Father, lord of life and death: *Abba.*

All three prayers, and many more, to a God who the story says is resurrected are contained within the prayer which is perhaps *the* Easter Saturday petition: *deliver us from evil.* For that, surely, is the prayer appropriately offered to the Trinity, in whom it has occurred that where sin and death increased, grace and life abounded even more.

Triune God, who loves in freedom and has chosen us from all eternity to be your creatures and your partners: in humility majestic and powerlessness almighty, you have made our humanity your own. In Jesus, you came closer to us than we are to ourselves, yet more like us though so greatly different from us; and in him, rejected by his own and destroyed by law, religion, politics, you lived our life, you died our death, and you occupied our grave.

God the Son, for us, between your dying and your rising, you lay buried in a tomb and descended into hell. Cursed for our sin and extinguished by our perishing, you suffered all our agonies of pain and judgment and abandonment, succumbing to the evil one who held us in the grip of fear and guilt, and our world in bondage to injustice and to death.

God the Father, for us you freely gave up your beloved Son, sacrificed and surrendered him to death; and thus bereft, you added to our tears of shame, bewilderment, and rage your own infinity of brokenheartedness and indignation at the tragic, proud estrangement of your children, and the wasteful corruption of your beautiful creation.

God the Spirit, for us you held together the forsaking Father and forsaken Son with unifying, resurrecting bonds of love, while death's hostility, our hearts of sin, and all the hatred of a crooked universe tore your divine family asunder. And still you groan beyond all utterance for creation's liberation, interceding for your church when our faith stumbles and our tongues fall silent before the continuing tyranny of evil.

God the Three-in-One, whose unity is realized in communal exchange between the Father, Son, and Spirit; eternal Lord, whose changeless, ever changing being is fulfilled in the dynamic of history and becoming: across the abyss of separation on the cross and in the grave you have reconciled the world and swallowed up our death, making space for our humanity within your own divine community. Hear our prayer for a world still living an Easter Saturday existence, oppressed and lonely, guilty of godlessness and convinced of godforsakenness. Be still tomorrow the God you are today, and yesterday already were: God with us in the grave, but pulling thus the sting of death and promising in your final kingdom an even greater victory of abundant grace and life over the magnitude of sin and death.

And for your blessed burial, into which we were baptized, may you be glorified for evermore. Amen.

Index